THE BLUE GUIDES

Countries
Austria
Belgium and Luxembourg
Channel Islands
Corsica
Crete
Cyprus
Egypt
England
France
Germany
Greece
Holland
Hungary
Ireland
Northern Italy
Southern Italy
Malta and Gozo
Morocco
Portugal
Scotland
Sicily
Spain
Switzerland
Turkey: Bursa to Antakya
Wales
Yugoslavia

Cities
Boston and Cambridge
Florence
Istanbul
Jerusalem
London
Moscow and Leningrad
New York
Oxford and Cambridge
Paris and Versailles
Rome and Environs
Venice

Themes
Churches and Chapels of Northern England
Churches and Chapels of Southern England
Literary Britain and Ireland
Museums and Galleries of London
Victorian Architecture in Britain

The original stalls from the old Flower Market are used for the daily market in Covent Garden

BLUE GUIDE

LONDON

Ylva French

Atlas, maps and plans by John Flower

A & C Black
London

WW Norton
New York

Fourteenth edition 1991

Published by A & C Black (Publishers) Limited
35 Bedford Row, London, WC1R 4JH

© A & C Black (Publishers) Limited 1991

Published in the United States of America by
W W Norton & Company, Incorporated
500 Fifth Avenue, New York, NY 10110

Published simultaneously in Canada by
Penguin Books Canada Limited,
2801 John Street, Markham, Ontario L3R 1B4

ISBN 0–7136–3277–1

A CIP catalogue record for this book
is available from the British Library.

ISBN 0–393–30729–8 USA

Ylva French was born in Sweden and came to England to study at
London University. She stayed and worked in the tourist industry. She
also lived and worked in Hong Kong for several years before
returning to London to work for the London Tourist Board promoting
London. She now has her own business as a marketing and public
relations consultant, and still writes about London.

Printed and bound in Great Britain by
William Clowes Limited, Beccles and London

PREFACE

The frenetic pace of development in London's Docklands is almost matched by the re-building of a large part of the City of London and its fringes, as well as pockets in the West End and Kensington. Visitors and residents struggling past building sites looking for familiar landmarks are still rewarded with some of the most spectacular and best-preserved historic and cultural treats available in Europe. Once completed, many new developments and refurbishments add a variety of pleasures: entertainment at Rock Circus in the London Pavilion, attractive riverside walks along the south bank at London Bridge City and Butler's Wharf, and an office environment on a human scale at Broadgate Square.

However, there is a price to pay for this accelerated pace of transformation: the loss of London's earliest history. Below the ground almost anywhere in this capital city there is something buried of London's past. In certain areas, the City and Southwark in particular, the trove will be especially rich, even where careless Victorians built before. The Museum of London's team of archaeologists, now expanded to 200, have seen their work snowball as developers press ahead with an ever-increasing number of projects. Fifteen years ago all they could do was to record what they found before the pile-drivers and excavators moved in. Today, a better organised system of negotiations usually allows the archaeologists enough time to record and rescue anything of interest on the site; recent developments where archaeological remains have been made a feature include Blackfriars priory site, Fenchurch Street Station, and Holborn Fleet Valley.

Yet there is no obligation on the part of the developer in London to allow for archaeological exploration unless it is made part of the planning permission, and this can only happen if there is a good reason to think there is something there worth investigating. There is no system of advance trial excavation and archaeological assessment of each site before planning permission is granted. The results of this haphazard way of approaching London's dwindling archaeological heritage were evident in 1989 in the case of Huggin Hill—a major find of the well-preserved remains of a Roman governor's palace. The best that could be achieved was a decision by the Secretary of State for the Environment not to schedule this site but to give consent for development to go ahead and to cover the remains below the new building 'for future generations'. The case of the Rose Theatre created even greater news interest with a long legal battle to ensure not only that the remains would be displayed, but that they would be shown in such a way that they could be fully appreciated and protected from futher damage during construction of the building above.

The really important sites are few and far between. The Museum of London estimates that out of 360 sites explored in recent years in the City of London only eight had remains that were worth preserving in situ.

So where can Londoners and visitors experience London's Roman and Saxon past? Of course the Museum of London itself, where a piece of the Roman wall is on display. From here there is the 'London Wall Walk' but the plaques at each point of interest are beginning to look rather tired and neglected. And that is the case with some of the most famous of London's preserved Roman remains including the Temple of Mithras with its out of date plaque, the Postern Gate at the Tower, and Winchester Palace with its remaining walls and window but no information. It's a case of divided responsibilities with the Museum of London as the archaeologists and English Heritage as the body responsible for public monuments. English Heritage is also responsible for scheduled monuments which remains on private sites but this is no guarantee of public access or proper presentation. The City of London, itself a local authority responsible for part of this treasure trove, has been caught in the development trap with the remains of a Roman amphitheatre on the site adjoining the Guildhall where the Corporation planned to build its new art gallery. The first plans were refused and a new scheme is now being put forward, including the display of the remains.

For it is, of course, a question of much more than just preserving a ruin and putting up a plaque. As London's museums have learnt the art of preservation, so those in charge of our archaeological remains must realise that today's public expect more. Yorvik, in York, is the obvious model, where an archaeological site has been developed into an entertaining and successful tourist attraction. In London there are some attractive presentations but most are not publicly accessible.

There are some hopes for the future: at Kingston where remains of a medieval undercroft and the original bridge are due to be incorporated in a new department store and at Merton Priory, where the Chapter House ruins preserved under a relief road may be enclosed in a museum. The overwhelming impression, though, is one of a muddle of inconsistencies, of a lack of direction and concern for London's past. Much could be done through the existing framework by incorporating archaeological assessments and directives in the planning procedure. London should also be declared an area of archaeological importance in the same way as York.

As the possibility of the responsibility for archaeology being dispersed to each of London's 33 boroughs is being discussed, or alternatively being taken over by English Heritage with its existing nationwide responsibilities, the outlook for a co-ordinated approach to preserving London's buried past and the future of the Museum of London's archaeological team looks uncertain.

Bibliography

History: 'A History of London', Robert Gray (1978); 'Everybody's Historic London', J. Keek (1987); The London Encyclopaedia, Weinreb and Hibbert (1987).

Other reading: 'Art and Architecture of London', Ann Saunders (1987); 'Blue Guide Museums and Galleries of London', Malcolm Rogers (1986); 'London Under London', Trench and Hillman (1985); 'The Buildings of England—London 1, 2', N. Pevsner; 'London Cemeteries', Hugh Meller (1981); 'The Black Plaque Guide to London', by Felix Barker and Denise Silvester Carr (1987); 'Ethnic London', by Ian McAuley (1987). 'Architecture of London', Woodward Jones, Weidenfeld & Nicholson (1989); 'London: Biography of a City', Chrisopher Hibbert, Penguin; 'London: 2000 years', Felix Barker.

For permission to reproduce the illustrations in this guide the publishers would like to thank Heather Waddell; David Clarke; the Trustees of the British Museum; Guildhall Art Gallery, City of London; the Museum of London; and the Wallace Collection.

The author would like to thank Andrea Mettarg, Gerald Parsons, Harvey Sheldon and many others in museums, attractions and galleries for their help in updating and rewriting this edition of Blue Guide London.

Ylva French, August 1990

A NOTE ON BLUE GUIDES

The Blue Guide series began in 1918 when Muirhead Guide-Books Limited published 'Blue Guide London and its Environs'. Finlay and James Muirhead already had extensive experience of guide-book publishing: before the First World War they had been the editors of the English editions of the German Baedekers, and by 1915 they had acquired the copyright of most of the famous 'Red' Handbooks from John Murray.

An agreement made with the French publishing house Hachette et Cie in 1917 led to the translation of Muirhead's London Guide, which became the first 'Guide Bleu'

Hachette had previously published the blue-covered 'Guides Joanne'. Subsequently, Hachette's 'Guide Bleu Paris et ses Environs' was adapted and published in London by Muirhead. The collaboration between the two publishing houses continued until 1933.

In 1931 Ernest Benn Limited took over the Blue Guides, appointing Russell Muirhead, Finlay Muirhead's son, editor in 1934. The Muirheads' connection with Blue Guides ended in 1963 when Stuart Rossiter, who had been working on the Guides since 1954, became house editor, revising and compiling several of the books himself.

The Blue Guides are now published by A & C Black, who acquired Ernest Benn in 1984, so continuing the tradition of guide-book publishing which began in 1826 with 'Black's Economical Tourist of Scotland'. The Blue Guide series continues to grow: there are now more than 40 titles in print with revised editions appearing regularly and many new Blue Guides in preparation.

'Blue Guides' is a registered trade mark.

CONTENTS

PREFACE   5
NOTE ON BLUE GUIDE   7
EXPLANATIONS   11
LONDON TODAY   12

BACKGROUND INFORMATION

ARRIVING IN LONDON   13
HOTELS   16
GETTING AROUND LONDON   17
EATING AND DRINKING, SHOPPING, CULTURE
AND SPORT   23
OPENING HOURS, PARKS   38
CALENDAR OF MAJOR EVENTS   44
USEFUL CONTACTS   46
GENERAL INFORMATION   49
CHRONOLOGY   52
OUTER LONDON TOURING TIPS   59

LONDON

I   **INNER LONDON: THE WEST END**

1   WESTMINSTER   61
2   WESTMINSTER ABBEY   64
3   THE HOUSES OF PARLIAMENT   81
4   VICTORIA EMBANKMENT AND WHITEHALL   88
5   CHARING CROSS AND TRAFALGAR SQUARE   93
6   THE MALL, BUCKINGHAM PALACE AND
    ST. JAMES'S PARK   100
7   PALL MALL AND ST. JAMES'S   107
8   PICCADILLY AND PICCADILLY CIRCUS   112
9   PARK LANE AND MAYFAIR   120
10 HYDE PARK CORNER, KNIGHTSBRIDGE,
    BELGRAVIA, HYDE PARK, MARBLE ARCH,
    AND BAYSWATER   123
11 KENSINGTON
    A. Knightsbridge, Kensington, Kensington
    Gardens, Holland Park and Bayswater   128
    B. The South Kensington Museums   137
12 VICTORIA, WESTMINSTER CATHEDRAL,
    PIMLICO, THE TATE GALLERY AND
    WESTMINSTER   148
13 CHELSEA   157
14 SHAFTESBURY AVENUE, SOHO, CHARING CROSS,
    LEICESTER SQUARE AND SEVEN DIALS   163
15 REGENT STREET, OXFORD STREET, WALLACE
    COLLECTION, MARYLEBONE, PADDINGTON AND
    MAIDA VALE   168
16 FITZROVIA, REGENT'S PARK, LONDON ZOO AND
    MADAME TUSSAUD'S   176
17 BLOOMSBURY
    A. Bloomsbury to Euston Road   182
    B. The British Museum and British Library   188
18 EMBANKMENT GARDENS, THE STRAND, THE
    COURTAULD INSTITUTE GALLERY AND
    THE ALDWYCH   197
19 COVENT GARDEN   202

II   THE CITY, NORTH EAST, EAST END AND DOCKLANDS

20   THE INNS OF COURT: LEGAL LONDON AND
     THE SOANE MUSEUM   208
21   FLEET STREET, BLACKFRIARS AND ST. PAUL'S
     A. Fleet Street and Blackfriars   215
     B. St. Paul's Cathedral and area   221
22   HOLBORN, SMITHFIELD AND CLERKENWELL   227
23   NEWGATE STREET, CHEAPSIDE, THE BARBICAN,
     THE MUSEUM OF LONDON   235
24   GUILDHALL, THE BANK OF ENGLAND, MANSION HOUSE
     AND THE STOCK EXCHANGE   243
25   CANNON STREET, THAMES STREET,
     THE MONUMENT   250
26   LOMBARD STREET, LEADENHALL STREET AND MARKET,
     LLOYD'S, ALDGATE AND PETTICOAT LANE   255
27   THE TOWER OF LONDON AND TOWER HILL,
     ST. KATHARINE'S DOCK   260
28   BISHOPSGATE, SPITALFIELDS, SHOREDITCH, BETHNAL
     GREEN AND WHITECHAPEL   270
29   LONDON'S DOCKLANDS: WAPPING, LIMEHOUSE,
     ISLE OF DOGS   277
30   LAMBETH, THE SOUTH BANK AND WATERLOO   283
31   SOUTHWARK, BANKSIDE, LONDON BRIDGE CITY AND
     BERMONDSEY   290
32   ISLINGTON AND CAMDEN TOWN   297

III   THE RIVER THAMES

33   WESTMINSTER TO THE TOWER; TO GREENWICH AND
     THE THAMES BARRIER   301
34   WESTMINSTER TO KEW; RICHMOND, KINGSTON AND
     HAMPTON COURT   308

IV   OUTER LONDON: SOUTH EAST, SOUTH AND SOUTH WEST

35   GREENWICH, BLACKHEATH, DEPTFORD, SURREY
     DOCKS, ROTHERHITHE, WOOLWICH, BEXLEY,
     ELTHAM   313
36   DULWICH, FOREST HILL, SYDENHAM, NORWOOD,
     STREATHAM, WANDSWORTH, BATTERSEA, BRIXTON,
     KENNINGTON, CAMBERWELL, PECKHAM,
     LEWISHAM   325
37   CROYDON, CARSHALTON, CHEAM, SUTTON,
     WIMBLEDON, MERTON, KINGSTON   336
38   RICHMOND, PUTNEY, BARNES, MORTLAKE, KEW, HAM
     AND PETERSHAM, TEDDINGTON, TWICKENHAM, THE
     HAMPTONS AND HAMPTON COURT PALACE   343
39   FULHAM, HAMMERSMITH, BRENTFORD, HOUNSLOW,
     UXBRIDGE, EALING, ACTON AND SOUTHALL   357
40   WINDSOR AND ETON   371

V   OUTER LONDON: NORTH WEST, NORTH EAST AND EAST

41   WEMBLEY, WILLESDEN, BRENT CROSS, HARROW,
     PINNER, STANMORE   376
42   HENDON, MILL HILL, BARNET, FINCHLEY   379
43   HIGHGATE, HAMPSTEAD, GOLDERS GREEN   384
44   WOOD GREEN, TOTTENHAM, STOKE NEWINGTON,
     HACKNEY, ENFIELD, LEA VALLEY, EPPING FOREST,
     WALTHAMSTOW   392

45 STRATFORD, BOW, NEWHAM, BARKING AND DAGENHAM, ROMFORD, HORNCHURCH, UPMINSTER   400

INDEX   405

MAPS AND PLANS

CENTRAL LONDON   At the end of the book
OUTER LONDON   At the end of the book
LONDON UNDERGROUND   At the end of the book
BRITISH MUSEUM   190–1, 194
GREENWICH   Atlas section
HAMPSTEAD AND HIGHGATE   Atlas section
HAMPTON COURT PALACE   354–5
HOUSES OF PARLIAMENT   82–3
INNS OF COURT   210
LONDON ZOO   180–1
NATIONAL GALLERY   96
NATIONAL MARITIME MUSEUM   Atlas section
ST. PAUL'S CATHEDRAL   222
SCIENCE MUSEUM   146
TATE GALLERY   154
THEATRES   32
TOWER OF LONDON   264–5
VICTORIA AND ALBERT MUSEUM   138–9, 142–3
WALLACE COLLECTION   173
WESTMINSTER ABBEY ENVIRONS   66–7
WESTMINSTER ABBEY   69
WINDSOR CASTLE   Atlas section

EXPLANATIONS

Type. The main routes are described in large type. Smaller type is used for branch-routes and excursions, for historical and preliminary paragraphs, and (generally speaking) for descriptions of greater detail or minor importance.

Asterisks indicate points of special interest or excellence.

Plans. References in the text (Pl. 1;1) are to the colour Atlas at the back of the book, the first figure referring to the page, the second to the square. There is a generous overlap between one page and another: the reference most convenient for the direction being described has been given. Ground Plan references are given as a bracketed single figure.

Abbreviations. In addition to generally accepted and self-explanatory abbreviations, the following occur in the Guide:

AA Automobile Association
Abp Archbishop
Adm Admission, Admiral
Bp Bishop
BH Bank Holiday
BR British Rail
BTA British Tourist Authority
c circa (about)
C century
DLR Docklands Light Railway
exc. except
GLC Greater London Council
incl. including
LB London Borough of ...
LCC London County Council
LRT London Regional Transport
LTB London Tourist Board
m mile(s)
MCC Marylebone Cricket Club
MSS manuscripts
NT National Trust
Pl. Atlas Plan
PLA Port of London Authority
pron. pronounced
RA Royal Academician
RAC Royal Automobile Club
Rest. restaurant
Rfmts refreshments
RHS Royal Horticultural Society
Rte Route
seq. sequentia, etc. (following)
SS Saints
St. Saint
St Street
YH Youth Hostel

LONDON TODAY

London, the capital of England and of Great Britain, is situated on the River Thames about 40 miles from the coast. Greater London consists of 33 separate local authorities and covers an area of 625 square miles. The population of London has declined gradually during this century and reached 6.7m in 1986; the majority are women (3.5m) and an estimated 30 per cent of Londoners were born elsewhere, including other Commonwealth countries, creating a heterogeneous mix which has done much to change London into the cosmopolitan city it is today.

London's three most important industries in terms of employment are retailing, the public sector and tourism, followed by banking and insurance, transport, communications and manufacturing.

Central London's population increases dramatically during weekdays and the number of people commuting to the centre to work has increased steadily during the '80s; in 1988 an estimated 1.25 million travelled daily, just over 1m by public transport and 162,000 by private car.

In 1988 an estimated 9.1m overseas and 12m British visitors stayed at least one night in the capital, spending over £4,000m. There are an estimated 130,000 beds in London's 1300 hotels and guest houses, registered by the London Tourist Board.

London's parks and open spaces are famous; there are some 387 parks over 20 acres in Greater London as a whole; the royal parks cover an area of 6000 acres, former GLC parks over 5000 acres and the London Boroughs' parks 28,000 acres. Even the City of London has more than 7000 acres of parkland but most of that consists of Epping Forest to the NE of the capital. Hampstead Heath now falls under the City of London's jurisdiction.

London is divided roughly into two halves by the River Thames: the southern area is traditionally more residential and industrial while the commercial and entertainment worlds are mostly located on the North Bank in the City and the West End. The City, which also incorporates much of Legal London, is expanding its commercial influence westwards into the Fleet Street area and Holborn and increasingly eastwards into the London Docklands, particularly the Isle of Dogs.

The West End includes the shopping areas and office districts of Victoria, Mayfair and Marylebone as well as the political world of Westminster. Bloomsbury retains its educational emphasis, with the University of London and the British Museum stamping their character on the area. Soho is losing some of its seediness and competes with trendy Covent Garden for the best restaurants; it remains London's principal so-called red-light district with the lively Chinatown to the south.

PRACTICAL INFORMATION

Arriving in London

Airports. London has two major international airports, Heathrow and Gatwick, two smaller airports, Luton and Stansted, which principally serve the charter trade (Stansted has been designated London's third international airport over the next 15 years), and a city-centre airport, London City Airport (opened October 1987).

Heathrow is 15m W of London along the M4 motorway (Tel. 081-759 4321). The first three terminals are within walking distance of each other, the 4th terminal is linked by shuttle bus. Public transport connections are excellent. Underground stations are Terminals 1, 2, 3 and Terminal 4, both on the Piccadilly Line. Services take 40–45 minutes to central London and operate 20 hours a day. Change at Hammersmith for the District Line. London Transport also operates two Airbus Services with pick-up points at all four terminals. One service operates to Victoria Station, via Earls Court Road, Cromwell Road (Forum Hotel), and Hyde Park Corner, the other to Russell Square via Euston Station, Holland Park Avenue (Kensington Hilton) and Bayswater. The trip takes 50–60 minutes, depending on traffic conditions. Green Line operates service 767 to and from Heathrow (45 minutes) and Victoria Coach Station via Hyde Park Corner and Kensington.

Connections with Gatwick. The two airports are linked by an Express Coach service (Speedlink) via the M25 motorway (c 50 minutes depending on traffic) or by Green Line Coach service No. 747.

Taxis. There are authorised (black cab) taxi ranks outside each terminal. Fares are shown on the meter and the drivers must accept rides of up to 20 miles from the airport, if they are in the rank. There are additional charges for luggage, extra persons, travelling after 20.00 and at weekends; these are also displayed on the meter. (Tipping, etc., see p 50.) Do not accept approaches from drivers of unauthorised taxis (so-called mini-cabs) as they are not metered.

Car Hire. All the major car hire companies are represented at Heathrow; many others will arrange for cars to be waiting for customers on arrival.

Car Parking. There are multi-storey car parks for each terminal to be used for up to 24 hours; for longer parking periods the long-term car parks are recommended. A shuttle coach service connects them with the terminals.

Information. The British Airports Authority has desks in each terminal providing information; announcements for missed contacts, lost children, etc., can be arranged. There are 24-hour banking facilities.

Hotel Bookings. Booking desks operate in all the terminals; the London Tourist Board operates a hotel booking and information service in conjunction with London Transport in Heathrow Underground Station.

Gatwick is situated 28m S of London on the M23 motorway (tel. 0293 28822). It has a main terminal (South Terminal), a satellite terminal, and a new North Terminal (1988). A high-speed train service (30-minute journey) connects Gatwick with Victoria Station in central London. Trains depart every 15 minutes during the day and hourly after midnight. There are also direct train services to East Croydon, Brighton, and other towns in SE England.

A Green Line Coach service (No. 747) connects Gatwick and Heathrow; another service 777 runs to Victoria Coach Station (journey time 70 minutes).

Taxis. A local taxi service is based at the airport; recommended only for short journeys. Central London is best reached by train.

Car Hire. Major car-hire companies are represented at the airport; others will arrange to meet customers.

Car Parking. There are three short-term and several long-term car parks with a shuttle service to and from the airport.

Information. The British Airports Authority has information desks in the terminals. There are 24-hour banking facilities.

Hotel Bookings. There is a reservation service based at the airport; alternatively use the service at Victoria Station; see below.

Victoria Station Terminal for Gatwick. This new terminal is situated on the W side of the station with direct access from Buckingham Palace Road. A separate taxi rank serves arrivals from Gatwick. Hotel booking services are available, including that of the London Tourist Board in the Tourist Information Centre in the station forecourt; see below.

Connecting Services. Regular scheduled services connect Heathrow and Gatwick with major cities in the UK and on the Continent. Quick check-in services between Heathrow and Edinburgh, Glasgow, Manchester and Belfast are provided by the British Airways shuttles.

London City Airport, King George V Dock, E16. 6 miles E of the City. 15–30 minutes by road. DLR access to the City by 1992. Scheduled services to European cities, Channel Isles and domestic flights. (Tel. 071-474 5555.) A River Bus service operates from Swan Lane Pier (City). Nearest BR station, Silvertown, connects with the District Line at West Ham.

Luton Airport (0582 405100), 30 miles N of London. Trains to Luton (35 minutes) run from St. Pancras and King's Cross Thameslink; taxi or bus to the airport from Luton (10 minutes). Luton and District coach service No. 757 operates from Buckingham Palace Road (70 minutes).

Stansted Airport, Stansted, Essex. (0279 502379). 32m NE of London. Train from Liverpool St to Bishops Stortford, then bus or taxi (1–1½ hours). (Do not take train to current BR Stansted.) Also Premier Coach service 738, approx every 2 hours, from Eccleston Bridge, Victoria (1½ hours). There is no left luggage facility at the airport. Considerable expansion is underway, and a direct rail link is due to connect Stansted with Liverpool Street Station in 1991.

Seaports. Major seaports with London connections are Tilbury (Fenchurch St Station), Harwich (Liverpool St Station), Dover (Victoria Station), Folkestone (Charing Cross Station) and Southampton (Waterloo Station). There are regular train services from all these port terminals to the London mainline stations. Hovercraft land at Dover and connect with trains to Victoria Station. **Arrival by Car.** Car-ferry services operate into the major seaports (see above) as well as Newhaven, Portsmouth and Plymouth.

Major Railway Stations. London's major termini serve different sectors of Outer London and the UK. The list below gives a general indication of the areas covered:

Charing Cross (071-928 5100). SE London and parts of S England.

Euston (071-387 7070). Liverpool, Manchester, NW England, Glasgow.

Fenchurch St (071-928 5100). Southend, Tilbury.

King's Cross (071-287 2477). Leeds, York, NE England, Edinburgh.

Liverpool St (071-928 5100). Harwich, Felixstowe, Ipswich, Cambridge, East Anglia.

Paddington (071-262 6767). Oxford, Bristol, SW England, Wales.

St Pancras (071-387 7070). Luton, Leicester, Sheffield.

Victoria (071-928 5100). Gatwick, Brighton, Dover, S and SE London.

Waterloo (071-928 5100). Southampton, S England, SW London.

Other useful British Rail services include *Motorail* to Scotland and SW England (tel. 071-387 8541); . Seat and sleeper reservations are available on Inter-city services; book through a travel agent or at the relevant London terminus. Personal callers are welcome at the British Travel Centre, 4-12 Regent St, London, SW1.

Coach Services. A national network of scheduled coach services (usually cheaper than rail) operates from Victoria Coach Station, Buckingham Palace Road. The Coach Station is c 400m from the Victoria Railway and Underground Stations. A minibus shuttle service operates. The Coach Station is at times severely overcrowded. General information on National Express services is available on 071-730 0202 (24 hours).

Passports, Visas. A valid national passport or alternative document must be produced on arrival in the UK. Visitors from some countries require a visa. At present there are no special vaccination requirements.

Quarantine. Animals and birds must be placed in quarantine on arrival in Britain (6 months for animals; 35 days for birds) as part of rabies control measures. *Attempts to circumvent the restrictions carry severe penalties.*

Customs. A red and green channel system operates at most points of entry. The green channel is for those with nothing dutiable to declare, or with only the permitted level of duty-free goods.

Foreign Exchange. The UK imposes no restrictions on the import or export of bank notes of any currency. The major London airports have 24-hour banking services with foreign-exchange facilities. Bureaux de change operate at London's major railway termini; check exchange rates and commission charges before entering into a transaction (see p 49). Most hotels also offer foreign exchange facilities.

Normal opening hours for banks are 09.30–15.30, Monday to Friday. Some West End and suburban bank branches now open longer hours and on Saturday mornings.

Hotels

London's wide range of accommodation includes everything from luxury hotels to *en famille* bed and breakfast, camp-sites to self-service apartments. From Easter to October it is advisable to book, although hotel rooms can be found for those who arrive without prior bookings through LTB's hotel accommodation service at the Tourist Information Centre, or other hotel booking agencies. However, this may not be in the area or price-range preferred.

A Book-A-Bed-Ahead Service is available between tourist information centres in major towns in England, including London. This operates on the same day but ensures that travellers around Britain have a room when they arrive in London and vice versa.

The English Tourist Board operates a grading and 'crown' classification system for hotels and other forms of accommodation, from one to five crowns depending on facilities. In London look for LTB membership and 'crowns' which ensures that minimum standards have been met. Complaints can be referred to LTB (see p 46).

'Where to Stay in London' lists a wide range of hotels, bed and breakfast establishments, and hostels. It is available from LTB (see above) and bookshops. (Hotel booking agencies, see p 47.)

Hotels are concentrated in Mayfair, Bayswater, Paddington, Bloomsbury, South Kensington, Earls Court, and Victoria. There are large international hotels at Gatwick and Heathrow Airports, and smaller hotels in London's suburbs.

Self-Service apartments are available throughout London; consult BTA's 'London Apartments' booklet or LTB's membership listing.

Camping and Caravan sites are listed in LTB's 'Camping and Caravan Sites' leaflet; *en famille* accommodation bookings are handled by a number of different agencies; contact BTA or LTB for an up-to-date list.

Hotel Charges. Hotels charge per person rates; either for a single or a twin-bedded room. VAT (at 15 per cent) should be included in the price quoted. Breakfast is usually included in the lower priced hotels. Service is mostly included in the total bill and no additional tipping is necessary except for personal services at the guest's discretion. A room reservation is a binding contract and hotels are entitled to hold on to a deposit or make a charge if a booking is cancelled and the room cannot be re-let. Prices of hotel rooms must be displayed and guests are entitled to see the room before agreeing to a reservation. Normally guests vacate their rooms before 12.00 on the day of departure. If arriving after 18.00 the hotel should be notified, or else they may release the room.

The *Youth Hostels Association* of Great Britain operates six hostels in London: Highgate (081-340 1831), Holland House (071-937 0748), Hampstead Heath (081-458 9054), Earl's Court (071-373 7083), Oxford Street, (071-734 1618) and Carter Lane (071-236 4965). A new hotel is being built in Surrey Docks (1991). Additional accommodation is made available during the summer in student halls of residence. Book by writing to the Youth Hostels Association, 36 Carter Lane, London EC4.

Membership of the Association is available for a small fee. Booking during peak periods is essential.

The YMCA maintains the Y-Hotel at 112 Great Russell St, WC1 (071-636 8616) and the London City YMCA, Barbican (071 628 0697). The YWCA Central Club, 16–22 Great Russell St, WC1 (071-636 7512) has 178 beds and leisure facilities.

Camping and Caravan information can be obtained from the Camping Club of Great Britain, 11 Lower Grosvenor Place, London SW1 (071-828 1012), and the Caravan Club, East Grinstead House, London Road, E Grinstead, Sussex (0342 26944).

Getting Around London

London Transport operates the Underground and bus services throughout Central London and to most parts of Outer London. In some areas individual bus routes have been privatised; these buses are a different colour from the familiar red London Transport buses. South-East, South and South-West London are served by British Rail's suburban rail services.

London's public transport system is busy through the day and evening. Most services end before six or at midnight. (For night-buses see below.) The rush-hour on both Underground and suburban railway services is at its height between 07.30 and 09.00 and 16.30–18.00. Traffic congestion can occur at any time in Central London and in the suburbs but is more likely during the rush-hour period, particularly on main roads in and out of Central London and on cross-London routes.

Travelcards offer discounts on underground, bus and rail travel. The Visitor Travelcard, available overseas and as part of a tour package, covers the underground network, including Heathrow, virtually all bus routes, suburban BR routes and the Docklands Light Railway. It is available for 1, 3, 4 and 7 days and includes discount vouchers to tourist attractions.

The regular Travelcard is available for 1 and 7 days from tourist information centres, London Transport travel information centres at Heathrow Central, Euston, King's Cross, Piccadilly Circus, Oxford Circus and Victoria, and Underground and BR stations. The card covers travel on underground, bus and suburban rail services. Travelcards for seven or more days require photocards; bring a passport-sized photograph when buying the ticket. The price varies according to the number of 'zones' covered. Note that the one-day card is available after 09.30 only, Monday to Friday; off-peak returns are also available on British Rail suburban services. More information from London Transport's 24-hour information service on 071-222 1234.

The *Underground* ('the tube') is the quickest and easiest way to travel around London and the network covers most of Greater London, except for the south-east and southern suburbs; there are some 250 stations in all on ten different lines now divided into a zonal fare system. Zone 1 is basically the area covered by and within the Circle Line. Tickets for individual journeys are available from ticket machines which now take a large selection of coins, or from a ticket-office (usually with a queue at busy stations); keep a large selection of coins or buy a discount card (see above). All tickets fit the automatic ticket barriers. Tickets are given up (or 'swallowed' by the machine) at the end of the journey. Return tickets are available on the Underground and are recommended for visits to Olympia and Earl's Court at exhibition time when there are usually large queues at the ticket office on return.

Disabled travellers in wheelchairs can use certain sections of the 'over-ground' Underground system where access is by stairs or lift; contact London Transport for details. Wheelchairs and push-chairs are not allowed, except if carried, on the escalators. Smoking is now banned on all Underground trains and Underground stations. Trains operate from 05.30 to 24.15, and 07.30 to 23.15 on Sundays; but check details of last trains to any particular part of outer London.

On the whole, the London Underground has a good reputation for safety and many new safety measures have been introduced in the last year. On certain sections and in the evening, women may feel comfortable with another person; alternatively choose a carriage near the guard, or the driver on a train without a guard.

Interchange between different lines is simple through the colour-code system and good signposting. However, at some stations long walks can be involved. If in doubt, when carrying heavy luggage for example, check with LRT.

Buses. London's famous red double-decker buses provide convenient central London services as well as a sightseeing service. Nos 11, 15 or 38 are good routes to catch for a 'tour' of London—sit on top at the front—smoking is now only allowed on the top-deck in the rear seats and may be banned altogether. (See also sightseeing tours, on p 20.) A queue system operates at bus stops, although it may easily break down if several buses arrive together; be prepared for some pushing in the rush-hour; sometimes only five standing passengers are allowed inside (downstairs) and drivers/conductors are normally fierce on this point. Push-chairs and limited luggage as well as dogs are carried at the conductor's/driver's discretion.

One-person driver-only buses, single and double-deckers, operate on several Central London routes and most routes in outer London and on the Red Arrow service between mainline stations and to Oxford St. The exact fare is usually required; carry 10p and 20p coins. A solid red sign at the bus-stop indicates request stop; hail the bus as it approaches; to get off ring the bell on the platform. Short bus journeys are cheaper than the Underground.

Nightbuses operate from Trafalgar Square from midnight and cover most parts of London. If travelling alone by bus at night, sit downstairs to be close to the conductor/driver; rowdiness is more likely on the top-deck.

British Rail, suburban network. South-East London (including Greenwich) is served from Charing Cross and London Bridge. South London (including Bromley, Orpington and Croydon) is served from Victoria Station. South-Western suburbs including those served by the District Line, (e.g. Wimbledon and Richmond as well as Kingston) are served from Waterloo. Services start from 06.00 and wind down from 22.30. Check last trains and weekend services carefully.

Commuter services to East Anglia (including Southend) operate from Fenchurch St and Liverpool St. Services to Hertfordshire (including St. Albans), operate from St. Pancras.

Taxis. The characteristic black London cab (known as a 'Hackney' carriage at one time—they were first built in Hackney) is gradually being replaced with a new style of cab based on the traditional design. It is accessible for disabled persons. The Hackney Carriage Office of the Metropolitan Police controls the licensing of taxis and of drivers who have to pass 'the knowledge' a detailed examination on London. Black cabs can be hailed in the street when the yellow 'For Hire' notice is illuminated. They are also available from ranks or by telephone: Computercab 071-286 0286; Dial A Cab 071-253 5000; Radio Taxi Cabs 071-272 0272.

Taxi-fares are generally increased once a year; there is a standard charge on the meter, to which additional charges are added for waiting time, additional passengers, luggage and after 20.00 and before 06.00 and at weekends. For long journeys (over 6 miles) to the suburbs or outside the Metropolitan area, it may be necessary to negotiate a fare (this does not apply to Heathrow— see p 000). Any dispute regarding fares should be referred to the Hackney Carriage Office of the Metropolitan Police; make a note of the cab number— inside the cab and also at the rear below the number plate—and if possible the driver's number; they wear a badge.

Mini-cabs are private cars, with untrained drivers, who operate taxi services mostly in the suburbs. They have to be adequately insured but their charges are not controlled or metered. Normally they work on mileage and a fare should be negotiated beforehand. They provide a useful alternative in the suburbs, which are poorly served by black cabs, except for major stations such as East Croydon. Look up mini-cabs in the 'Yellow Pages' telephone directory. They should not be hailed or used in central London (except possibly late at night)—in some cases visitors have been overcharged. In cabs and mini-cabs, pay the fare and add a discretionary 10 per cent as a tip. It is quite acceptable to round up or down to the nearest pound, if appropriate.

Driving. Visitors can drive in Britain on a current International Driving Permit or on a current domestic licence subject to a maximum of 12 months. No-one under 17 may drive a car, no-one under 16 may drive a motorcycle. Full details of Britain's road regulations are in the Highway Code (available from bookshops). Visitors to London are strongly recommended to leave their cars and to go sightseeing in London by public transport. If hiring a car for touring Britain, contact LTB for a list of car hire companies, located throughout London. Rates vary considerably.

Parking is controlled throughout central London and in suburban centres. Limited off-street car-parking is provided mostly by National Car Parks who can supply a useful guide to car parks. Contact a tourist information centre or National Car Parks on 071-499 7050. Meters apply on weekdays, on Saturday mornings in some areas and throughout Saturdays in others, from 08.00 to 18.30. Use 20p and 50p coins.

Parking on a single or double yellow line during weekdays, and on double yellow lines or in residents' parking zones without a permit at other times can result in a parking ticket—a fine to be paid—or in central London, in clamping, which means that the car cannot be moved. The clamp is removed once the fine has been paid at a nominated police station. Sometimes it will take several hours before the clamp is removed. The clamp is used against foreign-number-plated cars with just as much vigilance as British registered cars—only Diplomatic cars are exempt.

Two national motoring organisations look after the interests of motorists and offer touring information and breakdown services. Contact the AA (Automobile Association, Fanum House, 52 London Road, Twickenham, 081-891 1441 or the RAC (Royal Automobile Club, 89 Pall Mall, SW1) (071-839 7050), for details of membership. The BTA issues a free guide on Vehicle Hire and Driving in Great Britain (available from overseas offices only).

A good *map* is essential for touring Britain and Greater London; sign-posting except on motorways and major routes can be confusing. Follow road-numbers whenever in doubt rather than looking for the names of particular towns, or suburbs of London. Allow more time than distances on the map would suggest; most suburban roads and major and minor roads are congested, particularly through towns; major roads other than motorways may only be dual carriageway in patches and there is heavy traffic on routes to ports in particular.

Sightseeing. The ideal way to explore London is on foot; this guide is divided into routes which could take walkers up to half a day or more depending on how thoroughly each area is explored. There is a map section at the back of the book but an additional, more detailed map may be helpful. The most detailed are the 'A to Z' or the 'Streetfinder'; both show virtually every street in the Greater London area.

The *Silver Jubilee Walkway* is a 10-mile way-marked trail starting in Leicester Square and taking in the City, Bankside, South Bank, Westminster and back to Leicester Square. Redevelopments on Bankside (see p 290) have interrupted the trail but an alternative route can be taken. Use the Silver Jubilee Walkway Map, available from LTB tourist information centres. Two shorter, similar trails in the City are the *Heritage Walks*. Heritage Walk No. 1 starts in Threadneedle St by the Bank of England, and Heritage Walk No. 2 on the N side of St. Paul's Cathedral. These are also waymarked and a map and explanations can be found in the 'Visitors' Guide to the City of London' (50p) available from the City of London Information Centre. The London Wall Walk follows the Roman wall, see p 237.

Walking tours of London take place every day; these are organised by small groups of guides or small companies, such as Discovering London (0277 213704), London Walks (081-441 8906), and Citisights (081-806 4325), as well as various societies. They publish their own leaflets which can be found at tourist information centres; 'Time Out', 'What's On Where to Go', and 'City Limits' also carry daily listings. Tours on a theme such as 'Legal London', 'Jack the Ripper's London', the 'London of Charles Dickens' or geographical Hampstead or Mayfair usually start from a specified Underground station without pre-booking. There is a charge of between £2 and £4. Some tours end in a pub, while others are designed as pub tours (eg. the Londoner from Temple Underground every Friday at 19.30). These tours are particularly recommended for visitors on their own or those who want to meet Londoners; many go on these tours particularly in the off-peak periods.

By Car. Registered driver-guides (look for Blue Badge) offer individually designed tours for up to five people in private cars, limousines, or a black cab. Contact Prestige Tours, 10 Jacob's Well

Mews, W1 (071-584 3118), or the Driver Guides Association, 2 Bridge St, SW1 (071-834 2498). At first sight these may appear expensive, but, when several people are sharing, they are a very competitive alternative to a guided sightseeing tour with the advantage that the itinerary is flexible and caters for individual tastes. Tipping the guide, and sharing lunch would be expected on a full-day tour.

By Bus or Coach. Several companies run introductory London tours with or without commentary, covering most Central London sights without stopping and taking from 2 to 2.5 hours depending on traffic. London Regional Transport use the familiar red double-decker for their Original London Sightseeing Tour which starts from Victoria (Victoria St), Marble Arch, Piccadilly Circus and Baker St. Tours run frequently (every half hour) daily and are guided. There are also recorded commentaries in German and French (check with London Transport on 071-222 1234); London Pride operate a similar service from Coventry St with regular departures daily using their own style of double-decker bus. Cityrama, using distinctive blue double-decker buses, offer recorded commentaries in up to 12 languages with departures from Victoria (Grosvenor Gardens), Trafalgar Square and Piccadilly Circus. The above services require no pre-booking and operate on a first come first served basis from approx 09.30– 17.00 daily through the year, later in the summer. It may be necessary to let a bus go to get an upper deck seat on the open-topped buses used during the good weather in the summer.

Extensive programmes of scheduled sightseeing services are operated by several tour operators including Evan Evans Tours Ltd, 27 Cockspur St, Trafalgar Square, SW1 (071-930 2377), Frames Rickards, 11 Herbrand St, WC1 (071-837 3111), and London Transport (071-227 3456). These can be pre-booked at tourist information centres or through hotel porters in most hotels; there are usually several pick-up points for different tours and German, French and Spanish language tours are standard. The West End morning tour takes in the Changing of the Guard (if it is taking place that day), and Westminster Abbey as well as a general tour of the area; the City afternoon tour takes in the Tower of London and St. Paul's Cathedral as well as a panoramic drive through the City. The Whole Day London tour combines the two and includes lunch.

More adventurous tours combine a tour on the river with a visit to Greenwich; there are also Half Day and Whole Day tours to Windsor, Eton and Hampton Court. Tours go further afield to Oxford and Blenheim, Stratford on Avon, Cambridge, Stonehenge and Bath, Winchester and Broadlands, Leeds Castle, Arundel and Brighton. Full programmes and bookings at tourist information centres.

All these tour operators use Blue Badge, registered guides, trained and examined by the London Tourist Board. There are some 750 working guides in London speaking a variety of languages and offering some very special qualifications: in antiques, history, art, dealing with disabled visitors and so on. Contact the London Tourist Board (26 Grosvenor Gardens, SW1, 071-730 3488) for information on particular guide services.

By Coach. The excellent Green Line Coach network covers the South East. The coaches operate from Eccleston Bridge to a variety of destinations at competitive fares. Information from Green Line Coaches on 081-668 7261. A Golden Rover discount ticket which gives a day's unlimited travel is available.

By Bike or Scooter. Bicycles and scooters can be rented for the day or the week from several companies in London; the weekend is recommended as a gentle introduction to London's traffic! London drivers are not noted for their courtesy to cyclists. Try On Your Bike, 52–54 Tooley St, SE1 (071-378 6669), Saviles, 99 Battersea Rise, SW11 (071-228 4279) or Scootabout Ltd, 59 Albert Embankment, SE1 (071-

582 0055). Serious cyclists should contact the London Cycling Campaign Centre, Tress House, Stamford St, SE1 (071-928 7220) for a copy of 'On Your Bike'. For motorbikes, try Scootabout.

By Helicopter. Scheduled helicopter services no longer operate, but a helicopter sightseeing tour can be arranged by chartering a helicopter for 15 minutes to 1 hour. Contact Battersea Heliport Lombard Road, SW11 (071-228 3232).

By River. One of the most pleasant and peaceful ways of seeing London is on a river-trip. There are departures through the year to the Tower and Greenwich from Westminster Pier and Charing Cross Pier; and round trip services to the Thames Barrier also from Westminster Pier. Services in the winter operate between 10.30 and 16.00; in the summer between 09.30 and 17.30 at regular intervals.

In the summer there are also up-river scheduled services to Kew, Richmond, and Hampton Court from Westminster Pier. These services operate from Easter to September.

There are scheduled services between Kingston and Hampton Court from Easter to September; and between Greenwich and the Thames Barrier; there are also services around the Thames Barrier, from the Barrier Pier.

Check river services before departure by telephoning the London Tourist Board's Recorded River Service line (071-730 4812).

Circular cruises during the day and evening operate from Westminster Pier, usually with a bar on board. There are lunch cruises on Wednesdays, Saturdays and Sundays (book with Catamaran Cruisers on 071-839 3572). Several operators run evening disco cruises as well as music hall and dinner-dance cruises. Contact Catamaran Cruisers (071-839 3572), or Tidal Cruisers (071-839 2164). On most scheduled services a commentary is provided by the skipper. This is of varying quality and a tip is usually expected as passengers leave the boat. The River Bus operates to West India Pier and Greenwich via Charing Cross Pier and Swan Lane Pier (for the City). It uses high speed catamarans. Information 071-512 0555.

By Canal. London's Grand Union Canal and Regent's Canal are well worth exploring. Services operate from Camden Lock to Little Venice and back on Jenny Wren Cruises, 250 Camden High St, NW1 (071-485 4433) (April–Oct.); from Little Venice to Regent's Park and Camden Town on Jason's Trip, 60 Blomfield Road, W9 (071-286 3428) (April–Oct.); from Little Venice to London Zoo with the London Waterbus Company (071-482 2550) (March to Sept.); from Uxbridge Lock along the Grand Union Canal with Colne Valley Passengerboat Services, Adelaide Dock, Endsleigh Road, Southall, Middlesex (081-571 4428) (May to Sept.).

By Rail. Many towns of interest may easily be visited by train from London. They include Arundel, Brighton, Cambridge, Canterbury, Oxford, Salisbury and Winchester.

 A luxury train journey on the Pullman coaches of the Venice Orient Express can be enjoyed to visit Bath, Bristol, Hever Castle or Bournemouth. Champagne lunch or afternoon tea is served on board and one leg of the journey is usually by luxury coach. Bookings through a travel agent or contact Venice Orient Express, 20 Upper Ground, SE1 (071-928 5837).

Eating and Drinking, Shopping, Culture and Sport

Restaurants, Pubs and Wine Bars. Eating out and going to the pub or winebar are some of the greatest pleasures that London has to offer. The range and style of restaurants vary enormously—every month a new restaurant opens and somewhere else another closes its doors. Standards have in general improved and most first-class restaurants now offer an Anglicised version of nouvelle cuisine with emphasis on fresh vegetables and relatively small portions of meat or fish. Traditional English restaurants serving roast beef and steak and kidney pudding still survive but in the main it is the pub-restaurants and also carveries in many West End hotels, which are keeping this style of cooking alive.

It is the variety of food which is London's greatest asset; nearly every corner of the globe is represented. Some of the best Indian and Chinese restaurants in the world can be found here.

Fast food restaurants serving pizzas, hamburgers, or fish and chips are convenient stopping places for visitors; they usually stay open all day and into the evening and fit comfortably into sightseeing schedules. Many also welcome children and most hamburger restaurants will produce high-chairs. Children are not made to feel quite so welcome in restaurants which cater largely to a business clientele at lunch-time or in the evening; the exceptions are hotel coffee shops and Chinese and Italian restaurants with a tradition of serving families.

On the whole it is advisable to use a guide-book or recommendation when looking for a special lunch or dinner, and to book. A short list of a range of restaurants appears below, but the following restaurant guides are recommended: Time Out's 'Eating Out in London', 'The Good Food Guide', published by the Consumers' Association, and the 'Egon Ronay Guide'. Use the current edition.

Prices (including VAT) and menus now have to be displayed outside restaurants; increasingly service is also included in the final bill, so an extra tip is at the customer's discretion. Wine tends to be marked up approximately 100 per cent, and look for extra charges for vegetables which can increase the final bill substantially. Set price menus, common in some of the best hotel restaurants at lunchtime, offer exceptionally good value for money. Restaurants, in general, serve lunch between 12.30 and 15.00; and dinner from 18.30 or 19.30 until 22.30 or later. Restaurants which serve after 23.00 (for after-theatre suppers) have been starred in the list below.

Something has been happening to English pubs over the past 10 years; the rather dusty, dark, comfortable Victorian pub is giving way to a gleaming, high tech themed environment with bouncers on the door and vibrating disco music inside, serving cocktails rather than beer. Fortunately, this development is limited mostly to suburban pubs where the breweries are busy attracting a younger market, and the sheer number of pubs in Greater London ensures that many will survive in a more traditional form. The list below includes some well-known names; in most cases they are mentioned in the text where some of their history is given.

Pub-food varies in quality but if in doubt stick to the cheese or pâté and bread which (served as a traditional 'Ploughman's lunch') is a filling meal with a pint of best bitter; wine is generally available and more pubs are now serving coffee. Under present regulations children are only welcome in pubs·if there is a children's room or a separate area set aside for meals. Children of 14 and over may be admitted to a bar and consume non-alcoholic drinks with an adult at the landlord's discretion. Children are welcome in the garden or terrace area of pubs (these regulations also apply to wine bars).

The Cross Keys, Endell Street, Covent Garden

Pubs may now sell alcohol 11.00–23.00 Monday to Saturday, 12.00–15.00 and 19.00-22.30/23.00 Sundays, if they wish to do so. These hours may be shorter in the suburbs, and in the City of London most pubs close at 20.00 and stay closed at the weekend. These licensing hours also apply to wine bars and restaurants. In licensed hotels alcoholic drinks can be served at any time to hotel guests.

Wine bars offer a relaxing environment in which to enjoy a good selection of wine and some delicious food. As in pubs, the choice and freshness of the food tends to be more inspiring at lunchtime. Wine bars cater to a very local clientele in the same way as pubs and have their own character. A few have been mentioned below.

Most restaurants in London look after women customers just as well as men; only a few of the more traditional ones are likely to seat a lone woman by the door to the kitchen. Many are also getting used to women being hosts, tasting the wine and paying the bill, although a little prompting may be necessary. On the whole wine bars offer a more pleasant environment for women out on their own than pubs.

Soho, traditionally a centre of good restaurants, is improving again after years of decline. Covent Garden is the fashionable area where many new restaurants have opened in the last few years.

The list below has been divided into geographical areas.
£ = moderate
££ = expensive
£££ = very expensive
*Open after 22.30 (and taking orders)

West End and Soho

Amalfi, 31 Old Compton St, W1 (071-437 7284), Italian, £ (until 23.00)*

Anemos, 34 Charlotte St, W1 (071-636 2289), Greek, £

Arirang Korean Restaurant, 32 Poland St, W1 (071-437 6633), £ (until 23.00)*

Au Jardin des Gourmets, 5 Greek St, W1 (071-437 1816), French, ££ (until 23.00)*

Bentley's Oyster Bar, 11–15 Swallow St, W1 (071-734 4756), English, ££

Café Italien des Amis du Vin, 19 Charlotte St, W1 (071-636 4174), Italian, ££

Chez Gerard, 8 Charlotte St, W1 (071-636 4975), French, ££, (until 23.30)*

Chicago Pizza Pie Factory, 17 Hanover Square, W1 (071-629 2669), American, £ (until 23.30)*

Chuen Cheng Ku, 17 Wardour St, W1 (071-437 1398), Chinese, £, (until 23.45)*

Coconut Grove, 3–5 Barrett St, W1 (071-486 5269), American,£ (until 23.15)*

Delhi Brasserie, 44 Frith St, W1 (071-437 8261), Indian, ££ (until 24.00)*

The Dorchester Grill, Dorchester Hotel, Park Lane, W1 (071-629 8888), English, £££, (until 23.00)* (Reopening late 1990)

Dumpling Inn, 15A Gerrard St, W1 (071-437 2567), Chinese, £ (until 23.30)*

L'Epicure, 28 Frith St, W1 (071-437 2829), French, ££ (until 23.15)*

L'Escargot, 48 Greek St, W1 (071-437 2679), French, ££ (until 23.30)*

Fahkreldine, 85 Piccadilly, W1 (071-493 3424), Arab, £££ (until 24.00)*

The Gay Hussar, 2 Greek St, W1 (071-437 0973), Hungarian, ££

Le Gavroche, 43 Upper Brook St, W1 (071-408 0881), French, £££ (until 23.00)*

Hard Rock Café, 150 Old Park Lane, W1 (071-629 0382), American, £ (until 24.00)*

Kettners, 29 Romilly St, W1 (071-437 6437), Italian/American, £ (until 24.00)*

Langan's Brasserie, Stratton St, W1 (071-493 6437), French, ££ (until 23.45)*

Olive Tree, 11 Wardour St, W1 (071-734 0808), Vegetarian, £ (until 24.00)*

Pasta Fino, 27 Frith St, W1 (071-439 8900), Italian, £ (until 23.30)*

Rasa Sayang, 10 Frith St, W1 (071-734 8720), Malaysian, £ (until 23.45)*

Ritz Restaurant, Piccadilly, W1 (071-493 8181), International, £££

Le Routier, 29 Foley St, W1 (071-631 3962), French, ££

Soho Brasserie, 23–25 Old Compton St, W1 (071-439 3758), French, £ (until 23.30)*

Wheeler's, 19 Old Compton St, W1 (071-437 2706), Fish, ££

Covent Garden/Leicester Square/The Strand

Boulestin, 25 Southampton St, WC2 (071-836 7061), French, £££ (until 23.15)*

Le Café des Amis du Vin, 11–14 Hanover Place, WC2 (071-379 3444), French, ££ (until 23.30)

Café Pacifico, 5 Langley St, WC2 (071-379 7728), American/Mexican, £ (until 23.45)

Chez Solange, 35 Cranbourn St, WC2 (071-836 5886), French, ££ (until 24.15)*

Food for Thought, 31 Neal St, WC2 (071-836 0239), Vegetarian, £(until 20.00)

Joe Allen, 13 Exeter St, WC2 (071-836 0651), American, ££ (until 24.00)*

Joy King Lau, 3 Leicester St, WC2 (071-437 1132), Chinese, £ (until 23.30)*

Last Days of the Raj, 22 Drury Lane, WC2 (071-836 1628), Indian, £ (until 23.30)*

Mon Plaisir, 21 Monmouth St, WC2 (071-836 7243), French, ££ (until 23.15)*

The Neal St Restaurant, 26 Neal St, WC2 (071-836 8368), International, £££

Poons, 4 Leicester St, WC2 (071-437 1528), Chinese, ££ (until 23.30)*

Porters, 17 Henrietta St, WC2 (071-836 6466), English, £

Rules, 35 Maiden Lane, WC2 (071-836 5314), English, ££ (until 23.15)*

The Savoy Grill, The Strand, WC2 (071-836 4347), English, £££ (until 23.15)*

Sheekey's, 28–32 St. Martin's Court, WC2 (071-240 2565), Fish, ££ (until 23.15)*

Simpsons in the Strand, 100 The Strand, WC2 (071-836 9112), English ££

Terrazza Est, 109 Fleet St, EC4 (071-353 2680), Italian, ££ (until 23.30)*

Bayswater

Bombay Palace, 50 Connaught St, W2 (071-723 8855), Indian, ££ (until 23.30)*

Kam Tung, 59–63 Queensway, W2 (071-229 6065), Chinese, £

Mandarin Kitchen, 14 Queensway, W2 (071-727 9012), Chinese, £ (until 23.30)

Knightsbridge/Chelsea/Kensington

Borscht n'Cheers, 45 Beauchamp Place, SW3 (071-589 5003), Russian, ££, (until 01.00)

Capital Hotel Restaurant, 22 Basil St, SW3 (071-589 5171), French, £££ (until 22.30)

Drakes, 2A Pond Place, SW3 (071-584 4555), English, ££ (until 23.30)*

The English House, 3 Milner St, SW3 (071-584 3002), English, ££ (until 23.15)

Ma Cuisine, 113 Walton St, SW3 (071-584 7585), French, £££ (until 23.00)*

San Lorenzo, 22 Beauchamp Place, SW3 (071-584 1074), Italian, ££ (until 23.30)*

La Tante Claire, 68 Royal Hospital Road, SW3 (071-351 0227), French, £££ (until 23.00)*

Eleven Park Walk, 11 Park Walk, SW10 (071-352 3449), Italian, ££ (until 24.00)*

Hungry Horse, 196 Fulham Road, SW10 (071-352 7757), English, ££ (until 23.00)*

Parsons, 311 Fulham Road, SW10 (071-352 0651), American, £ (until 24.30)*

Belgravia/Victoria

Bumbles, 16 Buckingham Palace Road, SW1 (071-828 2903), English, ££ (until 22.45)

Ciboure, 21 Eccleston St, SW1 (071-730 2505), French, ££ (until 23.30)*

Gavvers, 61 Lower Sloane St, SW1 (071-730 5983), French, ££ (until 23.00)*

Ken Lo's Memories of China, 67 Ebury St, SW1 (071-730 7734), Chinese, ££ (until 23.00)*

Locket's, Marsham Court, Marsham St, SW1 (071-834 9552), English, ££ (until 23.00)*

Pomegranates, 94 Grosvenor Road, SW1 (071-828 6560), International, ££ (until 23.15)*

Dolphin Brasserie, Dolphin Square, SW1 (071-828 3207), French, ££

Tate Gallery Restaurant, Millbank, SW1 (071-834 6754), English, ££ (lunch only)

The City/Islington

Rudland and Stubbs, 35–37 Greenhill Rents, Smithfield, EC1 (071-253 0148), English, Fish, ££ (until 23.30)*

Baron of Beef, Gutter Lane, EC2 (071-606 6961), English, ££ (until 21.00)

George & Vulture, 3 Castle St, EC3 (071-626 9710), English, ££ (lunch only)

Sweetings, 39 Queen Victoria St, EC4 (071-248 3062), Fish, ££ (lunch only)

Frederick's, Camden Passage, N1 (071-359 2888), French, ££ (until 23.30)*

Serendipity, The Mall, Camden Passage, N1 (071-359 1932), International, £ (until 24.00)*

South Bank/Southwark

Archduke Winebar/Restaurant, Concert Hall Approach, SE1 (071-928 9370), English/French, £, (until 24.00)

Tall House Wine Cellar/Restaurant, 134 Southwark St, SE1 (071-401 2929), English/French, ££, (Restaurant - lunch weekdays only).

   More information from the Restaurant Switchboard on 071-444 0044.

A selection of **Wine Bars**:

West End/Soho
Tracks, 17A Soho Square, W1 (071-439 2318) (until 23.00)
Cork and Bottle, 44–46 Cranbourn St, WC2 (071-734 7807) (until 22.45)

Covent Garden
Brahms & Liszt, 19 Russell St, WC2 (071-240 3661) (until 23.00)
Crusting Pipe, The Market, Covent Garden, WC2 (071-836 1415) (until 23.00)

Belgravia/Victoria
Blushes, 52 Kings Road, SW3 (071-589 6640) (until 23.00)
Carriages, 43 Buckingham Palace Road, SW1 (071-834 8871) (until 23.00)
Tiles, 36 Buckingham Palace Road, SW1 (071-834 7761) (until 23.00)
The Footstool, St. John's Smith Square, SW1, (071-222 2779) (Lunch; and before and after concerts)

The City
Mother Bunch's Wine House, Old Seacoal Lane, EC4 (071-236 5317) (until 20.30)

A selection of **Pubs:**

Mayfair and Marylebone
Audley's, 41 Mount St, W1
Duke of York, 45 Harrowby St, W1
Guinea, 30 Bruton Place, W1
Prince Regent, 71 Marylebone High St, W1
Red Lion, 1 Waverton St, W1
Shepherd's Tavern, 50 Hertford St, W1
Thistle, 11 Vigo St, W1
Ye Grapes, 16 Shepherd's Market, W1

St. James's
Blue Posts, 6 Bennet St, SW1
Red Lion, 23 Crown Passage, Pall Mall, SW1

Trafalgar Square
Sherlock Holmes, 10 Northumberland St, WC2
Tom Cribb, Panton St, WC2

Covent Garden
Maple Leaf, 41 Maiden Lane, WC2
Lamb & Flag, 33 Rose St, off Garrick St, WC2
Nag's Head, 10 James St, WC2
Nell of Old Drury, Catherine St, WC2
Salisbury, St. Martin's Lane, WC2

Bayswater and Notting Hill
Victoria, 10 Strathearn Place, W2
Windsor Castle, 114 Campden Hill Road, W8

Knightsbridge and Belgravia
Duke of Wellington, 63 Eaton Terrace, SW1
Grenadier, 18 Wilton Row, SW1
Paxton's Head, 153 Knightsbridge, SW1

Victoria and Westminster
Albert, Victoria St, SW1
Orange Brewery, 37 Pimlico Road, SW1
St. Stephen's Tavern, Bridge St, SW1
Two Chairmen, 39 Dartmouth St, SW1

Bloomsbury and Holborn
The Lamb, 94 Lamb's Conduit St, WC1
Museum Tavern, 49 Great Russell St, WC1
Ye Olde Mitre, Ely Place, Hatton Garden, EC1

Fleet St
Old Bell Tavern, 95 Fleet St, EC4
Printer's Devil, 98 Fetter Lane, EC4
Seven Stars, 53 Carey St, WC2
Ye Olde Cheshire Cheese, 145 Fleet St, EC4
Ye Olde Cock Tavern, Fleet St, EC4

City
The Black Friar, 174 Queen Victoria St, EC4
Cock Tavern, The Poultry Market, Central Markets, EC1
Dirty Dick's, 202 Bishopsgate, EC2
Fox and Anchor, 115 Charterhouse St, EC1
Hand & Shears, 1 Middle St, EC1
Railway Tavern, 15 Liverpool St, EC2
Samuel Pepys, Brooks Wharf, Upper Thames St, EC4
Ye Olde Dr Butler's Head, Masons Avenue, Coleman St, EC2
Ye Olde Watling, 29 Watling St, EC4

East London
Black Lion, 57 High St, Plaistow, E13
Dickens Inn, St. Katharine's Way, E1
Grapes, 76 Narrow St, E14
Hayfield, 156 Mile End Road, Stepney, E1
Prospect of Whitby, 57 Wapping Wall, E7

South-East London
Anchor, 1 Bankside, Southwark, SE1
Angel, 101 Bermondsey Wall East, SE16
Phoenix & Firkin, Denmark Hill Railway Station, SE5
The George, 77 Borough High St, Southwark, SE1
Mayflower, 117 Rotherhithe St, SE16
Prince of Orange, 118 Lower Road, SE16
Trafalgar Tavern, Park Row, SE10
Yacht, Crane St, SE10

South-West London
Hand in Hand, Crooked Billet, Wimbledon Common, SW19
Ship, 10 Thames Bank, Riverside, SW14
Sun Inn, 11 Church Road, Barnes, SW13
Victoria, 10 West Temple, Sheen, SW14
White Horse on Parsons Green, 1 Parsons Green, SW6
Ye Old Windmill Inn, Clapham Common Southside, SW4

West London
Bull's Head, Strand on the Green, W4
City Barge, Strand on the Green, W4
Dove, 19 Upper Mall, W6

North and North-West London
Albion, 10 Thornhill Road, N1
Bull & Bush, North End Way, NW3
Eagle, 2 Shepherdess Walk, N1
Flask, 77 West Hill, Highgate, N6
Jack Straw's Castle, North End Way, NW3
Prince Albert, 11 Princess Road, NW1
Spaniards Inn, Spaniards Road, NW3

*The Michelin Building previously the Michelin headquarters,
now fashionable shops and restaurants*

Shopping. The main shopping areas are Oxford St/Regent St/Bond
St, Knightsbridge, Kensington High St and Covent Garden. Normal
Monday to Saturday shopping hours are 09.00 to 17.30. Shops in
Covent Garden Market stay open until 20.00 but open at 10.00.
Oxford St and area and Kensington High St stores and shops stay
open until 19.00 on Thursdays; Knightsbridge until 19.00 on Wednes-
days. More and more shops are staying open until 20.00 on late-
shopping nights. Shopping hours are extended in the period before
Christmas; Christmas illuminations in Regent St and Oxford St are
switched on in mid-November and continue until 6 January.

The proposed lifting of Sunday trading restrictions would allow
shops and stores in the West End to open all week if they wished. At
present it is mostly suburban do-it-yourself centres and garden
centres which open on Sundays. Late-night 7-day a week supermarkets can be found at Trafalgar Square, in the Strand, in Queensway,
in South Kensington, in Fulham Road and in King's Road. There are

several good shopping guides to London; a small booklet is available from the BTA, 'Shopping in London'.

Shopping generally gives good value for money but certain goods are particularly worth buying for visitors to Britain: antiques (Camden Passage, Bond St, King's Road); woollens (Marks & Spencer, Scotch House); books (Foyles, Dillons, Hatchards); records, tapes (Our Price, Virgin, HMV Shop); hi-fi and photographic equipment (Tottenham Court Road).

Under the Retail Export Scheme operated by most major stores, visitors to Britain receive a refund on VAT paid in this country for certain goods. Information on how this is done is available in the stores which operate the scheme or from the BTA overseas offices; nationals from some countries will have to pay tax in their own country if they reclaim VAT paid in Britain.

Theatre. London's claim to be the theatre capital of the world may be hotly contested by New York but no visit to London, even by New Yorkers, would be complete without at least one visit to the theatre.

The early years of the London theatre can be explored at the Shakespeare Globe Museum on Bankside not far from the site of the original Globe Theatre where some of Shakespeare's plays were originally performed. A replica of the Globe Theatre is now being built near the museum where his plays will be performed as close to the original as possible. Nearby are the remains of the Rose Theatre (see p 291). The theatre of the past 200 years is covered in the Theatre Museum, Covent Garden, where the fine Victoria and Albert Museum collection is displayed in the old Flower Market building with its entrance facing Russell St.

The living theatre can be enjoyed every night of the week (except Sundays) and at matinees at some 40 West End theatres and equally numerous suburban and fringe theatres. The range of productions is wide, from Shakespeare to modern drama and from musicals to light-hearted comedy.

The publicly funded theatre sector is dominated by the Royal National Theatre on the South Bank and the Royal Shakespeare Company's Barbican Theatre in the City, although some fringe theatres also receive public money. The programmes of these two giants amongst theatre companies contain a mixture of classical and modern drama and occasional large-scale musicals. The Royal National Theatre, which opened in 1976, reveals inside its forbidding concrete exterior unrivalled facilities with three auditoria: the Olivier, the Lyttleton and the Cottesloe. Tours of the building include these as well as the workshops where all scenery and costumes are made.

The Barbican Theatre opened in 1982 in another, larger, concrete block which also houses a fine Concert Hall. The theatre is as large as the Olivier and the RSC also has a workshop theatre, the Pit. Both these buildings have superb technical as well as good public facilities including bars, snack-bars, restaurants, lavatories, disabled access and induction loops for the hard of hearing.

The commercial theatres on the whole thrive in London's West End, changing hands regularly, as the historic buildings represent substantial property assets continually threatened by redevelopment. Most are members of the Society of West End Theatres, which publishes the fortnightly 'London Theatre Guide'. Many of the older commercial theatres are attractions in their own right, some saved from demolition or redevelopment by the Theatres Trust. Of particular interest is the Theatre Royal Drury Lane; the present theatre dates from 1812—the fourth on the same site—reputedly with its own ghost. Recently restored and reopened is the historic Old Vic theatre, whose decor now reflects its Victorian music-hall past. Other theatres worth a close look before the house-lights go out include the Theatre Royal, Haymarket, the Albery, the Palace, the Criterion, the Duke of York, Her Majesty's, the Shaftesbury, the Savoy and the famous Palladium.

In suburban centres, public money has funded a number of new theatres, mostly of little architectural distinction but serving local audiences with pre-West End and touring productions. The Greenwich Theatre and the Lyric Hammersmith both originate their own productions. The true 'fringe' as opposed to suburban theatres can be found all over London, including the West End, in pubs, halls, theatres and clubs. New and experimental plays and revues are performed nightly sometimes on Sundays, and at lunchtime, by professional actors and actresses. Pub-theatre is particularly enjoyable at the King's Head, Islington where a meal is served before the performance. At the Bush, Theatre Royal Stratford East, the Albany, the Orange Tree, and the Tricycle new playwrights are encouraged.

In summer theatre can be enjoyed out of doors at the Regent's Park Open Air Theatre where Shakespeare is magically performed under the trees and only the occasional aircraft on its way to Heathrow intrudes; Holland Park also has a theatre season in August.

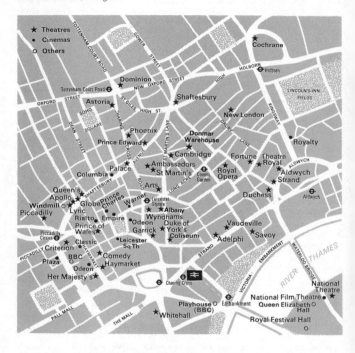

How to Book. Modern marketing techniques and new technology have combined to make it much easier to book for the theatre. (Theatre box offices are usually open from 10.00.) Telephone bookings using credit cards can be made on the theatre's own credit line or through a ticket agent (24 Hours), see below; most international cards are accepted. Tickets are posted or collected at the theatre.

Theatre ticket agents at stations, around Piccadilly Circus and in hotels can charge any price they like, although the original price of the ticket must be shown. Use Keith Prowse, Ticketmaster or First Call, all of whom charge a fixed set amount above the ticket price. Half-price tickets (plus a small commission charge) are available on the day of performance from the Half Price Ticket Booth in Leicester Square operated by the Society of West End Theatre. SWET also operates a discount scheme for pensioners at matinée performances and discounts are available for students at most theatres under the student standby scheme.

Evening performances start at 19.30 or 20.00; matinées are usually on Wednesdays or Thursdays and on Saturdays at 15.00 or sometimes at 17.00. 'The Observer', 'The Times', 'The Evening Standard' and 'The Independent' newspapers have good theatre guides. 'Time Out', 'What's On', and 'City Limits' provide weekly listings with descriptions of plays. Theatre tickets cost from £5 to £24 depending on the production; fringe theatres cost from £4 to £8; opera tickets cost from £12 upwards. Stalls and dress circles seats give the best views; boxes usually have a restricted view of the stage and the upper circle can be cramped and hot, especially in older theatres.

Keith Prowse, 081-741 9999.
First Call 071-836 3464.
Ticketmaster 071-379 4444.
Half Price Ticket Booth, from 12.00 for matinées; from 14.30 for eve. performances.
Society of West End Theatre, 071-836 0971.

Music, Opera and Dance.
Four symphony orchestras, three opera companies and two major ballet companies have their home in London in addition to numerous smaller orchestras, large and small choirs, and a variety of dance groups. The Royal Festival Hall on the South Bank has nightly performances of mostly classical music with a ballet season in the summer and at Christmas. The Queen Elizabeth Hall and Purcell Room are part of the facilities here and are used for recitals and chamber music concerts. The Barbican Concert Hall is the home of the London Symphony Orchestra which plays for three six-week seasons a year. Visiting orchestras complete the programme. In Croydon the Fairfield Halls with a purpose built concert hall has magnificent acoustics.

The magnificent Royal Albert Hall in Kensington is used for a variety of events including wrestling. But in July, August and September music takes over completely for the famous Henry Wood Promenade Concerts organised by the BBC; those with the stamina for standing can enjoy first class music inexpensively (seating is also available). The summer also sees outdoor concerts at Kenwood Lakeside and Marble Hill House.

The Greenwich Festival in June and the City of London Festival in July provide unique opportunities for enjoying music in unusual settings such as the Royal Naval Chapel at Greenwich and the livery halls in the City. Lunchtime and evening concerts can be enjoyed in smaller concert halls and churches; regular venues are St. John's Smith Square, the Wigmore Hall, St. Martin in the Fields and St. Bartholomew the Great (information from tourist information centres or newspapers). The periods before Christmas and Easter see a number of special performances of church music and carols in cathedrals and churches, including Westminster Abbey, St. Paul's Cathedral and Westminster Cathedral, in addition to their regular services and choir concerts.

At Covent Garden's Royal Opera House ballet and opera alternate. The audience cannot fail to be impressed with the splendid environments and professional performances. Gradually the 125-year old building is being extended and improved back-stage to provide the facilities required by today's opera companies. This may involve closing the Royal Opera House for several seasons in the early 1990s. The Coliseum in St. Martin's Lane offers opera in English and, at Sadlers Wells opera, operetta and dance make up a lively programme which features many visiting companies. The London Contemporary Dance Theatre and Ballet Rambert appear regularly at Sadlers Wells, The Place and other venues.

The musical variety on offer in London also includes traditional music hall entertainment at the Players' Theatre (a club), in some pubs and on Thames evening cruises. Jazz flourishes in pubs as well as clubs: Ronnie Scott's and the 100 Club are perhaps the best known. Good Jazz pubs are The Bull's Head, Barnes Bridge, SW13, Lord Napier, 111 Beulah Road, Thornton Heath, Surrey, and the Prince of Orange, 118 Lower Road, SE16. Try also Pizza Express, 10 Dean St, W1.

It is undoubtedly on the pop and rock scene that British artists have made their strongest international impact in recent years. Up-and-coming groups play in pubs and clubs. Established stars appear at bigger venues such as the Hammersmith Odeon, Wembley, London Arena and Earls Court (information in 'Time Out' or music papers).

Concert and opera tickets can be booked like theatre tickets. Pop concert tickets are offered by post in advance and some are made available from agents, particularly Keith Prowse and Premier Box Office. Note: pop and rock concerts and some popular musicals attract ticket-touts who sell tickets outside the doors or by small-ads in some newspapers at highly inflated prices. This is not illegal but occasionally the tickets are not genuine or are double-booked; the buyer should beware and stick to normal sources wherever possible.

Keith Prowse, 081-741 9999.
Premier Box Office, 071-240 2245.

Cinema. The cinema industry in London is going through a temporary boom despite the growth of home videos. Central London is particularly well served by large and small cinemas with a good selection of programmes; films are shown from early afternoon and several cinemas have late-night performances. Seats are usually bookable, at least direct from the box office, and most cinemas now ban smoking or allow it only in a limited section of the auditorium. The National Film Theatre (see p 287), with three auditoria and an interesting mix of films, welcomes temporary members. 'Time Out' and 'The Evening Standard' give details of film programmes; the former with a resumé of each film.

Art Exhibitions. At any one time there may be as many as 100 different art exhibitions in museums, and in major and minor galleries all over London. The big touring exhibitions are usually shown at the Hayward Gallery on the South Bank (see p 287) or at the Royal Academy of Arts (p 116). The Tate Gallery presents large scale exhibitions of individual artists' work and schools of painting in addition to its permanent exhibition. The National Gallery, the National Portrait Gallery, the British Museum and the Victoria and Albert Museum also stage art exhibitions. Items from the Queen's own collection are shown at the Queen's Gallery (see p 106). At the Serpentine Gallery, there is mainly modern art, and the Whitechapel Gallery offers an interesting programme of exhibitions including their own Open Exhibition for artists in the area.

The major open exhibition is of course the Royal Academy Summer Exhibition, held annually in June through to August. The Barbican Art Gallery has established itself as a major venue (see p 241) both for touring and its own exhibitions. Smaller galleries worth exploring are the Camden Arts Centre (see p 390), the Bankside Gallery (see p 291), the South London Art Gallery (see p 331), the Crafts Council Gallery (see p 108), the ICA Gallery (see p 101) and the Photographers' Gallery (see p 166).

A large number of private galleries display and sell paintings, prints, etchings and photographs. Many are concentrated in the area of Cork St, N of Piccadilly, Portobello Road also has a large concentration of galleries.

Art auctions take place at London's major auction rooms: Christie's, 8 King St, St. James's, SW1 (071-839 9060), Sotheby's, 34 and 35 New Bond St, W1 (071-493 8080), and Phillips, Son & Neale, Blenstock House, 7 Blenheim St, W1 (071-629 6602).

Spectator Sports. Main sports centres are at Crystal Palace, London Arena and Wembley where athletics, badminton, football, gymnastics, hockey, judo and swimming take place. Wembley Arena, Wembley, is used for show-jumping. Football and rugby finals are held at the main Wembley Stadium.

Athletics. The Amateur Athletics Association, Francis House, Francis St, SW1 (071-828 9326) organises major athletics events and can give information on clubs and facilities.

Badminton. The All England championships take place at Wembley in March. Contact the Badminton Association, National Badminton Centre, Bradwell Road, Loughton Lodge, Milton Keynes (0908 568822).

Basketball. Championships are held at Wembley and at the London Arena. English Basketball Association, Calomax House, Lupton Avenue, Leeds (0532 496044).

Boxing. Amateur championships are held in May at Wembley and the Royal Albert Hall. Events details from the London Amateur Boxing Association, Suite 68–69, Hop Exchange, 24 Southwark St, SE1 (071-407 2194).

Cricket. The cricket season begins in May and major matches take place at Lords and the Oval. Local cricket matches are played on 'greens' throughout suburban London and the South East. The Marylebone Cricket Club (MCC), the governing body, has its headquarters at Lord's, St. John's Wood Road, NW8 (071-289 1611); here test (international) matches, cup finals and Middlesex games are played. Surrey County matches are played at the Oval, Kennington Lane, SE11 (071-735 4911). First-class matches last for three days but there are now an increasing number of one day games.

Cycling. The Round Britain Milk Race (outside London) takes place in late May/June. There is a road circuit at Eastway Cycle Circuit, Lee Valley Park, Temple Mills Lane, E15 (081-534 6085). Contact British Cycling Federation, 16 Upper Woburn Place, WC1 (071-387 9320).

Association Football (soccer) is played from August to May. International matches and the finals of the FA (Football Association) Cup are held at Wembley. Tickets for cup finals are allocated through the clubs and sometimes sold through 'touts' at inflated prices, Beware! Local football matches take place on Saturday afternoons and some Wednesday evenings. Visitors are recommended to go in the stands with seating; any trouble at matches is more likely amongst standing spectators.

Arsenal FC, Highbury Stadium, Avenell Rd, N5 (071-226 0304); *Brentford FC*, Griffin Park, Braemar Rd, Brentford (081-560 2021); *Chelsea FC*, Stamford Bridge, Fulham Rd, SW6 (071-381 6221); *Crystal Palace FC, Charlton Athletic FC*, Selhurst Park, SE25 (081-771 6321) (Charlton is due to move back to the Valley at Charlton in 1990/91); *Fulham FC*, Craven Cottage, Stevenage Rd, SW6 (071-736 6561); *Millwall FC*, The Den, Cold Blow Lane, SE14 (071-639 3143); *Orient FC*, Leyton Stadium, Brisbane Rd, E10 (081-539 2223); *Queen's Park Rangers FC*, South Africa Rd, W12 (071-743 0262); *Tottenham Hotspur FC*, 748 High Rd, N17 (081-808 1020); *West Ham United FC*, Boleyn Ground, Green St, E13 (081-470 1325); *Wimbledon FC*, 49 Durnsford Rd, SW19 (081-946 6311).

Greyhound Racing. This takes place mostly in the evening with betting as the most important part of the proceedings. Tracks are at: *Walthamstow Stadium*, Chingford Road, (081-531 4255), *Wembley Stadium*, Empire Way, Wembley (081-902 8833), *Wimbledon Stadium*, Plough Lane, SW17 (081-946 5361), *Catford Stadium*, Adenmore Rd, SE6 (081-690 2261). Crayford Stadium, Crayford Road (0322 522262), Hackney Stadium, Waterden Road, E15 (081-986 3511) and Romford Stadium, London Road, Romford (0708 762345

Horse Racing. The flat-racing season lasts from March to November; in winter it is mostly hurdle racing and steeplechasing. The main events are the Derby at Epsom (14m SW of London) in early June—a great occasion with a good social mix on Epsom Downs, followed by the slightly more up-market and fashionable Ascot Week at Ascot Heath (5m SW of Windsor) to which the presence of the royal family adds glamour. Kempton Park (Sunbury on Thames), Lingfield Park (Lingfield Surrey), Sandown Park (Esher, Surrey), and Windsor, Berks, are convenient race courses for visitors staying in London. Details in the daily newspapers and from the Racing Information Bureau, Winkfield Road, Ascot, Berks (0990 25912).

Motor-Racing. The nearest circuit is at Brands Hatch, Fawkham, Kent (off the A20) (0474 872331). Stock-car racing takes place at Wimbledon Stadium, Plough Lane, SW17 (081-946 5361) on most Sundays.

Polo is played at Windsor Great Park; for details of matches contact the Hurlingham Polo Association (079 85 277).

Rowing. The most famous rowing event in the calendar is the Oxford and Cambridge Boat Race, usually rowed on a Saturday before Easter between Putney and Mortlake (4.25m); good viewing points from the banks and bridges (see p 310). The Head of the River Race, the largest of its kind in the world, is held in March. Doggett's Coat and Badge Race is more of a traditional event and rowed in July (see p 303). Contact the Amateur Rowing Association, 6 Lower Mall, Hammersmith, W6 (081-748 3632) for details of other events.

Rugby Union. Twickenham is the main venue for the amateur rugby union matches; local games take place at Blackheath, Richmond, Sunbury-on-Thames and Roehampton. The finals of the *Rugby League* take place at Wembley in May. The Rugby Football Union is at Whitton Road, Twickenham, Middlesex (081-892 8161).

Show Jumping. The two main events in London are the Horse of the Year Show at Wembley in October, and the Olympia International

Show Jumping Championships at Olympia in December. Contact the British Show Jumping Association, British Equestrian Centre, Kenilworth, Warwickshire (0203 552511).

Tennis. The All England Lawn Tennis Championships take place at Wimbledon for two weeks towards the end of June. Tickets are allocated in advance although some (usually at inflated prices) are available from ticket agencies, and tour operators. It is possible to go on the day and pay an entrance charge to watch matches on the outside courts, non-ticketed, and in the standing areas of the main courts. Wimbledon is preceded by the Queen's Club tournament and a week before that by the championships at Beckenham (see p 333) where some of the major competitors 'warm up' for the grass courts at Wimbledon. There are indoor tournaments at the Royal Albert Hall and Wembley. The sport is governed by the Lawn Tennis Association, Barons Court, W14 (071-385 2366). The All England Lawn Tennis & Croquet Club is at Church Road, SW19 (081-946 2244).

Participant Sports. Most of London's parks have sports facilities for the public (cricket, football, tennis, putting, golf, etc.). Apply for information to the Town Hall of the London Borough concerned, or the local library. Indoor sports facilities can be enjoyed by the public at the National Sports Centre, Crystal Palace, SE19 (081-778 0131) (small membership fee), and at Brixton Recreation Centre, Brixton Station Road, SW9 (071-274 7774), entrance charge. The London Docklands Arena also has indoor athletics facilities as well as catering for other sports. Contact the London Arena on 071-538 8880.

Cycling. See p 21 for information on hiring bicycles. For touring information contact the Cyclists Touring Club, 69 Meadrow, Godalming, Surrey, GU7 3HS (048 68 7217). The BTA also publishes a useful booklet.

Fishing. An extremely popular sport; join in by fishing along the canals, the Thames, and in Lee Valley Park. Information from the London Anglers Association, Forest Road Hall, Kervey Park Road, E17 (081-520 7477).

Golf. Played all the year round on a number of courses; many of the best are club courses and an introduction from a member is essential. But there are also many good public courses, some are listed here. Phone first to check on handicap, fees, weekend availability of course and clubs: Woodford Golf Course, Sunset Ave, Woodford Green, Essex, tel. 081-504 0553 (U Woodford); Bush Hill Park Golf Course, Winchmore Hill, N21, Tel. 081-360 5738 (BR Grange Park); Enfield Golf Course, Old Park Road, Enfield, Mx, tel. 081-363 3970 (BR Enfield Chase); Highgate Golf Course, Denewood Road, N6, tel. 081-340 3745 (U Highgate); Grims Dyke Golf Course, Oxhey Lane, Hatch End, Mx, tel. 081-428 4093 (BR Hatch End); Haste Hill Golf Course, The Drive, Northwood, Mx, tel. 09274 26485 (U Northwood); Northwood Golf Club, Rickmansworth Road, Northwood, Mx, tel. 09274 20112 (U Northwood); Beckenham Place Park Golf Course, Beckenham Place Park, Southend Road, Beckenham, Kent, tel. 081-650 2292 (BR Beckenham Junction); Surbiton Golf Course, Woodstock Lane, Chessington, Surrey, tel. 081-398 3101 (BR Hinchley Wood).

Ice Skating. There are now six ice rinks in the Greater London area: *Lee Valley Ice Centre*, Lea Bridge Road, Leyton E10 (081-533 3151); *Queen's Ice Skating Club*, 17 Queensway, W2 (071-229 0172); *Richmond Ice Rink*, Clevedon Rd, Twickenham (until Dec. 1990), *Romford Ice Rink*, Romford Valley Way, Romford, Essex (0708 724731); Twickenham (081-892 3646); *Streatham Ice Rink*, 386 Streatham High Rd, SW16 (081-769 7861); *Sobell Sports Centre Ice Rink*, Hornsey Road, N7 (071-607 1632).

Riding. There are riding schools throughout Outer London which welcome visitors. Riding in Hyde Park can be a little more difficult to arrange as horses are booked by regulars. Contact: *Richard Briggs Riding Stables*, 63 Bathurst Mews, W2 (071-723 2813), *Ross Nye's Riding Establishment*, 8 Bathurst Mews, W2 (071-262 3791), *Roehampton Gate Stables*, Priory Lane, SW15 (081-876 7089).

Skiing. Not a sport immediately associated with London! but there are dry ski slopes at Alexandra Park, N22, Crystal Palace, SE19, Woolwich, SE18 and Beckton, E6. The major event is the International Ski Show at Earl's Court in November.

Squash. Private squash clubs have sprung up all over London. Contact the Squash Rackets Association, Francis St, SW1 (071-828 3064) for details of clubs. The following welcome visitors: *The Oasis*, Endell St, WC2 (071-836 9555); *Wembley Squash Courts*, Empire Way, Wembley (081-902 9230), *Dolphin Square*, Grosvenor Road, SW1 (071-798 8686).

Swimming. Olympic-size pools are at Crystal Palace and Brixton Recreation Centre (see above). Many of London's public baths have updated their facilities and become health centres with a range of facilities; some have wave machines and waterslides. Swimming outdoors at the Serpentine (see p 125). The following welcome visitors: Chelsea Manor St, SW3 (071-352 6985); Ironmonger Row, EC1 (071-253 4011); Kensington New Pools, Walmer Rd, W11 (071-727 9923); Marshall St, W1 (071-439 4678); Oasis, Endell St, WC2 (071-836 9555); Porchester Baths, Queensway, W2 (071-798 3689); Seymour Pl, W1 (071-798 1421). Water Palace, Purley Way, Croydon.

Health and Fitness Centres. Several of London's hotels now offer facilities for guests (Grosvenor House, Le Meridien, Piccadilly, Kensington Close, Selsdon Park, the Rembrandt Hotel) and a number of commercial centres welcome visitors. *Fitness Centre*, 11 Floral St, WC2 (071-836 6544); *Westside Fitness & Leisure Club*, 201–207 Kensington High St, W8 (071-937 5386); *The Sanctuary and Dance Centre*, 12 Floral St, WC2 (071-836 6544); *Pineapple*, 7 Langley St, WC2 (071-836 4004), *Pineapple West*, 60 Paddington St, W1 (071-487 3444); *Dance Works*, 16 Balderton St, W1 (071-629 6183).

Opening Hours, Parks

The Sights. The table below gives opening hours of the most popular tourist attractions and indicates which have admission charges. In the text opening hours are given for all the attractions mentioned. In general, it should be noted that last admissions are usually half an hour before the stated closing time and most national museums and galleries are closed on Sunday mornings (usually they open at 14.30); they also close on Good Friday and New Year's Day. Commercial and all other attractions including museums and galleries close on Christmas Day; some also close on Christmas Eve and Boxing Day. Check with LTB. Season tickets for attractions are offered under the Great British Heritage Pass scheme, available for overseas visitors—details from the BTA Overseas Offices and tourist information centres.

English Heritage also offers a season ticket to monuments in its care; the National Trust operates a similar scheme for members.

Tours and lectures in museums and galleries are usually free of charge; special lectures are put on to coincide with special exhibitions. Pre-booking is not usually required.

Children's events are organised by all the major museums during the school holidays; details from each one or from tourist information centres.

Opening hours of cathedrals and churches vary greatly and have been entered in the text; City churches are usually closed at weekends and suburban churches are usually kept locked during the week.

HOURS OF ADMISSION

	Mon-Sat	Sundays	Notes
Apsley House	11.00–17.00	11.00–17.00	Closed Mon
Banqueting House	10.00–17.00	14.00–17.00	Closed Mon
Bethnal Green Museum of Childhood	10.00–18.00	14.30–18.00	Closed Fri
British Museum	10.00–17.00	14.30–18.00	
Cabinet War Rooms	10.00–17.50	10.00–17.50	
Carlyle's House	11.00–17.00	11.00–17.00	Closed Mon & Tues except BH Mon. Closed Nov–March
Chelsea Hospital	10.00–12.00 14.00–16.00	14.00–16.00	
Chiswick House	10.00–18.00		Oct–March shorter hours
Courtauld Institute Galleries	10.00–18.00	14.00–18.00	
Dickens' House	10.00–17.00		Closed Sun
Dulwich Gallery	10.00–13.00 14.00–17.00	14.00–17.00	Closed Mon
Florence Nightingale Museum	10.00–16.00		Closed Mon, Sun

	Mon-Sat	Sundays	Notes
Geffrye Museum	10.00–17.00	14.00–17.00	Closed Mon but open BH Mon 10.00–17.00
Ham House	11.00–17.00	11.00–17.00	Closed Mon
Hampton Court	9.30–18.00	9.30–18.00	Closed 16.30 in winter
Hayward Gallery	10.00–18.00 till 20.00 Tues, Wed	12.00–18.00	During exhibitions only
Imperial War Museum	10.00–18.00	14.00–18.00	
Johnson's House	11.00–17.30		Closed Sun 17.00 winter
Keats's House	14.00–18.00 Sat 10.00–17.00	14.00–17.00	Closed 17.00 in winter
Kensington Palace	9.00–17.00	13.00–17.00	
Kenwood	10.00–16.00	10.00–16.00	Longer hours in summer
Kew Gardens	9.30–dusk	9.30–dusk	Shorter hours in winter
London Zoo	9.00–18.00 or dusk		Shorter hours in winter
Madame Tussaud's	10.00–17.30 Sat 9.30–17.30	9.30–17.30	
Museum of London	10.00–18.00	14.00–18.00	Closed Mon
Museum of the Moving Image	10.00–20.00	10.00–18.00	Closed Mon
National Army Museum	10.00–17.30	14.00–17.30	
National Gallery	10.00–18.00	14.00–18.00	Wed in June, July, Aug 20.00
National Maritime Museum	10.00–18.00	14.00–18.00	Closed 17.00 in winter
National Portrait Gallery	10.00–17.00 Sat 10.00–18.00	14.00–18.00	
Natural History Museum	10.00–18.00	13.00–18.00	

	Mon-Sat	*Sundays*	*Notes*
Osterley Park House	11.00–17.00	11.00–17.00	Closed Mon Open some BH Mon
Queen's Gallery	10.30–17.00	14.00–17.00	Closed Mons except BH
Royal Academy	10.00–18.00	10.00–18.00	
Royal Mews	14.00–16.00		Wed & Thur only. Closed Ascot Week
St. Paul's Cathedral	10.00–16.00	Services only	
Science Museum	10.00–18.00	11.00–18.00	
Soane Museum	10.00–17.00		Closed Mon, Sun
Syon House	12.00–17.00	12.00–17.00	Closed Fri, Sat. Closed Oct–Easter Open Sun only in Oct
Tate Gallery	10.00–17.50	14.00–17.50	
Theatre Museum	11.00–19.00	11.00–19.00	Closed Mon
Tower Bridge	10.00–18.30	10.00–16.45	Until 16.30 in winter
Tower of London	9.30–17.00 (March–Oct) 9.30–16.00 (Nov–Feb)	14.00–17.00 (March–Oct)	Closed Sun (Nov–Feb)
Victoria and Albert Museum	10.00–18.00	14.30–18.00	
Wallace Collection	10.00–17.00	14.00–17.00	
Westminster Abbey	9.00–16.45 Sat 9.00–14.45, 15.45–17.45	Services	Until 20.00 Wed. Chapter House, Pyx Chamber shorter hours
Windsor Castle	10.30–16.30 March–Oct, 10.30–14.30 Nov–Feb		Precincts open daily Other times may vary

Parks and gardens are a special feature of London; they stay green all the year round and the Royal Parks Department (Dept of the Environment) and the individual London Boroughs maintain flower displays virtually all the year round. LTB runs a London In Bloom campaign and competition annually. The major parks are covered in the text; visitors with a horticultural interest should explore Kew Gardens, Chelsea Physic Garden, Dulwich Park, Golders Hill, Greenwich Park, Hall Place Gardens, Bexley, Ham House, Hampton Court Palace Gardens, Holland Park, Horniman Gardens, the Isabella Plantation, Richmond Park, Kenwood, Hampstead, Kensington Gardens, Kensington Roof Gardens, Queen Mary's Rose Garden, Regent's Park, and Syon Park Garden, Brentford.

A favourite with young and old, the Peter Pan statue in Kensington Gardens

Specialised Museums and Collections. Almost every interest or hobby can be studied in one of London's museums or specialist collections. The list below gives an indication.

Aircraft	RAF Museum (Hendon), Science Museum, Imperial War Museum
Art	National Gallery, Tate Gallery, Courtauld Institute . Galleries, Royal Academy of Arts, Dulwich Picture Gallery, Wallace Collection, Hayward Gallery
Antiquities	British Museum, Victoria and Albert
Chinese Ceramic	British Museum, David Percival Foundation of Chinese Art, Victoria and Albert
Clocks	Old Royal Observatory (Greenwich), Guildhall Museum
Craft	Crafts Council Gallery, Victoria and Albert,
Fashion	Victoria and Albert, Museum of London, Kensington Palace (Court Dress Collection)
Industrial Design	Science Museum, Victoria and Albert, The Design Centre, Design Museum
London History	Museum of London, London Transport Museum, Greater London Record Library
Manuscripts, Records, Charters	British Library, Public Record Office Museum, General Register Office, College of Arms
Maritime History	National Maritime Museum, Cutty Sark (Greenwich), Science Museum, HMS Belfast
Medicine	Science Museum (Wellcome Galleries), Hunterian Museum, Old Operating Theatre (Southwark), Florence Nightingale Museum
Musical Instruments	Horniman Museum (Forest Hill), Ranger's House (Blackheath), Fenton House (Hampstead), Musical Museum (Brentford), Royal College of Music, Victoria and Albert
Postal History and Stamps	National Postal Museum, British Museum, Bruce Castle Museum (Tottenham)
Private houses of the famous	Apsley House (Duke of Wellington), Dr Johnson's House, Linley Sambourne House, Dickens House, Keats House (Hampstead), Kensington Palace, Carlyle's House, Soane Museum , Freud Museum
Telephones & Technology	Telecom Technology Showcase, Science Museum
Theatre	Shakespeare Globe Museum (Southwark), Theatre Museum

Toys	Bethnal Green Museum of Childhood, London Toy and Model Museum, Pollock's Toy Museum
Sport	Cricket Memorial Gallery, Lords, Wimbledon Tennis Museum, Wembley Stadium Tours
War	Imperial War Museum, National Army Museum, Tower of London, Cabinet War Rooms, Royal Artillery Museum & Rotunda (Woolwich), HMS Belfast, RAF Museum, Guards Museum
Transport	London Transport Museum, Science Museum, The Heritage Motor Museum (Cars), Syon Park

Calendar of Major Events

Below are some of London's major annual events. For exact dates check with tourist information centres. (Traditional events marked *.)

January	International Boat Show, Earls Court *Charles I Commemoration, Trafalgar Square
February	Crufts Dog Show (poss. Birmingham) *Pancake Day Races, various locations
Jan/Feb	Chinese New Year, celebrations in Soho
March	Ideal Home Exhibition, Earls Court Oxford v Cambridge Boat Race Head of the River Race
Easter	*Butterworth Charity, St. Bartholomew the Great Easter Parade, Battersea Park *Harness Horse Parade, Regent's Park International Model Railway Exhibition, RHS Halls International Festival of Country Music, Wembley
April	Chelsea Antiques Fair, Chelsea Old Town Hall *St. George's Day, Shakespeare's Birthday, Southwark Cathedral London Marathon (Greenwich to Westminster) London Book Fair, Olympia
May *1st Mon*	Bank Holiday; Marches; May Festival FA Cup Final, Wembley Rugby League Final, Wembley Royal Windsor Horse Show, Windsor Park Biggin Hill Air Fair, Biggin Hill
Ascension Day	*Beating the Bounds, Tower of London (every 3 years: 1990,1993 etc.) Chelsea Flower Show Fine Art and Antique Fair, Olympia
End last Mon *29*	Open Air Theatre, Regent's Park—until August Bank Holiday *Oak Apple Day, Royal Hospital, Chelsea
June **2nd or 3rd Sat**	*Beating the Retreat, Horse Guards *Trooping the Colour, Horse Guards Parade: Queen's Official Birthday

The Derby, Epsom
Ascot week, Ascot
Greenwich Festival (two weeks)
Tennis Tournament, Queen's Club
Grosvenor House Antiques Fair
All England Lawn Tennis Championships, Wimbledon
Antiquarian Book Fair
*Garter Ceremony, St. George's Chapel, Windsor
London to Brighton Bicycle Race

July

Henley Regatta
Royal Tournament (three weeks)
City of London Festival (two weeks)
Henry Wood Promenade Concerts, Royal Albert Hall—until September
*Swan Upping; from Maidenhead
*Doggetts Coat and Badge Race
Metropolitan Police Horseshow, Imber Court, Surrey
Street Entertainers Festival

August

*London Riding Horse Parade, Hyde Park
Greenwich Clipper Weeks, Greenwich

last Mon

Bank Holiday: Westminster and Greater London Horse Show, Notting Hill Carnival
Fairs, Hampstead Heath and other locations

September

Chelsea Antiques Fair, Chelsea Old Town Hall
Burlington House Antiques Fair, Royal Academy
British Craft Show, Syon Park
*Horseman's Sunday, Church of St. John and St. Michael, W2
*Punch and Judy Festival, Covent Garden

October

Park Lane Antiques Fair, Park Lane
*Law Courts Open, Westminster Abbey
London to Brighton Road Running Race
Horse of the Year Show, Wembley
*Pearly Kings and Queens, Harvest Service, St. Martin in the Fields

21

*Trafalgar Day, Trafalgar Square
Motorfair, Earls Court
British Philatelic Exhibition, RHS Halls

November

*State Opening of Parliament (or late October)
London to Brighton Veteran Car Run (Hyde Park)

5

Guy Fawkes Day, fireworks, bonfires, various locations

Sun nearest 11th

*Remembrance Sunday

2nd Sat

*Lord Mayor's Show
Christmas Illuminations in West End

December

Royal Smithfield Show, Earls Court (4 days)
Christmas Tree illuminated, Trafalgar Square
Olympia International Showjumping Championships

25/26

Christmas Day/Boxing Day—public holidays

Useful Contacts

Tourist Information. Before arrival in London, information is available through the overseas offices of the **British Tourist Authority** in many countries. Make contact by telephone or post for up-to-date information. Below are listed some of BTA's offices:

Australia: BTA, 4th Floor, Midland House, 171 Clarence St, Sydney, NSW 2000 (29-8627).

Canada: BTA, 94 Cumberland St, Suite 600, Ontario M5R 3N3

Netherlands: BTA, Aurora Gebouw (5e), Stadhouderskade 2, 1054 ES Amsterdam (855051).

New Zealand: BTA, 8th Floor, Norwich Union Building, Queen and Durham Streets, Auckland (31446).

Ireland: 123 Lower Baggot Street,Dublin 2 (614188).

USA: BTA, John Hancock Centre, Suite 3320, 875 N Michigan Ave, Chicago, Ill. 60611 (7870490); Cedar Maple Plaza, Suite 210, 2305 Cedar Springs Rd, Dallas, Texas 75201 (720 4040); World Trade Center, 350 South Figueroa St, Suite 450, Los Angeles, CA90071 (628 3525); 3rd Floor, 40 West 57th Street, New York, NY 100102 (581 4700).

Tourist information in London is available through the services of the **London Tourist Board**, the official tourist board for London.

Tourist Information Centre, Victoria Station Forecourt, SW1. Open daily, summer 08.00–20.00; winter Monday–Saturday 09.00–19.00, Sunday 09.00–17.00. Services include tourist information, instant hotel bookings in London and throughout England, theatre and tour bookings, sales of tourist tickets, guidebooks and maps in extensive bookshop.

LTB, Tourist Information Centre, West Gate, Tower of London, EC3. Open daily Apr to Oct, 10.00–18.00.

LTB, Tourist Information Centre, Selfridges Department Store, Basement, Oxford Street, W1. Open store hours.

LTB, Tourist Information Centre, Harrods Department Store, Basement, Knightsbridge, SW1. Open store hours.

LTB, Tourist Information Centre, Liverpool Street Station. Open Mon to Sat 09.30–18.30; Sun 08.30–15.30.

LTB, Information Centre, Terminals 1, 2 3 Underground station concourse, *Heathrow Airport*. Open daily 08.00– 18.30. Services include tourist information, hotel reservations and tour bookings.

Telephone enquiries to LTB on 071-730 3488 (Monday–Friday 09.00–18.00). Riverboat information is available on 071-730 4812. Written enquiries should be addressed to LTB, Correspondence, 26 Grosvenor Gardens, London SW1W 0DU.

The City of London Information Centre is at St. Paul's Churchyard, EC4. Open 09.30–17.00 Mon to Fri, 09.30–12.00 Sat (071–606 3030).

An all-Britain Travel Centre is at 12 Regent St, SW1, (071-730 3400) open 09.00-18.30 Mon to Fri; 10.00-16.00 Sat; 10.00-16.00 Sun. (Extended hours in summer)

Local information is available from the following centres:

Bloomsbury Tourist Information Centre, 35-36 Woburn Place, WC1 (071-580 8284);*Clerkenwell Heritage* (Islington Visitor) *Centre*, 33–35 St. John's Square, EC1 (071-250 1039); *Croydon*

Tourist Information Centre, Katharine Street, Croydon (081-760 5630); *Greenwich Tourist Information Centre*, 46 Greenwich Church Street, SE10 (081-858 6376); *Harrow Tourist Information Centre*, Civic Centre, Station Road, Harrow (081-424 1103); *Hillingdon Tourist Information Centre*, 22 High Street, Uxbridge, (0895 50706); *Kingston-upon-Thames Tourist Information Centre*, Heritage Centre, Fairfield West, Kingston-upon-Thames (081-546 5386); *Lewisham Tourist Information Centre*, Lewisham Library, Lewisham High Street SE13 (081-690 8325); *Richmond Tourist Information Centre*, Old Town Hall, Whittaker Avenue, Richmond (081-940 9125); Tower Hamlets Tourist Information Centre,Mayfield House, Cambridge Heath Road, E2 (071-980 4831 ext 5313/ 5315); Twickenham Tourist Information Centre, Civic Centre, York Street, Twickenham (081-891 1411).

Other Information Services:

London Transport: 55 Broadway, SW1 (071-222 1234; 24 hrs).

British Rail: see p 15.

Airports: see p 13.

Artsline: information on access to the arts and venues for disabled people on 071-388 2277.

Kidsline: school holiday information for parents and children on 071-222 8070.

Metropolitan Police: 071-230 1212; use 999 for emergencies only.

Lost Property: for articles lost in taxis write to the Metropolitan Police Lost Property Office, 15 Penton Street, N1. For property lost on buses and the Underground contact the Lost Property Office, 200 Baker Street, NW1; open for callers Mon—Fri 09.30—14.00. For property lost on British Rail contact the appropriate main line station.

Children: Childminders, 67a Marylebone High Street, W1, 071-935 2049; Universal Aunts Ltd, 250 King's Road, SW3, 071-352 5413. Hotels may also have contacts.

Embassies, etc.: *Australia*, Australia House, Strand, WC2 (071-379 4334); *Canada*, Canada House, Trafalgar Square, SW1 (071-629 9492); *Irish Republic*, 17 Grosvenor Place, SW1 (071-235 2171); *New Zealand*, New Zealand House, Haymarket, SW1 (071-930 8422); *South Africa*, South Africa House, Trafalgar Square, SW1 (071-930 4488); *United States*, 24 Grosvenor Square, W1 (071-499 9000).

Hotel Bookings (other than LTB): Expotel Ltd, Banda House, Cambridge Grove, W6 (081-568 8765; telex 8811951); Room Centre, Kingsgate House, Kingsgate Place, NW6 (081-451 2311; telex 262059); British Hotel Reservations Centre, 10 Buckingham Palace Road, SW1 (071-828 2425; telex 916122); Concordia Ltd, 52 Grosvenor Gardens, SW1 (071-730 3467; telex 916988); London Reservation Service, 21 Blandford Street, W1 (071-486 3560). Note: these are correspondence addresses only.

Arts Council of Great Britain: 105 Piccadilly, W1 (071-629 9495) (moving to Tufton Street, SW1 in 1990/91); information about exhibitions and activities.

Tourist Boards: *British Tourist Authority*; Thames Tower, Black's Road, Hammersmith, W6 (081-846 9000). This is the head office of the BTA and the English Tourist Board. No public tourist information services are offered but trade and media enquiries are welcome. *Scottish Tourist Board*, 19 Cockspur Street, SW1 (071-930 8661); *Wales Tourist Board*, 34 Piccadilly, W1 (071-409 0969); *Northern Ireland Tourist Board*, c/o Ulster Office, 11 Berkeley Street, W1 (071-493 0601). (All-Britain Travel Centre—see p 46.)

English Courses: ARELS/Felco (Association of English Language Schools/Federation of English Language Course Organisers), 2 Pontypool Place, Valentine Place, SE1 (071-242 3136) provide information on English language courses in England.

English Heritage: Thames House,South Millbank, SW1 (071-211 8828) provides information on monuments in their care, and operates a season ticket scheme.

Museums Association: 34 Bloomsbury Way, WC1 (071-404 4767).

National Art Collection Fund, 20 John Islip Street, SW1 (071-821 0404). Membership gives access to National Art Library at the Victoria and Albert Museum.

National Trust, 36 Queen Anne's Gate, SW1 (071-222 9251). Information on events and stately homes; membership gives free admission to NT properties throughout the country.

The Victorian Society, 1 Priory Gardens, W4 (081-994 1019); lectures, walking tours and events.

British Waterways Board, Melbury House, Melbury Terrace, NW1 (071-262 6711); information on canals and cruising throughout Britain.

Civic Trust, 17 Carlton House Terrace, SW1 (071-930 0914); encourages a high standard of architecture.

Inland Waterways Association, 114 Regent's Park Road, NW1 (071-586 2510); organises walks along the Regent's Canal.

Royal Horticultural Society, Horticultural Hall, Vincent Sq., SW1 (071-834 4333); organises Chelsea Flower Show and other flower shows throughout the year.

Royal Institute of British Architects, 66 Portland Place, W1 (071-580 5533); exhibitions, library and lectures.

Local libraries and the Yellow Pages for different parts of London are good sources of local information.

General Information

Weather and The Seasons, a constant topic of conversation. English weather varies not just from day to day but sometimes from hour to hour. In general, winter temperatures rarely drop below freezing although there are occasional cold snaps with snow and deep frost. Fog on the outskirts of London and in the countryside can make driving hazardous. Spring is dominated by changeability with warm days (up to 15°C) and quite a lot of rain. The English spring with its array of blossom is probably one of the prettiest in the world—from March onwards the cherry trees blossom in London's suburbs and through Kent there are special apple blossom trails for motorists. The summer starts in May or June and coincides with the traditional London season into which all the major events of the social calendar were once crammed. This is no longer the case but the events list (p 44) shows the many traditional events which make up the London season, from the Royal Academy Summer Exhibition to the race meetings at the Derby and Ascot and the Regatta at Henley. July and August can be hot and dry with temperatures up to 25–28°C, or they can be cold and dismal months. The autumn, another attractive season in London's parks and countryside, starts at the end of September and is usually dry and sunny with more rain towards Christmas; temperatures are in 10 to 15°C range. Rain can occur at any time and the wise sightseer carries an umbrella or fold-away raincoat.

For up-to-date news on the weather tune into London's local radio stations before setting out in the morning: LBC, London's news station, offers news, traffic and travel information and weather forecasts every quarter of an hour. Capital Radio has much the same information interspersed with music and Greater London Radio London offers a third variation. The London Weather Line recorded information service is on 0898 500 401.

Summer Time. Between the end of March and October, Britain adopts Summer Time which means that clocks go forward one hour and then back in October to Greenwich Mean Time. Despite Britain's membership of the EC, it does not seem to have been possible to coincide these change-overs with those which also take place on the Continent. Visitors travelling in Europe should check their watches, airline timetables, etc. carefully, particularly during March/April and September/October.

Bank Holidays and Business Hours. Bank holidays were introduced in the 19C before statutory holidays to give working people a day off; they have survived as follows: New Year's Day, Good Friday, Easter Monday, first Monday in May (instead of 1 May); last Monday in May (instead of Whitsun); last Monday in August; and Christmas Day, Boxing Day and possibly 27 December, if one of those is a Sunday. In general not much business is done between Christmas and the New Year, but there is no general closing down in London during the summer months, as on the Continent. Business hours are from 09.00 to 17.30 with lunch between 13.00 and 14.00 (banks, see below) Monday to Friday. A fair amount of business is done over lunch and several hours may be spent. Restaurants catering for the business market tend to close on Sundays.

Money. The £1 sterling is divided into 100 pence. 'Silver' coins come as 50p, 20p, 10p and 5p; with copper coins worth 2p and 1p. The £1 coin, small and gold-coloured, has replaced the £1 note and a £2 coin has also been issued; other notes are £5, £10, £20 and £50. Banks are open Monday to Friday 09.30–15.30. In the suburbs some are open on Saturday mornings; at Heathrow and Gatwick there are 24-hour banks. Bureaux de Change with late hours and Sunday opening can. be found at or near major railway stations, at Piccadilly Circus and Leicester Square, South Kensington and Bayswater. Check the rate of exchange and commission charge (which can be very high) before entering into a transaction. Some post offices also operate a Bureaux de Change service (see below).

Tipping. In general service charges are now included on bills in hotels and restaurants. If in doubt ask, and only leave an extra tip if the service has been exceptionally good. If not included, add 10 to 15 per cent. Taxi drivers expect a tip of around 10 to 15 per cent; porters a minimum of 50p; cloakroom attendants 20 to 50p and barbers and hairdressers a minimum 50p. Barmen in hotel cocktail bars will expect something left on the plate, but otherwise do not tip in bars, cinemas, theatres, etc.

Post. Stamps are sold from Post Offices which are open Monday to Friday 09.00–17.30 and Saturday 09.00–13.00 (in some cases). Stamps can also be bought from some hotel desks. European mail goes airmail but airmail stickers and extra stamps are required for the service outside Europe. The Trafalgar Square Post Office is open Monday to Saturday 08.00–20.00. (There are stamp machines outside most post offices.)

Telephones. Britain's telephone system has been denationalised and is now operated by a public company, British Telecom PLC. But telephoning in Britain still remains a very costly activity. There are three scales for charges: Monday to Friday 09.00–13.00 (very expensive); Monday to Friday 08.00–09.00 and 13.00–18.00 (expensive); all other times including the weekend (less expensive). Overseas calls are subject to different bands. Charges vary with time and distance, and calls made in hotels (other than from a public telephone booth) are charged at a higher rate which includes the hotel's costs in providing the service. It is possible to direct dial from London to most places in the world; consult the telephone directory or dial 100 for the Operator. Telephone booths in the traditional red are being replaced with more functional boxes and new telephones have been introduced which take phone cards rather than coins. Cards can be bought at newsagents and bookstalls. Carry 10p and 50p for local calls. Credit cards can also be used in some public telephones. For emergency calls, fire, police, and ambulance dial 999.

In this book London telephone numbers have been shown with the new 081 and 071 codes, which replaced the old 01 prefix from 6 May 1990 allowing a greater capacity of telephone lines in Greater London. Those in the 081 area (Outer London) calling another number in the 081 area, dial the last seven digits. However, when calling a number in the 071 area (central London), dial the 071 first. Those in the 071 area follow the same procedure: just use the seven-digit number for a call within the 071 area, or 081 when calling a number in the 081 area. From outside London dial 071 or 081 as appropriate instead of the old 01.

Public Lavatories. London had a better range of public lavatories than most European cities. Unfortunately cutbacks in public spending have led to the widespread closure of traditional loos and the introduction of coin-in-the-slot French-style public lavatories in an ugly concrete box above ground. As alternatives use lavatories in department stores, tourist attractions, railway stations, restaurants, pubs, and hotels some of which have excellent lavatory facilities.

Facilities for Disabled Visitors. Some London hotels have bedrooms generally suitable, or adapted for disabled guests. A list is available from the Holidaycare Service or the London Tourist Board. In some cases these same hotels will also have suitable public lavatory facilities, which make them a good choice for dinner or meetings when disabled access is required. The Ramada Hotel, Berners St, W1, and the London Tara, Scarsdale Place, W8 are particularly recommended. Call or write to Holiday Care Service, 2 Old Bank Chambers, Station Road, Horley, Surrey RH6 9HW, tel. 0293 774535.

British Rail is improving facilities at stations for disabled travellers with dropped kerbs, toilet facilities and assistance if required. Both Heathrow and Gatwick Airports are well geared to the requirements of the disabled traveller and produce advance information (see p 13 for addresses). Tourist attractions, restaurants, and pubs vary in their accessibility, but most museums and galleries are accessible. Some theatres have induction loops and access for wheelchairs. More information from 'Access in London', published by Nicholson, and up-to-date advice from Artsline on 071-388 2277.

Medical Services. Visitors to Britain are able to use the accident and emergency services of the National Health Service free of charge. In central London casualty clinics can be found at University College Hospital, Gower St (entrance Grafton Way) WC1, St. Thomas's Hospital, Lambeth Palace Rd, SE1 and Westminster Hospital, Horseferry Rd, SW1. Boots The Chemist at Piccadilly Circus is open Mon to Sat 08.30–20.00, Bliss, 5 Marble Arch, W1 is open 09.00–24.00 every day, and John Bell and Croyden, 50 Wigmore St, W1 is open Mon–Fri 09.00–18.30, Sat 09.00–17.00.

The National Health Service charges for non-emergency treatment of visitors to Britain unless there is a reciprocal arrangement with the country of origin. Countries which have reciprocal arrangements are EC Countries, most other W European countries, Hong Kong, New Zealand, and the USSR.
   Visitors not from these countries (e.g. USA, Canada and Australia) are recommended to take out health insurance before travelling to Britain. Private medicine is provided by a growing number of clinics and hospitals. Information from the BTA/LTB.

People. London's population has fallen below 7m, but as many more live in the surrounding area but work within Greater London the numbers swell considerably during the week. Immigration mainly from Commonwealth countries since the Second World War (now severely curtailed) has produced a great cultural mix reflected in changes in some parts of London, the ethnic mix of restaurants, fashion and the music scene. Visitors will find people of many different national origins working in London's service industries, and a growing proportion of particularly smaller hotels owned by Asian families and companies.

Comments and Complaints. The British Tourist Authority and the London Tourist Board will deal with comments and complaints, in writing.

Chronology

AD 43	Growth of London began when invading Romans crossed the Thames close to the site of the later London Bridge. Population approx. 30,000.
60	London was severely damaged in conflict between the forces of Queen Boadicea and the occupying Romans.
200	London became a walled city in which trade flourished. Population approx. 45,000–50,000.
410	London reverted to a farming community following Roman withdrawal from Britain.
604	Thames became main artery for trade with the port of London.
836	London invaded by Vikings.
871	During the reign of Alfred the Great the office of alderman was created, in recognition of the growing dependence of the Crown on city wealth.
1014	London continued to be coveted by warring Saxon factions and was stormed for the last time by Olaf.
1052	Edward the Confessor removed his court to Thorney Island, W of the city, having been refused monetary support. Westminster Abbey was built on this site, once a Benedictine Abbey.
1066	Norman Conquest. City besieged. William I crowned. Charter established office of sheriff. Population approx. 14,000–18,000.
1087	William II crowned.
1097	White Tower of London completed as defensive bastion. Westminster Hall built by William II as part of the medieval palace of Westminster.
1100–1140	Henry I crowned. In return for supporting the Crown, city was allowed to raise its own taxes and elect its own governors.
1123	Saint Bartholomew's hospital built.
1135	Stephen, Count of Blois, crowned.
1154	House of Plantagenet began as Henry II was crowned.
1189	Jews banned from coronation of Richard Coeur de Lion were attacked. Population approx. 20,000–25,000.
1189	Henry FitzElywin chosen as first Mayor of London.
1199	King John crowned.
1215	King John, as a reward for financial support, recognised the authority of Lord Mayor and agreed to the election of 24 aldermen. City not satisfied and helped rebellious barons draft the Magna Carta.
1216	Henry III crowned.

1217	London Bridge rebuilt in stone and remained London's only bridge until the 18C.
1224	Westminster Hall became the chief law court of England.
1225	St. Thomas's Hospital established in Southwark.
1263	Trade guilds exercised their increasing power by wresting control of City from aldermen.
1269	New Westminster Abbey consecrated following dispute with city.
1272	Edward I came to the throne.
1280	Old St. Paul's Cathedral completed and displaced many inhabitants of the City.
1290	Jews expelled from England.
1301	Temple Bar gateway built to prevent sovereign from freely entering the city without Lord Mayor's permission.
1304	Recorder was elected by governors of city as spokesman. Buildings surrounding St. Paul's grew.
1307	Edward II came to the throne.
1326	Riots against the King result from city squalor.
1327	Edward III came to the throne.
1338	King made Palace of Westminster the regular meeting place of Parliament.
1348	Black Death halved the city's population to 30,000.
1377	Richard II crowned.
1381	Peasants' Revolt. Wat Tyler led army of labouring people to end feudalism and occupied London for two days. Tyler was killed by Mayor.
1394	Westminster Hall rebuilding began.
1399	City and Parliament combined to depose the autocratic Richard II. House of Lancaster began as Henry IV was crowned.
1400–1500	The increasing wealth of professional soldiers and merchants began to undermine feudalism.
1411	Construction of Guildhall in the City began.
1413	Henry V crowned.
1422	Henry VI came to the throne.
1430	Jack Cade led Kentishmen in protest against financial oppression and incompetence of King. Occupied London for three days.
1456	Riots against aliens.
1461	House of York took power under Edward IV, victor of the Wars of the Roses. In return for City's support many London citizens were knighted.
1483	Child King Edward V came to the throne and then replaced by Richard III.
1485	Tudor period began with crowning of Henry VII.
1499	Perkin Warbeck, Pretender to the throne, hanged at Tyburn.
1500–1600	London commerce increased substantially. Financial expertise and flourishing market established London as a major trading port with the Continent.
1509	Henry VIII crowned.
1510	St. Paul's School opened to provide secondary education in the City.

1533	Closure of monasteries during the Reformation increased land available for building. Wealthy merchant families became the new gentry.
1553–1558	Period of instability under the fiercely Roman Catholic Queen Mary. Executions took place at Smithfield in the city.
1558	Queen Elizabeth I came to the throne.
1562	Queen forbade any new building within three miles of the City, in response to the growth of slums.
1599	Globe Theatre built by Burbage on Bankside in Southwark.
1600	New landed families began to construct mansions on estates extending into the 'West End' and beyond.
1603	City began to resent the autocratic style of the Stuart King, James I, which did not improve with the accession of Charles I.
1605	Gunpowder plot to blow up Parliament and the royal family discovered.
1613	Globe Theatre burnt down.
1625	Charles I came to the throne.
1630	First square in London built at Covent Garden.
1637	Hyde Park became the first public park.
1642	Civil War began. City financed Parliament. Fortifications built and manned by citizens.
1649	Charles I beheaded in Whitehall and Commonwealth declared by Oliver Cromwell. Puritanism dominated social and political life.
1650	Population approx. 350,000–400,000.
1652	First Coffee House opened in St. Michael's Alley, Cornhill, and became centre for financial transactions.
1656	Jewish families re-entered London.
1660	Reaction against the constraints of fanatical religious egalitarianism lead London to support the return of Charles II. The Royal Society was founded.
1663	Theatre opened in Drury Lane. 'King's Performers' were the only company allowed in London.
1665	The Great Plague killed up to 100,000 and caused a major exodus of wealthy families to outlying districts.
1666	The Great Fire began in Pudding Lane and destroyed the medieval City of London.
1667	Act to allow rebuilding stipulated that stone should be used. City appointed commissioners to be responsible for sewers.
1675	Christopher Wren began construction of new St. Paul's Cathedral. Royal Greenwich Observatory built to mark meridian, celebrating Britain's supremacy in navigation.
1685	Religious intolerance forced French Protestants to seek refuge in England, many settling in London. James II crowned.
1689	William and Mary crowned.
1692	Chelsea Hospital, designed by Wren, was completed.
1694	Royal Charter established Bank of England to pay for war with France.
1696	Howland Great Wet Dock constructed, first wet dock in England, became Greenland Dock, on South Bank.

1700–1750	Wren's plans for developing London as the 'Venice of the North' defeated by complex ownership of land. Skyline of City, however, profoundly altered by the spires of 51 churches designed by him. Villages to the W of London engulfed by spread of building. Poorer neighbourhoods to the S and E notorious for high consumption of gin. Population approx. 600,000.
1702	Queen Anne crowned.
1711	Academy of Art opened.
1712	Handel settled in London.
1714	House of Hanover began as George I was crowned.
1720–1760	Many major London hospitals built; Guy's, London, St. George's, Westminster and Middlesex.
1727	George II crowned.
1732	Covent Garden Theatre opened.
1733	City commissioners no longer prepared to dredge Fleet River, so it was arched over.
1739	London's second bridge constructed at Westminster.
1743	Riots against Act to control the sale of gin.
1749	Bow Street Runners set up to prevent crime around the vicinity of legal centre of London.
1750	Population approx. 650,000.
1759	British Museum opened.
1760	George III came to the throne.
1770	First canal in London completed from River Lea to Thames.
1772	Battersea Bridge built
1774	Act created an embryonic office of district surveyor. Radical Whig reformer, John Wilkes, was elected as Mayor for the self-governing City.
1780	Gordon Riots. 850 lost their lives in protest against the repeal of anti-Catholic legislation.
1785	'The Times' newspaper began, then known as 'Daily Universal Register'.
1788	Bank of England moved to building designed by John Soane.
1798	Demands for parliamentary reform were suppressed when members of the London Corresponding Society were arrested.
1799	During the next few decades various acts were passed to allow the construction of commercial docks. Traffic on Thames remained in private hands creating considerable confusion and hardship throughout the next century.
1801	First census records 1,117,290, most of whom lived outside the City boundaries. London continued to be a centre for reform agitation. River Police established.
1803	Surrey Canal completed from docks to Peckham, improving local trade.
1810	Riots in support of radical MP Sir Francis Burdett. John Nash began to build terraces along Regent St northwards into London heathlands.
1811	Waterloo and Southwark Bridges designed by John Rennie.
1812	Regents Canal joined the Grand Union to link London with Midland industries.

1818	London still without effective local government. Act established system for voting-in parish officers.
1820	George IV came to the throne; coronation 1821. Plot to assassinate Cabinet uncovered, Cato Street conspiracy. Earth removed from new docks helped to stabilise land around Belgravia.
1822	Lambeth Bridge built.
1825	Buckingham House altered by Nash, later became residence of sovereign. London Bridge rebuilt to Rennie design.
1827	Hammersmith Bridge built, an early example on the suspension principle.
1829	Metropolitan Police force established. Area of operation did not include City. First regular horse-drawn bus service began along Marylebone Road. Construction of Trafalgar Square began.
1830	William IV came to the throne.
1831	Reform Riots in London. During the next 40 years Sir Thomas Wilson tried to enclose Hampstead Heath. Opposition to his schemes was based on free public access for urban families.
1832	Construction of National Gallery began.
1833	Police called to disperse reform protestors in Clerkenwell. First railway sanctioned by Parliament to run between London Bridge and Greenwich.
1834	Palace of Westminster destroyed by fire.
1835	London was exempted from Municipal Reform Act so many pressing public health problems could not be dealt with effectively. Cholera and destitution increased. City established its own police force.
1836	First railway opened between Deptford and Bermondsey. University of London established.
1837	Queen Victoria came to the throne. Geological Museum opened. London Bridge Station opened.
1838	Euston Station opened.
1840	Sir Charles Barry designed new Houses of Parliament in Gothic style. First station in City opened at Fenchurch St.
1841	Younger Brunel designed Hungerford Bridge.
1843	First tunnel under the Thames from Rotherhithe to Wapping.
1844	Width of streets in the entire metropolis controlled by new act.
1848	Women students admitted to University of London.
1849	'Morning Chronicle' published Mayhew's systematic survey 'London Labour and the London Poor'. Cholera killed 14,000. Harrods opened as a small grocery store.
1850	Brunel designed Paddington Station and asked Wyatt to design decoration.
1851	Great Exhibition held in the Crystal Palace, Hyde Park.
1852	Victoria and Albert Museum began in Marlborough House. King's Cross Station opened, designed in avant-garde style by Lewis Cubbitt.
1854	Great Western Hotel built at Paddington.

1855	Board of Works set up for London under new act. Disreputable Bartholomew Fair closed.
1858	The Great Stink, outside the Houses of Parliament, resulted in a bill for creation of a sewerage system for London. During the next 15 years many public health acts undertaken. Chelsea Bridge built.
1859	Vauxhall Gardens, once elegant pleasure gardens, closed
1860–1880	Many refugees from Eastern Europe entered London. They tended to settle E of City; Aldgate, Whitechapel and Spitalfields.
1860	Grosvenor Bridge, first railway bridge across Thames.
1863	First underground railway opened, Metropolitan Line.
1865	Blackfriars Bridge, designed by J. Cubbitt, opened on 18C site. St. Pancras, Charing Cross and Broad St stations opened. St. Thomas's Hospital moved to Lambeth.
1866	Riots developed when police tried to break up Reform League meeting in Hyde Park. The setting-up of Speaker's Corner resulted; Hyde Park has remained one of the most popular sites for large demonstrations to the present day.
1867	Clerkenwell Prison was bombed in an attempt to free Fenians (Irish Radicals).
1868	Gothic-style hotel built at St. Pancras.
1870	First tramcar service ran from Brixton to Kennington and Whitechapel to Bow.
1871	Hampstead Heath saved for the public.
1872	Bethnal Green Museum, part of V & A collection, opened.
1873	Albert Bridge built. Natural History Museum at South Kensington opened.
1874	Liverpool Street Station opened.
1880	Norman Shaw designed Bedford Park, Chiswick which became the forerunner of the garden city.
1884	Toynbee Hall opened in the East End as the first 'university settlement'.
1886	Tower Bridge opened.
1887	Black Sunday. Social Democratic Federation meeting in Trafalgar Square broken up by police, causing casualties.
1888	Series of murders in Whitechapel associated with 'Jack the Ripper'. New Unionism began with strike of badly paid women matchmakers.
1889	First London dock strike to protest at falling wages managed to unite a traditionally competitive workforce. Major act established strong local government for London, the London County Council.
1890	Battersea Bridge rebuilt.
1893	Tate Gallery construction began on site of the old Millbank Prison.
1894	First Lyons tea shop opened in Piccadilly.
1897	Queen Victoria celebrated her Diamond Jubilee as prosperity of London continued.

1899	Marylebone Station opened amidst controversy and local opposition.
1901	House of Saxe-Coburg began as Edward VII came to the throne. Population of London: Inner London 4,536,267, Greater London 6,506,889 and the City only 37,709.
1903	Water supply for London controlled by new Metropolitan Water Board.
1909	Port of London Authority took over running of docks.
1910	Privately-owned powered motor vehicles began to challenge horse-drawn public transport. House of Windsor began as George V came to the throne.
1911	Second London dock strike against insecurity of employment. Siege of Sidney St followed an unsuccessful robbery by Eastern European anarchists.
1912	New Waterloo Station construction began.
1914	Women operated many services in London during First World War.
1915	First Lyons Corner House opened on the Strand.
1920–1940	Clearance of slums allowed Modernist style estates to be built. Peckham Health Centre built as model for treatment of deprived inner-city children.
1928	Science Museum opened on present site.
1932	Green Belt established around London to control spread of suburbs.
1933	London Transport created.
1936	British Broadcasting Corporation began television broadcasting from Alexandra Palace, N London. Battle of Cable St; East Enders and anti-fascists prevented march of Oswald Mosley's Black Shirts through mainly Jewish districts. Edward VIII abdicated 325 days after coming to the throne. George VI succeeded him.
1939	Population of Greater London reached its peak at 8,615,050.
1940	City and East End severely damaged by bombs during the Blitz. Docks were targets for air raids.
1945	A mixture of private and public funds set aside for rebuilding of London.
1947	Legislation to protect buildings of historic and architectural importance began.
1951	Festival of Britain helps to revive the nation during post-war austerity. Battersea Park opens a funfair, a 'Dome of Discovery and Skylon Obelisk' were constructed on the South Bank and the Royal Festival Hall opened.
1952	Queen Elizabeth II was crowned.
1954	Temple of Mithras discovered as the City was rebuilt.
1956	'Pea soup' fogs of London finished after the Clean Air Act was passed.
1958	Race Riots in Notting Hill.
1960–1968	London becomes known as the 'Swinging City', as music and fashion develop.
1963	New Euston Station was built, destroying Victorian entrance arch.

1965	Greater London Council formed as strategic planning authority.
1967	Conservation areas identified and given statutory protection, over 300 have been established in London. East India Dock was closed in response to declining traffic and economic pressure. Old London Bridge sold and rebuilt in Arizona.
1968	Anti-Vietnam war demonstrations escalate into confrontation with police in Grosvenor Square. Ronan Point, tower block, collapsed after gas explosion.
1969	Greater London Development Plan proposed housing, open space and major road works in and through London.
1974	Covent Garden market moved to Nine Elms, South London. Existing buildings saved for redevelopment.
1976	Museum of London opened. National Theatre company moved from the Old Vic to new South Bank complex.
1981	Restored Covent Garden Market reopens as shopping and entertainment centre. London Docklands Development Corporation created by government to co-ordinate use of derelict docks.
1980	Listed Firestone Building demolished.
1981	Brixton Riots. Chelsea Barracks IRA bomb.
1982	Billingsgate market moved to West India Dock. Barbican Centre opened. Thames Barrier completed to prevent flooding of London. Hyde Park and Regent's Park bandstand IRA bombs.
1983	Population of London falls to 6,754,500. Harrods IRA bomb.
1985	London Regional Transport set up without GLC control.
1986	Greater London Council abolished.
1987	Docklands Light Railway opened. Heathrow Terminal 4 opened. King's Cross Underground Fire.
1988	Gatwick North Terminal opened.
1989	Tobacco Dock opened. Gates erected at entrance to Downing Street.
1990	ILEA (Inner London Education Authority) abolished Poll Tax Riots, Trafalgar Square. Courtauld Institute Gallery opens in Somerset House.

Outer London Touring Tips

Most Londoners know more about the attractions of the city centre than about those of their own area; good sources of information, apart from tourist information centres, are local libraries. These have information on local sights and facilities, and collections of literature compiled by historical and architectural societies.

Travelling between suburbs without a car can be difficult; rail and bus routes are designed largely to carry traffic into and out of London. Bus services between suburbs tend to be unreliable, where they exist at all.

Some suburban shopping centres retain early closing on one weekday (usually Wednesday or Thursday), but most purpose-built shopping centres and multiple stores are now open six full days a week. Sunday opening is less common in the suburbs than in Central London except for garden centres and DIY stores.

Due to vandalism, many churches are kept locked except when services are being held. Sometimes a sign on the door will indicate where a key-holder can be reached or when the church is open; otherwise ask at the local library.

There are many good restaurants in Outer London—consult a reliable restaurant guide. When in doubt look for a comfortable pub or winebar. Hamburger and pizza restaurants, including international chains, can be found in almost every High Street.

London High Streets are very similar architecturally— mainly Victorian or Edwardian, and with an overlay of multiple stores and shops with exactly the same frontage whether they are in Wembley or Bromley. To appreciate the quality and character of these buildings look up at the first and second storeys where original architectural details have usually been retained.

The 1960s saw the arrival of purpose-built shopping centres, often deteriorating into vandalised and wind-swept shopping plazas; the '80s have seen an improvement with covered shopping malls such as Brent Cross, Ealing Broadway, and the rebuilt Whitgift Centre in Croydon.

In residential areas, sudden gaps in rows of terraced Victorian houses filled with unattractive '50s blocks are usually the result of Second World War bombing. They are common in SE and E London, and much of Docklands. These areas were extensively damaged by bombing and a rash of new housing spread as the opportunity to carry out extensive slum-clearance was taken. Some of the high-rise housing put up in the process has quickly turned to slums and boroughs such as Newham are now demolishing tower blocks of flats.

I   THE WEST END, WESTMINSTER, AND KENSINGTON

The **West End** means different things to different people but broadly includes the areas of Mayfair, Westminster, Belgravia, Soho and Covent Garden; to some it means all the fashionable shopping areas including Knightsbridge and Kensington High St and to others, mainly theatre and restaurant land—the area around Piccadilly Circus and Leicester Square.

1   Westminster

Access: Underground, Westminster, St. James's Park.

The **City of Westminster** is the London borough covering most of the West End from its boundary with the City of London in the E, marked by heraldic dragons, to Knightsbridge and Belgravia in the W; N it stretches as far as Marylebone. Westminster itself refers to the political heart of London—the area around the Houses of Parliament and Whitehall. Parliament Square was created in 1926 as the first 'roundabout' in London. An ambitious plan by Westminster City Council would pedestrianise it from the S side. Whitehall and Trafalgar Square are to the N and to the SE are the dignified buildings of the *Houses of Parliament* with *Westminster Hall*. Due S are the towers of *Westminster Abbey*, beyond the picturesque *St. Margaret's Church*. The *Middlesex Crown Court* (formerly Middlesex Guildhall) and the *Royal Institute of Chartered Surveyors*, both dating from the beginning of this century, are on the W side, and on the N side along Parliament St is the flank of the huge *Government Offices Building*.

Round the lawn in the centre of the square are statues of eminent statesmen: *Field-Marshal Smuts* (1870–1950), by Epstein, *Lord Palmerston* (1784–1865), by Thos. Woolner, *Lord Derby* (1799–1869), by Matthew Noble, *Disraeli (Lord Beaconsfield)* (1804–81), by Mario Raggi, and *Sir Robert Peel* (1788–1850), by Noble. In front of the Middlesex Court stands *Abraham Lincoln* (1809–65), a replica of the statue by Saint-Gaudens at Chicago, and *George Canning* (1770–1827), by Sir Richard Westmacott. Disraeli's statue is annually decorated with primroses, said to have been his favourite flower, on 19 April ('Primrose Day'; the anniversary of his death in 1881). The NE corner is occupied by Ivor Roberts-Jones' bronze (1973) of *Churchill* (1874–1965) dramatically floodlit at night. A fountain is planned for the centre of the square, but before that it may become a building site for the extension of the Jubilee line to Docklands.

St. Margaret's Church, dating from 1485–1523, has been repeatedly altered and restored. Founded before 1189 as the parish church of Westminster, it is also (since 1621) the 'national church for the use of the House of Commons'. It is a fashionable church for weddings; Samuel Pepys was married here in 1655, Milton (for the second time) in 1656, and Winston Churchill in 1908. Sir Walter Raleigh, who was executed in 1618 in front of the Palace of Westminster, is buried in the chancel; and in the church or churchyard rest also William Caxton (1422–?91) and Wenceslaus Hollar (1607–77), the

*A popular image of Westminster: the Tower of Big Ben seen
from the statue of Queen Boudicca (Boadicea) on
Westminster Bridge*

Bohemian etcher who depicted London before the Great Fire. The
peaceful interior is adorned with unobtrusive Elizabethan and
Jacobean wall monuments

The font, in the S aisle, is by Nicholas Stone (1641). At the E end of
the S aisle is the notable tomb of Lady Dudley (died 1600), and on the
E wall, memorials to Caxton and Raleigh. Over the W door is a large
window dedicated by Americans to the memory of Raleigh (inscription by J.R. Lowell); while that at the W end of the N aisle, with an
inscription by Whittier, commemorates Milton. The richly coloured *E
Window, made in Holland before 1509, celebrates the betrothal
(1501) of Catherine of Aragon to Prince Arthur, Henry VII's eldest son.
It was bought for St. Margaret's in 1758. On the external E wall is a lead
bust of Charles I (c 1800). A blue sundial was added to the N face
of the tower in 1982 and the exterior has been recently cleaned.

Opposite St. Margaret's, in front of the Houses of Parliament, is
Westminster Hall with a statue of Oliver Cromwell by Sir Hamo
Thornycroft (1889). To the S opens OLD PALACE YARD (outside the
House of Lords) with an admirable bronze equestrian statue of
Richard I by Marochetti (1860). (See cover.)

Millbank follows the Thames S to the Tate Gallery (Rte 12). There
are fine views of the river from the flanking *Victoria Tower Gardens*.
Here are a bronze replica (1915) of a *Group by Rodin (erected at
Calais in 1895), representing the devoted *Burghers of Calais*, who
surrendered themselves to Edward III in 1340 to save their city from

destruction. There is also a fine memorial to the leaders of the suffragettes, *Mrs Emmeline Pankhurst* (1858–1928) and her daughter *Dame Christabel Pankhurst* (1881–1958), by A.G. Walker (1930), as well as a bronze replica of the prisoners' badge—over 1000 women were imprisoned between 1905–10.

Facing the Lords, across busy Abingdon St, beyond a pathway anciently connecting the Abbey with the Palace of Westminster, stands a memorial to *George V*, by Sir W. Reid Dick and Sir Giles Scott (1947), backed by fine plane-trees and the Chapter House. Immediately behind the attractive early 19C mansion flanking it is the low, moated **Jewel Tower** (1366), a survival of the medieval Palace of Westminster (open weekdays, 09.30–18.30 (summer) 09.30–16.00 (winter). Admission charge. Built by Edward III as a royal treasure-house, it served from 1621–1864 as the Record Office of the Lords, and thereafter until 1938 as an assay office of weights and measures. It retains fine original bosses in the vaulting and houses capitals (c 1090) from Westminster Hall, finds from the moat (Saxon sword), and medieval carvings from Whitehall Palace.

The ragstone wall of 1374 (10ft high) surrounds the Abbey precincts; cross Abingdon St Gardens (underground car park) past 'Knife Edge', a sculpture by Henry Moore (1967) and turn right into Great College St.

To the S are quiet Georgian streets popular with MPs as London residences. *Barton St* (where T.E. Lawrence lived at No. 14) and its continuation, Cowley St, lead to Great Peter St (new base for the Arts Council), and Lord North St goes on to *Smith Square* (1726; plaque on No. 5). Here are the headquarters of the Conservative Party (Central Office) and previously of the Labour Party too, at Transport House (now in Walworth Road). The eccentric shape of the baroque church of *St. John the Evangelist*, completed in 1728 by Thomas Archer, was likened by Dickens to 'a petrified monster on its back with its legs in the air'. The four angle towers are said to have been designed to ensure that the swampy foundations settled uniformly. Restored after bomb damage, it is used for concerts and lectures as St. John's, Smith Square with a wine bar/restaurant in the Crypt—the Footstool.

At the end of Great College St an archway (right) leads into DEAN'S YARD, once a portion of the Abbey Gardens. On the E side are entrances to the cloisters of the Abbey and to **Westminster School**, or *St. Peter's College*. This ancient monastic school, referred to as early as 1339, was refounded by Queen Elizabeth in 1560, and is now one of the great public schools. The school is built round *Little Dean's Yard*, on the site of the monks' quarters, relics of which remain. Visitors are admitted on written application to the bursar. The College Hall, with a fine hammerbeam roof, dates from the time of Edward III and was formerly the abbey refectory. The Great School Room was the monks' dormitory. *Ashburnham House* is the library and can be visited.

Ashburnham House, Dean's Yard, SW1 (Tel. 071-222 3116) is open during Easter school holidays (not Good Friday and Easter Monday) Mon to Fri 10.00–16.00. Admission charge. Access: Underground, Westminster, St. James's Park.

The red brick house dates from 1400 but was rebuilt in 1660, probably to a design by John Webb. Once the home of the Earls of Ashburnham it is now used by Westminster School. The unusual and impressive staircase (c 1665) is arranged around a spacious well. There are good ceilings and carved doorcases, portraits of Elizabeth I and former headmasters.

Westminster School now educates over 400 boys, and some girls. They enjoy certain privileges in connection with the Abbey, and shout the 'Vivats' at coronations. They attend a daily service there. On Shrove Tuesday 'tossing the pancake' takes place in the Great School Room, the boy or girl securing the largest fragment is rewarded with a guinea. In the long list of famous pupils are the names of Ben Jonson, George Herbert, Dryden, Locke, Wren, Cowper, Charles Wesley, Lord Mansfield, Warren Hastings, Gibbon, Southey, Lord Raglan, G.A. Henty, A.A. Milne, and Sir Henry Tizard.

On the S side of Dean's Yard is *Church House*, by Sir Herbert Baker (1937–40), the headquarters of the Canterbury Houses of Convocation, the House of Laity, the National Assembly of the Church of England, and over 50 Church societies. In 1940–44 it was used on several occasions as a meeting-place for Parliament. Later, it housed the Preparatory Commission of the United Nations, and the first sessions of the Security Council were also held here. The Assembly Hall, with its fine timber roof, and the Hoare Memorial Hall are sometimes open to visitors. On the W side is the *Abbey Choir School*, whose boys share the central green with Westminster School.

A passage at the opposite corner of Dean's Yard leads to BROAD SANCTUARY in front of Westminster Abbey. The name recalls the sanctuary to the N and W of the Abbey in which refugees were protected from the civil power by the church; a privilege abolished by James I. The Westminster Column, a Gothic memorial of red granite by Sir Gilbert Scott (1861), was erected in memory of Old Westminster boys who fell in the Crimean War and the Indian Mutiny. Opposite is the *Queen Elizabeth II Conference Centre*, opened by HM The Queen in June 1986, built on an empty site occupied until 1936 by the old Westminster Hospital. Architects Powell Moya and Partners have achieved an unobtrusive, even pleasing, building on a sensitive site. It incorporates high security and flexible conference facilities for up to 1200 in the Fleming and Whittle Rooms, and for 880 in the comfortable Churchill Auditorium.

At the corner of Tothill St rises the large domed *Central Hall* (open to visitors when not in use), built in 1912 (Lanchester and Richards) as the headquarters of the Methodist Church and also used for concerts and public meetings. In January 1946 it became the first home of the General Assembly of the United Nations. Despite French Renaissance trappings it has a steel frame and is one of the earliest examples of this method of construction in London.

2   Westminster Abbey

Westminster Abbey, Broad Sanctuary, SW1. Tel. 071-222 5152. Admission to Royal Chapels: weekdays 09.00–16.45, Sat 9.00–14.45; 15.45–17.45. Sun between services. Admission charge (Nave and precincts free). Chapter House open daily 09.30–17.45; Pyx Chamber/Undercroft Museum open daily 09.30–16.30. Admission charge. Super Tours (1½ hours) Mon to Fri 09.45, 10.15, 11.00, 14.15, 14.45, 15.30. Sat 10.00, 10.45, 12.30. Charge; (book at desk in South Aisle—includes Jericho Parlour and Jerusalem Chamber not otherwise accessible). The Abbey is closed or with restricted entry during special services. Regular services are held.

Brass Rubbing Centre in Cloisters. Open Mon to Sat 09.00–17.00. Tel. 071-222 2085.

Access: Underground, Westminster, St. James's Park.

Special services are held in the Abbey on the opening of the Law Courts in October, when judges in their robes walk in procession from the House of Lords, and on many other occasions. The annual Royal Maundy Service now takes place at a different church around the country and is no longer regularly held at Westminster Abbey.

The figures in italics after the monuments refer to the plan on p 69.

****Westminster Abbey** (Pl. 18; 2), more officially the *Collegiate Church of St. Peter in Westminster*, holds a unique position in English history as both the crowning-place and the burial-place of most English sovereigns. Though built at different periods, it is, with the exception of Henry VII's magnificent Perpendicular chapel at the E end and the 18C W towers, in the Early English style of which it constitutes one of the most beautiful and best preserved examples. Cleaning is revealing the details of external carvings and decorations.

W façade of Westminster Abbey dating from c 1390

According to tradition, a church built on *Thorney Isle* or Isle of Thorns, by Sebert, king of the East Saxons, was consecrated by Mellitus, first bishop of London in 616, but there is no authentic record of any earlier church than that of the Benedictine Abbey, founded here probably between 730 and 740, which was

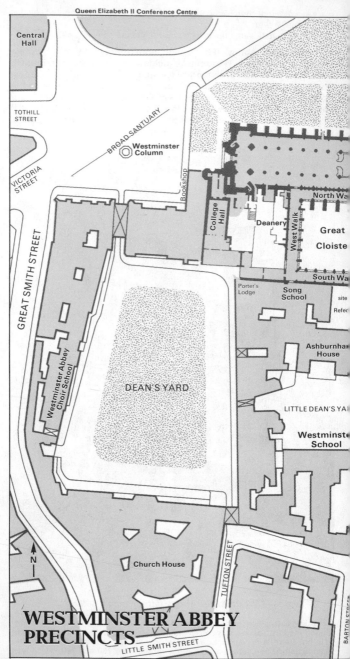

Queen Elizabeth II Conference Centre

Central Hall

TOTHILL STREET

BROAD SANCTUARY

Westminster Column

VICTORIA STREET

GREAT SMITH STREET

Bookshop

College Hall

Deanery

West Walk

North Wa

Great Cloiste

South Wa

Porter's Lodge

Song School

site

Refec

Ashburnha House

Westminster Abbey Choir School

DEAN'S YARD

LITTLE DEAN'S YA

Westminst School

N

Church House

TUFTON STREET

BARTON STREET

WESTMINSTER ABBEY PRECINCTS

LITTLE SMITH STREET

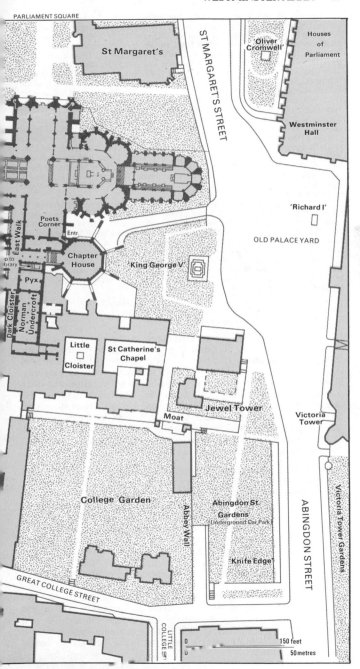

PARLIAMENT SQUARE

St Margaret's

ST MARGARET'S STREET

'Oliver Cromwell'

Houses
of
Parliament

Westminster
Hall

Poets
Corner

Entr.

East Walk

Dark Walk

p to
brary

Chapter
House

'Richard I'

OLD PALACE YARD

'King George V'

Pyx

Dark Cloister

Norman
Undercroft

Little
Cloister

St Catherine's
Chapel

Jewel Tower

Moat

Victoria
Tower

College Garden

Abbey Wall

Abingdon St
Gardens
(Underground Car Park)

Knife Edge

ABINGDON STREET

Victoria Tower Gardens

GREAT COLLEGE STREET

LITTLE COLLEGE ST

0   150 feet
0   50 metres

dedicated to St. Peter and received the name 'West Minster', or western monastery, probably from its position to the W of the City of London. Edward the Confessor (died 1066; canonised 1163) rebuilt the abbey on a larger scale, and in his Norman church, consecrated in 1065, the body of the sainted builder was placed in 1163. Within this church, or its successor, every English sovereign since Harold (except Edward V and Edward VIII) has been crowned. In 1220 a Lady Chapel was added at the E end, and in 1245 Henry III decided to honour St. Edward by rebuilding the entire church in a more magnificent style, as it appears today. The architects were Henry de Reyns (1245–53), John of Gloucester (1253–60), and Robert of Beverley (1260–84). The influence of French cathedrals such as Rheims and Amiens and of the Sainte Chapelle in Paris can be seen in the height of the nave and the arrangement of the radiating chapels around the apse. In 1269 the new church was consecrated. From this time until the reign of George III the Abbey became the royal burial-church. About 1388 Henry Yevele began to rebuild the nave for Abp Langham, and the work was continued after 1400 by William of Colchester; the design of Henry III's time was followed with even the details little changed. The nave-vault was completed by Abbot Islip in 1504–06. The new nave was hardly finished when the Lady Chapel was pulled down to make way for the magnificent Chapel of Henry VII (1503–19), attributed to Robert Vertue.

The lower part of the W façade dates from c 1390, but was altered by Hawksmoor; the towers (225ft high) were added by the same architect about 1739. The whole of the exterior was restored by Wren and Wyatt in 1697–1720. In 1875–84 the façade of the N transept was entirely remodelled by Sir Gilbert Scott and J.L. Pearson. The light and delicately shaped walls of Henry VII's Chapel remain the most pleasing part of the solemn heavily-buttressed exterior.

Elizabeth I made the church a 'Royal peculiar' under an independent Dean and Chapter, whose successors administer it today. The extant monastic buildings date mainly from the 13C and 14C, but there is Norman work in the Chamber of the Pyx and the adjoining Undercroft.

Measurements. The Abbey is 513ft in length, including Henry VII's Chapel, 200ft broad across the transepts, and 75ft broad across the nave and aisles. The Chapel of Henry VII is 104.5ft long and 70ft broad.

Enter by the W door, and pass below a gilded teak group of Christ between St. Peter and St. Edward the Confessor, by Michael Clark (1967). Visitors should allow the beautiful interior of the church to make its impact, before diverting their attention to the monuments. The architectural and sculptural details can be fully appreciated since the interior cleaning was completed in 1965. The height of the nave is at once striking; separated from the aisles by a tall arcade supported on circular columns round each of which are grouped eight slender shafts of grey Purbeck marble, it is the loftiest Gothic nave in England. Above the arches runs the double triforium with exquisite tracery and diaperwork and still higher, the tall clerestory.

Nave. Burial in the nave took place only after the Reformation. Many monuments throughout the church commemorate men who are not buried in the Abbey. A few paces from the W door in the middle of the nave a slab of green marble (*1*) is simply inscribed 'Remember Winston Churchill'. It was placed here 'in accordance with the wishes of the Queen and Parliament' on the 25th anniversary of the Battle of Britain. Churchill's body lies at Bladon, Oxfordshire. Immediately to the E, isolated by poppies, is the tomb of the *Unknown Warrior* (*2*): the body of an unidentified soldier was brought from Flanders and interred here on 11 Nov 1920, as representative of all the nameless British dead in the First World War, 'the bravely dumb that did their deed and scorned to blot it with a name'. He rests in earth brought from the battlefields. In contrast, a florid monument to *William Pitt* (1759–1806), by Westmacott crowns the W door. On the SW pier hangs a *Portrait of *Richard II* (*3*), the oldest contemporary portrait of an English monarch. Below is a memorial to the Earl and Countess Mountbatten (1985).

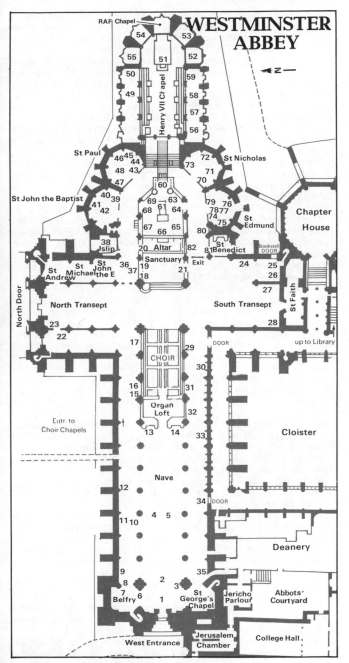

At the foot of the W piers are two fine bronze candelabra by Benno Elkan, representing the Old and the New Testaments (1940). A stone NE of the Unknown Warrior's tomb marks the spot where the remains of *George Peabody* (1795–1869), the American philanthropist, lay for a time before being removed to Massachusetts. The *Earl of Shaftesbury* (1801–85) and *Baroness Burdett Coutts* (1814–1906), likewise benefactors of London, are commemorated nearer the W door.—In the centre of the nave, further E, are the graves of *David Livingstone* (1813–73; *4*), African traveller and missionary, and of *Thomas Tompion* (1639–1713; *5*), 'father of English watch-making'.

North Aisle of Nave. Across the front of the NORTH-WEST or BELFRY TOWER (containing ten bells, recast in 1971) is a bronze effigy of *Lord Salisbury* (1803–1903; *6*). On the W wall are busts of *General Gordon* (1833–85), the defender of Khartoum, by Onslow Ford, and *Joseph Chamberlain* (1836–1914), by John Tweed. Among the crowded monuments is one (E side) to *Viscount Howe* (1725?–58; *7*) by Scheemakers, erected by the Province of Massachusetts while it was a British colony.—Behind it, in the next bay, called by Dean Stanley the 'Whigs' Corner', is a large monument to *Charles James Fox* (1749–1806; *8*). Floor-slabs commemorate *Earl Attlee* (1883–1967), *Ramsay MacDonald* (1866–1937), *Ernest Bevin* (1881–1951), and *Sidney* and *Beatrice Webb* (1859–1947; 1858–1943). On the wall is a monument to *Campbell-Bannerman* (1836–1908; *9*).—In the 3rd bay, a small stone in the pavement, inscribed 'O Rare Ben Jonson', marks the grave of the dramatist and poet *Ben Jonson* (1573?–1637; *10*); the original stone may be seen at the foot of the adjoining wall, beneath the monument to *Thomas Banks* (1735–1805; *11*), the sculptor. In the 4th bay is one of the earliest monuments in the nave, of unusual design, to *Mrs Jane Hill* (died 1631). In the 5th bay, at the foot of the window, *Spencer Perceval* (1762–1812; *12*), prime minister, who was shot by a madman in a lobby of the House of Commons; monument with a relief depicting the murder, by Westmacott.—A slab in the 7th bay marks the grave of *Sir John Herschel* (1792–1871); nearby is a memorial to *Sir William Herschel* (1738–1822; buried at Slough), like his son, an astronomer.

The choir screen (1828; re-gilded) is the work of Edward Blore. Set in to the W side are two impressive works by Rysbrack and Kent commemorating *Sir Isaac Newton* (1642–1727; *13*) and *Earl Stanhope* (1673–1721; *14*). Beside Newton's grave is that of *Lord Kelvin* (1824–1907), mathematician and physicist.

South Aisle of Nave. Several of the bays have interesting old coats of arms. To the left, in the 7th bay, *Major John André* (1751–80; *33*), hanged by Washington as a spy during the American War; the bas-relief shows Washington receiving André's vain petition for a soldier's death. Floor slabs in front of the next bay (usually covered by stalls) mark the graves of *Andrew Bonar Law* (1858–1923) and *Neville Chamberlain* (1869–1944), prime ministers. The 5th bay has unusual Morland monuments with trilingual inscriptions including Hebrew, Coptic, and Greek.—Above the W cloister door is a dramatic monument by Roubiliac to *Field-Marshal George Wade* (1673–1748; *34*), who provided the Scottish Highlands with roads and bridges in 1720–30. In the last bay is a small gallery of oak called the *Abbot's Pew* (*35*), erected by Abbot Islip (16C), and below, *William Congreve* (1670–1729), the dramatist.

The SW Tower, or Old Baptistery, is now the CHAPEL OF ST. GEORGE, dedicated to all who gave their lives in the World Wars and containing a tablet to the million British dead. In the wrought-iron screen is the trophy sent by Verdun to the Lord Mayor. Below is a tablet to *Lord Baden-Powell* (1857– 1941), founder of the Scout movement. In the floor, slabs mark the graves of *Lord Plumer* (1857–1932) and *Lord Allenby* (1871–1936), and on the S wall is an oak screen in memory of *Henry Fawcett* (1833–84), the blind statesman, and his wife, *Dame Millicent Fawcett* (1847–1929). Outside on the W wall is a plaque in memory of *President Franklin Roosevelt* (1882–1945).

THE NORTH CHOIR AISLE has fine examples of early heraldry on the N wall. A series of medallions under the organ (right) commemorate famous scientists, among them *Charles Darwin* (1809–82; tomb in N nave aisle) and *Lord Lister* (1827– 1912). Three matching diamonds in the pavement honour *Elgar, Vaughan Williams*, and *Stanford*. In the next bay *William Wilberforce* (1759–1833; *15*), one of the chief opponents of the slave-trade, and *Sir Stamford Raffles* (1759–1833), founder of Singapore, sit pensive in effigy above the tomb of *Henry Purcell* (1659–95; *16*), composer and organist at the Abbey. Beyond, a bust of *Orlando Gibbons* (1583–1625; buried at Canterbury) faces the tomb of *John Blow* (died 1708) and a memorial to *Dr Burney* (1726–1814), historian of music. At the entrance to the transept (right), *William Hesketh* (died 1605; *17*), with bright Jacobean decoration.

Sanctuary. The 18C roof of the lantern destroyed by incendiary bombs in May 1941 was replaced soon afterwards. The Sanctuary, or raised space within the altar-rails, where coronations take place, has a venerable pavement of Cosmati work laid by Master Odericus in 1268 (protected by carpets). On the left are the three most beautiful architectural *Tombs in the Abbey, dating from between c 1298 and 1325. The nearest one is that of *Aveline, Countess of Lancaster* (died c 1273; *18*), first wife of Edmund Crouchback. The others commemorate *Aymer de Valence* (died 1324; *19*), and *Edmund Crouchback, Earl of Lancaster* (died 1296; *20*), second son of Henry III and founder of the house of Lancaster. On the canopies of the two later tombs are representations of the deceased on horseback, and all three are adorned with rich painting and gilding (now much faded). The statuettes around Aymer de Valence's tomb are among the most exquisite small sculptures in England (better seen from the ambulatory; see below). —On the right side of the Sanctuary are sedilia dating from the time of Edward I, with paintings (1308) of Sebert, St. Peter and Ethelbert, and an ancient tapestry from Westminster School. On this is hung a Florentine triptych, by Bicci di Lorenzo (1373–1452), of the Madonna between SS. John Gualberto and Anthony of Padua (right) and SS. John the Baptist and Catherine of Alexandria; it was given to the Abbey in 1948 by Lord Lee of Fareham. Below is the tomb of *Anne of Cleves* (died 1557; *21*), fourth wife of Henry VIII. The 17C pulpit, replaced in 1935, is matched by a lectern (1949) in memory of William Carey (1761–1834), the missionary. The choir fittings were designed by Ed. Blore in 1830.

Transepts. The uniformity and proportions of the architecture have been upset by the host of monuments. In the N transept the E aisle is partially closed off, while in the S transept the E walk of the cloister accounts for the W aisle. Each transept is lit by a large rose-window (the glass in the N transept is the oldest in the Abbey, dating from 1721–22), below which are exquisitely carved censing angels, sculpted by Master John of St. Alban's c 1250; the S transept retains also two figures below the window.

The North Transept is the burial-place of several eminent statesmen. In the W aisle is a delicately carved monument to *Jonas Hanway* (1722–86; *22*), the philanthropist, and busts of *Richard Cobden* (1804–65; buried at West Lavington, W Sussex), the apostle of free trade, and of *Warren Hastings* (1732–1818; buried at Daylesford, Glos.), Governor General of India. On the wall behind, in the nave, is a huge monument to *William Pitt, Earl of Chatham* (1708–78; *23*), and statues of *Lord Palmerston* (1784–1865) and *Lord Castlereagh* (1769–1821). In the pavement are the graves of *Henry Grattan* (1746–1820), the Irish patriot and orator, and *C.J. Fox* (1749–1806). Towards the E wall, statues of *George Canning* (1770–1827), by Chantrey; *Benjamin Disraeli, Earl of Beaconsfield* (1804–81; buried at Hughenden, Bucks), by Boehm; *William Ewart Gladstone* (1809–98), by Brock; and *Sir Robert Peel* (1788–1850; buried at Drayton Bassett, Staffordshire), by Gibson.

The three chapels (usually locked) of ST. JOHN THE EVANGELIST, ST. MICHAEL, and ST. ANDREW occupy the E aisle of the N transept. At the entrance to the chapels is an overwhelming monument to *General Wolfe* (1727–59; buried at Greenwich), who fell at the capture of Quebec. To the left, is *Sir John Franklin* (1786–1847), lost in the search for the North-West Passage, with a fine inscription by Tennyson.—To the right, *Sir Francis Vere* (1560–1609), a distinguished soldier of Queen Elizabeth. This magnificent Renaissance tomb is modelled on that of *Engelbert II of Nassau* (died 1504) at Breda. *Lady Elizabeth Nightingale* (died 1731), a skilful but theatrical sculpture by Roubiliac. The large tomb in the next chapel is that of *Lord Norris* (1525?–1601) and his wife (neither buried here); the only one of their six sons who survived them may be distinguished by his attitude. On the N wall, *Sir James Young Simpson* (1811–70; buried in Edinburgh), who first used chloroform as an anaesthetic. *Mrs Siddons* (1755–1831) as the Tragic Muse, by Chantrey after Reynolds. *Sir Humphry Davy* (1778–1829; buried in Geneva), inventor of the safety lamp. *John Kemble* (1757–1823), the actor, designed by Flaxman. *Thomas Telford* (1757–1834), engineer and bridge-builder. On the right *Adm. Kempenfelt* (1718–82), who went down in the 'Royal George', by Bacon. South Transept, see below.

Choir Chapels. The choir-apse is rounded and contains the Chapel of St. Edward, so that the high altar is placed somewhat far forward, and the ritual choir extends into the nave. In the ambulatory are two fine brasses for *Abbot Estney* (1498; *36*) and *Sir John Harpedon* (1457; *37*). The three tombs in the Sanctuary are well seen here (see above).

The two-storeyed CHAPEL OF ABBOT ISLIP (lower storey not shown) contains the grave of *Adm. Sir Charles Saunders* (died 1775; *38*), who shared with Wolfe the glory of taking Quebec. On the carved screen appears the abbot's rebus: an eye with a slip of a tree or a man slipping from a branch. The upper chapel (adm. on application), with a too graphic window (1950), is now the Nurses' Memorial Chapel.

The CHAPEL OF ST. JOHN THE BAPTIST is entered through the tiny Chapel of Our Lady of the Pew. Above the entrance is a delicately carved alabaster niche from the demolished Chapel of St. Erasmus (15C). Traces of the painted vault remain from the late 14C; a statue of the Madonna by Sister Concordia was placed in the niche in 1971. To the right in the polygonal Chapel of St. John the Baptist are several 15C tombs of abbots, notably *William de Colchester* (died 1420; *39*). The huge tomb of *Lord Hunsdon* (died 1596; *40*), cousin and Lord Chamberlain to Elizabeth I, is a masterpiece of Elizabethan bombast.

The plain tomb by the NE wall of *Hugh* and *Mary de Bohun* (*41*), dates from 1304–05. Behind is a monument to *Col. Popham*; the inscription was removed because of his Parliamentarian activities. In the centre is a large monument to *Thomas Cecil, Earl of Exeter* (1542–1623; *42*), son of Lord Burghley, with his effigy and that of his first wife His second wife refused to accept the less honourable position on his left hand and was buried in Winchester Cathedral.

In the ambulatory opposite the chapel, the mosaics on the tomb of Henry III are well seen. The well-lit CHAPEL OF ST. PAUL is the easternmost chapel of the North Ambulatory and contains (right) the tomb of *Lord Bourchier* (died 1431; *43*), recently repainted, which forms part of the screen. On the monument of *Lord Cottington* (died 1652; *44*) is a bust of his wife (died 1633), by Le Sueur. On the site of the altar, *Frances Sidney, Countess of Sussex* (died 1589; *45*), founder of Sidney Sussex College at Cambridge. The fine monument to *Dudley Carleton* (died 1632; *46*) is by Nicholas Stone. Beyond good monuments to *Sir Thomas Bromley* (1530–87) and *Sir James Fullerton* (died 1631) is one to *Sir John Puckering* (1544–96; *47*), Speaker of the House of Commons. In the centre, *Sir Giles Daubeny* (died 1508; *48*) and his lady, with fine contemporary costumes. To the right of the exit, bust of *Sir Rowland Hill* (1795–1879), champion of the penny postage. In the ambulatory, opposite the exit from this chapel, note the *Grate of Queen Eleanor's tomb, an admirable specimen of English wrought-iron work by Thomas of Leighton, 1294. Beneath are traces of paintings by Walter of Durham. Above can be seen the Chantry of Henry V, forming a bridge over the ambulatory. The flight of steps leads to the Lady Chapel (Chapel of Henry VII), entered appropriately through a spacious barrel-vaulted vestibule, decorated with bright panelling.

**Chapel of Henry VII. Built in 1503–19, this chapel is the finest example in England of late Perpendicular or Tudor Gothic. Henry ordered it to be 'painted, garnished and adorned in as goodly and rich a manner as such work requireth and as to a king's work apperteyneth'. Of its profuse decoration the culminating glory is the superb fan vaulting, hung with pendants in the nave, and stretched as a canopy to accommodate the bay windows in the aisles. The beautiful tall windows, curved in the aisles and angular in the apse, are particularly ingenious. The carving throughout is of the highest quality, and includes a series of 95 (originally 107) statues of saints popular at the time, with a frieze of angels and badges below. The chapel was begun as a shrine for Henry VI, and carved stalls of the Knights of the Bath separate the nave from the aisles, which have separate entrances at the W end.

In 1725, it became the chapel of the Order of the Bath (reconstituted by George I) with the Dean of Westminster its perpetual dean. After 1812, however, no installation of knights was held until 1913, when the ceremony was revived with all its ancient pomp and the present banners placed in position.

NORTH AISLE OF HENRY VII'S CHAPEL. The tall canopied *Tomb in the centre of the aisle was erected by James I to *Elizabeth I* (1533–1603; *49*), who rests here in the same grave as her sister *Mary I* (died 1558); 'Consorts in throne and tomb, here we sisters rest, Elizabeth and Mary, in hope of the resurrection' (epitaph). The marble figure is the work of Cornelius Cure (1605–07).

The E end of this aisle (*50*) was called 'Innocents' Corner' by Dean Stanley, for here are commemorated two infant *Children of James I* (died 1607), one represented in a cradle which is the actual tomb; and in a small sarcophagus by the E wall are some bones, reinterred as those of *Edward V* and his brother *Richard, Duke of York*, the young sons of Edward IV, who were murdered in the Tower c 1483. Edward V had been born in the Sanctuary of the Abbey.

NAVE OF HENRY VII'S CHAPEL. The beautiful oak doors at the entrance, plated with bronze, date from the 16C. The heraldic devices that appear on them and recur elsewhere in the decoration of the chapel refer to Henry VII's ancestry and to his claims to the throne.

The Welsh dragon indicates his Tudor father; the daisy plant and the portcullis refer to the names of his Lancastrian mother, Margaret Beaufort; the falcon was the badge of Edward IV, father of Elizabeth of York, Henry's wife; the greyhound is that of the Nevilles from whom she was descended. The crown on a bush recalls Henry's first coronation on Bosworth field; while the roses are those of Lancaster and York united by his marriage. Other emblems are the lions of England and the fleur-de-lis of France.

Within, on each side, are the beautiful carved stalls of the Knights of the Bath, each with the arms of its successive holders emblazoned on small copperplates and the banner of the current holder suspended above. The lower seats are those of the esquires (no longer used as such) with their coats-of-arms. Beneath the seats are a number of grotesquely carved misericords (supports for monks when standing), one of which (8th stall on S side) dates from the 13C. At the W end is the naval sword of George VI, with which he conferred the accolade of the Order. The altar (1935) is a reproduction of the original, with a 15C altarpiece by Bart. Vivarini.

Beneath the pavement between the door and the altar reposes *George II* (died 1760; the last king buried in the Abbey), with *Queen Caroline* and numerous members of his family. Below the altar is the grave of *Edward VI* (died 1553). Behind it is the beautiful *Tomb (51)* of *Henry VII* (died 1509) and *Elizabeth of York* (died 1503), an important work by Torrigiani, completed about 1518. The noble effigies of the king and queen lie on a black marble sarcophagus, with a carved frieze of white marble and adorned with gilt medallions of saints. The fine grate is the work of Thomas Ducheman. *James I* (1566–1625) is buried in the same vault as Henry VII and his queen. The first apse-chapel on the S is filled by Le Sueur's monument to *Ludovick Stuart, Duke of Lennox and Richmond* (1574–1624; *52*) with a gilt canopy; in the next is buried *Dean Stanley* (1815–81; *53*), with a fine effigy by Boehm. Here too lies the *Duc de Montpensier* (1775–1807), brother of Louis-Philippe.

The E chapel is now the ROYAL AIR FORCE CHAPEL. The window by Hugh Easton, commemorating the Battle of Britain (July–Oct 1940), incorporates in the design the badges of the 63 Fighter Squadrons that took part. The Chapel keeps the Roll of Honour (facsimile in adjoining chapel) of the 1497 airmen of Britain and her allies who fell in the battle. Nearby is the grave of *Lord Dowding* (1882–1970), who commanded the air defence of Great Britain, and on the S side that of *Lord Trenchard* (1873–1956), 'father' of the RAF. In this chapel were buried *Oliver Cromwell* (1599–1658; tablet), *Henry Ireton* (1611–51), *John Bradshaw* (1602–59) and *Admiral Blake* (1599–1657). At the Restoration all were removed from the Abbey; Blake was reinterred in St. Margaret's churchyard, but the bodies of the others were treated with ignominy, and their heads were struck off at Tyburn and afterwards exposed on Westminster Hall. (See also Red Lion Square, p 188.)

In the next chapel is a vault (usually covered with an organ) with the graves of *Anne of Denmark* (1574–1619; *54*), queen of James I, and *Anne Mowbray*, the child wife of Richard, Duke of York, reburied here in 1965. In the last chapel is the large tomb by Le Sueur, of *George, Duke of Buckingham* (assassinated in 1628; *55*), the favourite of James I and Charles I, with statues by Nicholas Stone of his children. The low stone screen preserved here is in keeping with the originality of the design of the outer walls of the chapel.

SOUTH AISLE OF HENRY VII'S CHAPEL. At the end of this aisle are memorials to *Lord Cromer* (1841–1917), *Lord Curzon* (1859–1925), *Viscount Milner* (1854–1925), and *Cecil Rhodes*. In the centre, tomb of *Margaret, Countess of Lennox* (died 1578; *56*). Her son, Henry Darnley, was husband of Mary, Queen of Scots, and father of James I of England, and his figure among the effigies of her children on the sides of the tomb may be identified by the (restored) crown over his head (as Henry I of Scotland). Next, under a tall canopy, is a recumbent *Figure of *Mary, Queen of Scots* (1542–87; *57*), whose remains were removed here from Peterborough Cathedral in 1612 by order of her son, James I. The work of Cornelius and William Cure (1605–10), this was the last royal tomb erected in the Abbey.

The next *Tomb is that of *Margaret Beaufort, Countess of Richmond* (1443–1509; *58*), mother of Henry VII, patron of Wynkyn de Worde, and foundress of Christ's and St. John's Colleges at Cambridge. The beautiful recumbent figure in gilt-bronze, the masterpiece of Pietro Torrigiani of Florence, is noted for the delicate modelling of the hands. It is surrounded by a contemporary screen. On the wall to the N is a fine bronze bust of *Sir Thomas Lovell* (died 1524), also by Torrigiani. The statue of a Roman matron beside it, by Valory, commemorates *Catherine Lady Walpole* (died 1737).

The incongruous monument to *General Monk, Duke of Albemarle* (1608–70; *59*), restorer of the Stuarts, covers a vault containing the remains of *Charles II* (died 1685), *Mary II* (died 1694), her husband *William III* (died 1702), *Queen Anne* (died 1714), and her husband *Prince George of Denmark* (died 1708).

Cross a reinforced glass bridge (1971) past the tomb and beneath the CHANTRY OF HENRY V (1387–1422). His dispoiled effigy (*60*) rests on a slab of marble and was originally covered with silver-gilt plates stolen, together with the solid silver head, in the reign of Henry VIII. The head was replaced in 1971 in gilt bronze by Louisa Bolt. In the chantry (no adm. except for special services) *Katherine of Valois* (died 1437), Henry's 'beautiful Kate', lies beneath the altar; she was originally interred in the old Lady Chapel. On a beam still higher are a shield, saddle and helmet, probably made for Henry's funeral.

*Chapel of St. Edward the Confessor, is at the same time the most gorgeous and the most sacred part of the church. In the middle stands the mutilated *Shrine of St. Edward the Confessor* (died 1066; *61*), erected in the late 13C for Henry III by 'Peter of Rome', probably the son of Odericus (see above), and showing traces of the original mosaics. The upper part, now of wood (1557), was originally a golden shrine decorated with jewels and gold images of saints, all of which disappeared at the Dissolution. In the recesses of the base sick people used to spend the night in hope of cure. Roman Catholic pilgrims visit the shrine on St. Edward's Day (13 Oct). On the S side of the shrine is the tomb of *Philippa of Hainault* (died 1369; *63*), wife of Edward III, with the alabaster effigy of the queen by Hennequin of Liegè, sculptor to the king of France. The elaborate tomb of *Edward III* (died 1377; *64*) has niches in which were statuettes of his fourteen children, six of which remain (seen from S ambulatory); the contemporary wooden canopy is fine. The last tomb on this side is that of *Richard II* (died 1400; *65*) and his first wife *Anne of Bohemia* (died 1394), which is in the same style as that of Edward III. It is profusely decorated with delicately engraved patterns, among which may be distinguished the broom-pods of the Plantagenets, the white hart, the rising sun, etc.; the beautiful paintings in the canopy represent the Trinity, the Coronation of the Virgin, and Anne of Bohemia's coat-of-arms. At the W end is a beautiful screen (mid 15C) with 14 scenes of the life of Edward the Confessor. In front are remains of the Cosmati pavement, and the *Coronation Chair (66)*, made in oak by Walter of Durham c 1300–01. It has left the Abbey only thrice—when Cromwell was installed as Lord Protector in Westminster Hall, and for safety during the two World Wars. It encloses the famous 'Stone of Scone', carried off from Scotland by Edward I in 1297 and used for all subsequent coronations of English monarchs. Beside it are the *State Sword* (7ft long) and *Shield* of Edward III.

The *Stone of Scone*, on which the Scottish kings were crowned from time immemorial down to John Baliol, King of Scotland (13C) was regarded as the palladium of Scottish independence, and its character is supposed to have been vindicated when James VI of Scotland became also James I of England in 1603. A long but quite mythical history attaches to this block of reddish sandstone from central Scotland. It is traditionally identified with Jacob's pillow at Bethel, afterwards the 'Lia Fail' or 'Stone of Destiny' on the sacred hill of Tara, in Ireland. Historically, it is recorded as being used for the enthronement of Macbeth's stepson at Scone in 1057, and was certainly in use there earlier. On 24 Dec 1950, the stone was stolen by Scottish 'Nationalists' and taken to Arbroath; it was replaced on 13 April 1951.

On the N side is the plain altar-tomb, without effigy, of *Edward I* (died 1307; *67*); in 1744 his body (6ft 2in long) was found to be in good preservation, dressed in royal robes with a gilt crown. Beyond are the beautiful Gothic *Tombs of Henry III* (1207–72; *68*), and his daughter-in-law, *Eleanor of Castile* (died 1290; *69*), wife of Edward I. Henry's tomb was designed by Peter of Rome, and Eleanor's was executed by Richard Crundale with paintings by Walter of Durham; both the beautiful bronze effigies, the earliest cast in England, are by William Torel, a goldsmith of London. The canopy over Eleanor's tomb dates from the 15C, when the old one was destroyed by the erection of Henry V's Chantry.

The CHAPEL OF ST. NICHOLAS, off the S ambulatory, has a fine stone screen. On the right of the door, *Philippa, Duchess of York* is buried (died 1431; *70*). In the centre is the fine tomb of *Sir George Villiers* (died 1606; *71*) and his wife (died 1630), parents of the Duke of Buckingham. The large monument on the S wall, to the *Wife* and *Daughter of Lord Burghley* (c 1588; *72*), and that on the E wall, to the *Duchess of Somerset* (died 1587; *73*), widow of the Protector, are good examples of the Renaissance work. Below this chapel is the vault of the dukes of Northumberland, the only family with right of sepulture in the Abbey. In the Ambulatory, opposite this chapel, has been placed an oaken *Retable*, a precious example of French or English painting of c 1255, with rich decorations.

The CHAPEL OF SS. EDMUND AND THOMAS THE MARTYR is separated from the ambulatory by an ancient oaken screen. To the right, inside lies *William de Valence, Earl of Pembroke* (died 1296; *74*), half-brother of Henry III. This tomb consists of an oak coffin and effigy of the deceased, which were formerly coated with Limoges enamel, traces of which may still be seen. *Edward Talbot, Earl of Shrewsbury* (died 1617; *75*) and his wife, a handsome Jacobean tomb, to accommodate which, however, some of the arcading was destroyed. *Sir Richard Pecksall* (1571), master of the buckhounds. *Sir Bernard Brocas* (died 1395), Captain of Calais. Beyond the large monument to *Lord John Russell* (died 1584; *76*), with his infant son, is the seated figure of his daughter, *Lady Elizabeth Russell* (1576–1601), the earliest non-recumbent statue in the Abbey. In the floor, grave of *Edward Bulwer Lytton* (1803–73), the novelist. In the centre of the chapel are the tombs of *Robert Waldeby, Archbishop of York* (died 1397; *77*), the companion of the Black Prince, with a brass representing him in full eucharistic vestments, and of **Eleanor de Bohun, Duchess of Gloucester* (died 1399; *78*), in conventual dress, the largest and finest brass in the Abbey. Near the E wall, *Frances, Duchess of Suffolk* (died 1559), mother of Lady Jane Grey. Adjoining are the finely modelled but mutilated effigies of two children of Edward III (1340). Beside the door into the chapel, **John of Eltham* (1316–37; *79*), second son of Edward II; this tomb, with the earliest alabaster effigy in the Abbey, is especially interesting for the careful representation of the prince's armour. Opposite the entrance to this chapel is the outer side of Edward III's tomb, with beautiful little brass *Statuettes of his children, with enamelled coats of arms.

Between this chapel and the next a small altar-tomb (*80*) covers the remains of four children of Henry III and four of Edward I. Opposite is the CHAPEL OF ST. BENEDICT (no adm.), best seen from the S transept. Beside the railing on this side is the alabaster tomb of *Simon Langham* (died 1376; *81*), abbot of Westminster and afterwards archbishop and cardinal. In the ambulatory is the so-called tomb of *Sebert* (*82*) and his wife; then a tablet to Anne Nevill (1456–85), queen of Richard III. Above is the back of the sedilia in the sanctuary, with 14C paintings of Edward the Confessor and the Annunciation (mutilated). Outside the gate (right) is a monument to *Dr Richard Busby* (1606–95), a famous headmaster of Westminster School.

The South Transept is known as **Poets' Corner**, taking its name from the tombs of Chaucer and Spenser. The tombs of the poets have overflowed into the S end of the central aisle also. On the end wall of the transept are two magnificent wall-paintings of St. Christopher and the Incredulity of St. Thomas. Uncovered in 1936, they are ascribed to Walter of Durham (c 1280) and are outstanding examples of the Westminster school of painting.

On the left side of the E aisle is a bust of *John Dryden* (1631–1700), and on the pier opposite (right) is a bust of *William Blake* (1757–1827), by Epstein. By the next pillar (left) is a bust of *Henry Longfellow* (1807–82), placed by the English admirers of the American poet in 1884. Beneath the next window is the Gothic *Tomb of *Geoffrey Chaucer* (1340?–1400; *24*), the poet of the 'Canterbury Tales', erected 155 years after his death. The space at the end of the altar-tomb is perhaps a prayer recess. Further on lies *Michael Drayton* (1563–1631). Beneath the pavement in front of Chaucer's tomb is the grave of *Robert Browning* (1812–89), and memorials to *Alfred Tennyson* (1809–92), *T.S. Eliot* (1888–1965), and *Lord Byron* (1788–1824).

At the SE angle are two doorways. Outside that in the E wall is an ancient pathway going straight to the Palace of Westminster, and a tablet on the left marks the approximate site of Caxton's original printing press (1477), six years before he set up in larger premises in the Almonry. In the S wall is the entrance to the *Chapter-House Crypt* (no adm.), an eight-sided undercroft (1248) with a massive central column, once used as the royal treasury.

On the S wall, above the door to the crypt, is a medallion of *Ben Jonson* (1573?–1637; buried in the nave). Further on, *Edmund Spenser* (1552?–99; *25*), the poet of 'The Faerie Queene'; the present monument is a copy (1778) of the original. *John Milton* (1608–74; *26*; buried at St. Giles, Cripplegate), a memorial delayed by political feeling for over 60 years after the poet's death. Below, *Thomas Gray* (1716–71; grave at Stoke Poges). On the partition-wall, the remarkable monument to *Matthew Prior* (1664–1721), designed by Gibbs, executed by Rysbrack, with a bust by Coysevox. On the next pier, beyond a bust of Tennyson, *Adam Lindsay Gordon* (1833–70), the poet of Australia, and *Thomas Campbell* (1777–1844). In the floor a little to the N, gravestone of *Thomas Parr* (died 1635; 'Old Parr'), said to have lived 152 years and under ten sovereigns, while further S are those of *Dr Samuel Johnson* (1709–84), with a bust by Nollekens above it, *David Garrick* (1717–79), and *Sir Henry Irving* (1838–1905). On the W side of the partition-wall. *William Wordsworth* (1770–1850; buried at Grasmere); *Samuel Taylor Coleridge* (1772–1834; buried at Highgate); and *Robert Southey* (1774–1843; buried at Crosthwaite, Cumbria) epitaph by Wordsworth. *William Shakespeare* (1564–1616; *27*; buried at Stratford-on-Avon). On the monument, by Scheemakers, which was erected in 1740, are lines from 'The Tempest', and at the corners of the pedestal are carved heads representing Elizabeth I, Henry V, and Richard III. *John Keats* (1796–1821) and *P.B. Shelley* (1792–1822), both buried in Rome, are commemorated above. *James Thomson* (1700–48; buried at Richmond), author of 'Rule Britannia'. Above, *Robert Burns* (1759–96; buried at Dumfries). Below, the *Brontë Sisters*, with a line from Emily's 'Old Stoic': 'with courage to endure'. Above the door to the Chapel of St. Faith, *Oliver Goldsmith* (1728–74; date of birth given wrongly in the epitaph; buried in the Temple), with an epitaph by Dr Johnson.

The *Chapel of St. Faith* (c 1249 restored 1972), formerly the revestry, is used for private devotion.

To the right of the chapel, *Sir Walter Scott* (1771–1832; buried at Dryburgh), and above, *John Ruskin* (1819–1900; buried at Coniston). The monument to *John Campbell, Duke of Argyll* (1680–1743; *28*) is a fine work by Roubiliac. Above on the W wall, *George Frederick Handel* (1685–1759). Below is a memorial plaque to Jenny Lind (died 1887), the 'Swedish Nightingale'. A slab in the floor marks Handel's grave, and one beside it that of *Charles Dickens* (1812–70). In the floor are a tablet commemorating *Thomas Hardy* (1840–1928) and the grave of *Rudyard Kipling* (1865–1936). By the pier, *William Makepeace Thackeray* (1811–63; buried at Kensal Green). *Jos. Addison* (1672–1719). *Lord Macaulay* (1800–59). Recent additions to Poets' Corner are *Dylan Thomas* (died 1953), *D.H. Lawrence* (died 1930) *Noel Coward* (died 1973), *John Clare* (died 1864) and *Edward Lear* (died 1888). *Laurence Olivier* (died 1989), the great actor, will have a plaque here from 1990, close to Shakespeare.

South Choir Aisle. Opposite the E door into the cloisters are two good monuments to *William Thynne* (d 1584), and to *Sir Thomas Richardson* (died 1635; *29*), in black marble, by Le Sueur. To the left in the next bay is an inappropriate monument to *Sir Cloudesley Shovel* (1650–1707; *30*) between memorials to *Admiral Blake* (1599–1657) and *Robert Clive* (1725–74). Above is a monument to *Sir Godfrey*

Kneller (1646–1723; buried at Kneller Hall), the only painter comme-morated in the Abbey. In the 3rd bay (right), the tomb of *Thomas Owen* (died 1598; *31*), with a fine painted alabaster figure. On either side of it, are the tomb of *General Pasquale Paoli* (1725–1807), the Corsican patriot who died as a refugee in England, and a tablet to *William Tyndale* (1490–1536), translator of the Bible. Opposite, medallions to *John Wesley* (1703–91) and *Charles Wesley* (1707–88), both buried elsewhere, *H.F. Lyte* (1793–1847), author of 'Abide with me', with *Dr Isaac Watts* (1674–1748; buried in Bunhill Fields), the hymn writer, beneath. Under the organ loft is a monument to *Thomas Thynne* (1648–82; *32*), with a bas-relief depicting his assassination.

Cloisters and Conventual Buildings. The earliest parts of the present CLOISTERS date from the mid 13C, the remainder from 1344–70. The cloisters are connected with the church by two doors in the S nave aisle, affording convenient entrance and exit for conventual process-ions. Visitors should leave the church by the one to the E, entering the cloisters at their NE angle, the earliest and finest part. The external carving on the doorway should be noticed. In the *E Walk* a tablet on the wall in the second bay bears the touching inscription 'Jane Lister, dear Childe', with the date 1688. Between the entrances to the Chapter House and to the Chamber of the Pyx is the entrance to the Library and Muniment Room. The *S Walk* (14C) was the burial-place of the abbots for nearly 200 years after the Conquest. The three effigies beneath the wall seat are of Abbots Laurence (died 1173), Gilbert Crispin (died 1117), and William de Humez (died 1222). The recesses in the wall beside the old entrance to the Refectory served as towel-cupboards. The *W Walk* (14C) was used as the monastery school. On the wall is a memorial, by G. Ledward, to the members of the submarine branch of the Royal Navy who lost their lives in the two World Wars, and to members of the Commandos, the Airborne Forces and Special Air Service killed in 1939–45. In the *N Walk* (14C; being restored) is buried *General Burgoyne* (1722–92), who surrendered to General Gates at Saratoga in 1777.

Here is the Westminster Abbey Brass Rubbing Centre with an extensive collection of medieval and Tudor brasses.

The Chapter House open daily 0930–1745. Admission charge.

The *CHAPTER HOUSE is entered from the E Walk. Over the entrance are sculpted figures, much mutilated, of the 13C. The vaulted vestibule has fine bosses. At the top of the stairs *James Russell Lowell* (1819–91), the American writer, and *Walter Hines Page* (1855–1918), American ambassador, are commemorated. Opposite, the coffin-lid, with a cross in relief, is perhaps the only extant relic of Sebert's church; the Roman sarcophagus was buried in the green N of the Abbey. Note the original tiled *Pavement. The beautiful octagonal room, 56ft in diameter, was built c 1245–55 above the crypt of the Confessor's chapter-house. On the left is the Roll of Honour of the Royal Army Medical Corps. The lofty roof is supported by a single central shaft, 35ft high, and it is lit by six huge windows. These, destroyed by bombing in 1941, were reset in 1950 with some of the original glass; they show scenes from the abbey's history and the arms of benefactors. The tracery, like the roof, is modern, though copied from the blank window which escaped mutilation. The arcading on the walls is adorned with paintings (partly restored) of the life of St. John and of the Apocalypse, with a frieze of animals below, presented by John of Northampton (1372–1404), a Westminster monk. The beautiful Madonna and angel above the door date from 1250–53. The Chapter House is especially memorable as the 'cradle of representative and constitutional government throughout the world', for here the early House of Commons, separated from the House of Lords in the reign of Edward III, held its meetings down to 1547, when it migrated to St. Stephen's Chapel at the Palace of Westminster. From c 1550 to 1865 it served as a State muniment room.

Pyx Chamber/Treasury and Norman Undercroft Museum, Westminster Abbey, SW1. (Tel. 071-222 5152). Open daily 0930–1630. Admission charge.

The PYX CHAMBER AND TREASURY is entered from the E walk of the cloisters through a Norman archway and massive double door with six locks. It was part of the 11C undercroft beneath the Monks' Dormitory and became the royal treasury in the 13C. The Trial of the Pyx—the testing of new coins—once took place here. The exhibition, opened in April 1987 with financial support from English Heritage and the Worshipful Company of Goldsmiths, shows the Westminster Abbey plate dating from the 17C and the St. Margaret Church plate with two communion cups from 1551. The altar is the oldest in the Abbey.

The *Dark* or *Norman Cloister* (11C), leads to the UNDERCROFT Museum, an impressive, vaulted room which first became the Abbey Museum in 1908. The current exhibition was set up in 1987 and illustrates the history of the Abbey. It includes the famous royal effigies and is now run by English Heritage.

The carving on the capitals dates from the 12th century when the room may be have been used as 'a common room'—a calefactorium for the monks whose dormitory was above.

It used to be the custom to show the embalmed bodies of royal persons at their funerals; the actual bodies were later replaced by life-like effigies of wood, plaster, or, at a later period, wax. Notable among the wooden effigies or heads here are those of Edward III (perhaps the oldest in Europe) and Henry VII, both death-mask portraits. The plaster head of Mary II is less successful. Anne of Bohemia, Katherine of Valois, Elizabeth of York, and Anne of Denmark represent the queens-consort. The eleven wax figures are interesting both as portraits and for their costumes. The oldest is that of Charles II, the one of Elizabeth I having been remade in 1760; others include Lady Frances Stuart (the Duchess of Richmond and Lennox) dressed in the robes she wore for the coronation of Queen Anne and with her stuffed parrot by her side (possibly the oldest stuffed bird in England—they both died in 1702), William III and Mary II acquired in 1724—the king stands on a footstool to bring him nearer to the height of his very tall wife (nearly 6ft), and her sister Queen Anne (note the likeness). The figures of Nelson and Chatham are not funeral effigies, but were added to attract visitors to this exhibition first set up in Islip Chantry Chapel in 1779; they are outstanding as portraits.

Also displayed here are the royal writ and seal of Edward the Confessor and William I; a letter from John of Gaunt; the lease made out to Chaucer for premises in the garden of the old Lady Chapel; and the Coronation service book. A complete medieval arrow (unique), in the case opposite, was found in the top of Henry V's Chantry, possibly having been used as a pigeon scarer. Among other objects found in the Abbey are: the sword of Henry V; the ring of Bp Courtenay of Norwich (died 1415) found in his grave in 1953; the ring said to have been given by Elizabeth I to the Earl of Essex, and to have been intercepted by the Countess of Nottingham when Essex, on his condemnation, sent it back to the Queen in hope of pardon; a trunk thought to belong to Lady Margaret Beaufort; and the frater bell of the monastery.

Further on an arched passage on the left leads to the LITTLE CLOISTER, on the site of the monks' infirmary, a withdrawn and picturesque spot, though modernised and restored after damage in 1940–41. In the E walk survives the 14C doorway of *St. Catherine's Chapel* (1165–70; the infirmary chapel), the ruined arcades of which may be viewed through a doorway to the left. In the S walk a door leads to *College Garden* (open to visitors on Thurs 12.00–16.00 or 18.00; entrance also from Great College St). The Dark Cloister ends at the yard of Westminster School (p 64).

From the junction of the W and S walks of the great cloister a corridor leads to the W to Dean's Yard. Near its W end, on the right, is a passage admitting to the *Abbots' Courtyard*, lying between the Deanery, formerly the Abbots' Palace, on the right, and the College Hall, on the left. The steps at the end ascend to the *Jericho Parlour*, or panelled ante-room, to the **Jerusalem Chamber** (14C), the abbots' retiring room, now used as the chapter-room and shown only by special permission of the Dean. In this chamber Henry IV d in 1413, having had a stroke while praying at the shrine of the Confessor. (Only open on Super tours—see p 63.)

The *Library and Muniment Room* (adm. by special permission only), occupying part of the monks' dormitory, above the chapter-house vestibule and the Chamber of the Pyx, is entered from the E walk of the cloister by the original day-stairs. The library was founded c 1623 and contains contemporary bookpresses, as well as a priceless collection of books, charters, etc. For Dean's Yard, and the precinct wall, see Rte 1.

3 The Houses of Parliament

Access: Underground, Westminster

N.B. The Houses of Parliament and Westminster Hall are no longer open to visitors, except for those attending debates or visiting in an organised party arranged by a Member of Parliament or a peer. There is public access to the Central Lobby through St. Stephen's entrance for those who wish to lobby their Member of Parliament.

Admission to debates: to obtain a ticket for the afternoon session in the House of Commons, write to your own Member of Parliament or to your Embassy in London. Prime Minister's Question Time is on Tuesdays and Thursdays at 15.15. Those without tickets should queue outside St. Stephen's entrance and the head of the queue is usually admitted from 16.15 (11.30 on Fridays) for the House of Commons and from 14.30 for the House of Lords.

The House of Commons usually meets on Monday to Thursday at 14.30 and on Fridays at 11.00. After the Speaker's procession through the Central Lobby, there are prayers (public not admitted) and then Question Time. Public business usually begins at 15.30 and continues until 22.30 or later. On Fridays, private members' bills and motions are debated and the House rises at 16.30. Visitors to the public gallery may obtain the Order Paper from the doorkeeper as well as a pass for the cafeteria. The House of Lords usually meets at 14.30 and the sittings are shorter. The Houses of Parliament have short recesses at Christmas, Easter and Whitsun and a long summer recess from the

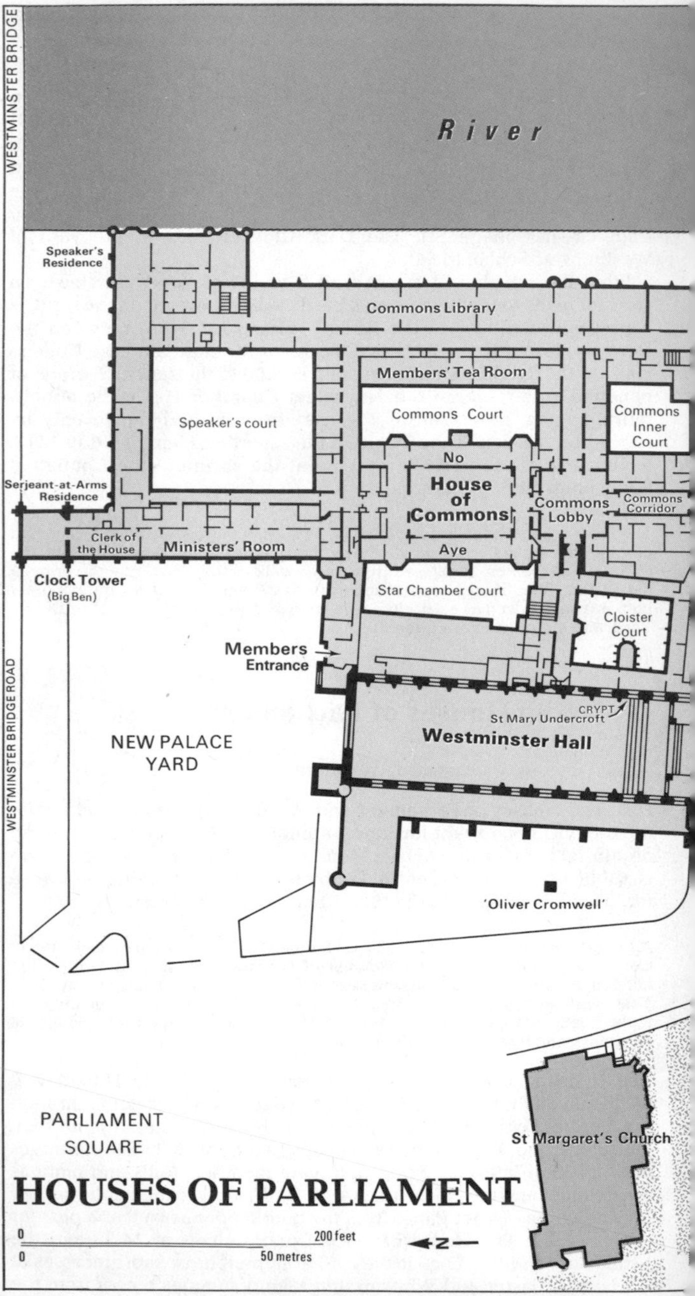

WESTMINSTER BRIDGE

River

Speaker's
Residence

Commons Library

Members' Tea Room

Commons Court

Commons
Inner
Court

Speaker's court

No

House
of
Commons

Commons
Lobby

Commons
Corridor

Serjeant-at-Arms
Residence

Clerk of
the House

Ministers' Room

Aye

Clock Tower
(Big Ben)

Star Chamber Court

Cloister
Court

Members
Entrance

WESTMINSTER BRIDGE ROAD

NEW PALACE
YARD

St Mary Undercroft

CRYPT

Westminster Hall

'Oliver Cromwell'

PARLIAMENT
SQUARE

St Margaret's Church

HOUSES OF PARLIAMENT

| 0 | 200 feet |
| 0 | 50 metres |

◄─Z─

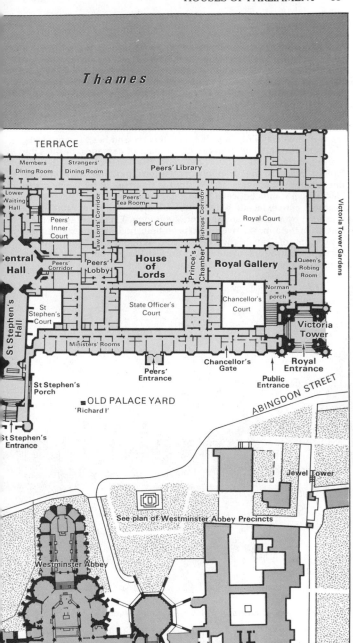

Thames

TERRACE

Members Dining Room

Strangers' Dining Room

Peers' Library

Lower Waiting Hall

Peers' Tea Room

Law Lords Corridor

Bishops Corridor

Royal Court

Peers' Inner Court

Peers' Court

Central Hall

Peers' Corridor

Peers' Lobby

House of Lords

Prince's Chamber

Royal Gallery

Queen's Robing Room

St Stephen's Hall

St Stephen's Court

State Officer's Court

Chancellor's Court

Norman porch

Victoria Tower

Ministers' Rooms

Peers' Entrance

Chancellor's Gate

Public Entrance

Royal Entrance

St Stephen's Porch

OLD PALACE YARD
'Richard I'

ABINGDON STREET

St Stephen's Entrance

Jewel Tower

See plan of Westminster Abbey Precincts

Westminster Abbey

Victoria Tower Gardens

end of July until the middle of October. The official State Opening of the parliamentary session usually takes place in early November.

The **Houses of Parliament** (Pl. 19; 1), or *Palace of Westminster*, a stately pile in an admirable late-Gothic style, rises close to the Thames. The rich external decoration of oriels, pinnacles, and turrets is well balanced by the imposing towers; recent cleaning and restoration have revealed the intricate details and a glorious sandstone colour. The building, which incorporates the ancient Westminster Hall and the crypt and cloisters of St. Stephen's Chapel, was designed by Sir Charles Barry, and was built in 1840–50. Augustus Pugin provided many of the detail drawings. It covers 8 acres and has 11 courtyards, 100 staircases, 1100 apartments, and 2 miles of passages. Besides the Houses of Commons, in the N half, and the House of Lords, in the S half, it contains the dwellings of various parliamentary officials (including the Speaker). The W front is interrupted by Westminster Hall, which stands between New Palace Yard and Old Palace Yard; but the E, or river façade, extends unbroken for a length of 940ft, and is preceded by a terrace on the river, 700ft long. This long façade (best seen from the opposite riverbank) is embellished with the statues and royal arms of British sovereigns from William the Conqueror to Victoria, while figures of the earlier English kings, from the Heptarchy to the Conquest, appear on the short N front.

The Houses of Parliament from the River Thames

Of the three towers, the tallest and the finest is the noble *Victoria Tower* (336ft high; 75ft square), at the SW angle, said to be the loftiest square tower in existence. The archway, 50ft high, below this tower, is the royal entrance to the building. The *Central Spire* (300ft) rises above the Central Hall and serves also as a ventilating shaft. The finial of the *Clock Tower* is 320ft from the ground. The clock (still wound by hand), an authoritative time-keeper, has four dials, each 23ft square; the figures are 2ft high and the minute-hands are 14ft long. The hours are struck upon 'Big Ben', a bell weighing 13.5 tons, named after Sir Benjamin Hall, First Commissioner of Works when it was hung.—A flag on the Victoria Tower by day and a light in the Clock Tower by night indicate that Parliament is sitting. MPs usually use the entrance in New Palace Yard (adorned with catalpa trees); beacons on the gate posts warn them of a division (comp. below). During the construction of an underground car park in 1973, successive fountains (12C and 15C) were unearthed.

The Houses of Parliament occupy the site of an ancient palace, and by virtue of that fact still rank as a royal palace and are in the charge of the hereditary Lord Great Chamberlain (not to be confused with the Lord Chamberlain of the Household). This palace was the chief London residence of the sovereign from the reign of Edward the Confessor (or perhaps earlier) until Henry VIII seized Whitehall in 1529. Old Palace Yard was an inner court of the palace, and until 1800 the House of Lords assembled in a chamber at its S end, which, in 1605, was the scene of the Gunpowder Plot. In 1512 the palace was very seriously damaged by fire, and it was never completely rebuilt. In 1547 the House of Commons transferred its sittings from the Chapter House of Westminster Abbey to St. Stephen's Chapel, and in 1800 the House of Lords moved to the old Court of Requests. In 1834 the entire palace was burned down, with the exception of Westminster Hall, the crypt of St. Stephen's Chapel, and part of the cloisters, but the rebuilding began at once, and the Lords took possession of their new chamber in 1847, the Commons theirs in 1852. During the Second World War the buildings were damaged on more than 12 occasions. The worst attack caused the almost complete destruction of the House of Commons on 10 May 1941, besides other damage.

On a pre-arranged tour visitors see some of the following features, following part of the line of route taken by HM The Queen when opening Parliament.

The INTERIOR of the building is handsomely decorated in a style characteristic of its period, with fine ceilings, friezes, mosaic pavements, and metal work. The *Royal Staircase* leads to the NORMAN PORCH, intended to be decorated with statues and frescoes illustrating the Norman period.

Around the QUEEN'S ROBING ROOM, used as the House of Lords in 1941–50, runs a series of carved panels, by H.H. Armstead, with episodes from the Arthurian legend, while frescoes above, by W.A. Dyce, illustrate the virtues of chivalry.

The ROYAL GALLERY is a fine hall, 110ft long, through which the sovereign passes on the way to the House of Lords. Here are portraits of George III and Queen Charlotte, George VI and Queen Elizabeth I, George V and Queen Mary (by Sir William Llewellyn), Queen Victoria and Prince Albert (by Winterhalter), and Edward VII and Queen Alexandra (by Luke Fildes). The two huge mural paintings by D. Maclise represent the Death of Nelson and the Meeting of Wellington and Blücher after Waterloo. The gilt statues of English monarchs are by B. Philip. A recess at the S end forms a War Memorial to Peers and their sons, by John Tweed. The floor of Minton tiles is noteworthy.

The PRINCE'S CHAMBER, which follows, is decorated in a more sombre tone, with dark panelling. In the recess opposite the entrance is a white marble statue of Queen Victoria, enthroned between Justice and Mercy, by Gibson. On the walls are portraits of the Tudor kings and their consorts (1485–1603). Below bronze reliefs depict events of their reigns.

The **House of Lords**, a lavishly decorated and colourful Gothic hall by Pugin (90ft long, 45ft wide, and 45ft high), was used by the House of Commons from the destruction of their own chamber in 1941 until the opening of the rebuilt House of Commons in 1950. The gilded ceiling was extensively repaired in 1984. The televising of proceedings in the House of Lords started in 1985 four years before the House of Commons.

At the S end, beneath an elaborate canopy, is the throne of the Sovereign. In front, separated from the throne by a gilded railing, the Woolsack, a plain cushioned ottoman stuffed with wool, is occupied by the Lord Chancellor as presiding officer of the House of Lords. It is said to have been adopted in the reign of Edward III as a reminder of the importance to England of the wool trade. At the N end is the Bar, where the Commons, headed by their Speaker, attend at the opening of Parliament, and lawsuits on final appeal are pleaded. Above it is the *Press Gallery* with the *Strangers' Gallery* behind. The six frescoes above are by Maclise, Cope, Dyce, and Horsley.

The PEERS' LOBBY, a handsomely decorated chamber, has a fine encaustic tiled pavement and good brass gates in the S doorway. Over the N and S doors are the arms of six dynasties of English rulers (Saxon, Norman, Plantagenet, Tudor, Stuart, and Hanoverian), with the initial letter of the dynastic name below each. In the PEERS' CORRIDOR, leading N to the Central Hall, are eight paintings, by C.W. Cope (1856–66), of the Stuart and Commonwealth periods.

The CENTRAL HALL (usually called the Central Lobby), an ornate octagonal vestibule, 60ft in diameter and 75ft high, separates the precincts of the Lords from those of the Commons. On the floor is the text, from the Latin Vulgate: 'Except the Lord keep the house, their labour is but lost that build it'. The ceiling is inlaid, between the massive ribs of the vaulting, with Venetian glass mosaic, showing various royal badges. Over the doorways, the patron saints of Great Britain and Ireland are represented in glass mosaic by Poynter and Anning Bell. In niches around the hall are statues of English sovereigns of the Plantagenet line and their consorts; and on pedestals are statues of eminent statesmen.

The **House of Commons**, approached by the COMMONS' CORRIDOR and COMMONS' LOBBY, lies to the N of the Central Hall. The original chamber was destroyed by fire on 10 May 1941; a new chamber (130ft long, 48ft wide, and 43ft high) designed by Sir Giles Gilbert Scott in a less inspired and more sombre interpretation of the late-Gothic style, was opened in Oct 1950. The structural oak and the stonework are English; many of the furnishings were gifts from Commonwealth countries. Televising of Commons proceedings started in the autumn of 1989 on an experimental basis.

The chamber is entered from the Commons Lobby through the CHURCHILL ARCH, built of stones battered and flaked by the fire of 1941, and flanked by statues of Churchill (1966; by Oscar Nemon) and Lloyd George.

The Speaker's chair (from Australia) is at the N end of the chamber. In front of the chair is the table of the House (from Canada), on which the mace rests during the sittings of the House. When the House is 'in Committee' the mace is placed 'under the table'. On either side are the 'front benches', the ministerial on the Speaker's right, the opposition on his left. On the floor of the House and in the side galleries are seats for 602 of the 630 members. Above the Speaker's chair is the Press Gallery, with 161 seats, and at the other end, facing the Speaker, is the gallery seating for *Distinguished and Ordinary Strangers*. The House is flanked on each side by *Division Lobbies*, into which the members file when a vote is b ing taken, 'Ayes to the right' (W), 'Noes to the left' (E).

To the W of the Central Hall is ST. STEPHEN'S HALL, the walls of which roughly correspond with the ground plan of St. Stephen's Chapel, founded by Edward I and completed by Edward III, 1292–1364. In this chapel, the chapel royal of the Old Palace of Westminster, the House of Commons met from 1547 until 1834. In the angles of the hall are figures of the early Norman kings, and on pedestals by the walls are statues of British statesmen. The panels beneath the windows illustrate The Building of Britain. ST. STEPHEN'S PORCH, leads to Westminster Hall. The beautiful large window on the left originally formed the S end of this hall, but was moved to its present position by Sir Charles Barry. The stained glass, by Sir N. Comper (1953), and the sculpture below, by Sir B. Mackennal (1922), are war memorials to Members and Officers of both Houses of Parliament.

The venerable and beautiful *Westminster Hall (239.5ft long, 67.5ft wide, and 92ft high), originally built by William Rufus, William II, in 1097, was rebuilt between 1397 and 1399 during the reign of Richard II when the magnificent oak hammer-beamed *Roof was added. Entirely bare of ornament and usually quite empty, the hall is one of the finest and largest timber-roofed buildings in Europe. The mason was Henry Yevele and the carpenter Hugh Herland. From the 13C until 1882 the chief English law courts sat at Westminster Hall, at first in the hall itself, afterwards in buildings (now pulled down) erected for the purpose on the W side. A thorough restoration of the roof was completed in 1923 and the war damage of 1941 has likewise been repaired.

Westminster Hall is perhaps specially memorable as the scene of the condemnation of Charles I in 1649. A brass tablet on the steps at the S end marks the spot where the king sat during his trial. But it has witnessed many other historic events and grave state-trials. Here Edward II abdicated in 1327, and, by the irony of fate Richard II, who rebuilt the hall, was deposed here in 1399, soon after its completion. A tablet on the E wall marks the position of the door through which Charles I passed in 1641 when he attempted to arrest the Five Members in their seats. Since then no sovereign entered the Commons until 1950, when George VI visited the rebuilt chamber. In 1653 Oliver Cromwell was installed as Lord Protector. Among those who have been condemned to death in this hall are William Wallace (1305), Lord Cobham (1417), Sir Thomas More (1535), Sir Thomas Wyatt (1554), the Earl of Essex (1601), Guy Fawkes (1606), and Strafford (1641). The last public trial in the hall was that of Lord Melville for malversation in 1806. Since the 19C the hall has been used for the lying-in-state of monarchs and eminent statesmen. The Opening Session of the American Bar Association was held here in 1985.

From the SE angle of Westminster Hall a staircase descends to *ST. STEPHEN'S CRYPT, the ancient crypt of St. Stephen's Chapel, now known also as the church of *St. Mary Undercroft*. The crypt, with its finely groined vaulting retaining most of the original bosses, has been restored and richly decorated and is still occasionally used for christenings and marriages in the families of Members of Parliament.

A doorway on the E side of Westminster Hall opens upon the beautiful *St. Stephen's Cloisters* built by Henry VIII, with a fan-tracery ceiling little inferior to that of Henry VII's Chapel in Westminster Abbey. A small oratory or chapel projecting from the W walk is traditionally said to be the place where the death-warrant of Charles I was signed.

4   Victoria Embankment and Whitehall

Access: Underground, Westminster and Embankment.

From Parliament Square (See Route 1), Bridge St continues to the Victoria Embankment which runs along the north bank of the Thames. Westminster Bridge is the second on the site, designed by Thomas Page and completed in 1862. (See also Route 31, p 290). The striking statue of Queen Boadicea or Boudicca (1902) driving her chariot (without reins) to victory against the Romans, accompanied by her two daughters is by Thomas Thornycroft. Below is Westminster Pier with regular sightseeing boat departures downstream (all the year round) and upstream (summer). (See p 301.) A new pier is planned. On the opposite bank is County Hall due to become an hotel (see p 206).

The Victoria Embankment was completed in 1870 to a design by Bazalgette and incorporating the District Line Underground service below. Norman Shaw, the architect, is commemorated in a medallion by Hamo Thornycroft (1914) inserted on the second floor frontage of the building which he designed as New Scotland Yard but which is now the Norman Shaw Building (see also p 90). The RAF Memorial in the shape of a gilded eagle at Whitehall Stairs is by William Reid Dick with the stone pedestal by R. Blomfield (1923). In front of the Ministry of Defence Building are statues of Viscount Portal of Hungerford (by Nemon, 1975) and further on General Gordon (1838–85) by Hamo Thornycroft transferred here from Trafalgar Square in 1953. Here is the surviving part of Queen Mary's Terrace, built for Mary II in 1691 with steps descending to the 17C waterlevel.

In the gardens beyond Horse Guards Avenue are statues of Air Chief Marshal Viscount Trenchard (by William Macmillan, 1961), William Tyndale, who translated the Bible (by Boehm, 1884), a bust of Samuel Plimsoll—'the sailor's friend'—showing the Plimsoll line (by Blunderstone, 1929), Sir Henry Bartle Frere (by Thomas Brock, 1888), and General Outram, who also made his name in India (by Matthew Noble, 1871), with Sir Joseph Bazalgette, the Embankment engineer, commemorated in a bust by George Simonds (1899) on the river-wall. Boats moored along here include the 'Tattershall Castle', a Clyde paddle-steamer, now a pub, and the 'Hispaniola', a restaurant. The Victoria Embankment continues on the other side of Hungerford Bridge. See Rte 18.

Return to Bridge St and Whitehall.

The brief half-mile known as **Whitehall** which separates Westminster from Charing Cross has been a thoroughfare at least since the 15C. In the 16–17C most of the area between Charing Cross and the present Westminster Bridge and between the Thames and St. James's Park was occupied by the ROYAL PALACE OF WHITEHALL, of which little now remains but the name and one building. The association of the area with government began as early as the 17C, and today it is the political centre of Great Britain, lined on the W side of the street with public offices, which range in date from 1725 at the N end, to 1919, at the S end. Recent cleaning has greatly enhanced their effect.

Whitehall Palace originated in a mansion purchased by Walter de Grey, Archbishop of York in 1240, which for nearly 300 years became the London residence, known as *York Place*, of his successors. When Card. Wolsey succeeded to the archbishopric he embellished the Palace (sited on the river side of the thoroughfare) with characteristic extravagance, and Henry VIII seized the desirable property in 1529. He renamed the palace 'Whitehall', a name then generally applied to any centre of festivities, and acquired more land towards St. James's Park, on which he erected a tiltyard, cockpit, and tennis courts. Whitehall became the chief residence of the court in London. Anne Boleyn was brought here on the day of her marriage to Henry in 1533, and in 1536 it was the scene of his marriage to Jane Seymour. In 1547 Henry died in the Palace. Masques by Ben Jonson, with sets by Inigo Jones and James Shirley were frequently presented at court in the time of James I and Charles I. Plans for a huge and sumptuous new palace for James I drawn up by Inigo Jones and John Webb were never carried out, although the new Banqueting House was completed in 1622 after a fire. Charles I was executed in 1649 in front of this hall. Oliver Cromwell died in the palace in 1658. Under Charles II, Whitehall became the centre of revelry and intrigue described by Pepys, and James II fled into exile from here in 1688. The offering of the Crown to William and Mary provided the last great ceremonial function here in 1689. In 1698 the palace was accidentally burned to the ground, and the royal residence transferred to St. James's Palace. The government offices already established here, such as the Horse Guards (1663), the Paymaster-General's Office (1676), the Admiralty (1694), and the Treasury (1698) remain to the present day.

From Parliament Square, Parliament St leads into Whitehall and on to Trafalgar Square. On the left (W) side are large blocks of government offices; the corner building (1907; by Brydon) is connected by a bridge over King Charles St with the Foreign and Commonwealth Office. During the Second World War an underground network of bombproof rooms was built for the War Cabinet underneath the western part of the building. They opened as a museum in 1984 under the care of the Imperial War Museum.

To reach the Cabinet War Rooms walk up Whitehall on the W side and turn into King Charles St; at the end of the street steps descend past a statue of Lord Clive by John Tweed (1912) to St. James's Park and the *Cabinet War Rooms*.

Cabinet War Rooms, entrance from Horse Guards Road. Open: daily 10.00–17.50 (last admission 17.15). Admission charge. Tel. 071-930 6961.

Nineteen underground rooms survive as they were when the Second World War ended. The total Cabinet War Room complex covered a huge area and was protected from bombs by a vast slab of concrete above. Among the rooms on view are the Cabinet Room, the Transatlantic Telephone Room, from which Churchill spoke to President Roosevelt in the White House, the Map Room and Churchill's bedroom. There is a shop selling postcards and wartime posters.

Before returning to Whitehall take a closer look at the façade of the *Foreign and Commonwealth Office* by Sir George Gilbert Scott (1872) in the style of Inigo Jones which can best be appreciated from Horse Guards Road. The building covers 5.5 acres and is undergoing a 15-year renovations programme. A statue of Lord Mountbatten of Burma (1900–79) (F. Belsky) was unveiled here by HM The Queen in 1983. Return to Whitehall.

In the middle of Whitehall rises the **Cenotaph**, commemorating in dignified simplicity the Glorious Dead of 1914–18 and 1939–45. The monument, designed by Sir Edwin Lutyens, was first erected in plaster as a saluting point for the Allied Victory March of 1919 and was rebuilt in stone and unveiled on 11 November 1920; the later inscription was unveiled in 1946. Every November the ceremony of

Remembrance Sunday takes place on the Sunday nearest to the 11th. Members of the royal family, the Government and Opposition, and representatives of Commonwealth countries lay 'poppy' wreaths around the Cenotaph and two minutes' silence is observed. The wreaths remain in place for two weeks.

On the right (E side) of Parliament St the Bridge St site is being redeveloped behind the listed façade; *St. Stephen's Tavern*, popular with Members of Parliament, is due to remain. The Norman Shaw S building which fronts Bridge St itself will be used as offices for MPs, Palace Chambers due to open in 1991. The Norman Shaw building just to the N, the former New Scotland Yard (1891), has already been converted into MPs' offices. (See above).

Facing Whitehall is the new Richmond House, housing the Department of Health and Social Security from 1988. William Whitfield, architect, has created a six-storey building partly behind the original Grade I Georgian façade (1822–25) with a dramatic Tudor-style infill elevation set back in a new courtyard.

On the left (W side) is the narrow DOWNING STREET, built in 1683–86 by Sir George Downing (who was the second graduate at Harvard in 1642) and famous out of all proportion to its appearance as the residence of British Prime Ministers since 1735. Access to the street is restricted by newly installed wrought iron gates (1989). *No. 10 Downing St* became the property of the Crown in 1732 and George II offered it as a gift to Sir Robert Walpole who accepted it for his office as First Lord of the Treasury. From that day it became the official residence of Prime Ministers, although many in the early years preferred to live in their own, probably grander, houses. William Kent redesigned the interior in 1732 and further alterations were made by Sir John Soane, who designed the impressive state dining room. The narrow front of the building belies its size and it contains offices as well as the Prime Minister's private apartment. *No. 11 Downing St* became the residence of the Chancellor of the Exchequer in 1805; No. 12 was first the Judge Advocate General's official residence but is now the Government Party Whips' office.

At the beginning of the street on the right is the office of the Judicial Committee of the Privy Council, the final Court of Appeal for countries of the Commonwealth without their own Supreme Court of Appeal. It was built by Soane in 1827.

Before Downing St became an official residence for the Prime Minister, other well-known people lived in it, including James Boswell who took lodgings here in 1762 and Tobias Smollett who set up a doctor's practice here c 1745–48.

Although it is possible to reach *Treasury Green* from Downing St, access is restricted, so the tall brick wall of Henry VIII's smaller tennis court of Whitehall Palace, revealed in 1961 and marked with a tablet, is best reached from Horse Guards.

The *Cabinet Office* and the *Old Treasury* front Whitehall from Downing St northwards; it was designed by Kent, Soane and Barry and completed in 1845. During restorations in the '60s remains of Henry VIII's Whitehall Palace were uncovered (see smaller tennis court, above). The building is best seen from Horse Guards. *Dover House* (1758) is now used by the Scottish Office; Lord Melbourne (1779–1843) was born here. The delicate portico and circular hall are by Henry Holland (1787). In Whitehall is an equestrian statue of Earl Haig (1861–1928).

The massive *Ministry of Defence* building, (1935–53; by Vincent Harris) dominates the right (E) side of Whitehall as well as the river-view (see p 88). In front, on the lawn facing Whitehall, known as Raleigh Green, is a statue of Sir Walter Raleigh (1552–1618) by

William McMillan (1959), and Field Marshall Montgomery (1887–1976) in combat uniform by Oscar Nemon (1980). A new statue of Field Marshal Slim (1891–1970) by Ivor Robert Jones, commissioned by the Burma Star Assn., was unveiled in 1990. The main entrance of the Ministry of Defence is in Horse Guards Avenue flanked by colossal sculptures (Earth and Water; 1949–53) by Sir Charles Wheeler.

Underneath the building is the King Henry VIII Wine Cellar, a brick vaulted undercroft of York Place. Its preservation involved moving it bodily in 1950, 43ft to one side and 20ft downwards.

Gwydyr House (1772), an attractive building in Whitehall on the E side, is now the Welsh Office.

Next to it is the **Banqueting House**, the main survival of Whitehall Palace. This superb example of Palladian architecture was erected in Portland stone by Inigo Jones 1619–22, on the site of a banqueting hall of 1607 burned down in 1619. The weathercock at the N end of the roof is said to have been placed there in 1686 by James II to show whether the wind was favourable or not to the approach of the Prince of Orange. The hall is open to visitors.

Banqueting House, Whitehall, SW1. (Tel. 071-930 4179). Open 10.00–17.00 (Tues to Sat) 14.00–17.00 (Sun). Admission charge. (Sometimes closed without prior notice.)

The lofty main hall (115ft long, 60ft wide and 55ft high) was completed in 1635 and extensively renovated in 1989. The nine allegorical ceiling paintings were designed for Charles I in 1629–34 by Rubens, who received £3000 and a knighthood, in return. The principal subject in the large central oval is the Apotheosis of James I; to the S, James is enthroned between Peace and Plenty and to the N is an allegory of the birth and coronation of Charles I.

Through a window of this hall Charles I passed in 1649 to the scaffold erected in the roadway in front of it (tablet beneath the lower central window; in fact it was probably a window in a N annexe, since demolished). From 1698 to c 1890 the hall was used as a Chapel Royal, and later as the museum of the United Service Institute. It is now used for government and other functions, including concerts, when not open to the public.

Beyond the Banqueting House on the right is a huge building by William Young (1906), formerly the War Office, now part of the Ministry of Defence. In front is a statue by Adrian Jones of the Duke of Cambridge (1819–1904), Commander in Chief of the British armies in 1856–95. The *Ministry of Agriculture and Fisheries* is next door in a building by John Murray (1910) and this is followed by *Great Scotland Yard*, the location of the headquarters of the Metropolitan Police until 1891. The street name originates in a mansion occupied before the 15C by the kings of Scotland and their ambassadors when in London. The stables of the Metropolitan Mounted Police remain here (appointment by request); the main establishment is now at Imber Court, East Molesey. (Tel. 081-398 1102.)

Also on the right (E) side of Whitehall is *Harrington House*, at Craig's Court, once the residence of Joseph Craig (1692); the façade is preserved.

Horse Guards on the left (W) side of Whitehall (1760, by Kent and Vardy) is a pleasant stone building with a central arch surmounted by a low clock tower, built on the site of a guard house of 1649 which stood on the old tiltyard of the Palace of Whitehall. It is now the office of the Commander in Chief of the combined forces. Two mounted troopers of the Life Guards or Royal Horse Guards (or Blues and Royals) are posted here daily from 10.00 to 16.00 and there are two dismounted sentries within the archway. The former are relieved hourly, the latter every two hours. At 11.00 (10.00 on Sundays), the guard on duty is relieved by a new guard of 12 men who troop from the Knightsbridge Barracks via the Mall.

The passage beneath the clock-tower leads to the large Parade Ground, Horse Guards' Parade and to St. James's Park. In May and June the *Parade Ground* is used for the ceremony of Beating the Retreat (public admitted, tickets from the Ticket Office, Bridge St, SW1), when military music and parades are performed under flood-light in the early evening, and Trooping the Colour, the Queen's Official Birthday parade on the second or third Saturday in June. Tickets by ballot only: write to Household Division HQ, Horse Guards, SW1, before March 1; two tickets per application only; those unsuccessful may receive tickets for the rehearsals on the two previous Saturdays.

The Trooping the Colour ceremony, at 11.00, is preceded by a parade along the Mall, when the Queen and other members of the royal household ride on horseback or by royal coach to Horse Guards. On the N side is the large *New Admiralty*, built in 1894–95, now housing a Government department. It is connected on the N to Admiralty Arch and on the W to the Citadel (see p 100). Looking back from the Parade, the elevation of Admiralty House, the former Paymaster General's Office, is to the left; the long rusticated façade of Horse Guards (by William Kent) opposite, Dover House (1758 by James Paine) to the right, the Portland stone façade of the Old Treasury (1736; William Kent) and then the barrel vaulted Treasury Passage to Downing St. To the right behind a statue by Tweed (1926) of Earl Kitchener (1850–1916) are the gardens of Downing St. (See also p 89.)

In front of the Horse Guards archway are equestrian statues of Viscount Wolseley (1833–1913) by Goscombe John, and Earl Roberts (1832–1914) by H. Bates, and a huge mortar from Cadiz presented by the Spanish Government in 1814 encased in a carriage made in Woolwich. On the edge of St. James's Park is the *Guards' Memorial* for 1914–19 by G. Ledward and H.C. Bradshaw.

Return to Whitehall; on the left going towards Trafalgar Square is the former *Paymaster-General's Office* (1732–33 by John Lane; now the Parliamentary Counsel); the flank of *Admiralty House* (1786–88; by S.P. Cockerell) is set back behind a wall and railing. Beyond is the *Old Admiralty* (by Ripley; 1725–28) with a tall classical portico in a small courtyard masked from the street by an attractive stone screen designed by Robert Adam in 1759. This was the Admiralty of Nelson's time and here his body lay in state in 1805; it is now used by the Home civil service. Immediately behind facing on to Horse Guards Parade is the *New Admiralty*, and then TRAFALGAR SQUARE.

Return to Whitehall with its souvenir shops, a pub and some restaurants and the *Whitehall Theatre* (1932) on the left, which gave its name to a 'trouser-dropping' style of comedy—the Whitehall farce—in the '50s and '60s but subsequently went into decline. It was restored in 1986 as part of the Maybox Theatre Group.

5   Charing Cross and Trafalgar Square
(National Gallery and National
Portrait Gallery)

Access: Underground, Charing Cross; Embankment.

Contrary to popular usage, *Charing Cross* is the irregular open space at the top of Whitehall just before Trafalgar Square; not the open space in front of Charing Cross Station. It was here that in 1291 Edward I erected the last of the series of thirteen crosses that marked the stages in the funeral procession of his wife Eleanor to Westminster Abbey. It was destroyed in 1647 and a replica later erected in front of Charing Cross Station. The cross gave its name to the ancient road junction which is now the site of the fine equestrian statue of Charles I by Hubert Le Sueur (1633) on a pedestal by Joshua Marshall, from a design by Wren. Those who risk their lives in the traffic to reach the small island will also note a tablet in the ground from which all mileages to and from Central London are measured.

At the entrance of Charles II to London in 1660, 600 pikemen were stationed here, and later in the same year it was the scene of the execution of Harrison and seven other regicides, witnessed by Pepys, who commented, 'Thus it was my chance to see the King beheaded at Whitehall and to see the first bloodshed in revenge for the blood of the King at Charing Cross'. In 1668 Punchinello, 'ye Itallian popet player', performed here. At the pillory set up near the statue, Defoe (1703) and John Middleton (1723) suffered. —On 30 January, the anniversary of the execution of Charles I, the statue is adorned with the wreaths by sympathetic adherents of the Royalist tradition.

To the E, beyond Charing Cross Station, runs the Strand (Rte 18), leading to Fleet St and the City. To the W, Admiralty Arch gives access to the Mall and St. James's Park (Rte 6). The wide Northumberland Avenue descends past the *Royal Commonwealth Society* to the Victoria Embankment (Rte 18). Grand Buildings on the corner has been rebuilt to a design by Sidell Gibson Partnership replicating the former building's Bath stone façade but with new octagonal towers. On the left in Northumberland Avenue (10 Northumberland St) is the Sherlock Holmes pub mentioned in 'The Hound of the Baskervilles', there called the Northumberland Arms Hotel. Upstairs is a perfect reconstruction of Holmes' study and in the bar are mementos and memorabilia relating to the hound and Sherlock Holmes; there is also a restaurant. The Playhouse Theatre has been completely restored and reopened in 1987, with a graceful 1907 interior by French architects Detmar Bow and Fernand Billerey. It originally opened as the Royal Avenue Theatre in 1882 and served as a BBC studio from 1951–75, when it closed.

Trafalgar Square (Pl. 14; 4), laid out in 1829–c 1850 at the suggestion of Nash, is said to have been described by Sir Robert Peel as 'the finest site in Europe'. Since the reign of Edward I the area had been a royal mews. Except when disturbed by the periodic political or social demonstrations for which the square is a traditional rendezvous, pigeons crowd the area by day and starlings take refuge in the surrounding buildings at dusk. This is the location for the annual New Year's Eve celebrations, more strictly controlled after two fatalities in 1983. From early December until Christmas Eve there are Christmas carols under the Christmas tree donated by the people of Norway in gratitude for help during the Second World War. During 1988 and 1989 the square was completely refurbished with new surface stones.

The NELSON MONUMENT, 172ft high, by William Railton (1841), carries a colossal statue of Lord Nelson (17ft), victor at the Battle of Trafalgar in 1805, by E.H. Baily (1840–43). The fluted granite column rises from a base guarded by four huge bronze couchant *Lions, beloved of children. These were modelled by Sir Edwin Landseer and cast by Marochetti in 1867. At the foot are four bronze reliefs cast from French cannon captured at the naval battles they depict. The monument is decorated on the anniversary of the Battle of Trafalgar, 21 October.

In the square are two fountains, designed by Lutyens in 1939 with fine sculptures by Charles Wheeler and W. McMillan. The statue of *Sir Henry Havelock* (1795–1857) is by Behnes (the stone pedestal conceals a police box), and that of *Sir Charles James Napier* (1782–1853) by G.G. Adams. At the NE corner an equestrian statue of *George IV*, by Chantrey, was intended to top the Marble Arch in front of Buckingham Palace. Against the N wall are bronze busts of *Lord Cunningham* (1883–1963) by Franta Belsky, *Lord Jellicoe*, (1859–1935), by W. McMillan, and *Lord Beatty* (1871–1936) by Sir Charles Wheeler. In the centre are the former Imperial standards of length, placed here in 1876.

Around Trafalgar Square are several large buildings: to the E, *South Africa House* (1933), designed by Sir Herbert Baker and to the W, *Canada House*, built in 1824–27 by Sir Robert Smirke. Streets lead to Pall Mall and the West End (Rte 7). Above the N side of the square rises the National Gallery (see below). On the grass in front are a bronze statue of James II in Roman costume by Grinling Gibbons, and a copy in bronze of Houdon's marble statue of George Washington at Richmond, Virginia.

The large church of **St. Martin in the Fields** (1722– 24), at the NE corner of Trafalgar Square, is perhaps the finest work of James Gibbs, with its richly decorated ceiling by Artari and Bagutti, a font (1689) from the previous church on this site, and a handsome 18C pulpit brought here after 1858. The side aisles, with canted walls and 'closet' pews, are particularly attractive. The *Crypt* refurbished in 1987, has a restaurant, bookshop and visitor centre. It is also the home of the London Brass Rubbing Centre, which moved here from St. James's Church. Off the S side opens the *Dick Sheppard Chapel* (1954), a memorial to the vicar who in 1914–27 began the tradition of social service still carried on by the church. The gateway to the chapel commemorates the 'Old Contemptibles' of the First World War. Behind the church is a crafts market.

In this church Bacon, Hampden, and Charles II were christened and Tom Moore married; while the burials of George Heriot, Nell Gwynn, Farquhar, Roubiliac, Chippendale, and John Hunter are recorded here. The first broadcast religious service took place here in 1924. A bust of Gibbs by Rysbrack is preserved in the Vestry Hall. The church provided the first home for the now world-famous Academy of St. Martin in the Fields Orchestra. The musical tradition continues with regular lunch-time concerts. The church is also the regular venue for memorial services of actors, actresses and politicians. Just beyond is the 'late-night' Post Office; see p 50.

On the 'island' in St. Martin's Place is a poignant monument by Frampton (1920) to Nurse Edith Cavell, who was shot at Brussels in 1915, and across Charing Cross Road on the side of the National Portrait Gallery is a statue of Sir Henry Irving (1838–1905) by Thomas Brock, 1910.

Charing Cross Road continues north, see Rte 14.

On the N side of Trafalgar Square is the **National Gallery**.

National Gallery, Trafalgar Square, WC2. Tel. 071-839 3321. Open Mon to Sat 10.00–18.00, Wed Jun, July and Aug till 20.00, Sun 14.00–18.00. Admission free.

Educational facilities; lectures, room talks or films Mon to Fri at 13.00 Sat at 12.00, free guided tours Mon to Sat at 1100 and 1500. Self-service restaurant. Bookshops with catalogues, guidebook, postcards, posters and Christmas cards. Access: Underground, Charing Cross, Leicester Square.

The National Gallery is one of the greatest art galleries in the world with a representative collection of masterpieces of all schools and of the greatest European painters from the 15th to the early 20C.

The idea of a national collection of paintings was first given effect in 1824 when Parliament voted £60,000 for the purchase of 38 paintings from the collection of the financier John Julius Angerstein (1735–1823). A regular grant for purchases followed in 1855 and since that date the policy of successive directors has been to build up a representative collection of Western European art.

The collection was first shown in Angerstein's house in Pall Mall (now the Reform Club) and moved to the present building in 1838. This was constructed by William Wilkins who used some of the columns from the demolished Carlton House in the façade. Extensions were later made by E.M. Barry and further extensions to the NW were opened in 1975.

The new Sainsbury Wing to the west is due to open in Spring 1991 to a design by Robert Venturi after the first proposals were rejected when described by the Prince of Wales as 'a carbuncle on the face of Trafalgar Square'. The new building features a dramatic glass elevation to the Square revealing the stone interior matching Wilkins' building and the grand staircase which will take visitors from street level to gallery level where the two galleries will be linked by a circular bridge across Jubilee Walk. A restaurant and cafeteria overlooks Trafalgar Square at mezzanine level.

On the E façade of the building is Flaxman's 'Minerva', originally made for Marble Arch. The Vestibule contains a series of mosaic pavements designed and executed by Boris Anrep (1952) illustrating abstract ideas, and showing eminent people in unusual settings, including Greta Garbo, Margot Fonteyn, Bertrand Russell and Winston Churchill. (A pamphlet on these mosaics is available in the bookshop.)

Here is a small selection of the paintings on view but a complete re-organisation is underway which will display the collection in chronological order, rather than schools as at present (1990), due to be completed in 1991. The Sainsbury Wing will house the Renaissance Collection and the new Annenberg Rooms, the Impressionist and Post-Impressionist Collection. Enter from the new Wing from Spring 1991.

Italian School: 13th to 15C: richly represented are Fra Angelico, Bellini, 'Doge Leonardo Loredan', c 1501, probably the most famous of all Venetian portraits, Botticelli, 'Venus and Mars', (1485), love triumphs over war. 'Mystic Nativity' (1500), with an inscription by the artist in Greek at the top—a personal prayer for peace; Leonardo da Vinci, 'The Virgin of the Rocks' (1483–1508).

Italian School: 16C: Leonardo da Vinci's cartoon 'The Virgin and Child with Saint Anne and Saint John the Baptist', damaged with a shotgun by a visitor in 1988 but now back on display after repair; Bronzino, 'An allegory with Venus and Cupid' (c 1550s), highly finished—a sophisticated defiance of naturalism; Michelangelo, 'The Entombment' (1506), unfinished, influenced by antique sculpture; Raphael, 'Pope Julius II' (1512), thought to be a copy but revealed by cleaning to be an original, very influential work, 'The Ansidei Madonna' for the family chapel in Perugia, a serene harmony; paintings by Tintoretto and Titian.

Early Northern: Van Eyck, 'The Arnolfini Marriage', signed and dated 'Jan van Eyck was here 1434', he may be glimpsed in the mirror of this

NATIONAL GALLERY

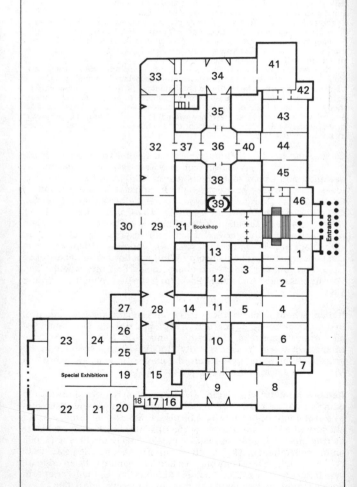

famous painting full of symbolic details; 'Man in Turban', signed and dated 21 October 1433 and inscribed with a Flemish proverb 'As I can, not as I would'.

Dutch School: Avercamp, 'Winter Scene' (1609). Cuyp, 'Maas at Dordrecht in a Storm' (mid 1640s)—a rare storm scene. Hals—a good group of portraits. Hobbema, 'The Avenue, Middelharnis', (1650s), one of the most famous Dutch landscapes with a marvellous illusion of distance. De Hoogh, 'Woman and Maid in a Courtyard' (1660), with the old town wall of Delft behind. Rembrandt—a large, representative group of works: note 'Self-Portrait' (1640), Rembrandt aged 34 and influenced by Titian, 'A Woman Bathing in a Stream' (1655), a sensuous study of his model and mistress Hendrickje Stoffels, 'Margaretha de Geer' (1661), a second portrait of the wife of Jacob Trip, this 40 years later. Vermeer, 'Young Woman standing at a Virginal' (1670).

Flemish School: 17C: Van Dyck, 'Equestrian Portrait of Charles I' (1630s), one of the most celebrated images of majesty—expressing his confidence as a horseman. An outstanding group of Rubens' work: note 'Rape of the Sabine Women' (late 1630s), 'The Watering Place' (1620s), which inspired Gainsborough to paint a similar painting, 'Judgment of Paris' (c 1600), painted after arrival in Italy, 'Samson and Delilah' (1610), influenced by Italy.

French School: 17C: Claude, a superb collection of the great French classical landscape painter's work, note 'Seaport, Embarkation of the Queen of Sheba' (1648). Poussin, 'Adoration of the Golden Calf' (late 1630s), a biblical variant of the bacchanals which were a favourite theme of the artist—after a recent attack it has been restored.

Spanish School: Goya, 'Dona Isabel de Porcel' (1805), apparently painted over a male portrait, but still very beautiful; El Greco, 'Christ driving the Traders from the Temple' (c 1600), one of many versions; Murillo, 'The Two Trinities', an altarpiece painted in 1681; Velasquez, 'Toilet of Venus/The Rokeby Venus', his only known female nude, named for the Yorkshire house where it hung in the 19C, damaged by a suffragette in 1914.

British School: Constable, 'The Haywain'—the picture which epitomises the rural landscape with a view of the River Stour near Flatford Mill in Suffolk—first exhibited in 1824 when it won a gold medal. Gainsborough, 'Mrs Siddons' (1785), an elegant portrait, and 'The Morning Walk' (1785), a poetic evocation of young love. Hogarth, 'Marriage à la Mode'—six canvases satirising the morals of high society. Lawrence, 'Queen Charlotte' (1789), Eton College is in the background. Reynolds, 'General Sir Banastre Tarleton' (1782)—in a striking pose. Stubbs 'The Melbourne and Milbanke Families' (1770s)—a glossy and formal composition. Turner, 'The Fighting Temeraire tugged to her last berth', with a characteristic Turner sunset.

Italian School: 18C: Canaletto, paintings of Venice and London, 'London, Interior of the Rotunda at Ranelagh' (1754), also 'Eton College'; and Tiepolo, an excellent group of small-scale works.

French School: 19C Impressionists and Post-Impressionists: Cézanne, 'Les Grandes Baigneuses' a late work (c 1904) foreshadowing Cubism; Degas 'Helene Rouart in her Father's study', unfinished painting towards the end of Degas' active period (1886),—'La-La at the Cirque Fernando' (1879); Gauguin, 'Flower Piece' (1896), painted in Tahiti;

Manet, 'Music in the Tuileries Gardens' (1862), including Manet and some of his friends; Monet, 'Water Lily Pond' (1899)—one of ten views of the bridge and pond in the artist's garden,—'Water Lilies', one of thirty of these huge canvases which Monet worked on between 1916 and his death in 1926, 'The Thames below Westminster' painted on his first visit to London (1871). Picasso, 'Fruit Dish, Bottle and Violin' (1914), the first abstract painting acquired by the National Gallery; Pissarro, 'Lower Norwood under Snow' (1870), 'The Avenue Sydenham' (1871); Redon, 'Ophelia Among the Bower', richly coloured pastels; Renoir, 'The Umbrellas' (1890s), painted in two stages, the girls and the woman (right) in an earlier style; Rousseau, 'Tropical Storm with a Tiger' (1891); Van Gogh, 'Sunflowers' (1888), one of six versions in that year.

Immediately N of and behind the National Gallery is the **National Portrait Gallery**.

National Portrait Gallery, St. Martin's Place, WC2. Tel. 071-930 1552. Open: Mon to Fri 10.00–17.00, Sat 10.00–18.00, Sun 14.00–18.00. Educational facilities, public lectures, temporary exhibitions, Bookshop. Access: Underground, Charing Cross, Leicester Square.

The National Portrait Gallery contains a most interesting and historically valuable collection, founded in 1856, of over 10,000 portraits (paintings, sculptures and drawings) of men and women of significance. The present building, in Italian Renaissance style by Ewan Christian, was donated by William Henry Alexander, and opened in 1896. It is now a little over-crowded and only a small proportion of the collection can be shown at any one time. An extension of the gallery into Orange Street is planned. The collection is arranged chronologically beginning on the top floor, level 5, with the Tudors and their predecessors; the rooms are decorated and lightly furnished so as to give a feeling of historical period. There are regular changes in displays; below are some of the highlights—chosen for their historical significance—to look out for. (Start on Level 5 and work down.)

Room 1, *The Tudors*. 16C portraits of early kings and queens: Henry VII by Michael Sittow (1505), painted for a prospective bride; Henry VIII in Holbein's large cartoon (c 1536–37) in black ink and coloured washes on paper. Henry VII also appears in this drawing for a fresco in Whitehall Palace (destroyed). Nearby is another portrait of Henry VIII after Holbein. Other portraits include Henry VII's wife Elizabeth of York, and three of Henry VIII's wives: Catherine of Aragon, Anne Boleyn and Catherine Parr. Elizabeth I and her marvellous costumes are portrayed in a group of paintings including 'The Coronation Portrait' formerly at Warwick Castle, by an unknown artist (c 1575), and 'The Ditchley Portrait', by Marcus Gheeraerts the Younger, painted in commemoration of the Queen's visit to Ditchley Park near Oxford. The Queen stands on the globe of the world, her feet planted on Oxfordshire. The first picture to be acquired by the Gallery was the 'Chandos' portrait of Shakespeare, attributed to John Taylor (1610) the only known contemporary portrait.

Room 2, *The Stuarts*. The early period is dominated by James I in full length by Mytens (1621), in a spectacular frame; his queen Anne of Denmark attributed to Larkin. Charles I in a full length portrait by Mytens (1631) with his queen Henrietta Maria in a portrait influenced by Van Dyck. The Civil War is recreated by portraits of Cromwell and his collaborators.

Room 3 continues with some of the smaller 17C portraits, miniatures, medals, engravings and portraits of writers.

Rooms 4 and 5, *Restoration and Late Stuart*: Charles II, a full-length by Hawker (c 1680), nearby his wife Catherine of Braganza by Stoop in the Portuguese costume which aroused much comment when she first arrived in England, and a group of his mistresses, including the Duchess of Cleveland (by Wright) and Nell Gwyn with a lamb (by Lely). Note Hayls' portrait of Samuel Pepys, mentioned in the latter's diaries in 1666. Pepys hired an Indian gown to wear for the portrait. James II in portraits by Kneller and Lely. William and Mary representing the Glorious Revolution.

Rooms 6 and 7, *Early 18C Arts and Sciences, the Kit-Cat Club*. Earl of Burlington, builder of Chiswick House and Burlington House, by Richardson (c 1717). Wren by Kneller (1711) and a group of Kneller's portraits of members of the Kit-Cat Club (see p 346 and p 391). The club took its names from 'kit-cats', the mutton pies served at the tavern near Temple Bar kept by Christopher Cat, where the Club met in the early days when it was run by publisher Jacob Tonson. There are 42 portraits in all and a selection is shown including Congreve, Vanbrugh, Tonson, Walpole and the Duke of Newcastle and the Earl of Lincoln.

Room 8, *Early Georgian Portraits* include the full-length portrait of George II from the studio of Hudson (1744), his wife Caroline of Anspach by Amigono (1735), their favourite composer Handel, by Hudson (1756), and the king's mistress the Countess of Suffolk.

Note the self-portraits of Hogarth (1758) and Thornhill (1725). There are more portraits in Room 9, Gainsborough (c 1759), William Jones by Hogarth (1740), recently acquired, and Reynolds (c 1754). Reynolds' portraits of Dr Johnson (1756) and Boswell (1785) are also here. *The British Overseas* in Room 10 are represented by Clive in a stiff portrait by Dance, and Captain Cook in a portrait painted at the Cape of Good Hope in 1776 by John Weber.

Room 11, *The Struggle for America*: George Washington, after Stuart, and representatives of both sides, including the 'Death of Chatham' (1780–81) showing Chatham's collapse in the House of Lords after speaking against withdrawal.

In Room 12, *England at War* is illustrated with a portrait of Nelson (1800–01) by Beechey and the portrait of his mistress Lady Hamilton by Romney (c 1785). And later an unflattering portrait of Wellington by Home, painted in India. Note also the political caricatures.

Room 13, *The Romantic Movement*. Representatives from literature include Burns by Nasmyth, Scott by Landseer (c 1824), Mary Wollstone-craft and her daughter Mary Shelley (1841) and Keats by Severn, Byron in Albanian dress by Phillips (1813) and Wordsworth by Haydon (1842). Artists are also represented.

Room 14, *Science and the Industrial Revolution* with portraits of inventors including Watts by Von Breda, Brunel by Drummond (c 1836) with the Thames Tunnel in the background. Chantrey's bust of Rennie (1818).

Room 15, *The Regency*, includes a number of theatrical portraits, the most striking that of Sarah Siddons by Beechey (1793). At the far end of the room is 'The Reformed House of Commons, 1833' by Hayter and William Cobbett (1831), unknown artist, and other parliamentary reformers. Note also Elizabeth Fry, the prison reformer, after Leslie. Among the miniatures, is Jane Austen by her sister Cassandra (1810), the only authentic likeness of the novelist.

1st Floor, Room 16, *The Young Victoria*, with Tweed's life-size plaster of 'Queen Victoria and Prince Albert as Ancient Saxons' (1868), just outside, as well as the full length portrait of the Queen by Hayter in her coronation robes.

In Room 17, Early Victorians include a number of well-known literary portraits: Tennyson by S. Laurence (c 1840), Thackeray by Frank Stone (c 1839), Dickens, by Maclise (1839), Charlotte Brontë and Mrs Gaskell in drawings by Richmond (1850 and 1850). The Brontë Sisters (c 1834) by their brother Branwell, a primitive but compelling portrait. Emile Brontë (1833) by Branwell. Jenny Lind, the 'Swedish Nightingale', a replica of a portrait by Magnus (1846) surrounded by opera bills and more theatrical portraits.

Room 19, *The Crimea, India and the Empire*—missionaries and explorers with a special display on the Crimea including Steel's bust of Florence Nightingale (1862). Room 20 continues the theme in *Victorian Science and Technology* symbolised by Prince Albert in a full length portrait by Winterhalter (1867) and engravings of the Great Exhibition. Room 21, more *Victorian writers and artists* including the Pre-Raphaelites, with portraits of Holman Hunt, Ruskin and William Morris. *Later Victorians* follow in Room 22 with well-known politicians, Disraeli and Gladstone by Millais (1881 and 1879).

Room 24, *Edwardian Arts*—theatrical and literary portraits. Note 'Ellen Terry as Lady Macbeth' by Sargent (1889). *Edwardian Arts and Politics* follow in Room 25.

Portraits of members of the royal family are on the landing and include Lavery's gracious 'Royal Family at Buckingham Palace' (1913) showing George V, Queen Mary, the Duke of Windsor and the Princess Royal. On the mezzanine are portraits of the present royal family including Annigoni's Queen Elizabeth II (1969); Bryan Organ 'The Princess of Wales' (1981), damaged but now repaired; Duke of Edinburgh (1983) also by Organ, and others.

On the ground floor is the 20C display with photographs, drawings and paintings mounted on moving turntables. Among the hundreds of famous faces are Churchill, sketches by Graham Sutherland, political caricatures by Beerbohm and Low, Elizabeth Frink's bust of Sir Alec Guinness, Rodrigo Moynihan's portrait of Margaret Thatcher, and Organ's portrait of Prince Charles.

From here continue with Route 14—Shaftesbury Avenue and Soho; or Route 18—The Strand and the Embankment; or Route 19— Covent Garden.

6   The Mall, Buckingham Palace and St. James's Park

(Changing the Guard)

Access: Underground, Charing Cross, Embankment.

Explore this area from Trafalgar Square, entering under *Admiralty Arch* with its striking view down the 'triumphal avenue' of the Mall with the Victoria Memorial and Buckingham Palace closing the vista. This massive triumphal arch was designed by Sir Aston Webb as part of the national memorial to Queen Victoria. On the left immediately beyond the Arch is a statue of Captain Cook (1728–79) by Brock (1914); on the right a memorial to the Royal Marines by Adrian Jones (1903). The conspicuous and grim-looking building on the left is the 'Citadel' covered in Virginia creepers. This 'cubist fortress' is often confused with the Cabinet War Rooms (see p89) but was built in 1941–42 as an extension to the Admiralty to provide bomb-proof protection for the communications room. It is now used as a naval radio communications centre. Horse Guards Parade is beyond.

The **Mall**, the spacious avenue lined with double rows of plane trees that skirts St. James's Park on the N, is so called from having been used in Charles II's time for the game of 'pail-mail' (from the Italian 'palla', meaning ball, and 'maglio', meaning mallet; a cross between croquet and golf). Overlooking it on the right is the bright *Carlton House Terrace* designed by Nash, a monumental terrace of mansions (entered from Waterloo Place, see Rte 7), with small gardens on the projecting podium below. Here are the entrances to the *Mall Galleries* of the Federation of British Artists, and, just before Duke of York's steps, at *Nash House*, to the Institute of Contemporary Arts (tel. 071-930 3647), with galleries, an auditorium, theatre, cinema, video-library and restaurant (open daily 12.00–23.00; galleries 12.00–21.00). Daily membership fee. Carlton House Terrace is interrupted by the Duke of York's Column and Waterloo Place, described on p 108. Opposite is a Royal Artillery Monument (by William Colton, 1910) in memory of the dead in the Boer War 1899–1902.

At the end of Carlton House Terrace is a double flight of steps designed by De Soissons. At the top a statue of George VI by W. McMillan (1955) fronts Carlton Gardens (p 109). The Mall now skirts the gardens of Marlborough House (see below), beyond which Marlborough Road passes between (left) St. James's Palace and (right) the Queen's Chapel and Marlborough House. The *Queen's Chapel* (open for services Easter–July Sun 10.45 for 11.15) was designed by Inigo Jones in 1623.

It was built as a private chapel for the Roman Catholic Infanta Maria of Spain whom Prince Charles, later Charles I, was expected to marry, and completed for Henrietta Maria, his eventual wife. With a temple-like façade, the classical double-cube hall has a superb elliptical coffered ceiling constructed of timber. The interior retains its 17C fittings, with an altar-piece of the Holy Family, by Annibale Carracci.

Marlborough House (Pl. 14; 6), concealed behind the chapel in a pleasant garden of 4.5 acres, and approached by an unassuming entrance at the W end of Pall Mall, is the base for the Commonwealth Secretariat. The staircases have mural paintings by Laguerre (restored), and a ceiling by Orazio Gentileschi was moved from Greenwich (Queen's House) in the 18C and inserted in the Blenheim Saloon.

Marlborough House, a good example of Wren's red brick work, was built in 1709–11 for the great Duke of Marlborough with bricks brought back as ballast from Holland after the Duke's military campaigns there. The third storey was added by Sir William Chambers in the 18C, and the porte-cochère and entrance in 1860–63. Here, next door to 'Neighbour George', the great Duchess Sarah lived for 22 years after the death of her husband at Windsor. Later occupants were Leopold I of the Belgians (before his accession), Queen Adelaide, and (as Prince of Wales) Edward VII and George V (1903–10). The last was born here in 1865. On the death of Edward VII it became the residence of Queen Alexandra (1844–1925). In 1936 Queen Mary (1867–1953) returned to her former home.—On the garden wall in Marlborough Road is an elaborate, finely wrought memorial (1932) to Queen Alexandra by Alfred Gilbert, and (on the Mall) a plaque to Queen Mary.

St. James's Palace (Pl. 14; 5; no admission), an irregular and picturesque brick building, encloses several secluded courtyards some of which are open to the public.

The palace stands on the site of a hospital for fourteen 'maidens that were leprous' which was dedicated to St. James the Less and is mentioned at least as early as 1100. Henry VIII acquired the hospital and its grounds in 1531, and built a palace here, of which only the Gatehouse, parts of the Chapel Royal, and the Old Presence Chamber (Tapestry Room) remain. Mary I died at St. James's in 1558. Charles I, most of whose children were born in this palace, spent his last days here. Charles II employed Wren to provide state apartments overlooking the park, and the palace became the principal residence of the Duke of York (afterwards James II). After 1698, when Whitehall was burned down, St. James's Palace became the official London residence of the sovereign, where all Court functions were held; the British Court is still officially known as the Court of St. James's, and the sovereign is proclaimed from the balcony in Friary Court. Among those born in the palace were Mary II (1662), Queen Anne (1664), the Old Pretender (1688), and George IV (1762). George IV employed Nash to restore and redecorate the palace. It is now occupied by 'Grace and Favour' apartments, the Gentlemen and Yeomen-at-Arms, and the Lord Chamberlain.—Sentries guard the palace in Ambassador's Court and outside the walls (unlike those at Buckingham Palace who now stand within the forecourt).

The open *Friary Court*, on the E side of the palace, takes its name from a Capuchin friary established by Henrietta Maria and demolished to make room for Marlborough House. The most attractive feature of the exterior is the fine 16C brick *Gatehouse*, to the N, facing St. James's St, with its four octagonal towers. The carving over the original doors which lead into the *Colour Court* (no adm.) shows the initials of Henry VIII and Anne Boleyn. Beyond the large restored N window of the Chapel Royal, an archway leads into the charming *Ambassador's Court* from which the Chapel is entered.

The **Chapel Royal** has been greatly altered since it was built for Henry VIII, and it was enlarged in 1837. It preserves a fine ceiling, probably designed by Holbein in 1540. The music here has always been noted for its excellence; among early organists were Orlando Gibbons and Purcell. The private choir of the sovereign is composed of 6 'Gentlemen' and 10 boys; the boys wear traditional Court costume. At Epiphany (6 Jan) an offering of gold, frankincense, and myrrh is made on behalf of the sovereign, on which occasion the service is conducted by the Bishop of London. Several royal marriages have been celebrated in this chapel including those of Mary, the daughter of Charles I and mother of William III (1641), William III and Mary II (1677), Queen Anne (1683), George IV (1795), Queen Victoria (1840), and George V (1893).—Visitors are admitted to the services held here Sun 09.15 and 11.00; open to the public from Oct–Good Friday.

An original passageway leads to Colour Court, and, on the S side, picturesque passages admit to Engine Court (both private). Opposite is *York House*, now the residence of the Duke and Duchess of Kent. Lord Kitchener lived here in 1915–16. The W wing (with some fine Adam details) has been restored for use as offices of the Crown.

To the W lies *Stable Yard*; the former stables (1661) remain in the N range. Facing them is the imposing entrance portico of **Lancaster House**, a massive palace built by Benj. Wyatt in 1825–27 for the Duke of York (the S façade is well seen from the Mall). It was continued in 1827–30 for the first Duke of Sutherland, earlier Marquess of Stafford, and enlarged to Wyatt's designs by Smirke and Barry in 1833–41 for the second Duke. The third Duke entertained Garibaldi here in 1864. It is now a Government Hospitality and Conference Centre. No public admission.

Known as *Stafford House* from 1842 to 1912, it was then presented to the nation by Lord Leverhulme (died 1921) and named Lancaster House. It was decorated in the Louis-Quinze style and reopened in 1950. Notable among the superb fittings are Barry's double staircase, and the ceiling paintings in the great first floor gallery (Assumption of St. Chrysogonus, by Guercino), and state anteroom (Cupid with the Graces, by Veronese).

A passageway which gives access to Green Park skirts *Warwick House* (1716; by Hawksmoor). On the E side of the Court is the *Lord Chamberlain's Office* in an attractive house with fine first floor windows.

On the N side of Buckingham Palace the tree-lined *Constitution Hill* (probably so named after the 'constitutionals' taken here by Charles II) leads due W to Hyde Park Corner (see Rte 10), with a sand-track for riders skirting Green Park. Here three attempts on the life of Queen Victoria were made (in 1840, 1842, and 1849), and here too, in 1850, Sir Robert Peel was fatally injured by a fall from his horse.

Green Park (53 acres), created in 1668 with fine expanses of grass and trees, extends N to Piccadilly. The decorative Dominion gateway opposite the Victoria Memorial, leads into a broadwalk, while the paved Queen's Walk, opened in 1730 and named after Caroline, wife of George II, skirts the E border of the park (see p 110). Ice houses were built here in 1660 by Charles II when the park was used for royal picnics. An ice-mound can be seen to the N, near Piccadilly. The only ornament is a small fountain near Hyde Park Corner (1954; by E.J. Clack). The Tyburn (comp. p 128), now channelled underground, still crosses the park, and can be heard near the centre. The railings along Piccadilly are hung with prints, paintings and souvenirs on Sundays—a colourful but not very aesthetic display—all for sale (Rte 8).

Return to the Mall by Stable Yard Road past the bright stucco flank of *Clarence House* built in 1825 by Nash for William IV when Duke of Clarence, restored in 1949 for Princess Elizabeth (Elizabeth II) and the Duke of Edinburgh, and the residence of Queen Elizabeth The Queen Mother. A piper plays in the garden every morning at 09.00 when the Queen Mother is in residence. The S façade of St. James's Palace extends eastwards and was built by Wren in the late 17C.

Opposite Marlborough Rd, across The Mall, a path, preceded by a fine wrought iron gate, leads to St. James's Park.

*St. James's Park (Pl. 14; 6; 93 acres) extends from the Horse Guards Parade, on the E, to Buckingham Palace, on the W, and is bounded on the N by the Mall, on the S by Birdcage Walk. Charmingly laid out in an aristocratic surrounding of palaces and government offices, and commanding a famous view in the direction of Westminster from the modern bridge, which replaced the earlier suspension bridge in the 1950s, this park is one of the most attractive in London. The lake in the centre (5 acres) is frequented by ornamental waterfowl, for which Duck Island at the E end is reserved as a breeding place. Among the 'great variety of fowle' described by Pepys are the pelicans first presented by the Russian ambassador in the 17th century, (their successors and more than 40 other species are best seen at feeding time, at 16.00 in summer or 15.00 in winter, near Duck Island). The flower-beds are beautifully maintained, and the trees, some dating from the Restoration, add an oriental flavour to the views over the lake.

Henry VIII laid out the land between his palaces at Whitehall and St. James's in 1532 as the first royal park in London. Under the early Stuarts it was the resort of the Court and other privileged persons, among them Milton (who lived in a house in Petty France overlooking the park; 1652–60). In 1649, Charles I walked across the park from St. James's Palace to Whitehall, on the morning of his execution and here in 1660 Pepys had his first view of Charles II on his return to London: 'Found the King in the parke. There walked. Gallantry great'. After the Restoration Le Nôtre was employed to make 'great and very noble alteracions', ˒nd the scattered ponds were united to form a 'canal'. The park was then opened ˒ the public, and remains the only large park in London which has not been enclosed by railings. It became a fashionable resort, where the king was frequently to be seen strolling unattended and feeding the waterfowl for which he established a 'volary' or aviary. The park was further altered and the form of the lake changed by Nash in 1827–29, as an appendage to Carlton House, then occupied by George IV. During the First World War the lake was emptied and its bed occupied by temporary government buildings.

From June to September a band plays in the park, daily exc. Sun 12.30–14.00, 17.30–19.00.—Since 1785 chairs have been on hire in the park. Refreshments in the Cake House.

Birdcage Walk skirts the park on the S side; the name recalls a royal aviary established here in the reign of James I. A small road across Birdcage Walk leads to *Queen Anne's Gate*, to the left, a quiet street of delightful houses, built by Charles Shales (who lived at No. 15) in 1704.

The houses have carved masks (or heads) on the keystones, and elaborately carved door cases with canopied hoods, unique in London. The statue of Queen Anne in state robes, first noted in 1708 is of unknown origin. Lord Palmerston (1784–1865) was born at No. 20, and Lord Haldane (1856–1929) lived at No. 28. William Paterson, 'founder' of the Bank of England, probably assisted Shales in building the street; he lived at No. 19 in 1705–18. At No. 40 three ornamental lead cisterns are fixed on the exterior, one dated 1745 (probably used inside the house). The SDP had its party headquarters here and so, supposedly, does MI5—the British secret service. At No. 36 is the headquarters of the National Trust.

Old Queen St, further W, presents a medley of domestic architectural styles, including Nos 9–15 dating from 1698–99. No. 14, possibly designed by Adam, was occupied by Charles Townley in 1777–1805 and here he entertained Reynolds and Zoffany at his renowned 'Sunday dinners'. The parallel Lewisham St is a narrow alley-way of unexpectedly tall industrial buildings. The old street lighting of the area survives.

Return to Birdcage Walk via Cockpit Steps between Queen Anne's Gate and Old Queen St, and head W, passing attractive houses with bay windows and balconies overlooking the park. Built in 1780, all are narrow and present pleasantly varied façades. Near the W end of Birdcage Walk are the *Wellington Barracks* originally by Hardwick (1834–59) but now rebuilt as the HQ of the Household Regiments, the new buildings spaciously laid out around the parade ground.

The **Guard's Chapel**, or *Royal Military Chapel*, is approached by a memorial cloister (1954–56), by H.S. Goodhart-Rendel, in honour of the Household Brigade in the Second World War. The chapel itself, opened in 1838 but completely transformed within in 1875–78 by G.E. Street, was wrecked by a flying bomb on 18 June 1944, during morning service, with the loss of 121 lives. The present chapel, opened in 1963, is by George, Trew and Dunn; its austerity sets off Street's ornate apse, which survives. At the end of the narthex opposite the memorial cloister is the *Household Brigade Cenotaph*, while the six S chapels are dedicated to the five regiments of Foot Guards and the Household Cavalry. The sculptured aluminium screens are by Geoffrey Clarke. The chapel is open Mon–Thurs 10.00–16.00, Sun for services 09.30–14.00. A statue of Earl Alexander of Tunis by James Butler was unveiled outside the chapel in 1985. Opposite is the new *Guards Museum* opened by Queen Elizabeth II in February 1988 and illustrating four centuries of history of the Foot Guards.

Guards Museum, Wellington Barracks, SW1 (entrance from Birdcage Walk). Tel. 071-930 4466 x3253. Open daily 10.00–17.00. Closed Fri.

The displays show the regiments in peace and war with imaginative tableaux and sound effects as well as original uniforms and personal effects from the past.

At the W end of the Mall and St. James's Park, a spacious circus with planted lawns surrounded by a stone balustrade opens before Buckingham Palace. In the centre rises the conspicuous **Queen Victoria Memorial** (1911) of white marble, crowned by a gilded bronze figure of Victory with Courage and Constancy at her feet, and surrounded by water.

The monument, designed by Sir Aston Webb, and well sculpted by Sir Thomas Brock, consists of the seated figure of Queen Victoria (E side), and groups illustrating Truth (S), Motherhood (W), and Justice (N). Other allegorical groups in dark bronze decorate the podium, representing Peace and Progress (E), Science and Art (N), Manufactures and Agriculture (W), and Naval and Military Powers (S).—The monument provides a good viewpoint for the changing the guard and royal processions.

Buckingham Palace (Pl. 14; 7), the residence of the Queen, stands between St. James's Park and a private garden of 40 acres. When the sovereign is in residence the royal standard is flown.

The E façade of Buckingham Palace, designed by Sir Aston Webb, 1913

The palace takes its name from *Buckingham House*, built on this site in 1703 by the Duke of Buckingham. George III purchased this house in 1762, and here the famous interview between him and Dr Johnson took place (1767). The building was altered and remodelled by Nash for George IV c 1825, and since that time it has been known as Buckingham Palace, although neither George IV nor his successor ever occupied it. Since the accession of Queen Victoria in 1837, however, it has been the London residence of the sovereign, and here Edward VII was born in 1841 and died in 1910. The W façade towards the garden remains largely as Nash designed it; the E wing, facing the park, was added by Blore in 1847, but in 1913 the entire E façade was replaced by a much more dignified design by Sir Aston Webb. The interior of the palace, never open to sightseers, contains many magnificent and sumptuously decorated apartments, besides a very fine gallery of paintings and other works of art. The Throne Room, 66ft long, has a marble frieze representing the Wars of the Roses. The royal apartments are in the N wing.

The palace gardens, the scene in July of royal garden parties, include a lake and one of the mulberry trees planted by James I after 1609 to encourage the silk industry. These *Mulberry Gardens* soon degenerated into a place of popular entertainment (c 1630–90), described by Pepys as 'a very silly place'.

Changing the Guard takes place at Buckingham Palace, daily April to August, every other day September to April, but not in wet weather or when other state occasions occur, and is normally carried out by the Brigade of Guards. The best vantage-point is the Queen Victoria Memorial, or near the centre gates of the palace. The ceremony involves the trooping of the Queen's colour from St. James's Palace to Buckingham Palace. At approx. 11.10 one contingent of the old guard parades in Ambassador's Court, St. James's (Pl. 14; 5), and then troops to Buckingham Palace. There they join the old Palace Guard at the left side of the centre gates at approx. 11.25.

The new Guard, accompanied by a band, marches from the nearby Wellington Barracks. They form up and are inspected in their barracks before coming on duty; at Wellington Barracks they are on parade by about 11.15. They enter the palace by the normal 'out' gate, and form up facing the old guard, slow marching to the right side of the centre gates. The officers of the old and new guard advance and touch left hands, symbolising the handing over of the keys, and at this point the guard is 'changed'. Eight men then peel off from the ranks to relieve sentries guarding St. James's Palace, Clarence House, and Buckingham Palace. Meanwhile music is played in the forecourt of Buckingham Palace. The old guard complete with the sentries march out of the centre gates at approx. 12.10 accompanied by the massed bands, turning right to return to barracks. The new guard is dismissed to go on duty at Buckingham Palace, while a small detachment of drums (or pipes and drums) leaves the palace by the right-hand gate to accompany the new guard back to St. James's Palace and Clarence House.

Buckingham Gate and its extension *Buckingham Palace Road* skirt the ornamental wall in front of the S wing of the palace. Here are the entrances to the Queen's Gallery and the Royal Mews.

Queen's Gallery, Buckingham Palace Road, SW1. (Tel. 071-930 4832) (open Tues to Sat 1100–1700, Sun 13.00–17.00, admission charge). **Treasures selected from the splendid royal collections are shown in specially mounted exhibitions, changing usually every two years.

The private chapel, in the S wing, was the part of the palace most seriously damaged in the air raids of 1940–44. It was rebuilt in 1961–62, and the W part adapted to form the Queen's Gallery.

Beyond a conspicuous pediment (with a scene of Hercules sculpted by William Theed) to the Riding House, designed originally by William Chambers in 1763, is the quadrangle (1824–25) and clock tower of the **Royal Mews** (Pl. 14; 7; adm. Wed and Thurs 14.00–16.00). Admission charge. (Closed Ascot week and on other ceremonial occasions). Here the Queen's horses and the royal equipages are on view. These include the magnificent Gold State Coach designed by Sir William Chambers in 1762 and painted by Cipriani, used for coronations, the Irish State Coach made in Dublin in 1852 and used for the State Opening of Parliament, and the Glass State Coach (1910) used for royal weddings. A new Australian-made state coach with hydraulic suspension and a heater was added in 1988. Among the cars is a three-ton Phantom Six Rolls Royce. In the old Carriage House is a charming frieze of the Coronation of William IV by R. Barret Davis (1782–1854).

On the opposite side of Buckingham Palace Road are the the *Girl Guides Association* (No. 17) and the *Scout Association* (No. 25) shops. Westminster Theatre in Palace St is described on p 149. In *Lower Grosvenor Place*, at the SW angle of the palace grounds, two attractive Regency shop fronts (Nos 5 and 6) remain, flanking an entrance to the paved Victoria Square. Victoria Station is just a little further along Buckingham Palace Road. For Victoria and the area to the S, see Rte 12.

7 Pall Mall and St. James's

Access: Underground, Green Park, Piccadilly Circus

Between St. James's Park and Piccadilly lies **St. James's**—an area of London where the street layout has remained virtually as it was planned in the 1670s by Henry Jermyn, Earl of St. Albans (1604–84), founder of London's West End, described by Pepys in 1660 as 'a fine civil gentleman'. St. James's has retained its gentlemanly air—the atmosphere of its 'gentlemen's clubs' and specialist shops survives among encroaching publishing and advertising offices.

St. James's was established as a residential district near St. James's Palace and Court and became famous in the late 18C for its bachelor lodgings. From the reign of William III the coffee and chocolate houses of St. James's (the forerunners of today's clubs) were the rendezvous of aristocratic and learned London society. Specialist shops set up to serve them as well as the Palace.

London's clubs are traditionally the preserve of men, although some now have women members and others welcome women as guests. Financial pressures have taken their toll on some clubs but others have adapted by offering overnight accommodation, health clubs, and in some cases merging with other clubs. There are no name plates on club front doors. The elaborate flambeaux which survive outside some of them are lit by gas on state occasions.

Explore this area from Piccadilly Circus: The HAYMARKET runs S from Coventry St to Pall Mall, parallel to Regent St (with British Travel Centre, see p 46). A hay market was established here in the 16C, providing hay for London's horses. The *Design Centre* at 28 Haymarket, is the showroom for the Council of Industrial Design with changing exhibitions of British-designed goods as well as an extensive register of designers, manufacturers and designs. For details of exhibitions tel. 071-839 8000. Further down is the *Haymarket Theatre* which opened in 1821. It has associations with Squire Bancroft and Beerbohm Tree, who later went to Her Majesty's across the road. Here Wilde's 'An Ideal Husband' was first played (1895). In an earlier theatre on this site, built a century earlier, Aaron Hill, Theophilus Cibber and Henry Fielding all appeared, and Charles Macklin and Samuel Foote produced plays. The massive brick columns of the present building, by Nash, extend over the pavement. Opposite, slightly further down, is *Her Majesty's Theatre*, elaborately decorated and crowned by a Baroque copper dome, founded by Sir Herbert Tree in 1897. The first theatre which opened in 1705 on this site was designed by Sir John Vanbrugh; it burned down in 1789 and the theatre was rebuilt three times.

In the 19C it functioned as an opera house and Bizet's 'Carmen' and Wagner's 'Ring' were both given their London premières here. The Royal Academy of Dramatic Art was founded at the theatre in 1904. During the 1920s there were performances of Diaghilev's Russian ballet and Noel Coward's plays. 'Phantom of the Opera' by Lloyd Webber has played here since 1986.

New Zealand House to the S was built on half the site occupied by a previous theatre. The 16-storey building has a roof terrace with magnificent views (New Zealand passport holders are admitted on request) and below is the Martini Terrace, used for receptions, with equally splendid views of the City and Westminster.

Adjoining it (entrance in Pall Mall) is the *Royal Opera Arcade* (1816) by Nash and G.S. Repton, lit by circular skylights and hung with lamps and flower baskets. This recalls the operatic past of Her Majesty's and was London's earliest shopping arcade; it runs through to Charles II St.

Pall Mall (Pl. 14; 6) runs from Trafalgar Square through to St. James's Palace. This end and Cockspur St, are the home of shipping companies and the Norwegian State Railway; also the Hong Kong Tourist Association and Cathay Pacific Airlines. A fine statue of George III by M.C. Wyatt (1836), 'a good horse ridden by a horseman', stands at the beginning of Pall Mall.

Like the Mall, Pall Mall takes its name from the game of 'pail-mail' played here in the 17C. It is famous for its clubs; the first building on the SE corner of Pall Mall and Waterloo Place is the former United Service and Royal Aero Club, now the headquarters of the *Institute of Directors*. The building by Nash (1827) incorporates the main staircase from the demolished Carlton House. It was remodelled by Decimus Burton in 1842 to match the Athenaeum opposite and the horseblocks in Waterloo Place were put in for the Duke of Wellington whose favourite club this was. The club, founded in 1815, was the earliest service club in London; it closed in 1976. The Royal Academy was established on part of this site in 1768–79.

Across Waterloo Place stands the *Athenaeum*, founded in 1823 as a club for 'scientific and literary men and artists' by Sir Humphry Davy, President of the Royal Society, Lord Aberdeen (Prime Minister 1852–55) and Sir Thomas Lawrence, President of the Royal Academy. The building by Burton (1830) features a replica of the Parthenon frieze by John Henning with a gilt statue of Athene by E.M. Baily above the entrance. It remains the leading club for academics and politicians. Thackeray wrote some of his works in the library.

Waterloo Place, which here intersects Pall Mall, is characterised by banks and insurance offices, and by numerous statues.

The group to the N of Pall Mall commemorates the Crimean War (1854–55). In the centre is the *Guards' Monument* by John Bell, with three guardsmen and a trophy of Russian guns. In front are statues of *Lord Herbert of Lea* (1810–61; by Foley), secretary of war during the campaign; and *Florence Nightingale* (1820–1910), by A.G. Walker. The fine street lamp dates from c 1830.

The Crafts Council Gallery is on the corner of Waterloo Place. Crafts Council Gallery, 12 Waterloo Place, SW1. Tel. 071-930 4811. Exhibitions of crafts with information library on British craftsmen and women. Open Tues to Sat 10.00–17.00, Sun 14.00–17.00. Waterloo Place opens into the S extension of Regent St.

S of Pall Mall is an equestrian statue of *Edward VII* (died 1910), by Sir B. Mackennal. To the left (E), *Captain Scott* (1888–1912), the Antarctic explorer, by Lady Scott (1915); *Colin Campbell, Lord Clyde* (1792–1863), the saviour of Lucknow, by Marochetti (its base damaged by a bomb in the Second World War); and *Lord Lawrence* (1811–79), Viceroy of India, by Boehm; to the right (W) *Sir John Franklin* (1786–1847), the Arctic explorer, by Matthew Noble, and *Sir John Burgoyne* (1782–1871), the Crimean General by Boehm.

At the S end of Waterloo Place rises the *Duke of York's Column* in Tuscan granite, 124ft high, designed by Benj. Wyatt and erected in 1834. It bears a bronze statue, by Westmacott, of the Duke of York (died 1827), second son of George III, and Commander-in-Chief of the British Army in 1795–1827. Every officer and soldier in the Army forfeited a day's pay to provide funds for the monument to 'the soldier's friend'. Beyond the column the *Waterloo* or *Duke of York's Steps*, with a fine view towards Westminster, descend to the Mall. *Carlton House Terrace*, once one of the most aristocratic places of residence in London, overlooks the Mall.

Carlton House, which stood on the site of Waterloo Place and the York Column, was built in 1709. George IV, when Prince of Wales, set up his household here in 1783, and here celebrated the news of his accession. Nash laid out Regent St to connect the house with Regent's Park to the N, but the house was demolished in 1829. On the left of Waterloo Steps. No. 11, built in 1831, was Gladstone's home from 1857 to 1875; it is now the headquarters of the *Foreign Press Association*. In Nash House are the offices of the *Association of Societies of Art and Design* (including the ICA; entered from the Mall, see p 101). Beyond the *Crown Estates Office* (No. 13), was *Crockford's* (No. 16), founded in 1827 (comp. p 121), London's most famous gambling club, recently removed to Mayfair. The British Council building occupies the site of Carlton Mews and Spring Gardens, formed in the reign of Elizabeth I; the new offices date from 1975.

Under a tree on the right (W side) of the York Column, the tombstone of the German ambassador's terrier (Giro; died 1934) recalls the Prussian and later German Embassy at No. 9, from 1849 until 1939. *The Royal Society*, one of the most famous scientific bodies in the world, has occupied Nos 6–9 (entrance at No. 6) since 1967. It originated from a group of eminent scholars who began to meet informally in London and Oxford in 1645. Its formal foundation dates from 1660 and its royal charter of incorporation from 1662. It now numbers about 760 fellows (FRS), with about 70 foreign members. The rooms contain many busts and portraits of distinguished Fellows, and also some interesting relics; Newton's telescope, watch, and sundial; MS of the 'Principia'; original model of Davy's safety lamp, etc. (Admission by appointment).

Beyond the Turf Club (No. 5; formerly the residence of Lady Cunard), No. 2 (*The Royal College of Pathologists*) was occupied in 1906–25 by Lord Curzon, a statue of whom stands opposite. The attractive S façades of clubs in Pall Mall are well seen across the gardens. In 1807 F. Albrecht Winzler erected 13 gas lamp-posts outside his house here, the earliest use of gas for lighting in London. By 1820 the whole parish of St. James's was lit by gas; the area retains some of the oldest and most closely spaced lamp-posts in the city.

Further W in *Carlton Gardens*, Lord Palmerston and Lord Balfour lived at No. 4 (rebuilt in 1933 by Sir Reginald Blomfield), where a tablet marks this as General de Gaulle's Free French headquarters from 18 June 1940. An attractive small square opens behind a statue of George VI (comp. p 101), and stairs descend to the Mall. No. 3 was designed by Decimus Burton. Lord Kitchener lived at No. 2 in 1914–15. No. 1 was occupied by Napoleon III (1840–41) and Lord Northcliffe (1920–22); it is now the Foreign Secretary's official residence. The well-proportioned Wool House (1967, by David Hodges) stands on the site of Nos 5 and 6.

Return to Pall Mall. Next to the Athenaeum in Pall Mall is the *Travellers' Club*, founded in 1819, and occupying a fine building (1829–32) by Barry, in an Italian Renaissance style. It draws many of its members from the Foreign Office. Next door is the imposing *Reform Club*, founded by Radicals and Whigs after the passage of the Reform Bill. It was established here in 1836 in a building also by Barry but on a larger scale, on the site of a house which contained the National Gallery from 1824 until 1834. Once noted for its cuisine because of the chef Alexis Soyer (1837–50) who assisted in planning the kitchens, it numbers many senior civil servants and media people among its membership, which includes women since 1981. The *Royal Automobile Club*, founded in 1897, with an Egyptian swimming pool and squash courts, has a long façade of 1911.

Opposite, the *Junior Carlton Club* (1966, by Norman Royce), was established in 1864 to accommodate the 'waiting list' for the Carlton Club. Benjamin Disraeli held political meetings here in 1868–74 round a circular table still owned by the club. To the W is the new building (1963) of the *Army and Navy Club*, familiarly known as 'The Rag', a contraction for 'rag and famish', a phrase used by a dissatisfied member in 1839 to characterise his meagre fare and referring to a nearby gaming house and brothel by that name.

Behind the Junior Carlton Club lies **St. James's Square** (Pl. 14; 6), id out by Lord St. Albans (who lived on the site of Chatham House in 1675–82). Nearly all the houses have since been rebuilt several times, and offices have displaced the former fashionable residences. In the garden of flowering trees in the centre is an equestrian statue of William III, by John Bacon the Younger (1808), based on designs by his father, and a seat designed by John Nash (1822).

Norfolk House (No. 31; rebuilt in 1939), was owned by the dukes of Norfolk from 1722 until 1937. Frederick, Prince of Wales, leased the property in 1737–41, and George III was born here. It was General Eisenhower's Allied Force headquarters in 1942 and again in 1944 (tablet). No. 32 was from 1771 till 1919 the town residence of the bishops of London. Across Charles II St (with a good view of the Haymarket Theatre), No. 4 (rebuilt by Hawksmoor in 1726–28, with an attractive garden behind) is occupied by government offices. From 1912 until 1942 this was the residence of Lord and Lady (Nancy) Astor, and in 1943–45 it was the London headquarters of the Free French forces; later it was the home of the Arts Council. The Libyan Embassy, formerly at No. 5, was under siege in 1984; a policewoman killed in the incident is commemorated with a simple stone on the E side of the square. No. 7 has an entrance porch rebuilt by Lutyens in 1911 (now the Royal Fine Arts Commission and the Museums and Galleries Commission). On this site was the showroom of Josiah Wedgwood from 1796 until 1830. No. 10 (linked with No. 9), *Chatham House, The Royal Institute of International Affairs*, has been occupied by three prime ministers: Chatham (1759–62), Lord Derby (1837–54), and Gladstone (1890). Cast-iron railings and lamp-holders adorn the entrance.
   Beyond a façade by Robert Adam at No. 11, the *London Library*, founded in 1841 by Thomas Carlyle, occupies No. 14. One of the largest private subscription libraries in Britain (more than one million books), it has served Dickens, Thackeray, George Eliot, T.S. Eliot, and E.M. Forster. No. 15 has a fine classical façade by James Stuart (1764); the original house was tenanted by the Duchess of Richmond ('La Belle Stuart') in 1678–79. The *East India (and Devonshire Sports) Club* has absorbed Nos 16 and 17. Queen Caroline lived at No. 17 during her trial in 1820, while Lord Castlereagh, then foreign secretary, lived next door (No. 18). No. 20 is a fine Robert Adam building (1771–74; the magnificent interior is well maintained by the Distillers Company). The steps and carving on the door can be enjoyed from the pavement. No. 21 which skilfully duplicates the façade of No. 20, was added in 1934–37, on the site of Winchester House.
   Return to Pall Mall.

On the S side of Pall Mall Gainsborough lived from 1774 till his death in 1788 in the W wing (No. 80) of *Schomberg House*, a 17C building of red brick with stone dressings (restored in 1956, when the rest of the house was rebuilt). No. 79 (rebuilt) was given to Nell Gwynn by Charles II, with whom, according to Evelyn, she used to talk over the garden wall. The cellars of the original house survive beneath the pavement. Opposite, Nos 48–49 are the headquarters of the *Royal British Legion*, concerned with the welfare of ex-servicemen. At No. 71 the *United Oxford and Cambridge Clubs* occupy a building by Sir Robert and Sidney Smirke (1830) refurbished in 1973. At the end of Pall Mall is the entrance to **Marlborough House** (p 101). *Cleveland Row* continues W past **St. James's Palace** (see Rte 6) to Green Park.

Three mansions (now offices) overlook the park. The Reform Bill of 1832 was drafted in *Stornoway House* (1794–96; rebuilt in 1959), which became the residence of Lord Beaverbrook in 1924 and housed his Ministry of Aircraft Production in 1940– 41. Beyond the delightful bow-front of *Selwyn House* (1895), the Italianate *Bridgwater House* (1841–49) with an elaborate two-storeyed hall by Barry, occupies the site of a house presented by Charles II to Barbara Villiers, duchess of Cleveland, who lived here in 1668–77.—Access to Green Park may be gained from Stable Yard (p 103), or further N off St. James's Place (comp. below).

Return to the bottom of **St. James's St** (Pl. 14; 5) which leads to Piccadilly. *Byron House* occupies the site of No. 8 where, in 1811 after the publication of the third Canto of 'Childe Harold', Lord Byron 'awoke one morning to find himself famous'. Berry Bros & Rudd, wine merchants, have traded at No. 3 since 1699; the shop-front retains a late-18C design. A passage at the side admits to the secluded *Picker* *ing Place* (c 1733); a plaque records that a legation from the Republic of Texas was set up here in 1842–45. Beyond, *Lock & Co. Ltd*, hatters, were established in 1759, with a delightful shop front dating, in part, from the previous century.

The shop window usually displays period headgear, including an original 'bowler' hat. This was designed for the Earl of Leicester's 'beaters'; the order was sub-contracted to Thomas Bowler & Co., who produced what later became, in a modified form, the fashionable London hat. Nelson's hat (on his wax effigy in Westminster Abbey) was made here.

On the opposite side of St. James's St is the former building of the Constitutional Club (at No. 86; with elaborate carvings), where it shared premises with the Savage Club. The *Carlton Club* (No. 69) was founded by the Duke of Wellington after the defeat of the Tories in 1831 and with the Marquess of Salisbury as its chairman was used as a centre for the Tory party organisation; it remains the leading Conservative Club and has admitted Margaret Thatcher as a special member. It was damaged by an IRA bomb in 1990. Beyond the lock and safe makers, Chubb, who patented a Detector Lock in 1818, the attractive *St. James's Place* diverges left.

At the end the incomplete N front of *Spencer House* by Vardy (1756–65; fine façade on Green Park, see below) faces a block of flats (1960) by Denys Lasdun. At No. 28 lived William Huskisson (plaque). On the site of Castlemaine House, Samuel Rogers, the wealthy banker-poet, lived from 1802 till his death in 1855, entertaining at his famous breakfasts the most eminent literary men of his day. A concealed narrow passage leads alongside No. 23 to Green Park. Here the attractive façades and gardens of the mansions skirting Queen's Walk are well seen. Among them is the striking Palladian front of Spencer House with graceful statues on the pediment, and a paved terrace raised on arches extending in to the garden.
    In *King St*, across St. James's St, pre-eminent among the art dealers and galleries in the area, is *Christie's* (No. 8), fine art auctioneers since 1766 (in King St since 1823). For details of sales, call 071-839 9060. The *St. James's Theatre*, now demolished, saw the first performances of 'Lady Windermere's Fan' (1892) and 'The Importance of Being Earnest' (1895). *Duke St*, the first street in London to have a pavement, runs N from King St to Piccadilly. In the parallel *Bury St*, Haydn lodged at No. 1 in 1794–95, and Thos. Moore at No. 28. The 17C *Crown Passage*, linking King St with Pall Mall, retains an unexpected 'village' atmosphere.

Continue up St. James's St past the raised white plaza of the *Economist building* (1964; by Peter and Alison Smithson). The offices on arcades varying in height form a striking group, and art galleries use the light ground floor premises. In *Blue Ball Yard*, opposite, attractive black and white stables survive from 1741–42. No. 14 Park Place houses the small Pratt's Club founded in the 1840s and the offices and club of the Royal Over-Seas League. *Brooks's* (No. 60), is a club founded in 1764. One of the earliest members was Charles James Fox who gambled on the faro table in the fine room overlooking St. James's St. It was the leading Whig club in the 18C and the rival of the Tory White's (see below). Other members included Burke, Gibbon, Hume, Garrick, Reynolds, and Palmerston. Opposite is *Boodle's* (No. 28), founded 1762–64, also patronised by Gibbon and Fox. The building, designed by John Crunden in the Adam manner in 1775–76, has been the home of the club since 1783. *White's*, the oldest club (1736) in London, which originated in White's Chocolate House (1693), was frequented by Swift, Steele, Gray and Pope. The building, probably designed by James Wyatt (1787–88), contains a famous bow window (1881) made the 'shrine of fashion' by Beau Brummell and his set. The proprietary clubs, Brooks's, Boodle's, and White's, were all distinguished in the 18C for fashion and gambling. Opposite was the former Devonshire

Club (No. 50), where Crockford's was opened in 1827 by a successful fish salesman. In Arlington St, Robert Walpole lived at No. 5 in 1742–45, and Horace Walpole was born on the site of No. 22. St. James's St. Before Piccadilly turn E into Jermyn St.

Jermyn St, one of the first streets to be built in the area, bears the Earl of St. Albans' family name.

On the corner of Duke St, the Cavendish Hotel recalls its predecessor managed by the formidable Rosa Lewis, an establishment featured in the novels of Evelyn Waugh. In the same street Benjamin Franklin lodged in 1725 as a journeyman printer. The Piccadilly Arcade and, further on, the Princes Arcade lead to Piccadilly and the main entrance of Fortnum and Mason. (Rte 8.) A Jermyn St Festival takes place in September with demonstrations in the shops and entertainment.

Note Alfred Dunhill's shop, then Floris the perfumers at No. 89, here since 1730 and with a magnificent mahogany showcase from the Great Exhibition. Paxton & Whitfield, cheesemongers, are at No. 93, established in 1740. Towards Regent St is Bates the Hatter and several shirtmakers.

In Jermyn St is the rear entrance to **St. James's Church** (Pl. 14; 3), a fine building by Wren (1676–84; rebuilt after damage in the 'Blitz' of 1940–41) on a spacious site. Keystones bear the arms of Lord St. Albans (see above). This was the most fashionable church in London in the early 18C, and three of its rectors became archbishops of Canterbury. The S entrance gate and railings date from c 1800. The church has a lively lunchtime and evening programme with political lectures and concerts. In the courtyard is a crafts market. The Wren Coffee Shop serves light, wholesome food.

The sumptuous *Interior* has galleries supported by elegant columns, and an ingeniously designed roof. The limewood altarpiece is a magnificent work by Grinling Gibbons. The marble font, at which Lord Chatham and William Blake were baptised, is attributed to Gibbons. The organ, from a chapel in Whitehall Palace, was presented to the church by Queen Mary in 1690 when John Blow and Henry Purcell supervised its installation. It was built by Renatus Harris and the splendid case is again the work of Gibbons. William Van de Velde the Elder (c 1610–93) and William Van de Velde the Younger (1633–1707), the marine painters, are buried here (plaque beneath the tower). A new stained glass window by Delia Whitbread commemorates Andrei Tarkovsky (died 1986). The courtyard towards Piccadilly commemorates Londoners of 1939–45; the gates were designed by Sir Reginald Blomfield (1937). A neo-Georgian rectory was built by Austin Blomfield (1955–57). The pleasant open garden with a fountain by A. Hardiman is a memorial to Lord Southwood (1873–1946), journalist and newspaper owner.

Re-join Piccadilly and Rte 8.

8   Piccadilly Circus, Piccadilly

Access: Underground, Piccadilly Circus.

Piccadilly Circus (Pl. 14;4) the hub of the capital, has been undergoing continuous redevelopment since 1984. The expansion of the subways and entrances of the Underground station has caused the greatest upheaval but was finally completed in 1989. For the next three years the S side, the Criterion building, is being redeveloped. Eros was repositioned in 1986, after refurbishment, on a new 'peninsula' on the S side facing the S extention of Regent St. The old Swan and Edgar department store was converted into offices with shops and restaurants on the ground floor and in the basement, opening up into the Underground concourse. The London Pavilion was rebuilt behind its original façade and became a shopping and entertainment complex in 1988/89.

Piccadilly Circus was originally a road-junction in Nash's Regent St. The circular pattern of buildings around it was destroyed by the building of Shaftesbury Avenue in 1886. Eros was unveiled shortly afterwards (1893) as a memorial to the philanthropist Lord Shaftesbury. The statue and fountain, designed by Alfred Gilbert, were intended to represent the Angel of Charity but soon became known as Eros. It was the first statue to be cast in aluminium and the fountain tended to overflow, as Gilbert's instructions were not followed. The statue was condemned by the critics and Gilbert, severely in debt, left the country for Belgium. But the public took to Eros and Piccadilly Circus has become perhaps the most famous meeting-place in the world. During the rebuilding of Piccadilly Underground Station in the 1920s the statue stood in Embankment Gardens; it was removed during the Second World War and is regularly boarded up for protection when large crowds are in London for football matches and other public celebrations.

The popularity of Piccadilly Circus was further enhanced with the arrival of illuminated advertisements; the first in 1910 and more in 1923. These can still be seen on the N side. The Circus was one of the locations for the massive VE celebrations of 1945. The circular Piccadilly Underground Station is one of the busiest in London.

On the S side stood the Criterion building with the *Criterion Brasserie*. This was the original Long Bar of the Criterion Restaurant built in 1874 by Thomas Verity using gemstone and gold leaf tiles. The restaurant's concert hall became the Criterion Theatre completely underground. The Long Bar which served as a Trusthouse Grill and Griddle, its mosaic covered by Formica, was restored and reopened in 1984 as a brasserie restaurant. The gilded ceiling and gemstone tiles are now valued at more than £1m. The Criterion building is being redeveloped as offices, and the Brasserie and the theatre will reopen in 1991–2. Four bronze horses by Rudy Weller will stand at the corner of Haymarket and Piccadilly Circus in front of the new neo-classical Criterion building due to be completed at the end of 1991.

The *London Pavilion* on the N side was a 19C music hall; the present building opened in 1885 and was first a theatre and then a cinema which closed in 1982. The original façade survives and was developed as part of the Trocadero complex. Escalators link the three floors of shops with the top floor restaurant and Rock Circus.

Rock Circus, Piccadilly Circus, Wl. Tel. 071-734 8025. Open Sun to Thur 11.00–21.00; Fri and Sat 11.00–22.00. This is a Madame Tussaud's exhibition with more than 50 waxworks recreating 30 years' of rock and pop music. The entrance charge includes head-sets through which the appropriate music is played as the head turns towards the 'performers'.

The **Trocadero** (entrances in Shaftesbury Avenue and Coventry St) opened in 1984 as a shopping, restaurant and entertainment complex. The architects Fitzroy Robinson have, behind the façades of the original Trocadero, Scott's Restaurant and Lyon's Corner House buildings, constructed an entirely new building with a central three-storey atrium. The Brent Walker Group took over the complex in 1987 and has made further structural changes.

The Trocadero takes its name from the Trocadero Palace which operated on the Shaftesbury site in the late 19C as a music hall. It continued as a popular place of entertainment throughout the '30s and became known as the Troc.

Guinness World of Records, Trocadero, Piccadilly Circus, W1. Tel. 071 439 7331. Open daily 10.00–22.00. Admission charge.

On the façade of Fortnum & Mason, Piccadilly, this clock, showing Mr Fortnum and Mr Mason greeting each other on the hour, was added in 1964

The exhibition on two levels illustrates the contents of the 'Guinness Book of Records'. The fattest man, the smallest woman, the longest fingernails—they are all here in actual size, with further illustrations of record-breaking attempts on video. Sporting achievements are reproduced and records stored on accessible microcomputers. The shop sells appropriate souvenirs and copies of the book.

Piccadilly Circus is a convenient starting-place for exploring the West End. Coventry St runs E to Leicester Square; the broad Shaftesbury Avenue, with its numerous theatres, leads NE through Soho to High

Holborn and New Oxford St; Regent St, interrupted by the Circus,
leads N to Oxford St and Regent's Park and S to Waterloo Place and
Pall Mall; while Piccadilly runs SW to Hyde Park.

Piccadilly runs from the top of Haymarket to Hyde Park Corner
(c 1 mile). Beyond Piccadilly Circus its initial section, to the S of
which is the region of St. James's, is occupied by airline offices,
banks, hotels, and some distinguished shops.

The name of Piccadilly is probably derived from 'Piccadilly Hall', the popular
name of a house built c 1611 near Windmill St by a retired tailor, Robert Baker,
who had made much of his fortune by the sale of 'piccadillies', apparently a
form of collar or ruff. The street was thus named by 1627–28 when building
began at the E end, and the name gradually extended westwards as building
progressed.

On the N side of Piccadilly is the former Piccadilly Hotel, now Le
Meridien, Piccadilly, with a bold colonnade on the upper storey
below which a conservatory-style restaurant has been added as part
of refurbishments in 1984. The former Masonic temple in the
basement has been transformed into a health club. Opposite, *Simpson's* was built in 1935–36 by Joseph Emberton. Beyond is the
forecourt of *St. James's Church*, described in Rte 7. The attractive
Midland Bank (1925) adjoining the garden was designed by Edwin
Lutyens. To the W the vast plate glass window of an office intrudes
into the lower storey of the former home of the Royal Institute of
Painters in Water Colours. The inscription and roundels remain on
the façade above; the busts are of Sandby, Cozens, Girtin, Turner,
D. Cox, De Wint, Barret, and W. Hunt. At No. 187 *Hatchards* (opened
here in 1801) is the sole survivor of the booksellers established in the
area at the end of the 18C. *Fortnum and Mason*, a luxurious
department store where the assistants in the grocery department
wear frock coats, was founded by Charles Fortnum, a footman in the
household of George III, in c 1770. A mechanical clock (1964; by
Thwaites and Red) crowns the entrance. The Soda Fountain
Restaurant—a popular meeting place—serves delicious afternoon
teas and lunches. Beyond, the *Piccadilly Arcade* (1909–10) has tall
glass shop-fronts. On the N side of Piccadilly is the Wales Tourist
Board's information centre and shop—further along a secluded
courtyard admits to *Albany* with an apartment block.

The house, designed by Sir William Chambers for Lord Melbourne in 1771–74,
was the birthplace of the second Viscount and future Prime Minister in 1779.
Frederick, Duke of York and Albany took possession in 1791 in exchange for
his own house in Whitehall (Dover House). Albany was converted to its present
use in 1803, when Henry Holland added two rows of chambers flanking a
covered passage which runs N to Burlington Gardens. Among the occupants of
these exclusive apartments have been Lord Byron (1814–15), Bulwer Lytton,
Macaulay (1840–56), 'Monk' Lewis, Canning, and Gladstone, in addition to the
heroes of many fashionable novels, and more recently, former Prime Minister,
Edward Heath.

Beyond is the imposing **Burlington House** (Pl. 14; 3), the home of the
Royal Academy. Three lofty archways of a façade in a somewhat
heavy Italianate style admit to a quadrangle built for various learned
societies in 1869–73 by R.R. Banks and Charles Barry. In the centre is
a fine statue of Joshua Reynolds by Alfred Drury (1931). On the N
side stands *Old Burlington House*. Its façade of 1719 was remodelled
by Sidney Smirke in 1872–74 when the top storey was added with
statues of Pheidias, Leonardo, Flaxman, Raphael, Michelangelo,

Titian, Reynolds, Wren, and William of Wykeham. The large block of exhibition galleries behind were added at the same time.

Burlington House, originally built in 1665, enjoyed its chief celebrity and splendour under the art-loving third Earl of Burlington (1695–1753), patron of Pope, Gay, and Arbuthnot; he redesigned the house with the aid of James Gibbs, Colen Campbell, and Kent.

Old Burlington House is now occupied by the **Royal Academy of Arts**, which here maintains its free School of Art. The annual *Summer Exhibition* shows contemporary works of painting, sculpture, architecture, and engraving which have not previously been exhibited and are selected by committee. The private view of the Exhibition is popular (open to Friends of the Royal Academy— details from Friends' Department); more exclusive is the Academy Dinner, held on the Wed before the opening of the Exhibition.

Royal Academy of Arts, Piccadilly, W1. Tel. 071-439 7438. Open daily during exhibitions 10.00–18.00. Admission charge (reduced on Sun mornings). Bookshop, cafeteria.

From the entrance hall with ceiling paintings by *Angelica Kauffmann* and *Benj. West*, the main staircase decorated with the works of *Seb. Ricci* (Diana and her Nymphs, and Triumph of Galatea) ascends to the galleries used for the main Exhibition. The permanent collections (not usually on view; shown sometimes on request) consist mainly of diploma works presented by Academicians elected since 1770, an interesting illustration of British art. Also good examples of the work of the original members of the Academy, including: *Reynolds* (Self-portrait), *Gainsborough*, and *Richard Wilson*; and 15 landscape studies and Dedham Lock, or the Leaping Horse, by *Constable*. The few notable earlier foreign works include the exquisite *tondo in low-relief by *Michelangelo* known as the 'Madonna Taddei' (c 1505), and a full-size copy of Leonardo da Vinci's Last Supper, at Milan, by his pupil *Marco d'Oggiono*.—The Sitters' Chair, preserved here, originally belonged to Sir Joshua Reynolds.

The Royal Academy of Arts, founded in 1768, with Sir Joshua Reynolds as its first president, had its abode first in Pall Mall, afterwards at Somerset House (1780–1838), and then at the National Gallery (1838–69). It consists of 40 Academicians (RA) and 30 Associates (ARA), and vacancies in the list are filled up by vote of the whole body of members. The distinguished honorary members included Sir Winston Churchill. The fine arts *Library* is open to scholars.

Burlington House accommodates various learned societies: in the E wing, the Linnean Society, the Chemical Society, and the Geological Society; in the W wing, the Society of Antiquaries, and the Royal Astronomical Society; the British Academy moved in 1982 to Regent's Park. Visitors are admitted by Fellow's introduction only.

The *Chemical Society*, founded in 1841, possesses one of the finest chemical libraries in the world. The *Geological Society* was founded in 1807 (and incorporated in 1825) for the purpose of 'investigating the Mineral Structure of the Earth'.

The *Society of Antiquaries of London*, founded c 1586, but not formally reconstituted until 1717, holds a charter of 1751. From 1781 to 1874 it occupied quarters in Somerset House. The rooms contain interesting paintings, MSS, etc. and a fine archaeological library. The *Royal Astronomical Society* was founded in 1820. The *Linnean Society* was founded in 1788 for 'the cultivation of the Science of Natural History in all its branches'. The Society possesses the collections of Carl Linnaeus (1707–78), the Swedish botanist who created the system of scientific nomenclature for plants and animals. Sir Joseph Banks, Sir Joseph Hooker, and Thomas Huxley have all been associated with the society, and it was here in 1858 that Charles Darwin and Alfred Russel Wallace read their first joint paper on evolution by natural selection.

The long *Burlington Arcade* (1818 by Sam. Ware; S façade of 1931; N end rebuilt 1952–54), a covered passage lined on both sides with mahogany-fronted fashionable shops, built by Lord Cavendish to stop passers-by throwing rubbish into his garden of Burlington House. The frock-coated Beadles are former guardsmen and enforce the rules against 'running', 'singing' and 'unseemly behaviour'. Near its N end, at No. 6 Burlington Gardens, is the Italianate building originally erected in 1866–67 by Pennethorne for London University. The Civil Service Examinations were later held here, and it now houses the *Ethnographic Department of the British Museum* renamed in 1972 the **Museum of Mankind**. Exhibitions are changed approximately every year and the collection illustrating the tribal and village cultures of the world is particularly strong in material from W Africa, Oceania, and America. The Department issues informative handbooks and guides in conjunction with exhibitions.

Museum of Mankind, 6 Burlington Gardens, W1. Tel. 071-437 2224, Open Mon to Sat 10.00 to 17.00, Sun 14.30–18.00. Access: Underground, Piccadilly Circus.

At the E end of Burlington Gardens is SAVILE ROW, a street synonymous with fashionable tailoring since the 1850s (neighbouring Cork St was already famous for its tailors in the previous century). Sheridan lived at No. 14 (tablet) and died in 1816 in the front bedroom of No. 17 (where George Basevi lived in 1794–1845). The *British Association for the Advancement of Science*, at Fortress House, stimulates public interest in science and technology and their relation to social problems and promotes the advancement of science to the benefit of the community. Cork St is the centre for the contemporary arts world with an annual street party in July involving galleries in the adjoining streets.

Return to Piccadilly via **Bond St** (Pl. 14; 3), the S portion of which is *Old Bond St*, while the N portion, running to Oxford St, is known as *New Bond St*. It was laid out by Sir Thomas Bond in 1686, and, forming the E boundary of Mayfair, is renowned for its fashionable shops and picture-dealers' galleries. The fine art auctioneers, *Sotheby's* (No. 34), founded in 1744, went into partnership with the Parke-Bernet Galleries of New York in 1964. Sales and previews Monday to Friday 09.00–16.00, tel. 071-493 8080 for details. At the corner of Bruton St is the Time-Life Building, with a sculpted screen by Henry Moore (1953).

Among noted residents of Old Bond St have been Sterne (No. 41), Sir Thos. Lawrence (Nos 24 and 29), and Boswell. In New Bond St lived Dean Swift, Nelson (at No. 147), and Lady Hamilton (at No. 150).

Return to Piccadilly. *Albemarle St*, leading (right) from Piccadilly, occupies the site of Clarendon House, sold after 1664 to George Monk, Duke of Albemarle, and pulled down about 1683. Behind a long façade of Corinthian columns at the N end of the street lies the *Royal Institution*, a society founded in 1799 for the diffusion of scientific knowledge, on the initiative of the cosmopolitan Sir Benjamin Thompson (1753–1814; Count Rumford of Munich), born in Massachusetts.

Here Campbell's lectures on poetry were delivered in 1812 and Carlyle's on heroes in 1840. Among the most popular of its lectures are those for children in the Christmas holidays. The Davy-Faraday Research Laboratory here commemorates two illustrious chemists closely connected with the work of the Royal Institution. In the basement is the *Faraday Museum*.

Faraday Museum, Royal Institution, 21 Albemarle St, W1. Tel. 071-409 2992. Open Tues to Thurs 13.00–16.00. Admission charge. Access: Underground, Green Park.

Michael Faraday's laboratory has been converted into a museum with a reconstruction of the Magnetic Laboratory where Faraday experimented with electromagnetism. Faraday's work on the discovery of benzene, alloy steels, magnetism and light is illustrated.

Opposite the Royal Institution is Brown's Hotel, founded by Lord Byron's butler and now a Trusthouse Forte hotel. In *Grafton St*, at the end of Albemarle St, Lord Brougham lived at No. 4 and Sir Henry Irving at No. 15A (tablet). The Hong Kong Government Offices are at No. 6.

Across Piccadilly, St. James's St descends to St. James's Palace (Rte 7). In *Dover Street*, the next street to the N, *Ely House* (No. 37) a fine mansion built in 1772 by Sir Robert Taylor, was the town house of the Bishops of Ely until 1909. No. 40 (restored) is the *Arts Club*. On the corner of Piccadilly and Dover St is a sculpture by Elizabeth Frink, 'Horse and Rider' (1975). On the S side of Piccadilly rises the large *Ritz Hotel* with an arcade over the pavement; the Portland stone exterior clothes one of the first steel-framed buildings (1904–06) in London. Its name inspired an American epithet for luxurious living. The ballroom in the basement is now the Ritz Casino. Opposite, between Berkeley St and Stratton St, a palatial block of shops and offices occupies the site of the ducal Devonshire House, one of the great Whig mansions (pulled down in 1924). The principal gateway, designed by Inigo Jones, was moved W to the N entrance of the Broad Walk in Green Park.

Berkeley St, with the office of Thomas Cook & Son, leads N to Berkeley Square (Rte 9). Beyond Stratton St the next three side-streets lead from Piccadilly to Curzon St, Mayfair (p 121). In *Bolton St* Henry James lived at No. 3 in 1875–86. *Clarges St* was the residence of C.J. Fox (No. 46), Lord Macaulay (No. 3; on the site of the Kennel Club), Edmund Kean (No. 12), and Lady Hamilton (No. 11); the last three houses are demolished. At the end of *Half Moon St*, where Boswell, Hazlitt, and Shelley lived, a Christian Science church (p 121) closes the vista.

Offices, clubs and luxurious hotels overlook Green Park which borders Piccadilly on the S. The *Naval and Military Club*, at No. 94, known also as the 'In-and-Out' from the instructions on the gate-posts, occupies an 18C building (damaged in the War) where Lord Palmerston lived from 1855 till his death in 1865. Beyond the *American Club* (No. 95), White Horse St diverges right for Shepherd Market. The building on the opposite corner was the site of the Public Schools Club—now offices and apartments. No. 105 Piccadilly was the home of *The Arts Council* due to move to Westminster in 1990. Next door is the new home for the Japanese Embassy. Beyond Down St, at No. 107, Blücher found a temporary home in 1804. The privately owned Park Lane Hotel was completed in 1927; it has a fine art deco ballroom. Opposite the *Cavalry and Guards Club* (No. 127), is a 'Porters' Rest' (1861), an unassuming relic of the past. Next door is the RAF Club. No. 138 was the house of the notorious Duke of Queensberry (died 1810).

The Hard Rock Café at No. 150, Old Park Lane, W1, Tel. 071-629 0382—an American hamburger restaurant—is easily London's most popular eating place with queues at most times of the day. A separate gift shop is now open.

The last house in Piccadilly ('No. 1, London') overlooking Hyde Park Corner, and now isolated by traffic, is **Apsley House** (Pl. 13; 6), the residence of the Duke of Wellington, and still in use as a family home. Acquired by the nation in 1947, and opened in 1952 as a

Wellington Museum, it contains relics and works of art acquired by the Iron Duke.

Wellington Museum, Apsley House, 149 Piccadilly, W1. Tel. 071-499 5676 (managed by the Victoria and Albert Museum). Open Tues to Sun 11.00–17.00. Closed Mon. Admission charge. Access: Underground Hyde Park Corner.
  Built of red brick between 1771 and 1778 by Robert Adam, for the second Earl Bathurst (Baron Apsley), this house was bought in 1805 by Marquess Wellesley and sold by him in 1817 to his younger brother, Arthur, the famous Duke of Wellington. In 1828–29 the mansion was faced with stone by Wyatt, who added the Corinthian portico and the Waterloo Gallery, in which the Waterloo Banquet was held annually until the Duke's death in 1852.
  In front of the house on a granite base stands Boehm's equestrian bronze statue of the Duke on his favourite horse 'Copenhagen' erected in December 1888. In Hyde Park NW of the house is Westmacott's Achilles statue which honours Wellington and his soldiers, paid for by the 'women of England'.

The interior has recently been renovated. In the Entrance Hall is a copy of Lawrence's whole length portrait of the Duke of Wellington, and 'His Last Return from Duty' (1853), by J.W. Glass, which shows the Duke on his horse 'The Brown Mare' leaving Whitehall for the last time as Commander-in-Chief. The monumental marble bust of Wellington is by Pistrucci (1832). To the right of the entrance door is a plaque commemorating the visit in 1810 of Simon Bolivar, the Liberator, when the house was used by the Foreign Secretary, Lord Wellesley. On the W side of the Hall is the Plate and China Room, including the Duke's orders, decorations and medals—The Garter, The Golden Fleece, the Danish Order of the Elephant are among them. Personal relics include the Duke's travelling canteen and dressing case.

The Inner Hall contains portraits of Wellington's contemporaries. In the Basement is an engraving showing the panorama of his funeral procession. In the Staircase vestibule is Canova's nude 'Statue of Napoleon Bonaparte' carved of one block of Carrara marble—it is 11ft 4ins high. Napoleon did not like it and the British Government bought it in 1816. The Piccadilly Drawing Room on the left was designed by Adam with apse and barrel vaulted ceiling—the decoration of frieze, doors and chimney-piece is inspired by Piranesi. The room is now hung with fine small Dutch 17C pictures, plus two English paintings, Wilkie's 'Chelsea Pensioners reading the Waterloo Despatch', commissioned by Wellington in 1816, and John Burnet's 'The Greenwich Pensioners commemorating Trafalgar' (c 1835).

The Portico Room was originally designed by Adam but transformed by Wyatt. The pictures include four large copies after paintings by Raphael or his followers which are now in the Prado. Francis Joseph's portrait of Spencer Percival was painted from a death mask after his assassination in 1812.

The Waterloo Gallery was designed by Wyatt in 1828 to house the Duke's fine collection of paintings. It is 90ft long with a superb white and gold ceiling. The eight windows have sliding shutters faced with mirror glass. This is where the Waterloo Banquets were held and an engraving of William Slater's painting of the banquet of 1836 shows how the room was arranged. Among the paintings are Goya's equestrian Portrait of Wellington (1812); Steen, 'The Egg Dance', one of his most elaborate; Coreggio, 'The Agony in the Garden' (1520s), an exquisite small panel, a treasured possession of the Duke; Velasquez, 'Two Young Men eating at a Humble Table' (1618–20), one of the artist's early genre scenes, and 'The Water-Seller of Seville'.

The Yellow Drawing Room was originally by Adam. Old Master paintings include works by Giordano, Vernet, Peyron, Pannini, Teniers and Platzer. The Striped Drawing Room was created by Wyatt and hung with crimson and buff striped silk tabouret with the banquettes en suite. This room has been referred to as the Valhalla, filled with portraits of the British commanders who fought with Wellington. Over the fireplace is Lawrence's portrait of Wellington (1814) and a silk tricolour standard (lent by the Queen), one of which is presented to the sovereign at each anniversary of Waterloo. These hang in the Waterloo Chamber at Windsor Castle, where the Waterloo banquets are now held. The Dining Room houses the oak chairs and dining-table from the Waterloo Gallery and in the centre of the table is the 26ft centrepiece of the Portuguese service presented to the Duke in 1816. On the walls are portraits of the allied sovereigns.

The traffic grinds slowly round around Hyde Park Corner outside, see Rte 10. Park Lane is to the north, Rte 9.

9 Park Lane and Mayfair

Access: Underground, Hyde Park Corner. Green Park, Marble Arch, Bond St.

Mayfair, bounded by Bond St to the E and Park Lane to the W, was once a fashionable residential area which took its name from a fair held annually in May, from the end of the 17C to the mid 18C when it was suppressed. The area retains an exclusive air. Many residences disappeared after the Second World War when temporary office planning permissions were granted to make up for the heavy loss of office space in the City due to bombing. Many of these leases expire in 1990 and the area may in future return to greater residential use. Unexpected pockets of less grand houses, often in individual architectural styles, may still be found, e.g. Shepherd Market, Mount Row, Waverton St, Bruton Place, Pitts Head Mews and Farm St. The grand houses which once occupied Park Lane have mostly gone and luxury hotels and offices have taken their place.

Park Lane runs N from Hyde Park Corner with Hyde Park on the W; its view of the park was screened by a high wall until the early 19C when it was replaced by iron railings. The road was widened after the great Hyde Park demonstrations of 1866 in support of the Second Reform Bill when the railings were trampled down. Most of the great houses had gone by the 1920s and Park Lane became a dual carriageway in 1963. Hamilton Place and Old Park Lane run parallel to Park Lane from Piccadilly and converge at the towering Hilton Hotel (1961–63) where the Roof Restaurant has one of the best views in London.

At No. 4 Hamilton Place is the *Royal Aeronautical Society*. The houses to the S occupied by the Duke of Wellington in 1814–15 were demolished in 1972. The Inn on the Park Hotel opened in 1970 and the Inter-Continental Hotel opened in 1975 (F. Gibberd and Partners); its top-floor supper-club overlooks Buckingham Palace Gardens. At No. 5 is Les Ambassadeurs Club in an impressive classical style (rebuilt in 1881).

The narrow Old Park Lane was relieved of its traffic congestion as Park Lane was widened. The Londonderry Hotel (next to the London Hilton) opened in 1967 and stands on the site of the Old Londonderry

House (Hertford St) designed in the 1760s by James Stuart and reconstructed by Wyatt in the 1820s for the Marquess of Londonderry. It had a grand staircase, magnificent ballroom and a fine collection of statues—it was demolished in 1962. The Londonderry Hotel reopened in 1985 after complete refurbishment.

In *Hertford St* (right) Gen. John Burgoyne lived and died (1722–92) at No. 10, subsequently occupied by Sheridan in 1796–1802. No. 20 was the residence of Sir George Cayley (1773–1857), 'inventor of the aeroplane'. At No. 14 (destroyed), Edward Jenner, the champion of vaccination, made an unsuccessful attempt to establish a practice in London. In Down St (right) *Christ Church* dates from 1865–68.

Continue N along Park Lane; past Curzon St to the right is the *Grosvenor House Hotel* which stands on the site of the Grosvenor family's London house; the family later became the Westminsters. The present Duke of Westminster still owns the freehold of most of the properties in the 300-acre estate which covers Mayfair and Park Lane, including the site of the American Embassy in Grosvenor Square. The Grosvenor's residence was the first of the grand houses to be demolished to make way for the hotel in 1928; the W façade is by Lutyens. The Great Room—London's biggest hotel banqueting venue—was used as a skating rink in 1929–34 and served as an American officers' mess in 1943. The Grosvenor House Hotel is now part of the Trusthouse Forte group.

The *Dorchester Hotel*, further N, opened in 1931 (designed by William Curtis Green) on the site of Dorchester House, later Hertford House; it served as the headquarters of General Eisenhower during the Second World War. Its luxury suites are popular with film stars; the hotel is now owned by the Sultan of Brunei and was completely refurbished in 1989 and reopened in 1990.

Benjamin Disraeli resided at No. 93 Park Lane from his marriage in 1839 until the death of his wife (to whom the house belonged) in 1872. The charming row of bow-fronted houses with 'Chinese' balconies (Nos 93–99) survive from the 19C. At No. 100, Dudley House was remodelled by Sir Basil Spence in 1970—these properties are now used as offices.

Curzon St, with fine older houses on the S side, runs E from Park Lane. At No. 19 Disraeli died in 1881. *Worcester House* (No. 30), a beautiful Adam House (1771) is now the Crockfords Casino Club which moved here in 1980. The Curzon Cinema (1933), which specialises in foreign and artistic films, is almost opposite *Crewe House* (in 1985 this became the Saudi Arabian Embassy), a stucco mansion set back from the road, designed by Edward Shepherd (c 1730, altered in 1813) and occupied by the Marquess of Crewe from 1899. Two archways lead S from Curzon St to the delightful *Shepherd Market*, established by Shepherd, retaining its 'village' atmosphere and 18C layout, with a somewhat dubious night-time reputation. The *Bunch of Grapes* pub (1882) has a restaurant. 'Elizabethan' entertainment can be enjoyed in the evenings in Tiddy Dols Restaurant.

At the end of Half Moon St is the large portico of the Third Church of Christ Scientist (1910). In Queen St, Mayfair, lived Harriette Wilson, the courtesan, whose threats prompted Wellington's famous 'publish and be damned' statement. Queen St leads to Charles St where a curious house with a timbered upper storey survives on the corner of Hays Mews. This is said to have been built by John Phillips, who worked as a carpenter in this area. The Chesterfield Hotel is next to the *English Speaking Union* in the former house of Lord Revelstoke, built from three older houses in 1890; original 18C panelling survives in one of the meeting rooms here, which are available to members and non-members. English Speaking Union, Charles St, W1. Tel. 071-499 7866. There is a club room, bar and library.

Charles St with attractive houses leads to **Berkeley Square**, once one of the most aristocratic of London squares, built c 1739 on part of the gardens of Berkeley House. The beautiful plane trees in the open garden in the centre (planted c 1789) dwarf the Pump House (c 1800) and a statue by A. Munro (1867).

Rebuilding in the 20C has practically destroyed its elegant character and it would be difficult to hear the nightingales above the traffic. Glamour returned once a year for the fashionable Berkeley Square Ball in July when champagne was served in elegant marquees erected for the occasion and dancing continued until the early morning. The last ball was held in 1989.

In the SW angle of the square *Lansdowne House* was demolished in 1985. It incorporated part of a house begun in 1762 by Robert Adam, and sold in 1768, before it was finished, to the Earl of Shelburne, the prime minister who conceded the independence of the United States and was created Marquess of Lansdowne in 1784. The new building is used for offices by Saatchi and Saatchi. The few remaining houses of interest in the square are situated on its W side. No. 50 is the so-called 'haunted house'. Winston Churchill lived as a child at No. 48, and at No. 47 William Pitt resided for a time with his brother, the Earl of Chatham. No. 45 was the scene of the suicide of Lord Clive in 1774, and here Lady Dorothy Nevill received Gladstone and Disraeli and the celebrities of their day. No. 44 (now the Clermont Club, a fashionable gambling den) was designed by Kent and possesses a beautiful interior staircase.

From the NW angle of the square Mount St return due W to Park Lane. Carlos St bears right past the *Connaught Hotel*— dating to 1896 when it was known as the Coburg. It was the headquarters of General de Gaulle in the Second World War; the restaurant is considered one of the best in London. Carlos St reaches **Grosvenor Square** (Pl. 13; 2), laid out in 1725 by Sir Richard Grosvenor on the site of Oliver's Mount, an earthwork hastily thrown up by the citizens in 1643, when Charles I was approaching London after the battle of Edgehill. It is dominated on the W side by the *American Embassy* (1957–58) by Eero Saarinen. The gilded aluminium eagle with a 35ft wingspan on the roof is the work of Theodore Roszak (1960). A memorial in the open 6-acre garden to Franklin Roosevelt, President of the United States in 1932–44, includes a statue by Reid Dick (1948). Opposite is a memorial to the Royal Air Force American Eagle Squadron in the form of a Portland stone pillar crowned by a bronze American bald eagle by Elizabeth Frink, unveiled in 1986. The monumental terraces, which now surround the square to house the diplomatic and other offices of the United States as well as two hotels, conform to a uniform style.

At the building in the NE corner of the square (No. 9) John Adams, American ambassador and later President, lived in 1785. No. 6 was the residence of W.H. Page while American ambassador in London (1913–18). No. 1 is the Sir John A. Macdonald building of Canadian offices. No. 20 (N side) was the headquarters of General Eisenhower in 1942 and 1944. In 1968 mounted police fought with demonstrators in the square.

North Audley St leads out of the NW corner of the square. Here Lord Ligonier lived in 1730–70 (No. 12). Beyond is the former American church of *St. Mark's* (1825–28), by J.P. Gundy, with a severe Greek classical porch and vestibule. The dark interior was remodelled by Blomfield in 1878. The church is redundant and various proposals have been made for secular use. Sydney Smith died at No. 59 Green St, opposite the church.

Brook St (where Handel lived at No. 25), and Grosvenor St, leading E to Bond St, are mostly offices.

South Audley St leads due S from the square. Across Mount St is the pleasant exterior of the independent *Grosvenor Chapel* (1730), the burial-place of Lady Mary Wortley Montagu (died 1762), and John Wilkes (died 1797), self-styled 'a friend of liberty' in his epitaph.

The U.S. armed forces used the chapel during the Second World War. A gate to the left admits to the quiet, public *Mount St Gardens*. In the secluded *Farm St* the Jesuit church of the Immaculate Conception (good music) by J.J. Scoles (1844–49) has a high altar by A.W.N. Pugin.

Rejoin Charles St (comp. above) by descending the pleasant Chesterfield Hill, or return W along South St. On the corner of South Audley St *Thos. Goode*, china and glass specialists, occupy an elaborate building of 1875–90, and, opposite, No. 71 has a fine doorway of 1736–37. No. 75 is the *Egyptian Embassy*. South St continues to Park Lane.

10   Hyde Park Corner, Knightsbridge, Belgravia, Hyde Park, Marble Arch and Bayswater

Access: Underground, Hyde Park Corner, Marble Arch, Bayswater.

Hyde Park Corner (Pl. 13; 6), the spacious area at the W end of Piccadilly and at the SE angle of Hyde Park, abandons itself to traffic. *Wellington Arch*, the triumphal arch at the end of Constitution Hill, dominates an open green reached by a maze of pedestrian subways. Designed by Decimus Burton in 1828 and crowned by a statue of Wellington, it originally stood opposite the main entrance to Hyde Park. Until recently it housed London's smallest police station. On top of the Arch, the fine bronze group of Peace and her Quadriga plus four horses, by Adrian Jones, dates from 1912. A statue of Wellington, mounted on 'Copenhagen' by Boehm (1888) faces Apsley House (p 119). To the right an heroic figure of David by Derwent Wood (died 1925), the *Machine Gun Corps War Memorial* was moved here in 1953. Close by rises the imposing*Royal Artillery War Memorial*, in white marble and bronze, finely sculpted by C.S. Jagger and Lionel Pearson.

To the W is the former *St. George's Hospital*, founded in 1719, in a building by Wilkins (1827; with later extensions). It is being rebuilt as a luxury Rosewood hotel. The hospital and medical school moved to Tooting, S London in 1980. *Grosvenor Place* leads S between Belgravia (see below) and the gardens of Buckingham Palace to Victoria Station (Rte 12).

On the N Side of Hyde Park Corner, a delicate screen with a triple archway by Decimus Burton (1828; reproduction of Parthenon frieze by Hemming) next to Apsley House (p 119) leads to Hyde Park. Immediately inside the Park is the statue of Achilles (see p 119) by

Westmacott (1822) in honour of the Duke of Wellington. On the right is a statue of Byron (not a good likeness) and his dog 'Bo'sun' by Belt (1880)—the pink marble slab was a gift from the Greek Government. Explore Knightsbridge and Belgravia before returning to the Park.

Knightsbridge from Hyde Park Corner to Old Brompton Road, is lined with elegant shops (for Harrods, see p 129). At Hyde Park Corner is the Pizza on the Park, popular jazz-venue, and closer to Knightsbridge Underground Station, the Spaghetti House Restaurant, site of a drawn-out siege in 1975 when a robbery went wrong and the staff were held hostage. The Hyde Park Hotel (1882) has a royal reputation: Queen Mary and the former King of Sweden were regular patrons. Guests can watch the Household Cavalry pass each morning from the restaurant overlooking the Park.

Now diverge right into *Wilton Place* which leads S to **Belgravia**. This fashionable residential area was developed in 1825–35 by Lord Grosvenor and Thomas Cubitt. The monumental white stucco mansions are well set off by delightful squares, and behind the spacious streets lie charming mews and less grand Georgian terraces. Beyond the fine light yellow stone façade of the Berkeley Hotel (1972, Brian O'Rorke) is *St. Paul's, Knightsbridge*, built in 1840, with an unexpected timbered roof. A tablet on the outside wall of the church commemorates 52 members of the Women's Transport Service who died in 1939–45. At the end, the unusual *Wilton Crescent* was built in 1827 by Seth Smith. In the mews behind are several pubs, including the *Grenadier* in Wilton Row, once an officers' mess for the Duke of Wellington; it claims a ghost. In Kinnerton St carriage archways admit to tiny subsidiary mews. In the Halkin Arcade (1971) and Motcomb St are antique shops and art galleries.

Motcomb St leads W from the Crescent past the doric columns of the Pantechnicon built in 1830 by Smith as fireproof warehouses, stables and wine vaults. It burned down in 1874. In West Halkin St, a former Presbyterian chapel (1880s) is now a private dining club, Mosman's.

To the SE lies **Belgrave Square** (Pl. 13; 5), built by Basevi in 1825 and now the home of many embassies which surround the beautiful sunken garden in the centre (c 10 acres). The philanthropic Earl of Shaftesbury died at No. 5 in 1885, and Seaford House (SE corner) was built by Hardwick (1842). Halkin St leads E out of the square past the Caledonian Club and Forbes House, set back amidst gardens. At the end (right) No. 6 was the residence of Sir Henry Campbell-Bannerman (1836–1908), Prime Minister in 1906–08.

Upper Belgrave St leads out of the SE corner of the square, with several pretty Georgian streets leading E to Grosvenor Place. Walter Bagehot (1826–77) lived at No. 12. At the corner with Eaton Square is *St. Peter's*, (by Hakewill, 1827; enlarged by Blomfield in 1875) the scene of many fashionable weddings. The church was severely damaged by fire in 1987, and the stained glass by John Hayward was destroyed. The rebuilding appeal is led by the Duke of Westminster, a resident of the long *Eaton Square* (Pl. 13; 8) with fine gardens flanked by two uniform rows of white stucco terraces. The new St. Peter's will reopen in 1991 with its exterior restored and a completely new interior designed by John and Nicki Braithwaite.

In Eaton Place, parallel to the N, No. 15 was the home of Lord Kelvin, and No. 29 that of Lord Avebury. On the doorstep of No. 36 Sir Henry Wilson was shot dead in 1922. In Lyall St, Thomas Cubbitt lived at No. 3, while building much of the area. On the corner of Eaton Place, a plaque at No. 88 records the first London recital given by Chopin (1848). Near the W end of the square, the animated Elizabeth St with interesting shops leads S past the peaceful Chester Square on the left, with *St. Michael's*. Matthew Arnold lived at No. 2, and Mary Shelley, widow of the poet, died at No. 24 in 1851.

At the W end of Eaton Square, Eaton Gate and Cliveden Place lead to *Sloane Square*, with the Royal Court Theatre, at the beginning of Chelsea (Rte 13). Turn N up *Sloane St* (Pl. 23; 7), a fashionable residential and shopping street, remarkably long and straight, bordered on the E by fine gardens. Near its S end *Holy Trinity* (1890) by John Dando Sedding is an outstanding representation of the arts and crafts movement with an E window designed by Burne-Jones, completed by William Morris, and elaborate art nouveau fittings. In Sloane Terrace (right) is the First Church of Christ Scientist in London. No. 44 Cadogan Place (across the gardens) was the home of William Wilberforce, the campaigner against slavery. No. 76 Sloane St, just before the intersection with Pont St, was the home of Sir Herbert Tree and Sir Charles Dilke (plaques). Strikingly seen at the far end of the red-brick gabled mansions of *Pont St* (1878) (left), described by Osbert Lancaster as 'Pont St Dutch', is the Scottish church of *St. Columba's*, well sited on a corner with a fine helm roofed tower, by Sir Edward Maufe (1950–55). Inside is a memorial chapel to the London Scottish regiment.

The *Cadogan Hotel* at No. 75 has a blue plaque to Lily Langtry; Oscar Wilde was arrested here. At No. 55 is the Danish Embassy designed by Arne Jacobsen (1978). The Chelsea Hotel is at No. 17–25. The Hyatt Carlton Tower (1961) Michael Rosenauer—since redeveloped, incorporates copper panels, 'Four Seasons' on the south face by Elizabeth Frink, and murals in the lobby by Topolski; the hotel overlooks Cadogan Place and its private gardens with statues by David Wynne.

Arnold Bennett lived for many years at No. 75 Cadogan Square, S of Pont St, and to the N, in Hans Place, with its thickly planted oval gardens, lived Jane Austen (at No. 23), and Shelley (at No. 41; both houses demolished).

Sloane St leads to the intersection of Knightsbridge past attractive boutiques.

Cross the busy intersection and enter Hyde Park through Albert Gate. Lying between Park Lane, Knightsbridge and Bayswater Road, and merging on the W with Kensington Gardens, the park has an area of 361 acres and measures 3.5m round the perimeter. Together with Kensington Gardens it forms one continuous park of over 600 acres, visually sadly reduced by tower blocks protruding above a sky-line once filled only with trees.

TRAFFIC. Private cars and taxicabs are admitted to the roads skirting the park, and to The Ring, which crosses it as the Serpentine bridge.

PARKING. N of the Serpentine bridge. An underground car park is entered from Park Lane and Marble Arch.

CHAIRS may be hired.

RESTAURANTS. Dell Café and Bar (E end of Serpentine); Serpentine Restaurant and Bar (by the bridge).

BOATS. Sailing dinghies and rowing skiffs may be hired.

BANDS at the bandstands.

SWIMMING. Mixed bathing May–Sept, daily from 10.00–19.00. Admission charge. Lido.

'DING. Bathurst Riding Stables tel. 071-723 2813; Richard Briggs Stables, tel. '1-723 2813.

HISTORY. The manor of Hyde belonged to the monks of Westminster Abbey from the Conquest to the Dissolution, when Henry VIII seized it and converted it into a royal hunting park. Under Charles I the place began to be a fashionable resort, though the deer were hunted until after the middle of the 18C and did not finally disappear until about 1840. In Charles I's reign the 'Ring', a circular drive and racecourse, was laid out, and was much frequented by fashionable carriages. During the reign of William and Mary and Queen Anne, the roads leading across the park were infested by 'footpads' (villains), and it became a favourite resort of duellists, but with the Georges its character improved. In 1851 the first *Great International Exhibition* was held in Hyde Park on a space of about 20 acres between Rotten Row (see below) and Knightsbridge. Sir Joseph Paxton's famous exhibition-building of glass and iron was afterwards re-erected at Sydenham as the Crystal Palace (see p 327).—The park contains several 'bird sanctuaries'. Some of the fine lodges by the numerous entrance gates are by Decimus Burton.

Enter the park through Albert Gate past Bowater House (1958-69) with the extraordinary group 'Pan' by Jacop Epstein, his last work (1959). Straight ahead is the carriage-road running along the S side of the park and to the right the Knightsbridge Barracks (see below).

Almost parallel with this is *Rotten Row*, the famous sand-track for riders (mounting blocks remain near many of the gates), also known as The Mile.

The long sweep of Rotten Row passes to the W, and past the site of the 1851 Exhibition (see above) and the conspicuous *Knightsbridge Barracks*. The angular buildings by Sir Basil Spence (1970) surround a tower block (310ft) which provides accommodation for men of the Household Cavalry; their horses (c 270) are stabled in the E wing. They exercise daily 6–8am in the park, and may often be seen at drill on Rotten Row. The guard for Horse Guards in Whitehall leaves the barracks beneath the fine pedimented portico daily at approx. 10.30; the old guard returns just before midday. In 1984, the IRA planted a bomb near Hyde Park Corner which killed several guardsmen and horses, not far from the Cavalry Memorial (by Adrian Jones, 1924) near the bandstand. To the W is Diana, a fine classical fountain by Feodara Gleichen (1906).

Stretching in a curve diagonally across the centre of both Hyde Park and Kensington Gardens is the *Serpentine*, an artificial lake of 41 acres (4.5–14ft deep), frequented by waterfowl. The portion within Kensington Gardens is known as the *Long Water*. It was in this lake that Harriet Westbrook, Shelley's first wife, drowned herself in 1816.

Straight ahead at the E end of the Serpentine—the Standing Stone marks a water conduit of 1861—is the rich vegetation of the *Dell*, watered by the Westbourne, and, nearby, on the shore of the lake, a pleasant open-air café. A small fountain The Colton Memorial (1896) is a replica of the original also known as 'Little Nell'. Beyond the boating pier, a road leads N to Ranger's Lodge, offices of the Park Superintendent, and a police station. The undulating *Buck Hill*, to the N, retains a pump and water-trough used when the area was pastureland (sheep still grazed here in 1937). A bird sanctuary and sunken area of green-houses lies behind a memorial 'Rima' (by Epstein; 1925) to W.H. Hudson (1841–1922). The fine bridge over the Serpentine (built in 1828 by the brothers Rennie), the last Rennie bridge still used in London, commands an open view to the towers of Westminster, and (NW) to the thin steeple of Christ Church (p 136) amidst the wooded dells of Kensington Gardens (Rte 11A). On the SW side of the lake stood the Serpentine Restaurant (1963; by Patrick Gwynne) demolished for redevelopment in 1989/90 (temporary restaurant in operation), and a Lido (surrounded by pavilions in summer), and fishing area, while further S, the *Serpentine Gallery* holds exhibitions of modern art all th year round supported by the Arts Council. The building, formerly a tea house, is by Henry Tanner (1908). The Arch by Henry Moore (1979) stands on the E bank of the Long Water.

Henry Moore's 'The Arch' (1979) overlooking the Long Water, seen from Kensington Gardens

Continue towards Kensington Gardens (Route 11A) or head NE towards Speaker's Corner at Marble Arch, where orators hold forth in the open air (on Sundays). Speakers' Corner was established as a result of the riots of 1866. Contrary to popular belief, the law has full jurisdiction over speakers here—only the free right of assembly applies. Extremists now tend to dominate. Broad Walk leads south back to Hyde Park Corner, past the modernistic 'Joy of Life' fountain, and the new East Carriage Ride—an extension of Rotten Row.

Beyond, the four important thoroughfares of Park Lane, Oxford St, Edgware Road, and Bayswater Road radiate from a broad open space. Here, between two elaborate, landscaped traffic islands (1961–62), rises the **Marble Arch** (Pl. 13; 1), designed by Nash more or less after the Arch of Constantine at Rome, and originally erected in 1828 in front of Buckingham Palace where it proved too narrow for the royal carriages. It was removed in 1850–51 to its present site, where it formed an entrance to Hyde Park until 1908. The gates are finely wrought; the reliefs on the north side are by Westmacott.

Marble Arch is close to the site of **Tyburn**, the famous place of execution, to which during many centuries victims were dragged through the centre of the city from the Tower or from Newgate. The first recorded execution took place here in 1196, the last in 1783. From 1571 to 1759 'Tyburn Tree', a permanent triangular gallows, stood on the spot now indicated by a stone slab on the traffic island opposite the site of the Odeon Cinema.

To the W, is the area of Bayswater with many hotels and guest houses. In Hyde Park Place, is the *Shrine of the Sacred Heart and Tyburn Martyrs* where 25 nuns say mass in memory of 'the glorious martyrs who laid down their lives in defence of the Catholic faith here on Tyburn Hill 1535–1681'. The chapel was built in 1961. At No. 10 is London's smallest house with a frontage of just 3.5 ft. Just beyond, new blocks of flats have been built on the site of a cemetery; the body of Laurence Sterne was removed from here to Coxwold. No. 2 Connaught Place, nearby, was the home of Lord Randolph Churchill in 1883–92.

(See Rte 11A for the rest of Bayswater.)

11 Kensington

A. Knightsbridge, Kensington, Kensington Gardens, Holland Park and Bayswater

Access: Underground, Knightsbridge, South Kensington, High St Kensington, Lancaster Gate, Queensway, Notting Hill Gate and Holland Park.

Kensington was made a royal borough at the wish of Queen Victoria in 1901, and was combined in 1965, much against its will, with Chelsea. The remarkable group of museums and educational institutions between Kensington Gardens and Cromwell Road was built on land purchased from the proceeds of the 1851 Exhibition.

The thoroughfare that continues the line of Piccadilly (Rte 8) W from Hyde Park Corner, along the S side of Hyde Park and Kensington Gardens, is known at first as *Knightsbridge* and further on as Kensington Road and Kensington High St.

From Knightsbridge Station (at the top of Sloane St, comp. p 125) *Brompton Road* (Pl. 13; 5), a wide and bustling thoroughfare, runs SW towards the South Kensington museums. It passes the huge terracotta edifice of *Harrods*, a superior department store where almost anything may be purchased. It was first established in 1849 by a tea-merchant, Henry Charles Harrod, as a small grocer's shop. The expanded store was destroyed by fire in 1883 and rebuilt in 1884; a huge depository was built at Barnes. In 1898 the first escalator in London was installed and the building was extended and rebuilt in 1901–5 by Stevens and Munt. In the magnificent food halls the listed tiled ceilings and walls include 'The Hunt' by Royal Doulton (1902) in the Meat Hall designed by W.J. Neatley.

With a staff of 5000 in 200 departments it is one of the world's largest stores. It was acquired by the House of Fraser in 1959; since 1986 this company has been owned by the Al Fayed brothers. There are several restaurants and afternoon tea is served between

W.J. Neatley's design of 'The Hunt' (1902) executed in Royal Doulton tiles in Harrods' Food Hall

15.30 and 17.00. There is a tourist information centre in the basement.

Beyond Harrods, opposite a stretch of raised pavement with trees, *Beauchamp Place* diverges left, its modest regency housing brightly transformed below iron balconies into fashionable boutiques and restaurants. The area to the N of Brompton Road retains some quiet residential streets (including Cheval Place, Rutland St, and Montpellier St, with Bonham's, the auctioneers). Beyond Brompton Square built in 1820 (where Stéphane Mallarmé, the poet, lived at No. 6 in 1863), an avenue of limes leads to *Holy Trinity* (1827; the chancel added by Blomfield in 1879), the rural parish church of Brompton. Across an open green behind is the colourful Ennismore Gardens Mews and St. The headquarters of the Independent Broadcasting Authority is in Brompton Road. The Visitors' Gallery was closed in 1987.

Brompton Oratory (Pl. 12; 8), or the *Oratory of St. Philip Neri*, is served by secular priests (housed in a building of 1853 to the W of the church) of the institute of the Oratory, founded by St. Philip Neri at Rome in 1575. The institute was introduced into England by Cardinal Newman in 1848 (his statue by Chavalliaud stands to the left of the entrance). The present church, a large and elaborate edifice in the Roman Baroque style, designed by H. Gribble, was opened in 1884, the façade and dome being completed in 1896–97. The interior, which is remarkable for the width of its nave (52ft), is heavily decorated with marble and statuary (including a series of Apostles from Siena, by Mazzuoli, c 1680). The huge Renaissance altar in the Lady Chapel (S Transept) come from Brescia.

Brompton Road branches left through an area of attractive squares and crescents (Alexander Sq, Thurloe Sq, Pelham Place and Crescent, etc.) built in 1820–40. Where Brompton Road meets the Fulham Road, Brompton Cross, stands the striking Michelin Building previously headquarters for the Michelin Tyre Co. designed by Francois Espinasse (1911) and featuring 34 ceramic-tiled decorative panels of racing cars. After refurbishing by Conran Roche and YRM Architects it re-opened in 1987 with shops, a bar and a restaurant, Bibendum, as well as offices.

Cromwell Road (Pl. 12; 7) continues due W, named from a vanished house of Henry Cromwell, son of the Protector. Though mainly lined with monotonous terraces of hotels, it begins with the long imposing Renaissance façade in stone and red brick by Sir Aston Webb (1909) of the *Victoria and Albert Museum*, the first of the **South Kensington Museums** described in Rte 11B. Opposite stands the new Islamic Cultural Centre in pink stone and glass (it includes the Zamana Art Gallery). Beyond Exhibition Road (with an entrance to South Kensington Stn), the *Natural History Museum* stands among plane trees.

In Cromwell Rd, opposite the Natural History Museum, is the *Institut Français du Royaume-Uni*, a centre of French culture in London with a lycée. In Cromwell Place, No. 7 was the home of Millais (1862–79). At the corner of Queen's Gate is *Baden-Powell House* (1959–61), headquarters of the Scout Association and a hostel for members, with a small museum devoted to Lord Robert Baden-Powell (1857–1941), founder of the international scouting movement. The displays illustrate the history of the founding of the Association with photographs and relics. Outside is Don Potter's statue of Baden-Powell.

Baden-Powell Museum, Baden-Powell House, Queen's Gate, SW7. Tel. 071-584 7030. Admission daily 07.00–20.00.

Further W in Cromwell Road, across Gloucester Road, Sainsbury's new superstore is located on the site of the former air terminal. Cromwell Hospital, private, is in the next block. No. 39 Harrington Gardens (parallel to the S) was built in 1881 for W.S. Gilbert; its terracotta decorations recall the Savoy operas.

Return to *Exhibition Road* which runs N, passing (left) the *Science Museum* (Rte 11B) and (right) a *Mormon Chapel* (1959–61) with a tapering spire covered in gold leaf. The elaborate organ is played 12.30–13.00 on most days. Beyond, on either side of the road, are the buildings of *Imperial College of Science and Technology*, a magnificently equipped group of associated colleges, incorporated in the University of London in 1907, for advanced training and research in science, especially in its application to industry. The open Prince's Garden (right) is surrounded by residential halls. On the left side of Exhibition Rd, unimaginative faculty buildings (1958–63) surround a huge *Campanile* by Thomas Collcutt (1887–93), preserved from the former Imperial Institute, erected as a national memorial to Queen Victoria's Jubilee and designed to exhibit and promote the resources of the Empire. The Campanile is open from July to September.

In Prince Consort Road which skirts the Royal School of Mines is the *Royal College of Music*, incorporated in 1883, but occupying a building opened in 1894. It contains the Donaldson Collection of ancient musical instruments (adm. on application to the Assistant Director of Studies, October to May) and the *Britten Opera Theatre* opened here in 1986, mainly for the use of students. Opposite, steps lead up past a bronze statue of Prince Albert, on a memorial to the Great Exhibition of 1851, to the former entrance to the Royal Albert Hall. To the left is the Union building of Imperial College, and to the W is the *Royal College of Organists*, with bright scraffito decoration. The grim yet individual building of the *Royal College of Art* (1960–61) is the last of this remarkable group of institutions devoted to science and art. Here are held periodic exhibitions. Adjoining it behind a Victorian parade is the new RCA studios opening in 1991.

The **Royal Albert Hall** (Pl. 12; 5), a huge amphitheatre roofed by a glass dome, was inspired by the Roman works of Provence and built in 1867–71. It is still privately owned and managed by the descendants of the original public investors in 1871. Each is entitled to a certain number of seats per year and membership now changes hands only occasionally, at a high price. The exterior, with a terracotta frieze by Minton, was cleaned in 1969–70, damaging the delicate surface which will now undergo further repairs; the frieze measures 273ft in length, 240ft in breadth, and 155ft in height. The interior (tours of the building daily include a special exhibition, a visit to the royal box and the 'real' Prince Albert) has an arena of 103ft by 68ft, holding up to 8000 for concerts, public meetings, balls, etc., and has a celebrated Willis organ. The famous Promenade concerts founded by Sir Henry Wood are held here from July to September.

The houses flanking the Albert Hall are known as *Kensington Gore*, from Gore House, which stood approximately on the site of the Albert Hall, and was famous for the salon held by Lady

Blessington (1836–49). At the beginning of the 19C it was the residence of William Wilberforce.

Kensington Road runs E to Knightsbridge (comp. p 128). On the corner of Exhibition Road (1 Kensington Gore, SW7, tel. 071-589 5466), is the *Royal Geographical Society* in a building by Norman Shaw (1874) adorned with statues of Sir Ernest Shackleton and David Livingstone. Admission to the small exhibition with relics of these and other explorers, and maps, is granted by the Director. The library is available to scholars. Across Exhibition Rd, at No. 14 Prince's Gate (now the Royal College of General Practitioners with a small private museum, tel. 071-581 3232), J.F. Kennedy lived while his father was ambassador to Britain (1937–40). Earl Haig (1861–1928) died at No. 21. No. 20 is the Polish Institute and Sikorski Museum (tel 071-589 9249) with Polish Art, historical archive and a library. The Iranian Embassy at No. 27 was partly demolished in the siege of April/May 1980. In Ennismore Gardens, the Russian Orthodox church of *All Saints*, in a curious mixture of architectural styles, contains sgraffito work by Heywood Sumner (1898). At 24 Rutland Gate in the former French consulate is the new Accademia Italiana devoted to promoting Italian art in London in a series of changing exhibitions. (Details on 071-224 3475). The Mitford sisters lived at 4 Rutland Gate Mews when in London. On the corner of Rutland Gardens is the Westminster Synagogue. Further on, opposite Knightsbridge Barracks (see p 126), Knightsbridge House is fronted by a pleasant bronze group, 'The Seer', by G. Ledward. The quiet streets to the S around Trevor Square are attractive.

W of the Albert Hall, beyond the wide Queen's Gate, with its equestrian statue of Lord Napier of Magdala (died 1890) by Boehm, is Hyde Park Gate. Here at No. 18 Epstein had his studio and died in 1959; Sir Leslie Stephen (1822–1904) lived at No. 22, and at No. 28 Winston Churchill died in 1965 (plaque). Beyond in De Vere Gardens, lived Browning (in 1887–89) and Henry James (in 1886–1901).

Facing the Albert Hall is the Gothic spire of the *Albert Memorial* (148 ft), the national monument to Prince Albert of Saxe-Coburg-Gotha (1819–61), consort of Queen Victoria, designed by Sir G. Gilbert Scott (1872). The statue of the prince (with the catalogue of the Great Exhibition) is by Foley. The pedestal is decorated with admirable marble reliefs of artists and men of letters by J.B. Philip (N and W sides) and H. Armstead. At the angles are allegorical groups (Agriculture, by Calder Marshall; Manufactures, by Weekes; Commerce, by Thornycroft; and Engineering, by Lawlor). At the foot of the steps are groups representing Europe, Asia, Africa, and America. The memorial is undergoing extensive repairs.

*Kensington Gardens (Pl. 12; 5), covering 274 acres, were once the private gardens of Kensington Palace (see below), and adjoin Hyde Park on the W. Although the Round Pond and Broad Walk were planned by George I, their present aspect is largely due to Queen Caroline, wife of George II, under whose direction they were laid out by Charles Bridgeman in 1728–31. The beautiful avenues of trees are a special feature.

At the N end of the *Long Water*, as the upper reach of the Serpentine is called (comp. p 126), is an attractive paved garden with a pavilion and fountains and a statue of *Jenner* by W. Calder Marshall (1858). Nearby is the charming *Queen Anne's Alcove* (originally at the S end of the Broad Walk), probably designed by Kent. The spot on the W bank of the Water, where *Peter Pan*, the hero of Sir J.M. Barrie's fairy play, first landed his boat, is marked by a delightful statue of him by Sir G. Frampton (1912). A little to the SW, a bronze cast of a fine equestrian figure by G.F. Watts (1903) represents *Physical Energy* (a replica forms part of the memorial to Cecil Rhodes at Groote Schuur, near Cape Town). An obelisk memorial to *Speke* (1827–64), the African explorer, lies to the N. A children's playgound with an 'elphin oak' occupies the NW corner of the park. And near Victoria Gate is the Pets' Cemetery started in 1880 but now full and closed to the public.

Behind the Albert Memorial the charming *Flower Walk* leads W to the *Broad Walk* which runs N between Kensington Palace and the *Round*

Pond (7 acres), noted for its model yachts in summer. In the private gardens on the S side of the palace is a statue of *William III*, presented to Edward VII in 1907 by William II of Germany; and on the E side is a fine marble statue of Queen Victoria by her daughter, Princess Louise (1839). The approach to the palace passes between a beautiful sunken garden, surrounded on three sides by a pleached walk of lime trees, and a group of bay and thorn trees in front of the brick *Orangery, built in 1704 by Hawksmoor and Vanbrugh, with ringed half-columns flanking the entrance. Inside (open daily 10.00–16.00, but often closed) the festoons on the elaborate entablature were carved by Grinling Gibbons. The marble crater with Roman reliefs of 2C AD was found, according to Piranesi, in Hadrian's Villa, Tivoli in 1760.

Kensington Palace was bought by William III from the second Earl of Nottingham in 1689, and from that time until the death of George II (1760) it was a residence of the reigning sovereign.

Kensington Palace, Kensington Gardens, W8. Tel. 071-937 9561. Access: Underground, High St Kensington. State Apartments open Mon to Sat 09.00–17.00, Sun 13.00–17.00. Admission charge.

The old house of 1605 was altered and added to by Sir Christopher Wren, and the exterior is much as he and Hawksmoor left it, but considerable interior alterations were made by William Kent in 1722–24. Mary II, William III, Anne, and George II all died in Kensington Palace. Queen Victoria was born here on 24 May 1819, and continued to live at the palace until her accession in 1837. Queen Mary was likewise born in this palace (26 May 1867). It is still the London residence of various members of the Royal Family, including Prince Charles and Princess Diana.

In 1984 the Queen's Court Dress Collection opened on the ground floor, including the room in which Queen Victoria was born. The uniforms and costumes date from the 18th to the 20C and include the wedding dress of the Princess of Wales.

The State Apartments on the first floor, virtually abandoned in 1760, were first restored and opened to the public in 1899. They were renovated and rehung from the royal collections in 1975.

In QUEEN MARY'S GALLERY the Vauxhall glass overmantels with gilded surrounds by Grinling Gibbons date from 1691. The fine portraits include *Adriaen Hanneman*, William III as a young man (1669); *William Wissing*, William and Mary as prince and princess; *Lely*, Anne Hyde; *Kneller*, Peter the Great. QUEEN'S DINING ROOM: *Lely*, Queen Mary aged 10 as Diana. DRAWING ROOM: *Kneller*, William, Duke of Gloucester, and *Michael Dahl*, Prince George of Denmark, Queen Anne's son and husband; paintings by *Van Dyck* and *David Teniers*. The BEDCHAMBER contains the bed belonging to James II and Mary of Modena, in which probably the 'Old Pretender' was born. The large 17C bowl in the hearth recalls Queen Mary II as a great collector of oriental porcelain. There follow two of the three rooms rebuilt in grander fashion in 1718–21 by Colen Campbell and decorated by *William Kent*. His also is the *trompe l'oeil* painting of the King's Staircase. The King's Gallery preserves the wind-dial made in 1694 by Robert Morden and (?) Thos. Tompion. Among the pictures, *Van Dyck*, Cupid and Psyche. Here Queen Victoria heard of her accession.

The following suite has been restored to near its appearance when occupied by the Duchess of Kent and Princess Victoria in 1834–36 with many personal mementoes. Here was Queen Victoria's bedroom which she shared with her mother. The KING'S DRAWING ROOM is hung with 17C pictures mainly acquired by Charles I or painted for Charles II. The COUNCIL CHAMBER, arranged as a memorial of the Great Exhibition of 1851, contains the ivory throne of the Maharajah of Travancore. In the CUPOLA ROOM Queen Victoria was christened.

On the S side of Kensington Gardens, W of the fine Palace gateway (late 17C), Kensington Road becomes *Kensington High St*, a busy shopping centre running through the residential district of Kensington. *Kensington Palace Gardens*, dubbed 'Millionaires' Row', was planned by Pennethorne in 1843, and remains a private road lined with fine mansions in gardens, many of them now used as embassies. Among the architects were Decimus Burton and Sidney Smirke, who used an entertaining variety of styles including the Eastern and the Italianate (best seen at N end). No. 8 was a primary interrogation centre for German prisoners during the 'Battle of Britain'. At the top on the left is the new Czechoslovak Embassy (see p 137). In *Palace Green* (S end; with an informal entrance to Kensington Palace), Thackeray died in 1863 at No. 2, a house designed by himself, and No. 1 was built by Philip Webb (1863).

Kensington Church St is the narrow main road N to Notting Hill (see above). On the corner stands the parish church of *St. Mary Abbots* (1869–81), a large church in 13C style with a conspicuous spire. It is the result of the combined efforts of Archdeacon Sinclair and Gilbert Scott. In Holland St (a charming street of early 18C houses built for the ladies-in-waiting at Kensington Palace), tablets mark the homes of Walter Crane (No. 13; 1845–1915), the artist, and Sir C.V. Stanford (No. 50A, 1856–1924), the musician. In Pitt St, to the N, Bullingham Mansions succeed the house where Newton died in 1727.

South of Kensington High St, *Young St* (where Thackeray lived at No. 16 from 1846–53 and wrote 'Vanity Fair') leads to *Kensington Square*, highly fashionable in the early 18C when the Court was frequently at Kensington Palace. Here Talleyrand lived after his escape from Paris in 1792. On the S side J.R. Green lived at No. 14, Hubert Parry, the musician, at No. 17, and J.S. Mill at No. 18. In the corner is the R.C. Convent of the Assumption, with a surprising façade of 1860. No. 33 (NT; no adm.) built in 1695, was the residence of Mrs Patrick Campbell (1865–1940), the actress. At No. 40 lived Sir John Simon, pioneer of public health, and next door, Burne-Jones. The Armenian church of St. Sarkis (1922) stands to the W in Iverna Gardens.

Just off Kensington High St in Derry St is the entrance to the *Kensington Exhibition Centre*, *Rainbow Suite* and *Roof Garden*.

This was part of the Derry and Toms department store which was founded in 1862 and which opened its new six-storey emporium in 1930 featuring the Rainbow Room and Roof Garden. It closed in 1973 and for a while Biba moved in, with an all-black decor, selling high-fashion clothes. It is now an exhibition centre and banqueting suite on two floors. On the sixth floor is the Garden, a disco/nightclub; there is public access to the Roof Garden during the summer, where flamingoes wander above the traffic fumes.

The famous Barker's department store has been converted (1989) into a shopping mall and offices for Associated Newspapers, including the 'Evening Standard' and the 'Daily Mail', featuring a spectacular 115 atrium with domed glass roof 115ft high. The Standard clock from its Fleet St building will be a feature on the Kensington High St façade while the 'Daily Mail's' Board Room (Lord Northcliffe's office) from Carmelite House has been rebuilt on the top floor.

.Opposite is the site of the old Town Hall, demolished by the local council in the teeth of a preservation order and now redeveloped as offices. The new Town Hall by Sir Basil Spence is in Campden Hill Road and features contrasting asymetrical blocks. It includes the Kensington and Chelsea Public Library and substantial exhibition facilities.

In this road Henry Newbolt, the poet, died at No. 29 in 1938, and Galsworthy lived at No. 78. In Campden Hill is the Holland Park School. Here, at Holly Lodge, Lord Macaulay died in 1859.

Aubrey Walk W leads to **Campden Hill** which descends steeply N to Notting Hill. It was a favourite place of residence in the 17C and a spa for taking the waters (the springs are still active); a few of the fine houses in spacious grounds survive, though the gardens of many were absorbed by Holland Park School. Swift, Gray, and Queen Anne (as Princess) were among its famous inhabitants. The peaceful Aubrey Walk, a colony of artists in Edwardian days, ends at the gates of Aubrey House which retains its spacious park. Aubrey Road leads into the delightful *Campden Hill Square* (Pl. 10; 1) which slopes steeply to the N. Here in the gardens while staying at Hill Lodge (on the corner of Hillsleigh Road), Turner painted the sunset. At No. 9 lived John McDouall Stuart (1815–66), the first explorer to cross Australia. The *Windsor Castle* pub at 114 Campden Hill Road has sloping floors, old beams and open fires. It dates from 1835 and has a large attractive garden.

Return towards Kensington High St down *Holland Walk*, parallel to Aubrey Road (entered down the hill left off Holland Park Avenue), a pleasant lane which skirts the park of **Holland House**, a beautiful and historic Tudor mansion, famous in the time of the third Baron Holland (1773–1840) as 'the favourite resort of wits and beauties, painters and poets, scholars, philosophers, and statesmen'. The house was badly damaged by bombs in 1941 and only the E wing remains, now forming an open quadrangle with the *King George VI Memorial Hostel* (1956–58). The gateway (with piers surmounted by griffins) was designed by Inigo Jones and executed by Nicholas Stone in 1629. The delightful formal gardens include a bronze statue The Boy and the Bear Cubs by John Macallan Swan (1902) and a monument to the third Baron Holland by G.F. Watts and E. Boehm (1872). Plays and concerts are performed here in the summer.

Built by John Thorpe in 1607 for Sir Walter Cope, Holland House passed by marriage to Henry Rich, created Earl of Holland (in Lincolnshire), who was executed in 1649. The house was then occupied for a time by the parliamentary generals Fairfax and Lambert, but was later restored to Lord Holland's widow. In the reign of Charles II William Penn probably lodged in this house, and in 1689 William III and Mary temporarily occupied it. Addison spent the last three years of his life here (died 1719). Lord Kensington, heir of the Rich family, sold the house to Henry Fox (father of Charles James Fox), who was made Baron Holland in 1763. The brilliant literary and political (Whig) circle, of which Holland House was the centre with Lady Holland as the hostess, is described in Macaulay's essay on Lord Holland. Lady Ilchester made the house a centre for parties during the Edwardian era.

The wooded *Holland Park (café and restaurant; free car park on W side, approached from Abbotsbury Rd) surrounds the gardens, frequented by peacocks. Beyond the Flower Garden, the *Orangery* (the statues are free copies of the famous Classical 'Wrestlers' in Naples) is used for exhibitions and concerts. The Belvedere Restaurant has been carefully restored after a fire. Near the car park is a children's 'Jungle'.

In *Melbury Road*, at the S end of Abbotsbury Rd, No. 2B was the residence of Sir Hamo Thornycroft (1850–1925), sculptor. To the E, *Tower House* (No. 29), an eccentric '13C' mansion, was designed by William Burges for himself in 1875. At No. 31 (by Norman Shaw) Sir Luke Fildes lived in 1878–1927, and Holman Hunt died in 1910 at No. 18. In *Holland Park Road* (S of Melbury Road). *Leighton House* (No. 12) was designed as the residence and studio of Lord Leighton (1830–96) who spent the last 30 years of his life here. Among the Victorian furnishings are ceramics designed by William de Morgan, and paintings by Burne-Jones and Leighton. In the charming garden is a bronze athlete by Leighton.

Leighton House Museum and Art Gallery, 12 Holland Park Road, W8. Open Mon to Sat 11.00–17.00. Admission Free. Access: Underground, High St Kensington. A plain red brick exterior hides an Oriental surprise designed for Lord Leighton by George Aitchison in 1866. The Arab Hall added in 1879 features a fountain in the mosaic floor, a stained glass cupola and tiles from Egypt and Greece. It is used for exhibitions and concerts.

At the S end of the park, approached from Kensington High St, is the *Commonwealth Institute*. The ungainly copper-sheathed roof hides a superb multi-level exhibition hall built in 1960–62 by Robert Matthew, Johnson-Marshall and Partners, listed in 1988. The instructive and now rather worn exhibits are provided by each Commonwealth government. There are also a changing exhibition, a cinema, a schools' reception centre, and a cafeteria/restaurant. A redevelopment programme is underway.

Commonwealth Institute, Kensington High St, W8. Tel. 071-603 4535. Open Mon to Sat 10.00–17.30, Sun 14.30–17.00. Free (except for some exhibitions). Access: Underground, High St Kensington.

To the W in Stafford Terrace is *Linley Sambourne House*, a charming Victorian house.

Linley Sambourne House, 18 Stafford Terrace, W8. Open March to October Wed 10.00–16.00, Sun 14.00–17.00. Admission charge. Access: Underground, High St Kensington.

The Victorian interior of this house, which belonged to the Punch cartoonist, Linley Sambourne, has been perfectly preserved and is now owned and operated by the Victorian Society.

To the W is Olympia with its exhibition halls. On the S side of the main road is *Earl's Terrace* where at No. 12 George du Maurier lived in 1867–70, and Walter Pater in 1866–93. Behind this long façade is the charming *Edwardes Square*, with small houses, built in the early 19C by Changier. Here Leigh Hunt lived at No. 32 in 1840–51, and G.K. Chesterton at No. 1 in 1901. *Earl's Court Road*, with many restaurants, leads S to *Earl's Court* and its Exhibition Halls. In Philbeach Gardens N of the Exhibition Halls in Warwick Road is St. Cuthbert Church with its dramatic decorative interior in the arts and crafts style designed by W. Bainbridge Reynolds in 1887.

To the S, across the Old Brompton Road (Access: West Brompton Underground Station) is *Brompton Cemetery* which covers 39 acres between Old Brompton Road and Fulham Road to the S.

Also known as the West London and Westminster Cemetery, this is one of the most interesting in London; it was first used in 1840. Surrounded by catacombs, it has a triumphal arch at the entrance. There are many soldiers buried here due to the proximity of Chelsea Hospital which has its own granite obelisk. Among others buried here are Emmeline Pankhurst (died 1928) the suffragette, Princess Violette Lobanov-Rostovsky (died 1932), Frederick Leyland (died 1892), patron of the pre-Raphaelites (his tomb is in arts and crafts funerary style), and Sir Samuel Cunard (died 1865), founder of the Cunard steamship company.

Hyde Park and Kensington Gardens are skirted on the N by *Bayswater Road* (see p 128 for the area around Marble Arch). N of the Park many of the residential white stucco terraces have been converted into hotels and guest houses. *Queensway*, is a busy street with shops and restaurants open late at night. The former Whiteleys department store (1911) re-opened in 1989 as a shopping 'mall' around a huge atrium with a striking glass dome incorporating the original grand staircase. At Nos 23 & 24 Leinster Gardens a false façade hides the underground cutting below. At Craven Hill is the London Toy and Model Museum with its miniature railway and collection of toy cars.

London Toy and Model Museum, 23 Craven Hill, W2. Tel. 071-262 9450. Open Tues to Sat 10.00–17.30, Sun 11.00–17.00. Closed Mon except Bank Holidays. Admission charge. Shop and cafeteria. Several private collections of commercially-made toys and models from 1850 onwards have been brought together in imaginative displays of trains, cars, planes, nursery toys etc. Working miniature railway in garden.

E, in *Lancaster Gate*, the conspicuous spire of Christ Church rises behind a memorial by Hermon Cawthra (1934) to the Earl of Meath. On Sundays the railings along Bayswater Road turn into a colourful and lively art market of dubious quality.

W of Queensway, No. 1 *Orme Square* was the residence of Sir Rowland Hill, inventor of the penny postage, in 1839–45. The next turning on the right, *St. Petersburgh Place*, leads N between the tall Eastern towers of the New West End Synagogue and the tapering spire of St. Matthew's Church to Moscow Rd and the Byzantine Greek *Cathedral of the Holy Wisdom*, with mosaics by Boris Anrep. Sir James Barrie lived at No. 100 Bayswater Rd in 1902–08. Beyond Kensington Palace Gardens (see below) and the Czechoslovak Centre and Embassy (1971, by Stramek, Bocon & Stapanski; No. 25), No. 57 Palace Gardens Terrace was the birthplace of Max Beerbohm (1872– 1956). Notting Hill Gate continues W.

Pembridge Road runs N from Notting Hill Gate to the famous street market at *Portobello Road* (left); the name commemorates the capture of Puerto Bello in the Caribbean by Adm. Vernon in 1739. Famous for its weekday vegetable and fruit market here since c 1870, it is known locally as 'The Lane'. The popularity of the Saturday antique market in the S section of the road has lead to its expansion northwards for a mile, as far as the A40 flyover, with crafts and fashion at Portobello Green. On the last weekend of August it is the location for the annual Notting Hill Carnival started by the local West Indian Community in 1966 and now the biggest event of its kind in Europe. Portobello Road and the surrounding streets has also developed into a lively area of art galleries with its own art fair in April.

To the W, *St. John's*, *Ladbroke Grove* (Pl. 10; 1) was built in 1845 on the site of a grandstand; only the shape of the housing terraces and Hippodrome Place recall the racecourse here in 1837–41. Near by, Pottery Lane survives from 'The Potteries', a once notorious area of brick-making and pig-keeping, described by Dickens in 1850 as 'a plague spot scarcely equalled for its insalubrity by any other in London'.

Holland Park Avenue continues the line of Notting Hill Gate to *Shepherd's Bush*.

B.   The South Kensington Museums

Access: Underground, South Kensington.

The ****Victoria and Albert Museum** (Pl. 12; 8) with its spacious and well-lit halls, galleries, and courts, contains perhaps the largest and finest collection of applied art in the world. The high standard of display and explanatory labels are most helpful, but repeated visits are necessary to do justice to its store of treasures.

The Victoria and Albert Museum, Cromwell Road, SW7. Tel. 071-938 8500. Open Mon to Sat 10.00–18.00, Sun 14.30–18.00.

Lectures Tues, Wed 13.15, Thurs 18.30, Sun 15.30. Gallery talks Sat 12.00 and 15.30, Sun 15.30. Voluntary admission charge. Self-service cafeteria. Bookshop. Craftshop.

The museum is continually improving the display of the collection as well as the fabric of the building. In 1982 the Henry Cole Wing opened in the adjoining building with its own entrance in Exhibition Road. The new cafeteria opened in 1986. The Boilerhouse Project, sponsored by the Conran Foundation, closed in 1986 and reopened at Butler's Wharf as a Museum of Design in 1989 (see p 296). The Pirelli Garden, in the Italian style, opened in the quadrangle in June 1987. Temporary exhibitions are held in the main museum and the Henry Cole Wing.

The National Art Library, housing over 650,000 volumes, occupies Rooms 77–78 and is open Mon to Fri 10.00–16.30, Sat 10.00–13.00, 14.00–16.30 (last book issued at 16.30). Regular users should apply for a reader's ticket from the Keeper.

The present museum originated in the Museum of Manufactures (later the Museum of Ornamental Art) established by the Department of Science and Art at Marlborough House in 1852, on the initiative of Prince Albert. It was founded with the object of developing decorative design in British manufactures, by providing models and samples of applied art, ancient and modern, for study by craftsmen and others. Gifts, bequests, and Government grants rapidly extended the museum, and the present unrivalled collection fulfils far more than its

VICTORIA & ALBERT MUSEUM

Lower Floors

Lower Ground Floor Rooms 1-9
Ground Floor Rooms 10-50
Upper Ground Floor Rooms 51-64

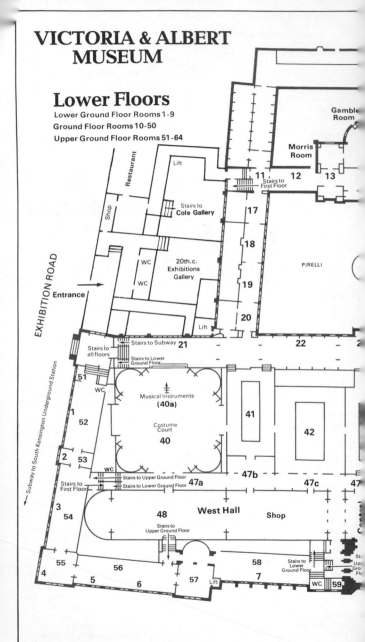

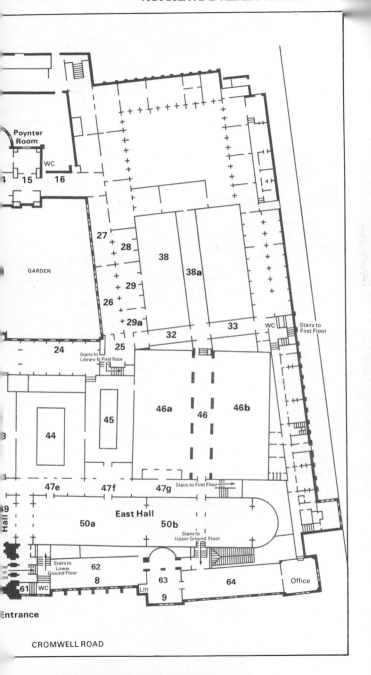

Poynter
Room

WC

15   16

27

28

38   38a

GARDEN

29

26

29a

33   WC   Stairs to
First Floor

24

25

Stairs to
Library & First floor

32

46a   46   46b

45

44

47e   47f   47g   Stairs to First Floor

Hall

East Hall

50a   50b

Stairs to
Upper Ground Floor

Stairs to
Lower Ground Floor   62

63   64   Office

8

61   WC   9   Lift

Entrance

CROMWELL ROAD

primary utilitarian function and appeals to every lover of art. The present ornate terracotta building by Sir Aston Webb opened in 1909 and features a 185ft central tower. Statues of Queen Victoria and Prince Albert by Alfred Drury decorate the entrance. Edward VII and Queen Alexandra are on either side, and other sculptures representing British artists are by students from the Royal College of Art. The displays are arranged into Art and Design Galleries and Materials and Techniques Galleries. The former present a rounded picture of the development of design and style within a broad historical framework. The first of these to have opened are the Medieval Treasury and the Toshiba Japanese Gallery.

Below is a selection of some of the highlights of the permanent exhibition starting from the main entrance.

The Medieval Treasury, in Room 43, is a new display from 400–1400 and including art objects and textiles; here is the Glouces-ter candlestick (c 1110) in gilt bell metal, Adoration of the Magi, a whalebone relief (Limoges; 13C), the Elternberg Reliquary in the form of a church, gilt copper enriched with enamel and set with walrus ivory carvings (Rhenish; 12C), Sion Gospels, with cover in gold cloisonné and precious stones (French or German; c 1000), and the Basilewski Situla (bucket) (Milan; c 980).

European Art, in Rooms 22–29, includes a collection of stained glass, note the Winchester College Window (c 1399). In Room 24, note the oak altar-piece probably from St. Bavon, Ghent (late 15C). In Room 26 the Campion Cup, hammered and engraved silver-gilt (English; 1500) and in Room 27 St. Mary, Salome and Zebedee (c 1506), wood-carvings of the highest order, Veit Stoss, the Virgins, boxwood statuette (c 1520) and other boxwood carvings.

On the N and W sides of the main quadrangle with the Pirelli garden are the galleries of *Italian Renaissance Art*, with fine pieces of sculpture complemented by cases of maiolica, cassoni, etc., start-ing in Room 16. Off Room 13 is the *Green Dining Room* or Morris Room, decorated for the museum by William Morris and Philip Webb in 1866. The stained glass and painted panels representing the months of the year were designed by Burne-Jones.

The *Gamble Room*, beyond, was designed in ornate Renaissance style by Godfrey Sykes and James Gamble, pupils of Alfred Stevens. The ceiling is in enamelled iron with a decorative frieze. The *Dutch Kitchen* has white and blue Minton tiles representing the seasons and stained glass windows.

Renaissance art continues in Room 17–21; the last room includes important sculpture. Danti, Leda and the Swan; Giambologna, large sketch models in red wax for the Grimaldi Chapel in San Francesco di Castelletto, Genoa (c 1579); Sansovino, Descent from the Cross, in gilt wax, and Giambologna's important group Samson slaying the Philistine (c 1565), made to adorn a fountain in the Casino of Grand Duke Francesco de' Medici in Florence.

Go down to Rooms 1–7 for the collection of *Continental Art* (1570–1800), arranged to convey the decorative ideas of the periods covered in a limited space, by combining furniture, textiles, sculpture, ceramics, carvings, and, in Room 2, Flemish, German and Italian ivories, and silver from Italy and Spain. Room 3A also features Old Master drawings with Rembrandt and Bernini repre-sented. Rooms 5–7 house 18C Continental Art including the Jones collection of French 18C art; furniture by Boulle is well represented.

Rooms 8 and 9 have been arranged in 19C style to show European and American art 1800–1900 including furniture, pottery and posters.

English Art is on the 1st floor in Rooms 52–58 and heavily weighted in favour of furniture. Note the Great Bed of Ware (c 1580) measuring 12ft by 12ft (mentioned by Shakespeare and Ben Jonson), in Room 54.

The following rooms are of particular interest to those exploring London's history as they contain rooms from many well-known London houses, now demolished. Room 57 incorporates a room from Henrietta Place designed by James Gibbs (c 1725) and also the Walpole Salver made for Sir Robert Walpole in 1728 with engraved decoration probably by Hogarth; note the embroidery and Spitalfields silk. Room 58 has a pine panelled room (c 1730) from Hatton Garden, Music Room from Norfolk House (1756).

On the floor above Rooms 126–118 display English Art 1750–1900, with mixed displays of furniture, textiles, china and glass, silver and paintings. In Room 125 is a chimney-piece from Winchester House, Putney (c 1750) and part of the Glass Drawing Room from Old Northumberland House, Charing Cross, designed by Adam (1773–74). Room 123 contains the Lee Priory Room from Strawberry Hill in Gothic style by James Wyatt (c 1785). In Room 122 is a bed by Chippendale (c 1775) from Garrick's villa at Hampton and also Garrick's tea and coffee service (1774–75). The Adam ceiling (c 1770) is from the great actor's drawing room at 6 Adelphi Terrace and the Adam mantelpiece from 5 Adelphi Terrace. Victorian Art continues in Rooms 120–118; note Scott's plaster model from the Albert Memorial (c 1863) in Room 120 and the furniture for the Great Exhibition. Room 119 is devoted to William Morris and his followers with wallpaper, carpet and tiles designed by Morris and furniture by members of his circle. Rooms 74–70 cover *British Art and Design* to the present day with work by members of the Omega Workshop, Heal and Son and sculpture by Eric Gill and Henry Moore.

Return to the ground floor and Rooms 41, 42, 44, 45 and 47 devoted to *Far Eastern Art* with a magnificent collection of Chinese Art from c 1550 BC to AD 1900.

Rooms 47c and 42 house the collection of *Islamic Art*; note particularly the carpets. The Chelsea carpet (16C) in Room 47c, often regarded as the most beautiful carpet in the world, was bought on the King's Road in the late 19C but its earlier history is unknown. Nearby is the enormous Ardabil carpet (1539–40) perhaps the most famous carpet in the world. Room 41 is opening in late 1990 as the Nehru Gallery of Indian Art (1550–1990) including objects from Moghul India include a white jade cup (1657) which once belonged to the Emperor Shah Jahan and a carpet from Lahore (1630) presented to the Girdlers' Company of London. Room 44—T.T. Tsui Gallery of Chinese Art (summer 1991) will cover Chinese art from 1550 BC–1900 AD. Room 45 is the Toshiba Gallery of Japanese interiors and includes lacquer, arms and armour, ceramics, kimonos and netsuke as well as the tea ceremony.

Room 40 is the *Costume Court* with a fine collection of English and Continental fashionable costume from c 1580 to the present day arranged in tableaux with supporting illustrative material. The *Musical Instruments Gallery* is on the mezzanine floor with some outstanding harpsichords and spinets.

The famous *Raphael Cartoons* in Room 48 are seven of the celebrated series of ten drawn by Raphael (1515–16) for Pope Leo X as designs in distemper on paper for tapestries to be woven in Brussels for the decoration of the Sistine Chapel on ceremonial occasions. They are among the most important surviving examples of High Renaissance art, distinguished by their imaginative force, clarity of structure, fresh

VICTORIA & ALBERT MUSEUM

Upper Floors

First Floor Rooms 65–117
Upper First Floor Rooms 118–131
Second Floor Rooms 132–145

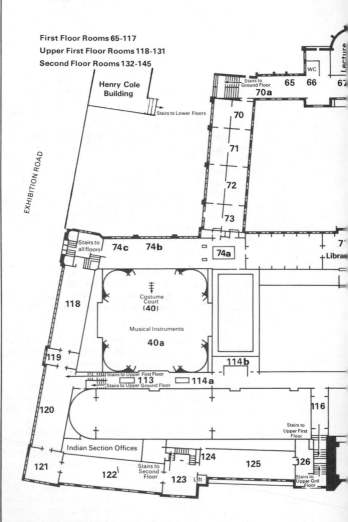

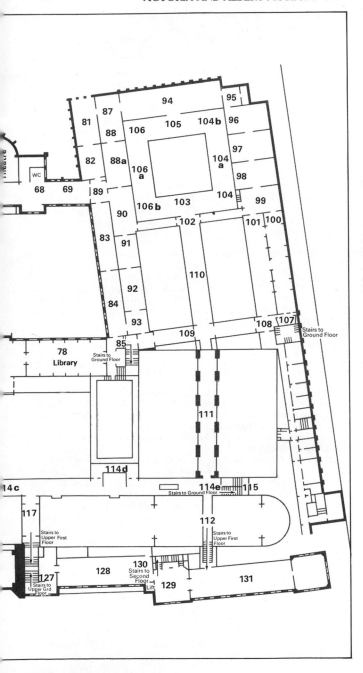

colour and serenity of mood. Charles I bought the cartoons in 1623 and they are on loan to the Victoria and Albert from the Queen. The tapestries are still in the Vatican. The subjects are a series of scenes from the Acts of the Apostles.

The *Henry Cole Wing*: approach by way of Room 11, Room 21 or direct via the new Exhibition Road entrance. In the entrance hall is a fine collection of sculptures by Rodin.

The Cole Building takes its name from the museum's first director, Sir Henry Cole (1808–82) and was, until ten years ago, used by Imperial College. It has been converted to make maximum use of the space available on six levels to house the Department of Paintings, Prints and Drawings and the collection of Photography as well as changing exhibitions. The Great Staircase (best seen from Level B) was designed by Major General Henry Scott (1882–83) who also designed the Royal Albert Hall. There is a bookshop on Level A.

In Room 403B is the outstanding collection of English and Continental portrait miniatures which include Holbein's 'Anne of Cleves' and 'Elizabeth I'. Room 419 features the Ionides Bequest of European paintings. On Level 6 are works by John Constable.

The **Natural History Museum** (Pl. 12; 7) originated in the scientific collections of Sir Hans Sloane, which were purchased for the nation in 1753 (comp. p 188). The present building, in an elaborate Romanesque style with fine terracotta detail in keeping with the function of the building, was erected in 1873–80 by Alfred Waterhouse, and the British Museum (Natural History)—its former title—transferred here from Bloomsbury.

The Natural History Museum, Cromwell Road, South Kensington, SW7. Tel. 071-938 9123. Open Mon to Sat 10.00–18.00, Sun 13.00–18.00. Admission charge. Lectures and film shows on some weekdays—cafeteria, bookshop with publications. Access: Underground, South Kensington.

The museum houses the national collection of fossil and living plants and animals, minerals, rocks and meteorites; it comprises five departments each with its own library and students' room—zoology, botany, mineralogy, palaeontology and entomology, with an increasing bias towards biology and man. Below are some of the highlights of the exhibition.

In the vast Central Hall on the ground floor, 170ft long, 97ft wide and 72ft high, the museum's most popular exhibits, the dinosaurs, are displayed. Note the 85ft-long plaster-cast skeleton of Diplodocus carnegii, 150 million years old and one of the largest land animals which ever lived. Nearby is the horned Triceratops prorsus and a head of Tyrannosaurus rex, Plesiosaurus and flying reptiles. In the North Hall is a temporary exhibition showing the giant panda Chi Chi who died in 1972 at London Zoo. The Bird Gallery in the West Wing contains a remarkable collection of stuffed birds, some in their Victorian display cases. The Discovering Mammals exhibition shows the skeletons and models of whales including the largest, the blue whale, 91ft long, and the white whale, sperm whale and dolphins.

The Hall of Human Biology explores all aspects of man's structures and functions with emphasis on reproduction, growth and perception. A new section opened in 1989 looks at human memory. Models, films, slide shows and games allow visitors to take an active part in the displays.

In the East wing is a new exhibition 'Creepy Crawlies' about the millions of insects, spiders and crustaceans which share the Arthropod kingdom, with interactive displays.

On the first floor (E Gallery) there is a display on Man's Place in Evolution; the Mineral Gallery shows part of the collection of 130,000 mineral specimens including a small case of items from Sloane's collection. In the Meteorite Pavilion are specimens from more than 1270 falls.

The Exhibition Road entrance to the Natural History Museum is close to the Geological Museum, now administered as part of the Natural History Museum.

The Geological Museum, Exhibition Road, SW7. Tel. 071-589 3444. Opening hours as Natural History Museum. Admission charge covers both Museums.

The **Geological Museum** was established in 1837 in Whitehall (Craig's Court). In 1851 the collection moved to Jermyn St, and in 1935 to the present building (designed by John H. Markham). In 1965 it became part of the Institute of Geological Sciences and in 1989 part of the Natural History Museum. Below are some of the highlights.

The central area of the main hall on the ground floor is devoted to a magnificent display of gems including diamonds, rubies, sapphires and emeralds in their natural state and at various stages of cutting. Models of some of the world's most famous stones, among them the Koh-i-nor and Cullinan diamonds, are included.

The Story of the Earth, an audio-visual display, is approached through a cleft in a simulated rock face 25ft high, modelled on a cliff in the NW Highlands of Scotland. It shows the origin of the earth and evolution. The earthquake simulator is particularly effective.

The first floor shows the regional geology of England, Scotland and Wales and a new exhibition on Britain's offshore oil and gas.

On the second floor is the world's largest display of metalliferous ores, including models of large gold nuggets and useful non-metallic minerals, as well as a model of Stonehenge.

Further N in Exhibition Road is the Science Museum.

The ****Science Museum** (Pl. 12; 7) occupies a handsome building opened in 1928. The museum, founded in 1856, is a remarkable collection of machinery and industrial plant, working models, and apparatus of every kind for scientific research and educational purposes.

The Science Museum, Exhibition Road, South Kensington, SW7. Tel. 071-938 8000. Open Mon to Sat 10.00–18.00, Sun 11.00–18.00. Admission charge.
    Public demonstrations daily, film shows, publications, educational facilities, cafeteria. Access: Underground, South Kensington.

The Science Museum houses the Wellcome Museum of the History of Medicine on the top floor—see below. These are some of the highlights of the collection. Special exhibitions are held at regular intervals.

On the left of the Entrance Hall is the Foucault Pendulum for demonstrating the rotation of the earth on its own axis. Galleries 2 and 3 are devoted to steam, oil, turbine and wind engines: included are an atmospheric boiler by Francis Thompson (1791), haystack boiler (1796), Boulton and Watts pumping engine (1777), compound beam engine (c 1838), Watts beam engine (1797) and the marine triple-expansion steam engine (1903).

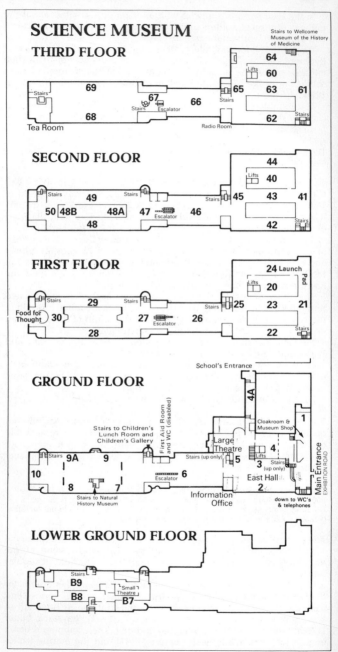

Gallery 6 is devoted to exploration in six areas on the fringes of present-day knowledge including spaceflight with the Apollo 10 capsule (on loan), which in May 1969 carried men around the moon, and a recreation of a moon base.

In Galleries 7 and 8 and the Centre Hall are railway locomotives and rolling stock, and relics of George Stephenson; the locomotives include Puffing Billy (1813), the oldest locomotive in the world, the Rocket Sans Pareil, and the remains of the Novelty, contenders at the Rainhill Trials of 1829.

On the lower ground floor is the Children's Gallery and small theatre with an introduction to basic scientific ideas through dioramas, working models and exhibits in which children can participate. Here also is the Bryant and May Collection of matches.

On the first floor is Launch Pad, a popular interactive space display with the Black Arrow satellite launch vehicle (1971). The new Sainsbury Gallery contains the exhibition 'Food for Thought' with hands-on displays, computer-driven exhibits and live demonstrations to show the impact of science and technology on every aspect of food. On the second floor, Gallery 44 is devoted to atomic physics and nuclear power with models demonstrating nuclear fission and Gallery 46 shows progress in computing, with participatory displays—one of the most crowded areas in the museum. In Gallery 49 are models of merchant steamers and battleships. Moving to the third floor, Gallery 60 is devoted to the history of photography with some early equipment including relics of pioneer photographer Fox Talbot (died 1877).

In Gallery 63 is the King George III collection of instruments formerly housed at Kew Observatory and used for the scientific education of the king's children and a philosophical table by George Adams (1762) used for lectures and demonstrations for the royal pupils.

Aeronautics from hot-air balloons to Concorde, are covered in Galleries 68–69 where the National Aeronautical Collection is housed. Among the early aircraft is the Vickers-Vimy aeroplane in which Alcock and Brown made the first direct transatlantic flight (1919), the De Havilland Gipsy Moth used by Amy Johnson on her flight to Australia (1930) as well as Second World War aircraft.

The *Wellcome Museum of the History of Medicine* moved here (fourth floor) from the Wellcome Institute in 1982 (see p 186) and was considerably augmented and improved. On the lower floor is a series of 40 tableaux and dioramas entitled 'Glimpses of Medical History' which show in great detail the development of medical practice from 'Trepanning in neolithic times' to 'Intensive Care in 1980'. Note Mr Gibson's pharmacy of 1905, Lister's ward, Glasgow, in 1868, at the dentist in the 1890s, and an ironlung in the 1950s. On the upper floor the display shows the history of medicine in chronological order with the emphasis on the scientific and social background, starting with tribal societies, oriental medicine, Classical Greek and Roman medicine, medieval medicine, the scientific revolution (Renaissance) and the developments during the 18th and 19th centuries with 20C health and community medicine. Curiosities include Napoleon's silver-gilt toothbrush, Florence Nightingale's moccasins, Dr Livingstone's medicine chest, and a microscope made for Lister.

12 Victoria, Westminster Cathedral, Pimlico, the Tate Gallery and Westminster

Access: Underground, Victoria, Westminster, St. James's Park, Pimlico.

Victoria St connects Belgravia and Victoria with Westminster; in the last 20 years it has been completely transformed with modern, clean-cut concrete and glass office blocks on either side with over-hanging colonnades to provide shelter. 19C blocks of flats survive to the S, and to the N is the wind-swept Stag Place on the site of a former brewery. Victoria St is part of the royal processional route for state visit arrivals at the Station. Many ordinary visitors to London and thousands of commuters arrive at Victoria Station every day.

Victoria Station (once two stations) is undergoing a great redevelopment programme finally merging the two historic termini, one which served the London, Brighton and South Coast Railway and the other the London, Chatham and Dover Railway; a wall still runs down the middle of the station and once they had separate entrances. The station was remodelled in 1908 and the adjoining Grosvenor Hotel rebuilt. New mosaic flooring in the Eastern hall was designed by Tess Jaray and laid by Italian craftsmen in 1984–85. Today Victoria Station is London's second busiest railway terminal serving commuters from Kent, Surrey and Sussex, cross-Channel travellers via Dover and Folkestone (the main Channel Tunnel terminal will be at Waterloo) and airline passengers using Gatwick Airport. An express rail service links Gatwick with Victoria and British Airways has a check-in facility at the Station in the new concourse, which also includes Victoria Place with telephones, fax, shops and a food-court. This provides a short cut to Victoria Coach Station in Buckingham Palace Road and Green Line Coach departures from Eccleston Bridge. Here is Victoria Plaza, a huge new glass edifice over the railway tracks designed by Heery Architects (1987) with a 55,000 sq ft trading floor for the international bankers, Salomon Brothers.

London's busiest tourist information centre, operated by the London Tourist Board, is located in the forecourt of the station and is open seven days a week. In front of the station is a large bus terminal.

Outside the station on the N side is the *Victoria Palace Theatre* built as a music-hall in 1911.

Here the original 'Me and My Girl', introducing the Lambeth Walk, ran from 1937 to '39; the Crazy Gang appeared here and the Black and White Minstrel Show started here before it became a television show. 'Annie' was a huge success in recent years.

On the traffic island opposite, Little Ben, a standing clock in the shape of Big Ben, was returned in 1981. The 30ft original stood near here for 70 years but was removed for street-widening. It was a traditional meeting place for travellers to or from the Station and the replacement clock was donated by a French oil company to mark the wedding of Prince Charles and Lady Diana Spencer.

The *Apollo Victoria Theatre* is in Wilton Road, opposite the side (E) entrance to Victoria Station; it was converted into a theatre in 1979 having started life as a

Westminster Cathedral (1895–1903), designed by J.F. Bentley in early-Christian Byzantine style

cinema. It stages large shows including most recently 'Starlight Express' for which the auditorium was transformed with rollerskating tracks.

Across Victoria St *Stag Place*, on the site of the former Stag Brewery, is a draughty and bare precinct dominated by the well-designed Portland House (1962), cigar-shaped and raised on arches, and a colossal sculptured stag. Beyond, in Palace St, is the *Westminster Theatre*, built in Welsh slate by John and Sylvia Reid in 1966. As a memorial to Peter Howard (1908–65), it is devoted to the cause of 'moral rearmament'.

N of Victoria Station GROSVENOR GARDENS forms a double triangle of trees. The equestrian statue here of Marshal Foch (1851–1929) is by G. Malissard, a copy of one at Cassel. The London Tourist Board has its offices here at No. 26 and the English Tourist Board/British Tourist Authority at No. 24. A cabmen's shelter has been restored in the N gardens. The Rifle Brigade's War Memorial is at the corner of

Grosvenor Gardens and Hobart Place with bronzes by John Tweed (1924). The S part of the Gardens provides the departure point for sightseeing tours and the A1 Airbus, see p 13.

Parallel to the N is Lower Belgrave St, with the *Plumber's Arms* pub near the former home of Lord Lucan at No. 46, the location of the family nanny's murder and his disappearance in the '70s. At No. 22 Ebury St is the doric portico (1830) of the former Pimlico Literary Institute. George Moore (1852–1933) died at No. 121, and Mozart composed his first symphony at No. 180 in 1764 at the age of eight. Opposite, Coleshill Flats, with an outside stair and balconies above shops, are amusing examples of 19C building.

From Victoria Station, Victoria St leads to Westminster Abbey, past another notable church, the Catholic **Westminster Cathedral* (Pl. 18; 3), set back to the S from Victoria St in a modern plaza with a small conference centre to the right. This is the seat of the Cardinal Archbishop of Westminster, and the most important Roman Catholic church in England, erected in 1895–1903. It was designed by J.F. Bentley (1839–1902) in an early-Christian Byzantine style, and the alternate narrow bands of red brick and grey stone of the exterior add to its exotic appearance. The church is oriented from NW to SE. The square campanile is 284ft high and commands an extensive **View* (lift in the entrance vestibule; fee). The (NW) façade is richly articulated in three receding stages. In the tympanum of the main entrance is a mosaic by Anning Bell (1916): Christ, St. Peter, Edward the Confessor, Our Lady, and St. Joseph. The detail of the dark interior is hard to see, except when lit during services.

INTERIOR. The brick walls are still partly bare, but the vast size and beautiful proportions of the church are remarkably impressive, especially when viewed from the W end, from between the two great columns of red Norwegian granite (emblematic of the Precious Blood of Jesus, to which the cathedral is dedicated). The church has a basilican plan roofed with four domes. In the apse beyond the raised Sanctuary at the E end is the still higher retrochoir; the Lady Chapel lies at the end of the S aisle. When the decorative scheme is completed the walls and piers up to the height of about 30ft will be covered with coloured marble, while the upper walls and the domes will be lined with mosaics. The total length is 342ft; the height of the main arches is 90ft, while the domes are 112ft above the floor. The nave is the widest in England (60ft; or, including the aisles and side-chapels, 149ft). On the piers are Stations of the Cross, carved in stone in low relief by Eric Gill. The great rood hanging from the arch at the E end of the nave is 30ft long; it bears painted figures of Christ and (on the reverse) the Mater Dolorosa, by Christian Symons. The pulpit with its Cosmati work was enlarged in 1934 by Cardinal Bourne (1861–1935), in commemoration of his 30 years as archbishop here.

The lateral CHAPELS are decorated with rich marbles and mosaics. The *Baptistery*, to the right of the main entrance, is divided from the *Chapel of SS. Gregory and Augustine* by a marble screen. The chapel was designed by J.F. Bentley, and contains mosaics referring to the conversion of England. Here is the tomb of Richard Challoner (1691–1781), bishop of Debra and Vicar-Apostolic of the London district, the most prominent Roman Catholic ecclesiastic of 18C England. The *Chapel of St. Patrick and the Saints of Ireland* is a memorial to the Irishmen who fell in 1914–18. Each regiment has its own marble tablet and 'Liber Vitae'. The gilded bronze statue of the saint is by Arthur Pollen. In the pierced marble screen near the aisle appear the shamrock of St. Patrick and the oak leaves of St. Bridget. Next is the chapel, in a faithful Byzantine style by Robert Schultz Weir, dedicated to *St. Andrew and the Saints of Scotland*. Scottish marbles and stone are largely employed in the decoration, with sculpture by Stirling Lee (lights to left of grille). The fine inlaid ebony choir stalls (c 1912) are the work of Ernest Gimson. The *Chapel of St. Paul* has a mosaic floor based on a design by the Cosmati.

Cross the South Transept with an early-15C Madonna in alabaster of the Nottingham School, and (above, on the pier) a bronze panel of St. Teresa of Lisieux by Giac. Manzu. The apse of the LADY CHAPEL, beyond, contains a mosaic of the Madonna by Anning Bell. The mosaics of the walls and vault are by Gilbert Pownall, as are those in the sumptuous *Sanctuary*. Here the altar table, flanked by double arcades of coloured marble, consists of a solid block of Cornish granite, 12 tons in weight. Above it rises a white marble baldacchino, with eight monolithic columns of yellow Verona marble on pedestals of *verde antico*. The throne of the archbishop, to the left, is a smaller copy of the papal chair on St. John Lateran at Rome.

On the left of the Sanctuary is the *Chapel of the Blessed Sacrament*, sumptuously decorated with mosaics (1956–62), by Boris Anrep, symbolising the Trinity and the Blessed Sacrament. Immediately to the left of it is the small *Chapel of the Sacred Heart*, while opening off the North Transept is the chapel of *St. Thomas of Canterbury*, or *Vaughan Chantry*, in which is a recumbent statue of Cardinal Vaughan (1832–1903; buried at Mill Hill), archbishop during the building of the cathedral. The chapels on this side of the nave, returning towards the exit, are those of *St. Joseph, St. George and the English Martyrs*, and the *Holy Souls*. In the first is the tomb of Cardinal Hinsley (1865–1943); in the second is the shrine of the Blessed John Southworth (1592–1654), the Jesuit martyr, while figures of St. John Fisher and St. Thomas More are seen in the altarpiece (1946) by Eric Gill. The Chapel of Holy Souls designed by J.F. Bentley, contains mosaics by Christian Symons.

The *Crypt* may be visited on request at the Sacristy (entered from the E end of the S aisle of the Lady Chapel). In the S wall of the semicircular crypt, or *Chapel of St. Peter*, are four relic-chambers, in which are preserved a mitre of St. Thomas Becket, some fragments of the True Cross, and other relics. A floor slab at the E end marks the tomb of Cardinal Griffin (1899–1956), and against the N wall is the tomb of Cardinal Godfrey (1889–1963). Off the W side of the crypt opens the *Shrine of St. Edmund*, a small chapel situated directly beneath the High Altar of the Cathedral and containing an altar under which is preserved a relic of St. Edmund (displayed on 16 Nov). In this chapel are the tombs of Cardinal Wiseman (1802–65) and Cardinal Manning (1808–92), the first two archbishops of Westminster (who were originally buried at Kensal Green).

Further along rises the characterless *Westminster City Hall* (1965). Beyond, the rebuilding of Victoria St has been more imaginative. The *Army and Navy Stores* has stepped upper storeys over arcaded pavements; the store was founded in 1871, and in 1891–1952 had branches in India. On the N side, the *Albert* pub, with a good Victorian interior, serves breakfast, lunch and dinner in its first floor restaurant.

Nearby is *New Scotland Yard*, the headquarters of the Metropolitan Police since 1967 (Chapman Taylor and Partners).

Broadway skirts New Scotland Yard and a solitary green with a memorial to women suffragettes (1970; by E. & L. Russell). In Caxton St (left) is Caxton Hall (1878), used for concerts, and weddings until 1977; now to be redeveloped as part of the St. Ermins Hotel with a conference centre. The former *Blewcoat School* (1709), with attractive brickwork, is the London shop of the National Trust. At the end of Broadway are *London Transport's Headquarters* (1929), in an ingenious

The Tate Gallery, a neo-classical building designed by Sidney J.R. Smith

building by Adam, Holden & Pearson with a lofty tower and remarkable sculptures by Jacob Epstein, Henry Moore, and Eric Gill. In Petty France to the W, Queen Anne's Mansions, by Sir Basil Spence (1976), house the *Home Office*, its fortress-like appearance suggesting the potential violence of the age. Here is the *Passport Office*. For Queen Anne's Gate and the area to the N skirting St. James's Park, see Rte 6.

The streets S of Victoria St beyond Strutton Ground are described on p 157.

The bend in the river between Lambeth Bridge and Chelsea Bridge SE of Victoria Station known as Pimlico is a residential area, popular with MPs and developed by Thomas Cubitt on drained marshland. The area's stucco houses with Tuscan doric columned porticos have frequently been converted into guest houses and flats. *Lillington Gardens*, a '60s housing estate by Darborne and Dark, (1969), features well-landscaped slate and brick buildings set back from the road with a pub and old peoples' home surrounding a Gothic church, parish hall and school by G.E. Street (1860).

Nearby in Vauxhall Bridge Road, with the offices of 'Today' newspaper at No. 70, is the *Queen Mother Sports Centre* with swimming pools and sports facilities. There is a small, lively street-market at Tachbrook St. In Warwick Square (No. 33) a plain neo-classical house has been converted into the Warwick Arts Trust (tel. 071-834 7856). It was built for the Victorian painter James Swinton and exhibitions are held in his studio and gallery; there are also evening recitals. Dolphin Square, in Grosvenor Road overlooking the river, was built in 1937, the largest block of flats in Europe at the time with 1250 flats. It has its own art deco swimming pool and public restaurant. Bessborough Square at the bottom of Vauxhall Bridge Road, has been completely transformed with new housing and office developments.

Just before *Vauxhall Bridge* (1906), which spans the river between Pimlico and Kennington, rises (right) the strangely coloured Rank Hovis McDougall House (1971, by Chapman Taylor), with a block of flats overlooking the river, and (left) a pile of cantilevered Government offices (1966), with a curious air-conditioning device in the forecourt.

In *Pimlico Road*, to the W, with its attractive shops, at a small 'square' of plane trees is the well-sited church of *St. Barnabas*, built in rusticated stone by Cundy and Butterfield in 1846. One of the earliest 'Ritualistic' churches, it was the first in London to open with all its seats free (other churches charged for some seats).

Turning E along *Millbank* past an attractive riverside garden, the setting for Henry Moore's 'Locking Piece' (1968) (damaged in the storms of January 1990—removed for repair) a plaque records the site of the steps down to the Thames used by prisoners from Millbank (the first national penitentiary built in 1812–21 on the site of the Tate Gallery) sentenced to deportation to Australia.

The **Tate Gallery**, see below, is flanked on the W by the *Royal Army Medical College*. The former Queen Alexandra Hospital is the site for the new Clore Gallery and further extensions planned by the Tate Gallery. Just to the E rises *Millbank Tower* (1959–62), the colour of the glass reflecting the changing daylight.

A delightful bronze protudes from corner building on the left just before Attenborough Place. It is 'Jete' by Enzo Plazotto (1975) modelled on the dancer David Wall and placed here in 1985.

Tate Gallery, Millbank, SW1. Tel. 071-821 1313. Open Mon to Sat 10.00–17.50, Sun 14.00–17.50. Admission free except for special exhibitions. Educational facilities including day-time and evening lectures, room-talks and films. Restaurant (see below) and cafeteria. Bookshop with guidebooks, publications, posters, postcards. Clore Gallery. Open same hours as Tate Gallery. Lecture room. Turner reference library.

The Tate Gallery, in a neo-classical building by Sidney J.R. Smith, opened in 1897 thanks to the generosity of Sir Henry Tate (1819–99), the sugar magnate. It houses the important national collection of British paintings and of modern British and foreign paintings and sculpture from the Impressionists to the present day. The gallery has been enlarged five times; in 1979 an air-conditioned extension on the NE side increased the gallery space by 50 per cent.

In April 1987 HM The Queen opened the new *Clore Gallery* housing the Turner Bequest, located on part of the site of the old Queen Alexandra Hospital. The distinctive 3-storey building designed by James Stirling is linked to the main gallery at first-floor level. Some 300 oil paintings and 20,000 sketches, drawings, notebooks, etc. comprise the Turner Collection, bequeathed to the nation and not seen together

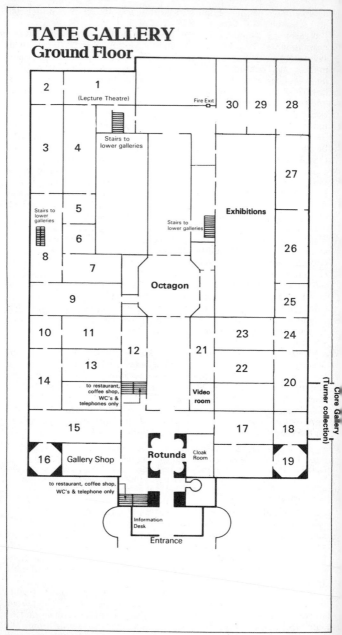

TATE GALLERY
Ground Floor

Entrance

since 1928. The display will change to allow all the paintings to be seen. The auditorium seats 200, and the classroom 50. The reference library is on the third floor.

The Tate Gallery Restaurant has become famous for its British style cuisine and good wine list; it is decorated with a wonderful mural by Rex Whistler and was refurbished in 1985. It is often used by politicians. Open for lunch only. Booking essential although individual guests are seated together at round tables.

The Gallery owns excellent groups of works by most of the major British artists, including Reynolds, Gainsborough, Constable, Blake and the pre-Raphaelites. It pursues an active policy of acquisition including purchases from the Royal Academy Summer Exhibition by the Chantrey Bequest, a fund bequeathed by the 19C sculptor. 20C European painting is well represented and the Gallery's special exhibitions are renowned, sometimes spreading into the Garden.

In 1990 the main Tate Gallery displays were completely reorganised into a new exhibition 'Past, Present and Future' on the basis of three new principles. Firstly, a simple chronological sequence provides a skeleton which can be followed backwards or forwards in time from the Tudors to the present, tracing the evolution of British art until Impressionism, and then the inter-relationship of British and Foreign art through the schools of Paris, New York and now continental Europe. Secondly, within that general sequence some artists and themes are presented in depth on a changing basis. Thirdly, the Gallery has introduced 'Cross-Current' displays, tracing certain themes through many generations of art. The galleries will change at planned intervals to allow more of the Tate Gallery's holdings to be shown.

This tour follows the chronological order of the displays in 1990 and 1991. Plans are available from the desk to the right in the entrance lobby.

From the central Rotunda (guided and recorded tours) the long perspective through the gallery is revealed by the new arrangement which has removed partitions. This is the sculpture gallery with a changing display of some of the Tate's major sculpture pieces—Rodin's 'The Kiss' (1901–4) and modern pieces. To the left is the shop. Walk through to the end where the new displays start with Room 1. Painting in Britain in the 16th and 17th Centuries, including John Bette 'Man in a Black Cap' (1545), Nicholas Hilliard's life-size portrait of Elizabeth I, Dobson's 'Endymion Porter painted in Oxford in 1640,' works by Lely, and Van Dyck's 'Lady of the Spencer Family' (1633–39). Room 2. The Age of Hogarth, the dominant figure in British Art from 1730 to 1764, with 'O The Roast Beef of Old England' and 'Portrait of the Painter and His Pug'. Room 3. The Grand Style—18th Century Painting with several important works by Gainsborough including 'Giovanna Baccelli' (c 1782), the Italian dancer, and 'Sir Benjamin Truman' (c 1773–74), the brewer, and Reynolds, 'Three Ladies Adorning a Term of Hymen'—the Montgomery Sisters. In Room 4 Landscape, Genre and Sporting Paintings of the 18C. Striking paintings by Stubbs include 'Mares and Foals in a Landscape' (c 1760–70). Continue to Room 8 and Constable and Early 19th Century Landscape Painting. 'Scene on a Navigable River, Flatford Mill' (1817), reflecting Constable's nostalgic affection for his childhood, and 'Chain Pier, Brighton', (1826–27) confirmed him as the greatest painter of skies in the whole history of landscape painting.

Room 5. Landscape Sketches 1770–1830 continues the sporting and animal theme. Room 6, William Blake and His Followers, illustrates this great visionary artist. The large colour prints of 1795 with subjects from the Bible, Milton, Shakespeare and the artist's own personal mythology are Blake's first mature works and the most vigorous. The prints are finished in pen and water-colour. Among the later works are the illustrations to Dante's Divine Comedy (1824–27). Room 7 continues the theme with The Romantic Imagination featuring Henry Fuseli, Richard Dadd, Loutherberg, James Ward and Edwin Landseer. Room 9. The 19th Century Academy and the Pre-Raphaelites with paintings by Rossetti, Hughes, Millais, Holman Hunt, and Madox Brown. Note Millais' 'Ophelia' (1851–2)—he spent several months on the bank of the River Hogsmill at Ewell in Surrey to get the background right. Rossetti's 'Beata Beatrix' (1864–70) is one of several based on his wife Elizabeth Siddal, who died of an overdose of opium in 1862. Room 10, Rural Naturalism and Social Realism is followed by Room 11, Impressionism in France and Britain, including Whistler's views of the Thames 'Nocturne in Blue and Gold: Old Battersea Bridge' and Gwen John, 'Nude Girl' (1909–10), Philip Wilson Steer, 'Boulogne Sands' (1888–91), who studied Monet, and John Singer Sargent, 'Carnation, Lily, Lily, Rose' (1885–6), plus a naturalistic bronze 'Little Dancer Aged Fourteen' by Edgar Degas (1880–81). Room 12, European Art around 1900 continues with post-impressionism and some outstanding works, Paul Gaugin, 'Faa Iheihe' (1898), Picasso, 'Girl in a Chemise' (1905) from the beginning of the rose period, Cezanne, 'The Gardener' (1906), Seurat, 'Le Bec du Hoc, Grandcamp' (1885) and Van Gogh, 'Farms near Auvers (1890). Room 13, The European Avant-Garde 1905–25, introduces works by Bonnard, Matisse, Picasso, Munch, Kirchner and Beckman. Room 14 returns to Britain to examine the work of the Camden Town group which included Sickert, Bloomsbury represented by Vanessa Bell, Roger Fry and Duncan Grant, and the Vorticists. Room 15, Stanley Spencer and his Circle highlights for the first time the work of this dominant, albeit traditional artist. Note 'The Resurrection, Cookham' (1923–7) set in his childhood village. Room 16, Constructivism and de Stijl features Mondrian and his comtemporaries.

Cross the sculpture gallery for the second half of the permanent exhibitions, where displays will change at intervals: Room 17, Dada and Surrealism; Room 18, Figurative Art between the Wars; Room 19, Paul Nash; Room 20, Neo-Romanticism and Henry Moore—British Art 1935–50; Room 21, Towards Abstract Expressionism; Room 22, Giacometti and the School of Paris 1945–60; Room 23, Abstract Expressionism American Art 1945–65; Room 24, Picasso, Matisse, Leger, Laurens—Later Works; Room 25, A New Beginning—Abstract Art in Britain 1945–56, Room 26 Anthony Caro and British Abstract Painting; Room 27, British Figure Painting; Room 28, Mark Rothko—Murals for the Seagram Building New York, 1958-9; Room 29, Minimal Art and Room 30, Recent European and American Art.

The **Turner Collection** in the Clore Gallery displays paintings from every period. Works from before his first visit to Italy in 1819 include the famous 'Snow Storm; Hannibal and his Army Crossing the Alps' (1810); Italian-inspired subjects include 'Bay of Baiae with Apollo and the Sibyl' (1823), 'Caligula's Palace and Bridge', (1831), and 'Decline of the Carthaginian Empire' (1817), where the sun sets on a great empire. Turner's later years are represented by 'Peace: Burial at Sea' (1842), a memorial to Turner's friend the painter Wilkie who died at sea in 1841 and was buried off Gibraltar; and further seascapes in Impressionistic style.

Millbank continues E to LAMBETH BRIDGE (1932) on the site of an ancient horse-ferry to Lambeth. *Horseferry Road* leads back to Victoria St, passing between Thames House and Imperial Chemical Industries House, and skirting the buildings of *Westminster Hospital* (founded 1719; present buildings of 1937), Smith Square (p 63) lies just to the E. The cohesion of the street has not been helped by the erection of three vast connected tower blocks to house the *Department of the Environment* in Marsham St. Only after a sharp bend at its W end do the buildings in the area become more interesting. Elverton St leads SW to the unexpected expanse of VINCENT SQUARE, once a bear garden, and now used as playing fields by Westminster School. To the right stands the heavy exterior of the main building (1904) of the *Royal Horticultural Society* (founded 1805). Regular flower shows are held here and in the second hall behind (1928; also used for exhibitions of stamps, model railways, etc.), with its curious barrel vaulted roof lit with stepped skylights. Contrast the neighbouring No. 86, with art nouveau details, and the nearby Maunsel St, a secluded terrace of early 19C cottages. Almshouses of the 19C survive off the N side of the square. At the end of Horseferry Rd in Greycoat Place are the pleasant buildings of the *Grey Coat Hospital* (1698, cupola added 1735; restored 1955), now a school for girls. From here Strutton Ground, which retains its lunchtime, Mon to Fri street market, leads back to Victoria St.

13   Chelsea

(From Sloane Square to Chelsea Harbour)

Access: Underground, Sloane Square.

Chelsea, a pleasant residential district, with picturesque 18th and 19C houses, extends for about 1.5 miles along the N bank of the Thames, W of Pimlico and S of Fulham Road. From the 16C on it was the residence of many eminent people and artists. Today, although most genuine artists have sought cheaper and quieter accommodation, Chelsea is popular with film and pop-music people, designers and others who like to be noticed; Prime Minister Margaret Thatcher had a home in Flood St for many years.

King's Road was in the height of fashion during the 'Swinging '60s' and recovered its popularity in the later '70s and the '80s when punk fashion was not only sold in many boutiques, basement shops, etc., but also paraded each Saturday to the delight of visitors.

Sir Thomas More settled here around 1520 with his large household in a mansion afterwards known as Beaufort House. Here he was visited by Erasmus and Holbein. In 1536 Henry VIII acquired the manor of Chelsea and built a palatial new manor-house (approx. at 19–26 Cheyne Walk) which he gave to Katherine Parr as a wedding present. Here Princess (afterwards Queen) Elizabeth seems to have spent the interval between her mother's death and her father's, and here Anne of Cleves, Henry's fourth wife, died in 1557. After the Restoration Chelsea became a fashionable resort much patronised by Charles II and his court. Sir Hans Sloane (1660–1753), the physician whose collections were the nucleus of the British Museum, bought the manor in 1712, though he did not take up residence in Chelsea until about 1742. Not long after his death the manor house was demolished. Thomas Carlyle (1795–1881), the 'Sage of Chelsea', lived in Cheyne Row from 1834 till his death. Turner (born 1775), the great landscape painter, died in Chelsea in 1851, but its reputation as a painters' 'village' is connected with names of a later date, such as D.G. Rossetti (1828–82), J.McN. Whistler (1834–1903), J.S. Sargent (1856–1925), P. Wilson Steer (1860–

Chelsea Bridge, one of three suspension bridges over the Thames

1942), and Augustus John. Ellen Terry (1847–1928) occupied No. 215 King's Rd in 1904–21. Smollett lived in 1750–62 in part of a house at No. 16 Lawrence St, where the celebrated Chelsea China Factory was active from c 1740 to 1784.

Busy *Sloane Square* (Pl. 17; 1), with the attractive Venus fountain by Gilbert Ledward (1953) beneath plane trees, is the home of the *Royal Court Theatre*. Many of G.B. Shaw's plays had their first performance here, and John Osborne's 'Look Back in Anger' was staged here in 1956. On the opposite corner stands Peter Jones, a department store in a building of 1936, by William Crabtree. *King's Road*, a private royal way from Hampton Court to St James's until 1829, is the haunt of young shoppers, especially on Saturdays. Some antique shops survive at its W end. The road leads SW through Chelsea past the *Duke of York's Headquarters*, built in 1801; here is the London Irish Rifles Regimental Museum (by appointment tel. 071-930 4466) with items and documents of the London Irish Rifles (TA) from 1859, and the Museum of the SAS and Artists Rifles dating from 1869. Further down King's Road on the same side is the *Chelsea Old Town Hall* by Brydon (1886) with murals on the subject of the arts, literature and science (1912), and opposite *Chelsea College of Science and Technology* (1964), and *School of Art* (1965).

Among the many restaurants along the King's Road, the most interesting is the former *Pheasantry*; the ornate façade and portico remain of the original building of 1881; earlier, pheasants were bred here. Princess Serafine Astafieva taught dance here (1916–34); among her pupils were Alicia Markova and Dame Margot Fonteyn. A club established in the basement was patronised by painters during the 1930s and '40s. It is now a bar and restaurant. The building was completely restored in 1983 and 1990.

Further along on the opposite side of the road, past Chelsea Old Town Hall, are the *Chenil Galleries*; a group of antique dealers under one roof in a beautifully decorated building with its own cafeteria.

From Sloane Sq., Lower Sloane St leads S to Chelsea Bridge Road which passes between Ranelagh Gardens and the *Chelsea Barracks* (1960–62). Just before *Chelsea Bridge* (700ft long; opened in 1858 and rebuilt in 1937), the attractive terracotta Lister Institute of Preventative Medicine has been embellished by the Wolfson wing opened in 1971.

The *Chelsea Embankment* (Pl. 17; 4), built in 1872, extends from Chelsea Bridge to Battersea Bridge, a distance of over a mile. This picturesque reach of the river is bordered on the S by Battersea Park. Just E of Chelsea Bridge the Grosvenor Canal passes under the embankment, near a Victorian pumping station and tall chimney. Turning W, past a memorial to the Carabiniers of the South African War, is an entrance to the *Gardens of the Chelsea Hospital* (open on weekdays; scene of the Chelsea Flower Show in May), which command a fine view of the beautiful brick buildings of the *Royal Hospital, Chelsea (Pl. 17; 3), built by Sir Christopher Wren in 1682–92. This refuge for old and disabled soldiers occupies the site of an unsuccesful theological college, founded about 1618. The foundation stone of the hospital was laid by Charles II; the real originator of the scheme was Sir Stephen Fox (1627–1716), and not Nell Gwynn.

The Royal Hospital, Chelsea, Royal Hospital Road, SW3. Tel: 071-730 0161. Open Mon to Sat 10.00–12.00 and 14.00–16.00. Free. Sunday service at 11.00. Grounds Mon to Sat 10.00–dusk, Sun, 14.00–dusk.

The central portion of the building, containing the Hall and the Chapel (see below), has a Doric portico flanked by a low colonnade with coupled columns, and is surmounted by a small tower and cupola. In the projecting wings, each enclosing a court, are the pensioners' dormitories and, at the S ends, the houses of the Governor (E wing) and Lieutenant-Governor (W wing).

It was damaged several times in 1940–45, and there were a number of fatalities. The in-pensioners, about 420 in number, are boarded, lodged, clothed, nursed when ill, and receive a small weekly allowance. In summer (from 29 May, Oak Apple Day) they wear long scarlet coats, exchanged in winter for dark blue ones.

From the colonnade of the *Centre Court* enter the vestibule off which open the Chapel (E) and Hall (W), in each of which a pensioner acts as guide (gratuities). The *Chapel*, on the right, is almost as Wren left it, with elaborate oak carving. The painting of the Resurrection, in the apse, is by Seb. Ricci (restored 1948). Over the dais at the W end of the *Hall* is a huge equestrian portrait of Charles II, by Verrio. Among the flags are some captured from the Americans in 1812–15; the portraits represent military heroes. Wellington lay in state here in 1852. In the middle of the Centre Court is a statue of Charles II, by Grinling Gibbons, which is wreathed with oak on 29 May, when the pensioners receive double rations in honour of Founder's Day. The grounds are beautifully maintained and adorned with early-18C lead flower tubs.

In the Secretary's Office Block, beyond Centre Court to the E, is the *Museum*, inaugurated in 1960. Here are photographs, prints, uniforms, medals, pewter, arms, etc., and the portrait of the pensioner William Hiseland, who served 80 years in the army and died in 1732 at the age of 112.

Immediately to the E lie the delightful *Ranelagh Gardens*, which now form part of the grounds of the Hospital and are entered from the E Walk. Nothing now remains of the spacious Rotunda which was erected here in 1742 and speedily made Ranelagh the most fashionable and frequented place of amusement in London. The gardens are home for the Chelsea Flower Show in May.

The E Walk emerges in *Royal Hospital Road* beside the graveyard (closed in 1854), where Dr Charles Burney, organist at the Hospital, is buried (d 1814). Turn left to reach the **National Army Museum**, in a modern building (1971).

National Army Museum, Royal Hospital Road, SW3. Tel. 071-730 0717. Open Mon to Sat 10.00–17.30, Sun 14.00–17.30. Free. Access: Underground, Sloane Square, Bus 11, 19, 22, 137, 239.

The collections, moved from Sandhurst and augmented by loans, cover the history of the British Army from 1485 to the Falklands. A vestibule with embroidered regimental colours leads up to the *Main Floor*, arranged chronologically to show phase by phase and campaign by campaign the developing function of the army, together with the changing nature of command, service, and conditions. This is achieved by personal relics, accoutrements, illustrations, and captured trophies, cleverly selected, with excellent explanatory labels and maps.

Second Floor. In the *Uniform Gallery*, army dress is displayed by periods in conjunction with furniture and pictures in contemporary surroundings. On a long wall are the orders and decorations of Field Marshals (Gough, Wolseley, Kitchener, and Roberts). Beyond in the *Art Gallery* portraits and battle scenes form a representative collection of British painting in the 18–19C, including works by Wootton, Reynolds, Romney, Beechey, Raeburn, and Lawrence.

The *Reading Room* (apply in writing to the director) has 20,000 books, the archives of many famous commanders, and the Col. Crookshank collection of battle prints (from the British Museum).

Tite St, which intersects Royal Hospital Road beyond the Museum, was the residence for 24 years of J.S. Sargent (1856–1925) who died at No. 31. No. 34 was the home of Oscar Wilde from 1884 to 1895. Opposite is the site of the White House, built for Whistler but occupied by him for a few months only in 1878–79; he lived also at No. 13 (in 1881–85) and No. 46 (in 1888). A tablet at No. 23 Tedworth Square, to the N, marks the London residence of Mark Twain (1835–1910). Margaret Thatcher lived in Flood St, which connects the Embankment with King's Road. She sold her house in 1984.

The walls of the *Chelsea Physic Garden* stretch all the way down to the Embankment. It opened to the public for the first time in 1983. The entrance is in Swan Walk.

Chelsea Physic Garden, Royal Hospital Road, SW3. Tel. 071-352 5646. Open mid April to mid October Wed and Sun 14.00–17.00; Bank Holiday Mondays and during the Chelsea Flower Show 12.00 to 17.00. Admission charge.

Sir Hans Sloane, whose statue by Rysbrack (1733) stands in the garden, presented the site to the Apothecaries' Society in 1722 (it has been established since 1676) on condition that 2000 specimens of distinct plants grown in the garden should be sent to the Royal Society 'well dried and preserved', in annual instalments of 50, a condition which has been amply fulfilled. In 1736 Linnaeus visited the garden to collect plants and specimens and Mrs Elizabeth Blackwell illustrated her 'Curious Herb' book by drawing plants here. The display of plants and herbs grown here is mostly of interest to specialists.

Continue to the Embankment, here separated by narrow public gardens from *Cheyne Walk* (Pl. 16; 6; pron. 'chainy'), an attractive row of red-brick Georgian houses, each with its own character. Original wrought iron railings and gates precede many of the gardens. No. 4 was occupied by George Eliot (died 1880) during the last three weeks of her life. No. 16, the *Queen's House*, erroneously connected with the name of Catherine of Braganza (died 1705), Charles II's queen, was built only in 1717. The fine railings are by Thos. Robinson. Rossetti lived here in 1862–82 and kept his menagerie in the garden. A memorial fountain to him in the Embankment gardens, with a medallion by Ford Madox Brown (1887), faces the house. In the gardens near the N end of *Albert Bridge* (1873), a statue of The Boy David by E. Bainbridge Copnall replaces one by Derwent Wood, stolen in 1963. A statue on the other side of the bridge is a memorial to Wood, its sculptor, placed here by members of the Chelsea Arts Club. Captain R.F. Scott, the polar explorer, lived at No. 56 Oakley St (tablet), leading N from Albert Bridge.

In the gardens on the Embankment to the W of the bridge is a fine statue of *Carlyle* (1882, by Boehm). In *Cheyne Row* (Pl. 16; 6), the quiet and unpretentious little street built in 1708 and running N from the river, behind Carlyle's statue, is the house (No. 24; formerly No. 5) in which Thomas Carlyle (1795–1881) and his wife (1801–66) lived from 1834 to the end of their lives.

Carlyle's House, 24 Cheyne Row, SW3. Tel. 071-352 7087. Open Wed to Sun 11.00–17.00 April to October. Admission charge. No electricity.

*Carlyle's House is preserved in the quiet and dignified simplicity impressed upon it by its famous tenants. The little rooms contain furniture used by the Carlyles. On the wall hang portraits of them and sketches and photographs of scenes and places connected with them, and in glass cases are exhibited books and MSS belonging to Carlyle and many interesting personal relics. On the top floor is the famous Attic Study with its double walls, added by Carlyle in 1853 at a cost of £169 in a vain attempt to ensure quiet. In the kitchen in the basement (not always shown), Carlyle and Tennyson smoked together, and in the garden 'Nero', Mrs Carlyle's dog, is buried.

To the E in Cheyne Walk, Shrewsbury House flats occupy the site of a house built c 1519, and demolished in 1813. The original garden walls surround the flats. At No. 21 Carlyle Mansions Henry James died in 1916 (tablet in the church).

*Chelsea Old Church, dedicated to *All Saints*, on the Embankment, was probably founded in the middle of the 12C. Severely damaged by a land-mine on 16 April 1941, it has been beautifully rebuilt by W.H. Godfrey, and was rededicated in 1958.

Chelsea Old Church, Old Church St. Open Sun, Tues to Fri 11.00–13.00 and 14.00–17.00, Sat 11.00–13.00. Tel. 071–352 5637 (check hours).

Interior. By the first window on the right are several old *Chained Books*, given to the church by Sir Hans Sloane, including two volumes of a fine edition of Foxe's 'Book of Martyrs' (1684). Close by is the large monument to *Lord and Lady Dacre*, erected in 1595. The *More Chapel*, almost undamaged by the mine, dates from 1325, and was restored by Sir Thomas More in 1528. In the corner, on the right, is the mutilated tomb of the *Duchess of Northumberland* (d 1555), mother of Robert Dudley, Earl of Leicester, mother-in-law of Lady Jane Grey, and grandmother of Sir Philip Sidney. The tomb, which resembles Chaucer's in Westminster Abbey, is probably not in its original position. The archway between the More Chapel and the *Chancel* dates from the 14C, but the capitals were recarved in Sir Thomas More's time, probably by French craftsmen. Near the W pillar is the finely carved pulpit (c 1679). To the right of the chancel is the *More Monument* (1532), designed by Sir Thomas More while still in royal favour, with a long epitaph composed by himself. On the left is the early 16C tomb of the *Brays*, the oldest in the church, now set into the wall under an arch. Above it is the late 16C monument of *Thomas Hungerford* and his family. To the N of the Chancel is the rebuilt *Lawrence Chapel* (1325), entered by an archway of 1563, an early example of the classic revival and a monument to *Richard Gervoise*. Henry VIII is said to have been secretly married here to Jane Seymour, some days before their public marriage. To the right is the unusual effigy of *Sara Colville* (d 1631), daughter of Sir Thomas Lawrence, and at the E end is the elaborate tomb of *Sir Robert Stanley* and two of his children (1632). To the right of this is the monument to *Sir Thomas Lawrence* and his family (1593). On the N wall of the nave *Jane Cheyne, Lady Newhaven* (1621–69), benefactress of church and neighbourhood, is commemorated in a large monument by Paolo Bernini (son of the great Gian Lorenzo).

The new tower, with clock and sundial, contains a small historical museum. In the graveyard are buried Jean Cavalier (1680–1740), leader of the Camisards in the Cévennes in 1702–04. Thomas Shadwell (1640–92), poet laureate, and Sir Hans Sloane (1660–1753).

Near the top of Old Church St is the old *Rectory* (No. 56), where Charles (1819–75) and Henry Kingsley (1830–76) spent part of their youth, when their father was rector. At No. 143 is the Chelsea Arts Club founded in 1891 for painters and sculptors and moved into its present premises in 1902. The thriving Club (women members welcome) has recently revived the annual Chelsea Arts Club Ball. In *St. Luke's* (1820–24), an early example of the Gothic revival, in Sydney St, N of King's Road, Charles Dickens was married in 1836.

Outside the church is a statue of Sir Thomas More (1969; by L. Cubitt Bevis). In Roper's Gardens (see below) is an unfinished bas-relief by Epstein on the site of his studio (1909–14), and a bronze 'Awakening', by Gilbert Ledward. Here stands **Crosby Hall**. Brought from Bishopsgate in 1910 and re-erected so far as possible with the careful retention of its most beautiful features, it is now a college hall of the British Federation of University Women. (Tel: 071-352 9663. Open Mon to Sat 10.00–12.00, 14.15–17.00; Sun 14.15–17.00; closed for functions at short notice. Admission free.)

Crosby Hall was the great hall of Crosby Place, a mansion built in Bishopsgate in 1466 by Sir John Crosby, a London grocer and alderman, and occupied by the Duke of Gloucester (1483), later Richard III. Sir Thomas More, whose Chelsea garden once included the site on which the hall now stands, seems to have bought the house in 1523, and his son-in-law William Roper occupied it. Roper's Gardens are now laid out on the site of Sir Thomas More's orchard. In the 16C the mansion was considered sumptuous enough to be the abode of various ambassadors. When Crosby Place was burned in the 17C the hall escaped to meet a chequered fate, finally becoming a restaurant before its purchase in 1908 by the University and City Association of London. It was used as a reception centre by the Chelsea War Refugees Committee during the First World War. The hall retains a fine oriel window and the original roof, and contains a copy of Holbein's lost group of Sir Thomas More's family, c 1527.

At 20A Danvers St Sir Alexander Fleming (1881–1955), discoverer of penicillin died; in the '30s the unrelated Peter Fleming, explorer-writer, occupied the flat above.

Battersea Bridge, an iron structure (1890) crossing the river at the end of Beaufort St, replaced the picturesque old wooden bridge of 1771–72, which was a favourite subject with Whistler and other artists. The river, with new blocks of flats opposite, here bends S, and offers moorings for house-boats.

To the W of the bridge are several interesting old houses in *Cheyne Walk*. Mrs Gaskell (1810–65) was born at No. 93 (tablet). Whistler lived at No. 96 in 1866–78, and No. 101 was his first home in Chelsea (1863–66). *Lindsey House* (NT), named after the Earl of Lindsey, the only 17C mansion in Chelsea, is divided into Nos 97–100; a tablet on No. 98 marks the home of the Brunels, father and son, both engineers. P. Wilson Steer died at No. 109 in 1942. At No. 118 J.M.W. Turner lived in anonymous retirement from 1846, and died here in 1851. George Meredith wrote 'The Ordeal of Richard Feverel' at No. 7 Hobury St, a little to the N, and Henry Tonks (1862–1937) died at No. 1 The Vale, further E.

At the end of Cheyne Walk is Lots Road, with a huge London Transport power-station (due for closure in the 1990s). Chelsea Wharf has been converted into workshops and has a restaurant. The gates in the adjoining gardens are from Cremorne Gardens. Cremorne Rd, crossing the site of the old *Cremorne Gardens* (1845–77), leads on the right to *King's Road*, and SW along Lots Road to the new **Chelsea Harbour**. On 29 acres of derelict land used as coal depot, P & O has financed a new development designed by Moxley, Jenner and Partners including 480 luxury homes, a 75-berth marina, a Conrad Hilton hotel, shops, restaurants and offices. A river service links Chelsea Harbour with Charing Cross and the City. The focal point is a 20-storey luxury block surmounted by a red tide-ball.

Development is now going ahead on the adjoining old Fulham power station site (to the SW) which will include council and private housing as well as light industry and an indoor tennis centre.

14 Shaftesbury Avenue, Soho, Charing Cross Road, Leicester Square and Seven Dials

Access: Underground, Piccadilly Circus, Leicester Square, Tottenham Court Road.

Shaftesbury Avenue, with theatres and restaurants, runs from Piccadilly Circus through Cambridge Circus, and was built in 1886 as a deliberate slum-clearance move in what was then a less salubrious part of London. It is named after Lord Shaftesbury, see p 113. It soon superseded The Strand as London's theatre district and offers a mixture of comedy and popular drama. On the NW side are four theatres: the Lyric (1889, designed by C.J. Phipps but refurbished in the '30s), the Apollo (1901, in ornate French Renaissance style), the Globe (1906, designed by W.G.R. Sprague in the ornate Louis XVI style) and the Queen's Theatre (1907, also by Sprague but bomb-damaged—the new exterior is by Hugh Casson). The Shaftesbury

Theatre (1911, ornate French Renaissance style—carefully restored) is confusingly located at the very top of Shaftesbury Avenue where it meets High Holborn.

Soho, is the area boarded by Regent St, Leicester Square, Charing Cross Road and Oxford St. The name Soho, first recorded in 1636, probably derives from an ancient hunting cry used when the area was mostly parkland.

Soho retains much of its cosmopolitan atmosphere with continental restaurants, patisseries and delicatessen shops among the sex-shops and drinking clubs. French refugees settled in Bateman St soon after the Revocation of the Edict of Nantes in 1685. For a time it became a fashionable residential area, with great houses alongside those of French craftsmen and traders. Artists and writers began to settle here in the 18th and 19th centuries but an outbreak of cholera in the mid 19C drove the better-off residents away. The residential population has now declined considerably. The area has attracted the film, music and advertising industries and there are some attractive office developments. More recently fashion boutiques have appeared in the area but most of the original buildings have been destroyed or demolished.

Westminster City Council's environmental improvement programme for Soho includes a pedestrianised route from Argyll St near Oxford Circus, along Carnaby St, Broadwick St, Berwick St, Rupert St, Old Compton St, Mead St and Gerrard St, some of which has already been implemented.

Soho retains its reputation of illicitness although stringent efforts are being made by Westminster City Council to control the number of sex-shops, strip clubs, clip-joints and so-called near-beer clubs—drinking clubs without alcohol licences.

Explore Soho from Piccadilly Circus along Shaftesbury Avenue past the Trocadero, see Rte 8. The area to the S has in the last two decades become London's Chinatown with many settlers from the New Territories of Hong Kong opening restaurants, bakeries and supermarkets. The pedestrianisation of Gerrard St and the addition of Chinese street furniture by the Council has improved the appearance of the area taken over at Chinese New Year (January/February) by lion and dragon dances, Chinese pop-singers and families from all over the country.

In Gerrard St, Dryden lived from 1687 until his death in 1700 (No. 44, rebuilt; tablet on No. 43). In 1900 G.K. Chesterton and Hilaire Belloc first met in a French restaurant here.

Follow Wardour St N to *St. Anne's Soho*. Only the tower of the church (1685, partly by Wren) remains, the rest was destroyed in 1940. A garden has been laid out around it. The heavy steeple (1801–03) is by S.P. Cockerell and below is the monument of William Hazlitt (1778–1830). Wardour St was once occupied by furniture makers including Thomas Sheraton in 1793–95 at No. 103, later at No. 147. The music publishers Novello & Co. had a building here designed by Frank Louborough Pearson in 1811, now occupied by the British Library including the delightful galleried Novello Room (main entrance in Sheraton St).

Old Compton St retains a few of the delicatessens which made Soho famous, and leads S to join Berwick St, a street market popular with office workers. Fruit, vegetables, and fabrics are sold (best at lunchtime).

GOLDEN SQUARE, to the W, is traditionally a centre for film companies. Angelica Kauffmann lived at No. 16, Cardinal Wiseman at No. 35, and John Hunter, the surgeon, at No. 31 (all rebuilt). The statue in antique costume in the centre of the square represents George II. In Warwick St, nearby, a R.C. church survives from 1789.

N of Beak St is Broadwick St the birthplace of William Blake (1757–1827) who lived at No. 74 (demolished); inscription in Marshall St. Shelley took lodgings at No. 15 Poland St nearby in 1811 after his expulsion from Oxford.

Return to Old Compton St via Lexington St. *Dean St* runs parallel with Wardour St. Karl Marx lived at No. 28 from 1851–56 above the present Leoni's Quo Vadis Restaurant, in two cramped rooms with five children, his wife and maid. He had no regular employment and lived in great poverty. From here he walked daily to the British Museum Reading Room. The rooms may be seen on request. Nearby is the newly established Groucho Club for journalists, publishers etc. The pub *The French House* has served served emigré French since 1914 as well as famous artists and poets including Augustus John and Dylan Thomas.

In *Frith St* is the well established Ronnie Scott's Jazz Club. Here at No. 6 (1718 partly rebuilt) Hazlitt died in 1830 and at No. 22 J.L. Baird staged his first television demonstration in 1926 (plaque in upstairs room of restaurant). Kettner's in Romilly St is one of London's oldest surviving restaurants; it was established in 1868 and is now a brasserie with a champagne bar.

To the N lies SOHO SQUARE, laid out in 1681 (though only one 18C house survives), and now a centre of the music trade. In 1764 Mozart (then lodging at No. 20 Frith St) taught music in the house (No. 22) of Lord Mayor William Beckford, brother of Richard (see below). The statue of Charles II is by Cibber (1681). On the E side of the square, the Italianate *St. Patrick's* church (R.C.) was opened in 1793 (rebuilt, 1891–93). The French Protestant church (ring for adm. at door on right) dates from 1893.

The square was first surrounded with large mansions, including one belonging to the Duke of Monmouth, who chose 'Soho' as his password at the Battle of Sedgemoor (1685). It soon became a fashionable area, and Sir Roger de Coverley had his town quarters here. In the 18C it was a favourite residence of ambassadors. No. 32 (rebuilt), where Sir Joseph Banks came to live in 1777, was the centre in London for the scientists of the time (Cavendish, Priestley, and others) and the inaugural meeting of the Royal Institution was held there.

In the SE corner of the square the *House of St. Barnabas-in-Soho* (open Wed 14.30–16.15, Thurs 11.00–12.30; donations welcome), a mansion built in the late 1740s, has been occupied by a charity for the destitute (founded by Dr Henry Monroe in 1846) since 1862. It was the home of Richard Beckford in 1754, and he was probably responsible for the fine rococo plasterwork, wood carving, and ironwork in the interior. The chapel dates from 1862. The meeting between Dr Manette and Sidney Carton in Dickens' 'Tale of Two Cities' occurred in the rear courtyard (comp. Manette St, entered by an archway in Greek St); an old mulberry tree survives. *Greek St* is named after a colony of Greeks from Melos whose church (founded c 1680) was in Charing Cross Road, parallel to the E. Some fine restaurants here include L'Escargot, established early this century and with the founder George Gaudin represented riding a snail outside –'slow but sure' was his motto. The modern Prince Edward Theatre has been both a cinema and musical theatre (1930). Recent successes include 'Evita' and 'Chess'.

CHARING CROSS ROAD is divided in two by Cambridge Circus; bookshops still dominate in the northern section and theatres to the S toward Leicester Square. *Foyles*, 'the world's largest bookshop', is at No. 113–19.

It was founded in 1906 by two brothers who sold off their textbooks after failing their civil service examinations and realised they had the start of a good business. They now stock some six million books in a new five-storey building; the original building at No. 121/123 was demolished in 1966. Foyles is now run by Christina Foyle, daughter of one of the brothers.

No. 84 Charing Cross Road, home of the second-hand bookshop made famous by the American writer Helen Hanff, closed in the '70s. A play based on the book ran in the West End for three years from 1979. The Phoenix Theatre opened in 1930 with Coward's 'Private Lives'.

The undistinguished *Cambridge Circus* is being redeveloped by Westminster City Council. The terracotta façade of the *Palace Theatre* (1888, by T.E. Colcutt) is being restored by its new owner, composer Andrew Lloyd Webber; already the gilt and marble of the interior has returned to its former appearance.

It opened as the English Opera House in 1891 with Sir Arthur Sullivan's 'Ivanhoe'. Anna Pavlova made her first London appearance here. Andrew Lloyd Webber intends to create a 'palace of music' and has made a successful start with 'Les Miserables' which opened in 1987.
To the S in Charing Cross Road is the octagonal lantern of the Welsh Presbyterian Chapel (1887, by James Cutbitt); now the Limelight Club, a disco, entrance in Shaftesbury Avenue. In Great Newport St to the E is the Photographers' Gallery (open Tues to Sat 11.00–19.00; 071-240 5511), and the small Arts Theatre, established in 1927 as a club theatre with a reputation for 'avant-garde' plays. In 1967 it became the home of the children's Unicorn Theatre—mostly daytime performances—and still stages some 'fringe' productions in the evenings.

Cranbourn St leads W from Charing Cross Road to Leicester Square past Leicester Place, on the N side and the French church of *Notre-Dame de France*, burned in 1940, and completely rebuilt in 1955 save for its circular wall (a relic of Burford's 'Panorama' established in 1793). In the interior is a mural by Jean Cocteau (1960), and over the altar an Aubusson tapestry.

LEICESTER SQUARE was notorious by 1700 as a scandalous centre of entertainment and well-known throughout the world from the First World War song 'It's a long way to Tipperary'.

Over the next few years part of the Square is blocked off during the construction of an electricity sub-station.

It was laid out in the 1670s, and named after Leicester House which stood on the N side in 1631–35. In the central garden is a statue of Shakespeare, a 19C copy of the monument by Sheemakers in Westminster Abbey. In the four corners are busts of famous local residents: Hogarth, Reynolds (painters), Hunter (doctor) and Sir Isaac Newton (scientist). The statue of Charlie Chaplin by Doubleday, unveiled in 1981, is now in the garden.
In the 18C the area was much frequented by artists. From 1753 until his death in 1764 Hogarth had his town house at the SE corner (No. 30), Sir Joshua Reynolds lived at No. 47, on the W side, from 1760 till his death in 1792; this was the first house to acquire an official commemorative plaque (1875). Charles d'Agar lived at Nos 22 and 29, Philip Mercier at No. 40, and Michael Dahl at No. 49. Swift had rooms here in 1711. At No. 28 John Hunter built a museum for the famous Hunterian Collection, later moved to the College of Surgeons.

Here three famous 19C music halls gave place to 'super-cinemas' presenting first runs of films. First to change in 1920 was the *Empire* (rebuilt 1927) which had shown moving pictures as early as 1891. Later the *Warner* succeeded *Daly's*, where the Carl Rosa Opera had introduced 'Hansel and Gretel' to England and later musical successes included 'The Merry Widow' and 'Maid of the Mountain'. The *Odeon* occupies the site of the *Alhambra* (1854–1936), where the eclectic entertainment ranged from the 'Bing Boys' to the distinguished Diaghilev season of 1921. The Leicester Square Theatre is also a cinema.

Three large cinemas, the Empire (formerly a ballroom, now a disco) and the restored Hippodrome (formerly the Talk of the Town) carry on the entertainment tradition of Leicester Square. The Society of West End Theatre operates a *Half Price Theatre Ticket Booth* from a pavilion in the Square; tickets are available after 12.30 for matinees and after 14.30 for evening performances—all for same day; a charge is made. The Dental Hospital at the S side of the Square has been converted into an elegant hotel, the Hampshire (1989).

In St. Martin's St, leading out of the square on the SW side, the admirable *Westminster Reference Library* (free; open weekdays) replaces the house occupied by Sir Isaac Newton (1710– 27) and Dr Burney (1774–94). Here Fanny Burney wrote 'Evelina'. Irving St leads SE from the Square to Charing Cross Road and St. Martin's Lane with more theatres (Pl.14; 4). The *Coliseum Theatre*, with its prominent globe, became in 1968 the new home of Sadler's Wells, now the English National Opera Company. It was built (1904) as a music hall by Sir Oswald Stoll, and Ellen Terry, Lily Langtry, and Sarah Bernhardt all appeared on its elaborate stage. The *Duke of York's* (1892) saw the first performance of Barrie's 'Peter Pan'. It has been restored and is now owned by Capital Radio. A tablet on No. 6 marks the site of Chippendale's workshop from 1753; in 1764 Mozart lodged in *Cecil Court* (left) now lined with print and second-hand book shops; while *Goodwin's Court* (right) preserves some charming 17C shop-fronts; further N is St. Martin's Court with Sheekey's fish restaurant and oyster bar dating from 1896 and New Row with delightful shops.

The Albery family continues its involvement with the Albery Theatre and six other theatres in the Albery group, including the Donmar Warehouse. St. Martin's Lane continues N as Monmouth St through *Seven Dials*, once a notorious thieves' quarter known as St. Giles. A Doric pillar topped by a clock with seven faces was erected here in 1694 at the junction of seven streets. It was taken down in 1773 when it was falsely rumoured that treasure was buried beneath it. It now stands on the green in Weybridge in Surrey. After a local appeal, a replica of the monument was unveiled in 1989 by Queen Beatrix of Netherlands. The Sundial Pillar has been made by trainee masons and stands in an area which has been imaginatively redeveloped as the Comyn Ching Triangle by Terry Farrell with workshops and shops and an open space with an oriental slant. (See also p 207). To the N the former Shaftesbury Hotel has been refurbished as the Mountbatten Hotel with some family memorabilia on display. The Cambridge Theatre (1930) is on the S side.

From here explore Covent Garden Route 19, or return to Cambridge Circus via Earlham St and small street market.

15   Regent Street, Oxford Street, Wallace Collection, Marylebone, Paddington and Maida Vale

Access: Underground, Piccadilly Circus, Oxford Circus, Baker St.

REGENT STREET, 1 mile long, a main N–S thoroughfare through the West End, is an important shopping street. It leads from Waterloo Place to Piccadilly Circus and continues N to Oxford Circus and Langham Place. It was laid out as part of Nash's impressive West End design intended to unite the Prince of Wales' Carlton House with Regent's Park in 1813–20, but was never completed. The curved section from Piccadilly Circus to Oxford Circus was known as the Quadrant; colonnades protected shoppers and above, balconies fronted lodging houses. The new façades designed by Blomfield in 1925 omitted the colonnades but retained an elegant unity. The stores and restaurants formed an association in 1925 and arrange elaborate Christmas decorations each year illuminated from the middle of November to Twelfth Night.

The Swan and Edgar store at the Piccadilly Circus end of Regent St closed in 1982 but many other well-known names survive, including Austin Reed, Aquascutum, Lillywhites, Garrard, Wedgwood, Mappin & Webb, Hamleys—the world's largest toy-shop which is now in a new building on six floors—Jaeger, Laura Ashley, and Dickins and Jones. Liberty with its St. George and the Dragon Clock is in two parts—the mock-Tudor building of 1924, stands in Great Marlborough St. Among the famous restaurants is Veeraswamy's, one of London's first Indian restaurants (No. 99), Verrey's (No. 233) established in 1848, mentioned by Sherlock Holmes, but popular with Victorian politicians including Disraeli, and the Café Royal. This opened in 1865 and the Domino Room was used by artists and writers including Beardsley, Oscar Wilde, Whistler, Max Beerbohm and Sickert between 1890 and 1920 (see painting inside by Adrian Allinson, c 1916). The future Edward VIII was a regular customer. The Café Royal was rebuilt in 1925 and the present Grill Room became the meeting place of another generation of writers including T.S. Eliot, J.B. Priestley and Compton Mackenzie. Today the Café Royal has five floors of banqueting and meeting rooms, and two restaurants; the original wine cellar is available for wine tastings and private boxing matches take place occasionally.

Explore Regent St from Piccadilly Circus; Vigo St on the left (W) side of Regent St leads to *Savile Row* where much of London's bespoke tailoring industry still survives; further up on the right (E side) Beak St and Great Marlborough St lead to Carnaby St, now a pedestrianised revamped reminder of the swinging '60s when this was the mecca. This is part of Westminster City Council's Soho improvement scheme, see also p 164.

W of Regent St lies *Hanover Square*, with a bronze statue of William Pitt the Younger (1759–1806), by Chantrey (1831). No. 21 was occupied by Talleyrand in 1835. *St. George's, Hanover Square*, to the S, was built in 1713–24, and three of the E windows contain 16C stained glass from Malines placed here c 1843. The two cast-iron dogs in the porch are said to be by Landseer. Concerts are held here, particularly during the annual Handel Festival.

The registers contain entries of the marriages of Sir William Hamilton and Emma Lyon or Hart (1791), Benjamin Disraeli and Mrs Wyndham Lewis (1839), 'George Eliot' and Mr J.W. Cross (1880), Theodore Roosevelt and Edith Carow (1886), and H.H. Asquith and Margaret Tennant (1894); also of the remarriage of Shelley and Harriet Westbrook in 1814 confirming the Scottish marriage of 1811.

Parallel with Regent St at the N end is Argyll St to the E with the London Palladium theatre (1910) designed by Frank Matcham in white and gold with warm red seating and a Palm Court in Norwegian rose granite. With 2300 seats, it is one of London's largest theatres famous for its Christmas pantomimes, the televised Sunday Nights at the London Palladium of the '60s and royal variety performances.

Oxford Circus marks the junction of Oxford St and Regent St. On the line of a Roman road, Oxford St today is possibly the busiest shopping street in the world with stores and shops from the Marble Arch (W) end to Tottenham Court Road in the E. It is partially closed to cars during the day and plans have been made for further pedestrianisation of the street. The Oxford St Association organises illuminated Christmas decorations. Among the famous names here are two Marks and Spencer stores, John Lewis, House of Fraser, HMV, and Selfridges, which is, after Harrods, London's largest store. It was founded by American Gordon Selfridge in 1909; the impressive Ionic façade of the building (1928) designed by American Daniel Burnham features a giant art deco clock 'Queen of Time' by Gilbert Bayes. Opposite Balderton St leads S to Brown Hart Gardens (1903)—a raised Italian garden hiding a huge electricity supply station in a small residential area.

Although known as the 'Road to Oxford' and 'The Tyburn Way' Oxford St, established in the 18C, took its name from the Earl of Oxford, Edward Harley who married Lady Henrietta Cavendish-Holles; their daughter married the Duke of Portland and the three families' names appear on streets throughout the area. In the late 19C it developed into a shopping street and in the last decade several of the large stores have been converted into shopping malls although the famous names remain.

In Regent St N of Oxford Circus is the *Polytechnic of Central London*, founded in 1882 for the mental, moral, and physical development of youth. The line of Regent St is prolonged to the N by the curving *Langham Place* where the tower and needle-like spire of *All Souls' Church* were built by Nash in 1823–24 and almost detached from the church in order to close the vista up Regent St. In the portico is a bust by Behnes of the architect.

Langham Place is continued northward towards the green expanse of Regent's Park by *Portland Place*, one of the broadest streets in London. At its foot (right) rises *Broadcasting House*, the headquarters of the BBC, a huge edifice by Val Myer and Watson Hart (1931), with a sculptured group of Prospero and Ariel by Eric Gill. The BBC has purchased land at White City where the new headquarters are now under construction. See p 370. The future use of Broadcasting House is uncertain.

The Langham, opposite, vacated by the BBC in 1986 has been redeveloped by Hilton Hotels into a 400 bedroom luxury hotel, due to open in 1991, retaining some of the features of the original building designed in the style of a Florentine palace by Giles and Murray, which opened in 1864 as a hotel. Its lavish suites were frequented by the famous including the exiled Napoleon III, Mark Twain, Toscanini and Haile Selassie. It was partially destroyed when a bomb hit its giant water tanks in 1940.

The Adam houses in Portland Place (1776–80) have gradually yielded to larger modern structures. At No. 28 is the *Royal Institute of Public Health and Hygiene*. No. 66 is the *Royal Institute of British Architects*, a striking building by G.G. Wornum (1934).

The RIBA Library of architectural books, journals etc. is open to the public at 66 Portland Place, Mon 10.00–17.00, Tues to Thurs 10.00–20.00, Fri 10.00–19.00 and Sat 10.00–13.30.

Monuments in the roadway commemorate *Quintin Hogg* (1845–1903), founder of the Polytechnic (see above) by George Frampton (1906); *Sir George White* (1835–1912) an equestrian statue by John Tweed, (1922), Field Marshal, Governor of Gibraltar and Commander-in-Chief in India, defender of Ladysmith (opposite No. 47, once the house of Lord Roberts); and *Lord Lister* (1827–1912), the surgeon and founder of antiseptic medicine, the bronze bust is by Thomas Brock. Lister lived nearby in Park Crescent.

The attractive and fashionable area to the W of Portland Place (known generally as Harley St—see below) is best-known for the many physicians and surgeons, homoeopaths and others in alternative medicine, as well as dentists, who share consulting rooms here to benefit from 'the right address'; their main surgeries are often at hospitals elsewhere. *Cavendish Square* (Pl. 6; 5; underground car park) dates from about 1717; the columned façades of two of the houses on the N side are relics of a great mansion begun in 1720 for the Duke of Chandos. The archway connecting the two wings is adorned with a Madonna by Epstein. Nelson lived at No. 5 in 1787. At No. 20, blue plaque, is the former home of H.H. Asquith (1852-1928), Prime Minister. Dr Brown-Sequard (1817–94; born in Mauritius), a pioneer in many fields of medicine, was also a resident in the square. In the garden is a statue of Lord George Bentinck (1802–48), politician, by Thomas Campbell (1851). In *Holles St* which leads S to Oxford St (S) Lord Byron (1788–1824) was born at No. 21, now the site of John Lewis department store, with a sculpture by Barbara Hepworth on the SW wall. At the end of Chandos St (NE corner of the square), the fine *Chandos House* built by Robert Adam in 1771 is part of the Royal Society of Medicine.

Wigmore St, an attractive shopping street with restaurants and coffee shops. Henrietta Place lead out of the Square W. Chamber music recitals are held in *Wigmore Hall* (tel. 071-935 2141) with popular 'coffee' concerts on Sunday mornings. In Wimpole St, S, is the *Royal Society of Medicine*, with its famous library. Opposite *St. Peter*, *Vere St*, a neat little church by Gibbs (1721–23) has unusual capitals inside. In *Stratford Place* further W, the 18th C Stratford House, now the Oriental Club, remains in a small cul de sac where once the Lord Mayor's Banqueting House stood; gates separated it from Oxford St and a single gate-pier topped by a Coade stone lion remains. At No. 10 is the Royal Society of Musicians.

St. Christopher's Place links Wigmore St with the busy Oxford St to the S, just before James St. This pedestrianised Victorian shopping street has been restored to its 19C appearance with small boutiques, hanging signs, flower baskets, outdoor cafés and restaurants. It also links with Barrett St and Giles Court.

In *Welbeck St*, leading N from Wigmore St, Anthony Trollope died at a house on the site of No. 34 in 1884. Thos. Woolner lived at No. 29 and Thos. Young, 'man of science' at No. 48 (plaque).

Edward Gibbon published the first volumes of his great history while living at No. 7 Bentinck St off Welbeck St in 1772–83 and Sir James Mackenzie lived at No. 17 (plaques). During the Second World War Guy Burgess and Anthony Blunt, later unveiled as spies while the former worked for British intelligence, shared a flat at No. 5 Bentinck St. Berlioz stayed at No. 58 Queen Anne St (on the E side of Welbeck St) in 1851 when he was a judge at the Great Exhibition competition for makers of musical instruments.

Parallel to the E is Wimpole St where Henry Hallam lived in 1819–40 at No. 67, 'the long unlovely street' of Tennyson's 'In Memoriam', written in commemoration of A.H. Hallam (1811–33). From No. 50 (rebuilt), her home since 1836, Elizabeth Barrett stole secretly in 1846 to be married to Robert Browning in Marylebone church and again a few weeks later to accompany him to Italy. More recently (1963) No. 17 Wimpole Mews was associated with the Christine Keeler/Profumo affair which shook the Macmillan government; here was the home of Dr. Stephen Ward where Keeler and later Mandy'Rice Davies lived for a time.

Turner, the landscape-painter, lived for many years at No. 64 Harley St, parallel to the E with Wimpole St, and was also the eccentric tenant of a house in Queen Anne St (close by) from 1812–51 (house rebuilt; tablet on No. 23). No. 73 Harley St was occupied by Gladstone from 1876–82 (rebuilt). *Queen's College* (43 Harley St), founded in 1848, is the oldest college for women in England. Wilkie Collins, who died at No. 82 in 1889, was born in 1824 at No. 11 (demolished) New Cavendish St. In this area note the many mews, narrow streets parallel with the main streets, once the place for horses and coaches, later garages for smart cars, and increasingly sought-after homes and offices.

New Cavendish St leads E to Marylebone High St, the continuation of the winding Marylebone Lane to the S, the original heart of the village of 'St. Mary's by the bourne'—later Marylebone, next to Tyburn Stream. The attractive High St, a relic of the old village, with boutiques, patisseries and the studios of Greater London Radio leads N to the Church of *St. Marylebone* (1813–17), (in Marylebone Road) by Thos. Hardwick, the church in which Robert Browning was married in 1846 (a Browning Room here contains relics of the poet). The Schulze swell organ was formerly in Charterhouse School. In a chapel in the N aisle is a painting of the Holy Family, by Benjamin West.

The site of the 18C parish church (demolished in 1949), a successor to that in which Francis Bacon was married (1606) is now laid out as a Garden of Rest in Marylebone High St. Lord Byron (1788) and Nelson's daughter Horatia (1801) were baptised in this church; Sheridan was married here to Miss Linley (1773). The graves of Charles and Samuel Wesley (died 1788 and 1837), James Gibbs (died 1754), John Rysbrack (1770), Allan Ramsay (1784) and George Stubbs (1806) remain in the Garden.

On the corner of Marylebone High St, and Marylebone Road to the E, a carved panel (1960, by E.J. Clack) shows Dickens and characters from six of his works written in 1839–51 when he lived in a house on this site. Opposite is the *Royal Academy of Music*, founded in 1822. For Madame Tussaud's, see below p 182.

Return along Marylebone High St to George St where at No. 85, Thos. Moore had his first lodgings in London. On the N side is the large R.C. church of *St. James's, Spanish Place* in a pure Early English style (by Goldie, 1885–90). Spanish Place (where a tablet at No. ·3 marks the house of Capt. Marryat) leads S to the secluded **Manchester Square**, built about 1770–88, and retaining some pleasant houses. At No. 2 lived Sir Julius Benedict, No. 3 was the home of John Hughlings Jackson, the neurologist, and No. 14 the residence of Lord Milner (plaques). In Duke St, just out of the S side of the square, Simon Bolivar stayed in 1810 (No. 4).

Hertford House, once the residence of the marquesses of Hertford and afterwards that of Sir Richard Wallace (d 1890) and of Lady Wallace (d 1897), lies on the N side. The ****Wallace Collection** (Pl. 5; 7) is the most important single collection in London for the lover of art in its various manifestations; in the choiceness and variety of its contents it resembles and rivals the Château of Chantilly in France. The great charm is in the arrangement, the beautiful furniture, porcelain, sculptures, and innumerable small works of ornamental art being admirably exhibited in the rooms containing the paintings. It is notable especially for its French paintings, furniture, and porcelain and for its European arms and armour.

The Wallace Collection, Hertford House, Manchester Square, W1. Tel. 071-935 0687. Access: Underground, Bond St. Open: Mon to Sat 10.00–17.00; Sun 14.00–17.00. Free.

All items on display are identified; a catalogue/guide is available. Below are some of the highlights. (Most of the important pieces are on the 1st Floor.)

The collection was started by the first Marquess and the foundation was laid by the second Marquess (1743–1822). The third Marquess figures as Lord Steyne in Thackeray's 'Vanity Fair' and as Lord Monmouth in Disraeli's 'Coningsby'. The fourth Marquess of Hertford (1800–70) resided chiefly in Paris and bequeathed the collection to his natural son, Sir Richard Wallace (1818–90), who removed it to London, added to it the collection of arms and armour, besides many pictures and Renaissance works of art, and changed the name of the house to Hertford House. In 1897 the priceless collection was bequeathed to the nation by Lady Wallace. The present gallery was opened in 1900.

Entrance Hall: Family portraits of the Hertfords by Reynolds and others. Room 1: British 18th and 19C paintings, French 18C furniture. Room 2: fine Boulle furniture, Sèvres porcelain and important European paintings including Murillo, 'Virgin and Child' and Rubens, 'Christ on the Cross'. Rooms 3 and 4: Medieval and Renaissance sculpture and works of art. Limoges enamels are on display. Room 4, originally the Smoking Room, houses an important collection of Italian maiolica, from the main centres of production; note the dish signed by Maestro Giorginio Andreoli of Gubbio dated 1525, one of the most important pieces of surviving maiolica. Original Minton tiles have been uncovered in the E alcove. Rooms 5–7: European armour, displayed in reverse chronological order (earliest pieces in Room 7); Oriental arms and armour in Room 8.

Room 9 was formerly the Housekeeper's Room and is now the shop, with paintings by Lawrence, 'Sally Siddons', and Landseer, 'Looking for crumbs from the rich man's table'.

Room 10 used to be the Breakfast Room; here is an important group of paintings by Richard Bonington, a British artist who worked in France (1802–1828).

Room 11 is the former Billiard Room: among the paintings are Lemoyne, 'Time revealing the Truth'—the artist committed suicide a few hours after completing the painting. Room 12, the Dining Room, has more superb Sèvres porcelain, and a collection of 18C French gold boxes.

The white marble staircase leading to the first floor is flanked by wrought-iron and bronze balustrades made for the Palais Mazarin in Paris. At the top of stairs canvases by Boucher, designs for Gobelins tapestries. Room 13: paintings by Guardi and Canaletto. Room 14: more Canaletto and imitators. In the Londonderry library cabinet Sèvres porcelain. Note the 'régulateur' clock with four dials, surmounted by figures of Time and Cupid; it belonged to Madame de Pompadour's godfather.

Room 15: three paintings by Murillo, a group of oil sketches by Rubens, and Rembrandt, 'Self-Portrait in a Cap'.

Room 16: figurative 17C Dutch paintings. Room 17: more small 17C Dutch pictures, mainly landscapes and seascapes including works by Van de Velde II and Hobbema. Room 18: mainly 17C Dutch Italianate paintings. Room 19: the largest room, 118ft long and housing the finest paintings including Murillo, 'Holy Family with St. John the Baptist', Van Dyck, 'Isabella Waerbeke', Rembrandt, 'Titus', Hals, 'The Laughing Cavalier', Rubens, 'Holy Family with Sts Elizabeth and

WALLACE COLLECTION

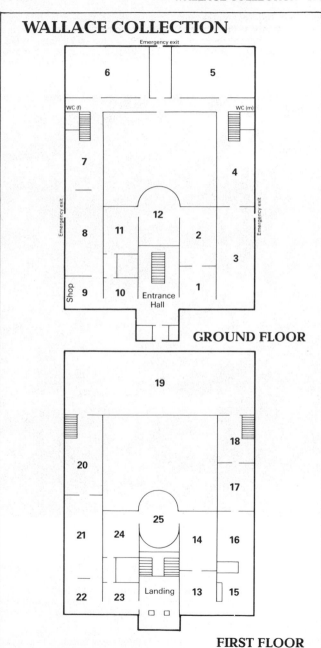

GROUND FLOOR

FIRST FLOOR

John the Baptist', Velasquez, 'Don Baltasar Carlos in Infancy',
Poussin, 'Dance to the Music of Time', and others.

Room 20: French paintings from 1820–60. Room 21: fine French
18C paintings and furniture including Watteau, Lancret, Pater and
Boucher, and a rococo style chest of drawers in kingwood and
mahogany made in 1739 for Louis XV's bedroom at Versailles.

*Gilles and his family, by Antoine Watteau (1684–1721), part of
the Wallace Collection*

Room 22: formerly Lady Wallace's bedroom. Fine paintings by
Boucher. Room 23: late 18C French and English paintings.

Room 24: still life paintings. Boule furniture and clocks. Room 25:
the Oval Drawing Room with later 18C French furniture, sculpture
and paintings, including a roll-top desk by Riesner with marquetry.
Collection of gold snuff boxes.

BAKER STREET (Pl. 5; 5), a busy thoroughfare which runs N to S, links
Marylebone Rd and Oxford St. Here are the headquarters of Marks

and Spencer plc. Bulwer Lytton was born at No. 68 in 1803. No. 82 was the headquarters of the Special Operations Executive (SOE) in 1940–45. Arnold Bennett died in 1931 at Chiltern Court (No. 97). In *Gloucester Place*, parallel with Baker St on the W, Wilkie Collins lived at No. 90 (now No. 65) in 1863–76 and 1883–88. To the W is Marylebone Station. Overlooking Marylebone Road, opposite the station, are the former offices of British Rail, built in 1800 as the Grand Central Hotel. The building is now being returned to its original use and will open in 1991 as the Windsor—a Ritz-Carlton luxury hotel.

At the N end of Baker St (see also p 182) are the offices of the Abbey National Building Society which reputedly employs one secretary just to deal with Sherlock Holmes' post. This is the site of the fictional 221B Baker St where Sherlock Holmes had his rooms. A 'Sherlock Holmes House' is opening to the public further along Baker Street at No. 239.

On the W side of Baker St lies *Portman Square*, in a sought-after area dating back to 1760. Here is the luxurious church of *St. Paul's, Portman Square* opened in 1970. *__Home House__* (No. 20) is the best surviving example of a Robert Adam town house (c 1773–76). The delightfully shaped rooms and staircase are decorated with paintings by *Zucchi*. Also here is a painting (unfinished) of the Holy Family by *Perino del Vaga*. The house belonged to the *Courtauld Institute of Art* of the University of London, founded by Samuel Courtauld in 1931, which owns the Witt Library of c 950,000 reproductions of European paintings and drawings from the Renaissance to the present day. The Institute has moved to Somerset House (see p 200). 21 Portman Square, a house designed by James Adam in 1772, is since 1972, the art department of the Royal Institute of British Architects. The *Heinz Gallery* contains a changing exhibition of architects' drawings, while the library consists of over 200,000 European architectural drawings (comprehensive photographic service).

Heinz Gallery, Portman Square, W1. Tel. 071-580 5533. This is an exhibition gallery for the Royal Institute of British Architects. Open during exhibitions Mon to Fri 11.00–17.00, Sat 10.00–13.00. Exhibitions are based on RIBA's collection of more than 200,000 architectural drawings; photographic exhibitions are also held here.

In *Seymour St*, to the W, a tablet at No. 30 marks the house of Edward Lear, now a small hotel by the same name. New Quebec St, with some pleasant shops, leads N to the attractive *Montagu Square* where Anthony Trollope lived (at No. 39) in 1873–80. The Swedish Embassy is in Montague Place. On the corner of George St and Seymour Place is Bryanston Court where Mrs. Wallis Simpson lived while entertaining the Prince of Wales between 1933–36. She later moved to Cumberland Terrace, Regent's Park.

George St leads W to Edgware Road (Pl. 4; 8) which runs N from Marble Arch in an almost straight line towards Edgware (7 miles), following ancient Roman *Watling St*. Off Harrowby St, a turning on the E side, an archway leads into the narrow *Cato St*, once notorious as the meeting-place of the 'Cato St Conspirators' (hanged at Newgate in 1820), whose object was the wholesale murder of the ministers of the Crown at a Cabinet dinner in Grosvenor Square. To the N, in Old Marylebone Road, the R.C. *Church of the Holy Rosary* makes interesting use of the arch. In Chapel St and Church St further N there are lively street markets.

Paddington Station (approached by Praed St) lies to the W. The Metropolitan Railway Company opened the first underground railway in the world in 1863 from Paddington to Farringdon. Paddington Station will be the London terminus for a new Heathrow rail link.

Marylebone Flyover takes the A40 (here motorway) across Edgware Rd to forge W through an area of '60s and '70s redevelopment, including the high security Police Station, 1971. On the edge *Paddington Green* (reached by sub-way) survives the church of *St. Mary* (1791), the successor of the church in which Hogarth was secretly married in 1729. Thomas Banks (died 1805) and Joseph Nollekens (died 1823), sculptors, and Benj. Haydon (died 1847), painter, have their tombs here. The actress Mrs. Sarah Siddons is buried at the N end of the churchyard. In the adjoining recreation ground there is a statue of Mrs. Siddons (1755–1831) in a dramatic pose based on the Reynolds portrait, in white marble by L.J. Chavalliaud (1897). In 1829 the first London omnibus service pulled by three horses started from the Green on its journey to the Bank of England along the Marylebone Road.

To the NW at the REGENT'S CANAL is a tranquil green oasis (left) named **'Little Venice'** by Browning and Byron. House-boats and bright Victorian houses line the canal. In *Bloomfield Road* (No. 60) is the starting-point of Jason's canal cruises which, in summer, make trips through Regent's Park to Camden Town, and then back to Little Venice. This triangular stretch of water became known as 'Browning's pool and Island'. Water-buses (London Waterbus Co) to the Zoo depart from Warwick Crescent (tel. 071-482 2550). Opposite the station (Warwick Avenue) a bas-relief by D. Thackway (1965) commemorates Browning, who lived at No. 19 Warwick Crescent, now demolished. Katherine Mansfield stayed at No. 2, a hostel, in 1908–9. The tow-path from Lisson Grove (Pl. 4; 3) to Regent's Park and Camden Town has been opened for walkers.

For about a mile beyond the Regent's Canal the Edgware Road is known as MAIDA VALE, and is flanked by pleasant dwellings and large blocks of flats. The name (the pronunciation of which time and gentility have corrupted) recalls the battle of Máida, by which the British under Sir John Stuart expelled the French from Calabria in 1806. On the right extends St. John's Wood (comp. p 179) and on the left north of Elgin Avenue is Paddington Recreation Ground with playing fields.

16 Fitzrovia, Regent's Park, London Zoo and Madame Tussaud's

Access: Underground, Oxford Circus, Baker St, Bus 74 for Regent's Park and London Zoo.

To the NE of Oxford Circus fashion workshops and wholesalers survive against the tide of increasing rents and environmental improvement. In *Great Portland St*, Boswell died at No. 122 (rebuilt). The *Central Synagogue* (left), N of New Cavendish St, was rebuilt in 1958. The huge new glass science building of the London Polytechnic dominates New Cavendish St to the N. Margaret St runs E to *All Saints Church*, a brick building by Butterfield (1849–59), with a fine tower and spire, important to the development of Gothic revival architecture.

Mortimer St, where (at No. 44) Nollekens, the sculptor, lived for fifty years, leads to the *Middlesex Hospital*, a noted teaching hospital founded in 1755. Here Kipling died in 1936. Behind the hospital is Foley St where Sir Edwin Landseer lived at No. 33 and Henry Fuseli No. 37. At 82 Great Tichfield St (demolished), parallel with Gt Portland St, Samuel Morse, the American pioneer of electric telegraphy, and C.R. Leslie, the Philadelphia artist, had rooms, in 1811, before moving to No. 8 Buckingham Place, now No. 141 Cleveland St, nearby. In *Charlotte St*, the main axis of a literary and Greek area to the E with many publishers, Greek and other more fashionable restaurants; in Goodge St, No. 76 was leased by Constable in 1822 until his death in 1837, and the Rossettis lived at No. 50 in 1847 (both houses demolished).

Pollock's Toy Museum in Scala St is based on Benjamin Pollock's shop which sold his toy-theatre sheets in Islington in Victorian times. The museum moved here in 1969 (the houses date from 1760); the collection appeals more to adults than children. A shop continues on the same premises.

Pollock's Toy Museum, 1 Scala St, W1. Tel. 071-636 3452. Open Mon to Sat 10.00–17.00; admission charge.

To the NE, the *British Telecom Tower*, formerly the Post Office Tower, used for television and satellite broadcasting and receiving, opened in 1964 and is 619ft high, including the 39ft-high mast. Its viewing platform and a revolving restaurant closed in 1975 after a bomb incident.

The compact *Fitzroy Square* was begun (E and S sides) by the Adam brothers in 1792. Ford Madox Brown lived at No. 37 where he entertained members of the pre-Raphaelite Brotherhood between 1867–82. Lord Salisbury, Prime Minister, lived at No. 29 (plaque); later Bernard Shaw occupied the same house from 1887–98. Roger Fry established the Omega Workshops at No. 33. This is the heart of 'Fitzrovia', a term used to describe this area, popular with writers, artists and academics.

Portland Place emerges in *Park Crescent*, a fine composition (1812–22) by John Nash. Outside the International Students' House (No. 1) is a copy of a bust of President Kennedy by J. Lipchitz (1965), original in the Library of Congress.

Cross Marylebone Rd (see below) and skirt Park Square Gardens to reach **Regent's Park** (Pl. 5; 4). Roughly circular in shape, the park has an area of 472 acres, and within its precincts is London Zoo.

Cars are admitted to the Inner Circle, (via Chester Road and York Bridge). Cafeteria in Queen Mary's Gardens and on Broad Walk.

An *Open Air Theatre* (with buffet) in Queen Mary's Gardens holds performances of Shakespeare plays in summer. *Bands* and puppet shows in summer.

Boats may be hired at the boat house near Hanover Gate (NE end of lake). Children's boating pond. For boats along Regent's Canal, see p 176.

Marylebone Park was claimed by Henry VIII as a royal hunting ground, and continued as such until Cromwell's day. It was laid out in its present style as an aristocratic 'garden suburb' from 1812 by Nash, and named after the Prince Regent, who contemplated building a country house here.

The park is encircled by a carriage-road known as the *Outer Circle*, the S half of which is flanked by fine monumental Regency *Terraces in the classical style, mainly by Nash. From S to N, across the E half of the park, runs the *Broad Walk* (1m) leading straight to the Zoo. In the SW portion of the park is an artificial lake of 22 acres (with many wildfowl), while to the N runs the Regent's Canal laid out by Nash in the 1820s. Near the S end of the Broad Walk are beautifully kept flower gardens; the fine greensward covering the greater part of the park is used for cricket, American football and other games.

York Gate to the S leads to the Inner Circle. To the W, beyond the bridge, stands the former buildings of Bedford College, a School of London University, founded in 1849 to provide women with a liberal education in secular subjects; it moved here in 1913 and to Surrey in

1985. The Holme is now residential and the College buildings now belong to Rockford College, Illinois, a private university. The buildings were rebuilt in 1948–50 after war damage.

The circular *Queen Mary's Gardens* (18 acres; entered by elaborate gates of 1933–35), within the Inner Circle, occupied from 1840 to 1932 by the Royal Botanic Society, is now one of the prettiest little public parks in London, with a rosery, a lily-pond, the Mermaid fountain (by W. McMillan, 1950), and the open-air theatre, see above.

St. John's Lodge, with a secluded rose-garden on the N side of the Inner Circle, was also part of Bedford College, now a private residence. It was enlarged by Barry in 1846–47 and altered in the '90s by Robert Weir Schulz. *Winfield House*, on the Outer Circle to the W, was built for Barbara Hutton in 1936, and is now the residence of the American Ambassador. Residents of Nash's *Hanover Lodge* (c 1827), across the road, included Thos. Cochrane, Joseph Bonaparte, king of Naples, and Adm. Earl Beatty. Lutyens' additions were swept away in 1961–64 when the building became a hall of residence for Bedford College. Nuffield Lodge is also in private ownership. *Regent's Lodge*, by Hanover Gate, houses the Islamic Cultural Centre next to the *Central Mosque* (1977). Visitors welcome at certain times. H.G. Wells (1866–1940) died at No. 13 Hanover Terrace, and Ralph Vaughan Williams (1872–1958), the composer, died at No. 11. The last home of Sir Edmund Gosse (1849–1928), the critic, was No. 17. In Sussex Place, turning S along the Outer Circle, beyond the new building of the Royal College of Obstetricians and Gynaecologists, the *London School of Business Studies* (founded in 1965; c 250 students) occupies a pleasant modern building in yellow stone (1970, by Westwood, Piet & Partners) concealed behind the fine Nash façade on the park. *St. Cyprian*, in Glentworth St to the S, has a light interior by Ninian Comper (1903). *York Terrace West* (now entered from the pleasant road to the S) has been faithfully rebuilt to Nash's design. At Park Square E is the surviving façade of the Diorama opened by Daguerre in 1823, closed in 1854. A restoration appeal was launched in 1990. Pugin designed the exterior for Nash.

On the E side of the park, the monumental terraces by Nash (Chester and Cumberland Terrace, 1825–26) facing the Outer Circle have their backs to Albany St. At the S end is the Royal College of Physicians, a fine building (1962–64) by Denys Lasdun. *St. Katharine's* church at the N end, formerly the chapel of St. Katharine's Royal Foundation (see Rte 27), was built in 1823. Restored in 1950–52, it is now the church of the Danish community in London. It has fine carving on the ceiling, two wooden figures of saints (by C.G. Cibber, 1696) from the old Danish church at Limehouse, and above the windows, 39 shields of arms of the Queens of England from Matilda to Queen Mary. In Albany St are territorial barracks, the Whitehouse and Christ Church (1837, by Pennethorne) where the Rev. William Dodsworth was the first vicar.

London Zoo in Regent's Park (officially the *Zoological Society of London*) was founded by Sir Stamford Raffles and Sir Humphry Davy (1826). Situated at the N end of Regent's Park, it is bounded on the N by Prince Albert Road and on the E by Broad Walk, and intersected by Regent's Canal and by the Outer Circle. Changing attitudes towards city-based zoos have led to the transfer of many animals to the more spacious Whipsnade Zoo in Bedfordshire. Recently the Zoo has received some direct Government funding to upgrade facilities for both animals and visitors and a major redevelopment programme is now underway.

London Zoo, Regent's Park, NW1. Tel. 071-722 3333. Open daily 09.00–18.00 (March to October); 10.00 to dusk (winter). Admission charge.

Access: Underground to Baker St, Bus 74; Underground, Camden Town. From April to Sept Zoo Waterbus from Little Venice. The main entrance is in the Outer Circle; car and coach park in Outer Circle Albany Road; Cafeterias, restaurant, shops, meeting rooms and lecture hall

The Zoological Gardens opened in five acres of Regent's Park to members of the Zoological Society only, in 1825. Decimus Burton laid out and designed the enclosures; the Raven's Cage, Giraffe House, the old Camel House/Clock Tower and the East Tunnel still remain. The public was admitted in 1847 and during the Great Exhibition thousands flocked to the Zoo. Peak attendance came in 1950 and reached 3 million a year but has since declined. The Zoo pioneered the exhibiting of exotic animals, including reptiles, insects, chimpanzees and giraffes. More recently, in 1974, the Zoo received two giant pandas (one has died) and one is in Mexico.

The striking aviaries on the N side of the Zoo were designed by Lord Snowdon; they can be seen from Regent's Canal. The Charles Clore Pavilion for Mammals (1967) incorporates reversed lighting so that nocturnal animals can be observed by day. The Penguin Pool designed by Lubetkin in the '30s and considered his finest work was refurbished by Peter Palumbo in 1988. The Mappin Terraces (listed) are due to be redeveloped providing a home for the giant panda and Chinese flora and fauna. The acquarium below will feature floor to ceiling display tanks including sharks. The refurbished Victorian parrot house will be home to invertebrates and there will be a new gorilla house. Already open is the Elephant Satellite Tracking Station and the Lifewatch Centre, both illustrating the Zoo's links with the conservation of animals in the world.

Institutions based here include the Wellcome Institute of Comparative Physiology, an animal hospital, the Nuffield Institute of Comparative Medicine, as well as the Zoological Society itself with a lecture room and library.

To the N of Regent's Park, separated from the Zoological Gardens by Prince Albert Road (where in 1855 Wagner lodged and completed 'Die Walküre'), rises *Primrose Hill*, a park of 61 acres. The top of the hill (219ft) commands a fine view. To the W of it is **St. John's Wood**, a residential district extending to Maida Vale, and once a favourite area with artists, now a wealthy residential area. Many of its attractive villas standing in large gardens have been replaced by large blocks of flats. Among its many distinguished residents were Sir Edwin Landseer, George Eliot, Thomas Hood, Charles Bradlaugh, Thomas Huxley, and Herbert Spencer. At the junction of Prince Albert Road, Park Road, St. John's Wood Road and Wellington Road to the NW of Regent's Park is the church of *St. John*, in which Joanna Southcott, the religious fanatic, (1750–1814) is buried (under the name of Goddard). J.S. Cotman (1782–1842), the painter, is buried in the churchard. *Grove House*, was built by Decimus Burton in 1823–24.

Wellington Road leads NW to St. John's Wood Station and Finchley Road. The Riding School (1825) of the Royal Horse Artillery barracks (rebuilt) off Wellington Road has been restored to use. St. John's Wood Road runs SW from the church to Maida Vale passing **Lord's Cricket Ground**, property of the Marylebone Cricket Club (the MCC) and headquarters of the English national game. The Museum of Cricket at Lord's Cricket Ground (open during matches only (10.30–17.00), or by appointment—tel. 071-289 1611 houses mementoes of the game including the original urn that contained the 'Ashes' (1882–83). the new stand with its 'floating roof' was designed by Michael Hopkins and opened in 1987.

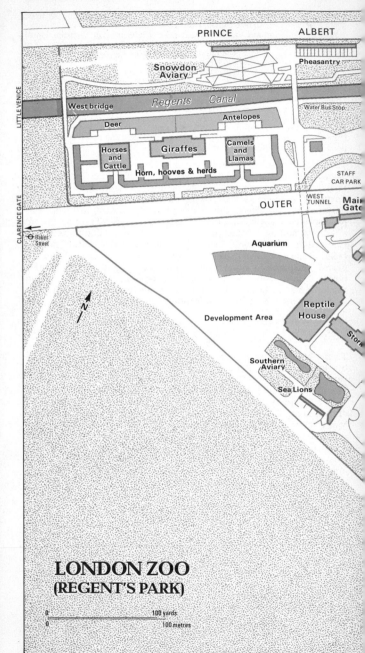

PRINCE   ALBERT

Pheasantry

Snowdon
Aviary

LITTLE VENICE

West bridge   Regents   Canal   Water Bus Stop

Deer   Antelopes

Horses
and
Cattle   Giraffes   Camels
and
Llamas

Horn, hooves & herds

STAFF
CAR PARK

OUTER   WEST
TUNNEL   Mai
Gate

CLARENCE GATE

Baker
Street

Aquarium

Reptile
House

Development Area

Stork

Southern
Aviary

Sea Lions

N

LONDON ZOO
(REGENT'S PARK)

0   100 yards
0   100 metres

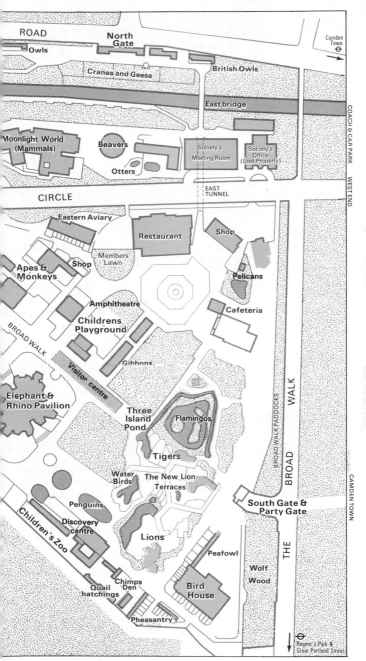

Grove End Road leads N from St. John's Wood Road to Abbey Road and the pedestrian crossing made famous by a Beatles' album cover, picturing them crossing the road from the EMI Studios on the (W side) where many of their recordings were made in the 1960s. The *Saatchi Gallery* of modern art is at 98A Boundary Road, NW8 (tel. 071-624 8299), in a former paint factory, further along Abbey Road.

Park Road leads S to Baker St (See p 174), and Marylebone Road with the conspicuous buildings of *Madame Tussaud's Waxworks* and the *London Planetarium.*

Madame Tussaud's, Marylebone Road, NW1. Tel. 071-935 6861. Access: Underground, Baker St. Open Mon to Fri 10.00–17.30, Sat and Sun 09.30–17.30. Admission charge (an inclusive ticket with the London Planetarium is available, see below). Crowded in summer; go early or late.

Madame Tussaud (1761–1850) was employed at the court of Louis XVI to make wax-figures. She was imprisoned during the Revolution and took models from the heads of guillotine victims. She fled to London in 1802 with many of her original moulds; those beheaded in the French revolution can be seen in the Chamber of Horrors. The first exhibition opened in Baker St in 1835. The present building opened in 1884 and was restored after bomb-damage. The exhibition is continually updated with popular figures of the day from the world of politics, the arts and sports. Pop and rock stars are now featured at the new Rock Circus, see p 113.

London Planetarium incorporating the Laserium, Marylebone Road, NW1. Tel. 071-486 1121. Access as above. Open 11.00–16.30; Planetarium presentations at intervals; Laserium in early evening. The Planetarium was built in 1958 and features a Zeiss projector with 20,000 separate parts to create 9000 stars. Lectures are held on a variety of subjects. Laser shows with pop and classical music use the same equipment plus lasers.

Opposite are the huge buildings (1971, by Kinner) of the architecture and town planning departments, etc. of the London Polytechnic.

17 Bloomsbury

A.   Bloomsbury to Euston Road

Access: Underground, Tottenham Court Road, Holborn, Warren St (for this walk start at Tottenham Court Road).

The green squares of **Bloomsbury** (Pl. 7; 3) date mainly from the 18C and early 19C. Their modest well-proportioned terraced houses have gradually disappeared as extensions to London University, hotels and offices encroach on the area. Many smaller hotels occupy houses in the formal streets. Bloomsbury is linked with the names of Virginia and Leonard Woolf, Clive and Vanessa Bell, Lytton Strachey, and others, who before the First World War, began here, an eccentric association of intellectual and artistic interests later known as 'The Bloomsbury Group'.

St Giles Circus (Pl. 6; 6), is dominated by the notorious Centre Point (1963–67; R. Seifert and Partners)—this speculative tower stood empty for many years on its sterile, windswept traffic island—due to be transformed at ground level. *Tottenham Court Road*, running N, noted for its furniture, hi-fi and camera dealers, has something of a run-down appearance. The undistinguished Dominion Theatre (1929) on the NE corner is used for ballet and also as a cinema. This site may be redeveloped. On the corner of Gt Russell St (comp. below) *stands the Y Hotel* (1976), with a splendid recreation and sports club (annual membership fee) of the YMCA. Oxford St is continued E from St. Giles Circus as *New Oxford St.*

Before New Oxford St was constructed in 1849 through the poverty-stricken and congested area known as the 'rookery of St. Giles', the main thoroughfare E followed the shallow curve on the S (now one-way W), via St. Giles High St to High Holborn. A hospital for lepers (named after their patron saint St. Giles) was founded here in 1101 by Matilda, Queen of Henry I: Shaftesbury Ave and St. Giles High St follow the line of the walls. One of the first cases of the Great Plague in London occurred among Flemish weavers in the parish in 1664.

In High St the church of **St. Giles in the Fields**, built in 1731–33 by Flitcroft, and well restored in 1954, still preserves a 'rural' setting in the face of continuous traffic. Above the W gate is an oak relief of the Resurrection carved in 1687. Inside, the Father Smith organ (1671; partly remodelled), and the pulpit (1676) survive from an earlier church. In the S aisle the upper part of a pulpit used by John and Charles Wesley in 1743–91 (formerly in West St Chapel) is preserved. In the S porch is the tombstone of Richard Penderel (died 1671), the woodman who guarded the 'royal' oak and thus secured the escape of Charles II after the Battle of Worcester. In the N aisle George Chapman (died 1634), translator of Homer, has an appropriate tomb said to have been designed by Inigo Jones, and here too Andrew Marvell (died 1678), the poet, is commemorated. The recumbent effigy of Lady Frances Kniveton was carved by Joshua Marshall. A memorial to Flaxman (carved by the sculptor) was placed in the porch in 1930. In the churchyard is an architectural monument to Sir John Soane. The baptism is recorded in the parish register of Milton's daughter Mary in 1648, and in 1818 of Allegra, daughter of Byron, and of Shelley's children, William and Clara.

Bloomsbury St and Bloomsbury Way branch N from New Oxford St. In *Bloomsbury Way* the church of *St. George's, Bloomsbury* was built by Hawksmoor in 1716–31. The Corinthian portico is impressive, and the steeple is surmounted by a statue of George I. Anthony Trollope was baptised in the church, which was the scene of the 'Bloomsbury Christening' in Dickens' 'Sketches by Boz'.

Bloomsbury St (or the parallel Museum and Coptic Sts with bookshops and antique dealers) lead to the **British Museum** (see p 188). At the corner of Great Russell St is the home of the *Trades Union Congress* (1958). Bloomsbury St runs through the E side of **Bedford Square**, built around 1776, and presenting some characteristic examples of the style of the Adam brothers.

The *Architectural Association* is housed in Nos 34– 36; Lord Eldon (1751–1838), the reactionary Lord Chancellor, lived at No. 6, and Henry Cavendish, the natural philosopher, died in 1810 at No. 11.

N of the square, in Store St, are the *Department of Oriental Manuscripts and Printed Books* of the British Library and the *Building Centre* (No. 26), founded in 1930 'to provide a permanent exhibition and information service for the free use of all interested in good building' (open Mon to Fri 09.30–17.15, Sat 10.00–16.00). Across Tottenham Court Rd, the *Whitefield Memorial Church* (by E.C. Butler; 1956–58) was built on the site of the chapel erected for George Whitefield (1714–70), the famous preacher.

The severe and rectilinear *Gower St* continues N past the *Royal Academy of Dramatic Art*, founded by Sir H. Beerbohm Tree (d 1917), to University College (see below), and Euston Road.

At No. 2 a tablet commemorates Millicent Fawcett (1847–1929), a pioneer of women's rights. On the right, at the corner of Keppel St, is the *London School of Hygiene and Tropical Medicine*, established in 1922. At No. 69 William de Morgan (1839–1917) was born, and George Dance the Younger (1741–1825) lived and died at No. 91. No. 105 is the Royal National Institute for the Deaf. The Biological Department of London University (E side) occupies the site of a house where Charles Darwin lived in 1838–42. Giuseppe Mazzini's home was at No. 183 (N of Euston Rd) in 1837–40.

Turn E along Montague Place between the N façade of the British Museum and the Senate House of the **University of London**. Many of the administrative buildings here dominated by the central tower of the Senate House, begun in 1933, are by Charles Holden. Much of the University's work of instruction and research is carried on in institutions far removed from the administrative centre; but a number of departments and dependencies are concentrated in the area in new buildings or in the terraced houses in neighbouring squares. The fine Senate House Library is accessible to visiting scholars.

London was the last of the great European capitals to found a university. In 1836 a charter was granted constituting a University of London, with the power of granting academic degrees, without religious tests, to students of University College, King's College, and certain other affiliated institutions. In 1858 the examinations were thrown open to all students without restriction, and twenty years later (in 1878) the University of London became the first academic body in the United Kingdom to admit women as candidates for degrees on equal terms with men. Hitherto a purely examining body, it was reconstituted in 1898–1900 as a teaching university, instruction being given in existing colleges and schools. University College and King's College were incorporated as 'integral parts' of the University; these and other institutions are 'Schools of the University', each controlled by its own governing body; while others have teachers 'recognised by the University'. Students attending these colleges are known as 'internal students'; those presenting themselves for examination only are 'external students'.

Birkbeck College, founded in 1823 as a scientific and technical institute, now offering part-time degree courses for mature students, is in Malet St. The first part of the building of the *Students' Union*, adjoining on the N, was opened in 1955, while on the E side are the *School of Oriental and African Studies* (SOAS) and the *Institute of Historical Research*. Other institutes occupy temporary quarters in Russell Sq., to the SE. Between Russell Sq. and Woburn Sq. new buildings by Denys Lasdun house the *Institutes of Education and Law* and an extension to SOAS.

RUSSELL SQUARE (Pl. 7; 3) laid out in 1801, is the largest square in central London, with the exception of Lincoln's Inn Fields. On the S side of the garden is a statue of the fifth Duke of Bedford (1765–1805) by Westmacott. The *Royal Institute of Chemistry* (by Sir J.J. Burnet) is at No. 30. Over the entrance is a seated figure of Priestley. The attractive *Bedford Place* connects the square with BLOOMSBURY SQUARE (Pl. 7; 5; underground car park), one of the earliest squares in London (c 1665). The statue of Charles James Fox (1749–1806) in its garden is by Westmacott. No. 17, occupied and refaced by Nash in 1782–83, was the home of the *Pharmaceutical Society* since 1841, now in Lambeth.

To the NW of Russell Square new buildings for the University of London intrude into *Woburn Square*. In *Christ Church* Christina Rossetti (d 1894) is commemorated by a reredos with paintings by Burne-Jones.

On the W side of the square is the **Courtauld Institute**, previously the location of the Courtauld Institute collection of paintings, which has now moved to Somerset House, see p 200. The *Warburg Institute* (Woburn Square), beyond the Courtauld Institute, faces Gordon Square. A relief panel of nine muses which decorated the original building at 1 Gordon Square has been retained in the entrance hall. The Institute, which is part of the University of London, is concerned with the study of the classics, European art and iconography. It has a large library and photographic collection. Facing the Institute is the *Church of Christ the King*, in Byng Place, a huge Gothic revival church, built in 1853 for the sect known as the Irvingites but now used by the University. At 53 Gordon Square is the unique **Percival David Foundation of Chinese Art**.

Percival David Foundation of Chinese Art, 53 Gordon Square, WC1. Tel. 071-387 3909. Open Mon to Fri 10.30–13.00, 14.00–17.00. Admission free. Access: Underground, Euston Square.
    Sir Percival David presented his collection of Chinese ceramics and his library to the University in 1951 and a further bequest was made by Mountstuart Elphinstone. The collection on three floors includes Sun, Yuan, Ming and Ch'ing porcelain (AD 960–1912) and the library may be used by scholars, on application.

Virginia Woolf lived at No. 46 Gordon Square before her marriage and Lytton Strachey and Clive Bell also lived in the Square.

    Backing on to Gordon St are the buildings of **University College** (main entrance in Gower St). It was founded in 1826 and opened in 1828, with the title of University of London, by Lord Brougham, Thomas Campbell, James Mill, and other friends of religious liberty, with the object of affording, on non-denominational lines, and 'at a moderate expense the means of education in literature, science, and art'. In 1900 it became a 'school' of the University of London, with which it was incorporated in 1907. The central building with its Corinthian portico and fine dome was designed by W. Wilkins; on all sides are extensions and additions. In the hall beneath the dome is the *Flaxman Gallery* (open by appointment only), containing original models and drawings by John Flaxman (1755–1826). In the cloisters below is the 'Marmor Homericum', with Homeric subjects in marble niello by Baron Triqueti, presented by Grote, the historian.

Flaxman Galleries, University College, Gower St, WC1. Tel. 071-387 7050. Jeremy Bentham's embalmed body, now a clothed skeleton with a wax head, is shown on application and during term time.

The *Petrie Museum of Egyptian Archaeology*, open Mon to Fri 10.00–12.00, 13.15–17.00, closed 4 weeks in summer, is a university teaching collection in cramped premises which includes outstanding archaeological finds from prehistoric to Coptic periods.
    Also at the University College in the South Wing is the Mocatta Library and Museum of the Jewish Historical Society. The Gustave Tuck Lecture Theatre is by Albert Richardson (1954).

The central *Collegiate Building, Union* and *Theatre* are in new buildings in Gordon St. The *Slade School of Art*, established under the will of Felix Slade (1790–1868) the art collector, is part of the college. The *Bartlett School of Architecture* is now part of the School of Environmental Studies. In Gower St is the *University College Hospital*, founded in 1834 but the present medical school dates from 1906. The first operation in Europe under ether was performed at the Hospital in 1846.

East of Gordon Sq. lies *Tavistock Square* (Pl. 6; 4) with a statue of Mahatma Gandhi (1869–1948) by Fredda Brilliant (1966). Off the NE corner of the square the HQ of *British Medical Association* stands near the site of Tavistock House, occupied by Dickens in 1850–60. Here he wrote 'Bleak House' and 'Little Dorrit'. Opposite is *Woburn House*, a Jewish centre.

Jewish Museum, Woburn House, Upper Woburn Place, WC1. Tel. 071-388 4525. Access: Underground Russell Square; Open Tues to Thurs (Fri during summer) 10.00–16.00, Sun (Fri during winter) 10.00–12.45. Closed Jewish holidays. Admission free.

This collection consisting of ritual objects was founded in 1932 to show the richness of the Anglo-Jewish heritage. On display are ceramics, embroidery, manuscripts, silverwork, and an Ark in which the scrolls of the law are kept.

Tavistock Place leads E to Hunter St where the house (No. 54) in which John Ruskin (1819–1900) was born was demolished in 1969.

Endsleigh St, with the first headquarters (1922) of the National Union of Students (No. 3), leads out of the NW corner of the square to Endsleigh Gardens. Turn left to reach the *Wellcome Institute* (entrance on Euston Rd), an important scientific foundation established in 1913 by Sir Henry Wellcome (1853–1936). The dioramas showing the history of medicine were transferred to the Science Museum in 1980, and the Wellcome Institute's Library and facilities are now available to doctors and students on application only. To the E, *Duke's Road* and *Woburn Walk* preserve quaint 18C shop-fronts. W.B. Yeats lived at No. 5 Woburn Walk in 1895–1919.

EUSTON ROAD (Pl. 6; 2), the N boundary of Bloomsbury, continues the line of Marylebone Rd E to King's Cross. It forms part of the 'New Road' laid out in 1754–56 to connect Islington with Paddington, and now bears the heavy traffic of the Inner Ring Road. *Friend's House* (1926, by H. Lidbetter), the headquarters of the Society of Friends, contains documents relating to William Penn and the foundation of Pennsylvania. To the E of *Euston Square* is **Euston Station** rebuilt in 1963–68, when, against considerable opposition, the old classical entrance arch was demolished. The statue in the forecourt is of Robert Stephenson who, with Philip Hardwick, designed the original station in 1836. Across Eversholt St rises the 'new' *St. Pancras Church*, built in 1819–22 by Inwood (restored in 1951–53) in a 'Grecian' style, a pastiche of various buildings in Athens. On the N side of Euston Rd huge new office buildings (1968–70) tower above the *Elizabeth Garrett Anderson Hospital* and the *St. Pancras Library* and *Shaw Theatre* (1971).

The Shaw Theatre, Euston Road, NW1, (founded in 1971), tel. 071-388 1394, is part of a complex which includes a library. It was named after George Bernard Shaw and is used by the National Youth Theatre, touring theatre companies and the fringe.

The new British Library is being built on the former rail goods yard here adjoining Midland Road. Completion is scheduled for 1993 and the transfer of books from the British Museum and other storage will start in 1991. Designed by Prof. Colin St John Wilson and commissioned by the PSA, the new building will rise in steps from the piazza on Euston Road with an entrance in brick and marble. It will provide four levels of storage below ground with some 15km of shelving (accessible) and 280km (closed access) and cater for over 600 readers at a time. An exhibition area and conference centre form part of the development.

St. Pancras Station and Chambers, a Gothic fantasy, tower above the modern **King's Cross Station**. The station, completed in 1867, was one of the wonders of Victorian engineering, a 100ft-high glass and iron structure. The adjoining *Midland Grand Hotel* was designed by George Gilbert Scott and based on his rejected plans for government offices in Whitehall. It was described as one of the most sumptuous hotels in the Empire and features an imperial staircase. Used as offices since 1935 and known as St. Pancras Chambers, it is now being redeveloped as a hotel.

In *Pancras Road*, which leads NW, is (900 yards) *St Pancras Old Church*, of very ancient foundation, but practically rebuilt in 1848. The church is kept locked because of vandalism; the attractive interior may be seen at the services. In the old graveyard, now a public garden entered through elaborate gates, Mary Godwin is said to have first met Shelley in 1813 beside the grave of her mother, Mary Wollstonecraft (died 1797), whose remains were transferred to Bournemouth in

1851. John Flaxman (died 1826), and John Christian Bach (died 1782) are buried here, and Sir John Soane (died 1837), with his wife, in the mausoleum he designed for her in 1815. An ash tree offers protection to a curious mass of gravestones. To the E the GRAND UNION CANAL (with a nature reserve) flows behind King's Cross Station. This is the site for one of the largest redevelopment projects currently planned in London on 134 acres of mostly derelict land. Norman Foster and a team of international architects have designed the project for the London Regeneration Consortium, with a mix of offices and homes, including a large park and leisure complex. Part of the scheme will be the new, largely underground, Channel Tunnel Terminal between Kings and St. Pancras stations. Building could start in 1991.

Pentonville Road leads E towards the Angel, passing on the N the former *St. James's Churchyard* where Joseph Grimaldi (1779–1837), the famous clown, was buried. A memorial garden has been created on the site.

A plaque at the back of the Royal Scot Hotel at 100 King's Cross Road marks a house in Percy Circus where Lenin stayed in 1905. A memorial designed by Lubetkin for Lenin is now buried in the ground underneath a block of flats. Lenin also lived in Holford Square in 1902 (near King's Cross) and frequented the former *Pindar of Wakefield* pub, Gray's Inn Road, now the home of Aba Daba and renamed Water Rats Pub and Music Hall (regular evening performances).

Gray's Inn Road, a long and uninteresting commercial thoroughfare, leads S from King's Cross to Holborn. Here are the former offices of 'The Times' (established 1785) which moved so dramatically to Wapping in January 1986 (see p 279). Independent Television News will move from Wells St into the redeveloped building in 1990. A more pleasant route S diverges to the right opposite St. Pancras into Judd St. Hunter St continues down to *Brunswick Square*, overpowered by the harsh Brunswick Centre of flats and shops. At No. 40 are the headquarters of the **Thomas Coram Foundation for Children** (formerly the *Foundling Hospital*), founded in 1739 by Captain Thomas Coram (d 1751), which still cares for unfortunate children, in Berkhamsted. The Foundling Hospital occupied the site of Coram's Fields (see below) from 1724–1926.

Thomas Coram Foundation, 40 Brunswick Square, WC1 Tel. 071 270 2424. Open Mon to Fri 10.00 16.00, admission charge. (Sometimes closed at short notice; telephone to check.)

The present house contains many relics of the old building, including part of the oak staircase and the beautiful Court Room, re-erected here with the original woodwork, ceiling, and plaster decoration; also interesting paintings by Hogarth (*March to Finchley; Portrait of Coram), Kneller (Portrait of Handel), Gainsborough, etc.; sculptures by Rysbrack and Roubiliac; and a cartoon by Raphael. Other mementoes include a MS. score of the 'Messiah' and other Handelian relics, and a number of 'tokens' formerly left with abandoned infants. Handel and Hogarth both took a great interest in the hospital and its children, and readers of 'Little Dorrit' will remember that Tattycoram was a 'Foundling'.

To the SE extend **CORAM'S FIELDS**, a playground with Georgian colonnades, owned by the Foundation and open to children under 18 years (9–dusk). To the N the delightful *St. George's Gardens* occupy a disused cemetery. Across the Fields at the corner of Guilford St and Doughty St stands *London House*, a hostel and centre of collegiate life for male students from overseas, by Sir Herbert Baker. In the undulating *Doughty St*, with the vista at each end closed by trees, Sydney Smith lived at No. 14 in 1803–06. **Dickens House** (No. 48), the home of Charles Dickens in 1837–39, the period of 'Oliver Twist' and 'Nicholas Nickleby', is now a museum of great interest.

Dickens House Museum, 48 Doughty St, WC1. Tel. 071-405 2127. Open Mon to Sat 10.00–17.00; last admission 16.30. Admission charge. Access: Underground, Chancery Lane; Russell Square.

Besides the most comprehensive Dickens library in the world, the museum contains numerous portraits, illustrations, signed letters, and personal relics.

The Suzannet Gift (1971) includes parts of the MSS of 'Pickwick Papers' and

'Nicholas Nickleby', Dickens' correspondence, illustrations for the novels, etc. In the basement is a reproduction of the 'Dingley Dell' kitchen. On the first floor is Dickens' Study. The Drawing Room has been arranged as it would have appeared in Dickens' time. The House combines well its role of a museum while recreating the atmosphere of the home of the writer.

Lamb's Conduit St leads S from Coram's Fields and crosses *Great Ormond St*, which retains several attractive houses of the Queen Anne period. At its W end are the *Hospital for Sick Children* founded in 1851, and the *Royal London Homoeopathic Hospital*. No. 23 was the home of John Howard (1726–90), the philanthropist.

The Home Office Department for Alien's Registration is in Lamb's Conduit St; in the Victorian *Lamb* pub, at No. 94, Hogarth prints decorate the walls and the original snobscreens remain.
    In the quiet QUEEN SQUARE, with a statue that may represent Queen Charlotte, Queen Anne, or Mary II, William Morris had his residence and workshops in 1865–81 at No. 26 (rebuilt, now the *National Hospital for Nervous Diseases* founded in 1860). Nearby is the *Italian Hospital* (1884), and the church of *St. George the Martyr*, founded in 1706, which once provided annual Christmas dinners for 100 apprentice sweeps.

Beyond Theobald's Road (where at No. 22 Benjamin Disraeli was born in 1804) Lamb's Conduit Passage leads to RED LION SQUARE, named after the Red Lion Inn, now the *Old Red Lion* at 72 High Holborn, where the bodies of Cromwell, Ireton and Bradshaw were laid out in 1661 after being disinterred from Westminster Abbey. They were taken the next day to Tyburn where the bodies were desecrated and heads placed on poles at Westminster Hall. The Square was laid out in 1684 and the W side is now occupied by the former Holborn College, now part of Central London Polytechnic.
    On the S side is No. 17, in which D.G. Rossetti lodged in 1851 and where Morris and Burne-Jones lived together in 1856–59. John Harrison (1693–1776), inventor of the chronometer, and Jonas Hanway (1712–86), who has the reputation of being the first habitual user of an umbrella in London, also lived in the square. At the NE corner is *Conway Hall* (1929) the seat of the South Place Ethical Society, a pioneer of religious-humanist thought (chamber concerts on Sundays in October to April). There is a bronze bust of Bertrand Russell by Marcelle Quinton (1980), and a bronze statue of veteran international peace campaigner Lord Brockway was erected in the square in 1985.

In SOUTHAMPTON ROW, to the W, the *Central School of Art and Design* uses the theatre named in honour of Jeannetta Cochrane who taught at the school from 1914 to 1957. Many productions for children are staged here in the Jeannetta Cochrane Theatre. On the corner of Catton St, to the S, the Baptist Church House has a statue of Bunyan.

The streets leading S from the square run into **High Holborn** (comp. Rte 20).

B.   The British Museum and British Library

The ****BRITISH MUSEUM** (Pl. 6; 5), unrivalled in the world for the richness and variety of its contents, is entered from Great Russell St in Bloomsbury, a few yards N of New Oxford St, or from Montague Place, on the N. In the pediment of the colonnaded main façade (S) are allegorical sculptures by Westmacott.

The British Museum was founded in 1753, its nucleus being the Cottonian and Harleian MSS and Sir Hans Sloane's collections. These, with subsequent additions, including the Egyptian Antiquities, the Elgin Marbles, and the King's Library (i.e. George III's), were contained until 1852 in *Montagu House*, built by Robert Hooke in 1686 on the site of the existing edifice and opened as the first public secular national museum in the world in 1759. In 1823 the main building was begun by Robert and Sydney Smirke, and in 1852 Montagu House was demolished and the present S front completed; the monumental neo-classical screen was built in the 1840s. The Reading Room (by Sydney Smirke) and Library were opened in 1857, the SE wing in 1884, and the King Edward VII Building in 1914.

The S façade of the British Museum, started in 1823, by Robert and Sydney Smirke

In 1973, the British Library formed from the library departments of the British Museum and various other national libraries became a separate institution. Pressure on space has increased and a new building near St. Pancras Station is now under construction and occupation will start in 1991 with completion of phase 1 in 1993. The removal of the British Library will release space for the British Museum to expand which may mean further changes to the layout which has already changed considerably in the last few years. In this description, the contents of the British Museum and British Library are therefore treated separately, although for the time being they may be viewed together, and only the highlights of each collection have been mentioned. Several visits would be necessary to do justice to the enormous range and variety of items on display.

British Museum, Great Russell St, WC1. Tel. 071-636 1555. Open Mon to Sat 10.00–17.00, Sun 14.30–18.00. Admission free, except for special exhibitions. Access: Underground, Holborn, Tottenham Court Road. Lectures, Mon to Sat 13.15, Gallery talks, Mon to Sat 11.30. Bookshop, guide books, self-service café.

BRITISH MUSEUM

Ground Floor

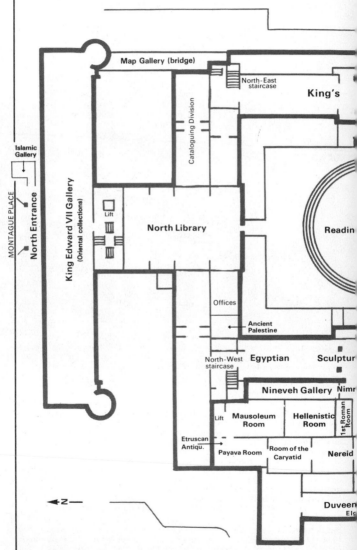

Map Gallery (bridge)

North-East staircase

King's

Cataloguing Division

Islamic Gallery

North Entrance

King Edward VII Gallery (Oriental collections)

MONTAGUE PLACE

Lift

North Library

Readin

Offices

Ancient Palestine

North-West staircase

Egyptian

Sculptur

Nineveh Gallery   Nimr

Lift   Mausoleum Room   Hellenistic Room

1st Roman Room

Etruscan Antiqu.   Payava Room   Room of the Caryatid   Nereid

◄Z—

Duveen
Elg

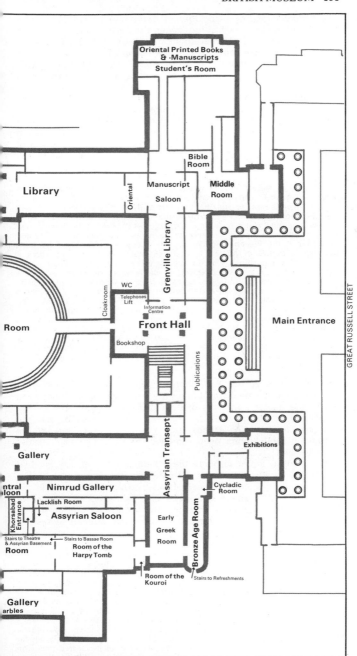

The *collection of Greek and Roman Antiquities* is arranged in the West Wing in chronological order from the Early Bronze Age to the Roman Imperial Period, from Room 1 to Room 15. In Room 8 is the Duveen Gallery, containing the famous *Elgin Marbles*, named after Thomas Bruce, seventh earl of Elgin, Ambassador to the Porte, who in 1801–03 collected numerous sculptures which he saw being destroyed daily at Athens, and in 1816 sold them to the British Government for £35,000, i.e. half what they had cost him to remove. The collection includes other sculptures from the Erechtheion and elsewhere, and casts from marbles which were left *in situ*. The most important of the Elgin Marbles are the sculptures of the Parthenon or temple of Athena Parthenos (the Virgin), the patron goddess of Athens, which stood on the Acropolis, and was dedicated in 438 BC.

The sculptures were carved between 447 and 432 BC, when Pericles was leader of Athens. Pheidias, the sculptor, supervised his great building schemes, Ictinus was the principal architect of the Parthenon, and Callicrates was the second architect or perhaps the contractor. The gold and ivory (chryselephantine) statue of Athena, 40ft high, which stood in the temple, was made by Pheidias, and is believed to have been finished in 439 BC and dedicated at the Panathenaic Festival the following year. The Parthenon remained a temple of Athena for the next nine centuries, after which it became a Christian church. The E Pediment was ruined by the builders of the Byzantine apse. At the fall of Athens to the Turks it was converted into a mosque. In 1674 a draughtsman, probably Jacques Carrey of Troyes, made drawings of the architectural and sculptural remains of the Parthenon. These form an invaluable record, as in 1687, during the siege of Athens by the Venetians, the centre of the temple (then used as a powder magazine by the Turks) was destroyed through an explosion caused by a shell from the besiegers' army. The W Pediment was shattered in falling during its attempted removal by Morosini.—The S Slip Room, left of the entrance to the Duveen Gallery, contains models, drawings and photographs illustrating the structure, sculptures, and history of the Parthenon. 'Sound guide'-commentaries are available.

The sculptures of the Parthenon are generally held to be the greatest ever executed. In London are preserved 15 metopes from the S side, major fragments of both pediments, and 247ft (rather under half) of the frieze. What survives of the remainder is in the Acropolis Museum in Athens, that part hitherto *in situ* on the Parthenon itself having been removed in 1976 to prevent further deterioration.

The Central Room displays the **FRIEZE alone at eye level. It represents in low relief the Panathenaic procession up to the Acropolis, the greatest Athenian festival, which culminated in the investiture of the image of Athena in a sacred violet 'peplos' or robe. This frieze ran above the porches and around the outside of the cella wall, and must have been curiously difficult to see. Its condition varies greatly.

The W FRIEZE (right of door) shows horsemen preparing to take part in the Panathenaic procession. As the procession, which started at the SW corner, approaches the NW corner it gathers speed, and the two leading horsemen (2, 3) on the last slab are already cantering. N FRIEZE (turning left and passing the NW angle). The procession moves forward at a trot, the number of horses increases; the fine leading *Horsemen are seen on slab XXIV (NE angle). On the left of the slab is the inside of the rim of a shield and an arm holding it (belonging to a chariot on the opposite wall which continues the N frieze) which indicates that chariots have now joined the procession, followed by citizens and animals being led to sacrifice. E FRIEZE. Girls carrying vessels for use in the sacrifices, magistrates, and the ceremony of the sacred peplos in the presence of deities and attendants. The S FRIEZE is much more fragmentary, but the rendering of cattle and galloping horses on slabs XXXVIII and XXX (SW end of wall) is especially noteworthy (S frieze continued on SE end of opposite wall).

In the N Transept in the centre is the **E PEDIMENT GROUP. These sculptures are in the round and had a correspondingly projecting architectural frame. The subject represented was the birth of Athena, fabled to have sprung fully armed from the brain of Zeus.

The central group probably consisted of Zeus with Athena and Hephaistos on either side. At the left (S) end is Helios (A), the sun-god, driving his chariot out of the sea at daybreak; in front are two heads of horses from his team (B, C). Facing Helios is a male figure (D) of wonderful power and grace, seated on the skin of a lion or panther; he is thought to be Heracles, or to personify Mount Olympus, or to be Dionysos, the wine god. The head (the only remaining one in the group), though damaged, heightens the noble impression of the figure and justifies the fame of the Pheidian School. Two draped and seated female goddesses (E, F) are Demeter and her daughter Persephone. The young girl running towards them (G) is Iris or Hebe, the cup-bearer, who starts back in alarm at the miraculous event which has just taken place. The identity of the group of three figures (K, L, M) is doubtful; the Clouds, Thalassa (the sea) in the lap of Gaia (the earth), Aphrodite in the lap of her mother Dione, or the three Hesperid nymphs, are suggestions that have been made. The sculpture in the extreme right angle is one of the horses of Selene, goddess of the moon, descending into the waves.
On the walls are metopes XXVI–XXXII (see below).

In the S Transept in the centre are fragments from the **W PEDIMENT GROUP, which represents the contest between Athena and Poseidon for the land of Attica.

According to the myth, Poseidon with his trident made a salt spring gush from the rock of the Acropolis; Athena caused the first olive to grow and was awarded the victory. The olive tree probably filled the centre of the pediment. Athena and Poseidon have been conducted to it by Hermes and Iris, the two torsos (H, N) to the left and right of the centre. Iris is identified by holes for the wings and by the short robe. The figure (A) in the N (left) angle of the pediment is a river god of Athens, either Kephisos or Ilissos; it has suffered less damage and is one of the most beautiful of the sculptures. The torso to the right of Iris (O) is the driver of Poseidon's chariot (as may be seen from Carrey's drawing), perhaps Amphitrite, his wife. The figure (Q) to the right may have been a sea nymph.

On the walls are *METOPES II–IX, square panels carved in high relief, which alternated with the triglyphs above the architrave all round the building. The 15 originals (eight here and seven in the N Transept) together with 41 still remaining (much decayed) in Athens and one in Paris, are all that remain of the original series of 92. The metopes represent the battle of the Lapiths (a Thessalian people) and the Centaurs, one of whom tried to carry off the bride of Peirithoös, the Lapith king.

The Etruscan antiquities in Room 11 include remarkable painted wall panels, and a polychrome terracotta sarcophagus with a reclining figure.

In Room 14 is the famous *Portland Vase* (late 1C BC, or early 1C AD) of blown glass in two layers, white on cobalt blue, the white layer cut away like a cameo to leave a frieze of figures. It takes its name from the Dukes of Portland who owned it. The vase was deliberately shattered by a madman in 1845 but pieced together. The decoration probably shows the wooing of the sea nymph Thetis by the mortal Peleus. In 1989 the vase was deliberately broken, reassembled and restored closer to its original appearance.

From here stairs lead down to the basement and the Wolfson Galleries and several rooms of Greek and Roman sculptures, including the collection of 18th century dilettante Charles Townley. Note the pair of greyhounds in marble in Room 83.

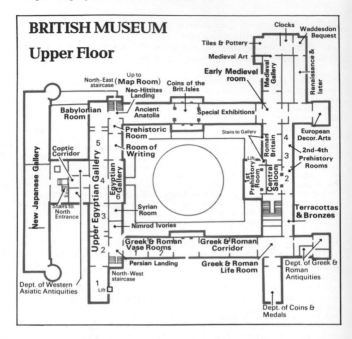

The *Western Asiatic Collections* start in Room 26 nearest the main entrance but room numbering and chronology do not coincide. In the Nimrud Gallery (Room 19) are imposing reliefs from the palace at Calah (Nimrud) including a black obelisk of Shlmaneser III. Reliefs from the palace of Nineveh are in the Assyrian Saloon (Room 17A). Assyrian sculpture and the Ishtar Temple remains are in the basemented galleries 88A and 89.

The *Egyptian Collections* start in Room 25 in a new display. The entrance is flanked by two black granite seated figures of Amenophis III from his mortuary temple at Thebes (c 1400 BC). On the left the famous **Rosetta Stone**, with a small accompanying display. It is named after a town near the mouth of the Nile where it was found by the French in 1797. It bears a priestly decree, inscribed twice in Egyptian (first in hieroglyphs, the writing of the priests, and secondly in ordinary, secular characters) and also in Greek translation. This triple inscription gave scholars the key to the Ancient Egyptian language and script and in turn to the whole of Egyptian culture.

Note also the so-called 'false doors' from tombs (particularly that from the tomb of Ptahshepses, Middle Kingdom, XI–XIII Dynasties) through which the spirit of the deceased passed from the burial chamber to the chapel where food offerings were presented; a fine black granite statue of Sesostris III (c 1850 BC) (one of three), and considered to be one of the best pieces of sculpture in the gallery; the wooden figure of Ramesses I (c 1218 BC), one of the few to survive; and in the tomb-like slip-rooms on the E side smaller funerary objects are well lit and displayed.

After the Egyptian Galleries on the ground floor, it may be convenient to take in the British Library collection, as currently displayed; see below under British Library.

There are further Egyptian Galleries on the 1st floor; first the *Chinese Antiquities* (Room 33; these may also be approached directly via the N entrance to the Museum in Montague Place) are seen. These are arranged chronologically beginning with the Neolithic period. The collection of the ceramics of the Sung (960–1279), Yuan (1280–1368) and Ming (1368–1644) dynasties is unrivalled in the West and includes many world-famous pieces. The W half of the Gallery is devoted to Indian antiquities, mainly comprising sculpture and bronzes from temples in India and SE Asia.

The Egyptian Rooms on the 1st floor in the N wing of the main building contain the collection of mummies and other objects found in tombs (Rooms 60–66).

The British Museum's collection of *Prints and Drawings* is displayed in thematic changing exhibitions in Room 90.

A new Japanese Gallery is opened in 1990 in Rooms 92/94 with changing exhbitions from the Museum's extensive Japanese collection and loan exhibitions from Japan and includes Jomon pottery, 10,000 BC–400 BC, 19th and 20thC prints. Note 16C tea bowl 'Horinji'.

Prehistoric and Romano British Antiquities begin in Room 35 with a large 4C mosaic pavement from Hinton St. Mary, Dorset. In Room 39 is the Battersea Shield, the finest example of early Celtic art in Britain (mid 1C BC). In Room 40 is the MILDENHALL TREASURE, a sumptuously decorated set of 4C Roman silver tableware, including a great dish weighing 24lbs with embossed decorations of the highest quality. At the centre is a mask of Neptune, surrounded by sea-creatures and a frieze of Bacchic revels. The set, which was discovered in 1942, is one of the finest to be found anywhere in the Roman empire and must have belonged to a high official.

In Room 41 is the SUTTON HOO TREASURE, a 7C royal ship-burial, probably that of King Redwald of the East Angles, excavated in Suffolk in 1939, and the richest and most varied burial of its kind yet found in Europe. It includes: gold and garnet strap-fittings, a sword with jewelled mounts, a magnificent helmet (restored 1971) and shield, ceremonial whetstone surmounted by a finely cast bronze stag, drinking horns and bottles with silver-gilt fittings, hanging bowls, massive bronze cauldron and iron cauldron chains. This room also contains the treasures from the Taplow Barrow.

Room 45 displays the **WADDESDON BEQUEST, amassed by Baron Ferdinand de Rothschild in the tradition of the Renaissance merchant-princes. Exquisite and often exotic *objets d'art* of the 14–17C include silver plate, cups and caskets, Limoges enamels, a Mantuan dama-scened shield of 1554, and a magnificent collection of gold and jewelled pendants, outstandingly the Lyte Jewel.

In the long Renaissance gallery, No. 46, note the 'magic mirror' used by Dr John Dee, the Elizabethan alchemist, the English pottery including Lambeth Delft and Fulham stoneware and the Battersea enamels.

For the time being still housed within the Museum, the **British Library** is due to start moving in 1991 with the new Library at St. Pancras opening in 1993.

British Library, Great Russell St, WC1. Tel. 071-636 1544. Open as British Museum. Admission to the Reading Room and the Students' Rooms is by ticket only (apply in writing to the Director at least two days in advance; applications must be accompanied by a letter of recommendation from a person of recognised position). Tours of the Reading Room daily (weekdays) on the hour between 11.00 and 16.00. Admission free.

The British Library contains over 8,000,000 volumes. Though now surpassed in size by the Library of Congress at Washington and the Lenin State Library, it still ranks as one of the most important libraries in the world, and it is especially rich in books in foreign languages. These and older books are provided from a Treasury grant and by donation, while, by law, a copy of every book, newspaper, and so forth published in the United Kingdom must be deposited at the British Library, where it must be accepted and preserved. The university libraries at Oxford and Cambridge and Dublin, and the national libraries of Scotland and Wales have the right to demand copies of books, etc., without the statutory duty to preserve them.

On the N side of the Main Entrance Hall is the circular **Reading Room**, tickets of admission to which are granted for purposes of research and reference which cannot be carried out elsewhere. The dome (140ft in diameter and 106ft high) is, after that of the Pantheon in Rome (142ft), the widest in the world. The superintendent's raised desk occupies the centre, and from it a service passage leads into the library; it is ringed round with desks holding the General Catalogue, which, including the Maps and Music Catalogues, is in well over 2000 volumes. The groundfloor shelves are occupied by a large library of reference books, which may be consulted directly by readers; other books are requisitioned by filling in forms.

Newspapers are held in the collection at Colindale (see p 381).

While still at the British Museum permanent and changing exhibitions are held in the Grenville Library, Manuscript Saloon and King's Library.

The *Grenville Library*, Room 1, houses English and Continental illuminated manuscripts. In the *Manuscript Saloon* is the Library's collection of historical and literary manuscripts. Among the autographs are those of Raleigh, Spenser, Ben Jonson, Bacon, Hobbes, Milton, Wren, Locke, Defoe, Pepys, Dr Johnson, Pope, Garrick, Sarah Siddons, Keats, Wordsworth, Byron and Shelley, Elizabeth and Robert Browning, Charlotte and Emily Brontë and Jane Austen. Note the unique manuscript of Beowulf (c 1000), and the earliest known history of England in English, the Anglo-Saxon Chronicle. Many famous continental painters and writers also have their autographs here including Luther, Goethe, Voltaire, Michelangelo, Rembrandt, and Titian. Scientific names include Galileo, Newton and Leonardo da Vinci. The most famous display is perhaps the MAGNA CARTA with two original copies, as well as the Articles of Barons sealed at Runnymede in 1215. There are royal signatures, too, including that of Elizabeth I, and those of prime ministers.

In the *King's Library* (Room 32) are early books including the Gutenberg Bible, and famous books including 'Das Kapital', written by Karl Marx mainly in the Reading Room here. Note also Roubiliac's life-size statue of Shakespeare (1758) which stood at Garrick's Temple at Hampton. The Tapling Collection of postage stamps of the world and other stamp collections are also on display.

18 Embankment Gardens, the Strand, the Courtauld Institute Gallery and the Aldwych

Access: Underground, Charing Cross, Embankment.

The STRAND originally bordered on the Thames and provided the vital road-link between the City and Whitehall Palace at Westminster. The embankment of the Thames created a narrow roadway with grand houses on either side, later followed by commerce, entertainment and hotels. The music-hall song 'Let's Go Down the Strand' recalls the hustle and bustle of the past; today the Strand is mostly lined with uninteresting offices enlivened by some good stamp shops, including Stanley Gibbons, three theatres and three large hotels.

It.is still occasionally used as a processional route to the City and St. Paul's Cathedral, most recently for the wedding of the Prince of Wales to Lady Diana Spencer, in 1981.

Charing Cross Station (Pl. 15; 3), near its W end, was built in 1863 on the site of *Hungerford Market*. The town house of Walter (first Baron) Hungerford was erected here in 1422–23, and a descendant opened the market (later destroyed by fire) in 1682. The Gothic Cross (by E.M. Barry; 1865) in the station forecourt is a memorial, but not a copy, of Eleanor's Cross. (cf. Charing Cross p 93). The Charing Cross Hotel, entrance from the station forecourt, was designed by E.M. Barry (1864)—one of the first buildings to be faced with artificial stone. On the N side of the Strand, the Nash façade and eccentric turrets of the Coutts's Bank building by Smirke have been incorporated using large glass screen covers in a three storey building. The old Charing Cross Hospital site has been redeveloped; the hospital moved to Fulham in 1973. *Zimbabwe House*, on the corner of Agar St, was designed by Charles Holden (1908); the mutilated statues on the second floor are by Epstein.

Craven St skirts the W side of Charing Cross Station to reach the Embankment. (See below) Benjamin Franklin lived at No. 36 (1757–62) and there are plans to restore the house into a museum, library and conference centre by the Friends of Benjamin Franklin House (tel. 071-629 2149); the German poet Heinrich Heine at No. 32; Henry Flitcroft, the architect, at No. 33. The old Craven Passage and the Arches market for coins and medals have disappeared in the comprehensive redevelopment project above and below the station designed by Terry Farrell, which will give direct access to Hungerford Bridge and the South Bank from the Station. Villiers St will be partly pedestrianised and Embankment Gardens opened up to the N. This new development (partly open from 1990) incorporates offices, shops and the famous Players Theatre Club in new premises within the historic vaults. The Players Theatre started in 1946 underneath the arches where a Victorian music hall flourished. The Players reverted to this formula after a success with 'The Boy Friend' in the '50s. On the site between Villiers St, E of the station, and the parallel Buckingham St, George Villiers, Duke of Buckingham, partly rebuilt (in 1624) *York House*, the birthplace in 1561 of Francis Bacon. The old *Water-Gate survives at the end of Buckingham St; built by Nicholas Stone in 1626, it shows where the Thames reached at that time. Victoria Embankment Gardens descend to the Embankment.

Across the busy Embankment is Charing Cross Pier with regular departures up and downstream including the fast River Bus service. See p 22. On the wall of the Embankment is a bronze medallion to W.S. Gilbert 'playwright and poet' (George Frampton, 1913); Gilbert and Sullivan operettas were regularly performed at the nearby Savoy Theatre. In the delightful Embankment Gardens there is a bandstand and cafeteria (summer) and statues to Scottish poet Robert Burns (1759–96) by John Steell; Lord Cheylesmore, (1848–1925) by Edwin Lutyens; the temperance campaigner, Sir Wilfrid Lawson by David McGill (1909); as part of a fountain there is a medallion of the blind Post-Master General Henry Fawcett, a campaigner for female suffrage, with his wife Millicent, by Mary Grant 1886, the fountain is by Basil Champneys; Robert Raikes, who started the first Sunday School in 1780, by Sir Thomas Brock, 1880; and Sir Arthur Sullivan, composer and part of the Gilbert and Sullivan team, as a bronze bust by William Goscombe John, 1903, with a weeping girl against his stone plinth.

On the Embankment is the oldest monument in London, Cleopatra's Needle which dates from 1450 BC, originally one of a pair at Heliopolis (the other is in Paris). Emperor Augustus had them moved to Alexandria after Cleopatra's death. Mohammed Ali, Viceroy of Egypt presented one to the British and it had a treacherous journey towed through stormy seas in 1878 and was abandoned twice. The bronze sphinxes are by George Vulliamy, 1882 with bomb scars from the First World War. Buried underneath the pinkish obelisk (cleaned in 1979) is a collection of memorabilia from 1878 including a railway guide, coins, and a picture of Queen Victoria. Next to Waterloo Bridge is the 'Queen Mary', a former 1933 pleasure steamer and now a pub/restaurant.

Return to Villiers St where Sir Richard Steele lived from 1721 to 1724, and which was Rudyard Kipling's first London home in 1889–91 (No. 19, now No. 43). Pepys occupied No. 12 Buckingham St in 1679–88; while No. 14 bears a tablet recording its tenancy, in its various transitions, by Pepys (in 1688–1700), Robert Harley, Earl of Oxford, William Etty, the painter, and Clarkson Stanfield, the marine painter. Burdett House opposite (rebuilt as the headquarters of the Royal National Pension Fund for Nurses) was occupied by Peter the Great in 1697–98. The names of David Hume, Rousseau, and Henry Fielding were also associated with this house.

John Adam St, parallel to the Strand on the S, runs through the region known as *The Adelphi*, named after the four Scottish brothers Adam who planned a residential area on the land sloping down to the river in 1768. The ambitious scheme involved the building of streets, houses and terraces supported on an embankment of arches and subterranean vaults. The main brick terrace overlooking the Thames was directly inspired by the Palace of Diocletian at Split. A lottery was authorised by Parliament in 1773 to rescue the enterprise from financial disaster. A few fine Adam houses survive.

Among artists and writers who came to live here were David Garrick, Rowlandson, Tom Hood, Charles Dickens (whose youthful experiences in this area are described in 'David Copperfield'), Bernard Shaw, Sir James Barrie, H.G. Wells, and John Galsworthy. Robert and James Adam lived in Robert St Nos. 1–3 (built in 1772; plaque) Later Hood, Galsworthy and Barrie lived here. Some remaining vaults can be seen in Lower Robert St but the main part of the Adelphi was demolished in 1936–38 and replaced by a building of the same name by Colcutt and Hemp, re-aligning the streets and renumbering many of the houses.

The *Royal Society of Arts* occupies a fine Adam building at 8 John Adam St. The Society was established in 1754 to foster art, manufacture and trade. The hall contains mural paintings by James Barry (1777–83), illustrating the benefits of civilisation. A conference centre and restaurant opened here in 1990 (tel. 071-930 5115). No. 7 Adam St is one of the most attractive remaining Adam houses.

The *Gilbert and Sullivan* pub in John Adam St was damaged in a fire and its collection of memorabilia has been moved to the Old Bell in Wellington St, now also called the *Gilbert and Sullivan*. W.S. Gilbert was born in Southampton St on the N side of the Strand; Richard d'Oyly Carte lived at No. 4 Adelphi Terrace while producing the Gilbert and Sullivan comic operas at the Savoy Theatre.

The *Savoy Theatre* in the Strand was built in 1881 by Richard d'Oyly Carte for Gilbert and Sullivan's operas. It was the first public building in London to be lit by electricity. It opened with 'Patience'. After 1893 it was used for comic operas; plays and comedies were also staged. A severe fire damaged the interior in 1990. The *Savoy Hotel* adjoining the theatre opened in 1889, also financed by Richard d'Oyly Carte. This was one of the first hotels to have many private bathrooms, electric lifts and electric lights. Cezar Ritz was the first manager and Escoffier the first chef; his pots and pans remain at the hotel. One part of the hotel has been converted into apartments. The forecourt is the only street in London where traffic must keep to the right. A statue of Count Peter of Savoy, see below, by American F.L Jenkins (1904), tops the covered canopy. Many famous people have stayed here including Henry Irving and Sarah Bernhardt.

Savoy St leads S to the Thames Embankment past the garden of the **Chapel of the Savoy**, erected in the late-Perpendicular style in 1505, on part of the site of Savoy Palace. Entered from Savoy Hill, it is open on Tues to Fri, 11.30–15.30 (closed Aug/Sept), and for services on Sunday.

Savoy Palace, built in 1246, was given by Henry III to his wife's uncle, Peter, Earl of Savoy and Richmond (died 1268), and afterwards passed into the possession of John of Gaunt. King John of France, taken prisoner at the Battle of Poitiers (1356) died in the palace in 1364. Geoffrey Chaucer and John Wyclif here enjoyed the patronage of John of Gaunt. The palace was burned down by Wat Tyler in 1381, and the manor made over to the Crown in 1399 by Henry IV. It was rebuilt as a hospital and chapel by Henry VII in 1505. Here in 1661 the famous Savoy Conference for the revision of the Prayer Book took place.

The chapel was restored by Queen Victoria after a fire in 1864. It is the Chapel of the Royal Victorian Order, and the stalls of the knights are marked by small copper plates emblazoned with the arms of the holder. A stained glass window commemorates Richard d'Oyly Carte (1844–1901; see above).

Opposite in Savoy Hill at what is now the Institute of Electrical Engineers, the BBC started the first daily radio programmes in 1922 as station 2LO. The BBC moved to the new Broadcasting House from here in 1932.

In the Strand is the traditional *Simpsons in the Strand* restaurant founded in 1848. The present building designed by T.E. Collcutt opened in 1904 and still prides itself on its roast beef; the lunchtime clientele is still male-dominated (tel. 071-836 9112). On the N side of the Strand is the *Adelphi Theatre*, opened in 1806 and rebuilt twice, famous for melodramas during the 19C (one actor was shot outside the theatre in a real drama) and more recently musicals, including 'Me and My Girl'. The much smaller *Vaudeville Theatre* dates from 1870. The undistinguished Strand Palace Hotel (1930) has a useful 'all-night' coffee shop.

The *Lyceum* in Wellington St has a chequered history. Founded as a concert and exhibition hall in 1771, it staged Madame Tussaud's first wax-work exhibition in London in 1802; it was destroyed by fire in 1830 and rebuilt a little further W in 1834 as an opera house. From 1874 it became synonymous with the brilliant actor Henry Irving who staged many of Shakespeare's plays here with Ellen Terry as his leading lady; the last was Coriolanus in 1901. The former LCC acquired the building in 1939 for future road development, but from 1945 it functioned as a dance-hall. The Lyceum closed in 1985; its future is uncertain.

The busy *Lancaster Place*, on the right, forms the approach to Waterloo Bridge, passing the W façade of Somerset House. Beyond, Aldwych, taking the eastbound traffic, forms a wide crescent to the N (see below). Continue along the Strand, to the N façade of **Somerset House** (Pl. 15; 3) and the Courtauld Institute Galleries in the Palladian building erected by Sir William Chambers in 1776–86. The E wing (King's College) was added by Sir R. Smirke in 1829–34, the W wing by Sir James Pennethorne in 1852–56. The chief *Façade, nearly 600ft long, fronting the Thames, stands on a terrace 50ft above the Embankment. Three medallions of George III, his wife Queen Charlotte and son, later George IV, by Joseph Wilton feature on the Strand façade of the building. Its basement arcade originally rose straight from the river, and the great central arch was the water-gate.

The present building occupies the site of a palace begun by the Lord Protector Somerset c 1547, but left unfinished at his execution in 1552. The palace then passed into the hands of the Crown. Elizabeth I lived here for a time during the reign of her sister Mary. The body of Oliver Cromwell lay in state here in 1658.
Somerset House was until recently mainly occupied by Government offices. In the W wing is the *Board of Inland Revenue*, which deals with stamps, taxes, death duties, and land values duties. The *Principal Probate Registry* (in the S wing), which formerly housed also Prerogative Court of Canterbury (PCC) wills from 1382 (transferred to the Public Record Office), now only holds wills and testaments registered in England since 1858. A copy of any will can be seen for a fee (Mon to Fri, 10.00–16.30). Other wills (pre-1858) are preserved elsewhere. The *Fine Rooms* (interior by Chambers) in the N wing have become the new home of the **Courtauld Institute Collections** which moved here from Blooms-bury in 1990 after £10m restoration of the partly dilapidated building. (See p 184). The vaults have been imaginatively restored to house the Witt Library.

Courtauld Institute Galleries, Somerset House, The Strand, WC2. Tel. 071-837 2777. Open Mon to Sat 10.00–18.00, Sun 14.00–18.00; until 20.00 on Tues. Admission charge. Access: Underground, Temple, Aldwych. Bookshop. Cafeteria.

The collection originated in 1931 with Samuel Courtauld's (1865–1949) French Impressionist and Post-Impressionist paintings with later additions including the collection made by Lord Lee Fareham (1868–1947) of 14–18C art, the Roger Fry Collection, the Witt Collections of Old Master Drawings, the Mark Gambler-Parry Bequest (1966) of early Italian paintings and the Count Antoine Seilern bequest (1978) of paintings and drawings by Rubens and Michelangelo. In its former premises at Woburn Square only 35 per cent of the collection could be shown. In the new galleries 80 per cent of the collection is on view in 11 galleries on two floors. These are some of the highlights. Gallery 1–2: Renaissance and Rubens; Gallery 3: Rubens drawings; Gallery 4: Tiepolo drawings; Gallery 5 and 6: French Impressionists and Post-impressionists including Cézanne's 'Card Player, Degas 'Two Dancers on the Stage', Gauguin 'Nevermore', Monet 'Le Déjeuner sur L'Herbe' and 'Bar at the Folies-Bergère', Modigliani 'Nude', Pissarro 'Lordship Lane Station', Renoir 'La Loge', Seurat 'Young Woman at a Powder Table', Toulouse-Lautrec 'Jean Avril' and Van Gogh 'Portrait of the Artist with Bandaged Ear'. (Note the plasterwork in Gallery 5, repainted in

original colours of pink, lavender and green.); Gallery 7: 18C paintings and portraits, the Chambers medal cabinet (open) and Huguenot
silver; Gallery 8: the Great Room, once used by the Royal Academy
for its annual open exhibitions, 19C and 20C works: Gallery 9 and 10:
20C paintings, Gallery 11: 14C, 15C, 16C Flemish and Italian
paintings.

To the E of Somerset House is the new façade (1972) of **King's
College**, one of the incorporated colleges of the University of London.
Following a public meeting in 1828 with the Prime Minister (the Duke
of Wellington) in the chair and the Abps of Canterbury and York in
attendance, it was opened in 1831.

The names of the next series of streets leading from the Strand to the
Embankment commemorate the sites of the town houses of Thomas Howard,
Earl of Arundel, Surrey, and Norfolk (c 1585–1646), and of Robert Devereux, Earl
of Essex (1567–1601). Off Surrey St is an alleged *Roman Bath*, fed by a rivulet
(tel. 071-798 2063; open Wed 13.00–17.00, by appointment); the bricks used are
small and non-porous, of an unusual kind, the Roman origin of which is by no
means certain. Adjacent are the remains of an Elizabethan bath, said to date
from 1588. On neighbouring sites are a hotel, and an extension to King's. During
building in 1973 part of a Roman frieze from Pergamon was found, having been
shipped to England in 1627 by the Earl of Arundel, and abandoned in his garden.
Marochetti's statue of Isambard Kingdom Brunel (1877) stands on the corner of
Temple Place and Victoria Embankment.

In the middle of the Strand stands the finely proportioned church of **St.
Mary-le-Strand**, with an Ionic portico and graceful steeple, built by
James Gibbs in 1714, and consecrated in 1724. The barrel vault has
fine plasterwork, and the pulpit is usually attributed to Gibbons. The
fabric of the church is being restored. The space in front was the site of
the famous Maypole where the first hackney carriage rank stood in
1634; it was removed in 1718 and bought by Sir Isaac Newton as the
stand for a telescope at Wanstead House. Thomas Becket was once
lay-rector of the parish and Charles Dickens's parents were married
in the church in 1809.

Further E, the church of **St. Clement Danes** forms another island in
the Strand. Designed by Wren and built in 1680–82 on the site of a
much earlier building, it is traditionally believed to be the burial-
place of Harold Harefoot and other Danes. The tower, added by
James Gibbs in 1719–20, is 115ft high and contains a famous and
tuneful peal of bells ('Oranges and lemons, say the bells of St.
Clement's'). In 1941 the church was gutted by fire and it has been
beautifully restored as the headquarters church of the Royal Air
Force. A statue of Lord Dowding (1882–1970) by Faith Winter was
erected in front of the church in 1988, near the impressive *Gladstone
Memorial*, by Hamo Thornycroft (1905).

The interior has bright white and gilt stucco decoration, and a Father Smith
organ (restored). The floor is inlaid with unit and squadron badges, and Books of
Remembrance line the aisles. The altarpiece is by Ruskin Spear. A fine staircase
descends to the crypt which is decorated with ancient tomb slabs. William Webb
Ellis, the inventor of Rugby Football in 1823, was rector here (memorial tablet).
Dr Johnson was a worshipper in this church and is commemorated by a statue by
Percy Fitzgerald outside the choir.

The Strand is continued by Fleet St towards the City (see Rte 21) and
the Law Courts. Turn NW into **Aldwych**, which takes its name from an
old colony (ald-wych) of Danes in this vicinity before the Conquest.

On the S corner of the Aldwych facing the Strand is *Australia House*
built in 1911–18 as the office of the Commonwealth of Australia. The

groups flanking the entrance represent Exploration, and Shearing and Reaping; high above are the Horses of the Sun. Across Melbourne Place, *Bush House*, a massive pile of offices, begun in 1920 by Harvey Corbett, occupies the greater part of the area between Aldwych and the Strand. Here are located the External Services of the BBC. There is a shop selling English language and BBC publications. The entrance facing Kingsway is a huge archway surmounted by a colossal group, by Malvina Hoffmann (1925; damaged by a flying bomb), symbolising the friendship of Britain and the United States. Across Aldwych, in Houghton St, are the premises of the *London School of Economics and Political Science*. Sidney and Beatrice Webb participated in its establishment in 1895, and Harold Laski, when Professor of Political Science here in 1926, instilled some of the left-wing views for which it is celebrated. In 1968 there was a lengthy sit-in by students which ended in violence. *Kingsway* (Pl. 15; 1) runs N to High Holborn (comp. Rte 22). On the corner stands *St. Catherine's House*, with the Office of Population Censuses and Surveys (General Register Office). The records of Births, Marriages, and Deaths in England since 1837 have been moved here from Somerset House.

Beyond Bush House, *India House* (1930) designed by Sir Herbert Baker, is the office of the High Commissioner for India. The fine interior is decorated in the Indian style and largely by Indian artists. On the last building on the island (now a bank) tablets record the site of the Gaiety Theatre, home of musical comedy in London in 1903–39, and the Broadcasting Station of Marconi's Wireless Telegraph Company from 11 May to 15 Nov 1922, when it became the first station of the BBC.

On NW side is the *Aldwych Theatre*, built as a pair with the Strand Theatre to the S in 1905 by W.G.R. Sprague. At the Aldwych musical comedies were followed by the famous Ben Travers farces from 1925 to 1933. From 1960 to 1982 the theatre was the London home of the Royal Shakespeare Company now at the Barbican Centre. Between the two is the Waldorf Hotel (1908) with its elegant art deco Palm Court (afternoon tea and tea-dances).

Continue N to Covent Garden, see below or E to Fleet St and the City, see p 208.

19 Covent Garden

Access: Underground, Covent Garden, Leicester Square.

From the Underground Station, Covent Garden, turn S from Long Acre down James St past the new, rear façade of the Royal Opera House to Covent Garden Piazza.

Since the restored buildings of the Covent Garden Market opened in 1981, the area has quickly established itself as one of the liveliest in London, at the hub of theatreland, with wine bars, restaurants and a variety of shops.

The area derives its name from the convent garden of the monks of Westminster Abbey. After the dissolution of the monasteries, the first Earl of Bedford, John Russell, received the land from Henry VIII in 1536 and it stayed in the Bedford family until 1918. Bedford House faced the Strand to the S with gardens which produced fruit and vegetables just as the monks had done. These gardens were where the present Piazza is today. In the 17C the fourth earl decided to take advantage of the growing demand for property and appointed Inigo Jones as architect to plan a new square. Jones was influenced by Italian town-planning (notably at Leghorn), and the Piazza became one of the first and finest of its kind in London, focussed on the portico of St. Paul's Church on the W side. The N and E sides of the Piazza were made up of porticoed houses with an arcaded walk underneath—the present buildings to the N are a pale imitation. The S side was bounded by the wall and terraced walk of Bedford House gardens. The Piazza was gravelled and later a Doric column with a gilded sun-dial was added in the middle—this only remained for 100 years. Trading continued against the S wall and later as Bedford House was demolished and the gardens built over, market stalls began to appear in the centre of the Piazza creating a nuisance for the fashionable residents who began to leave the area. The sixth earl decided that the market needed a proper building and commissioned Charles Fowler to design the Central Market building.

The neo-classical *Central Market Building* straight ahead transformed the open square when it was completed in 1830. The iron and glass roofs were added by Cubitts between 1875 and 1889. The Doric columns and Coade stone sculpture at the E end as well as the roofs have been magnificently restored by the Greater London Council after the vegetable market moved to Nine Elms in 1974. By then the market activities had grown to such proportions that they were causing intolerable congestion in the centre of London. The fashionable shops and restaurants now have original shop fronts and individual hanging shop signs. The Opera Terrace in the style of a conservatory has been added on the first floor level overlooking Russell St. In the Apple Market inside the Market Building people sell their goods from the original stalls from the Flower Market.

St. Paul's Church on the W side of the Piazza, known as the actors' church, has a side entrance in King St and its main entrance in Bedford St. The impressive Tuscan portico, fronting the Piazza (well-known from the flower-girl scene in 'My Fair Lady') is just a false front. During construction of the church the Bishop of London protested at the unorthodox location of the altar against the W wall and Inigo Jones had to move it to the E wall. Although this is the highlight of Inigo Jones's Covent Garden, very little money could be spent on it as heavy fees were extracted from the Bedfords by Charles I. Jones, when asked to keep costs down, promised to build 'the handsomest barn in England'. Most of the building was destroyed by fire in 1795 but reconstructed by Thomas Hardwicke to the original design. Inside the walls are filled with memorials to the artistic—Grinling Gibbons is buried here and a carved wreath by him from St. Paul's Cathedral was added as a memorial in 1965. Others include Samuel Butler, Sir Peter Lely, William Wycherley; a silver casket holds the ashes of Ellen Terry. Marie Lloyd, Clement Dane, Ivor Novello and Vivien Leigh are all commemorated here.

A plaque in the portico marks the site of the first recorded performance of a Punch and Judy show, witnessed here by Pepys in 1662; the pub opposite in the Central Market has taken his name and there are regular Punch and Judy performances in the Piazza as well as an annual Punch and Judy Festival in the otherwise quiet churchyard. The tradition of street entertainment continues with live performances under the portico every day and music inside the Market.

During the 18 and 19C Covent Garden coffee houses attracted the writers and artists of the day. One well-known house was Bedford's Coffee House in the NE corner and others were Will's, Button's and Tom's. The tradition continued in Garrick St (branching NW from King St) where the *Garrick Club* has attracted actors and writers since 1831. Rose St runs through to the *Lamb and Flag* pub which dates back to 1638 although the present building is 18C. Poet John Dryden was nearly assassinated here by opponents to his writings in 1679. At No. 5 King St is the Royal School of Needlework with a shop and classes (tel. 071-240 3186). Opposite at No. 38 is the Africa Centre with a shop and restaurant (tel. 071-836 1973).

The *Jubilee Hall* at the SW corner of the Piazza was built in 1908 to house the imported fruit market. It has now been redeveloped behind the original façade into offices, houses and a sports and leisure centre. The seven-day-a-week Jubilee Market fronting the cobbled Piazza offers crafts (Sat, Sun), antiques (Mon) and general goods (Tues to Fri). The stall-holders are joint owners in the new market which was officially opened by HM The Queen in August 1987. A café overlooks the colourful stalls.

The *Flower Market Building* in the SE corner of the Piazza was added in 1872 as activities at the market expanded and represents a Victorian classical design in brick and stone with some excellent glass and iron work towards the Piazza and Tavistock St. It now houses the *London Transport Museum* and the *Theatre Museum*—the National Theatre of the Performing Arts.

London Transport Museum, The Piazza, Covent Garden, WC2. Tel. 071-379 6344. Open daily 10.00–18.00. Admission charge. Access: Underground, Covent Garden. Shop with London Transport posters, models and postcards, cafeteria.

The collection was formed in the 1920s and '30s by the London General Omnibus Company and constitutes a unique record of public transport from c 1830 to the present day. The collection moved here from Syon Park in 1980 and augmented its display with a number of additional features, including an informative display of photographs, documents and maps showing the impact on London of a growing transportation network.

The collection of London Transport posters includes the work of some of the leading British graphic artists of the 20C and special exhibitions take place regularly. Visitors may take the controls of an underground train, a bus, and a tram, and operate points and signals. Among the most important exhibits are: a replica of the Shillibeer Horse Omnibus (1829–34), a Knifeboard Horse Bus (c 1850–1900), and a Garden Seat Horse Bus (c 1885–1914). The earliest motor bus on show is the Type B Bus (1910–27) and the earliest railway vehicle, a Metropolitan Railway Class A locomotive (1866).

Turn W into Russell St; at No. 8 was the bookshop of Tom Davies where Boswell first met Johnson in 1763. Boswell's coffeeshop, a recent addition, marks the place today.

The entrance to the **Theatre Museum** is in Russell St.

Theatre Museum, Russell St, WC2. Tel. 071-836 7891. Open Tues to Sun 11.00–19.00 (shop, café and box office until 20.00). Admission charge. Library.

The impressive lobby features the old box office from the Duke of York's Theatre, the gilded figure of the Spirit of Gaity from the demolished Gaiety Theatre in the Aldwych, and some elaborate boxes from the Palace Theatre, Glasgow. The cafeteria on this level is fashioned as a stage set. A long ramp (disabled access) descends to the basement level which, as well as the exhibition galleries, includes a plush theatre-bar and a rather curious theatre seating some 70 people with a sloping wooden stage. For the first time since the closure of the Leighton House exhibition in 1971, the V. & A. collections of theatre memorabilia can now be seen, elegantly displayed in darkened galleries. Temporary exhibitions are held in two galleries. The library is open by appointment.

Russell St leads E to Drury Lane where to the S stands the impressive Theatre Royal Drury Lane, entrance in Catherine St. The present theatre was designed by Benjamin Wyatt in 1811–12; the portico was added ten years later and the colonnade in 1830. The pillars came from Nash's Quadrant in Regent St. The auditorium which seats 2245—one of London's largest theatres—was remodelled in 1921. A ghost is said to haunt the Upper Circle. The theatre has an illustrious 300 year history and is now used mostly for musicals, recently the successful '42nd St' and 'Miss Saigon' (since 1989).

The first theatre on the site was built in 1663 under a royal patent for Thomas Killigrew's 'King's Company'—the first to be granted after the Restoration. Charles II was frequently in the audience and here he met and fell in love with the actress Nell Gwynne who had lodgings in Drury Lane. The theatre burnt down in 1671 and was rebuilt in 1674 to a design by Wren. The theatre's stormy history includes riots and the attempted assassinations of two kings, George II and George III. During David Garrick's management from 1747 Shakespeare revivals became popular. When Sheridan took over in 1776 it became a theatre of comedy, including his own 'School for Scandal'. In John Kemble's period the theatre was declared unsafe and had to be closed. It reopened in 1794 but was destroyed by fire only 15 years later. Sheridan watched the flames while sipping a glass of port in a coffee-house across the road and said 'Surely a man may take a glass of wine by his own fireside'. The present theatre contains statues, busts and paintings of its famous actors, owners and managers. On the wall near the entrance is a bronze bust and stone plaque commemorating Sir Augustus Harris, manager-owner from 1879 to 1897, set in an elaborate fountain by Thomas Brock.

The tiny but perfect Duchess Theatre in Catherine St in Tudoresque style dates to 1929.

Continue northwards along Drury Lane hich is still residential in character, having once been the address of aristocratic families including Sir Thomas Drury who gave it his name. In the 18C the area deteriorated and by the end of the 19C it was one of the worst slums of London.

The Peabody Estate on the E side was one of the many estates built for the poor during the 1860s and '70s by the wealthy American-born philanthropist George Peabody, in an attempt to eradicate some of the worst slum housing. This estate stands on the site of original Cockpit Theatre (1616–64), also known as the Phoenix Theatre. Further N on the E corner of Drury Lane and Great Queen St is the huge *Freemason's Hall* (entrance in Great Queen St), the second on the site and completed in 1933 by H.V. Ashley and F. Winton Smith. It is the Headquarters of the United Grand Lodge of England, established in 1768, and houses an exhibition of the history of English Freemasonry, open Mon to Fri 09.00–17.00. Adjoining it are the *New Connaught Rooms*, which incorporate some parts of the original Freemason's Hall including the fine banqueting hall designed by F. Cockerell, available for functions.

Drury Lane continues N past the New London Theatre and the Talk of London cabaret restaurant, in a new building which opened in 1973 on the site of the Winter Garden Theatre, a place of entertainment since Elizabethan times. The theatre (seating 1102) was used initially for television until the longest running musical in West End history, 'Cats', opened in 1981.

Turn back S along Drury Lane and then W along *Long Acre*, past new housing estates to the N, part of the renovation of the Covent Garden area. Long Acre was originally a path through the monks of Westminster's huge gardens. In the mid 17C as the area became built up, coach and cabinet makers, including Chippendale, settled here. Today glass-blowers can be seen at work at the Glasshouse, 65 Long Acre (open Mon to Fri 10.00–18.00, Sat 10.00–16.00).

Turn S into *Bow St*, which takes its name from its shape of a bent bow. Immediately to the W is the impressive portico of the **Royal Opera House**, Covent Garden, home of the Royal Ballet and Opera companies. The present theatre, the third on the site, was designed by E.M. Barry and completed in 1860. It is dominated by the Corinthian style portico and the sculptural embellishments by Flaxman and Rossi salvaged from the previous building. The magnificent auditorium which seats 2158 is decorated in white and gold with a plaster relief by Raffaelle Monti over the proscenium. The elegant foyer and Crush Bar are equally celebrated. The cramped back-stage facilities are being improved in a ten-year programme; the first phase completed in 1982 took the building along Floral St to James St (to the W) in a matching design. A further extension is planned towards the Covent Garden Piazza when sufficient money has been raised and the design agreed. It will involve the reconstruction of the adjoining *Floral Hall*, opened in 1860. It formed an extension to the Opera House and was used for balls and even ice-skating. It now provides storage space and workshops and in the new plan becomes the main foyer. The Royal Opera House advance box office is in Floral St. The Opera House may close for two to three years in the '90s, to allow redevelopment to take place.

The first Royal Opera House was designed by Edward Shepherd and opened in 1732. The actor and manager John Rich had a triumphant opening with a revival of Congreve's 'The Way of the World'. There was lively rivalry with the Theatre Royal Drury Lane over the next 150 years until the Opera House became the place for Italian opera. In the 18C a disastrous fire destroyed the theatre and Handel's organ. The second theatre on the same site was modelled by Robert Smirke on the Temple of Minerva. When it opened in 1809 prices were raised, sparking off the so-called 'Old Price riots' which continued for two months until prices were reduced. Another fire followed in 1855 leaving only Flaxman's frieze undamaged.

Opposite the Royal Opera House is the Bow St Magistrate's Court and Police Station, completed in 1880 but representing a link with law and order that dates back to the first courthouse on the site in 1740. Here the famous Fielding brothers (Henry and John) established the Bow St Runners from 1749 to catch thieves and villains; forerunners of the Metropolitan Police which followed less than 100 years later. In the Police Station is the *Metropolitan Police Historical Museum* which recreates the history of London's police force with photographs, uniforms and set-piece reconstructions. (Open by appointment only; write to Metropolitan Police Museum, 28 Bow St, WC2.) At the entrance to Broad Court is a delightful sculpture by Paolazzi of young ballet dancers.

Floral St leads back to James St and Covent Garden Underground station. Across Long Acre is Neal St with new shops and restaurants in former market premises. On the corner of Earlham St, Neal St and Shelton St is Smith's Galleries with changing art exhibitions and a restaurant in the basement. Opposite is the Donmar Warehouse Theatre and the galleries of Contemporary Applied Arts. Just off Short's Gardens is Neal's Yard, an attractive courtyard with a bakery, craft shops and a wholefood snack-bar. In Endell St parallel with Neal St craftspeople can be seen at work in Endell St Market.

Short's Gardens leads on to *Seven Dials*. See p 167. Endell St leads N to St. Giles, see p 183 and High Holborn.

II THE CITY, THE NORTH EAST, EAST END AND DOCKLANDS

The **City of London**, one of the most important commercial centres in the world, covers just one square mile from the Royal Courts of Justice in the Strand (Temple Bar) to Aldgate in the E and from the Thames in the S to City Road in the N. Nearly one third of this tightly built-up area was destroyed during the Second World War and has now been completely rebuilt. The surviving City churches and livery company halls, as well as the financial institutions and 'legal' London, contain much of interest for visitors, but most of the intimate alley-ways and courts which once characterised the City have disappeared in the shadow of huge tower blocks. The demolition of architecturally interesting buildings in the path of efficient glass and concrete office blocks has been allowed to progress further within the City, which has its own planning authority, than anywhere else in London, although the mid 1980s has seen a change of heart which has saved the City from such proposed developments as Mansion House Square—a windswept plaza surrounded by tower blocks intended to replace the existing buildings around Mansion House.

The Corporation of London has survived recent local government reforms to retain much of its independence, and its own police force. It is the only part of the United Kingdom which has councillors elected by commercial interests. These councillors form the Court of Common Council which meets at Guildhall. The Court of Aldermen forms an additional tier within the structure from which the Lord Mayor is elected. The Lord Mayor of the City of London takes up his/her

The late Roman gateway at Aldersgate seen from outside the City, c AD 375. Reconstruction drawing by Peter Jackson

appointment in November. The Lord Mayor's Show is the official procession to the Law Courts where the Lord Mayor takes the oath of office (see p 244); he or she is accompanied by Sheriffs, Aldermen, the Sword Bearer and the Common Cryer. The population of the City once numbered over one million, but it declined rapidly during the 19th and 20th centuries to just 5000 people, augmented each day by hundreds of thousands (approximately 350,000) who work within the Square Mile.

The *City Information Centre*, open Mon to Fri 09.30–17.00, Sat 09.30–13.00 (tel. 071-606 3030), is in St. Paul's Churchyard. It supplies information on the City, open days of livery halls, City churches, etc.

The City of London Festival takes place during two weeks of July with concerts at the Barbican Centre, St. Paul's Cathedral and in livery halls and churches. The extensive fringe programme includes open-air dancing and music, trails, and street-theatre.

20   The Inns of Court: Legal London and the Soane Museum

Access: Underground, Chancery Lane, Temple. Bus 11 from Victoria or Trafalgar Square.

The district between the Thames on the S and Theobald's Road on the N, bounded (roughly) on the E and W by lines running through Fetter Lane and Lincoln's Inn Fields, may be fairly described as 'Legal London', including as it does the Royal Courts of Justice, the four great Inns of Court, and the chambers of the leading solicitors and barristers.

Where the Strand and Fleet St meet (comp. p 215) stand the **Royal Courts of Justice** (Pl. 15; 2) or **Law Courts**, an imposing Gothic pile, erected in 1874–82 for the Supreme Court of Judicature, established in 1873. The architect was G.E. Street (1825–81), who died about a year before the completion of his work, and it was finished by Sir Arthur Blomfield and A.E. Street. The main feature of the interior is the fine Central Hall, 238ft long by 38ft wide, and 80ft high, with a mosaic pavement designed by Street (admission Mon to Fri 10.30–16.30). A small exhibition of legal costume is displayed in a room off the hall. The public entrances to the courts and to the galleries of the hall are in the towers flanking the main entrance. Extended several times to cope with the growth in the law, the latest 12-storey extension at the rear is linked to the Thomas More building in Carey St, where the Bankruptcy and Companies Courts are situated.

The four great **Inns of Court** (*Lincoln's Inn, Inner Temple, Middle Temple*, and *Gray's Inn*) have the exclusive right of calling persons to the English Bar. They originated in the 13C, when the clergy ceased to practise in the courts of justice, giving place to professional students of law. The members of the Inns comprise Benchers, Barristers, and Students. Senior barristers appointed as Queen's Counsel wear silk gowns; others wear 'stuff' gowns. Each Inn has a dining hall, library, and chapel, the Temple Church (see below) serving in the last capacity for both the Temple Inns. The Inns provide lectures for law students and examine candidates for admission to the Bar. The students may pursue their legal studies elsewere, but to become a member of an Inn they must 'keep term' or 'commons' by dining so many times in hall.

Visitors are practically always admitted freely to the quaint and quiet precincts of the Inns of Court (closed on Ascension Day) among which only Lincoln's Inn survived the Second World War without extensive damage.

From the Strand just past the Law Courts turn N into Bell Yard. Across Carey St, synonymous in England for bankruptcy proceedings (see above), attractive archways admit to the dignified 17C quadrangle of *New Square*, part of **Lincoln's Inn** (Pl. 15; 2). It probably takes its name from Henry de Lacy, Earl of Lincoln (died 1311), adviser to Edward I in matters of law and a great proponent of legal education; the Inn is not on the site of his London mansion, which lay E of Barnard's Inn. A body of lawyers is known to have occupied the present site from c 1292, though no formal records exist earlier than 1424. Visitors should call at the Porter's Lodge, 11A New Square, (open 08.00–19.00) or tel. 071-405 6360 for admission to the halls and chapel.

Between New Square and the *Old Buildings* to the E is the *Old Hall* (c 1492; S bay of 1624), with good exterior brickwork and fine open roof, well restored in 1926–28. It served as the Court of Chancery from 1733 to 1873, within which period falls the famous fictional case of Jarndyce v. Jarndyce (in Dickens' 'Bleak House'). The *Chapel* (open Mon to Fri 12.00–14.30), probably by John Clarke (1620–23), has been restored and enlarged; the crypt used to serve, like the Temple Church, as a rendezvous for barristers and their clients, and in the Second World War it acted as a shelter from air raids. The side windows contain glass by Bernard van Linge (1632–34). The replica of the *Gatehouse* into Chancery Lane was originally built in 1518 by Sir Thomas Lovell (whose arms it bears). To the N are the classical range of *Stone Buildings* (1774–80) and the attractive Gardens. The imposing *New Hall and Library* (to the W) is a successful red-brick edifice in the Tudor style, by Philip and P.C. Hardwick (1843–45). The hall contains a large mural painting by G.F. Watts ('Justice—a Hemicycle of Lawgivers'; 1853–59), and many legal portraits. The brilliant heraldic glass dates from 1954. The Benchers' Rooms also contain fine paintings, including a small work by Holbein. The library is the oldest in London (1497) and contains the most complete collection of law books in England (70,000 vols), but these may be visited only with a member of the Inn.

Among the eminent names associated with Lincoln's Inn are those of Sir Thomas More, Donne, Penn, Pitt, Horace Walpole, Newman, Macaulay, Canning, Disraeli, Gladstone, Morley, Asquith, Galsworthy, and Newbolt.

An archway at the NW corner of New Square leads into **Lincoln's Inn Fields** (Pl. 15; 2; fine plane trees), the largest square in central London, the old houses surrounding it are mainly occupied as solicitors' offices. It was laid out in 1618 by Inigo Jones, who is said also to have built some houses on the W and S sides (now practically all gone). On the S side, beyond the *Land Registry Office* and *Nuffield College of Surgical Sciences*, the **Royal College of Surgeons** occupies a large building with an Ionic portico, erected in 1806–13 by G. Dance, Junior. It was modified with great skill by Sir Charles Barry (1835–37), whose library and entrance hall survive. New buildings replace Second World War damage.

The College contains the *Hunterian Collection*, the remnants of what was the greatest medical museum in the world, founded by the

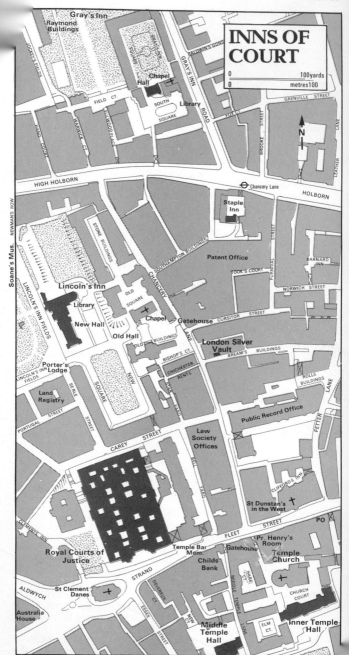

INNS OF COURT

| 0 | 100 yards |
| 0 | metres 100 |

Gray's Inn
Raymond Buildings
JOCKEY'S FIELDS
Hall
Chapel
FIELD CT.
SOUTH SQUARE
Library
GRAY'S INN
BALDWIN'S GARDENS
GRAY'S INN ROAD
GRENVILLE STREET
BROOKE STREET
LEATHER LANE
N
WARWICK CT.
HAND COURT
JOCKEY'S FIELDS
FULWOOD PLACE
HIGH HOLBORN
Chancery Lane
HOLBORN
Soane's Mus. NEWMAN'S ROW
Staple Inn
STONE BUILDINGS
SOUTHAMPTON BUILDINGS
Patent Office
TOOK'S COURT
FURNIVAL STREET
BARNARD INN
NORWICH STREET
Lincoln's Inn
Library
New Hall
Old Hall
CHANCERY LANE
OLD SQUARE
Chapel
Gatehouse CURSITOR STREET
London Silver Vault
BREAM'S BUILDINGS
ROLLS BUILDINGS
LINCOLN'S INN FIELDS
Porter's Lodge
LINCOLN'S INN FIELDS
NEW SQUARE
BISHOP'S CT.
CHICHESTER RENTS
STAR YARD
Land Registry
PORTUGAL STREET
SERLE STREET
STREET
Public Record Office
FETTER LANE
Law Society Offices
CAREY STREET
BELL YARD
CLIFFORD'S INN
St Dunstan's in the West
PO
CLEMENT'S INN
Royal Courts of Justice
Temple Bar Mem.
Childs Bank
STRAND
Gatehouse
Pr. Henry's Room
Temple Church
HARE CT.
CHURCH COURT
MIDDLE TEMPLE LANE
ALDWYCH
St Clement Danes
DEVEREUX CT.
ESSEX STREET
NEW COURT
Middle Temple Hall
ELM CT.
Inner Temple Hall
Australia House

celebrated surgeon John Hunter (1728–93). Many of its specir
were destroyed during bombing in 1941.

Hunterian Museum, Royal College of Surgeons, Lincoln's Inn Fields, WC2. Te
071-405 3474. Access: Underground, Holborn. Open to professional media
people only. Mon to Fri 10.00–17.00, by written application only. Closed during
August. Children not admitted. Free.

Next door is the large new building of the *Imperial Cancer Research
Fund* which extends into Portsmouth St, where an old shop survives
claiming to be Dickens' 'Old Curiosity Shop'; the original of the novel
was located near the site of Irving's statue in Charing Cross Road.
However, this may well be the oldest surviving shop in London,
dating back to 1567. Today it sells memorabilia and souvenirs.

On the W side of Lincoln's Inn Fields, *Lindsey House* (Nos 59, 60) is
attributed to Inigo Jones (c 1640); Nos 57–58 are imitations built in
1730, and altered by Soane. *Powis House*, at the NW corner, is a fine
brick building of 1684–89 (restored). Among famous residents were
Lord Brougham (1778–1868), Spencer Perceval (1762–1812; No. 60),
John Milton, Lord Tennyson (1809–92) John Forster (1812–76; No.
58), and Nell Gwynn (1650–87).—Before their enclosure the gardens
were a favourite duelling-ground and a great haunt of thieves. The
pillory was often erected here. Lord William Russell was executed in
Lincoln's Inn Fields in 1683. Memorials on the N side of the garden
commemorate Mrs Ramsay MacDonald (died 1911), who lived at No.
3 Lincoln's Inn Fields, and Lord Hambleden (1868–1928) head of the
book-distributing organisation of W.H. Smith & Son. There is a bust of
Hunter (1979) in the SW corner.

The N walk of the gardens has been named *Canada Walk*, to
commemorate the establishment here of the headquarters of the
Royal Canadian Air Force in 1940–45 (tablet beside a memorial maple
tree). In the middle of the N side of the square (where most of the fine
houses have been demolished) No. 13 survives as ***Sir John Soane's
Museum**, founded by Sir John Soane (1753–1837), architect of the
Bank of England. Owing to the stipulation of the founder that his
collections should be neither augmented nor disturbed, the museum
has the unusual interest of retaining the character of a private house
of the period (1813), though admittedly somewhat eccentric. The
arrangements to make the most of the room available are exceedingly
ingenious and the effect of space is enhanced by a clever use of
mirrors. Several rooms have recently been returned to their original,
rather unusual, colour scheme. An extension into the adjoining
building is planned. The museum includes some objects that no
visitor to London should miss, pre-eminently the paintings by William
Hogarth and the sarcophagus of Seti I.

Sir John Soane's Museum, 13 Lincoln's Inn Fields, WC2. Tel. 071-405 2107.
Access: Underground, Holborn. Open Tues to Sat 10.00–17.00. Free.

The PICTURE ROOM on the ground floor contains two admirable series
of paintings by *William Hogarth* (1697–1764), the *Rake's Progress
(eight scenes; 1735) and the *Election (four scenes; 1754–57), excellent examples of his satirical humour, harmonious colouring, and able
composition. Here also are The Passage Point by *Callcott*, and a
Design for the Ceiling of the Queen's State Bedchamber at Hampton
Court, by *Thornhill*. Descend to the SEPULCHRAL CHAMBER with the
*Sarcophagus of Seti I, King of Egypt c 1370 BC and father of
Ramesses the Great.—Return to the ground floor and the first room

the plaster casts, in which are *Turner*'s *'Admiral Tromp's
.e entering the Texel after his defeat of Blake in 1652', and
...naletto's *'View of the Grand Canal'. Ascend to the FIRST FLOOR
.enovated in 1970) where a connecting door admits to the
.djoining house (No. 12) built by Soane for himself in 1792, and
now used as a library for students (see above: location of planned
extention). The numerous small works of art, antiquities, casts, and
furniture, etc., throughout the Museum include many objects of
great interest. The fine doors of mahogany and ebony deserve
notice, and many of the windows are filled with old stained glass.

Leave the square by Newman's Row (at the NE corner) and emerge
in High Holborn (see p 188). Turn E, cross, and turn N into Fulwood
Place to reach **Gray's Inn** (Pl. 7; 6). Originally in the buildings of
the manor of Portpool, it is known to have been occupied by
lawyers before 1370 and takes its name from the former owners of
the site, the Lords Grey de Wilton. The Inn was very seriously
damaged in 1941, the Hall, the Chapel, and the Library being
burned out. It has been restored in a harmonious style. Both the
Chapel and Hall are usually open when not in use. Pass through an
archway (right) to the squares either side of the *Hall* (1560), rebuilt
in 1951, with a second oriel presented by the American Bar
Association. It preserves its stained glass and much of the fine
carved screen. Shakespeare's 'Comedy of Errors' had its first
performance here in 1594, and the Court of Exchequer was held in
this hall in the 18C. The *Chapel* was reconsecrated on the 19th
anniversary of the fire; it preserves a stoup from the 14C manor
chapel. The *Library*, in South Square, is a building by Sir Edward
Maufe (1956). The *Gardens* (entered from Field Court through a
gate of 1723), with their ancient catalpas, were thought to have
been laid out by Francis Bacon (whose statue stands in South
Square). *Raymond Buildings* (1825) and *Verulam Buildings* (1811)
skirt the gardens on the W and E in long terraces.

The great name of Gray's Inn is Francis Bacon, who became Treasurer of the
Inn and retained his chambers here from 1577 till his death in 1626. Among
other members were Sir William Gascoigne, the judge traditionally thought to
have committed the Prince of Wales (later Henry V) to prison, Sir Thomas
Gresham, Thomas Cromwell, Nicholas Bacon, Burghley, Abp Laud, and Lord
Birkenhead. The Council of Legal Education occupies a building in Gray's Inn
Place where Sun Yat-Sen, the 'Father of the Chinese Republic', lived during
his political exile from his country in the 1890s—a privately erected plaque
marks the site.

Return across High Holborn to *Chancery Lane* (Pl. 7; 6) which runs
S to Fleet St.

The nine **Inns of Chancery** differed from the Inns of Court in being of minor
importance and subordinate character. It was long the custom for students of
law to enter first an Inn of Chancery and then graduate to an Inn of Court, but
this practice had become obsolete by the beginning of the 17C. The Inns of
Chancery were then abandoned to the attorneys, and by the middle of the
18C they had practically ceased to have any legal character.
   Clement's Inn, *Clifford's Inn* (the oldest and most important of the Inns of
Chancery), *Thavie's Inn*, and *Furnival's Inn* now exist merely as names of
modern buildings. *Lyon's Inn*, *New Inn*, and *Strand Inn* have completely
disappeared. The legal history of *Staple Inn* goes back to the reign of Henry V
(1413–22), that of *Barnard's Inn* to the time of Henry VI (1422–61).—The two
Serjeants' Inns were independent bodies, composed solely of serjeants-at-law
('servientes ad legem'), an order of the highest rank of barristers. The society

was dissolved in 1877, but the buildings of one of their inns survived 1941.

Chancery Lane skirts the E side of Lincoln's Inn (p 209). To the E r Southampton Buildings, and the entrance to the *London Silver Vaults* (Mon to Fri 09.00–17.30, Sat 09.00–12.30), storing and selling a copious stock of antique silver, etc.

Further on is the *Patent Office Library* now Holborn Division of the British Library (British Science Library) (tel. 071-323 7919), housing the finest collection of technical and scientific works in England. It is adjoined on the N by the small garden of Staple Inn.

Further S in Chancery Lane rises the **Public Record Office**, one section of the chief repository of the state archives of England, a fortress-like building in a Tudor style (1851–66, by Pennethorne, and 1891–96, by Sir John Taylor), very reminiscent of the 19C parts of the Tower of London from which many of the archives were removed. Here are the legal and judicial records from the Conquest; 16–18C papers of Secretaries of State; and 19C census returns (see also Kew, p 347).

Public Record Office Library, Chancery Lane, WC2. Tel. 071-405 0741. Open Mon to Fri 09.30–17.30; entry by Reader's Ticket (proof of identity required).
Public Record Office Museum (as above). Free. Open Mon to Fri 10.00–17.00.
The ***Public Record Office Museum**** occupies the exact site and area of the old Rolls Chapel. Three of the monuments, erected in the old chapel, are still in their original positions on the N wall. Adjacent is the most important object in the museum, the *Domesday Book* (2 vellum vols.), containing the results of the statistical survey of England made by order of William the Conqueror in 1086. The so-called *Domesday Chest*, with its triple lock, is likewise shown. The glass cases contain a remarkable series of famous and interesting historical documents and records.

Almost opposite the Record Office are the massive offices of the *Law Society*, which controls the education, membership, and discipline of the solicitors' branch of the legal profession. At the foot of Chancery Lane cross Fleet St to enter the **Temple** (Pl. 7; 8) by North's fine *Gatehouse* (1684), which opens from Fleet St near Temple Bar.

The *Temple Bar* marks the boundary between the City of London and the City of Westminster. See p 201.

The general name of the Temple covers two Inns of Court, the *Middle* and the *Inner Temple*, extending from Fleet St to the Thames, and named after their topographical relations to the City proper. The Outer Temple, merely a piece of ground belonging to the Templars, was absorbed at an early date by private owners.
The Temple was originally the seat in England of the famous Order of Knights Templars. On the dissolution of the Order in 1312 the Temple passed to the Crown and later into the possession of the Knights Hospitallers of St. John, who leased it in the reign of Edward III (c 1338) to certain professors of the common law. The first trustworthy mention of the Temple as an Inn of Court is found in 1449. The church (see below), and the crypt and buttery of the Inner Temple Hall are the only edifices going back to the Middle Ages, the other old buildings dating mainly from the reign of Elizabeth I or just after the Great Fire of 1666. Widespread destruction in 1940–41 has been repaired, and new buildings in traditional style have been erected by Sir Edward Maufe, Sir Hubert Worthington, and T.W. Sutcliffe. Buildings belonging to the Inner Temple bear the device of the Winged Horse, those of the Middle Temple the Lamb and Flag.
Among famous members of the Inner Temple may be mentioned Granville, Hampden, Jeffreys, Lyndhurst, Thurlow, and Hallam; of the Middle Temple,

ndon, Raleigh, Pym, Congreve, Wycherley, Sheridan, Blackstone, Fielding,
.. Moore, De Quincey, Burke, Dickens, Blackmore, Eldon, Havelock, and
xett.

ne *Temple Church**, or *Church of St. Mary the Virgin*, belonging to
.he Middle and Inner Temple in common, is the most important of the
five remaining round churches in England. (Open 09.30–16.00, closed
Aug, Sept.) It is a 'peculiar', i.e. exempt from episcopal jurisdiction.
The round part of the church was consecrated in 1185, and is in the
transition-Norman style, with handsome ornamentation. The Norman
W doorway survives. The chancel ('oblong'), an admirable example of
Early English, was added in 1240. The whole building was very
seriously damaged in 1941, but the final touches of restoration were
completed in 1961.

The chancel, entered by a new S porch, is borne by clustered piers of
Purbeck marble, from the same quarry as the originals. The reredos,
designed by Wren in 1682, was removed as a modification in 1840, and
so escaped damage. The stained glass of the beautiful E windows,
given by the Glaziers' Company, the Middle Temple (N), and the
Inner Temple (S), is by Carl Edwards.—In the churchyard is a noble effigy of a
13C ecclesiastic, and near the S door (beneath a glass slab) is the
gravestone of John Selden (1584–1654), the jurist. In the round church
are nine *Monuments of Associates of the Temple* of the 12–13C, with
recumbent marble figures (damaged) in full armour. The two arresting
coloured *Monuments* are to Richard Martin (1618; S side) and
Edmund Plowden (1585; N side).

The lawyers used to await their clients in 'the Round', just as the
serjeants-at-law did in St. Paul's Cathedral. The *Master's House*, the
home of the incumbent of the Temple Church, NE of the church, was
re-erected after the Great Fire and totally destroyed in 1941 but has
been rebuilt in its 17C form.—In the churchyard, N of the choir, is a
slab (now covered) marking the grave of Oliver Goldsmith (1728–74).

To the S of the church is a cloister built, by Maufe, in accordance
with Wren's original design. Beyond is the **Inner Temple Hall** and
Library, by Worthington (1952–56) replacing the 19C range destroyed
in 1941. The refaced buttery at the W end and the crypt below it date
from the 14C. To the E is *King's Bench Walk*, with two houses ascribed
to Wren (Nos 4 and 5), popular locations for film companies. Towards
the river lie the *Inner Temple Gardens* (no adm.); and on the other side
of Middle Temple Lane are the *Middle Temple Gardens* (no adm.). In
one of these, according to a scene in 'Henry VI' (Pt I, ii, 4), were
plucked the white and red roses, assumed as badges in the Wars of the
Roses.

On the W side of the Middle Temple Lane is *Middle Temple Hall**
(open Mon to Fri 10.00–16.00. Closed Aug. Free. Tel. 071-353 4355), a
stately Elizabethan chamber of 1562–73 (100ft long, 42ft wide, 47ft
high), the interior of which, heavily damaged in 1941–44, is now
rebuilt and restored (inscription on the E gable). Shakespeare is said to
have taken part in a performance of 'Twelfth Night' in this hall on 2
Feb 1601.—The *Middle Temple Library*, which lost some 65,000
volumes, is housed in Middle Temple Lane, below the hall. Middle
Temple Lane is still lit by gas.

At No. 2 Brick Court, Middle Temple Lane (destroyed), Oliver
Goldsmith died. Blackstone, the celebrated jurist, occupied the rooms
below Goldsmith, and complained of the noise made by his 'revelling
neighbour'. Thackeray (1853–59) and Praed also had chambers in this
building. Crown Office Row, where Charles Lamb was born (1775)
and spent his first seven years (at No. 2), has been rebuilt. Later he

lived with his sister within the Temple from 1801 to 1817, first at ⋮ Mitre Court Buildings and (after 1808) at 4 Inner Temple Lane (both houses pulled down). Dr Johnson occupied rooms at 1 Inner Temple Lane, replaced by Johnson's Buildings. Thackeray had rooms at 10 Crown Office Row from 1848–50. In *Fountain Court* to the N of Middle Temple Hall, the fountain, dating from 1681, was restored in 1919 to its original condition.

21   Fleet Street, Blackfriars and St. Paul's

A.   Fleet Street and Blackfriars

Access: Underground, Temple; Buses 11 or 15 from Trafalgar Square.

Where the Strand ends at the Royal Courts of Justice and meets Fleet St the *Temple Bar Monument* marks the boundary between the City of London and the City of Westminster. It was erected in 1880 on the site of old Temple Bar; designed by Sir Horace Jones, the statues of Queen Victoria and Edward VII (as Prince of Wales) are by Boehm. The bronze griffin is by C.B. Birch. The bronze reliefs show Queen Victoria in a state coach passing through the old Temple Bar on her way to the Guildhall.

The original **Temple Bar** was erected by Wren in 1672, after the Great Fire, but its wooden predecessor is known to have stood here in 1501, and some kind of a bar or chain, on the boundary between Westminster and the City proper, seems to have existed as far back as the 12C. From the top of the gate projected a number of iron spikes, on which the heads of felons and traitors were exhibited (e.g. those of the rebels of 1745). The gate was removed to Plumstead Marshes in 1878, and ten years later was re-erected by Sir Henry Meux as an entrance to Theobalds Park, near Waltham Cross. Plans are periodically mooted to rescue it from its rural decay (see p 396). When the sovereign of England visits the City on state occasions, the ancient custom of obtaining permission from the Lord Mayor 'to pass Temple Bar' is still observed and the Lord Mayor presents the Pearl Sword to the sovereign, which he then carries before the royal procession.

The George pub just opposite the Royal Courts of Justice was once a coffee house. The long, beamed bar serves snacks and there is a restaurant upstairs. Nearby is London's narrowest shop, *Twining's*, of 1787; earlier premises date to 1716. The *Wig and Pen Club* (members only but overseas visitors can apply for instant membership) just W of Temple Bar (230 Strand) occupies a quaint building of 1625 with a bar and restaurant, providing a meeting place for journalists and lawyers.

Fleet St, the busy continuation of the Strand, leads from Temple Bar to Ludgate Circus. The 'Street of Ink' or 'Street of Shame' as it was also known was the centre of Britain's newspaper industry until 1987. All the major newspapers were at one time printed off the streets, squares, and courts on either side of Fleet St. The neighbourhood was especially lively between 21.00 and midnight, when the dailies went to press with their first editions. All national newspapers have now moved their printing plants and editorial offices to Docklands and other locations. Fleet St derived its name from the Fleet River or Fleet Ditch (now an underground sewer) which rises amid the heights of Hampstead, flows through the Holborn Valley and joins the Thames near Blackfriars Bridge. This is now an area in transition as City banks

..d offices move westwards to take over many of the former
·ewspaper headquarters and the pubs adjust to a new clientele.

Immediately below the Temple Bar Memorial, at No. 1 Fleet St is
Child's Bank, one of the oldest in London (founded 1671), now
amalgamated with Williams and Glyn's Bank. On its books were the
names of many royal persons as well as Oliver Cromwell, Marlborough, Nell Gwynn, Prince Rupert, Pepys, and Dryden. At the former
Devil Tavern, on this site, Ben Jonson reigned supreme in the 'Apollo
Club'.

Middle Temple Lane, beyond Child's Bank on the same side, leads
through N Gateway to the *Temple* (Rte 20), and just beyond is another
passage (Inner Temple Lane) leading to the Temple Church. No. 17
Fleet St, above this latter archway, is an interesting specimen of a
timbered house of 1610, with a projecting upper storey. On the first
floor is *Prince Henry's Room*, with a decorated ceiling, referring to
Prince Henry, elder son of James I. Here is a collection of memorabilia
of Samuel Pepys, including an original letter to Charles II.

Prince Henry's Room, 17 Fleet St, EC4. Tel. 071-353 7323. Free. Access:
Underground, Temple. Open Mon to Fri 13.45–17.00, Sat 13.45–16.00.

The *Cock Tavern*, at No. 22, preserves some internal fittings and other
interesting relics of the old tavern, which stood opposite till 1887 and
was frequented by Pepys, Dickens and Tennyson, who wrote 'O
plump head-waiter at the Cock'. The original sign carved by Grinling
Gibbons is preserved in the bar on the first floor.

On the N side of Fleet St, beyond a branch of the Bank of England,
Chancery Lane (comp. p 213) runs N to Holborn. Beyond, *Clifford's
Inn Passage* leads through the old gatehouse of the Inn of Chancery to
a building which has appropriated the name. The octagonal church of
St. Dunstan in the West, by John Shaw (1831–33) was well restored in
1950; it stands on the site of an earlier building. The fine tower ends in
an open-work lantern. The figure of Queen Elizabeth I (1586) over the
E (vestry) porch, and the statues of King Lud and his sons within it,
came from the Ludgate, which stood half-way up Ludgate Hill and
was pulled down in 1760. The fine clock (1671) with 'striking Jacks',
from the old church, was returned from St. Dunstan's Lodge in
Regent's Park in 1936. It is the oldest performing clock in London.

On the S front are a bust of Lord Northcliffe (1865–1922), and a tablet to J.L.
Garvin (1868–1947), journalist and editor. Inside, the chapel on the left contains
a quaint brass to Henry Dacres, 'merchant taylor and alderman of the City of
London', and his wife (1530). The chapel to the left of the altar is now closed by
an iconostasis from Autim monastery, Bucharest, dedicated in 1966 to mark the
chapel's second use by the Roumanian orthodox congregation. A stained glass
window in the chapel, and a tablet to the right of the entrance porch,
commemorate Izaak Walton, a vestryman of the parish. On the wall beneath are
plaques to George Calvert, Lord Baltimore (1580?–1632), founder of Maryland,
who was buried in the old church, and to Daniel Brown of Connecticut, the first
Anglican clergyman to be ordained for America (1723). The communion rail was
carved by Grinling Gibbons while John Donne was vicar here (1624–31).
Sweeney Todd, the fictional barber who made pies out of his customers,
supposedly had his shop next to the church.

Hoare's Bank, No. 37 Fleet St, on the S side, founded in 1672 by
Richard Hoare, a goldsmith and the son of a successful horse-dealer,
moved to Fleet St in 1690. It is the only remaining 'private' bank in
London. *El Vino's* wine bar, haunt of generations of newspaper men,
is still fussy about dress and serving women. *Fetter Lane*, diverging to
the N (left) beyond St. Dunstan's and leading to Holborn, derives its

name either from the 'faitours' (i.e. beggars) with which it used to swarm, or from a colony of 'feutriers' (felt-makers).

A little further, on a bend in Fleet St reveals a celebrated view of St. Paul's. On the N side is a series of small courts and alleys (dating from the late 17C and probably originating as gardens), all redolent of literary and historical associations. *Crane Court* was the home of the Royal Society from 1710–80. In *Johnson's Court*, Dr Johnson lived from 1765–76; in allusion to his residence here he jokingly called himself, when in Scotland, 'Johnson of that ilk'. From 1776 till his death in 1784 he lived in *Bolt Court* (both houses demolished).— Wine Office Court was another resort of Dr Johnson and the *Old Cheshire Cheese* pub and restaurant (rebuilt in 1667; entrance 145 Fleet St), in which it is likely that Johnson's circle met; followed later by Dickens, Tennyson, Carlyle, Reynolds, Thackeray and after that of Mark Twain, Theodore Roosevelt, Conan Doyle and others reliving Johnson's 'Cheese'. The 14C Crypt of the Whitefriars monastery can be seen in the basement and is available for functions.—Johnson's Court and Bolt Court both lead into *Gough Square* and **Dr Johnson's House** (No. 17), where he lived from 1749 to 1758, engaged in the production of 'The Rambler' and of his famous 'Dictionary'. His wife died here in 1752.

Dr Johnson's House, Gough Square, EC4. Tel. 071-353 3745. Access: Underground, Blackfriars, Temple. Open Mon to Sat 11.00–17.30, May to September, 11.00–17.00 October to April. Admission charge.
    The house was built c 1700 and restored in 1948 and 1990. Among relics of Dr Johnson are an early edition of the 'Dictionary' and signed letters. The portraits include Dr Johnson by J. Opie, and James Boswell by Joshua Reynolds. The most notable room is the large attic in which Johnson and his six amanuenses worked at the 'Dictionary'.

On the S side of Fleet St, behind No. 49, a pleasant brick quadrangle (1956) is entered by the old iron gate of *Serjeants' Inn*. Here an archway through Mitre Court Buildings admits to the Inner Temple (comp. p 214). Beyond Bouverie St, *Whitefriars St* perpetuates the name of the Carmelite monastery founded about 1241 and dissolved in 1538. Here were the offices of News International: the 'Sun' and the 'News of the World', which relocated to Wapping in January 1986. The huge Kumagai Gumi's Whitefriars projects involved demoliton of the News International building and lifting the clear the 4m square underground chapel of the 1420 Carmelite Crypt which has been preserved in the new building.

The privilege of sanctuary was claimed in 1580 for the area within the precincts of the Whitefriars Monastery after the monastery was dissolved by Henry VIII. It became known as *Alsatia*, and debtors, criminals, and lawless characters of all kinds gathered here until 1697. (The name was apparently taken from the province, Alsace, contested by France and Germany).

On the N side of Fleet St are the former offices of the 'Daily Telegraph' (moved to the Isle of Dogs in 1987) now redeveloped as the headquarters for the Wall St investment house, Goldman Sachs, and the distinctive glass-front of the listed former 'Daily Express' building (1931). The 'Evening Standard' moved from here to new editorial offices in Kensington High St. The Express Newspapers moved in 1989 to a new building in Blackfriars Rd. A bust of T.P. O'Connor (1848–1929), journalist and parliamentarian, marks the offices of the long-since defunct 'News Chronicle'. No. 85 on the S side is the headquarters of Reuters (moving to Blackwall Yard, Docklands) and ne Press Association. Brides Passage leads S to the church of **St. Bride** (open Mon to Sat 08.30–17.30, Sun 08.30–20.00), rebuilt by Wren in 1671–75, and seriously damaged in 1940. The *Spire (1703), called by Henley 'a madrigal in stone', was originally 234ft high, but was struck by lightning in 1764 and rebuilt 8ft shorter. It is still, however, the tallest of Wren's steeples, an inspiration for wedding cakes—see below—and has survived the damage to the rest of the church. Restoration, by Godfrey Allen, was carried out in 1953–57, with woodwork (stalls and reredos) in the style of Wren and Grinling Gibbons, by Alfred Banks. The reredos is a memorial to Edward Winslow, the Pilgrim Father, a parishioner. At the W end are statues of St. Bride and St. Paul, by D. MacFall, while the E end has been painted by Glyn Jones, in a *trompe-l'oeil* manner, to create the effect of an apsidal ending. There are lunchtime concerts.

The old church was the burial-place of Weelkes (1623), the madrigalist, and of Lovelace (1658), the Cavalier poet. The parish registers include entries of the baptism of Samuel Pepys (1633; born in Salisbury Court, overlooking the churchyard, where his father was a tailor). The crypt of the much-rebuilt medieval church which Wren incorporated into his own church is open to the public. Excavations have revealed a Roman ditch (15–16ft wide) and the pavement of a Roman building, the first recorded outside the wall of London. Evidence of a late Saxon cemetery was found, and remains of earlier churches on the site (the first built in the mid-11C). The coffin of Samuel Richardson (died 1761), author of 'Clarissa Harlowe', who carried on his business as a printer in the adjacent Salisbury Square, is preserved here. A small exhibition illustrates the development of printing in Fleet St and the church has a special connection with newspapers and the printing industry.

Bride Lane, passing St. Bride's Church, contains (right) the *St. Bride Institute* (1894), an educational association for the printing industry. New Bridge St leads S to Blackfriars bridge and railway bridge, past the site of the notorious old prison, *Bridewell.*

Some kind of castle, taking its name from the holy well of St. Bride (above) and occasionally occupied by English sovereigns, stood here in early Norman times. Henry VIII restored it so as to form the 'stately and beautiful house' which was the residence of himself and Queen Catherine during her trial. Edward VI granted it to the City of London, and in 1556 it became a prison for vagrants and immoral women. Partly destroyed in the Great Fire, it was rebuilt in 1668. New Bridewell, built in 1829, was pulled down in 1864.

Tudor Street leads W to the site of the former *City of London School for Boys* which has been redeveloped behind its façade as the London home of Wall St's Morgan Guaranty Corporation. The school moved to a new building in Queen Victoria St in 1986. The City of London School opened in 1837 in Milk St and moved to the Embankment in 1883. Lord Asquith was educated here. Further on, overlooking the Embankment are the Gothic buildings of *Sion College and Library* designed by Sir Arthur Blomfield (1886) who incorporated the original timber roof from London Wall.

Sion College (adm. on application), founded in the City in 1624, exists for the benefit of the Anglican clergy. Its chief glory is the Library (300,000 vols), which possesses many rarities, but suffered considerable war damage.—The City Livery Club is also accommodated here.

The 'Daily Mail', which had its offices in Carmelite St, moved its printing plant to Surrey Docks and editorial offices to Kensington High St in 1989. The buildings are due to be redeveloped. Further W are the *Temple Gardens*, outside which two heraldic dragons (from the demolished Coal Exchange) mark the boundary of the City. On the river two ships are moored: the 'Wellington', serves as the livery hall of the Master Mariners' Company, and the 'President' is a training ship.

On the corner of the Embankment and New Bridge Street is the huge *Unilever House* (1932) with a new 35ft fountain sculpture of St. George slaying the Dragon by M. Sandle (1987).

The district of **Blackfriars** was so called from the Dominicans (who wore black habits) who settled here in the 13C and erected extensive monastic buildings. Remains of a site to the N along Carter Lane were found during excavations in 1989. In the monastery, in 1382, an assembly condemned as heretical 24 Articles deduced from the teachings of Wyclif. It was here that a decree of divorce was pronounced against Queen Catherine of Aragon (1529; 'Henry VIII', ii. 4; Shakespeare). In 1596 James Burbage established the first covered theatre in London here, in which Shakespeare (who owned a house in the district) probably performed. The name of *Playhouse Yard* commemorates its existence.

On the corner of Queen Victoria St is the distinctive *Blackfriar* pub (opposite the station) in a triangular building. The unique art nouveau interior has recently been restored; note the beaten bronze bas-reliefs of the monks at work. In the side chapel-bar there are red marble columns, an arched mosaic ceiling and decorative figures. A new building by John Outram behind the pub will disguise the railway line leading to the new St. Paul's Thameslink station replacing Holborn Viaduct; see below.

To the N in *Blackfriars Lane* stands the charming **Apothecaries Hall**, dating partly from 1670, partly from 1786, with portraits of James I, Charles I, John Keats (licentiate of the Hall), and others.

At Puddle Dock, S, is the *Mermaid Theatre*, established by Bernard Miles in 1956. The Mermaid Theatre reopened in 1982 after further rebuilding. Here by the river in 1963 a 2C Roman boat was uncovered. It had sunk with its cargo of building stone brought via the Medway from Maidstone to build the city walls (comp. p 237).

In nearby *Baynard House* a Museum of Telecommunications opened in 1982.

Telecom Technology Showcase, 135 Queen Victoria St, EC4. Tel. 071-248 7444. Open Mon to Fri 10.00–17.00. It illustrates the history of Britain's telecommunications and also looks to the future with many up-to-date and potential gadgets on view.

During reconstruction in 1972, part of Baynard Castle was temporarily exposed. The castle was first built by William the Conqueror, and named after a follower. When the Dominicans took over the area (now Blackfriars) in 1278, a second castle was built a little to the E. A 15C successor to this castle was uncovered including the prominent towers and wall along the old line of the river (shown in Hollar's 'View of London'). The castle, which extended to the N of Upper Thames St, was destroyed in the Great Fire, and warehouses (often following the line of the old walls) were built on the site. It was intended that the castle wall be exposed permanently in the precinct of the new City of London School for Boys on the river front.

In Printing House Square to the N of Queen Victoria Street, 'The Times' used to be printed before it moved to Grays Inn Road, and the King's Printing House was established in 1667. Nearby is *St. Andrew by the Wardrobe*, rebuilt by Wren in 1685–95, and restored in 1961 after serious war damage. It took its name from the proximity of the King's Great Wardrobe, used as an office for the keepers of the king's state apparel. 'The Observer' had its offices at St. Andrew's Hill and moved to Battersea in 1987. The *Faraday Building* (1933) in Queen Victoria St was the first building in the City allowed to go higher than the London Building Act then normally permitted, and thus the first obtrusive precursor of many into the city townscape.

The **College of Arms** is the seat of the official heraldic authority for England, Ireland, and the Commonwealth. The Heralds of the kings of England were first incorporated by Richard III in 1484, and in 1555 Queen Mary I gave them a new charter and the site of the present College.—The Court Room is open to the public Mon to Fri 10.00–16.00.

Free. The Earl Marshal's throne is used on ceremonial occasions. The reredos is early 18C.

The original building was burnt down in the Great Fire of 1666; the present one, by Maurice Emmett (1671–88), is a good example of the period. Splendid 19C wrought iron gates, apparently made for Goodrich Court, Herefordshire, were given to the College in 1956.

The Officers of Arms, who are members of the Royal Household, are still appointed directly by the Crown, by letters patent under the great seal, on the advice of the Duke of Norfolk as hereditary Earl Marshal. They consist of three kings of Arms (Garter, Clarenceux, and Norroy and Ulster), six heralds (Windsor, Lancaster, Somerset, York, Chester, and Richmond), and four pursuivants (Bluemantle, Portcullis, Rouge Croix, and Rouge Dragon). The titles of the heralds are taken from Royal duchies, earldoms and castles, while those of the pursuivants are taken from national badges (Rouge Croix), royal badges (Portcullis and Rouge Dragon), and the blue mantle of the Order of the Garter. For many centuries the kings of arms have been authorised by the sovereigns to grant arms to eminent men, subject to the approval of the Earl Marshal.

The heraldic and genealogical records and collections are unique, and the registers of recorded pedigrees include many families who have settled in the other parts of the world.

In Bennet's Hill, to the S (footpath), is the now isolated brick church of *St. Benet* (restored after damage by arson in 1971). It was rebuilt by Wren in 1677–83, and is now used by a Welsh congregation. Henry Fielding was married here in 1748 and Inigo Jones (1573–1652) was buried in the earlier church.

At 101 Queen Victoria St is the international headquarters (1962) of the *Salvation Army*, founded by William Booth, a Methodist, in 1865. A Christian movement organised in a quasi-military style, it is concerned with all in need. Beyond, to the N, is the church of *St. Nicholas Cole Abbey* (originally 'Cold Abbey'), rebuilt by Wren in 1671–77 and reopened in 1963 after being burnt out in 1941. A striking feature of the interior is the richly coloured glass of the E windows by Keith New. The font and the ornamental woodwork were saved and behind a panel on the S wall is a sculptured head from the medieval church.

New Bridge St leads back to *Ludgate Circus*, formed by the junction of Farringdon St, Ludgate Hill, and Fleet St. On the NW side is a tablet with a relief portrait of Edgar Wallace (1875–1932), novelist and journalist.

Farringdon St, leads N under the Holborn Viaduct. To the E beyond Seacoal Lane, is the site of the historic *Fleet Prison*, which stood on the E side of the Fleet River, and was used for those committed by the Star Chamber and for debtors. The prison was twice rebuilt, after its destruction in the Great Fire (1666) and in the Gordon Riots (1780), and it was finally pulled down in 1844–46. This was the prison in which Mr Pickwick was supposedly confined.

Branching to the W is Shoe Lane with the *International Press Centre* where many overseas newspapers, radio and TV stations have their London HQs. *The Cartoonist* on the ground floor is a modern pub with a wonderful collection of original cartoons.

Beyond Ludgate Circus *Ludgate Hill* (Pl. 8; 5), rises towards St. Paul's Cathedral, the ugly railway viaduct has been demolished; see below. To the N diverges the *Old Bailey*, which leads to Newgate St and the Central Criminal Court (see Rte 22). Further up Ludgate Hill, to the left, is the church of *St. Martin Ludgate*, the slender spire of which shows up well against the dome of St. Paul's. This church was rebuilt by Wren in 1677–87 and has fine oaken *Woodwork, and a Father Smith organ. Captain (later Adm. Sir) William Penn, father of the

founder of Pennsylvania, was married in the former church in 164
The old church stood just within the Roman wall close to Lud Gate, th
first curfew gate in London to be closed at night (comp. p 237).

At No. 3 Ludgate Hill lived William Rich (1755–1811), a pastry cook
who modelled his wedding cakes on the steeple of St. Bride seen from
his window, starting a fashion still followed. *Ave Maria Lane* diverges
left just before St. Paul's. Here is the *Stationers' Hall*, the guildhall of
the Stationers' Company, the members of which (unlike those of most
City Guilds) have some actual connection with their nominal trade.

The Hall was built soon after the first Great Fire of London in 1666, but was
stone-faced in 1800, and a wing was added in 1887. It was severely damaged in
1940, but the hall has now been restored. It contains a fine screen and panelling
of the late 17C, the work of Stephen Colledge.

The Stationers' Company, founded c 1402, was incorporated by royal charter
in 1557, and for a time it preserved the sole right of printing in England (apart
from the presses at Oxford and Cambridge), while it had a monopoly of the
publishing of almanacks down to 1771. Until the passing of the Copyright Act of
1911 every work published in Great Britain had to be registered for copyright at
Stationers' Hall. In 1933 the company was amalgamated with that of the
Newspaper Makers. A plane tree in the court behind the Hall marks the spot
where seditious books used to be burnt.

Among the buildings spared by the bombing of this area is *Amen
Court*, a curiously quiet little nook in the heart of London, entered
from Ave Maria Lane. It contains the dwellings of the Canons
Residentiary of St. Paul's, which Wren is thought to have built.

Beyond the ugly, projecting Juxon House (1964) at the top of
Ludgate Hill (due to be redeveloped with Paternoster Square, see
below is the entrance to St. Paul's Cathedral. In front stands a statue of
Queen Anne.

B.   St. Paul's Cathedral and area

St. Paul's Cathedral, EC4. Tel. 071-248 2705. Access: Underground, St. Paul's,
Mansion House.

The area around St. Paul's Cathedral was heavily bombed during the Second
World War and insensitively rebuilt. Plans are now underway for substantial
redevelopment to give Wren's creation a worthy setting.

The churchyard (now a public garden) surrounding the cathedral is enclosed
by massive railings. In the NE angle are the foundations of *Paul's Cross*, an
open-air pulpit where sermons were regularly preached. On the S side of the
church are a few fragments of the cloisters and chapter house, destroyed in 1666.

The street skirting the S side of the cathedral is called *St. Paul's Churchyard*. In
Dean's Court, leading S, is the *Deanery*, built by Wren c 1670. Adjoining it, in
Carter Lane, is the *Choir House*, with the old Choristers' School (see below; now
a Youth Hostel). A tablet in Carter Lane, a few paces to the E, records
Shakespeare's connection with the Bell Tavern which stood here. Further E,
beyond the *City of London Information Centre* (this may move to the Juxon
House redevelopment), extends *Old Change Court*, now flanked by modern
offices. The stepped *St. Peter's Hill* reveals a view of the Thames across Queen
Victoria St.

Across Cannon St the pleasant *St. Paul's Garden* is adorned with a fountain,
and a statue by Georg Ehrlich. To the N the tower (and restored spire) of *St.
Augustine's* has been incorporated in the new *Cathedral Choir School*, designed
in 1962 by Leo de Syllas and built after his death, with four linked buildings. The
church was rebuilt by Wren in 1683 and destroyed in 1941.

The area to the N of the cathedral was devastated by fire in 1940; only the
Chapter House by Wren (re-opened in 1957) survived. The plaza of the brutal
'60s Paternoster Square will be replaced with a sequence of public spaces, a
urved shopping arcade and offices to a maximum of eight storeys designed in

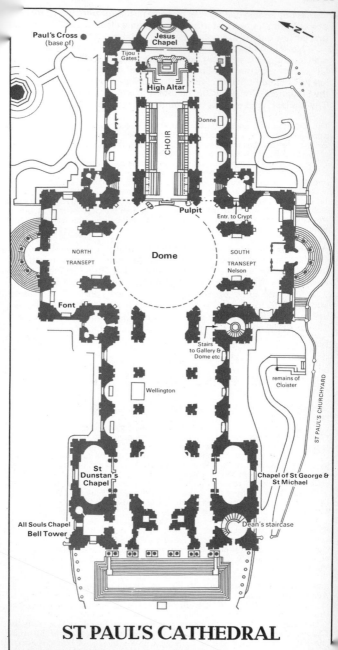

ST PAUL'S CATHEDRAL

the classical style by Arup Associates. A garden and small museum form part of the plan with rebuilding starting possibly in 1990.

The ecclesiastical character of the district survives only in some street and place-names; Ave Maria Lane, Amen Corner and Cathedral Place. Panyer Alley, so named from having formerly been largely occupied by basket-makers, has been replaced by *Panyer Alley Steps* which lead down to Newgate St (N; comp. p 235). The old relief (1688) of a boy seated on a 'panier', marking the highest ground in the City, has been placed on the steps.

In front of St. Paul's Cathedral is the statue of Queen Anne in whose reign the cathedral was finished. The present statue is a copy (1886) of the original by Francis Bird (1712).

Cathedral open Mon to Sat 08.00–18.00. No sightseeing on Sun. Galleries, Crypt, Ambulatory open Mon to Sat 10.00–16.00 Admission charge to each section.

Educational facilities and guided 'super tours' Mon to Sat at 11.00, 11.30, 14.00 and 14.30. Charge. Tour includes crypt, ambulatory, etc. Bookshop.

Services are on weekdays at 08.00 and 10.00, 12.30 (Wed and Fri) and 16.00. There are prayers every hour; on Sun at 08.00, 10.30, 11.30, 15.15 and 18.30. Matins and Evensong daily and the services at 12.30 on Wed and Fri and at 11.30 on Sun are choral.

*St. Paul's Cathedral (Pl. 8; 6), the largest and most famous church in the City, stands at the top of Ludgate Hill. The cathedral of the Bishop of London, it is the masterpiece of Sir Christopher Wren, a dignified edifice in a Renaissance style, dominated by the famous dome. The Portland stone of which it is built was picturesquely bleached and stained by London's climate and smoke, until cleaning in the 1960s disclosed its golden colour and the beautiful detail of the carved stone work.

The tradition that a Roman temple dedicated to Diana stood on the commanding site now occupied by St. Paul's was repudiated by Wren, and there is no evidence to support this theory. A Christian church, said to have been founded here in the 7C by Bp Mellitus was endowed by Ethelbert, King of Kent. Its second successor was burned down in 1087 and its Norman successor was partly destroyed by fire in 1136 but immediately restored. In the 13C the steeple was rebuilt and the choir extended eastwards. This was the noble church of *Old St. Paul's*, in which John Wyclif was tried for heresy in 1377, and Tyndale's New Testament publicly burned in 1527. It was the longest cathedral in England (600ft). The central tower was surmounted by a steeple, which, at the lowest estimate, was 460ft high, but was destroyed by lightning in 1561 and never re-erected. For a long period the church was sadly neglected, but restorations were begun under Charles I. Inigo Jones added a classical portico to the W front, one of his objects being to banish from the church the secular rabble that for over a century had used the middle aisle of the nave ('Paul's Walk') as a place of business and intrigue. In 1666 the cathedral was practically burned down in the Great Fire. Sir Christopher Wren planned an entirely new cathedral and building began in 1675. The first service was held in the choir in 1697 and the last stone was placed in position in 1710. (A model of Old St. Paul's and Wren's model are in the Crypt.) Between 1666 and 1723 the amount spent on the cathedral was about £748,000, most of which was raised by a tax on sea-borne coal entering London. Wren's original ground plan, designed in the form of a Greek cross, was modified at the demand of the Court party, some of whom may have looked forward to the restoration of the old religion, for the ceremonies of which a long nave and side-chapels were required. In 1941 the E end and the N transept received direct hits from high-explosive bombs; another, which did not explode, was dug out with great heroism from beneath the W end. Throughout the war the building was guarded from fire by the coolness and efficiency of its Night Watch.

MEASUREMENTS. The exterior length of the cathedral is 515ft; its W front, with two towers each 212.5ft high, is 180ft wide. Internally it is 479ft long and 227.5ft wide across the transepts. The nave, 125ft across (including the aisle), is 92.5 ft high. The dome is 122ft in diameter, and the total height from the pavement of the church to the top of the cross above the ball is 365ft. The area of St. Paul's is 87,400 sq. ft; that of St. Peter's in Rome 163,181 sq. ft.

The **Exterior** of St. Paul's consists throughout of two orders, the lower Corinthian, the upper Composite. On the N and S sides the upper order is merely a curtain-wall, not corresponding with the height of the aisles and concealing the flying buttresses that support the clerestory of the nave. The balustrade along the top was added against the wishes of Wren, who cynically remarked of it that 'ladies think nothing well without an edging'. The *W Front*, approached by a broad flight of steps, and flanked by towers, has a lower colonnade of twelve columns and an upper one of eight columns. In the NW tower is a peal of bells, and in the SW tower are the clock and 'Great Paul', a bell weighing nearly 17 tons (hung in 1882), which is rung daily for five minutes at 13.00. In the pediment of the *S Front* is a Phoenix, typifying the rise of new St. Paul's from the ashes of the old, and recalling also the incident when Wren sought a stone from the ruins to mark the centre of the new dome-space a fragment of an old tombstone was brought to him bearing the word 'Resurgam' ('I shall rise again'). The sculpture in the W Pediment and Portico and the statues above the North Pediment are by Francis Bird.—The famous *Dome lifts its cross 365ft above the City below. The outer dome is of wood covered with lead, and does not bear the weight of the elegant lantern on the top, which rests upon a cone of brick rising between an inner brick dome and the outer dome. The ball and cross date from 1721.

The **Interior**, though 'classical' in detail, has the general ground plan of a Gothic church: nave and aisles with triforium and clerestory, transepts, and choir, with, however, the great dome-space at the crossing. Against the massive piers rise Corinthian pilasters, and stone enrichments relieve the wall-spaces. Wren no doubt contemplated the use of colour in the decoration, but, though Thornhill's paintings in the dome were finished in 1720, nothing more was done until the dome and choir mosaics were added in 1863–97.

The visitor on entering St. Paul's should first walk up the centre of the NAVE to the great space beneath the dome, where the huge proportions of the church are especially impressive. The candelabra at the W end are by Henry Pegram. At the entrance to the nave is a memorial in the floor to 'St Paul's Watch', who 'saved this cathedral from destruction' (1939–45). A Falklands War memorial by David Kindersley was unveiled in 1985.

The DOME, the inner cupola of which is 218ft above, rests upon twelve massive supports, of which the four chief ones, at the angles, afford room in their interiors for the vestries and the library staircase. In the spandrels of the dome are mosaics executed by Salviati of Venice. Those on the W, designed by Alfred Stevens and partly executed by W.E.F. Britten, represent (from S to N) Isaiah, Jeremiah, Ezekiel, and Daniel; the others represent SS. Matthew and John (by G.F. Watts) and SS. Mark and Luke (by Britten). In the quarter-domes, at a lower level, are more recent mosaics by Sir W.B. Richmond (d 1921).—Above the arches is the Whispering Gallery, above which again are recesses with marble statues of the Fathers of the Church. The cupola, above, was decorated by Sir James Thornhill with eight scenes in monochrome from the life of St. Paul.

To inspect the monuments in the church, eloquent of the nation's history, return to the W end, and start the tour at the NW door, leading to the NORTH NAVE AISLE. On the left is *All Souls' Chapel*, dedicated in 1925 to the memory of Field Marshal Earl Kitchener of Khartoum (died 1916) with a recumbent figure by Reid Dick and a roll of honour of the Royal Engineers. Next is the *Chapel of St. Dunstan*. The memorial under the first window is to Lord Leighton (died 1896), painter and sculptor. The great monument to the Duke of Wellington (1796–1853) is by Alfred Stevens. Above the pediments at either end are groups representing Truth plucking out the tongue of Falsehood, and Valour thrusting down Cowardice. The equestrian statue on the top was executed by Tweed in 1912 from a sketch-model by Stevens. On the opposite side is the monument to General Gordon; further down on the left is the memorial to Lord Melbourne (died 1848) with Two Angels at the Gate of Death by Marochetti. A bust by Tweed of Lord Roberts (1833–1914) is on the wall.

NORTH TRANSEPT. This transept was severely damaged by a bomb in April 1941, when the transept dome and the whole of the North Porch, with the famous inscription from Wren's tomb: 'Si monumentum requiris, circumspice' ('If you would see his monument, look around you'), fell into the crypt below. Here are commemorated *Sir Arthur Sullivan* (1842–1900), the composer, *Lord Rodney* (1718–92), and *Sir Joshua Reynolds* (1723–92), the last by Flaxman. The W aisle of this transept is now the *Baptistery*. Before the entrance to the NORTH CHOIR AISLE (note the Jean Tijou gates c 1712) is the statue of Samuel Johnson (died 1784), in a Roman toga, by Bacon. The choir-screen, formed of the original altar rails, is also by Tijou. On the left is a carved wooden pulpit (1964), designed by Lord Mottistone. The Chapel of the Modern Martyrs is at the E end of the aisle, commemorating Anglican martyrs since 1850.

The *American Chapel*, which occupies the apse of the cathedral, is the memorial to America's fallen in the Second World War, with a roll of honour containing 28,000 names of those who fell in operations based on Britain.

At the end of the S choir aisle, with fine iron gates by Jean Tijou is the Lady Chapel (1959). The figure (clad in a shroud) of *Dr John Donne* (1573–1631) (Nicholas Stone), poet and Dean of St. Paul's is the only comparatively uninjured monument to have survived the destruction of Old St. Paul's, and it still shows traces of fire.

SOUTH TRANSEPT: on the E wall, *Lord Hower* (1726–99), by Flaxman. On the left, farther on, *Sir Henry Lawrence* (1806–57). Opposite is the entrance to the Crypt, beyond which, at the angle of the dome-space, is a statue of *John Howard* (1726–90), the prison reformer, the first monument admitted into new St. Paul's.

On the S wall of the E transept aisle, *J.M.W. Turner* (1775–1851), the painter, and *Lord Collingwood* (1750–1810), Nelson's successor.

In the WEST AISLE are monuments to *Sir Ralph Abercromby* (1734–1801) and to *Sir John Moore* (1761–1809), who died at Corunna. To the left, above, is a memorial by Princess Louise to the *Colonial Troops* who fell in the South African War. On the W wall of the transept, *Monument of Lord Nelson* (1758–1805), by Flaxman; the reliefs on the pedestal represent the Arctic Ocean, the North Sea, the Nile, and the Mediterranean.

SOUTH NAVE AISLE: on the right in the S aisle hangs 'The Light of the World', a painting by Holman Hunt. At the E end of the aisle is the ticket-office for the upper part of the church. The chapel at the W end has been since 1906 the *Chapel of the Most Distinguished Order of St. Michael and St. George*, with the banners of the Knights Grand Cross (CGMG). The order (instituted in 1818) is conferred for distinguished services in colonial or foreign affairs. The prelate's throne is a memorial of Lord Forrest (d 1918) of Bunbury, Western Australia, the first Australian peer.

On the left is the door to the Geometrical Staircase—a spiral of 92 stone steps and an iron balustrade by Tijou.

Return through the centre of the nave to the choir.

Enter the CHOIR proper. Above the High Altar is a carved and gilded baldacchino of marble and oak, by Godfrey Allen and S.E. Dykes Bower, replacing the reredos damaged in 1941 and serving as a memorial to the Commonwealth people of all creeds and races who lost their lives in the two World Wars. The tall bronze *Candlesticks* in front are copied from four now in St. Bavon's, in Ghent, which were made by Benedetto da Rovezzano for the tomb of Henry VIII at Windsor, but were sold under the Commonwealth.—The beautiful carved *Choir Stalls* and the *Organ Case* are by Grinling Gibbons. The organ was originally built in 1695 by Father Smith to John Blow's direction, and played by Jeremiah Clarke at its inauguration. Although a bomb struck the E end of the choir, bringing down tons of masonry on to the Sanctuary, the priceless carvings escaped almost undamaged.

The *Mosaics* with which the vaulting of the choir is decorated were designed by Sir W.B. Richmond and were executed in 1891–1912. In the central panel of the great apse is Christ in majesty, seated upon the rainbow. In the shallow cupolas above the choir proper are (from W to E) the Creation of the Beasts, of the Birds, and of the Fishes.

The *CRYPT (entrance in the S transept) corresponds in size with the upper church. Here are the graves of many of those whose monuments are above, as well as many additional monuments and graves. In the crypt below the S choir-aisle, at the foot of the staircase is (right) a bust of *Sir John Macdonald* (1815–91), premier of Canada. In the second bay (right) monuments to *Sir Edwin Landseer* (1802–73) and *Reginald Heber* (1783–1826), by Chantrey. In the pavement is the tomb of *Sir Lawrence Alma-Tadema* (1836–1912). In the next bay is the tombstone of *Sir Christopher Wren* (1632–1723), above which is the original tablet with its famous epitaph (see above). This bay, and the one to the N, are known as 'Painters' Corner', for here rest *Lord Leighton* (1830–96), *Benjamin West* (1738–1820), *Sir Thomas Lawrence* (1769–1830), *Landseer* (1802–73), *Millais* (1829–96), *Turner* (1775–1851), *Reynolds* (1723–92), *Opie* (1761–1807), and *Holman Hunt* (1827–1910), while on the walls are memorials to *Randolph Caldecott* (1846–86), *William Blake* (1757–1827), *Van Dyck* (1599–1641), *Constable* (1776–1837), *Wilson Steer* (1860–1942), *Lutyens* (1869–1944), and *Muirhead Bone* (1876–1953). *J.S. Sargent* (1856–1925), buried elsewhere, is commemorated by a relief-group of the Redemption which he designed.—The Chapel at the E end of the crypt, formerly called *St. Faith's*, was dedicated in 1960 as the *Chapel of the Order of the British Empire*. Further W a wall-tablet marks the grave of *Sir Alexander Fleming* (1881–1955), discoverer of penicillin.

In the W portion of the crypt is Wellington's colossal porphyry sarcophagus and further on a memorial to *Florence Nightingale* (1820–1910). Below the centre of the dome *Lord Nelson* rests in a coffin made from the mainmast of the French ship 'L'Orient', enclosed in a sarcophagus of black and white marble originally designed for Cardinal Wolsey. In recesses to the S, *Lord Beatty* (1871–1936), *Lord Jellicoe* (1859–1935), *Lord Keyes* (1872–1945) and his son, *Lt-Col Keyes*, VC (1917–41), and *Lord Napier of Magdala* (1810–90). To the N, *Lord Wolseley* (1833–1913), *Lord Roberts* (1832–1914), and a bust of *Lawrence of Arabia* (1888–1935). A plaque commemorates 5746 men of the garrison of Kut (Iraq) who died in 1916. In the adjoining recess: *R.J. Seddon* (1845–1906) and *W.M. Hughes* (1864–1952), prime ministers of New Zealand; *Sir Stafford Cripps* (1889–1952; fine bust by Epstein). Opposite: bust of

George Washington near a tablet to P/O William Fiske, RAF, who los. his life in the Battle of Britain, 'an American citizen who died that England might live'. Here too are memorials to *George Cruikshank* (1792–1878), the caricaturist and *W.E. Henley* (1849–1903; *Bust by Rodin), the poet and critic. In the nave: *Wilson Carlile* (1847–1942), founder of the Church Army; *R.H. Barham* (1788–1845), of the 'Ingoldsby Legends'; *Sir W. Besant* (1836–1901) and *Charles Reade* (1814–84), the novelists; and *Sir Alfred Duff Cooper* (1890–1954), the statesman.

Further W (1st bay N side) are memorials to the brothers *Sir Charles* (1782–1853) and *Sir William Napier* (1784–1860). By contrast, the next bay contains five mutilated monuments from Old St. Paul's. Next a monument to the historian *Henry Hallam* (1777–1859); opposite is one to *Lord St. Vincent* (1735–1823).

The TREASURY in the N side of the Crypt is a small museum opened in 1981 as part of the Diocesan Treasuries Scheme of the Goldsmiths' Company. The first section shows ecclesiastical vestments, altar frontals and plate belonging to St. Paul's. In the second section ranged round St. Paul's Jubilee cope, stole and mitre designed by Beryl Dean (1977), is silver on loan from the parishes of the diocese.

There is an audio visual display on the history of St. Paul's in the Crypt and near it is Wren's model of St. Paul's. The model of Old St. Paul's is also on display in the Crypt.

The **Upper Parts** of the cathedral are reached by a staircase from the S aisle (adm. see p 223). An easy ascent of 143 steps leads to the S *Triforium Gallery*.

Continue the ascent to the WHISPERING GALLERY, 112ft in diameter, within the lower dome, where words whispered near the wall on one side can be distinctly heard at the other side. This gallery is the best point from which to see Thornhill's paintings on the dome.—The STONE GALLERY, the exterior gallery round the base of the dome, commands a fine *View of London, which is still more extensive from the *Golden Gallery*, at the base of the lantern above the dome. The total ascent to the Golden Gallery involves 627 steps.

22 Holborn, Smithfield and Clerkenwell

Access: Holborn, Underground, Chancery Lane; Smithfield, Underground, Farringdon; Clerkenwell, Buses 19 and 38 from Piccadilly Circus.

Holborn (Pl. 8; 5), beginning at the S end of Gray's Inn Road, continues the line of Oxford St and High Holborn to the City. The W limits of the City (Holborn Bars) are indicated by stone obelisks near Chancery Lane Underground Station and opposite Staple Inn. In the roadway stands the *War Memorial of the Royal Fusiliers* (City of London Regiment), by Albert Toft (1924). Holborn derives its name from the Fleet River which flowed through the valley here and was known as the 'Hole-Bourne', or stream in the hollow.

To the S, opposite Gray's Inn Road, is ***Staple Inn**, the picturesque gabled and timbered façade of which, dating from 1586 (last restored in 1950), is a unique survival of its kind in a London street. The inn, which seems to have been a hostel of the wool-staplers in the 14C, was an Inn of Chancery from the reign of Henry V until 1884. It consisted of two little quadrangles, with houses dating mainly from the 18C, but was severely damaged in 1944, when the fine 16C hall was demolished. This has now een rebuilt (with much of the old material) and is occupied by the *Institute of Actuaries* and the courtyard can be entered. Dr Johnson lived here for a time in 1759–60, and here he is said to have written 'Rasselas' in the evenings of a single week, to pay for his mother's funeral. The second court now contains a pleasant garden.

In Brooke St, to the N, Thomas Chatterton (1752–70) poisoned himself at No. 39. Just beyond Brooke St rises the *Prudential Assurance Co.*, a huge Gothic edifice of red brick (by A. Waterhouse; 1879–1906, altered in 1932). It occupies the site of *Furnival's Inn*, in which Charles Dickens was lodging when he wrote the first part of the 'Pickwick Papers' (memorial tablet and bust by Percy Fitzgerald (1907) in the building). A passage down its E flank leads to Leather Lane market.

Leather Lane market (Monday to Friday) is mainly a lunchtime market geared to office and shopworkers. The name has nothing to do with leather but probably comes from the 14C 'Lyverlane'. It is best for glassware, plants, some clothes, fruit and vegetables. There is usually a stall selling genuine chamois leather.

On the other (S) side of Holborn, near the corner of Fetter Lane, is the entrance to *Barnard's Inn*. The old *Hall (late 14C), the oldest surviving secular building in the City, has 16C panelling and good heraldic glass. It is now a restaurant (Tel. 071-405 5233, to view the building).

From 1894–1959 the inn, mainly rebuilt, was occupied by the *Mercer's School*. The school founded about 1450, had Dean Colet and Sir Thomas Gresham among its pupils. The device of the Mercers' Company still survives above the gateway.

Beyond Fetter Lane, where the corner bank's elegant cupola emphasises the brash, obtrusive mass of the 'Daily Mirror' building (1958–61), Holborn reaches *Holborn Circus*. In the middle is a delightful equestrian statue of *Prince Albert* doffing his plumed hat by Charles Bacon (1874).

Hatton Garden, to the NW, now occupied largely by diamond merchants, takes its name from the garden belonging to the house of Sir Christopher Hatton, Lord Chancellor to Queen Elizabeth. A tablet with a bas-relief portrait and a device of clasped hands commemorates the residence at No. 5 of Giuseppe Mazzini, who while living in this house from 1836 inspired Italy to struggle for freedom. Later in 1864 Garibaldi visited London and this area known as 'Little Italy' has now its focus in St. Peter's Italian Church in Clerkenwell Road to the N, founded by the Italian Community in 1863; Caruso performed here. Once a year in July there are street processions on the Feast of Our Lady of Mount Carmel. There is an Italian school and social club in Back Hill, EC1 and the Italian Hospital has closed. For Clerkenwell, see below.

At the beginning of Charterhouse St (left) opens *Ely Place* (1772), occupying the site of the town house of the bishops of Ely, where John of Gaunt died in 1399. The garden was famous, and is mentioned in 'Richard III' (iii, 4). When forced to cede these grounds to Sir Christopher Hatton (at the picturesque yearly 'rent' of a red rose, ten loads of hay, and ten pounds), the Bishop reserved in perpetuity the right to walk in the gardens and to gather yearly twenty bushels of roses. *Ye Olde Mitre Tavern* in Ely Court (the quaint passageway on the left) was built in the 18C on the site of a 16C tavern. The sign probably comes from the bishop's gatehouse. Medieval tiles were exposed during roadworks in 1985. Ely Place is guarded at night by its own watchman.

The only relic of the bishop's house is the beautiful little ***Ely Chapel** (*St. Etheldreda's*), a gem of 13C Gothic (1290), with an old chestnut roof. The tracery of the E and W windows and the arcaded statue-niches are superb. The notable glass and statues of English martyrs are by Charles and May Blakeman (1952–64), who also adorned the vaulted *Crypt* (1252) which stands

on Roman foundations. In the entrance is a fine carved escutcheon from the t.
of Charles I which, until 1874, hung over the communion table. St. Etheldred.
was the first pre-Reformation church in the country to return to the Roma
Catholics (purchased 1874).

In *Saffron Hill*, parallel to the E, was Fagin's Thieves' Kitchen in 'Oliver Twist',
while the name of Bleeding Heart Yard, off Greville St (left) is familiar to readers
of 'Little Dorrit'.

To the S, just beyond Holborn Circus, is the church of *St. Andrew*,
built by Wren in 1684–87, ruined in 1940–41, and restored in 1960–61.
The interior of the medieval tower, dating from 1446 and unaltered by
Wren, survives.

The tomb of Captain Thomas Coram was designed by Lord Mottistone (1962);
the organ was originally presented by Handel to the Foundling Hospital (p 187.
In this church William Hazlitt was married to Sarah Stoddart in 1808 (Mary Lamb
was bridesmaid and Charles Lamb the best man). In 1817 Benjamin Disraeli (at
the age of 12) was here received into the Christian Church.

Beyond St. Andrew's is the *City Temple* (Congregational), opened in
1874, under Dr Joseph Parker, for a congregation founded in 1640.
Burnt out in 1941, it was rebuilt (apart from the façade) by Seely and
Paget in 1956–58. *Atlantic House* (1951), opposite, is the headquarters
of *H.M. Stationery Office*.

Holborn Viaduct is 1400ft long and 80ft wide, constructed at the
cost of over 4000 dwellings in 1867–69, designed by William
Haywood to carry the thoroughfare over the depression of the
'Hole-Bourne'. The two bronze figures at each end represent Agriculture and Commerce by H. Bursill and Science and Fine Arts by
Farmer and Brindley (1868). Beyond the bridge stood *Holborn Viaduct Station* now being redeveloped as offices. The new station below
ground is St. Paul's Thameslink; trains continue through the Snow
Hill Tunnel, linking S London with Kings Cross and Watford.

At the end of Holborn Viaduct, to the N, at the corner of Giltspur St
(leading to Smithfield) is the church of **St. Sepulchre**, the history of
which goes back to the days of the Crusaders (12C), though it was
rebuilt in the 15C, altered within by Wren in 1670–77, over-restored in
the 19C, and more carefully repaired in 1950. Down to 1890 the bells
of St. Sepulchre were tolled on the occasion of an execution at
Newgate, and before 1774 it was the custom to present a nosegay
here to each condemned criminal on his way to Tyburn.

In the *Musicians' Chapel* in the N aisle windows commemorate Sir Henry Wood
(died 1943) who, at the age of 12, deputised for the organist here, Dame Nellie
Melba (died 1931), and Dr John Ireland (died 1962). The organ (1670) is by
Renatus Harris. A musical service is held on 22 November, St. Cecilia's Day; St.
Cecilia being the patron saint of music (admission by ticket). In the same chapel
an Easter sepulchre is thought to mark the tomb of Roger Ascham (1515–68),
tutor to Queen Elizabeth I. Captain John Smith (1580–1631), 'sometime
Governor of Virginia and Admiral of New England' is buried in the S aisle. On a
pillar nearby is displayed a handbell which the bellman of St. Sepulchre's used
to ring outside the condemned cell at Newgate at midnight preceding an execution, at the same time reciting the inscribed verses. The S aisle and chapel and
the garden serve as a memorial to the Royal Fusiliers.

Adjoining in Giltspur St is the rebuilt *Watch House* (1791; 1962), with
a bust (1935) of Charles Lamb moved from near the site of Christ's
Hospital School in Newgate St (see below), where Lamb was
educated.

Opposite St. Sepulchre's, at the corner of the *Old Bailey*, rises the
curved façade of the **Central Criminal Court** (1905). This occupies the

. of Newgate Prison, some of the stones of which have been used in e rustic work of the lowest storey.

The *Central Criminal Court*, or *Old Bailey*, is the chief criminal court for Greater London, and parts of Surrey, Kent, and Essex. The bronzed figure of Justice stands on a ball atop the building, wearing a five-pointed star on her head, holding a sword and a pair of scales, by F.W. Pomery (1907). He also sculpted the figures over the main entrance—The Recording Angels and Fortitude and Truth. An extension (by McMorran and Whitby), with an impressive exterior in Old Bailey, was opened in 1970. This stood up well to a terrorist bomb in 1973. The public are admitted to trials (no children under 14): the 12 courts in the new building are entered from Old Bailey, and the six courts in the old building from Newgate St.

Visitors may see part of the medieval wall in *Warwick Slip* which connects Old Bailey and Warwick Lane (parallel to the E). Milton's writings justifying the execution of Charles I were burned by the common hangman in the Old Bailey in 1660.

Newgate Prison, long the chief prison of London, was begun in 1770 and completed in 1782, after having been partly destroyed by the Gordon Rioters in 1780. It was finally demolished in 1902. Public executions, previously carried out at Tyburn, took place in front of Newgate from 1783 to 1868, and then within the prison down to 1901. Among the prisoners confined here were Anne Askew, Daniel Defoe, Jack Sheppard, Jonathan Wild, Titus Oates, William Penn, and Lord George Gordon (who died of gaol fever in 1793). Mrs Elizabeth Fry's successful efforts to improve the conditions of prison life in Newgate (1817) laid the foundation of prison reform throughout Europe.

Below the new office block opposite, archaelogists discovered the remains of a Romano-Celtic temple in 1988; located outside the Roman wall the temple covered 502 sq m.

From St. Sephulchre's church at the E end of Holborn Viaduct, Giltspur St runs N to Smithfield, dominated by the *Smithfield Meat Market*. Plans are mooted from time to time by the City of London, which operates the market, that it may be moved to a less central location. In the meantime empty warehouses and other industrial buildings in the area are being restored for office use.

A small gilt figure of a naked boy on the corner-house of *Cock Lane*, on the left, marks *Pye Corner*, where the Great Fire of 1666, which started at Pudding Lane, near the Monument, is generally said but erroneously said to have stopped.

Smithfield (Pl. 8; 3), more particularly known as West Smithfield to distinguish it from the less important East Smithfield near Tower Hill, is a place of great historic interest. Originally a spacious 'smoothfield' or grassy expanse just outside the City walls, it was the scene of various famous tournaments, and from 1150 to 1855 it was the chief horse and cattle market of London. From an early period until the reign of Henry IV it was a usual place of execution, and here Sir William Wallace, the Scottish patriot, suffered in 1305. In 1381 the rebel Wat Tyler was slain here by Sir William Walworth, the Mayor, in the presence of Richard II. Under the Tudors many people were burned at Smithfield for their religious convictions. Anne Askew perished here in 1546. Memorials on the exterior wall of St. Bartholomew's Hospital commemorate the Scottish Patriot, William Wallace, 'hanged, drawn and quartered' here in 1305, and the Protestant martyrs burnt at the stake in the reign of Mary I. From 1133 till 1840 Smithfield was the scene of Bartholomew Fair, held every year for several days at the time of the Feast of St. Bartholomew (24 August), and the Royal Smithfield Show (now held at Earl's Court) had its origins at Wooton's Livery Stables here in 1799.

On the SE side of Smithfield is **St. Bartholomew's Hospital**, whic together with a priory for Augustinian canons, was founded in 112 by Rahere, a favourite courtier of Henry I, in fulfilment of a vow made by him when lying sick in Rome. It is the oldest charitable institution in London that retains its original site. Whittington, the famous mayor, bequeathed money for its repair in 1423. At the Dissolution, the hospital was spared by Henry VIII, who is regarded as its second founder. The fine gateway (1702) is by Edward Strong the Younger. The buildings in the great quadrangle were built by James Gibbs in 1730–70. Inside the gates to the left is the small octagonal church of *St. Bartholomew the Less*, rebuilt (except for the striking 15C tower) in 1823–25 and well restored in 1950. Inigo Jones (1573–1652) was baptised here. The Stairway and Hall—entrance from the Quadrangle—are open Mon to Fri 09.00–17.00.

Harvey, who discovered the circulation of the blood, was chief physician of the hospital in 1609–43; Abernethy, the surgeon, was a lecturer from 1791 to 1827 at its famous medical school ('Bart's') The Hospital houses an anaesthetics museum (appointment only).

By far the most interesting building at Smithfield is the church of **St. Bartholomew the Great*, which belonged to the priory founded in 1123 by Rahere, and is, after the chapel in the White Tower, the oldest church in London. It is approached from the E corner of Smithfield (to the N of the hospital), through a small gateway, once the W entrance, to the S nave-aisle. Above the gateway is a house, with an Elizabethan half-timbered façade, brought to light by a Zeppelin bomb explosion in 1915 through the loosening of the tiles that long concealed it. The site of the nave, which was completed in the 13C, is now occupied by the churchyard. Enter the church by a modern porch beneath a brick tower built in 1628 to take the place of the tower over the crossing. The five bells date from 1510. The church, noted for its music, is open from 09.00–16.30; Sun services at 09.00, 11.00, and 18.30.

At the Dissolution the conventual buildings and much of the church were pulled down or alienated, and of the original priory-church there stands only the choir, built by Rahere, with the crossing and one bay of the nave, added before 1170 by his successor. The restoration of the church, begun in 1863, was resumed in 1886, with Sir Aston Webb as architect.

On Good Friday, in accordance with a custom dating from 1686, 21 poor widows each receive an old sixpence, which is laid on a flat tombstone in the churchyard. The sixpence is now supplemented by a hot cross bun and a share in the proceeds of the collection, mainly for children.

The INTERIOR of the church, the choir of Rahere's priory-church, is most impressive, with its heavy columns, piers, and round arches in the pure Norman style. The clerestory was rebuilt early in the 15C, and the Norman triforium is interrupted on the S side by *Prior Bolton's Window*, a beautiful oriel (once communicating with the prior's house) added by Prior Bolton (1506–32), whose rebus, a bolt and a tun, it bears. The apsidal ending of the choir, with its stilted arches, was built in 1886 by Sir Aston Webb in place of the previous square ending, which is supposed itself to have been an innovation of the 15C. On the N side of the sanctuary is the **Tomb of Rahere* (died 1143), with a coloured effigy beneath a rich canopy (c 1400; perhaps by Yevele).—In the *South Transept* stands the 15C font at which Hogarth was baptised in 1697. In the *South Ambulatory* is the alabaster tomb of Sir Walter Mildmay (died 1589), founder of Emmanuel College, Cambridge. The *Lady Chapel*, rebuilt in 1896 and retaining little of the original fabric of the 14C, is separated from the E end of the choir by a beautiful modern iron screen. It was at one time used as a printing office and then as a fringe factory; it now serves as the chapel of the Imperial Society of Knights Bachelor. The *N Transept* was at one time occupied by a blacksmith's forge. The stone screen at its W end dates from the beginning of the 15C. The

een beneath the organ has painted panels (1932) illustrating the life of Rahere.
A Norman doorway, with the original 15C oaken doors, at the W end of the S
ambulatory, admits to the E walk of the old *Cloister*, built c 1405 and
reconstructed in 1905–28. The arches in the wall mark the entrance to the former
chapter-house. A few ancient fragments and relics are exhibited here.

To the S of the church is *Bartholomew Close*, in which Milton sought
hiding after the Restoration in 1660. Hogarth was born here in 1697,
and here Benjamin Franklin lived while working in the printing office
in the Lady Chapel. Washington Irving also lodged here. At Nos 87–88
is *Butchers' Hall* (1959). *Cloth Fair*, skirting the N side of the church,
marks the site once occupied by the booths of drapers and clothiers at
Bartholomew Fair. At Nos 41 and 42 the Jacobean houses (1614) have
been well preserved and restored. In Cloth Lane is the new livery hall
for the Worshipful Companies of Farmers and Fletchers by Michael
Twigg Brown (1987).

In the middle of the square is a small public garden with a large
fountain and a figure of 'Peace' by J.B. Philip (1873). The N side of the
square is filled with the elaborate building of the *Central Meat Market*
(built in 1867 by Sir Horace Jones); the *Poultry Market* (1963) with a
vast barrel vault, lies to the W. The largest dead meat, poultry and
provision market in the world, it covers 10 acres, and has a 'shop
frontage' of nearly two miles. Enormous, refrigerated lorries arrive
from 20.00 to unload the carcases which are then prepared by 'cutters'
ready for selling at 05.00. The scene remains animated until midday
when the wholesale market closes.

In Charterhouse St, skirting the N side of the market, is the *The Fox
and Anchor* one of the many pubs with early opening hours serving the
meat market. It has an art nouveau façade and serves a full breakfast
(open 06.00–15.00). The *Smithfield Tavern*, 105 Charterhouse St is
open 06.30–09.00 and at lunchtime. NB: only market workers can buy
alcohol outside normal licensing hours.

Charterhouse St leads E to the quiet *Charterhouse Square*. Here is
the 16–18C gatehouse of the *Charterhouse**, founded in the 14C as a
monastery, but since 1611 a hostel for poor gentlemen. The buildings,
dating mainly from the 16C, were badly damaged in 1941 and have
been restored. Visitors are admitted on application to the Master,
usually at 14.45 on Wed in April to July. Admission charge.

In 1371 the Carthusian priory of the Salutation of the Mother of God was founded
here by Sir Walter de Manny, a distinguished soldier under Edward III, on a
burial-ground where 50,000 victims of the Black Death had been interred. This
was the fourth English house of the Carthusians; the name Charterhouse is a
corruption of the French name Chartreuse. Sir Edward North, afterwards Lord
North, to whom the property was granted in 1545, built a mansion on the site of the
Little Cloister. This passed later to the Duke of Northumberland who was
executed in 1553 for his attempt to put Lady Jane Grey (his daughter-in-law) on
the throne. The property was considerably altered by a later owner, the fourth
Duke of Norfolk who was executed for complicity in a plot to put Mary, Queen of
Scots, on the throne. Elizabeth I paid four visits to the mansion (then known as
Howard House). James I was entertained here prior to his coronation in 1603 by
Thomas Howard, later Earl of Suffolk, to whom the property had passed in 1601.
In 1611 the Charterhouse was bought for £13,000 by Thomas Sutton, a shrewd
Elizabethan soldier, probably also a merchant-adventurer, who founded the
'Hospital of King James in Charterhouse' here, including a hospital for 80 poor
brethren and a free school for 40 poor boys. (See also p 394.)

The average number of 'poor brethren' is now 30—pensioners with a
professional or military background. They occupy chambers in Master's Court
and Wash-House Court. The *British Records Association* also has offices here.

The *Charterhouse School* rapidly developed into one of the chief public schools
of England, and in 1872 it was transferred to Godalming in Surrey. Thackeray, a
former pupil, in 'The Newcomers' describes the Charterhouse under the name of

'Greyfriars'. From 1875 to 1933 the site of the school, mainly around the Gr
Cloister, was occupied by the *Merchant Taylors' School*, founded in 1561
Suffolk Lane, Upper Thames St, where Spenser, Lancelot Andrewes, Clive, an.
Gilbert Murray were pupils. This school is now at Moor Park (see 'Blue Guide
England'), and the buildings here, with large new extensions, are occupied by
St. Bartholomew's medical school.

The *Chapel* was perhaps originally the chapter house of the monastery, and
portions of the S and E walls belong to the 14C structure. The ante-chapel was
built in 1512. The N arcade, the N aisle, the pulpit, communion table, and seats in
the middle of the church date from about 1614. The elaborate tomb of Thomas
Sutton (died 1611), with a recumbent effigy, was designed by Nicholas Stone
and Bernard Jansen. Above rises a low tower containing a vaulted chamber
(perhaps the monks' treasury). This is provided with a round squint affording a
view of the high altar of the original church (to the S), which was demolished by
Lord North to build his hall, and the site of the tomb of the founder, Sir Walter de
Manny (died 1372), was located in 1947, in front of this now vanished altar. The
Chapel Cloisters (1613) contain memorials to famous 'Carthusians', including
John Wesley. On the N side of the *Master's Court* are the *Great Hall*, and (on the
first floor) the *Great Chamber*, both of the 16C, with 17C alterations, restored to
something very near their original splendour by Lord Mottistone and Paul Paget
(1956). To the W is the *Wash-House Court*, the best preserved part of the
monastic buildings as rebuilt in the 16C, and to the N are two courts of 1826–39.
The *Great Cloister*, with traces of the monks' cells, lay to the E.

Some fine Georgian houses, 1700–1775, survive in the Square. Carthusian St
leads E out of the Square to Aldersgate and the Barbican, see Rte 23.

From Charterhouse St opposite the Central Meat Market, St. John St
runs N to the Angel at Islington, through **Clerkenwell**. Clerkenwell's
history is based on the well, Clerk's Well, which supplied Charterhouse. The connection with water continued when Hugh Myddleton established the New River Head water supply just above Clerkenwell (see p 395) in 1613. During the 17C newcomers including French
Huguenots settled here (they were not allowed in the City of London)
and established Clerkenwell's reputation as a centre of clock-makers,
jewellers and opticians. The area enjoyed a period of prosperity with
several fine houses built for merchants but decline followed in the
19C as slum-housing took over and in the 20C when the area was
deserted by residents. It became a centre of radicalism during the 19C
and Clerkenwell Green became a political meeting place and scene
of Chartist marches.

The London Borough of Islington, of which Clerkenwell is now part, is engaged
in a programme of revitalising the area by encouraging crafts workshops and
other developments. A Heritage Centre has been established at 33 St. John's
Square (tel. 071-250 1039) and there are guided tours of the area.

W of St. John St before Clerkenwell Road, **St. John's Gate** (erected in
1504) spans St. John's Lane. This is the S gate of the once famous and
wealthy priory of the Knights Hospitallers of the Order of St. John of
Jerusalem, which was founded about 1130 but later suppressed by
Elizabeth I.

The priory was later the residence of Edmund Tilney (died 1610), Master of the
Revels, who licensed 30 of Shakespeare's plays. In 1731–81 the gatehouse was
the printing office of the 'Gentleman's Magazine', conducted by Edward Cave,
to which Dr Johnson contributed articles. The premises are now occupied as the
Grand Priory in the British Realm of the *Venerable Order of the Hospital of St.
John of Jerusalem*, revived in 1831, which devotes itself to ambulance and
hospital work. An entirely voluntary organisation 'in the service of mankind', it is
supported by public donation.

The *Museum of the Order of St. John*, St. John's Lane, Clerkenwell, EC1. Tel.
071-253 6644. Open Tues, Fri, Sat 10.00–18.00. Conducted tours of the Grand
Priory Church and St. John's Gate at 11.00 and 14.30 on those days. Reference
Library open by appointment. Access: Underground, Farringdon.

The collection, arranged in glass cases, relates mainly to the Order of St. John
nd includes the Rhodes Missal of 1504, an Annunciation by Luigi Gentile

48), a small oil on copper, arms and armour used by the knights, crosses
played on the fronts of houses belonging to the Order, and some examples of
.e crafts and light industries of the area of Clerkenwell including clockmaking,
brewing, printing and toolmaking.

In St. John's Square, across Clerkenwell Road, lies the **Priory Church
of St. John** built about 1720 and incorporating the choir-walls of the
ancient priory church, probably destroyed c 1381 when Wat Tyler
burned the priory. The area of the original circular nave is indicated
by a line in the road. In 1930 this again became the priory church of
the order, and it has been sympathetically restored after its destruction in 1941. The altarpiece consists of two wings of a Flemish triptych
(15C) probably removed at the Dissolution and recovered in 1932. The
lion-head handles on the church doors were found in the ruins of the
Muristan, the site of the original hospice of the order in Jerusalem.
Below is an interesting and well-preserved *Crypt, the three W bays
of which date from about 1140; the two E bays and the side-chapels
were added about 1185. Monuments here include a *memento mori*
from the tomb of Sir William Weston (died 1540), last Prior of the
Order, and a fine alabaster effigy (16C) of a knight of the Order,
brought from Valladolid.

Among former residents in Clerkenwell were Izaak Walton (1650–
61), John Wilkes (born here in 1727), Christopher Pinchbeck, inventor
of the alloy that bears his name (1721), and Emanuel Swedenborg (d
1772). The old 'Clerks' Well' (on the site of 14–16 Farringdon Road, to
the E, the former offices of the 'New Statesman') mentioned as early
as 1174, where the parish clerks of London used to perform miracle
plays, gave name to the district. Apply to visit through Finsbury Public
Library, tel. 071-278 7343 ext. 21.

In *Clerkenwell Green* N of Clerkenwell Road is the old *Middlesex
Court of Sessions* (1779–82), designed by John Rogers with reliefs by
Nollekens, now used as a Masonic conference centre. At No 37A is
the *Marx Memorial Library*, a pointer to the area's radical history (tel.
071-253 1485—usually open in the afternoons). Built in 1730 it housed
a Welsh charity school, later a radical working men's club and a
socialist press. William Morris spoke here, and Lenin edited 'Iskra'
from here 1902–3. It was established in 1933 to commemorate the 50th
anniversary of Marx's death and contains well over 100,000 books
and periodicals. In Clerkenwell Close is the Parish Church of *St.
James's* with its graceful steeple by James Carr; 1788–91. There are
memorials to the Protestant Martyrs burned at Smithfield and the
remains of the medieval Benedictine nunnery of St. Mary which
stood on this site can be seen in the gardens behind the church.
Nearby are the Clerkenwell Workshops, London County Council's
former furniture stores, now converted into 140 workshops. In Clerkenwell Road there are craft workshops in Pennybank Chambers.
Further along to the NW is the Greater London Record Library at 40
Northampton Road, EC1. Tel. 071-633 7132. Open Tues to Fri 09.30–
16.45, housing the records and maps of London. Farringdon Road,
with a secondhand book market (best Mon to Sat lunchtime) of which
just a few stalls remain, leads S towards Holborn or N to Rosebery
Avenue and Sadler's Wells.

Sadler's Wells in Rosebery Avenue also recalls the area's richness
in water. The first music hall here, built in 1683, was a side attraction
to a medicinal well on this site. Grimaldi played here in 1781–1805.
During the 19C a period as a Shakespearian theatre under Samuel
Phelps was followed by use as a skating rink, a boxing arena and then
a pickle factory. It re-opened as a music hall in 1893 but soon closed

The present theatre dates to 1931. It was founded by Lilian Bay and Sir Reginald Rowe and became part of the Bayliss theatre whr included the Old Vic; ballet and opera dominated but the oper company moved to the Coliseum in 1968. Sadler's Wells still stages opera, ballet and music, performed mainly by visiting companies from overseas. The original well can still be seen under a trap door. A smaller theatre, the Lilian Bayliss Theatre, opened in 1988.

Also in Rosebery Avenue are the former offices of the Metropolitan Water Board, *New River House* (1920), now the Thames Water Authority. This is being redeveloped, possibly as part of a new, larger Sadler's Wells. Further SE, at *Mount Pleasant*, is the largest letter and parcel sorting office in the United Kingdom, built in 1900 on the site of the Coldbath House of Correction, a prison from 1794 to 1877. It is one of the key stations in the fully automated underground railway which carries most of London's post connecting the Post Office headquarters at King Edward Building with Mount Pleasant and railway stations. It was completed in 1927.

23 Newgate Street, Cheapside, the Barbican, the Museum of London

Access: Underground, St. Paul's and Barbican

Newgate St continues the line of Holborn and leads towards the heart of the City. Past the Old Bailey (see Rte 22) to the S in Warwick Lane stands *Cutlers' Hall*, with terracotta reliefs by Benj. Creswick (1887). Opposite Warwick Lane is the rebuilt steeple of *Christ Church*, built by Wren in 1667–91 (original steeple added in 1704) on part of the site of the great Church of the Grey Friars, second only to St. Paul's in size in the City, and destroyed in the Great Fire. Wren's Church was destroyed in the 'Blitz' of 1940–41. The steeple was re-erected in 1960 from the original stonework. Lawrence Sheriff (died 1567), founder of Rugby School, was buried in Christ Church. To the N of the church stood *Christ's Hospital*, the famous 'Blue Coat School', founded by Edward VI in 1552 and removed to the country (near Horsham in Sussex) in 1902 (plaque). The site is now occupied by buildings of the Post Office and St. Bartholomew's Hospital.

(Pl. 8; 6). In King Edward St is *King Edward Building*, in which ordinary postal business is transacted. Outside is a statue of Rowland Hill by E. Onslow (1882 Royal Exchange, moved here in 1923). It also houses the **National Postal Museum**.

National Postal Museum, King Edward Building, King Edward St, EC1. Tel. 071-432 3851. Access: Underground, St. Paul's. Open Mon to Thurs 09.30–16.30, Fri 09.30–16.00. Free.
The museum was established in 1965 when Reginald M. Phillips donated to the nation his unique collection of artists' drawings, proofs, and stamps of the Queen Victoria issues of Great Britain. This collection and the comprehensive range of specimen stamps of the world, received by the Post Office through the Universal Postal Union since 1878, are displayed. Temporary exhibitions of specialised material from the postal archives are mounted and a reference library is available by appointment.

The *Post Office North*, opposite, contains the offices of Postal Head-quarters including the library. An extensive network of tunnels carries the Post Office Railway. See also above. Started in 1913, it was

pleted after the First World War and opened in 1927. Tours by
ppointment: contact the Post Office Controller, King Edward
uilding, EC1.

Until 1913 the General Post Office proper stood on the E side of St.
Martin's-le-Grand, a street commemorating the church, college, and
sanctuary of St. Martin, dissolved in 1548. The former burial-ground
of Christchurch, Newgate St, has been laid out as *Postman's Park*. To
the W Little Britain, a narrow winding street, reflects something of the
'old' City. Milton lived here in 1662; Benjamin Franklin stayed here in
1742.

On the S side of Newgate St is Paternoster Square (see p 221).
Newgate St is continued towards the E by *Cheapside* (Pl. 8; 6), a short
and busy thoroughfare formerly known as the *Chepe* (from Old
English 'ceap', a bargain). The names of the cross-streets indicate the
position of the different traders' booths during medieval times: bakers
in Bread St, goldsmiths in Goldsmiths Row, fishmongers in Friday St,
dairymen in Milk St etc. The 'prentices of Chepe were long notorious
for their turbulence' (Chaucer). Offices line the street, the most
prominent of which is the curving neo-Georgian block of offices
extending S to Watling St.

In Foster Lane to the N stands the church of *St. Vedast* (see below), and in Gutter
Lane, the next turning N from Cheapside, is the entrance to *Saddlers' Hall*
(1958); the first hall on this side dated from the 14C. The Saddlers' Guild is
thought to have its origin in Anglo-Saxon times. On the same side, at the corner
of Wood St, a plane tree grows on the site of the church of St. Peter destroyed in
the Great Fire of London; one of the Eleanor crosses stood here.

In Cheapside, near the corner of Bread St to the S, stood the *Mermaid
Tavern*, famous for the club founded by Ben Jonson in 1603 and
frequented by Shakespeare, Raleigh, Donne, Beaumont, and
Fletcher.—John Milton (1608–74) was born in *Bread St*, to the right,
and Sir Thomas More (1478–1535) in *Milk St*, nearly opposite. Milton
is commemorated by a tablet (with Dryden's famous lines) on the
exterior W wall of Bow Church. In the churchyard is a statue of
Captain John Smith, founder of the Colony of Virginia, a copy of the
statue in Jamestown by William Couper, erected in 1960. He is buried
in St. Sepulchre, Newgate (see p 229).

*Bow Church, or *St. Mary-le-Bow*, in Cheapside, was begun by
Wren in 1670 and completed with the steeple in 1683, but was badly
damaged 1941. It succeeds the older church of 'St. Marie de Arcubus',
'the first in this city built on two arches (bows) of stone'. Saxon finds
indicate that a church must have existed on this site before the crypt
was built. The beautiful *Steeple, a very fine Renaissance campanile,
is 222ft high.

The restoration by Laurence King was completed in 1971. The exterior has been
restored to its original design, but the interior has been redesigned to suit the
needs of 20C worship. The beautiful E windows are the work of John Hayward.
The NE window represents the bombed City churches grouped round Mary who
holds the church of St. Mary-le-Bow in her arms. There are two pulpits, both
used in the service.
   The Norman *Crypt*, built about 1090, is the oldest ecclesiastical structure in
the City. Also restored, it has an etched glass entrance screen by John Hayward.
It contains the chapel of the Holy Spirit, built in the part formerly used as a
burying place, which was once the meeting-place of the ecclesiastical *Court of
Arches*.
   In 1914 an ancient stone from the crypt of Bow Church was placed in Trinity
Church, New York, in reference to the fact that William III granted to the vestry
of that church the same privileges as those of St. Mary-le-Bow.

Anyone born within the sound of Bow Bells is a 'cockney', i.e. a Londoner and simple. The bells that (according to the old story) called back [Whittington to be three times Mayor of London, perished in the Great Fire; th successors were destroyed in 1941 but new ones have been recast from thos salvaged.

A Roman public bath (c AD 100) was found in 1955 on the other side of Cheapside.

Beyond Bow Church *King St* and *Queen St* diverge to the N and S, the former leading to the Guildhall, the latter to Southwark Bridge. At the corner of Ironmonger Lane, just beyond King St, stands *Mercers' Hall*, the livery hall of the Mercers, one of the richest of the City companies and first in order of civic precedence, still committed to education and also involved in property. It was rebuilt in 1958 to a design of Sir Albert Richardson incorporating fittings from the 17C hall and carvings by Grinling Gibbons.

In Ironmonger Lane to the N is the tower of *St. Olave's*, Old Jewry, a relic of a Wren church demolished in 1888, now used as offices. There is a Roman mosaic pavement beneath No. 11.

Old Jewry was the area set aside for Jews in the 12C where they suffered extortionate taxation, murder and ransacking before being expelled by King Edward I in 1291. The *The City of London Police Headquarters* are at No. 26 Old Jewry. The continuation of Cheapside is known as *Poultry*, from its early occupation by the shops of poulterers. It is dominated by the Midland Bank headquarters by Lutyens.

From the top of Cheapside, Foster Lane leads N past the church of *St. Vedast*, rebuilt by Wren in 1670–73, and restored in 1962. Within is a richly decorated ceiling, fine carving, and a splendid sounding organ, built by Renatus Harris in 1731 and now restored. The poet Robert Herrick was christened here. Further on, on the corner of Gresham St, stands the *Goldsmiths' Hall*, a handsome Renaissance edifice (1835) rebuilt by Philip Hardwick, containing some interesting portraits and a fine collection of plate. The Goldsmiths' Company, which was incorporated in 1327, has the duty of assaying and stamping gold and silver plate. Its hall-mark is a leopard's head.

Across Gresham St N *St. Anne and St. Agnes*, a Wren church (1680), restored in 1963–68, became a Lutheran guild church in 1954. At the end of Noble St a new *Plaisterers' Hall* (1971) faces London Wall.

It is slightly longer but more interesting to turn E along Gresham St, passing Staining Lane with the entrances to the *Haberdashers' Hall*, part of an office block designed by A.S. Ash (1956) on the site of the first 15C hall, and (in Oat Lane) to the neo-Georgian *Pewterers' Hall* (1961; the original hall was built in 1496), and turn N up Wood St. Here stands the tower of *St. Alban*, built by Wren in 1682–98, now converted into an unusual office block. Beyond the police station is London Wall.

London Wall (Pl. 8; 6), though here realigned, still follows, more or less, the site of the old **City Wall**. Parts of the wall have been exposed in this area. The *London Wall Walk*, with information panels and directional signs, can be followed from the Tower to the Museum of London (or vice versa). The Walk starts just outside Tower Hill Underground Station and follows the line of the City Wall. (See p 260.)

The **Roman Wall** around the city was 2 miles long, usually 8ft thick, and probably 20–25ft high. The best preserved section is exposed near the Tower (comp. p 260). It was built c AD 190–225 with stone shipped along the river Medway from Maidstone; one of the ships sank near Blackfriars and has been excavated. The five gates were Aldgate, Bishopsgate, Cripplegate, Newgate, and Ludgate. A sixth, Aldersgate, was added later. The fragments of wall now visible show the

ı substructure with its characteristic bands of tiles, and, above, additions
ɛ to these foundations in the succeeding centuries.
    eceding the City Wall in date was a **Roman Fort**, built AD 120–30, and
covered in 1950. Its N and W boundaries were later strengthened and
corporated into the city defensive wall. Cripplegate was on the site of the N
ɡate of the fort. Sometime after the 13C a system of semicircular bastions was
constructed outside the walls: a number of these are now visible.

London Wall was rebuilt with brutal '60s office blocks some now
demolished; the first new building to reopen in 1990, Alban Gate,
spans the road in an adventurous design by Terry Farrell. Beyond
lies the **Barbican** (Pl. 8; 4) where a 60-acre area, heavily bombed in
the last war, has been rebuilt to provide housing for over 5000
people and an arts and conference centre. Designed in massive concrete in derivative styles in which medieval fortification and Le
Corbusier seemingly predominate, the residential blocks are linked
by raised walkways. An artificial lake, part of the air-conditioning
system, and the residents' gardens help to alleviate the concrete
harshness.
    Walkways cross London Wall to podium level at the SW corner
(partly interrupted by the rebuilding programme). Here the
**Museum of London, opened by Queen Elizabeth II on 2 December
1976, presents the history, the social and domestic life, and the
manners of the capital from the earliest habitation to the most recent
past. It combines the former Guildhall and London Museums.

Museum of London, London Wall, EC2. Tel. 071-600 3699. Access:
Underground, St. Paul's, Underground and BR Barbican. Open Tues to Sat
10.00–18.00. Sun 14.00–18.00. Lectures, temporary exhibitions. Cafeteria.
Excellent guidebook and bookshop.
    The Guildhall Museum was founded by the Corporation of the City of
London in 1826 as an adjunct to the Guildhall Library. The London Museum
was a national museum formed in 1911. Before 1939 it had been in Lancaster
House. After 1945 both museums had temporary quarters: the Guildhall
Museum in the Royal Exchange and the London Museum in Kensington
Palace.
    The new building, by Powell, Moya and Partners, with interior by Higgins,
Ney and Partners, surrounds a central court and is on two levels connected by a
glazed ramp. As part of the redevelopment of this area, the museum will be
partly rebuilt in the next few years.

The exhibition, on the continuous open plan, consists of chronological tableaux incorporating 'bygones' of every kind, presented as an
illustrated social history of some brilliance. Later centuries are
accompanied by discreetly played period music. Costume is particularly well represented. Exhibits come from all social levels, inevita-
bly with some imbalance, since Tudor relics tend to survive from
court and church circles, while for the 19C, equally a period of high
material progress and endeavour, poverty and trivia are perhaps too
preponderant, and the early 20C appears quaint rather than inno-
vatory.
    Highlights of the exhibition include the Lord Mayor's ceremonial
Coach and a representation of the Great Fire of London. Recent
additions include a pair of 17C models of English warships from
Trinity Green, finely carved in white marble, and the new 18C
gallery opened in 1989. The Second World War gallery has also been
refurbished.
    The Museum of London's archaeological department is engaged
in a number of projects around the City and new finds are incorporated in existing displays or shown separately according to space
and suitability.

The arrangement is in general anti-clockwise and from the w. the centre. Displays are numbered consecutively and documented.

PREHISTORIC. A relief model of the Thames Valley faces an imaginary sectie through a City cellar to demonstrate archaeological levels. Flint and bone toor from riverine gravel terraces; Neolithic bowl from the Heathrow excavation; leaf-shaped swords of the Bronze Age; finds from a temple site (6C BC) found at Heathrow during airport construction; early British coins; iron dagger; the Brentford Tankard (1C) of bronze-mounted oak with an ornamental handle; a replica of the Battersea Shield.

ROMAN from AD 43 (when Claudius's soldiers crossed the Thames). Stone figure of a Roman soldier; soldiers' accoutrements; commercial wax letter tablet addressed Londinio; inscribed gravestones; a tile from the state tile works stamped P.P. BR. LON; head of Hadrian and other fragments of bronze statues.

A vantage window overlooks the remains of the 2C Roman fort; house reconstruction comprising 1C and 4C dining-rooms and kitchen grouped round a 3C tessellated pavement from Bucklersbury; leather 'bikini' trunks (one from a well in Queen St), probably worn by dancing girls.

Marble sculpture (mainly 2–3C) found on the Mithraic temple site, including *Heads of Mithras and Serapis, a colossal hand, and a 3C Bacchic group; note also the late-Roman decorated silver box containing a strainer; clay jug inscribed Londini; sarcophagus from Lower Clapton.

SAXON AND VIKING from c 400. The tunnel leading into the gallery illustrates the Dark Age of London before the Angles and Saxons arrived. Scramasaxes, the large knives from which the Saxons are thought to have taken their name; brooches from Saxon cemetery at Mitcham; Celtic bell (?8C) found in the Thames at Mortlake; spear-heads, axes, and other Viking weapons; Viking grave slab (11C) with runes, from St. Paul's churchyard.

MEDIEVAL until 1484. Models of William the Conqueror's White Tower and Old St. Paul's; 15C City chest of solid iron; chain-mail hauberk; sculptured panel in elm (from a chest) with Chaucerian scene; huge 13C storage jar; heraldic fragments of the Cheapside Eleanor Cross; earliest known swinging cradle (15C); coin hoard (temp. Edward III) from Upper Norwood; costrels, tallybag in leather with inscription of the Calais garrison. A 15C carved door frame from the church of St. Ethelburga-within-Bishopsgate, flanked by the four Civic Virtues from the medieval Guildhall.

TUDOR 1485–1602. Above coats of arms of City Livery companies; the *Cheapside Hoard, probably part of the stock-in-trade of a 16C jeweller. In wall-cases: leather clothing preserved from a Moorfields rubbish dump; *Copper plate engraved with part of the earliest known survey of London (c 1558); characteristic flat cap with ear-pieces; Ming bowl mounted on silver-gilt stand, said to have belonged to Mary, Queen of Scots; of Thos. Gresham's *Steelyard and weighing bell; fashionable Gloves and leather hat; lace shirt; cups and apostle spoons.

EARLY STUART LONDON 1603–1666. The transition from Tudor to Stuart is marked by scale models of Tudor London and Whitehall Palace. Relics of Charles I (vest worn on scaffold) and Cromwell (death mask); oil painting showing entry of Charles I into the City; swords from a factory at Hounslow; *Armour made at Greenwich c 1630 and worn by John Dymoke as hereditary King's Champion at George III's coronation. Panelled room from Wandsworth with embroidered hangings; Mercers' Company silver flagon; plague bell; the 'Great Fire Experience', an audio-visual representation of the Great Fire of 1666, with a reading from Pepys' Diary.

A ramp leads down to the *Lower Floor.*

LATE STUART 1667–1713. Cross section of St. Paul's; William Morgan's Map of London; Pepys' chess set and backgammon board; shop and tavern signs: Gerard the Giant, Ape and Apple, etc. Trumpet of 1666; playing cards illustrating the murder and other facets of the 'Popish Plot'; panelled room from 15 Buckingham St, with a pair of virginals by James White, 1656; sedan chair.

18C GALLERY 1714–1800. Shops and shop windows including pawnbroker's; Spitalfields silk dresses; printing press; Lambeth Delft pottery; Chelsea and Bow porcelain; Battersea enamels; debtor's cell from Wellclose Square Lockup (visited and described by John Howard, the penal reformer); Newgate Gaol exterior including Debtor's Door and cell; Lady Hamilton's guitar; Lord Nelson sword.

…ENTH CENTURY HALL. Pass under the sign of the Bull and Mouth Inn
…0) from St. Martin's-le-Grand. Model of Euston Arch and Crystal
…ce; the Woolsack from the old House of Lords; Dickens's chair;
…ges' fire engine of 1862; school room of 1870.

…PERIAL LONDON 1881–1910. 'Popularity', a panorama of stage artists by
…V.H. Lambert; two groups of shops and offices including a cooper's,
haberdasher's, grocer's, chemist's, and tailor's shop interiors; section of
banking hall; Hansom cab.

THE TWENTIETH CENTURY. Suffragette poster; broadcasting studio of 1932;
Woolworth's 3d and 6d counter; lifts from Selfridge's; model Y Ford car.
Second World War Gallery with Anderson Shelter and Blitz experience.

CEREMONIAL LONDON. The Lord Mayor's *State Coach, built in 1757 and
used in the annual Lord Mayor's Show; it is decorated with allegorical
scenes in a London setting by Cipriani. Model of the last Lord Mayor's
barge (1807).—In the TREASURY, opposite, reminders of the coronation
ceremony.

In Nettleton Court next to the Museum of London a John Wesley Memorial
was unveiled in 1981. It marks the spot of Wesley's conversion in 1738.
The memorial is in the shape of the leaf of his journal and stands 15ft
high.

Aldersgate St, which skirts the Barbican on the W, takes its
name from the old N City gate (pulled down in 1761). The road
follows a Roman alignment; recent excavations revealed a
sequence of eleven subsequent roads on its course. The decorative *Ironmongers' Hall*, almost hidden among the new buildings,
is the successor (1925, Sydney Tatchall) of the old hall in Fenchurch St, which suffered bomb damage in 1917. *St. Botolph
without Aldersgate*, slightly damaged by the Great Fire, was
entirely rebuilt in 1790 and contains a transparancy in the E window by J. Pearson 'The Agony in the Garden'.

On the SE corner of Beech St and Aldersgate St stairs lead to the
podium and walkways of the Barbican Centre to the N of a small
artificial lake, passing the *City of London School for Girls*, founded in Carmelite St in 1894, moved here in 1964 and the Guildhall School of Music. On the other side is the the paved piazza
around the church of **St. Giles without Cripplegate**.

The stone tower (with a brick top storey added in 1682 by John Bridges)
and the nave belong to the church built in 1390. After a fire in 1545 and
alterations in the 17–18C, the edifice was badly damaged by bombs in
1940. In 1960 it was restored; the E and W windows were renewed in
1967–68, and the fine organ (incorporating an 18C case) installed in 1969.
  In this church Shakespeare attended the baptism of his nephew in 1604
while lodging nearby in Silver St with Christopher Montjoy, a Huguenot
and 'tire maker' whom he had known 'for the space of tenne yeres or
thereaboutes'. Oliver Cromwell was married here in 1620.

In the S aisle is a monument (restored in 1971) over the burial-
place of John Speed (1552–1629), topographer, and an epitaph to
Thamas Stagg (1772) ending with the curt phrase 'That is all'. At
the W end of this aisle a plaque records the burial here of John
Milton (who died in Bunhill Row in 1674) in the same grave as
his father. The bust is by John Bacon (1793). 'Paradise Lost' was
sold by Milton to an Aldersgate printer; the poet occupied
several houses in the area from 1643–47, and after the Restoration. A plaque to the right of the entrance door recalls other
'Men of Mark' connected with the parish, who include Sir Martin
Frobisher (died 1594), seaman and explorer, John Foxe (died
1587), martyrologist, John Bunyan (died 1688), and Daniel Defoe

(died 1731; the parish register records his burial in Bunhill Field
The Great Plague was at its worst in the parish of St. Giles, and plag
burials fill nearly a folio volume of the parish register (1665). The
documents are now in the Guildhall Library.

Outside, tombstones have been set in to the paving, including
some curious mummy-shaped tombs dating from the early 19C. A
bastion built outside the City wall sometime after the 13C is prominent to the S.

The **Barbican Centre** can be approached via the walkway system.
Follow the signs and yellow markings.

The Barbican Arts and Conference Centre, Silk St, EC2. Tel. 071-638 4141.
Access: Underground/BR Barbican, Underground, Moorgate, St. Paul's. Car
parks.
    The plans for rebuilding the residential area of the Barbican included a modest
arts centre and premises for the Guildhall School of Music and Drama. By 1964
these plans had grown to accommodate the Royal Shakespeare Company, the
London Symphony Orchestra, a library and an art gallery. At the same time the
City of London Corporation aimed to give the development a commercial use by
incorporating first-class conference and exhibition facilities. The complicated
structure on eight levels, half of which are underground, was eventually opened
by HM The Queen in March 1982; the work had taken over 25 years and the cost
was £157m.

The *Concert Hall* seats 2000; it is panelled in light wood and has
comfortable seating and multi-lingual interpretation facilities. The
London Symphony Orchestra and others perform here in a programme scheduled around mainly daytime conference activities. The
Royal Shakespeare Company Theatre has the highest flytower in
Europe, at 110ft, and 1100 seats on four levels, none further than 65ft
from the centre of the stage. The *Pit Theatre* below is used for
smaller-scale works. There is a comfortable cinema which seats 300
and also doubles as a lecture theatre.

The *Barbican Art Gallery* on two levels houses the City of London's
outstanding collection of paintings which is shown at regular intervals
interspersed with the changing exhibitions of modern artists. (See
also foyer, below.)

Barbican Art Gallery, Level 8; details as above. Open Tues to Sat 10.00–18.45,
Sun 12.00–17.45. Admission charge/free depending on exhibition.

The *Barbican Library* combines the two libraries of the City of London
with a reference section and lending library for residents and people
working in the city.

The *Barbican Exhibition Halls* (8000 sq m) are in Golden Lane, off
Beech St, and are used for special exhibitions, trade and public.
Access: Underground, Barbican.

The Barbican Centre also features a Conservatory and a sculpture
court. There is a carvery restaurant, a cafeteria, an outdoor cafeteria
by the lake in the summer, bars and sandwich stalls in the foyers
during performances. There is music on Sundays and early evenings
in the foyers and a foyer exhibition gallery. A statue by Elizabeth
Frink, 'The Running Man', stands on the terrace by the lake.

Near the Barbican Centre, in Chiswell St, are the *Chiswell St Vaults*, a
pub and restaurant in the cellars of the buildings of the Chiswell St
Brewery, part of which has been restored and opened to the public
(closed at weekends). On the S side is the original Whitbread brewery
building, now converted to the Porter Tun Room with one of the best
hammer-beam roofs in London (available for functions); below was

location for the Overlord Embroidery before it was moved to rtsmouth in 1984. On the N side are stables for the 14 dray-horses vhich are still used for delivering beer in the City and which pull the Lord Mayor's coach (see Museum of London) in the Lord Mayor's Procession each November. Beer is no longer brewed on this site, but the horses can be seen Mon to Fri 11.00–12.30 & 13.30–15.00 (tel. 071-606 4455 for appointment). Gift shop.

Elizabeth Frink's 'The Running Man' on the Barbican terrace

To the S in Monkwell Square is the *Barber Surgeons' Hall* (1969) by Kenneth Cross on the original site dating to mid 15C. The W Gate of the Roman Fort (comp. above) is entered from London Wall (Mon to Fri 12.30–14.00; other times by arrangement at Museum of London). On view are remains of the N guardroom, a gravelled roadway, and the central piers of the gate (closed during London Wall redevelopment'

Off Wood St, N of London Wall, is the sunken garden of *St. Alp*
where another fine section of the city wall has been exposed. Above
Roman level (part of the N wall of the early fort), the additions in g
stone date from c 1350, and the red brick top was added c 1477. Near
are the remains of the N porch of *Elsing Spital* (enter through car park), a
priory church founded in 1329 'for the sustentation of a hundred blind
men'.

Cross London Wall, by walkway, redevelopment permitting. To the E
of *Brewers' Hall* in Aldermanbury Square, on this site since 1420 and
rebuilt in 1960 after its destruction in 1940, is the *City Business Library*
(formed from the Commercial Reference Room and the Newspaper
Room of the Guildhall Library). In the garden of Brewers' Hall is a
charming statue, 'The Gardener', by Karin Jonzen (1971). The *Girdlers'
Hall* (1961) in Basinghall Avenue to the E has an 18C mulberry tree in
the garden. S in Aldermanbury is the *Chartered Insurance Institute*
(1934), with its fire-marks and fire-fighting equipment collection.

Chartered Insurance Institute (fire engines) Museum, Aldermanbury, EC2. Tel.
071-606 3835. Open Mon to Fri 10.00–17.00. Free. Access: Underground,
Moorgate.
    There is a small museum on the second floor of this building on the theme of fire,
marine, life and accident insurance with early fire-fighting equipment including
hand-drawn fire-engines, firemen's helmets, leather buckets, etc. The firemarks
are particularly interesting; the fire brigades owned by the insurance companies
would only fight fires at properties bearing their company's marks.

In Guildhall Piazza is another delightful sculpture by Karin Jonzen
'Beyond Tomorrow' (1972); a flight of steps descends right to a coloured
glass fountain by Allen David.

Across *Aldermanbury* a pleasant garden surrounds the site of the
Wren church of *St. Mary*, bombed in 1940 and removed in 1968 to the
campus of Westminster College, Fulton, USA as a memorial to Winston
Churchill (who made his famous Iron Curtain speech at the College).
The memorial to the editors of Shakespeare's First Folio, Heminge and
Condell, church-wardens, remains. Judge Jeffreys was buried here,
having died in the Tower in 1689. The registers recording Milton's
second marriage (1656) are now in the Guildhall Library.

On the corner of Aldermanbury and Gresham St stands St. Lawrence
Jewry, built by Wren in 1671–77 and effectively restored by Cecil
Brown (1956–57) after substantial war damage, as the official church of
the City Corporation. The painting in the heavy Renaissance style
reredos is by the architect. A Trumpeter's gallery is used on ceremonial
occasions and there is a Commonwealth Chapel. Pepys records a visit to
the church 'for curiosity' and his disappointment with the sermon. Sir
Thomas More deliverd a series of lectures here. The church has been
adopted by the New Zealand Society. Guildhall Yard and the Guildhall
is to the NE. See Rte 24.

24 Guildhall, Bank of England, Mansion House and the Stock Exchange

The attractive **Guildhall**, the base of the City Corporation of London, is
best approached from Gresham St through to Guildhall Yard. To the E
work is under way on an extension to house the City of London art
collection. The remains of a Roman amphitheatre, the first discovered
in London, was found on the site in 1987, holding up the redevelopment.

ll, EC2. Tel. 071-606 3030. Access: Underground, Bank. Open Mon to
.00–17.00 Sun (May to Sept), Bank Hols, summer 10.00–17.00. Free
ed at short notice for functions; Crypt not always open—ask at the desk.)
Court of Common Council of the City of London (see p 207) meets every
.d Thursday; the public is admitted.

The *Hall of the Corporation of the City of London* dates from c 1411–35, though its external appearance is substantially due to the design of George Dance, Jr (1788–89). Over the porch is the City coat-of-arms, with the motto 'Domine dirige nos'. The lower part of the great hall, the porch, and the crypt are medieval. Much damage was caused by fire in 1666 and 1940 but the interior was beautifully restored by Sir Giles Scott in 1952–54.

The GREAT HALL (151.5ft long, 48ft wide, and 89ft high) was restored in 1668–71 and in 1866–70, but its 19C timber roof was destroyed in 1940 and has been replaced by stone arches with a panelled ceiling (1954). The hall is used for Court of Common Council meetings, the ceremonies of the City such as the election of the Lord Mayor and Sheriffs, and the state banquets hosted by the Corporation. The most important of these last is the banquet given in November, by the new Lord Mayor and Sheriffs, for the members of the Cabinet when the Prime Minister makes an important speech. At an earlier period the hall was used also for major trials (recorded on a panel). Against the walls are a statue of *Churchill*, by Oscar Nemon, and monuments to *Nelson* (inscription by Sheridan), *Wellington*, *Chatham* (inscription by Burke), *William Pitt* (inscription by Canning) and *Lord Mayor Beckford*; the popular wooden figures of *Gog and Magog*, by David Evans (above at the W end), replace those burned in 1940.

The Crypt is a very interesting survival of the building of 1411–35. The *Eastern Crypt* is borne by six clustered columns of Purbeck marble; restored in 1961.

The **Guildhall Library and Art Gallery** is reached either by a corridor running W from the porch of the Guildhall or from an entrance in Aldermanbury. The library contains about 140,000 printed volumes and pamphlets and over 30,000 MSS. It is especially rich in works on London and Middlesex, and includes several important special collections. The Commercial Reference, and Newspaper Libraries now form the City Business Library. The Art Gallery is due to reopen in its new extension in 1991. It will house the Corporation's collection of London topographical work, pre-Raphaelite works and paintings by Matthew Smith, which it shares with the Barbican Art Gallery.

The *Guildhall Clock Museum* (Aldermanbury, EC2. Open Mon to Fri 09.30–17.00. Free) is one of the most important horological collections in the country, bequeathed to the Museum by the Clockmakers' Company established in 1631.

In Gresham St to the E stood Gresham College (now in the Barbican Centre as part of the City University), founded by Sir Thomas Gresham in 1579 for the delivery of lectures in Latin and English on 'divynitye, astronomy, musicke, geometry, law, physicke, and rethoricke' by seven professors. The lectures are now all given in English.

At the end of Gresham St, Prince's St, skirting the huge wall of the Bank of England (see below) leads S to the Mansion House. Opposite the Bank a driveway admits to *Grocers' Hall*, virtually destroyed by fire in 1965. A new hall was completed in 1970, the fifth to be built on

this site. It preserves part of the 17C ironwork from the sec#
and the oldest bell in the city (1458; recast since the fire). The C#
or 'Pepperers' was first mentioned as a guild in 1180 and incorpo#
in 1428.

Prince's St emerges at the Mansion House and the Bank of Englar#

The triangular space overlooked by the Bank, the Royal Exchange
and the Mansion House may fairly claim to be the heart of the City;
from it radiate eight important streets. Nearby are the headquarters of
all the big banks.

Access: Underground, Bank.

The **Bank of England** (Pl. 9; 5) covers about three acres between
Lothbury, Bartholomew Lane, Threadneedle St, and Prince's St. A
museum opened in 1988. The Bank was founded in 1694 by William
Paterson, backed by powerful City men. From 1694 till 1734 the bank
operated in Grocers' Hall. Its first building was erected by George
Sampson in 1732–34, but the bank's later aspect (one-storeyed in
appearance) was due to Sir John Soane, who built the massive
external wall (windowless in the interests of security) with its
Corinthian columns, from 1788 onwards. It was rebuilt by Sir Herbert
Baker in 1925–39 and rises seven storeys above ground within
Soane's original outer wall and has three floors below ground. The
sculptures are by Charles Wheeler; in the pediment appears the 'Old
Lady of Threadneedle St', as the bank is popularly known.

Bank of England Museum, Bartholomew Lane, Threadneedle St.EC2. Tel.
071-601 4387. Open summer: Mon to Fri 10.00–17.00; also Sat, Sun 11.00–17.00
in summer.

The Museum tells the story of the bank's incorporation and includes the Royal
Charter of 1694, under which, and another of 1946, it now operates. The first joint
stock bank in England, it had an original capital of £1,200,000, later increased to
£14,553,000, which is held by the Treasury. Its affairs are managed by a Board
consisting of a Governor, a Deputy Governor and 16 Directors appointed by the
Crown. The Bank is the Government's banker and, on its behalf, manages the
National Debt and the Note Issue of which it has the sole right in England and
Wales. It is also the bankers' bank and the central bank of the country. All
important overseas central banks have accounts on its books but for many years
it has not undertaken new commercial banking business. After the Gordon Riots
(1780) the Bank was protected nightly by a picket mounted by the Brigade of
Guards until 1973.

The Museum is guarded by a 'gatekeeper' in the traditional pink tailcoat and
top hat worn by bank officials. From a traditional banking hall, the displays
include the development of the bank note, gold bars, the bank's own collection
of silver and interactive visual displays on the financial markets.

Opposite the Bank, in the angle formed by Threadneedle St and
Cornhill, stands the **Royal Exchange**, erected by Tite in 1842–44. It is
the third building of its kind on this spot. The first Exchange, erected
by Sir Thomas Gresham in 1564–70, was burned down in 1666 and
the second in 1838. The present owners, Guardian Royal Exchange,
are adding another two storeys to the building; the work is due to be
completed in 1991/92, until then part of the building is covered. The
tympanum group above the Corinthian portico represents Commerce
holding the charter of the Exchange and attended by the Lord Mayor,
British merchants, and natives of various foreign nations. The campanile, 180ft high, with a peal of bells, has a statue of Gresham on its E
face and a gilded vane in the form of a grasshopper (Gresham's crest).

The forecourt features 12 Victorian-style lamps—donated by 12
livery companies. Here stands an equestrian statue of *Wellington*, by
Chantrey (1844). A *War Memorial* (1920), by Aston Webb and Alfred

...mmemorates London Troops. Around the building the shops
...e reinstated as redevelopment work is completed. On the
...needle St sidewall of the Royal Exchange there are statues to
...ugh Myddleton (1845) and Richard Whittington (1845). At the
...r is an granite column topped by a statue of Baron Paul Julius
...euter who founded the Reuter's News Agency at the Royal
...xchange in 1851, by Michael Black (1976). Across the passage is a
seated figure of *George Peabody* (died 1869), facing a charming little
fountain-group by Dalou (1878).

The inside of the Royal Exchange has been the base of the the London
International Financial Futures Exchange since 1982, with its trading floor
constructed as a separate shell within the existing building. This makes it
difficult to see the Turkish pavement from the first Exchange and the interior
paintings, particularly the well-known wall panels painted by Lord Leighton and
others and the important statues: A bust of Abraham Lincoln by Andrew
O'Connor (1930); Queen Victoria in marble by William Hamo Thornycroft
(1895); and Prince Albert, who laid the foundation stone, by J.C. Lough (1847);
Queen Elizabeth I (1847) by M.L. Watson; by the clock a stone statue of its
founder Sir Thomas Gresham by William Behnes (1845); and Charles II by
John Spiller (installed in 1844). The wall paintings and statues can be seen by
appointment with LIFFE, Royal Exchange, Threadneedle St, EC2.
However, LIFFE provides its own entertainment for those interested in the
workings of the financial markets. There are three 'pits' in which deals are done
in gold, currency and government securities—all to be completed in the future.
The Visitor's Gallery is open Mon to Fri 11.30–14.45. Admission free. Leaflets are
available to explain the activities. N.B. LIFFE may move in 1991, see p 247.

The forecourt of the Royal Exchange provides a fine view of the
Mansion House to the S, Lutyens Midland Bank and the Bank of
England, as well as straight ahead between Poultry and Queen
Victoria St, the controversial site owned by Peter Palumbo where
Mappin & Webb and other buildings were to be demolished to make
way for an office complex designed by Stirling, now rejected. On the
corner at 39 Queen Victoria St is *Sweetings*, London's oldest fish
restaurant, first established in 1830 and in the present building since
1906. Oysters, prawns and other shellfish are served from the counter
and lunchtime diners queue for places at the cramped tables.

The **Mansion House**, the official residence of the Lord Mayor, is to
the S. It is a Renaissance edifice, with an imposing Corinthian portico,
erected by George Dance the Elder in 1739–53, with a pediment
sculptured by Sir Robert Taylor. (Closed during refurbishment.)

The chief feature of the interior (visitors admitted on certain Saturdays, written
applications to the Secretary) is the *Egyptian Hall*, the scene of banquets, balls,
and other functions, as well as numerous public meetings. Dance modelled it
after the so-called Egyptian Hall of Vitruvius, which, however, bore no
resemblance to Egyptian architecture. It contains some 19C sculptures. The
Long Parlour, with a remarkable ceiling, the *Saloon*, adorned with tapestry and
sculpture, the *State Drawing Room*, are shown also. Visitors enter by the door in
Walbrook.

The colourful *Lord Mayor's Show* is held on the second Saturday in November,
when the new Lord Mayor is taken by coach through the streets of the City to be
sworn in at the Royal Courts of Justice, preceded by a procession with a theme
chosen by the Lord Mayor, but always traditionally including the defence
services, and made especially spectacular by the presence of the Hon. Company
of Men at Arms and the Household Cavalry.

In Walbrook, just behind the Mansion House, is the church of **St.
Stephen**, rebuilt by Wren in 1672–79. The noble *Interior, with its
circular dome (63ft high) supported on eight arches, is one of the
architect's masterpieces, and has been carefully restored since its
partial destruction in 1941. The dome represents, on a small scale,

Wren's original design for St. Paul's. The font is by Thomas Stro~
with a fine cover by William Newman, and the rich pulpit is by Th~
Creecher. To the left a tablet commemorates Dr Nathaniel Hodge~
appointed by the Lord Mayor in 1665 to combat the spread of the
Plague, which had started in Mansion House Place. The fine sword
rest dates from 1710, and the organ (by Hill) from 1906. A glass mosaic
in the S wall commemorates John Dunstable (died 1453), 'the father of
English harmony', and a tablet serves as memorial to John Lilburne
(died 1657), the political agitator. In the vaults lies Sir John Vanbrugh
(1664–1726), playwright and architect.

Controversy surrounds the new altar by Henry Moore in the shape
of a large round 'cheese' installed in the church in 1986.

To the E of the Bank, beyond Bartholomew Lane, the **London Stock
Exchange**, the headquarters of the dealers in negotiable securities,
occupies a tall tower and buildings at its foot (1972). The site may be
redeveloped in 1993 as the buildings are no longer suitable. The
Stock Exchange has occupied part of the site since 1802. The public
are admitted to the Visitors' Gallery (Mon to Fri 10.30–15.30) and to a
cinema where films explaining the working of the Stock Exchange
are shown. Since the 'Big Bang' in October 1986 which removed the
distinction between jobbers and brokers and introduced com-
puterised dealing, the trading floor of the Stock Exchange is only used
by the London Traded Options Market. The London International
Financial Futures Exchange is merging with LTOM and forming a
new market, the London Derivatives Exchange, in 1992. It will move
to Cannon Bridge, Cannon St.

Member companies of the London Stock Exchange have to be approved by the
Stock Exchange Council; since 1986 foreign companies have been admitted. An
independent dealer must have worked for a member company for at least three
years, be sponsored by two members and pass an examination in order to be
admitted. Dealing is now carried out mostly via computer terminals. A fall in
prices leads to a 'bear' market, a rise to a 'bull market'. The Stock Exchange
Index and the Financial Times Index measure the average price changes.

In Lothbury, on the N side of the Bank, is the church of *St. Margaret Lothbury*,
rebuilt by Wren in 1686–90. It contains an exquisite, carved font, pulpit, and
canopy ascribed to Grinling Gibbons, and a fine chancel screen from All Hallows
the Great, probably English work of c 1689. The elaborate sword-rests date from
the late 18C. The bust of Sir Peter le Maire (died 1631), at the W end of the nave,
is perhaps by H. le Sueur.—Opposite, in an alcove in the wall of the Bank, is a
statue of Sir John Soane.

In Throgmorton St, just N of the Stock Exchange, is *Drapers' Hall*,
dating in part from 1667 but practically rebuilt in 1866–70 (restored
1949; entrance in Throgmorton Avenue). It contains a handsome
staircase, and a famous mulberry still flourishes in the garden.—In
Austin Friars, close to Drapers' Hall, stands the *Dutch Church*, by
Arthur Bailey (1950–54). This lofty church with its graceful flèche,
replaces the 13C building—originally the nave of a priory of Augustinian friars—that was assigned by Edward VI in 1550 to Protestant
refugees and was ultimately left exclusively to the Dutch. The old
church was completely destroyed in 1941, and the great W window,
by Max Nauta, shows Edward VI and Princess Irene of the Netherlands, who laid the foundation stone of the new church. Beneath the
Communion table is the altar-stone of the priory church (1253).

Old Broad St, diverging on the left from Threadneedle St, leads to
Liverpool St Station and Broadgate Square, see Rte 28. On its E side
the elegant *City of London Club*, by Philip Hardwick (1834), only just
saved from demolition to make way for the **National Westminster**

ver, (1980, by Richard Seifert) then the tallest office block in rope at 600ft and 52 storeys. The original development envisaged demolishing not only the Club but also the Banking Hall, designed by John Gibson (1864–65), which now adjoins the Tower and is used for conferences, banquets, etc. The National Westminster Tower houses the headquarters of the banking concern. There is a viewing area at the top from which the Thames Estuary, the Chilterns and the South Coast can be seen on a clear day but it is only open to guests and invited customers of the Bank.

Further S in Threadneedle St (No. 30) is *Merchant Taylors' Hall*, the largest of the livery company halls, incorporated in 1327, damaged by the Great Fire of 1666, gutted by fire in 1941, and reopened in 1959. A 14C crypt survives. The company, incorporated in 1327, maintains a large public school for boys. The activity of the Merchant Taylors and the needlemakers (whose hall was nearby) probably gave the name to 'Threadneedle' St. In Threadneedle St (N side), stood the old South Sea House, built in 1711 for the South Sea Company, where Lamb was a clerk in 1789–92 and where the 'South Sea Bubble' burst in 1719. The British Linen Bank was built over part of the site in 1902. Threadneedle St ends at Bishopsgate, see above.

From the Royal Exchange junction, *Moorgate* (Pl. 9; 5) runs N from Princes St past the Bank of England. To the E, in Great Swan Alley, is the *Chartered Accountants' Hall*, a Renaissance-style building by John Belcher (1890–93; extended 1930), with sculptures by Hamo Thornycroft and H. Bates, was redeveloped with a new Great Hall by William Whitfield in 1970. The Moorgate, a postern gate in the City Wall built in 1415, and pulled down in 1761, stood at the junction with London Wall. To the W in London Wall stands *Armourers' Hall* (1841), founded 1453. The Barbican beyond is described in Rte 23. To the E in Throgmorton Avenue is *Carpenters' Hall*, rebuilt 1956–60, and, further on, the church of *All Hallows London Wall* by the younger Dance (1765–67), with a fine plaster ceiling and blue and gold decorations, well restored in 1962. The monumental pulpit is entered through steps from the vestry. Part of the medieval city wall may be seen in the churchyard.

Moorgate continues N beyond London Wall; parallel to the W, *Moorfields* preserves the memory of the marshy district outside the old Moorgate, once the resort of archers, washerwomen, and (later) of booksellers. Here the Royal London Opthalmic Hospital was established in buildings by Robert Smirke in 1821. In 1899 Moorfields, as it came to be known, outgrew its premises and moved to City Road. John Keats was born in 1795, the son of a livery stable keeper, on the site of No. 85 Moorgate (public house; tablet). Opposite is the School of Business Studies of the City of London Polytechnic. To the E opens *Finsbury Circus* (bowling green), with Britannic House by Lutyens, next to the new River Plate House. In Ropemaker St, W of Moorgate, Daniel Defoe died in 1731. From here the line of Moorgate is continued by *Finsbury Pavement* to the unexpected expanse (reminiscent of Continental cities) of *Finsbury Square* (underground car park) laid out by George Dance the Younger but with none of the original building surviving including Lackington's bookshops 'The Temple of Muses'. To the W runs Chiswell St, at the end of which is *Whitbread's Brewery* (see p 242).

N of the square begins the long *City Road*. Here is the entrance to the drill-ground and headquarters (*Armoury House*, 1737) of the **Honourable Artillery Company** of the City of London, the oldest military body in the country, having been incorporated by Henry VIII in 1537 under the title of the Guild or Fraternity of St. George.

It has been established at its present home since 1642, and since 1660 the captain-general has usually been the Sovereign or the Prince of Wales. Officers for the Trained Bands of London were supplied by this company, in whose ranks Milton, Wren, and Pepys served. The HAC has the rare privilege of marching through the City of London with fixed bayonets.

A small museum on the history of the HAC is now open to the public. The facilities are available for functions. Tel. 071–606 2521.

Bunhill Fields, a nonconformist cemetery, disused since 1852

Visitors should note the Long Room; and the Court Room with a fine suit of armour (Greenwich; c 1555) and a unique leading-staff of 1693.—In 1638 Robert Keayne, a member of the London company, founded the Ancient and

nourable Artillery Company of Boston, in the United States, the oldest
litary body in America. On 15 Sept 1784, Lunardi made a balloon ascent
rom the HAC ground and became the first aerial traveller in the English
atmosphere.

The adjoining castellated building is a Territorial Force headquarters.
Immediately to the N, between the City Road and Bunhill Row
(formerly Artillery Walk), lie **Bunhill Fields**, the famous cemetery of
the nonconformists, disused since 1852, the earliest burial on record
being 1623. Possibly this is the site of a Saxon burial-ground which
gave these two fields the name of Bon or Bone-Hill Fields. Here are the
graves of *John Bunyan* (died 1688; recumbent effigy; restored 1950), in
the second turning to the S from the main walk; *Daniel Defoe* (died
1731; obelisk erected in 1870 by boys and girls of England), to the N of
the main walk, close by (renovated 1949); *Dr Isaac Watts*, the
hymn-writer (died 1748; altar-tomb), to the E of Defoe (renovated
1951); *William Blake* (died 1827), 25 yards NW of Defoe; and *Susannah
Wesley* (died 1742), mother of John Wesley (renovated 1957).

Milton wrote 'Paradise Regained' and died in 1674 at a house (No. 125;
demolished) in Bunhill Row. In the *Friends' Burial Ground*, across
Bunhill Row, laid out as a garden in 1952 and surrounded by new flats,
is the grave of George Fox (1624–91), founder of the Society of Friends.
  On the opposite side of City Road stands *Wesley's Chapel*, built in
1777, with a statue of John Wesley (1703–91), the founder of
Methodism, in front of it and his grave behind. The chapel still retains
Wesley's pulpit. **Wesley's House** (tablet; adjoining the chapel), where
he moved in 1779, contains the simple room in which he died 12 years
later. Here also are mementoes of his brother, Charles Wesley.
Margaret Thatcher, Prime Minister 1979– , was married here.

Wesley's House and Chapel, City Road, EC1. Tel. 071-253 2262. Open: Chapel
Mon to Sat from 08.00–17.00, weekdays. Sunday Service at 11.00. House, Mon to
Sat 10.00–16.00. Admission charge. Access: Underground, Moorgate, Old St.

The Foundry, nearby, used by Wesley as a headquarters in 1739–78
before he built the chapel, is commemorated by a plaque in Tabernacle St (No. 21), just to the E.—A little further on City Road crosses *Old St*
(busy roundabout) which leads right (E) to Shoreditch and left (W) to
Clerkenwell, passing the partly demolished church of *St. Luke* with its
obelisk steeple by Hawksmoor and John James (1727–33). Here
William Caslon (1692–1766), the type-founder, is buried.
  City Road continues past *Moorfields Eye Hospital* where HM the
Queen opened a new £15m building in 1988, to the *Angel*, a busy road
junction named after a long-demolished but once famous coaching
tavern, and Islington, See Rte 32.

25 Cannon Street, Thames Street, and The Monument,

Access: Underground, Cannon St, Mansion House.

Cannon St (Pl. 8; 8) runs E through an area once occupied by
wax-chandlers; its name is a corruption of Candlewick St. Starting
from Mansion House Station, to the W in Cannon St is the former
Financial Times building, *Bracken House* (1960), a striking pink

building with an interesting astronomical clock, now listed bu
being redeveloped internally by its new Japanese owners. The
Financial Times has moved to Southwark Bridge, south of the River.

In Bread St to the N, stood *St. Mildred's* church (1677–83, by Wren), where
Shelley and Mary Godwin were married in 1816. It was destroyed in the last
war. A memorial to Adm. Phillip (1738–1814), governor of the first colony of
British settlers in Australia (1788), who was born in Bread St, has been moved
to Gateway House in Cannon St.
    To the SW in Queen Victoria St is Huggin Hill where a palatial Roman bath
was excavated during 1989 and then buried under the new building, Dominant
House, for future generations. To the N in Queen Victoria St is the church of
St. Mary Aldermary, so called, says Stow, because 'elder than any church of St.
Marie in the City'. It was rebuilt by Wren after 1681 (tower 1704). The plaster
fan-vaulting is especially noteworthy. Milton married his third wife, Elizabeth
Minshull, here (1663). The *London Chamber of Commerce* (1934) offices are to
the E at the corner of Queen St and Cannon St. In Dowgate Hill to the S, just
before Cannon St Station, are the decorative entrances to the halls of the
Tallow Chandlers (No. 4), the *Skinners* (No. 8), with a fine series of panels in
the dining hall by Frank Brangwyn, and the *Dyers* (No. 10), the first two rebuilt
soon after the Great Fire and Second World War damage and the third dating
to 1842. Beyond Queen St is the huge *Bucklersbury House* (1958) occupying
most of the triangle (right) between Queen Victoria St, Cannon St, and
Walbrook. In the forecourt of Temple House are the remains of a TEMPLE OF
MITHRAS, unearthed in 1954 beneath the foundations of Bucklersbury House,
about 80 yards to the SE, adjoining Walbrook. Built shortly before AD 200, it is
58.5ft long and 26ft wide and has the triple W end characteristic of Mithraic
temples. The bases of two rows of pillars and the walls supporting them have
survived. The important sculptural finds from the site are now in the Museum
of London.

Upper Thames St runs parallel with Cannon St to the S.
    High Timber St joins Upper Thames St on its ancient line just E of
the surviving tower of *St. Mary Somerset*. The rest of the church,
built by Wren in 1695, was taken down in 1871.
    Although the warehouses and wharves have now gone, some
narrow lanes bearing historic names still run down to steps into the
Thames. In Brooks Wharf the quaint *Samuel Pepys* pub, with views
over the river, occupies a 19C warehouse. Queensbridge House and
Queen's Quay have superseded *Queenhithe Dock*, once an important harbour for the City, the property of Isabella of Angoulême, and
the earliest fish market in London. From the evocative cobbled lane
to the E its shape and extent are still apparent. *Vintners' Hall*, near
the corner of Queen St, was rebuilt in 1671, after the Great Fire,
though the Court Room (1446; panelled in 1576) was preserved. The
company, incorporated in 1437, owns valuable tapestries and a
painting of St. Martin by the school of Rubens (see also Swan
Upping, p 304). In Vintners' Lane a statue of a Vintry Ward school
boy (1840), in Coade stone, survives. Next to Southwark Bridge,
Vintry House has been demolished to give way to a new building
projecting 35ft over the river with a Buckingham Palace-style
frontage.
    The picturesque Garlick Hill once devoted to the fur trade with a
view of the tower of St. Mary-le-Bow is N of Upper Thames St. Here
the church of *St. James Garlickhithe* (open for services) is so called,
according to Stow, because garlic was sold on the Thames nearby.
The attractive steeple, attributed to Hawksmoor, dates from 1714–
17. The interior, by Wren (1676–83), with good wood-carving and
ironwork, and an organ attributed to Father Smith (1697), has been
pleasingly restored. In Little Trinity Lane to the W lies the *Hall of
the Painter-Stainers*, rebuilt after the Great Fire of 1666, restored
after damage in 1941, and extended in 1961. Nearby stood the head-

ıarters of the Hudson's Bay Company, established as fur-traders in ∟ondon since 1870; now closed down and the building demolished.

Queen St to the E forms the approach to *Southwark Bridge* (Pl. 8; 8), originally the work of John Rennie in 1813–19 but entirely rebuilt in 1913–21 (good view of the river). Beyond Queen St, on the N side of Upper Thames St, Whittington Gardens commemorate Richard ('Dick') Whittington (died 1423), three times Mayor of London, who lived in College Hill (named from a college he founded), to the N. He rebuilt and was buried in *St. Michael Paternoster Royal*, again rebuilt by Wren in 1686–94, with a steeple of 1713. It was beautifully restored (with fine windows by John Hayward) and rededicated in 1968 as the chapel and headquarters (offices in the tower) of the Missions to Seamen, a society 'ministering to the needs of seamen throughout the world'.

To the E of Southwark Bridge (1988), excavations have unearthed evidence of the Roman quay and removed the remains of three Saxon ships and other Roman and Saxon finds before building started on the Thames Exchange site.

To the NE is **Cannon St Station** (Pl. 9; 7), rebuilt except for its decorative riverside turrets. Beneath Bush Lane House excavations in 1965 revealed traces of a Governor's Palace built c AD 80–100 beside the mouth of the Walbrook stream, overlooking the Thames. At a lower level timber foundations suggested this was the earlier site of a Roman fort. Further excavations in 1988/89 have revealed a late Roman building. Evidence has also been found of the Hanseatic League's trading colony with remains of a 14C guildhall. Opposite in Cannon St is the *Bank of China*, built on the site of *St. Swithin's*, a church rebuilt by Wren and destroyed in 1940–41 (the churchyard is now a garden in Salters' Hall court). Immured in the wall of the bank is LONDON STONE, generally believed to have been the Milliarium of Roman London, from which the distances on the Roman high roads were measured. This is the stone which Jack Cade struck with his staff, exclaiming 'Now is Mortimer Lord of this City'. In St. Swithin's Lane is *Founders' Hall* (No. 13), dating to 1877–8.

In Abchurch Yard, off Abchurch Lane, the next side-street to the E, stands *St. Mary Abchurch* (i.e. 'up' church, from its high site), rebuilt by Wren in 1681–86 and the least altered, containing wood carvings by Grinling Gibbons. The dome, with its paintings by William Snow (1708), is an architectural tour de force; considerably damaged in Sept 1940, it has been finely restored (1948–53). The 14C crypt is plain and vaulted. To the S, in Laurence Pountney Hill, two houses (Nos 1 and 2) survive from 1703.

Cannon St ends at a busy crossroads where King William St converges with Gracechurch St and *Eastcheap*, on a site believed to have been occupied by the 'Boar's Head Tavern' where Falstaff and Prince Hal caroused. *St. Clement Eastcheap*, to the N, was rebuilt by Wren in 1683–87. It contains a handsome carved pulpit, possibly by Grinling Gibbons, and font-cover, and a fine organ of 1695.

On the Thames waterfront to the S is Mondial House, the International Telephone Centre, and Angel Passage or Swan Lane lead (right) to a terrace overlooking the Thames. Here, opposite the graceful pinnacles of Southwark Cathedral, the moored paddle steamer 'Princess Elizabeth', now a bar/restaurant (Mon to Fri), affords a fine view of London Bridge. **London Bridge** (Pl. 9; 7) was rebuilt in 1967–73 by Harold Knox King, remaining open to traffic throughout the operation. Borne on three arches of pre-stressed concrete faced with granite, it is 105ft wide. The former bridge designed by John Rennie, begun in 1825 by his sons John and George Rennie and completed in 1832, was sold for £1,025,000. It was dismantled into 10,000 granite slabs which were numbered and shipped to Lake Havasu City, Arizona, where it was re-erected over an artifical lake.

A wooden bridge across the Thames existed by the 1C AD. This probably survived until 1176, having been repaired by the Saxons. The popular rhyme 'London Bridge is falling down' may date from this time, when it was resolved to 'Build it up with stone so strong'. The new bridge, about 100ft W of the old, was begun in 1176 by Peter of Colechurch, at the instance of Henry II, but it was not completed until 1209 in the reign of King John. It stood close to the W end of the church of St. Mary Magnus. Rows of wooden houses sprang up on each side, and in the middle was a chapel dedicated to St. Thomas Becket. At each end stood a fortified gate, on the spikes of which the heads of traitors were exposed. It was notoriously difficult to navigate because of the narrow passage between the starlings and the force of the ebb tide. After a fire in 1758 the houses were demolished and the bridge partly reconstructed and opened in 1763. This bridge, the only bridge over the Thames until 1729, was removed after the completion of Rennie's bridge 100ft upstream.

London Bridge divides the Thames into 'above' and 'below' bridge. Downstream is the Port of London, the reach immediately adjacent to the bridge being known as the *Pool*, while upstream is the *King's Reach*.

Fishmongers' Hall stands at the N end of London Bridge (entrance from the viaduct across Upper Thames St which carries King William St on to London Bridge). With a fine classical façade on the river, it was erected in 1831–34 by Henry Roberts and Gilbert Scott. It was badly damaged in September 1940, when it was the first of the City Halls to catch fire; similarly, a previous Fishmongers' Hall on this site was the first to burn during the Great Fire of 1666.

The Fishmongers' Company is one of the richest as well as one of the oldest of the 12 great livery companies. Its origin is lost in remote antiquity but it is unquestionable that the Company existed before the reign of Henry II. The fine interior has been restored in its former style. It contains the Annigoni portrait (1955) of Queen Elizabeth II (the model for stamps and bank-notes), a painted wooden figure of Sir William Walworth, the Mayor who killed Wat Tyler in 1381, and a fine dagger he is supposed to have used; also a richly embroidered pall of the Tudor period.

On the other side of London Bridge to the E is *Lower Thames St*, which retains its cobbled surface and was once redolent of fish from end to end. Geoffrey Chaucer is said to have lived in this street from 1379 to 1385, during part of which period he was Comptroller of the Petty Customs in the Port of London. To the S is *St. Magnus Martyr*, rebuilt by Wren in 1671–76. The *Steeple, 185ft high, one of Wren's masterpieces, was not completed till 1705. The passage beneath the tower was from 1763 to 1832 part of the footpath of Old London Bridge. Miles Coverdale (died 1569), author of the first complete English version of the Bible (1535), was rector of St. Magnus in 1563–66 and is buried in the church.

To the N, at the top of Fish St Hill, rises the **Monument**, a fluted Doric column, 202ft high, erected from the designs of Wren in 1671–77, to commemorate the Great Fire of London which broke out on 2 September 1666, in Pudding Lane, at a point alleged to be exactly 202ft from the Monument. A winding staircase (of 311 steps) ascends to the upper gallery, which commands a wide and striking view. The flaming gilt urn surmounting the Monument is 42ft high.

The cage enclosing the gallery was added to prevent suicides. The allegorical relief by C.G. Cibber shows Charles II and the Duke of York encouraging the stricken city.

The Monument, Monument St, EC3. Tel 071-626 2717. Open April to Sept, Mon to Fri 09.00–18.00, Sat, Sun 14.00–18.00; Oct to March, Mon to Sat 09.00–14.00 and 15.00–16.00. Admission charge. Access: Underground, Monument.

A little further on is the former **Billingsgate Market** which moved to West India Docks in 1982. It took its name from an old gate, supposedly called after Belin, a legendary king of the Britons and claimed to be the only market in which every variety of fish was sold—'wet, dried, and shell'.

Billingsgate Wharf, said to be the oldest on the river, was used from very early times (perhaps from the 9C) as a landing-place for fishing boats and other small vessels. The striking blue glass building on the adjoining site is linked to the old building which was converted into offices in 1988 and is now occupied by Citicorp.

The narrow Lovat Lane, opposite Billingsgate leads N to the church of *St. Mary at Hill* rebuilt by Wren in 1670–76 from the medieval church destroyed in the Great Fire. Another fire in 1988 destroyed the noteworthy woodwork and much of the box pews and other interior features including the sword rests the organ by William Hill and the ceiling which dated from 1849. Plans are afoot to restore the church which was the venue for the annual Sea Harvest Thanksgiving Festival. A narrow passage skirts the church on the S and emerges beneath a grim gateway surmounted by a skull and crossbones in St. Mary at Hill. Here to the (right) is the attractive *Hall of the Watermen and Lightermen* (1776–80) with improvements in 1951 and 1961 after Second World War damage. The Watermen and Lightermen's Company still examines and approves all apprentices who wish to work on the River. At the corner of St. Mary at Hill and Lower Thames St a *Roman Bath* was discovered in 1969 which belonged to a private house of c AD 200. Finds on the site showed the house to have been occupied until the second half of the 5C.

Beyond Billingsgate is the **Custom House** in Lower Thames St, a large classical edifice (1814–26), the fine river façade of which is well seen from London Bridge. The first custom house was established here in 1275 to collect duty on trade on the River. St. Dunstan's Hill, opposite, leads up to the church of *St. Dunstan in the East*, rebuilt in 1671 by Wren, who added the fine square lantern tower in 1698. The body of the church was severely damaged in 1941 though the shell remains and has been beautifully planted by the Worshipful Company of Gardeners as a public garden. A fig tree commemorating the coronation of George VI in 1937 survives outside the S wall. In Harp Lane, a little further E, is the *Bakers' Hall* (No. 9; 1963) with windows by John Piper commemorating the burning of the former halls.

Turn E along Great Tower St past the church of *St. Margaret Pattens* (restored 1956), built by Wren in 1684–87, with a fine tall spire. It is thought to be named from the pattens (shoes with iron rings attached to the soles to protect the wearer from muddy roads) once made and sold in the lane. The font and the reredos are fine works; the altarpiece is by Carlo Maratti. The two canopied pews are unique in London.

The S pew has on its ceiling the engraved monogram C.W.; possibly Christopher Wren himself occupied this pew. N of the altar is the original Beadle's pew and a punishment bench. The church is a Christian Study Centre, with conference rooms in the gallery.

Continue to the Tower (Rte 27).

26 Lombard Street, Leadenhall Street and Market, Lloyd's, Aldgate and Petticoat Lane

Access: Underground, Bank, Aldgate.

From the junction at *Bank Station, King William St.* and *Lombard St* (Pl. 9; 5) to the SE have for centuries been one of the chief banking and financial centres of London. Lombard St derives its name from the 'Lombard' money-lenders from Genoa and Florence, who during the 13–16C took the place of the Jews in this profession. The church of **St. Mary Woolnoth** forms a monumental bastion between King William St and Lombard St. A building of great originality, it was erected by Nicholas Hawksmoor in 1716–24 and altered in 1875. It was the only City church to remain intact throughout the air raids of 1940–45. It is a guild church.

The interior contains an elaborate reredos, and ornamental woodwork. From the pulpit John Newton (1725–1807; tablet on N wall) helped to inspire William Wilberforce, Claudius Buchanan, and Hannah More to their philanthropic pursuits. On the S wall is a memorial to Edward Lloyd (p 257); and (end of the S aisle) the armour of Sir Martin Bowes (died 1566), a Lord Mayor of London, is preserved. The 'Spital Sermon' is preached here in Easter week, attended by the Lord Mayor and aldermen.

The adjacent post office occupies the site of the General Post Office from 1678 till the move to St. Martin's in 1829. Post Office Court also houses the *Bankers' Clearing House*, in which, four times daily, the mutual claims of the various banks against each other in the form of cheques and bills are compared and settled by cheques on the Bank of England.

In *Change Alley*, to the N, there were scenes of wild speculations during the South Sea Bubble excitement in 1720. A restored pump of 1799 recalls a predecessor of 1282 and drinking water still flows from a fountain of classical inspiration (1859) a few paces away. Change Alley leads to Cornhill, named from a long extinct grain-market; a Roman building for storing grain has been discovered here. No. 39 Cornhill occupies the site of the house (burned down in 1748) in which Thomas Gray (1716–71), the poet, was born. St. Michael's Alley to the E reveals the unexpectedly tall tower of *St. Michael's*, rebuilt by Wren and Hawksmoor in 1670–1724, and restored by Sir G.G. Scott in an incongruous Gothic style in 1857–60. At the end of the Alley a tablet on the Jamaica Wine House recalls the opening of the first London coffee house in 1657.

To the S is the church of *St. Edmund the King and Martyr*, completed by Wren in 1679 (steeple, 1708). In George Yard, a pleasant Neptune fountain in bronze fronts the *George and Vulture*, (Castle Court), a tavern known to all readers of 'Pickwick', now a restaurant and pub, bookings on 071-626 9710. Beyond to the S in Lombard St is the striking grey *Lombard Bank* building, and, on the corner of Grace-church St are the headquarters of *Barclays Bank* (1959) with sculptures by Sir Charles Wheeler.

Gracechurch St leads N to Leadenhall Avenue and Market.

St. Peter's, to the W in Cornhill opposite, stands on a high point of the City, occupied in Roman times by the administrative Basilica (comp. below), wrongly supposed by later tradition to have been the

rliest Christian church in London. The existing structure, rebuilt by
Vren in 1677–81, contains a carved wooden choir-screen, one of the
only two known to be by Wren himself. The organ is by Father Smith
(1681); Mendelssohn (1840 and 1842) played on the former keyboard
(now in the vestry). The old bread-shelf (W wall) and the illuminated
MS of the Vulgate made for the church in 1290 are interesting, and
there is a monument to the Fifth Army.

Leadenhall Market to the E has been restored and still includes
traders selling traditional meat and game, as well as croissant and
coffee shops; in 1663 Pepys bought 'a leg of beef, a good one, for
sixpence' here. The medieval street plan was retained when the
elaborate arcaded buildings were erected in 1881 by Sir Horace
Jones. The small area remains congested and lively. The buildings
were built over part of a Roman Basilica and Forum erected in AD
80–100, one of the largest buildings of its kind in the whole Roman
Empire. The London Metal Exchange is just off Leadenhall Market.

The 28-storey block of *Commercial Union Insurance* and the 12 storey
P & O Building are set in an open piazza off Leadenhall St with the
church of St. Helen's to the N. This attractive modern development
was designed by Collins, Melvin and Ward.

At the corner of St. Mary Axe stands the church of *St. Andrew
Undershaft*, built in 1520–32. The name is derived from the ancient
practice (discounted in 1517) of erecting a 'shaft' or maypole, taller
than the tower, in front of the S door.

At the E end of the N aisle is the alabaster monument of *John Stow* (1526–1605),
the antiquary. The pen in Stow's hand is annually renewed by the Lord Mayor in
March or April. On the same wall, further to the W, is the monument of *Sir Hugh
Hamersley*, Lord Mayor in 1627, notable for the fine figures of the two
attendants. In the S aisle is a tablet recording that Holbein (1497–1543) was once
a resident of this parish. The font, by Nicholas Stone, dates from 1631, and the
organ (restored in 1969) was built by Renatus Harris in 1696. The spandrels are
adorned with 18C paintings, and the roof was restored with its 16C bosses in
1950.

In St. Mary Axe (in an area with the offices of many shipping
companies) is the **Baltic Exchange**, the headquarters of a body of
merchants and brokers who deal in floating cargoes, consisting of
grain, timber, oil, coal, and other commodities, and now also in air
charter. Visits by appointment. This institution is an amalgamation of
the old Baltic (which sprang from 'The Virginia & Baltick Coffee
House') and the Shipping Exchange (the modern representative of
the old 'Jerusalem Coffee House'). The name 'Baltic' is now
misleading.

To the S in Lime St is the striking new glass and steel edifice of
Lloyd's of London (Pl. 9; 6), designed by Richard Rogers and opened
by HM the Queen in 1986. It stands on the site of the 1928 building
designed by Sir Edwin Cooper and demolished in 1979. On the other
side of Lime St is the second Lloyd's building by Terence Heysham
(1952–58), now used as offices. The Underwriting Room, Lutine Bell
and a new Visitors' Gallery are in the new building.

Lloyd's of London, Visitors' Gallery, Lime St, EC3. Tel. 071-623 7100. Open Mon
to Fri 10.00–14.30. Exhibition. Shop and Cafeteria on ground floor.

Visitors enter the gallery via one of the outside lifts, to level 5. The exhibition
traces the history of insurance and there is a view over the Underwriting
Room—a hub of activity.

The new Lloyd's building concentrates the services of the building in si. towers which contain lifts, staircases, lavatories, etc. The eight columns support the 12 floor-high atrium, linked to the fourth floor level by escalators. The Underwriting Room extends from the ground floor to the fourth floor level and firms occupy 'boxes' based on the original coffee-house booths. The Lutine Bell is strikingly positioned in the centre; it was recovered from HMS 'Lutine' which sank in 1799. Once the bell was sounded for every loss at sea, now it is used only on ceremonial occasions—two strokes for good news, one for bad. Historic rooms

Lloyd's of London, designed by Richard Rogers and opened in 1986

ansferred here from the old building include the Committee Room, originally
rom Bowood House in Wiltshire, the old Library from the 1928 building, the
Special Dining Room, the Lutyen's War Memorial erected at the Leadenhall
Market end of Green Yard, and the Nelson Collection.

Lloyd's Underwriting Rooms, an association of underwriters and insurance
brokers transacting most kinds of insurance, arose from a gathering of merchants (1688) in Edward Lloyd's coffee-house in Tower St (later in Lombard St
and in the Royal Exchange); its original business was marine insurance.

On the site of Lloyd's stood (till 1862) East India House, where Charles Lamb
(1792–1825), James Mill (1819–36), and John Stuart Mill (1822–58) were clerks
in the service of the East India Company.

In *Leadenhall St*, further E is the church of *St. Katherine Cree* (i.e.
Christchurch, from a priory founded by Maud, queen of Henry I in
1108), rebuilt in 1628–30, with a mixture of Gothic and Renaissance
detail.

This church was consecrated by Laud, then bishop of London. The cover of his
prayer book is kept in the vestry. The chapel in the SE commemorates both Laud
and Charles I and contains the tomb of Sir Nicholas Throckmorton (died 1570).
The E window, with stained glass of 1630?, is in the form of a catherine-wheel.
The font dates from c 1640. The organ was built by Father Smith (1686). At the
SW angle a pillar of the old church projects 3ft above the floor, the level of which
is said to have risen 15ft. An unverified tradition has it that Holbein (died 1543)
was buried in the earlier church. The annual 'Lion Sermon' (on 16 Oct)
commemorates the escape of Lord Mayor Gayer, who held office in Charles I's
time, from a lion. The church was restored in 1962; the Industrial Christian
Fellowship has offices in the N and S aisles.

Leadenhall St ends in a junction with Aldgate and Fenchurch St.

Off *Fenchurch St* to the S is *Mincing Lane*, named from the
'Minchens' or nuns of St. Helen's, was the headquarters of the
wholesale tea trade. The *Hall of the Clothworkers*, rebuilt in 1958 on
the E side after its destruction in 1941, is the sixth hall on this site since
1456. The archives and the plate, among which is a loving cup
presented by Samuel Pepys, Master of the Company in 1677, were
saved. A pleasant oasis of green to the W marks the churchyard of St.
Gabriel Fenchurch (destroyed 1666). At the corner of *Mark Lane* (i.e.
Mart Lane) is the Institute of Marine Engineers. Nearby is the 15C
tower of *All Hallows Staining*, adjoining which is a 12C crypt brought
brought from a bastion of the city wall, near Cripplegate, and rebuilt
here by the Clothworkers in 1872. Near the S end of the Lane is the
principal seat of the grain trade, now a commodity market, with the
Corn Exchange established here in the mid-18C; the new building
was opened in 1953 (tel. 071-480 6610 to view).

In Hart St, leading E from Mark Lane, the *Ship* has a painted stucco
façade. Here is the church of *St. Olave, one of the few churches that
escaped the Great Fire of 1666. Seriously damaged in 1941, it was
sensitively restored in 1951–54, when Haakon VII of Norway laid the
'King's Stone' in front of the sanctuary recalling the Norwegian birth
of the patron saint, and incorporating a stone from Trondheim
Cathedral. Samuel Pepys (1633–1703) the diarist, who lived in the
adjacent Seething Lane, was a regular attendant at this church (the
entrance to his Navy Office pew may be seen in the churchyard; a
plaque was erected within the church in 1883). Mrs Pepys (1640–69) is
commemorated with a charming bust, attributed to John Bushnell (N
side of the chancel), erected by her husband. Both are buried beneath
the high altar. There is an annual Pepys memorial service in June.

Below the monument to Mrs Pepys is a fine monument to the Bayning brothers
(died 1610 and 1616). Over one of the pillars on the S side of the nave is a plaque
to John Watts (1780), 'President of the Council of New York'. Other fine
monuments include: (S aisle) Sir James Deane (died 1608); (N aisle) Peter

Capponi (died 1582), a Florentine merchant who died of the plague; and Andrew Riccard (died 1672). The pulpit and altar rails are noteworthy. From the W end of the S aisle (light on left) narrow steps descend to a small *Crypt* (probably late 12C), with an ancient well. Here are displayed finds from the churchyard and well, and sculptural fragments of the 15–18C. The skulls over the churchyard gate in Seething Lane (Dickens's 'St. Ghastly Grim') are supposed (somewhat doubtfully) to refer to the burials during the Plague in 1665.

When Pepys was Secretary of the Admiralty the Navy Office stood in *Crutched Friars* (i.e. 'Crossed Friars', from an old monastery), the prolongation of Hart St to the E. *Crutched Friars House* (No. 42) is one of the few surviving City residences of the early 18C. It is now the residence of the Director of Toc H, the brotherhood established to perpetuate the memory and devoted spirit of the Talbot Houses of Poperinghe and Ypres. The first Toc H (i.e. T.H. in the army signaller's alphabet) opened at Poperinghe in 1915, was named in honour of Lieutenant Gilbert Talbot.

In Railway Place, is **Fenchurch St Station** (1840), the first to be built in the City, redeveloped in 1987 when part of the Roman wall and bastion was revealed. At the corner of Fenchurch St and Lloyd's Avenue is **Lloyd's Register of Shipping**, a society (distinct from Lloyd's, see above) founded in 1760 and reconstituted in 1834. The roof is surmounted by an appropriate gilt weathervane.

Its primary object is to secure an accurate classification of merchant shipping, but it now discharges many other important functions for which 'surveyors' are maintained in the chief ports of the world. The Register Book contains full particulars of all sea-going merchant vessels of 100 tons and upwards. The highest class for steel and iron vessels is 100 A1, and for wooden vessels A1, the letter A referring to the hull and the figure 1 to the equipment.

Aldgate, to the NE, a short street taking its name from one of the old City gates. A draught (draft) on *Aldgate Pump* (still standing at the beginning of the street) was once a cant expression for a worthless bill. Geoffrey Chaucer leased the house above the Aldgate from the City of London in 1374 (tablet).

Jewry St, to the S, was once an area of mainly Jewish shops and residents, which extended eastwards to Whitechapel and Mile End. In Duke's Place, just N of Aldgate, stood the 17C Great Syngagoue. Here is the *Sir John Cass Foundation School*, founded in 1710 by a charitable alderman (died 1718; buried in St. Botolph's) and rebuilt in 1909 (playground on the roof). Off Bevis Marks, in Heneage Lane, is the handsome *Spanish and Portuguese Synagogue* moved here in 1701 from Creechurch Lane and the oldest in use in England.

Aldgate High St, continuing Aldgate, forms part of a complicated traffic system round large modern buildings, where only the *Hoop and Grapes* on the S shows the former scale—a pub with foundations dating to the 13C, the oldest in the City. The building is probably late 17C. Beyond Houndsditch is *St. Botolph Aldgate*, built by George Dance the Elder in 1741–44, and restored in 1966–71, after a fire. In the octagonal vestibule beneath the tower is a handsome font and cover. Here have been placed a memorial to Sir John Cass (1661–1718), and the monuments of Robert Dow (died 1612; with an anxious portrait bust), and Thomas Darcy and Sir Nicholas Carew, beheaded on Tower Hill in 1538. The organ, a gift from Thos. Whiting in 1676 (plaque), was built by Renatus Harris. Thomas Bray, founder of the SPCK and SPG, was vicar from 1708 to 1722. William Symington (1763–1831), pioneer of steam navigation, is buried here (tablet on W wall). In the S aisle is a finely carved panel of David playing the harp which, together with the lectern, dates from the early 18C. Daniel

efoe was married here in 1683, and Jeremy Bentham christened in
he church in 1747. The founder of the Sir John Cass School is
commemorated in February.

Houndsditch, runs NW from Aldgate to Bishopsgate (see below)
and forms the E boundary of this part of the City. Further E is
Middlesex St or 'Petticoat Lane', one of London's most popular tourist
attractions.

Petticoat Lane, Aldgate, E1. Open Sun 0800—1400 (adjoining street markets
operate through the week). Take care with handbags and wallets. Access:
Underground, Aldgate, Aldgate East, Liverpool St.

During the 15C this was Hog Lane which a century later started its association
with cloth and clothing as traders were moved from London Bridge; particularly
dealers in second-hand clothes. A map of the area dating from 1603 refers to it as
Petticoat Lane because of its clothes stalls. Jewish immigration during the 18C
gave further impetus to the market's growth, as they were allowed to trade on
Sundays. In 1870 the name was changed to Middlesex St although the market
has continued to thrive under the of name Petticoat Lane.

Today half the stalls in Middlesex St and adjoining Goulston St still sell
clothing but kitchen and household goods are also available. In the side streets
the market continues, each has its own character. Note particularly Cutler St
specialising in gold and jewellery.

In nearby Whitechapel High St is the famous Blooms Jewish delicatessen and
restaurant.

The *Minories*, running S from Aldgate to the Tower, was formerly
famous for its gun-makers. Its name is derived from an old convent of
Minoresses ('Sorores Minores'), or nuns of St. Clare. Off St. Clare St,
within the convent precincts, was found (1964) the tomb of Anne
Mowbray (died 1481), wife of Richard, Duke of York (comp. p 74).—In
America Square, just W of the Minories, was the home of Nathan
Meyer Rothschild (1777–1836), founder of the English branch of the
family. No. 100 (rebuilt in 1969) houses the *School of Navigation* of the
City of London Polytechnic (which incorporates the Sir John Cass
College). The new Docklands Light Railway operates from here
(Tower Hill); one branch to Stratford and the other to Island Gardens.

Aldgate High St is continued E to Whitechapel. On the corner of
Whitechapel High St and Aldgate High St are the glass-clad offices of
the Sedgwick Group which incorporate a conference centre based on
the 300-seater Chaucer Theatre (also used for recitals, concerts and
ethnic plays and music).
See Route 28.

27 The Tower and Tower Hill, St. Katharine's Dock

Access: Underground, Tower Hill; by boat to Tower Pier from
Westminster Pier or Charing Cross Pier, all the year round.

The area is dominated by the Tower of London, and Tower Bridge
opened as an attraction in 1982, All Hallows by the Tower and St.
Katharine's Dock add further interest to this historic part of London.
From April to October there is a tourist information centre at the
Tower of London.

A large section of the Roman and medieval wall of London (with a
reproduction of a Roman funerary inscription found nearby and a
Roman bronze statue) can be seen in *Wakefield Gardens*, beyond the

Underground station. Another stretch may be seen in the courtya
the bank in *Cooper's Row* (explanatory tablet). It is here 35ft high,
upper part, pierced with windows and with a sentry walk along
top, was built in the 12C. The medieval postern gate on the N edge
the Tower was excavated in 1979 and can be seen at the S end of the
Tower Hill underpass. This is the start of the London Wall Walk (see p
237).

To the NE of the Tower was the former *Royal Mint* (1810–12 Sir R.
Smirke). The Mint, first established within the Tower in 1275–85, has
been moved to Llantrisant, near Cardiff. During reconstruction of the
listed building the 14C Cistercian Abbey remains were excavated
and may be included in the new building by RMJM (London) as a
museum. Barclays Bank is now occupying part of the building.

TOWER HILL is a small area just behind All Hallows by the Tower
(see below); this was an execution area from the 14C onwards with as
many as 100 eminent people losing their heads here. At the execution
of Lord Lovat in 1747 a public stand collapsed killing several people; a
gallows here was used during the Gordon Riots in 1780. A stone in the
pavement in the *Trinity Square Gardens* on the other side of the road
marks this gruesome site. Tower Hill has since been used for public
gatherings, speeches and performances. It is now being redeveloped.

Close by is the *Mercantile Marine War Memorial*, by Lutyens
(1928), extended by Maufe with sculptures by Wheeler (1955).
Beyond the gardens rises a massive building by Sir Edwin Cooper
(1922; until 1972 the offices of the Port of London Authority): **Trinity
House**, adjacent, was erected by Samuel Wyatt in 1793–95 for the
'Guild, Fraternity or Brotherhood of the most Glorious and Undivided
Trinity', the first charter of which was granted by Henry VIII in 1514.

The corporation consists of a Master (at present the Duke of Edinburgh), a
Deputy Master, Wardens, Assistants, and Elder Brethren, besides a large
number of Younger Brethren, and its object is the safety of navigation and the
relief of poor mariners. Pepys was Master here in 1676 and 1685. The building,
badly damaged in the Second World War, was restored by Sir A.E. Richardson
and reopened in 1953. In the main hall are statues of Captain Maples, by Jasper
Latham (1683; the first lead statue known to have been made by a British
sculptor), and of Capt. Sandes, by Scheemakers (1746), both formerly in the
courtyards of Trinity Almshouses (p 276).

To the W is London's most visited 'parish church', **All Hallows by the
Tower**.

All Hallows by the Tower, Byward St, EC3. Tel. 071-481 2928. Undercroft open
Mon to Fri 09.30–18.00; Sat, Sun 10.00–17.00, except during services. Free
except for groups. Access: Underground, Tower Hill.
    Founded in the 7C, it was largely destroyed in the Second World War but the
brick tower, from which Pepys watched the progress of the Great Fire, is the only
surviving example of Cromwellian church architecture in London. The spire in
the manner of Wren was added during restoration in 1958. This restoration
revealed an important Saxon arch, set now in the N wall of the new baptistery
(1960). The font is of Gibraltar rock and the font-cover of limewood was carved
by Grinling Gibbons (1682).
    The tombs and the fine series of brasses in the sanctuary survived. In 1922 All
Hallows became the guild church of Toc H (p 259); and in the sanctuary, with a
15C Antwerp painting, probably by Jan Provost, is the tomb of Alderman John
Croke, with a casket containing the parent Lamp of Maintenance from which are
lit all Toc H lamps around the world. In front of the sanctuary is a memorial
bronze, by Cecil Thomas, to elder brethren of Toc H. In the S aisle is the
Mariners' Chapel, with a 16C Spanish ivory crucifix. Stairs descend to the
Chapel of St. Clare, a 17C vault, and a mid-14C crypt chapel.
    The *Undercroft* is of the greatest interest. Entering from the W end note
fragments of Roman remains, including some of two pavements, pottery and
ashes of Roman London burned by Boudicca in AD 61, and a model of Roman

. There are also fragments of Saxon crosses, one of unusual type, later
.e Danish occupation (c 1027–50). At the E end is a memorial chapel
.ining the ashes of members of Toc H. The plain crusading altar is from
.ard I's castle at Athlit in Palestine. In front of it is the tomb in which the
.nains of Abp Laud rested (1645–63) before they were removed to St. John's
.ollege, Oxford. William Penn (1644–1718), born on Tower Hill, was baptised in
.ll Hallows and here John Quincy Adams, sixth president of the United States,
was married to Louisa Johnson in 1797.—Kitchener's Omdurman sword is
preserved in the Vestry. There is a *Brass Rubbing Centre* in the crypt.

Tower Hill Pageant, an underground exhibition of the history of London and its
port is planned for the vaults, due to open in 1991. Information from the Museum
of London.

Continue downhill to the entrance to the **Tower of London** (Pl. 21; 2) **and Royal Armouries**.

Open March to Oct Mon to Sat 09.30–17.00, Sun 14.00–17.00, Nov to Feb, Mon to
Sat 09.30–16.00 (closed Sun). Admission charge. The Crown Jewels are included
in the admission charge. They are usually closed in January for maintenance.
Changing of the Guard on Tower Green 11.00 daily summer, alternate days in
winter. Ceremony of the Keys every night at 22.00; applications in writing to the
Governor, Tower of London, EC3. Shops.

Long queues for admission may be experienced in summer (especially on
Sundays). Yeoman Warders give frequent guided tours on fine days which begin
at the Middle Tower, and include the Chapel Royal of St. Peter ad Vincula
(otherwise kept locked; the Sunday services at 09.30 and 11.00 are open to the
public).

The Tower of London, a fortress of surpassing interest from its intimate
connection with English history, the excellent preservation of its Norman and
medieval buildings, and the many illustrious people who have suffered within its
walls, occupies a site across the old City wall and covers an area of nearly 18
acres. The outer wall is surrounded by a deep *Moat* (drained in 1843 and now
beautifully planted as a public garden). Between the outer wall and the inner
wall lies the narrow *Outer Ward*, and near the centre of the spacious *Inner Ward*
rises the massive square *White Tower*. The entrance is near the SW corner, at the
foot of Tower Hill.

A Wall Walk opened to the public in 1982 linking the towers of the Inner
Wall—look for signs. Enter from Wakefield Tower and descend at Martin Tower.

The Tower, in its day a fortress, a royal residence, and a state-prison, is still
maintained as an arsenal, with a garrison, and during both wars its former use as
a prison was revived. The Constable for the Tower, always an officer of high
dignity, is assisted by the Lieutenant; the duties of governor are now performed
by the Major of the Tower, who is Resident Governor. Quite distinct from the
garrison are the *Yeoman Warders* ('honorary members of the Queen's
Bodyguard of the Yeomen of the Guard'), a body of about 40 men chosen from
retired warrant and non-commissioned officers of the army. They wear historic
costume, said to date from the time of Henry VII or Edward VI and are familiarly
known as 'Beefeaters', a sobriquet probably derived from the rations anciently
served to them. Black ravens have always lived at the Tower and according to
legend 'the kingdom would fall should the ravens leave the Tower'; this may
date to the time of Charles II when he tried to get rid of the ravens but was
warned against doing so.

History. The White Tower, the oldest part of the fortress, dates from the reign of
William the Conqueror, when the Roman Wall formed the E boundary of the
precinct. Of Richard I's additions only some work in the Bell Tower remains, and
it was in the reign of Henry III (1216–72) that the 'small castle' was turned into a
great concentric fortress. The outer curtain and the moat were added in 1275–85
by Edward I.

Built by William to overawe the citizens of London, the Tower has never been
seriously assaulted, and its gloomy history is more that of a state-prison than of a
fortress. Sir William Wallace (executed in 1305), King David II of Scotland
(1346–57), and King John of France (1356–60) were confined here under Edward
I and Edward III. James I of Scotland spent part of his long imprisonment in
England (1406–24) at the Tower. In the same century the Tower witnessed the
secret murders of Henry VI (1471), of the Duke of Clarence, brother of Edward IV
(1478), and of Edward V and his brother, 'the little Princes in the Tower' (?1483).
Henry VIII (1509–47) was married to Catherine of Aragon and to Anne Boleyn
here. Anne Boleyn, after a trial in the Great Hall of the palace, was beheaded

here in 1536. Other victims in this reign were Bishop Fisher and Sir Tho
More (both beheaded 1535) and Queen Catherine Howard (beheaded 154
Among the many prisoners of Mary's reign (1553–58) were Lady Jane Gr
and her husband, Lord Guildford Dudley (both beheaded 1554), Elizabet
(afterwards queen), who was rigidly confined for two months; Cranmer and
Sir Thomas Wyatt (beheaded 1554), by whose followers the Tower had been
attacked, for the last time in its history.

In Elizabeth's reign the Duke of Norfolk, who was beheaded in 1572 for
intriguing in favour of Mary, Queen of Scots, and the Earl of Essex (beheaded
1601) were imprisoned here. Sir Walter Raleigh was thrice confined in the
Tower—1592, in 1603–16, and again in 1618, just before his execution. In
1605–06 Guy Fawkes and his companions were tortured in the dungeons of
the White Tower. James I (1603–25) was the last monarch to reside in the
Tower. The Earl of Strafford and Abp Laud both passed through the Tower to
the scaffold (in 1641 and 1645), followed, after the Restoration, by Viscount
Stafford (1680), Lord William Russell (1683), and the Duke of Monmouth
(1685). Charles II (1660–85), who passed the night here before his coronation
in 1661, was the last monarch to sleep in the Tower. Lord Lovat, one of the
prisoners brought to the Tower after the Jacobite risings of 1715 and 1745,
was the last person beheaded in England (1747). Later prisoners in the Tower
were John Wilkes (1763), Lord George Gordon (1780), Sir Francis Burdett
(1810), and the Cato St conspirators (1820). During the two World Wars
several spies met their doom within its walls.

The modern entrance bridge passes over the pit of the *Drawbridge*
built by Edward I. On the right is a shop, on the site of the former
Lion Tower, where the King's menagerie was kept until 1834.
Started by a gift of leopards from Frederick of Hohenstaufen to
Henry III, and augmented in 1255 by an elephant from St. Louis of
France, the collection finally formed the nucleus of the London Zoo.
The tame ravens which haunt the inner ward are perhaps a relic of
this collection. Pass through the *Middle Tower* (also built by
Edward I) and cross over the *Moat* to the *Byward Tower* (late 13C;
14C additions). Opposite us rises the *Bell Tower* (late 12C), the
prison of Fisher, More, and Monmouth, where curfew is still rung at
sunset. Follow the *Outer Ward* or *Outer Bail* (comp. the Plan) to the
E. On the right, further on, is *St. Thomas's Tower*, above the
Traitors' Gate, the old water-gate, through which many illustrious
prisoners little deserving the name of traitor have entered the
Tower. Both tower and gateway date from Edward I's reign. Opposite are the Bloody Tower and the *Wakefield Tower* (c 1225),
traditionally thought to be the murdering place of Henry VI in 1471.
A tablet in the floor marks the spot and flowers are laid on the
anniversary of his death (21 May) by students of Eton and King's
College, Cambridge. Pass under the Bloody Tower into the *Inner
Ward*, dominated by the White Tower. On the right of the ascent is
a portion of the medieval wall of the Inner Bailey, and part of
Coldharbour Gate (1240).

The *White Tower, the oldest part of the whole fortress, was
begun about 1078 for William the Conqueror, by Gundulf, also the
builder of Rochester Cathedral. The Tower stands on a slope and
rises to a height of 90ft on the S side. It measures 118ft from E to W,
107ft from N to S, and has walls 12–15ft thick. The exterior was
restored by Wren, who altered all the windows except for four on
the S side. The interior is still very much as it was in Norman times.
Beneath an external staircase on the S side, removed during the
restoration, the bones of the Little Princes were found in 1674.

Enter via the external staircase at the NE corner to the First Floor.
The interior contains **The Royal Armouries *Collection** (an
independent national museum with its own Board of Trustees)
started by Henry VIII, based on the Tower arsenal and a workshop

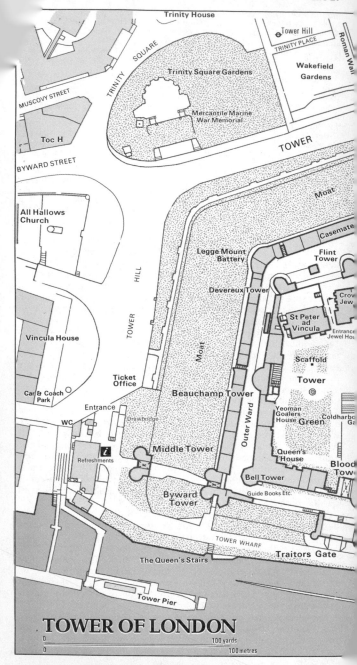

TOWER OF LONDON

| 0 | 100 yards |
| 0 | 100 metres |

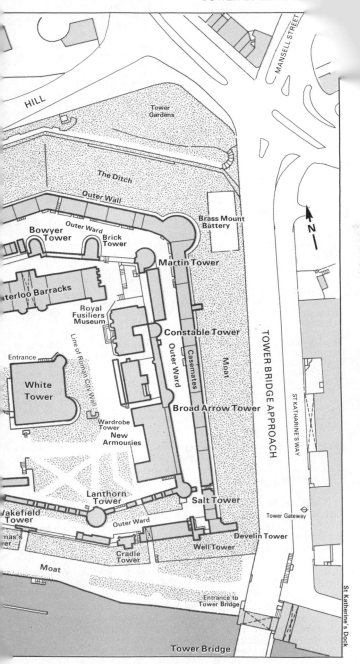

MANSELL STREET

HILL

Tower Gardens

The Ditch

Outer Wall

Outer Ward

Bowyer Tower

Brick Tower

Brass Mount Battery

N

Martin Tower

terloo Barracks

Royal Fusiliers Museum

Constable Tower

TOWER BRIDGE APPROACH

Entrance

Line of Roman City Wall

Outer Ward

Casemates

Moat

ST KATHARINE'S WAY

White Tower

Broad Arrow Tower

Wardrobe Tower

New Armouries

akefield Tower

Lanthorn Tower

Salt Tower

Tower Gateway

nas's er

Outer Ward

Develin Tower

Cradle Tower

Well Tower

Moat

Entrance to Tower Bridge

St Katherine's Dock

Tower Bridge

nwich which made armour for himself and his court. During
.gn of Charles II it opened here to the public.

first gallery shows *Hunting and Sporting Weapons* from the cross-bow to the
phant gun.—The *Tournament Gallery* contains superbly displayed and
pelled exhibits which include: armour made for the Court of Emperor
Maximilian I (Innsbruck, c 1490); a suit made in Augsburg, c 1590 (most of the
arms and armour for jousting was made at Greenwich, c 1610–25, and at
Augsburg, 16–17C); great wood saddle covered in rawhide (German, late 15C);
half-armour made for the Elector Christian I of Saxony (1591); fascinating relics
of exhibitions mounted in the past; wooden heads and horses (one carved by
Grinling Gibbons) used for the 'line of Kings' set up in armour in 1680; supposed
trophies from the Armada; Jacobite trophies from Culloden; case of Victorian
'medieval' forgeries. Near the E end is the small cell in which Raleigh is said to
have spent his final term of imprisonment. There is a shop on the Crypt of St.
John's Chapel.

On the Banqueting Floor level is *St. John's Chapel, the oldest church
in London and a splendid example of pure Norman architecture.
Henry IV created 46 Knights here in 1399, and the institution of the
Order of the Bath remains closely connected with the Chapel. The
further gallery displays arms and armour from Anglo-Saxon times to
the 15C. Also displayed here is a MS volume of the Making of
Gunpowder and its use in the late Middle Ages (German, c 1450). At
the end of the room is one of about five surviving examples of
complete Gothic armour for the horse (German, c 1480). The
adjoining gallery displays Renaissance armour, a superb array
including an astonishing suit for a giant.
    On the Third or Council Floor is the Stuart and Tudor collection
from the English Royal Armour Workshop founded by Henry VIII at
Greenwich, which operated from 1511 to 1642.

On the right of the entrance, Grotesque helmet presented to Henry VIII by
Maximilian I (1514, Innsbruck); horse armour traditionally thought to be a
present from Maximilian to Henry (1515, Flemish); armour, including magnificent horse armour, made for Henry at Greenwich (1520–35); the suits of Robert
Dudley, Earl of Leicester, and of William Somerset, 3rd Earl of Worcester, both
made at Greenwich (1575); and a German suit with English decoration (c 1580)
made for Sir John Smythe.—The adjoining room displays infantry arms and
armour of the 17C (including fabric and leather buff coats). Also, two suits
probably made for Charles II (1640, and 1643, ?French); and armour belonging to
James II.

From the Council Floor 114 steps descend to the Dungeons, where
16–19C weapons are displayed, including bronze mortars and
cannon. In the Cannon Room, with a well 40ft deep, are bronze guns
cast for Henry VIII, and many others, some of which are trophies of
war.
    The Royal Armouries Collection is also on view in the New Armour-
ies, Waterloo Barracks and Bowyer Tower. See below.
    The *Sub-Crypt* of St. John's Chapel is entered by a doorway
traditionally regarded as the cell called 'Little Ease', where Guy
Fawkes was confined, tied by his ankles and wrists to a ring in the
floor.
    To the N of the White Tower is the long range of *Waterloo Barracks*,
built by the Duke of Wellington (1845). In the W wing the *Crown
Jewels* (included in admission charge; queues in summer) have been
displayed since 1967. The ancient regalia were dispersed during the
Commonwealth, and in consequence the present regalia date mostly
from the Restoration when they were first publicly exhibited for a fee.
The first room contains 19C banqueting *Plate*; silver gilt *Maces*; the
Great Sword of State (1678; used at the opening of Parliament);

insignia of the various *Orders of Knighthood*; silver State *Trump* and the robes worn at Coronations since 1821.

Descend to the vaults protecting the Crown Jewels. The *Sword Spiritual Justice*; *Sovereign's Sceptre with Dove*, called also the Rod o Equity and Mercy; the *Sword of Temporal Justice*.—The *Exeter Salt* and the *Plymouth Wine Fountain* were accession gifts to Charles II.—Orbs made for Charles II and Mary II are displayed near the *Crown of Queen Elizabeth*, consort of George VI, with the famous Koh-i-Noor diamond, a spoil from the fall of Lahore presented to Queen Victoria in 1850 by the East India Company.—The *Queen Elizabeth Salt* dates from 1572–73; the font (1660) was first used for George IV's christening.—Jewelled *State Sword*, made for George IV; *St. Edward's Crown*, made for Charles II.—The *Imperial State Crown*, made for Queen Victoria's coronation, set with innumerable gems, including the large uncut ruby given to the Black Prince by Pedro the Cruel in 1367 and worn by Henry V at Agincourt, and one of the 'Stars of Africa' (317 carats), cut from the 'Cullinan' diamond, and worn by Queen Elizabeth II at her coronation; *Sovereign's Sceptre with Cross*, containing the largest of the 'Stars of Africa' (530 carats), the largest cut diamond in the world; the *Coronation Ring* made for William IV.—The *Anointing Spoon*, of the late 12C, and the *Ampulla*, in the shape of an eagle, which dates probably from Henry IV (both restored for Charles II), are the only relics of the ancient regalia.—The *Maundy Dish* holds the Maundy money distributed by the sovereign on Thursday in Holy Week.—The display ends with the *Curtana* or point-less *Sword of Mercy*.

The *Old Waterloo Barracks*, built in 1845, also houses the Oriental Gallery, part of the Royal Armouries, and the Heralds' Museum, the latter open from April to September. The Oriental Gallery houses a striking display of arms and armour from Persia, China and Japan as well as North Africa, Turkey and the Balkans. Note the complete set of elephant armour (late 17C or early 18C) probably captured by Clive at the Battle of Plassey (1757) from the Nawab of Bengal. The Heralds' Museum illustrates the significance of heraldry in British history and society with a changing exhibition including the work of the Heralds and the College of Arms and its connection with the Orders of Chivalry.

Outside Waterloo Barracks, to the W, lies TOWER GREEN. A brass plate marks the *Site of the Scaffold*. Here suffered Anne Boleyn (1536), Catherine Howard (1542), Lady Jane Grey (1554), and the Earl of Essex (1601).—To the N is the *Chapel Royal of St. Peter ad Vincula* (adm. see above), rebuilt by 1307 and restored in 1512, and again in 1971.

Within the altar rails are buried Anne Boleyn, Catherine Howard, Lady Jane Grey, Essex, Monmouth, and other illustrious victims. In the crypt lie St. John Fisher, Sir Thomas More (bust by Raphael Maklouf, 1970), and the Jacobite lords executed in 1746; and there are many more recent memorials to distinguished soldiers. In the N aisle is the sumptuous monument of the Duke of Exeter (1447), formerly in St. Katharine's, Regent's Park.

Across Tower Green is the semicircular *Beauchamp Tower* (1281). The walls are covered with inscriptions and carvings by former prisoners, many brought here from other parts of the Tower. On the first floor are displayed some Roman tiles, etc. and medieval pottery found in the Tower. In the adjoining *Yeoman Gaoler's House* Lady Jane Grey was imprisoned; more recently Rudolf Hess was incarcerated here (May 1941). The top of the wall behind is *Princess Elizabeth's Walk*.

the SW corner of the Green is the unpretentious Tudor
Queen's House (no adm.), the residence of the Governor, incorporating the Bell Tower. In the council chamber of this house Guy
Fawkes and his accomplices were examined in 1605. Adjacent is
the *Bloody Tower* (begun probably by Henry III as a water-gate
and completed by Edward I). Its portcullis is still in working order.
This tower was the prison of Cranmer, Raleigh, and Laud, and of
Judge Jeffreys, who died here of delirium tremens in 1689. The
winding staircase ascends to the room in which the Little Princes
are said to have been smothered by order of Sir James Tyrrell at
the instigation of Richard III. Outside is *Raleigh's Walk*, where Sir
Walter, during his second imprisonment, was permitted to take
the air.

On the opposite side of the Inner Bailey is the *Regimental
Museum of the Royal Fusiliers* (the City of London Regiment),
with uniforms, medals, equipment and relics relating to the history
of the regiment from 1685 to the present. Separate admission
charge.

Skirt the E side of the White Tower, passing the scanty remains
of the *Wardrobe Tower* (late 12C), built against the Roman city
wall, of which a fragment adjoins. Beyond, in an attractive late
17C building is the Board of Ordnance Gallery showing small
arms.—Opposite, a HISTORY GALLERY opened in 1978 illustrates
the history of the Tower in documents and models. (Shop).

The Outer Ward towers include the *Byward Tower*, on the second floor of
which an early 14C wall-painting of the Last Judgment was discovered in
1953. In the NE part of the ward, several German spies were shot. In the
Bowyer Tower the Duke of Clarence is said to have been drowned in a butt
of malmsey in 1478. *Instruments of torture are displayed on the ground
floor of the *Lower Martin Tower*, the scene of Col. Blood's bold and nearly
successful attempt to carry off the state crown (1671). The *Constable*, *Broad
Arrow*, and *Salt Towers* (the last with interesting inscriptions by prisoners)
follow, ending with the Lanthorn Tower.

Tower Wharf (open daily), between the Tower and the Thames, with four
old cannon, affords a good view of the river. Here royal salutes are fired by
the HAC (see p 249) on state occasions. HMS 'Belfast' (and the Design
Museum) can be reached by ferry in the summer from Tower Pier.

*Tower Bridge spans the Thames immediately below the Tower.
The bridge, about 800ft long between the abutment towers, was
designed by Sir Horace Jones and Sir John Wolfe Barry, and was
built in 1886–94 at a cost of £800,000 (including the approaches
£1,500,000). The tall towers rising from massive piers in the
stream are connected with each other near the top by a lattice-
work footbridge. The carriageway is formed by two bascules or
drawbridges, 29.5ft above high-water, each weighing about 1000
tons and raised in 90 seconds to permit the passage of vessels
through the bridge. The original steam pumping engines used to
provide hydraulic power were replaced in 1975 by electric motors.

The *Tower Bridge Walkway* opened to the public in 1982 having closed in 1909 after it had become known as a haunt for
prostitutes and villains.

Tower Bridge, SE1. Tel. 071-403 3761. Open April to Oct 10.00–18.30; Nov
to March 10.00–16.45. Admission charge. Museum, gift and bookshop.

The entrance is in the NW tower; lift or stairs. On the 2nd floor there is
an exhibition illustrating the design of the bridge. There are excellent views
upstream and downstream from the two walkways which are 60ft above
ground-level. In the S tower there is a display of the City's bridges and a
model of Tower Bridge. Outside the S Tower there is a separate entrance t

the museum in which the original steam engines which operated the brid,
on view.

St. Katharine's Dock can be reached from the Tower, from Tow
Wharf on the riverside by the Tower and a subway under Towe
Bridge; or from Tower Bridge by steps on the N side.

*Ivory House at St. Katharine's Dock with the marina
in the foreground*

...harine by the Tower is the first completed transformation of one of ...n's docks into a commercial and leisure centre (see Docklands, Rte 29). ...St. Katharine Foundation dates to 1148, established on this land near the ...ver under the patronage of Queen Matilda. By the end of the 18C some 3000 ...ople worked and lived in the precincts of the convent, which escaped ...ssolution thanks to Catherine of Aragon who remained its patron. Thousands more settled here, turning it into a slum. In 1825 the area was taken over for development as a dock and the inhabitants were unceremoniously evicted except for the Foundation which was found land off Regent's Park (see p 178).

St. Katharine's Dock, built by Telford, consisted of two basins and a range of attractive warehouses by Philip Hardwick; the docks specialised in tea, rubber, marble, ivory, sugar and other valuable commodities. After considerable Second World War damage the docks closed in 1968 and the redevelopment plans of Taylor Woodrow Ltd were approved by the Greater London Council. Further development has now taken place and the view over the Thames lost with the addition of more offices.

The remaining original buildings are *Ivory House* (1854), an attractively restored warehouse, converted into self-service apartments, with shops on the ground floor, and the Beefeater cabaret restaurant located in the vaults in the basement. The *Dickens Inn*, another warehouse from the site moved and converted into a pub and restaurant opened in 1976. In 1988 Marble Quay was added with flats, more restaurants and offices. The *Dockmaster's House* by Philip Hardwick was demolished to make way for Devon House, an office building with views over the Thames. The gates towards East Smithfield adorned with two elephants raising their trunks remain, while Hardwick's other warehouses were destroyed by fire during the war or during the redevelopment. The new buildings of the London World Trade Centre have been built to match the old warehouses and include Europe House, 1960, and International House, 1982. Next to Tower Bridge is the 826-room Tower Hotel (1973), designed by the Renton Howard Wood Partnership with good views from the Princes Room Restaurant over the Thames. Commodity Quay, 1987, houses the London Futures and Options Exchange—London Fox.

The *St. Katharine's Yacht Haven* provides mooring for visiting and permanent yachts and launches; Thames sailing barges moored here are available for hire. The Coronarium overlooking the W Basin marks the site of St. Katharine's church; it opened in 1977 to mark the Silver Jubilee of HM The Queen.

Public housing by the Greater London Council and private houses by Taylor Woodrow overlook the E Basin, where until 1987 the Maritime Trust's *Historic Ships Collection* was on display. This has now been broken up and the ships moved, except for the Lighthouse Ship Norse in the W Basin. RRS 'Discovery' is in Dundee; the schooner 'Kathleen & May' can be seen on Bankside; see p 292.

28   Bishopsgate, Spitalfields, Shoreditch, Bethnal Green, Whitechapel

Access: Underground, Bank, Liverpool St; Bus No. 22.

Bishopsgate (Pl. 9; 5), beginning at the junction of Cornhill and Leadenhall St, runs N to Shoreditch. To the W rises the *National Westminster Tower* (600ft), by Richard Seifert (1978); at the time, the tallest occupied building in Europe (see p 248). To the E is Great St. Helen's, leading to **St. Helen's** (open 09.00–17.00, closed weekends, except for services), one of the largest and most interesting of the City

churches, shaded by huge plane trees. The church is dedicated
Empress Helena, and legend asserts that the Emperor Constar.
himself erected the original edifice in honour of his mother.

The present church belonged to a priory for Benedictine nuns, founded c 1210.
has two parallel naves (one the 'nuns' choir'; N), a S transept, and two chapels
added about 1374.

The chief interest of the wide well preserved medieval interior is in the
monuments of City worthies. N Aisle: John Robinson (died 1599) with his nine
sons and seven daughters; altar tomb of Hugh Pemberton (died 1500); (beneath
nave arches) William Kirwin (died 1594); altar tomb of Sir Thomas Gresham
(died 1579); Sir Andrew Judd (died 1558), founder of Tonbridge School; and the
elaborate marble monument of Sir William Pickering (died 1574). In the N wall
may be seen the nuns' night staircase, an Easter Sepulchre and a 'squint'
(peep-hole). In the chancel are some fine 15C stalls brought from the nuns' choir
(the front stalls are mid 17C), and a rare wooden sword-rest (1665). Beyond the
tomb of Sir John Crosby (died 1475), the Chapel of the Holy Ghost contains 15C
glass. The monument to John de Oteswich and his wife probably dates from the
early 15C.

The fine brasses in the church (15–16C) include a lady in a heraldic mantle (c
1535). Among several monuments removed from the demolished church of St.
Martin Outwich is one to Richard Staper (died 1608; S wall of the nave). Beside
the S entrance is the fine restored monument of Sir John Spencer (died 1609).
The Jacobean font, pulpit, poor box, and doorcases (W end) are noteworthy.

In St. Helen's Place, further N, is the elaborate entrance-way to the
hall of the *Leathersellers' Company*, rebuilt 1949–59, and incorporated in the 14C. Just beyond is the ragstone façade with an 18C turret
surmounted by a weathervane (1671) of *St. Ethelburga*, one of the
smallest and most ancient churches in London. It escaped the Great
Fire and dates in its present form from c 1400. Henry Hudson (died
1611), commemorated by three stained-glass windows, took Communion here before starting on his first voyage in search of the
North-West Passage. A shrine honours Blessed John Larke (1504–42),
rector of the parish, executed by Henry VIII. Above the altar is a mural
painting by Hans Feibusch (1962). The fine 17C font cover came from
St. Swithin's. The tiny garden with loggia and fountain is charming,
and has become a refuge for birds.

The old Bishopsgate (pulled down in 1760) stood at the point where
Camomile St leads E and Wormwood St W. It is commemorated by a
bishop's mitre in the wall. Beyond, to the W, opens a garden
surrounding the pleasant church of *St. Botolph Bishopsgate* (1728).
The light interior has an unusual design. Keats was baptised here in
1795. Adjacent is the church hall (1861) with two charming statues
(1821) of charity children. The garden contains a tennis court.

Across Liverpool St is the Great Eastern Hotel and the huge
Liverpool St Station (Tourist Information Centre), a tour de force of
Victorian Gothic. Constructed of cast-iron and brick, it has been
extensively redeveloped, incorporating Broad St Station, now gone.
In the booking-hall is a memorial to Captain Fryatt, master of the
railway steamer 'Brussels' who was shot by the Germans at Brussels
in 1916. The site was occupied by the Hospital of St. Mary of Bethlem
(see also p 284). The massive Broadgate development to the W takes
in part of the hospital's burial ground, used as a car park since the
Second World War. The 10-acre site includes Broadgate Square
designed by Arup Associates, opened by HRH Prince of Wales in
1987, providing over 1 million sq. ft of office space. The circular rink at
its centre is used for open air performances and ice skating in the
winter. The brown-glazed buildings and tiered walkways are over-
hung with greenery and there are several outdoor sculptures; restaurants and shops line the lower ground floor which leads through to the

.. The second phase includes a massive office block spanning the
.ay track.

.Bishopsgate (at No. 202) is one of London's most famous pubs, *Dirty
.cks*. It takes its name from 18C recluse Nathaniel Bentley who
.ccording to the ballad closed his house on the death of his fiancée and
stopped washing. The cellars of the present pub of 1870 are part of the
original house and synthetic cobwebs and mice skeletons add to the
atmosphere. There is a restaurant upstairs (tel. 071-283 5888). The
Bishopsgate Institute (No. 230) was opened in 1894. The Library (open
by appointment, tel. 071-247 6844) contains a fascinating collection of
plants of old London.

At the end of Brushfield St, past Spitalfields Market, Hawksmoor's
masterpiece, **Christ Church, Spitalfields** overlooks Commercial St.
The Spitalfields Festival of Music in June/July each year provides an
opportunity to see the church at its best. It has a massive portico
supported by Tuscan columns, and an unusual octagonal tower. The
1720 interior, including the flat coffered ceiling, has been partly
restored and there are monuments by Thomas Dunn and John
Flaxman. The church was supported by the Huguenot refugees who
settled in this area and many of the 18C gravestones carry French
names.

Spitalfields wholesale market was first established under Charles II
in 1682. It is now run by the City Corporation and new market buildings
opened in 1928. Trading starts at 05.00 and comes to an end in late
morning. The market is due for redevelopment in the near future.

The area of Spitalfields, once occupied by silk-weavers largely descended from
Huguenot refugees who arrived after the Edict of Nantes in 1685, takes its name
from the priory of St. Mary Spital, founded in 1197, where the 'Spital Sermon' (now
delivered at St. Mary Woolnoth) was first preached. Some of the fine Georgian
buildings of the prosperous 18C survive in Fournier St and Elder St. Many houses
have been restored for private use and at 18 Folgate St visitors can see a house of
the period without electricity and with the top-floor weaving room set up as it
would have been in the 18C. (Contact Dennis Severs, tel. 071-247 4013, to make an
appointment for a tour; charge.) In the 19C the area went into decline aggrevated
by the 'Jack the Ripper' murders (see p 275). The building of large blocks of
artisans' dwellings followed, most of which were occupied by the many Jewish
immigrants who arrived from the 1880s onwards. Clothiers and furriers became
established here and the Jewish community has now been followed by Asian
immigrants mainly from Bengal and Pakistan.

Bricks were made in Brick Lane (parallel with Commercial St to the E).
Here among the Bengali shops and workshops stood the *Truman
Brewery*, established in the 17C and formerly known as the Black Eagle
Brewery, taking its name from Black Eagle St. Beer was still brewed
here up until February 1989 in an attractive adaptation of the old
building by Arup Associates (1976). The site will now be redeveloped
with some of the listed buildings retained as offices and workshops.

There is very popular market here every morning; it is particularly
active on Sundays; also some excellent Bengali/Indian restaurants.

Brick Lane Market (and surrounding streets), Sunday morning. Access:
Underground, Liverpool St, Buses 8, 47, 149.
The market grew up during the 18C as farmers sold some of the livestock and
produce outside the City boundary along Club Row, near Whitechapel. (The trade
in pets and small animals which continued in this section of the market has been
curtailed.) The Brick Lane Market itself offers an interesting mix of fruit and
vegetables, new clothes, household goods; there are stalls selling political
literature, a reminder of the radical past and present of the East End. Some of the
side streets offer genuine antiques, second-hand clothes, and bric-a-brac, but
unsuspecting visitors should be wary of buying goods from individuals without
stalls as these might be stolen goods.

Bishopsgate is continued N by *Norton Folgate*. Here a griff.
the City boundary. *High St Shoreditch* leads N through Shorec
area once famous for its boot-makers and furniture makers, to (.
busy intersection outside **Shoreditch Church** (*St. Leonard's*).
large church, rebuilt c 1740, was restored in 1930. James and Rich.
Burbage (see below) are buried here. The stocks and whipping-po
are preserved in the churchyard.

In *Curtain Road*, parallel with High St on the W, *The Curtain
Theatre* (tablet on Nos 86–88), the first theatre in London, was erected
in 1576 by James Burbage (died 1597), father of Shakespeare's friend,
Richard. In 1598, owing to a dispute about the lease, the wooden
structure was hurriedly pulled down at night by Burbage's sons, and
the materials transported to construct the Globe Theatre in
Southwark.

The once densely populated district of **Hoxton** lies to the NW. W of
Hoxton St is the attractive Waterloo church of *St. John*, built after the
Battle of Waterloo. In *Pitfield St* new buildings for Walbrook College
have incorporated the façade of almshouses of 1825. The area is being
gentrified.

Kingsland Road leads N to (c ¼m) the **Geffrye Museum**, with its
detailed displays of the history of the domestic English interior.

Geffrye Museum, Kingsland Road, E2. Tel. 071-739 9893. Access: Underground,
Liverpool St, then Bus 22 or 48. Open Tues to Sat 10.00–17.00, Sun 14.00–17.00.
Educational facilities. Special exhibitions. Cafeteria.

The museum occupies the old *Geffrye* or *Ironmongers' Almshouses* (1715), a
group of fourteen one-storey houses ranged round a forecourt. The central foyer
occupies the old almshouse chapel and the whole collection is most attractively
arranged. A series of period rooms in chronological order from 1600 to the 50s,
provides a background not only to the history of English furniture styles, but also
to the history of England and English family life. Guides and charts on display
provide additional information.

*The Geffrye Museum, the history of the domestic English interor
on display in converted almshouses*

of Hoxton lie the relatively uninteresting areas of *Hagger-
ngsland* and to the NE *Dalston*, part of the London Borough of
ey. Holy Trinity, Dalston contains portraits of famous clowns
ne statuette of Grimaldi formerly in St. James's, Pentonville Rd.
annual Clown's Service is held here in February. De Beauvoir
wn between Hoxton and Kingsland, W of the busy Kingsland Road,
eatures well-maintained neo-Jacobean villas with Flemish-style
gables dating from 1840 built on land which belonged to the de
Beauvoir family. After a period of prosperity the houses fell into
decline and during the '50s and '60s the local council, Hackney,
demolished the southern part and built tower blocks along the
Regent's Canal. The De Beauvoir Association fought back and many
houses are now listed.

For Hackney itself, see p 394.

To the E of Kingsland Road S of Haggerston is Bethnal Green, part
of the London Borough of Tower Hamlets.

Bethnal Green, E of Shoreditch, was one of London's most crowded
and poorest areas during the 19C. Here the Victorian social reformers
built huge blocks of working-class dwellings; later efforts of slum
clearance by the then London County Council created among others
the Boundary Estate, a somewhat better environment. Now the area is
a soulless mixture of old and new, with a large immigrant community.

In *Bethnal Green Road*, a general market dating back to 1853
survives (Monday to Friday). More interesting is the *Columbia Road
Sunday Market*, famous for plants (best approached from Hackney
Road, E from the junction with Shoreditch High St).

On this site was the huge Columbia Market built in 1869 by the Victorian
philanthropist Baroness Burdett-Coutts to provide cheap and nourishing food for
the local community. It failed and the building was finally pulled down in 1960.
The plant market flourishes and garden tools, bulbs, seeds, plants, and pots are
all on sale, according to season.

Club Row at the western end of Bethnal Green Road was part of the
Brick Lane Market. The trade in pets here has stopped. At the E end
of Bethnal Green Road at the junction with Cambridge Heath Road
is *St. John's*, a church built by Soane (1824–28); the parish church of
St. Matthew's is to the S and was built by George Dance (1743–46),
rebuilt internally in 1859 and repaired after bomb damage, in 1961.

To the N in Cambridge Heath Road is the **Bethnal Green Museum
of Childhood**.

Bethnal Green Museum of Childhood, Cambridge Heath Road, E2. Tel. 081-980
2415. Open Mon to Thurs and Sat 10.00–18.00, Sun 14.30–18.00. Closed Friday.
Free (part of Victoria and Albert Museum). Access: Underground, Bethnal
Green. Educational facilities, art room, temporary exhibitions, lectures,
bookshop.
    The unusual building is based on a prefabricated structure of iron and glass
similar to that of the Crystal Palace, erected in 1856 in South Kensington as the
forerunner of today's Victoria and Albert Museum. It was removed here in 1872
and the brick exterior added by James Wild; the scraffito panels were executed
by students of the new Royal College of Art and designed by F.W. Moody.
    The interior comprises a central hall with two gallery levels and a basement;
part of the museum has recently been refurbished and the displays improved.
    The collection of toys includes toy trains, rocking horses, board games and a
superb group of dolls' houses, among them a Nuremburg dolls' house (1673), a
Dutch miniature kitchen (1709), the Tate baby house (English, c 1760), and a
house of 1887 owned and furnished by Queen Mary. The collection of costumes
includes children's clothes and wedding dresses from 1770 onwards. There are
visual toys in the basement including puppets and a marionette theatre and
marionettes, possibly for the Palazzo Carminati in Venice (early 18C).
    Cambridge Heath Road leads S to Whitechapel Road, see below.

Old Ford Road going E leads to **Victoria Park** (217 acres),
blished in 1845; some of the grounds belonged to the for
Manor of Stepney. A comprehensive redevelopment program.
aimed to restore the park to its Victorian splendour began .
1988. It includes restoring a Chinese pagoda (the original of 184?
was used as scrap metal during the last war) on the island in the
boating lake, the reintroduction of gas lamps, and the restoration
of the Burdett-Coutts memorial; the open-air Lido will also reopen
and a floodlit fountain introduced in the lake. The canal skirts the
W edge of the park and the towpath leads N to Shoreditch and
the Kingsland Basin, and S to Mile End and Limehouse. The park
was used by Mosley for fascists' meetings in the '30s.

Whitechapel (Access: Underground, Aldgate East, Whitechapel),
immediately E of the City of London, is now part of the London
Borough of Tower Hamlets.

At the end of the 19C Charles Booth described it as 'the Eldorado of the
East, a gathering together of poor fortune seekers; its streets full of buying
and selling, the poor living on the poor'. Waves of immigration brought
Jewish settlers here through the 19C, most of whose successors have now
moved on to other parts of London to make way for the Bangladeshis. At
the end of the 19C there were 80 synagogues here, now there are seven
and a huge new mosque in Whitechapel Road. Irish dock-workers, German
sugar refinery workers, a lively market in hay and straw and the old clothes
trade (see Petticoat Lane, p 260) added colour to the area which achieved
national notoriety in 1888 with the Jack the Ripper murders of some six
prostitutes. The first murder happened just off Whitechapel Road and others
in alleyways in the area, including Mitre Square. The murders stopped but
the villain was never caught; the London Police Commissioner resigned in
disgrace.

Political confrontation came to Whitechapel in the 1930s with the Cable St
'battle' when the Fascists led by Mosley marched through the East End.
Windows in Jewish shops were smashed; see mural 'Battle of Cable St' by
local artists at St. George's Town Hall.

Today Whitechapel is a mixture of old and new. Office developments are
creeping in from the City, Asian shops predominate; Jewish families have
moved to the suburbs and much of the original 'Cockney' community has
moved out to new housing estates in East London and Essex. Uneasy relations between the different communities continue throughout this area.

Whitechapel High St continues E as Whitechapel Road and
presents a mixed picture of old neglected buildings and some new
developments. However, there are some buildings of interest to be
explored. Elizabeth Garrett Anderson (1836–1917) who founded
the first hospital for women is commemorated at her birthplace, 1
Commercial St, E1, now the London College of Furniture.

At 28 Commercial St is *Toynbee Hall*, the first 'University Settlement' founded in 1884 and named after Arnold Toynbee (1852–
83). The *Attlee House* settlement was built by public subscription
in 1971 (in memory of Earl Attlee, 1883–1967). The Curtain Theatre forms part of the community centre here. Behind, in contrast,
the housing in Wentworth St was provided by the East End
Dwellings Company in 1890. Petticoat Lane extends here (see p
260).

Beyond Blooms, a popular Jewish restaurant at No. 90, is the
Whitechapel Art Gallery.

Whitechapel Art Gallery, Whitechapel High St, E1. Tel. 071-377 0107. Open
Tues to Sun 11.00–17.00 (until 20.00 Wed). Admission charge. Access:
Underground, Aldgate East. Publications, coffee shop. Open only during
exhibitions.

The gallery was founded in 1901 and the striking building, recently
extensively renovated, with its art nouveau façade is by Harrison Townsend.

lery focuses on work by living artists; the Whitechapel Open Exhibition
, February/March is an opportunity for artists living in this and neighbour-
oroughs to exhibit.

djacent is the Whitechapel Library with a decorative frieze.

To the S Adler St leads to the church of *St. Boniface* (German R.C.;
1959) with a tall concrete bell tower. Within, the florid decoration
includes plants tumbling down from the choir loft. At 32–34
Whitechapel Road is the *Whitechapel Bell Foundry*, established in
1570. It moved here in 1738, and still occupies part of an inn building
of c 1670. Here bells have been made for Westminster Abbey since
1583, and for many churches in the City, Britain, and America. A small
museum is housed in the front office. The foundry (partially rebuilt in
1970) may sometimes be seen by appointment.

A little further on, across Davenant St (left) *Booth House* was built in
1968 by the Salvation Army. The East London Mosque is at 84–92
Whitechapel Road (1985) with three towering minarets, a crescent
moon atop the tallest, and an austere interior; telephone 071-247 1375
to view.

A quarter of a mile further on the pavement widens and on the S rise
the buildings of the *London Hospital*, founded in 1759. The remains of
John Merrick, the Elephant Man, who lived at the hospital are kept
here. A helicopter landing pad has been added to the roof (1990) for
the newly established Helicopter Emergency Medical Service.
Behind is a colossal bronze statue of Queen Alexandra, by Wade.
Opposite is a memorial to Edward VII, erected by the Jews of E
London.

Brady St diverges to the N; here is one of the four Jewish cemeteries of the area,
dating to 1761 and closed to burials (since 1858). It is a peaceful oasis behind a
high brick wall. Nathan Rothschild (d 1836), founder of the family bank in
London, is buried here. Other prominent Jewish families are buried in the
Jewish Cemetery at Alderney Road, E1 (also United Synagogue). There are two
Sephardi Cemeteries in Mile End Road; the 'old' founded in 1657, is also a
garden for a students' hostel. The flat marble tomb stones of the Sephardim
merchants are set into the ground with Spanish or Hebrew inscriptions and skull
and cross bone symbols. The 'new' cemetery was established to the E in 1733
and served the Anglo Sephardim community for over 100 years until the Golders
Green cemetery was opened. Queen Mary College has built on some of the
ground (some remains were moved to Brentwood) and only 19 and 20C
tombstones, some with well-known names, can still be seen.

The impressive main entrance to the *Watney Mann Brewery* in
Whitechapel Road, corner of Cambridge Heath Road dates to 1902.
Further on *Cambridge Heath Road* leads N towards Bethnal Green.
Immediately opposite is Sidney St, notorious for the 'siege' in 1911 of a
cornered gang of anarchists against whom Winston Churchill, then
Home Secretary, had called out the army. *Mile End Road* begins here
1m from the old City Wall through the area known as Stepney to the S
and Mile End to the N. There is a bronze bust commemorating
William Booth (1829–1912), from whose open-air services in this
neighbourhood in 1865 sprang the Salvation Army. A replica of the
statue of him at Denmark Hill (see p 332) was added in 1979 to mark
the 150th anniversary of his birth. The picturesque *Trinity Almshouses* were established in 1696 for master mariners and mates and
their wives or widows. Damaged during the last war, they have been
restored and now house a rehabilitation centre. The attractive chapel,
known as Captain Cook's Church, is a welfare centre. Opposite, No.
88 was the residence of Captain Cook after 1764 (plaque erected on
site in 1970). Beyond Cleveland Way the ungainly upper storey of the

former Empire Music Hall survives above shops; it is re
the cobbled Assembly Passage opposite. In *Stepney Gree*
charming houses (c 1700) is the London Jewish Hospita
Green ends at the large churchyard of *St Dunstan's* (res
1946–52), mostly 15C, with early 16C tombs. A Saxon *rood-p*
(early 11C) decorates the 13C chancel. In the wall of the S aisle
a stone with an inscription (1663) stating it was brought from
Carthage.

On the N side of Mile End Rd, before Stepney Green Station
are *Charrington's Anchor Brewery* (established in 1757) and the
Mile End Municipal Baths. No. 253, formerly the Spanish and
Portuguese Jews' Hospital, is now an old people's home. Behind
is a small disused Jewish cemetery, granted to the Jews by Oliver
Cromwell in 1656 and the oldest Jewish cemetery left in Britain.
Beyond Queen Mary College is a larger Jewish cemetery opened
in 1725 (see above).

The new buildings of **Queen Mary College**, a school of London
University, are to the N; beyond Bancroft Road its great hall occupies the site of the *People's Palace*, opened in 1887 and intended
as a realisation of the 'Palace of Delights' in Sir Walter Besant's
novel 'All Sorts and Conditions of Men' (1882). It was rebuilt after
a fire in 1936 and again in 1953– 56, with sculptures by Eric Gill.
Just beyond is the beautifully simple University of London chapel
of *St. Benedict*.

Mile End Road crosses the Grand Union Canal and is prolonged
by the slightly more attractive Bow Road to Bow and Stratford.
For Bow see p 401. Burdett Road leads S to Limehouse, see Rte
29.

29 London's Docklands: Wapping, Limehouse and the Isle of Dogs

Access: Underground Tower Hill, Wapping; Docklands Light
Railway from Tower Hill Gateway (from Bank 1991) to Island
Gardens (closed weekends); Minibus from Tower Hill to Tobbacco
Dock; from Tobacco Dock to Isle of Dogs.

'The most important inner city development in Europe' is taking
place in London's docklands. The designated area covered by the
London Docklands Development Corporation, set up in 1981,
stretches from Tower Bridge in the W to well past the Thames
Barrier at Woolwich in the E; altogether some 5000 acres of land
and water-filled docks on both sides of the River. Many developments are commercial and residential and the description below
covers the heritage of the area as well as some noteworthy new
projects. More information from London Docklands Development
Corporation, Visitor Centre, 3 Limeharbour, E14. Tel. 071-515
3000.

London's prosperity during the 16th and 17th centuries depended on its
growing port based on quays along the Thames, e.g. Billingsgate and
Queenhithe and some deep water moorings at the Tower, Wapping and
Puddle Dock. Most moorings were in the Pool of London itself, the area of
water below (E of) London Bridge. Apart from two small wet docks there
were no enclosed docks until the 19C when trade, and pilfering, had
increased enormously. The City Corporation which operated the Pool
resisted the building of docks which were developed piecemeal by private

n the marshy land below Tower Bridge. The first to be completed
ndia Dock (1802). The London Docks followed in 1805, then the East
. Surrey Docks on the S bank, St. Katharine's in 1828 (see p 269), Royal
(1855), Millwall (1868), Royal Albert (1880) and King George V (1921) in
yal Group of Docks. Each of the docks specialised in a particular type of
and security was tight with high walls, gates and even a drawbridge at
t India Docks.

During the second half of the 19C the docks struggled in competition with the
ailways, rivalry with Liverpool and difficulties with labour. The formation of the
Port of London Authority in 1909 removed some of the destructive competition
between the various London docks but by the 1960s trade had declined to such a
level that docks began to close due to the arrival of larger, container ships,
served better at Tilbury and Felixstowe, labour problems, particularly restrictive
practices, and slowness in modernising. Most of the London docks are now
closed; the London Docks and part of Surrey Docks have been filled in but in the
main the planned redevelopment will incorporate the large expanses of water of
the original docks. The high walls surrounding the old docks have come down
and visitors are encouraged to come and see, for the first time, the dockland
landscape, previously only visible from the river. The Docklands Light Railway
which runs overground from Tower Hill to Island Gardens, with a second branch
to Stratford, opened in 1987. It is being expanded to take more passengers and
also to connect directly with the underground at Bank. An extension of the
Jubilee line to the Isle of Dogs is also planned, linking Waterloo with Canary
Wharf and Stratford by 1996. The road network is also being expanded. This
exploration covers Wapping and Limehouse and the Isle of Dogs. For the Royal
Docks, see Newham, p 402. For St. Katharine's Dock see p 269, and for the area
from London Bridge to Rotherhithe, including Surrey Docks, see p 320.

Wapping High St winds its way along the narrow river-front of
Wapping, bounded on the N by the former, filled-in London Docks
and on the river-front by redeveloped wharves and warehouses. At
one time there were 36 taverns in this street serving sailors and
dockworkers, only a handful has survived.

Near the attractive tower of *St. John* (1760; the church was
destroyed in the Second World War) is *Wapping Pierhead* with houses
built in 1811–13 for senior dock officials. The Wapping Old Stairs of
the ballad still exist next to the *Town of Ramsgate* pub where Judge
Jeffreys was arrested in 1688, disguised as a sailor, on his way to
France, and brought to the Tower. Further on is a modern police
station for river police built on the site of the original police station of
1797. Beside *Tunnel Pier* is the site of Execution Dock, where Captain
Kidd (died 1701) and other notorious pirates were hanged. A landscaped area overlooks the River at Wapping New Stairs. At *Wapping
Station* a plaque commemorates the tunnel, the first for public traffic
to be built beneath a river, designed by Marc Isambard Brunel and
completed in 1843. It was used by pedestrians until 1865 when its
present use as a railway tunnel for the Metropolitan Line, now East
London Line, began. (See also Rotherhithe, p 320.)

Wapping Lane leads N past (W) the development area of the former
London Docks to The Highway, past the *Three Swedish Crowns* pub,
at Wapping Lane and the church of St. Peter's, in Victorian Gothic
style (1865), bomb damaged, repaired in 1949.

Ahead to the W is *Tobacco Dock*, entrance from Wapping Lane or
The Highway (car parking, DLR station Shadwell; minibus from
Tower Hill; open 7 days a week).

Tobacco Dock was built in 1811–14 by D.A. Alexander to house
tobacco up to the 1860s, wool, wine and spirits later, linked by a
passage to the Eastern Dock of the London Docks. These closed at the
end of the 1960s and Tobacco Dock's Grade I listed buildings stood
empty before being redeveloped into a shopping and restaurant
complex (1989) to a design by Terry Farrell, which uses the original

vaults, cast iron columns and timber trusses to support t□
open roof. Shops and restaurants surround a cobbled courtya□
further shops in the four acres of wine-vaults below. Outside □
S side are two full size replica sailing ships 'The Three Sis□
housing an exhibition of piracy through the ages and 'The Sea L□
with an exhibition on 'Treasure Island'.

The site between Tobacco Dock and The Highway will be developed. Cross The Highway to reach *St. George in The East*, in
Cannon St Road to the N, opposite Tobacco Dock. This fine Hawksmoor church (1726) has a massive 160ft tower. Gutted in 1941, it has
been ingeniously restored by Arthur Bailey (1960–64) with a modern
interior. Close by in *Swedenborg Square* (council flats) stood the
Swedish Church in which the body of Emmanuel Swedenborg
(1688–1772), mystic and philosopher, rested until it was removed to
Sweden in 1908. There was a Danish Church in Welclose Square
further along but this was demolished and another built to the N on
Commercial Road on the corner of Yorkshire Place.

S of The Highway, in Pennington St next to Tobacco Dock, are the
headquarters of News International, publishers of 'The Sun' and
'The Times', known as 'Fortress Wapping' after the demonstrations
when 'The Times' moved here in 1986. The plant has been expanded in the last year.

Turn E towards the Shadwell Basin with a boating club and new
housing. Garnet St leads S to *Wapping Wall*; turn E for Metropolitan
Wharf, previously an artists' colony, now housing/offices, and the
popular *Prospect of Whitby* pub and restaurant, overlooking the
river, at 57 Wapping Wall, E1 (tel. 071-481 1095). Built in 1520, its
reputation was reflected in the name the Devil's Tavern because of
the smugglers and thieves who drank here. The 'hanging' Judge
Jeffreys was a customer as were Samuel Pepys and later Dickens
and Turner. Its current name was taken from a ship in 1777.

Opposite is the last working hydraulic pumping station in London
(Grade II), now closed.

King Edward Memorial Park (1922) marks the site of the old
Shadwell fish market and contains a memorial to Willoughby,
Frobisher and other 16C navigators. Note the ventilation shafts for
the Rotherhithe Tunnel.

Rejoin The Highway via Glamis Road. To the W overlooking
Shadwell Basin is *St. Paul's* church, built in 1820 by John Walters.
Here Captain Cook's son James and Walter Pater were baptised.
The massive Free Trade Wharf to the S retains two of the original
saltpetre warehouses in a mixed residential/commercial development. Continue E along The Highway and turn N into Butcher Row.
Here are the buildings of the *St. Katharine's Royal Foundation*,
completed in 1925. St. Katharine's Royal Hospital was originally
founded near the Tower in 1148 by Queen Matilda; in 1273 Queen
Eleanor, wife of Henry III, took the wardenship into her own hands
and reserved the patronage for ever for the queens of England
personally. The foundation was removed to Regent's Park in 1825,
when the St. Katharine's Docks were excavated; it returned in 1950.
The funds are now administered for social welfare work. A cloister,
with monuments from the Regent's Park chapel (comp. p 178),
admits to the plain but effective *Chapel* (1952), containing stalls,
with misericords (c 1370), and other woodwork (15C and 17C),
including the Jacobean pulpit. The 18C *Warden's House* occupies
the former rectory of St. James's church, which was destroyed in the
Second World War.

the area known as Ratcliff where, in the Ratcliff Highway,
of drinking dens, the Ratcliff murders took place in 1811
even victims, leading to demands for a professional police

urn S along Narrow St past the entrance of the Grand Union
anal to Limehouse Basin and on to the *Grapes* pub at No. 76 (tel.
071-987 4396), set among redeveloped wharves and warehouses,
immortalised by Dickens as The Six Jolly Fellowship Porters in 'Our
Mutual Friend'. There is a good view up and down the river from
the verandah; fish is served in the restaurant. To the N is *Limehouse
Basin* with new homes under construction, supported by leisure and
shopping facilities. Limehouse Cut was built in 1770 to link the
River Lea with the Thames and in 1820 the Regent's Canal Dock
opened linking the Port of London with England's inland waterway
system at Limehouse Basin. Canal tours along the system take place
in the summer. See Camden Lock, p 300. It is possible to walk by the
Regent's Canal from Tomlins Terrace off Salmon Lane, to the N on
the other side of Commercial Road. Here Stonebridge Wharf has
been landscaped as a *Canalway Park*. The walk leads N towards
Mile End and Victoria Park (see p 275).

Limehouse Causeway, once the heart of a notorious Chinatown,
continues E to meet the West India Dock Road. Good Friends, a
well-known Chinese restaurant in Salmon Lane, N of Limehouse
station, carries on the tradition.

Limehouse was one of London's main shipbuilding centres during
the 18 and 19C but declined as the area became more populous with
labourers serving the West and East India Docks. The Chinese
community established itself here in the 1890s and the area's
reputation for vice and opium-dens was enhanced and romanticised
by writers (including Oscar Wilde) and the press. London's Chinese
community is now centred on Soho, but there is still a sizeable
Chinese population in this area.

At Limehouse Town Hall in Commercial Road a National Museum
of Labour History was established in 1975 and closed in 1987 after
the local council withdrew its support. The museum is now established in Manchester. Outside the library in Commercial Road is a
new bronze statue of Clement Attlee (former Prime Minister and MP
for Limehouse) by Frank Forster unveiled by Harold Wilson in 1988.

Nearby is the church of *St. Anne* by Hawksmoor (1714–30) with the
highest church clock in London. It was damaged by fire in 1850 and
restored by John Morris and Philip Hardwick in 1857. They also
designed the font and the pulpit. The stained glass window of the
Crucifixion at the E end is by Clutterbuck. The dominating feature is
the W tower with an apse as an entrance.

West India Dock Road leads S to the **Isle of Dogs**. Some way
further on, just before the railway bridge, is the unusually shaped
plain brick *Danish Seamen's Church* and mission by Holger Jensen
(1959). The interior, in wood and brick, with an attractive glass
mosaic, contains two wooden figures (from an earlier church) of SS.
Peter and Paul, by G.G. Cibber (died 1700), father of Colley Cibber.
In Branch Road, opposite, begins the N approach to **Rotherhithe
Tunnel**, c 1.25 miles long, which passes beneath the Thames to
Rotherhithe.

Isle of Dogs, Access: Underground to Mile End then bus D13 (in Burdett Road);
Docklands Light Railway from Tower Hill Gateway or Bank.

The **Isle of Dogs** is the heart of the new docklands; here a headquarters of the London Docklands Development Corpor and the Enterprise Zone which gives planning and tax incentive developers.

The marshy peninsula of the Isle of Dogs, known as Stepney Marshes, remained relatively unpopulated until the docks were built here in the 19C bringing employment and industrialisation. The name probably comes from the royal dogs kept here for Henry VIII and other inhabitants at Placentia Palace across the river who came here on hunting trips.

The first West India Docks opened in 1802 and a canal was cut across the peninsula in 1805, later incorporated in the South West India Dock. Millwall Docks followed. In the current redevelopment many features of the early dock period are being retained (consult the LDDC visitor map).

Explore the area from the main dock gates in West India Dock Road. Just outside in Garford St is a row of constables' cottages built in 1819. The Salvation Army building in a Scandinavian 'Queen Anne' style was opened in 1902 as a mission for Scandinavian seamen. The *Dockmaster's House* (1807; designed by Thomas Morris) was once the Jamaica Tavern but reverted to use as the dock manager's office. It now houses the Docklands Business Research and Information Centre.

The original gate posts remain at the main entrance and there was also a ditch and a swing bridge which had to be left open at night. There was a *Round House* housing a gunpowder magazine and a matching building on the other side was used as a lock-up for thieves caught at night.

The attractive *Ledger Building* just inside the gates was designed by George Gwilt in 1803; it now serves as offices for the LDDC. The original dock wall can be seen at the rear of the building. To the W along Marsh Wall are the *Cannon Workshops*, erected in 1825 and designed by Sir John Rennie to be used as stores, workshops and a cooperage. An original forge remains; since the docks closed in 1980 the building has been converted into offices and workshops for small businesses. Under the entrance arch a cast-iron plaque marks Trinity High Water. In 1989 part of the workshops were demolished to make way for a new road access to Canary Wharf, see below. New workshops were established at Poplar Business Park. To the E overlooking the first dock is the listed *Sugar Warehouse*, Port East, due to be developed as a leisure facility, possibly with a 12-screen cinema complex, plus shops, restaurants, hotels, a museum and workshops as part of the Canary Wharf development opposite. George Gwilt designed this in warehouse 1802 and John Rennie added the cast-iron columns in 1814.

On the same side further E is the new *Billingsgate Market* which moved here in 1981. This is London's main wholesale fish market, established in the City (see p 254) from the 9C and based on the wharf at Billingsgate. The new market building offers modern freezing and storage facilities. There is a space for a restaurant on the top-floor; tours by appointment (tel. 071-987 1118).

Further S is *Canary Wharf* on a narrow piece of land between two docks, which once handled the trade with the Canaries. It is the site for the most colossal of redevelopments involving 12 million square feet of offices, hotels, restaurants and shops. Olympia and York, the Canadian developers, aim for completion of Phase 1 in early 1991 with the 'Beaux-Arts' Canary Wharf Tower by Cesar Pelli at 200m high dominating the East London skyline. Six interlinking buildings are also part of the first phase with two further towers to the E in the phase on the site of the former Limehouse Studios (closed At *Blackwall Basin* to the E Mercury owns two satellite dishes. *Heron Quay*, which divides the second and third dock, an active low-rise redevelopment incorporates office and residential commodation as well as shops: further development is planned ere. The Dockland Light Railway crosses the three West India Docks with a station in between each.

Marsh Wall turns E past South Quay with a new hotel planned at Arrowhead Quay. To the S in Millharbour is 'The Guardian' printing plant, while further to the SW are the editorial offices and new printing plants for the 'Daily Telegraph'. Telegraph staff enjoy their meals on a floating restaurant in the dock—the 50 year old Scottish ferry 'Celtic Surveyor'. At Crossharbour on the other side of Millwall Inner Dock is the London Arena, see below. Marsh Wall leads to the end of Millwall Dock and the *Pierhead Cottages* (1860) from which the dockmaster supervised the work of the dock.

Turn S into Westferry Road past the former St. Paul's Presbyterian Church (1856) now in industrial use. Further on is *Burrell's Wharf* where the 'Great Eastern'—the wonder and failure of her age—was launched. Isambard Kingdom Brunel and John Scott Russell designed the 629ft-long ironship which was built between 1853–58. It took three months to float her broadside on to the Thames. She was a failure as a cargo and passenger ship, too slow, but was used to lay Atlantic cables before being broken up in 1888. Some of the original buildings survive and have been incorporated in the planned residential Burrell's Wharf complex. The Eastern slipway is being preserved by English Heritage. The *Lord Nelson* pub dates to 1859 and had a stabling block for horses. Nearby is the *Ferry House* pub, once the only building on the southern end of the Isle of Dogs (apart from the chapel where Chapel House Estate now stands), with a lookout tower for the ferry from Greenwich. A new Island Gardens Pier is at the end of East Ferry Road and along Ferry St is the entrance to the *Greenwich Foot Tunnel* at *Island Gardens*. The tunnel opened in 1902 and replaced the ferry. The walk to Greenwich under the river takes approximately five minutes and includes a ride in the Victorian lifts, due to be replaced in 1990/91. Here is the last stop of the Docklands Light Railway; good views of Greenwich from *Island Gardens*, laid out in 1895.

Saunderness Road leads NE to the *Waterman's Arms* (1 Glenaffric Avenue). Nearby is the *Church of Christ and St. John*, designed by F. Johnstone in 1850 for William Cubitt. Stones from the old London Bridge were used in the construction. To the N is the former industrial area of *Cubitt Town* with housing built by the Cubitts for the workers in the docks, shipyards and factories. East Ferry Road leads N past Millwall Park where the railway viaduct dates to 1872 when a service operated to North Greenwich; it closed in 1926 but is now used for the new light railway. Further N is the 'Mudchute' so-called from the artificial landscape created by the silted mud from the dock. An urban farm is located here and some new housing. East Ferry Road passes the ASDA Superstore opened in 1983, considerably improving the area's shopping facilities. Further along to the E is the Docklands Visitor Centre and, opposite, the London Arena on the site of the former *Olsen Shed*. It opened in February 1989 with a 200-metre indoor running track and seating for up to 12,000 for concerts. A 250-room hotel will form part of the development.

Limeharbour continues N past the massive Harbour Exchange development (offices); Marsh Wall leads E to Prestons Road across

the Blue Bridge at the entrance of West India Dock. To the E
Coldharbour and the *Gun* pub, in a street of mainly 19C house
overlooking the river. Lord Nelson and Lady Hamilton are said tc
have met here. *Nelson House* and the northernmost houses here date
from the early 19C. Nelson House was built in 1824 by Rennie who
also built the *Bridge House* (1819) at the next bridge to the Blackwall
Basin in Preston's Road.

The Satellite Dishes and Billingsgate Market are over to the W (see
above). Preston's Road leads to Cotton St, past the Poplar Business
Park to the W. The DLR station here (Poplar) serves Tower Gateway or
Stratford; the new line towards the Royal Docks (see p 402) crosses
Cotton St; it is due to open in 1992. East India Dock and the River Lea
estuary are still to be developed to the E. This includes the demolition
of the Blackwall Power Station. East India Dock Road leads E to
Canning Town, past the new award-winning 'Financial Times'
printing plant by Terry Farrell and on to the the Royal Docks; see
Route 45, Newham; or W back to Commercial Road.

30 Lambeth, the South Bank and Waterloo

Access: for the South Bank: Underground, Embankment and
Hungerford footbridge; or Waterloo; for the Imperial War Museum:
Lambeth North; for Lambeth Palace and the Museum of Garden
History, Bus No. 507 from Victoria or Waterloo.

Cross Lambeth Bridge to the South Bank. To the NE is St. Mary's
Church and Lambeth Palace. At the gate of the palace is the church of
St. Mary Lambeth, now a museum devoted to gardening, based on the
connection with the Tradescants, father and son, both of whom are
buried in the churchyard (John Tradescant died 1638)—as is Admiral
Bligh (died 1817) of the 'Bounty' who lived at 100 Lambeth Road. The
churchyard has been converted into a delightful botanical garden.

Museum of Garden History, St. Mary at Lambeth, Lambeth Palace Road, SE1.
Tel. 071-261 1891. Open Mon to Fri 11.00–15.00, Sun 10.30–17.00. Closed
December to March. Bookshop, souvenirs. Access: Underground, Westminster;
Bus, 77, 159, 170, or 507 from Victoria.

The church retains its 14C tower but was rebuilt in 1851 and is now owned by
the Tradescant Trust (set up in 1977). The Tradescants were gardeners to
Charles I and introduced many rare plants to Britain. The church features
displays on them and their work and other aspects of garden history. Temporary
exhibitions and fund-raising events are held regularly.

The well-restored church includes at the E end of the S aisle the Pedlar's
Window, commemorating the bequest to the parish of the Pedlar's Acre, a piece
of ground originally worth 2s 8d but sold to the LCC as the site for County Hall for
£31,000. The existing window is a replacement of 1956.

Lambeth Palace has been the London residence of the archbishops of
Canterbury for seven centuries. The building was begun by Abp
Langton (1207–29) but few of his successors failed to add to or alter it;
the residential part was built in 1829–38. The palace was damaged in
1941. Erasmus, Thomas More, and Cranmer (who wrote the English
Prayer Book here) are known to have visited the Palace. (Small parties
by arrangement only.)

The entrance is by *Morton's Tower*, a noble red-brick gatehouse
erected c 1490. In the courtyard is a memorial to Abp Lord Davidson
(1848–1930). The *Great Hall*, rebuilt in medieval style by Abp Juxon
n 1663, has a roof 70ft in height, resembling that of Westminster Hall.

ow houses the *Library*, the nucleus of which was bequeathed to e see by Abp Bancroft in 1610. It is thought to be the oldest free ublic library in the country. It is open to readers by appointment only (exhibitions), and contains nearly 1500 MSS, many finely illuminated, letters of Francis Bacon, Gladstone's diaries, six Caxtons, Edward VI's Latin grammar and Elizabeth I's prayer book. The *Guard Chamber*, with a 14C roof (reconstructed), contains a fine series of portraits of the archbishops since 1503, by Holbein, Van Dyck, Hogarth, Reynolds, Romney, Lawrence, and others. The beautiful *Crypt* beneath the chapel is the oldest part of the building, dating possibly from c 1200. The small *Chapel* (c 1230), rededicated in 1955, preserves stalls and other fittings provided by Abp Laud (1634). From 1273 down to the present day many English bishops have been consecrated in this chapel, and in 1787 Bp White of Pennsylvania and Bp Provost of New York were consecrated here by Abp Moore. The chapel was the scene of the second trial of Wyclif in 1378. The picturesque *Lollards' Tower* (1434–45) derives its name from the belief that the Lollards, followers of Wyclif, were imprisoned in it. In the stair-turret is the 'Lollards' Prison'.

Archbishop's Park, a portion of the palace grounds opened to the public in 1900, extends to the NE and provides a good view of the Palace (entrance in Lambeth Road).

From Lambeth Bridge, Lambeth Road runs E to St. George's Circus passing to the S *Lambeth Walk*, popularised by the '30s musical 'Me and My Girl'. At No. 124 is Morton Place, where a tablet on No. 6 marks the residence of Miss Cons and Miss Bayliss (see Old Vic, below).

In Hercules Rd (left) the *Central Office of Information* building has a huge mosaic mural of the Labours of Hercules. Cross Kennington Road where Charles Chaplin lived as a boy (at Nos 261 and 287 and at No. 3 Pownall Terrace; in one of these he may have been born in 1889). For Kennington, see p 331. Set in a park across the road is the building occupied from 1815 to 1930 by Bethlem Hospital ('Bedlam'; now near Croydon; see p 337). The central portion of the old hospital (by Lewis, 1812; dome by Smirke, 1846, restored after fire) now houses the **Imperial War Museum** (Pl. 19; 4). Opened in 1920 at the Crystal Palace, it was housed in 1924–36 in the Imperial Institute. It is concerned with all aspects of the two World Wars and with other British military operations since 1914.

The Imperial War Museum, Lambeth Road, SE1. Tel. 071-416 5000. Open daily 10.00–18.00. Access: Underground, Lambeth North. Educational facilities, Library and Photographic Records Dept by appointment Mon to Fri 10.00–17.00. Film shows. Bookshop with guidebooks, souvenirs. Café. Admission charge; free on Fridays.

The museum launched an appeal during 1985 to extend and improve facilities, including the addition of an in-fill building in the centre of the structure, designed by Arup Associates as a steel-framed atrium exposing the inner brick walls and original Georgian windows. It reopened to the visitors in July 1989. In Stage 2, the redevelopment plans include an extension to the in-fill building to include an education and conference centre, plus additional gallery space, and a roof-top restaurant.

On the lawn in front of the museum are the last two surviving 15-inch British naval guns from the battleships 'Ramillies' and 'Resolution', cast in 1915 and 1916. The obelisk of 1771 in the grounds used to stand at St. George's Circus and was removed here in 1907.

The new entrance hall at the Imperial War Museum

The grounds surrounding the museum were acquired by Lord Rothermere in 1926 and named the *Geraldine Mary Harmsworth Park* in memory of his mother. Below is a description of some of the highlights of the museum, following the new layout.

The main entrance leads into the 77ft high main exhibition gallery. Suspended in the atrium: First World War Sopwith Camel, American P51 Mustang; a Battle of Britain Spitfire. In the centre German V2 rocket and Polaris missile. Also 13-pounder gun from First World War; tanks; Argentinian anti-aircraft gun from the Falklands.

Lower Ground Floor galleries exhibition tells the story of war in the 20C, starting with the First World War followed by the Inter-War Years, Second World War and Post-War conflicts presented thematically using interactive videos and 'experiences' for the public—a First World War front-line trench and a blitzed London street. Also on display is material from the Spanish Civil War; the Munich Agreement signed by Chamberlain and Hitler in 1938; escape aids from Colditz; German surrender documents from Lüneberg Heath in 1945; the Burma-Siam railway and relics from Hiroshima.

Victoria and George Crosses are in the southern galleries, to be developed in stage 2. Here are also Montgomery's caravans, and post-1945 exhibits.

museum's important art collection is displayed in two new art galleries on second floor, presented thematically and including First and Second World oils and watercolours. The ground floor art galleries are used partly for nporary exhibitions.

On the corner of St. George's Road and Lambeth Road, on the very spot where the 'No Popery' rioters assembled in 1780, stands St. George's Cathedral of the RC diocese of Southwark, built by Augustus Pugin in 1840–48, wrecked by bombs in 1941 and freely rebuilt by Rommilly Croze using the original design. A spacious edifice, brick outside and stone inside, it mixes a profusion of Gothic styles without loss of dignity.

Christ Church, at the corner of Kennington Road and Westminster Bridge Road, has been rebuilt into an office block. The tower of 1876, which survived wartime bombing and on which appear the Stars and Stripes, was erected by subscription from Americans as a memorial to President Lincoln.

Westminster Bridge Road runs NW from St. George's Circus past *Morley College*, founded in 1885. *Westminster Bridge* (Pl. 15; 7) has been guarded since 1966 by a colossal Lion. In Lambeth Palace Road to the S, opposite the Houses of Parliament, is the new *St. Thomas's Hospital*, begun in 1960. The hospital, founded in 1213, was moved here from Southwark (comp. p 290) in 1868 and built on the 'pavilion' plan devised by Florence Nightingale, who had established the first English school of nursing at St. Thomas's in 1860. The pavilions were demolished after being damaged in the Second World War. A *Florence Nightingale Museum* opened at the hospital in 1989.

Florence Nightingale Museum, 2 Lambeth Palace Road, SE1, Tel. 071-620 0374; open 10.00–16.00 Tuesday to Sunday. Admission charge. Underground, Waterloo or Westminster; Bus 507.
   The entrance to the museum is directly from the road (near the bus stop). It is located on the lower ground floor of one part of the hospital. The imaginative displays illustrate the history of nursing and the role of Florence Nightingale, including her years in the Crimea. Memorabilia include Florence Nightingale's medicine chest, childhood books, and a lamp from the Crimean War. The conditions of the war are graphically illustrated and an audio-visual presentation gives additional information.

To the north, across Westminster Bridge Road is the former County Hall and Belvedere Road. Hereabouts was the factory for artificial stoneware started by Eleanor Coade (1733–1821) in 1759. The factory closed in 1840 and the secret of manufacture was lost. A lion, sculptured in the stone (1837), which formerly adorned the Lion Brewery, demolished in 1950, stood outside Waterloo Station in 1951–66 before being moved to its present site on the bridge outside County Hall.
   County Hall was the headquarters of the London County Council from 1912 and its successor the Greater London Council from 1965 until 1986. This huge Renaissance edifice, by Ralph Knott and W.E. Riley, has a river-façade (1932) 750ft long. The sculptures on the exterior are by Ernest Cole and A.F. Hardiman.
   The Greater London Council was abolished in 1986 and its powers transferred to the London boroughs, various boards and government departments. The Inner London Education Authority continued to occupy part of the building including the extension on the 'island' at the end of Westminster Bridge until it was abolished in 1990

Redevelopment plans which would retain the exterior include a 450 room luxury hotel (due to be operated by Hyatt) and offices.

The **Greater London Council** was constituted in 1965 when some 70 local authorities were combined into 32 new boroughs, and the boundaries of the County of London extended deep into Essex and Surrey and incorporated Middlesex. It was the ruling authority for the Greater London area with direct elections, save the jurisdiction exercised by the City Corporation within the City of London. Since 1986, in the absence of an overall authority for London the 32 London boroughs and the City have set up boards and committees to deal with London-wide matters such as planning, fire services and voluntary organisations. Local boroughs are responsible for libraries, rubbish collection, parks, most roads, local planning matters and education. In 1990 the Inner London Education Authority, which had responsibility for schools in the inner boroughs (with direct elections), was abolished and responsibility passed to individual boroughs.

Beyond *Jubilee Gardens*, laid out for the Queen's Silver Jubilee in 1977, to the E, on a 7.5 acre site between York Road and Belvedere Road are the two massive blocks of the *Shell Centre* (1957–62) linked by a tunnel, and when built one of the largest office blocks in Europe.

Belvedere Road continues to the **South Bank Centre**, representing the cultural institutions S of the Thames. Developments here started with the Festival of Britain in 1951; a large exhibition was laid out on derelict ground in the area between Westminster Bridge and Waterloo Bridge with the then new Royal Festival Hall as its focus. Improvements extended to Battersea Park (see p 330). The area now includes three concert halls, an art gallery, the National Film Theatre, the Museum of the Moving Image and three theatres within the Royal National Theatre. Concerted efforts were made by the Greater London Council during 1983–85 to brighten up and counteract some of the sterility created by the 1950s and '60s concrete 'bunker' style of architecture. The South Bank Board was set up in 1986 to take over and manage the GLC's South Bank assets. It is financed by the Arts Council. Further proposals have been made by architect Terry Farrell which would transform the area by including commercial activities such as shops and restaurants and demolishing the concrete walkways. Work could start in 1992.

The South Bank can also be reached via Hungerford footbridge from the Embankment and the redevelopment includes upgrading this route. See also p 197 (Charing Cross).

Royal Festival Hall, Belvedere Road, SE1. Tel. 071-928 8800 (box office).

The main concert hall seats 3000 in this complex designed by Sir R.H. Matthew and J.L. Martin (1949–51) and completed by Sir Hubert Bennett (1962–65). There is a small recital room and the main stage will hold a choir of 250. The large ballroom/foyer is used for exhibitions and there are several eating areas including a self-service cafeteria and a wine bar, with free lunch-time music. The Arts Council Poetry Library is located here. The nearby *Queen Elizabeth 'Hall* opened in 1967 and seats 1100. The *Purcell Room*, used for recitals, seats 330. Both were designed by G. Horsfall.

The **Hayward Gallery** just behind was designed by the GLC Architects Dept. It stages major modern art exhibitions.

Hayward Gallery, Belvedere Road, SE1. Tel. 071-928 3144. Open during exhibitions: Mon to Wed 10.00–20.00; Thurs to Sat 10.00–18.00, Sun 12.00–18.00, admission charge. Access: Underground, Waterloo.

The **National Film Theatre** (tel. 071-928 3232) was established in 1953 and moved to its present site under Waterloo Bridge in 1958. There are four auditoria, a restaurant and bar, as well as library facilities. The London Film Festival is organised by the British Film Institute and centres on the National Film Theatre in November each year.

The *Museum of the Moving Image*, MOMI, opened in 1988 on two floors below Waterloo Bridge, in glass and steel by Aver Associates.

Museum of Moving Image, South Bank, Waterloo, SE1. Tel. 071-401 2636. Open Tues to Sat 10.00–20.00; Sun & BH 10.00-18.00. Underground, Waterloo; Admission charge. Shop, café.

This award-winning museum covers the history of moving pictures from the magic lantern to satellite television. The first galleries include a fantasmagorie and phenakistoscope discs which introduced moving pictures. This is followed by early experiments in photography including the work of Eadweard Muybridge, August and Louise Lumiere's work in Paris leading into the early years of the cinema, and the greats of Hollywood, illustrated on a spectacular Temple of Gods which leads to the second floor. Chaplin has his own display, in the silent era. The work of Eisenstein, including the Battleship Potemkin, is shown in a railway carriage. Mae West's lipstick couch introduces Hitchock and talking pictures. Documentaries and newsreel are covered with excerpts and an REO 1930 Newsreel Van. In the section dealing with animation children can draw their own cartoons. A look at the Hollywood Dream Factory is followed by the British cinema and wartime coverage. The arrival of television includes a line of TV-sets, the earliest showing a wide range of popular early programmes, and also advertising. Cinema stages a comeback with wide screens, and 3D. Individual countries' film industries are illustrated. The exhibition ends in a large TV studio where visitors can join in the making of a news programme or a film.

To the E is the **Royal National Theatre**, opened in 1976, and containing three auditoria: the open-staged *Olivier* seating 1160, the *Lyttelton* (seating 890) with a proscenium stage, and the rectangular *Cottesloe* with adjustable seating (up to 400), used for more experimental productions.

Royal National Theatre, South Bank, SE1. Tel. 071-928 2252. There are self-service cafeterias and bars, as well as a wine bar restaurant, Ovations. Exhibitions and musical entertainment take place in the foyers which also have bookstalls. In the summer the terraces provide a fine view over the Thames.

The idea of a National Theatre for Britain was first put forward in 1848, but not pursued seriously until 1904 when a National Theatre Scheme and Estimate were prepared by several leading actors and playwrights led by H. Granville Barker; appeals raised enough funds to purchase a site in Cromwell Gardens in 1930. The Second World War intervened and in 1944 the London County Council made a site on the South Bank available to the Shakespeare Memorial National Committee; Sir Laurence Olivier and Norman Marshall were appointed joint Chairmen and Denys Lasdun architect. In 1951 the foundation stone was laid. The National Theatre Company under Sir Laurence Olivier was set up in 1962 and took over the Old Vic as a temporary home, opening with Peter O'Toole in 'Hamlet'. In 1969 building finally started and Sir Peter Hall was appointed artistic director for the opening in 1976. The Royal National Theatre is subsidised by the Arts Council.

Beyond are the headquarters of London Weekend Television and IBM (see below).

Waterloo Road continues S across a roundabout. The church of *St. John* by Francis Bedford (1823–35) was restored in 1950 to serve the Festival of Britain. It had been badly damaged in the Second World War and only the walls, portico, steeple and 18C Italian marble font survive of the original church.

To the SW is **Waterloo Station** (Southern Region, rebuilt in 1912–22), already London's busiest mainline terminal, handling an average of 2000 trains a day and serving the S coast as well as the commuter belt of Surrey and Hampshire and due to become considerably bigger as the main Channel Tunnel Rail Terminal in London. The station opened in 1848; in 1899 the direct 'tube' link with the City (to Bank Station) opened and still operates, popularly known as 'the Drain'. Terry Farrell has designed the new extension to the W of the existing station with five international platforms, departure area above, and arrivals area below due to open in 1996.

The Cut street market, just outside the station, which also spreads into Lower Marsh, has declined since its heyday in the 1870s when it was a popular S London meeting place. Since much of the residential character of this area has been lost, the market functions now mostly as a lunch-time shopping area for office workers and is most famous for a stall run by a one of the former Great Train Robbers.

The Old Vic: there has been a theatre on this site since 1817

On the corner of the Cut and Waterloo Road is the *Old Vic Theatre*, beautifully restored in 1984 by Canadian millionaire Ed Mirvish, and now operating as a repertory theatre, tel. 071-928 7616 (box office)

It was built in 1817 as the Royal Coburg Theatre. Rebuilt in 1833, it changed its name to the Royal Victoria and reopened in 1871 as the New Victoria, later becoming a temperance music-hall for the working class. Lilian Bayliss arrived in 1900 and took over the management in 1912, raising the standard of productions, particularly of Shakespeare, and making it one of London's leading theatres. It was damaged in 1941 but reopened in 1950. In 1963 it

came the temporary home of the National Theatre (see above). After it left for
new home on the South Bank, the Old Vic went through a difficult period until
dramatically rescued by Ed Mirvish who has invested £1m in returning the
building to its Victorian splendour.

The *Young Vic*, further along in the Cut, occupies an octagonal
building (1970) seating 450 and has a small studio seating 100. It has
its own independent board of management and aims to provide good
theatre for young people at reasonable prices. Tel. 071-928 6363.

Between Roupell St and Stamford St to the N of the Cut is the Lambeth
Preservation area with preserved 18C cottages, now gentrified.

A large part of the South Bank between Stamford St and Upper Ground to the N
was derelict for many years while a planning battle took place between the local
community and property developers. Known as the Coin St site, it includes river
frontage between Kent House and King's Reach. The property developers
withdrew their scheme in 1984 and the community's redevelopment plan has
now gone ahead, financed partly by the former GLC. This includes housing,
workshops, a riverside park with gigantic animal shapes, and the retention of the
local landmark, the *Oxo Tower* (Ali Moore; 1928), created to defy a ban on
outdoor advertising. This will open to the public when refurbished together with
Stamford Wharf. It will include exhibition space, crafts workshops, shops and
restaurants on the top floor with a view over the Thames, due to open in late1991.
(Coin St tel. 071-620 0544).
    An open-air market, Gabriel's Wharf, with crafts workshops, is already open
Fri, Sat, Sun on the river-bank. The South Bank Riverside Walk continues to
Blackfriars Bridge and the *Doggett's Coat and Badge* pub, named after the
famous race (see p 303).
    Stamford St leads E past Kings Reach Tower, the offices of IPC magazines, and
the London Nautical College with its ceremonial entrance—the portico of the
demolished Unitarian Chapel of 1823, to Blackfriars Rd. To the S is the site of the
Surrey Theatre, owned in its days as the 'Royal Circus' by Charles Dibdin, author
of 'Tom Bowling'; and further on that of the old round Surrey Chapel, famous
under the Rev. Rowland Hill (1744–1833). At 197 Blackfriars Road is the India
Office Library, part of the British Library, with books, manuscripts and letters.
    On the E side of Blackfriars Bridge overlooking the River are the new offices of
Express Newspapers, Ludgate House, designed with distinctive banding in
glass and grey granite by John Fraser (1989) on the site of a demolished part of
Blackfriars railway bridge.
    This is Southwark, see Route 31.

31 Southwark: Bankside, London Bridge City and Bermondsey

Southwark, on the S side of London Bridge, has as long a history as
the City of London itself; archaeological excavations continue to
reveal Roman and pre-Roman finds, some of which are on display at
the Museum of London and the Cuming Museum. It was the main
entry point from the S, and coaching inns, such as the existing *George
Inn*, flourished. During the 16C it became a place of entertainment
with bear-baiting, cock-fighting and eventually the theatre—all of
which were banned from the City of London. The Rose Theatre was
built in 1587 and Shakespeare's Globe Theatre opened here in 1599.
The area was well-known for its brothels and its prisons. In 1556 it
came under the jurisdiction of the City of London and was known as
Bridge Ward Without to distinguish it from the Bridge Ward Within—
the London Bridge and the area to the N—but it continued to enjoy its
freedom from City restrictions on entertainment and other 'vices'.
Wharves and warehouses were built along the Thames in the 18 and

19C but with the decline in the trade on the river, Southwark wε
neglected. Today the London Borough of Southwark stretches as far S
as Dulwich (see p 325) and encompasses the inner city decline of
Southwark itself and the prosperity of a leafy suburb. Regeneration of
the river-bank now under way is bringing this historic part of London
back to life.

Access: Underground, London Bridge (also British Rail), or for this description
approach from Rte 30, or across Blackfriars Bridge.
    From Blackfriars Road (see 290) turn E into Southwark St and then N in
Hopton St past the Hopton St Almshouses of 1752 still in use by pensioners.
There is a 100-year old cattle-trough outside. Further on is the *Bankside Gallery*,
home of the Royal Society of Painters in Watercolours and the Royal Society of
Painter-etchers and Engravers. As well as open exhibitions for the two societies
there are changing exhibitions, mostly of prints. The gallery was designed by
Fitzroy, Robinson and Partners.

Bankside Gallery, 48 Hopton St, SE1, 071-928 7521. Open during exhibitions
Tues to Sat 10.00–17.00, Sun 13.00–18.00. Admission charge. Access:
Underground, Blackfriars.

This modern housing/office development includes the *Founder's
Arms*, a pub, built on the site of a bell foundry where the bells of St.
Paul's were cast. From the terrace, bar and restaurant there are good
views of St. Paul's.

A riverside walk leads E past the redundant Bankside Power Station
built in 1963 by Sir Giles Gilbert Scott on the site of Great Pike
Gardens which supplied fish to ecclesiastic houses in the area in the
14C. Plans (1989) for the site includes an opera house.
    This is **Bankside** (Pl. 20; 2) which covers an area of great interest as
the site of the early theatres where Shakespeare's genius found
expression. Here, too, in the Liberty of the Clink, were the 'stews',
largely inhabited by Dutch or Flemish women, and numerous bear-
gardens, used also for prize-fights. Bankside commands a view of St.
Paul's, especially fine at sunset, although partly blocked by new office
blocks. An inscription on a 17C house (restored) on Cardinal's Wharf
marks the house where Wren used to watch the building of his
cathedral. Across the narrow Cardinal Cap Alley, dating from the 17C
with a secluded garden, the Cathedral Provost's Lodgings have
occupied a building of 1712 (restored) since 1958.
    The river-walk passes the site of the new Globe Theatre; the
original was in Park St, see below. Shakespeare was a shareholder
and acted at the Globe for many years. Fifteen of his plays were
produced at the theatre, built by the Burbages and opened in 1599,
which was a small but lofty circular building ('this wooden O'). It
burned down in 1613, and the second theatre was demolished in 1644.

The Shakespeare Globe Trust, headed by American actor and film producer
Sam Wannamaker, has started construction of the third Globe Theatre, modelled
closely on the second theatre. It is due for completion in 1992 and will have been
built using traditional building methods. It will hold 1500 people for Shakespeare performances under open skies and in natural light, with a smaller indoor
theatre, the Inigo Jones, for 300 people, as well as a permanent exhibition on the
theatre of the 16th and 17th century. Contact, see below.
    Until the new development is complete the International Shakespeare
Globe Centre is based in Bear Gardens to the E at the *Shakespeare Globe
Museum* of Elizabethan Theatre History.

Shakespeare Globe Museum, (formerly Bear Gardens Museum), Bankside, SE1.
Tel. 071-928 6342. Open Mon to Sat 10.00–16.30, Sun 13.30–17.30. Admission
charge. Access: Underground, London Bridge. (International Globe Centre, tel.
071–620 0202)
    The museum occupies a 19C warehouse which retains its old machine driving

ar. It is devoted to the Elizabethan and Jacobean theatre; exhibits include a
il-size working replica of the Cockpit Theatre (1616) (used for workshop
roductions), models of the first and second Globe Theatres and the Swan, a
recreation of a frost fair which used to take place on the Thames at Southwark
and early maps and engravings of the area.

This was the site of the *Hope Theatre* (1614–56) where Ben Jonson's
'Bartholomew Fair' was first performed. Bear-baiting began on the site before
1550 and continued in the theatre. Performances in Davies' Amphitheatre here
from 1662 to 1682 were visited by Evelyn and Pepys ('After dinner, with my wife
and Mercer to the Bear Garden where ... I saw some good sport of the bull's
tossing of the dogs, one into the very boxes. But it is a rude and nasty pleasure',
Diary, 14 Aug, 1666).

Rose Alley parallel to the E recalls the *Rose Theatre* put up by Philip
Henslowe in 1587. The plays of Shakespeare, Marlowe, and Kyd were
performed here, and Edward Alleyn was a leading actor. The remains
of the theatre were discovered in 1989 during archaelogical excavations before the building of a new office block alongside Southwark
Bridge. These show that the 16-sided theatre was enlarged to hold
2400 before it closed in 1605. After considerable pressure, the
developers have agreed to retain the remains of the theatre, build a
special floor above to protect them, and open them to the public,
possibly in conjunction with the new Globe.

On the other side of Southwark Bridge are the new offices of the
'Financial Times'. In Park St, E of the Bridge, is the plaque on the wall
marking the approximate site of the original Globe Theatre; remains
were found during excavation in 1989.

Just before Cannon St railway bridge in Bank End is the *Anchor
Inn*. Of 15C origin, the present building dates to the 18C and has
recently been restored. There are bars, a restaurant, a minstrel's
gallery and old oak beams. It once belonged to Henry Thrale, friend of
Dr Johnson. There is a good view of St. Paul's and a model of the
Globe Theatre.

Clink St leads E and was named after the manor of 70 acres attached
to Winchester House and known as the '*Liberty of the Clink*', where a
pleasure-quarter sprang up outside the jurisdiction of the City under
the control of the Bishops of Winchester in Southwark. *Winchester
House*, built in the 12C, was the town residence of the bishops of
Winchester down to 1626; it is recalled in the names of the streets to
the S. It was burned down in 1814.

The *Clink Prison*, partly located below the palace, which stood on
the bank of the Thames, was used initially by the bishops as a place of
detention for heretics from the 16C, and later for thieves and ruffians.
The name may have come from 'clinch' or 'clench', rivets hammered
in a clinching iron which held prisoners to the wall or floor. It was
burned in the Gordon Riots of 1780; a plaque commemorates the
Clink, which gave its name to prisons in general. A temporary
exhibition opened in an old building on the site in 1989, tel. 071-403
6515. Open daily 10.00–18.00; admission charge. Nearby are the
remains of the 14C great hall including a rose window of Winchester
Palace which has now been incorporated in a warehouse wall.

In this area of yellow-brick buildings in 'warehouse' style are offices
and the Southwark Heritage Centre, open Mon– Fri 0900-1700. Tel.
071-407 5911. At *St. Mary Overie Dock*, said to date from the time of
Winchester Palace is a pub/restaurant overlooking the Thames, and
in the dock the 'Kathleen & May' schooner owned by the Maritime
Trust, open daily 10.00–16.00 (summer), 11.00–15.00 (winter). Admission charge.

Cathedral St leads to Southwark Cathedral.

Southwark Cathedral, Borough High St, SE1. Tel. 071-407 3708. Services: M.
Fri 12.30 Matins; 12.45 Holy Communion, 17.30 Evensong; Sun 09.00 F
Communion; 11.00 Eucharist; 15.00 Evensong; Sat 11.30 Matins; 12.00 H
Communion; 16.00 Evensong. A new Chapter House, including a restaurant an.
cafeteria opened in 1988.

Officially the *Cathedral and Collegiate Church of St. Saviour and St. Mary
Overie, Southwark*, it has been the seat of a bishop since 1905. Often rebuilt and
repaired it remains the finest Gothic building in London after Westminster
Abbey.

According to legend, a nunnery was founded on this site by a ferryman's
daughter called Mary, whence is derived the former title of the church, St. Mary
Overy, which is explained as 'St. Mary of the Ferry' or 'St. Mary over the Ie'
(water). In 852–862 this nunnery was changed by St. Swithin, Bp of Winchester,
into a house for canons regular of the Augustinian order. In 1106 a church was
erected, of which few traces survive. The present choir and retro-choir were built
by Peter des Roches, Bp of Winchester, in 1207; the transepts were remodelled in
the 15C. The nave, which had collapsed about 1838 and been replaced by a
temporary erection, was entirely rebuilt by Sir Arthur Blomfield in 1890–96. Over
the crossing rises a noble 15C tower, 164ft high.

Interior (open all day). NAVE. At the entrance is a memorial to those
who died in the Marchioness boat disaster in 1989 (see p 301). In the
SW corner is a portion of 13C arcading; in the NW corner a case of
splendid bosses from the 15C roof. The stained glass, mostly destroyed
in 1941, is modern. Under the 6th window is the *Tomb of John Gower*
(1330–1408), the friend of Chaucer. Behind the door into the Vestry
may be seen the jambs of a Norman door and an ancient holy-water
stoup.

TRANSEPTS. In the North Transept has been placed a dresser given
to the church in 1588. The monuments here include one to John
Lockyer (d 1672), pill-maker, with an amusing hyperbolical inscription. To the E of this transept is the *Harvard Chapel*, restored and
decorated in 1907 in memory of John Harvard, founder of Harvard
University, Mass., who was born in the parish and baptised in this
church (1607). During the restoration a Norman shaft (left of the altar)
was disclosed. The stained-glass window (restored 1948) was presented in 1905 by Joseph H. Choate (died 1917). On the right a tablet
commemorates the playwright and lyricist, Oscar Hammerstein
(1895–1960).

CHOIR. This and the retro-choir represent perhaps the earliest
Gothic work in London. The altar-screen, erected by Bp Fox in 1520, is
a magnificent piece of work, though much mutilated and restored. The
statues in the niches date from 1912. The fine tombs in the choir aisles
include: (N Aisle) two handsome Jacobite monuments to John
Trehearne (died 1618), gentleman-porter to James I, and Richard
Humble (died 1616), Alderman, and the wooden effigy of a Knight
(1280–1300; restored); (S Aisle) fine tomb of Lancelot Andrewes
(1555–1626).

The beautiful aisled RETRO CHOIR is now used as the parish church.
The Lady Chapel, which extended to the E, was pulled down in 1830.
Here Gardiner and Bonner held the consistorial courts in the reign of
Queen Mary, and condemned Hooper, Rogers, Bradford, Saunders,
Ferrar, and Taylor to the stake. Bishop Bonner later died for his beliefs
at Marshalsea (see below) in 1569.

The SOUTH TRANSEPT was rebuilt in the 15C by Cardinal Beaufort,
whose niece, Joan Beaufort, was married to James I of Scotland in this
church (1423). On the W wall is a monument in miniature to William
Emerson (died 1575), supposedly an ancestor of Ralph Waldo Emerson. Above, John Bingham (died 1625), saddler to Queen Elizabeth
and King James. Near by is a touching inscription to Mistress Margaret
Maynard (died 1653, aged 13 years). In the S aisle of the nave, beneath

‗morial window to Shakespeare (by C. Webb, 1954), is a
‗mbent alabaster figure of the playwright (1911).

ohn Fletcher and Philip Massinger, the playwrights, Edmund
‗1akespeare (died 1607), the younger brother of the poet, and Henry
‗Sacheverell (chaplain in 1705–09), are buried in St. Saviour's, but
their graves are unidentified.

S of the Cathedral is *Borough Market*; a street market has existed in this part of
London since the 13C. It was established at its present site in 1756 and now
functions as a wholesale fruit and vegetable market trading from early to
mid-morning.

To the E is Borough High St and London Bridge. Thousands of
commuters walk across London Bridge each day from the British Rail
station to work in offices in the City, repeating the journey made by
millions of Londoners and others in history over the many different
bridges on this site (see p 253). To the E is London Bridge City (see
below); to the W is Bankside and straight ahead is *Borough High St.*

The High St has from earliest times been the great highway to the SE of England
and the Continent. It was the scene of countless processions and pageants in the
Middle Ages, and was trodden by the feet of many pilgrims to the shrine of St.
Thomas Becket at Canterbury. It abounded in hostelries, the old buildings of
which, however, have almost entirely disappeared.

To the E is the approach to *London Bridge Station*, on the W is
Southwark Cathedral, see above. St. Thomas's St skirts the S side of
the station. Here is the remarkable *Old Operating Theatre.*

Old Operating Theatre, Museum & Herb Garret, 9A St. Thomas St, SE1. Tel
071-955 4791. Open Mon, Wed, Fri, 12.30–16.00. Admission charge.

The S wing (1842) of the original St. Thomas's Hospital which stood
here from 1225 to 1865 is occupied by telephone engineers (behind
post office façade). The church of *St. Thomas* (1702–03), formerly
Southwark Chapter House, in St. Thomas's St, is another relic of the
hospital. In the roof space is the Old Operating Theatre of 1821,
rediscovered in 1956 and restored. It is the only known example of a
Victorian operating theatre in existence. In this vicinity lived Robert
Harvard, the father of John Harvard (1607–38), who attended St.
Olave's Grammar School, of which his father was a governor. A little
further on in St. Thomas's St stands **Guy's Hospital**, founded in 1725
by Thomas Guy, a City bookseller, who made a fortune by his
speculations in South Sea stock. The hospital contains one of the
largest medical schools in England. John Keats studied here in
1815–16. In the courtyard is a brass statue of Guy, by Scheemakers
(1733), and in an inner quadrangle is another of Lord Nuffield, by
Maurice Lambert (1949).

The pattern of yards and alleys along the E side of Borough High St
survives from the Middle Ages when most contained coaching inns.

Opposite Southwark St the *King's Head* was called Pope's Head
before 1540. Next door stood the White Hart, Jack Cade's headquarters in 1450 (Shakespeare, 'Henry VI', Part II, V. iv. 8: 'Hath my sword
therefore broke through London Gates that you should leave me at
the White Hart in Southwark?'), and where Mr Pickwick first met Sam
Weller. In a courtyard beside George House is the *George Inn* (NT),
the last surviving galleried inn in London. It is still a public house and
restaurant, and preserves a rare 'inn-keeper's' clock inside; the
façade dates from c 1676. Shakespeare plays are sometimes performed here in summer. On the site of Talbot Yard stood the most
celebrated hostelry of all, the Tabard Inn, the 'Gentil hostelrye that

highte the Tabard, faste by the Belle', the starting-point of Chau
Canterbury pilgrims. It survived (as the Talbot Inn) until 1875-76

The *Queen's Head Inn* stood in Queen's Head Yard and w
owned by the family of John Harvard. The sale of this propert,
before his emigration to America in 1637 augmented his fortune, half
of which (with his library) he left to Harvard University when he died
the following year. In Newcomen St, off the High St, the *King's Arms*
(rebuilt 1890) appropriated the sign from the Great Stone Gate (1728)
on London Bridge when it was demolished in 1760.

Horsemonger Lane Gaol, in which Leigh Hunt was confined for
two years for libelling the Prince Regent as a 'fat Adonis of 50' (1812),
stood in Union Road, to the W.

A tablet in the High St recalls the original old prison of the **Marshalsea**, first
mentioned in 1377 and abandoned in 1813, when the name was transferred to
the New Marshalsea (see below). Here Ben Jonson was imprisoned for sedition
in 1597. Adjoining the Marshalsea on the S stood the old **King's Bench**, the
prison to which Judge Gascoigne is said to have committed Prince Henry
(afterwards Henry V). Tobias Smollett was imprisoned here in 1739 for libel. In
1758 this prison was superseded by the new King's Bench, at the corner of
Newington Causeway. Here John Wilkes was held for libel in 1768-70, and
many debtors were imprisoned, though they were often allowed to live in
lodgings near by, 'within the rules of King's Bench' (comp. Dickens's 'Nicholas
Nickleby'). Mr Micawber found a 'temporary haven of domestic tranquility and
peace of mind' at the King's Bench. The prison was partially burned in the
Gordon Riots (1780; see Dickens's 'Barnaby Rudge'), disused in 1860, when
imprisonment for debt was abolished, and finally pulled down.

At 207 Borough High St a small part of the walls survive of the *White
Lion* or *Borough Gaol*, a 16C prison; to a later building on this site the
name of the Marshalsea was transfered. Here Dickens's father was
confined in 1824, and Little Dorrit, 'the child of the Marshalsea' was
born and brought up. In *St. George's* church (first mentioned in 1122,
rebuilt in 1734-36 by John Price, and since restored) Little Dorrit was
christened and married. Marshalsea Road, running W from the
church, leads to *Mint St*, in which was St. George's Workhouse,
usually accepted as the workhouse in which Oliver Twist asked for
more (though that was not in London). The workhouse copper is
preserved in the Cuming Museum. In *Lant St*, the next turning to the
W from the High St, Charles Dickens lodged as a boy, while his
father was in the Marshalsea and he himself worked at Hungerford
Market. Here, too, lodged Bob Sawyer, the medical student in
'Pickwick'.

Great Dover St branches left from the High St to join the Old Kent
Road (p 332). At No. 75 lived C.H. Spurgeon (see below) in 1854-56.
Here is the *Pilgrim Fathers Memorial Church* (1956), the second
successor to the oldest Congregational church in London (1616). In
the area, Dickens Square, Merrick Square, and Trinity Church
Square date from the early 19C; in the last, opposite the Henry Wood
Memorial Hall, once Holy Trinity Church, is a statue of King Alfred,
said to come from Westminster Hall.

The Borough High St is continued to the S by Newington
Causeway, in which is *London Sessions House*. Beyond is the
Elephant and Castle (Pl. 20; 6), (named after a former tavern)
redesigned in 1957-64 as two roundabouts linked by Newington
Butts, with a revamped shopping centre. Facing this are the London
College of Printing and the Baptists' *Metropolitan Tabernacle*
(rebuilt with a modified façade 1959), the successor of the tabernacle
(burned down in 1898) in which C.H. Spurgeon preached from 1861
until his death in 1892, living at No. 217 New Kent Road.

n N to **London Bridge Station**, the first railway terminus in the
tal, opened in 1837 to serve the first steam railway, to Deptford.
1840 a proper station had replaced the wooden platform and
rved Croydon and Brighton. The station was completely rebuilt
after extensive Second World War damage. Tooley St is to the N of the
station. After a disastrous fire in Tooley St in 1861 in which James
Braidwood, first chief of the 'London Fire Engine Establishment' lost
his life, the service was reorganised as the Metropolitan Fire Brigade,
now the London Fire Brigade. Here is the London Dungeon.

London Dungeon, 28–34 Tooley St, SE1. Tel. 071-403 0606. Open 10.00–17.30
daily (April to Sept), 10.00–16.30 (Oct to March) Admission charge. Not suitable
for children under 10.
    An exhibition in the dank vaults underneath the railway arches of the horrors
of the Middle Ages including the plague, torture and executions.

Opposite is the entrance to London Bridge City, stretching E from
London Bridge to Tower Bridge—part of the rejuvenation of London's
docklands (see Rte 29).

The first phase, completed in 1987, includes office blocks, a private hospital, and
the Hay's Galleria, created from Hay's Wharf (Cubitt, 1856), filled, stripped of its
exterior cladding to reveal the 19C brick-work, and spanned by an iron and glass
roof structure. Restaurants, bars and shops here cater for office workers and
visitors. The *Horniman* pub commemorates the travels of tea merchant Frederick
John Horniman in a magnificent frieze above the bar and a collection of
artefacts. (See also p 326.) Cottons, a striking office block with three atria to the
W is by Michael Twigg and Brown. A riverside walk from London Bridge will
eventually lead to Tower Bridge, passing the second phase of the development
over which there has been some dispute (1989). More offices and a public park
are planned. Excavations on the site revealed the remains of 'Rosary', Edward
II's moated 13C palace directly opposite the Tower.
    Further E along the River Walk is the entrance to HMS 'Belfast', a
Southampton-class cruiser (1936–38) saved from the scrapyard and opened as a
museum in 1971 by the Imperial War Museum.

HMS Belfast, Vine Lane, SE1. Tel. 071-407 6434. Open 10.00–18.00,
summer, 10.00–16.30, winter, daily. Access: Underground, London
Bridge, Tower Hill. Ferry from Tower Pier, daily in summer, weekends in winter. Admission charge. Educational facilities.
    Boarding by gangway to the Quarterdeck, tour the ship following
the arrows (some confined spaces and steep ladders). The highlights
are the main gun turrets, the navigation bridge, the cruiser exhibition
detailing the ship's fighting history (Battle of North Cape, Normandy
D-Day, Korea), the mess decks, bakery and machine shop. Special
exhibitions are held regularly.

The riverside walk will continue to Tower Bridge when the rest of
London Bridge City is complete. Tooley St leads E to Tower Bridge
Road, with Tower Bridge to the N.

On the E side of Tower Bridge redevelopment of the Courage
Brewery/Butler's Wharf site is nearing completion. Offices, work-
shops, shops, a hotel and housing form part of this complex site. The
Design Museum on a water front site opened in 1989.

Design Museum, Butler's Wharf, Shad Thames, SE1. Tel. 071-403 6933; open
Tues to Sun 11.30–18.30. Open Bank Holidays. Library Tues to Sat 11.30–18.30
until 21.30 on Thurs.; admission charge. Restaurant, bookshop. Access:
Underground, Tower Hill, London Bridge.
    The Design Museum, created by the Conran Foundation as an educational
charity in 1981, started life as the Boilerhouse Project at the Victoria and Albert
Museum. The new museum in a white-painted, converted '50s warehouse,
strikingly positioned overlooking the Thames, contains a study collection

temporary exhibitions, reviews of new products, a library, lecture theatre and restaurant. 400 objects are included in the permanent exhibition illustra the design influences on every-day products; interactive computer-aided des. programmes simulate the design process. On the first floor the Boilerhou. exhibitions examine the relationship between ideas and objects; the Inter national Review looks at new products.

In this area a number of new residential schemes in striking styles are nearing completion including The Circle and Horsleydown Square.

Tooley St leads E to Jamaica Road and the area of **Bermondsey**. *St. Saviour's Dock*, to the E of which lay Jacob's Island, scene of Bill Sykes' death in 'Oliver Twist', is part of the new development. New Concordia Wharf, attractive workshops and flats, have already been completed on this site. The Angel pub (16C) in Bermondsey Wall has a restaurant and balcony over the River. Here, Samuel Pepys paused on his journeys to and from Deptford Dockyard. (See p 319). Jamaica Road continues E to Rotherhithe and Surrey Docks, see p 320.

Tower Bridge Road leads S from Tower Bridge underneath the great brick arches of London's earliest railway station (Bermondsey; 1836) passing the 19C buildings of the former *St. Olave's Grammar School* (founded in 1560), and the *New Caledonian Market* at Bermondsey Square, SE1. (Access: Underground, Borough; Buses 1, 42, 78 and 189). Open Fri 07.00–10.00.

The new Caledonian Market opened in here in 1949, moved from its pre-war site at Copenhagen Fields in Islington (see p 299). There are some 200 pitches and the standard of antiques is generally high. Dealings start unofficially before dawn and the public is welcome from 07.00. By mid-morning the serious traders have gone. The market spills over in the surrounding streets; the so-called Bermondsey Antique Market is under cover in Long Lane.

The church of *St. Mary Magdalen* here (rebuilt in 1680) has original woodwork and preserves some 12C capitals from Bermondsey Abbey, a large and powerful house founded in 1087, in which the widows of Henry V and Edward IV died. Remains of a gatehouse can be seen at 7 Grange Walk, nearby. The name, Tanner St, recalls the area's past as the site of London's leather and tanning industry.

32 Islington and Camden Town

Islington, within easy reach of the City of London, was heavily developed for housing during the 19C; thousands of clerks would walk from here to their offices in the City. Much of this terraced housing has now been restored after a period of decline during the early part of the century and Islington has become gentrified. Since the 18C, the Irish have settled here and there are still many Irish pubs with Irish music.

Access: Underground to the Angel; by road from the City via City Road.

The Regent's Canal passes unnoticed through Islington; from the City Road Basin just to the S of the Angel, where the Islington Boat Club is now established, the canal enters the longest tunnel on its route—960 yards—opened in 1816. There is no towpath and the towing horses were led along Chapel St (a market then—see below) while the bargees propelled their boats lying on their backs and pushing against the wall with their feet; a steam tug was introduced in 1826 and used until the 1930s. The canal emerges again at Muriel St (where the gardens of the Barnsbury Estate made an attractive backdrop) and continues to Camden Town, Regent's Park and Paddington (see p 22 for canal tours).

Islington High St which leads due N from the Angel soon splits into the long, still drab *Liverpool Road* and *Upper St*. Liverpool Rd runs NW past Chapel Market (see below) to Holloway. To the W among interesting terraces and squares is Cloudesley Square with *Holy Trinity Church* in the centre, built by Barry in 1826 and inspired by King's College Chapel, Cambridge. To the N is the collegiate-style Lonsdale Square by R.C. Carpenter (c 1842–45). Parallel to Upper St

E, where Kate Greenaway lived between c 1851 and c 1884, is ...den Passage (see below). Further E are the attractive Colebrooke ...w and Duncan Terrace. Charles Lamb came to live at No. 64 ...ancan Terrace in 1823 'never having had a house before'. It was on ...eaving this house that his friend George Dyer walked into the New River and nearly drowned. Its course is indicated by the garden in front of Duncan Terrace. It was carried across Regent's Canal (also underground).

At 25 Noel Road overlooking the Canal lived the playwright, Joe Orton ('Loot') with his lover Kenneth Halliwell, who murdered Orton here in 1967 and then committed suicide.

Chapel Market, N1 (White Conduit St, Grant St, Baron St); Tues to Sun (mornings only Thurs and Sun); Access: Underground, Angel. There has been a street market at least since the middle of the 19C and probably longer; it is now busiest at the weekends and offers fruit, vegetables, general household goods. The *Royal Agricultural Hall* (1862) in Liverpool Road was used for cattle shows, world fairs, circuses and the Royal Tournament. It closed in 1976 and after restoration opened in 1986 as the **Business Design Centre** with permanent showrooms, a large exhibition floor and three restaurants. Tel. 071-359 3535.

In Upper St is the *King's Head* theatre and pub (115 Upper St, N1, tel. 071-226 1916). The theatre is at the back and dinner is served at narrow tables before the play, review or cabaret starts; there is live music in the bar. Prices are in old pence and shillings.

Camden Passage has grown to include not only the Passage with its shops and stalls, the latter trading on Wednesday, Thursday and Saturday, but also two indoor markets. It is London's foremost antique and bric-a-brac market for individual buyers (Bermondsey is geared more to the trader) and developed during the early 1960s. There are good restaurants, such as Fredericks, but the famous Carrier's restaurant closed in 1984.

At *Islington Green* Essex Road diverges NE. On the Green is a statue of Sir Hugh Myddelton (died 1631) who projected the New River scheme for supplying London with water (comp. above). Continue N along Upper St passing (right) *St. Mary's Church* with a tall tower and spire which remains from the previous church begun in 1754. The church was restored in 1962 and contains striking mural paintings. Behind the church, with entrance from Dagmar Passage off Cross St, is the *Little Angel Theatre*, one of only two permanent puppet theatres in England.

Beyond the Town Hall, Canonbury Lane diverges right into the fashionable district of **Canonbury**, with the charming Canonbury Square, begun in 1790. Further on, fronting Canonbury Place (with stuccoed houses of c 1770) is **Canonbury Tower**, a red-brick tower 66ft high and 17ft square, the chief relic of a 16C house of the priors of St. Bartholomew's. (Open by appointment tel. 071-359 4900.) On the W side are two old three-storeyed buildings, in the first of which are the beautiful oak-panelled Spencer Room and Compton Room. The house came into the possession of Sir John Spencer, Lord Mayor of London, in 1594–95, and in 1616–25 Sir Francis Bacon was the lessee of 'Canbury House'. In the 18C the buildings were let out in lodgings and among the noted people who stayed here was Oliver Goldsmith (in the Compton Room). The tower commands an extensive view, and behind it is a pleasant garden. The buildings (with the modern hall adjoining) are occupied by the Tower Theatre. The old octagonal garden-houses that marked the SE and SW corners of the garden of the 16C house are still to be seen in Alwyne Villas (1824) and Al▪ Place (mostly late Georgian), to the S. From Alwyne Road pleasant New River Walk leads to St. Paul's Road.

Continue along Upper St past handsome Compton Terrace wit. the incongruous Victorian *Union Chapel* (it contains a piece of the rock upon which the Pilgrim Fathers landed from the 'Mayflower'), to **Highbury**. In Highbury Place (with fine terraces of c 1774–79), on the SE side of Highbury Fields, Sickert had a studio at No. 1 and No. 25 was the frequent lodging of Wesley and was the residence of Joseph Chamberlain in 1845–54 (tablet). The attractive Highbury Terrace (1789) skirts the N side of the Fields. Off Highbury Hill is the *Arsenal Football Ground*, removed here in 1913 from Woolwich, where it had been founded at the Royal Arsenal Factory in 1884 (hence the sobriquet, 'the gunners').

From *Highbury and Islington Station* the wide Holloway Road leads to the NW through *Holloway*, with a well-known women's prison. It was built in 1852 by James Bunning as a House of Correction for the City. The 20ft-high perimeter walls were demolished in 1971. To the W, in Caledonian Road, is *Pentonville Prison* built in 1840. Within this prison Roger Casement was hanged for high treason on 3 August 1916, the first person hanged in England for this offence since the execution of the Cato St Conspirators in 1820. On the opposite side of the road is the former site of a cattle market transferred here from Smithfield in 1855, and occupying 50 acres in what was formerly Copenhagen Fields. It became the famous Caledonian Market in 1924; this in turn was transferred to Bermondsey after the Second World War and a housing estate built here—the market taverns and clock tower remain.

N of Islington is **Tufnell Park**, an undistinguished Victorian suburb, where in 1968 a brave attempt was made by the actor George Murcell to create a Shakespearean Theatre with true 16C atmosphere, in a converted church. *St. George's Theatre*, 49 Tufnell Park Road, N7, occupies a church dating to 1866, modelled on a 15C crusaders' church. The theatre finally opened in 1976 with a series of Shakespeare plays and has faced continual financial problems. Tel. 071-607 1128.

To the W is **Kentish Town** with a mixed residential population; council housing and substantial private houses. Karl Marx and his family came to live at No. 9 Grafton Terrace, Fitzroy Road (now No. 46 Grafton Terrace) in 1856 from their cramped rooms in Soho. Later they moved to 1 Maitland Park Road nearby (the house was demolished in the Second World War) and a block of flats now occupies the site. In 1875 they moved to 41 Maitland Park Road (also gone) where Karl Marx died in 1881.

Camden Town is to the S. The London Borough of Camden is very diverse, stretching from Hampstead in the N to St. Pancras and Bloomsbury in the S. Somewhere in the middle, just NE of Regent's Park, is Camden Town, a mixed residential area with well-cared-for houses and blocks of flats towards Primrose Hill and Regent's Park.

The once rural aspect of Camden was changed dramatically by the building of the Regent's Canal and the wharves established at Camden Lock in the 1820s. The growing residential population suffered further upheavals with the building of the London, Birmingham and Midlands railways. Today Camden takes full advantage of its position on the Canal and an attractive market/craft workshop area with restaurants has been established at Camden Lock since the '60s.

n Camden Town Underground Station Camden High St leads
d joins with Chalk Farm Road. Before Camden Lock Market and
. past the bridge over the Regent's Canal there is a smaller market
ostly trading in very fashionable clothes and bric-a-brac.

Camden Lock Market, Chalk Farm Road, NW1. Access: Underground, Camden
Town; BR, Camden Road. Market trades on Saturday and Sunday.

Camden Lock Market itself is located around Dingwalls, formerly an
old timber warehouse at Camden Lock, which now offers pop and
rock music and food. Workshops and showrooms of the craftspeople
who work here through the week are in the buildings to the back of
the market; on Saturdays and Sundays traders set up their stalls, some
under cover, selling fashion, arts and crafts, and home-made sweets
and other foods. There are two restaurants within the complex and, of
course, the Canal at one end. The facilities are being expanded with a
two storey market hall by 1991

The 'Fair Lady' cruising restaurant on a traditional canal barge departs from here
daily for lunch and dinner cruises (booking essential on 071-485 4433); during
the summer (April to October) the 'Jenny Wren' operates cruises from here along
the Canal to Little Venice and back.

The new offices of TV-AM (the breakfast TV station) are to the E,
designed by Terry Farrell. Note the eggcups. Next to the High
Victorian, St. Michael's Church, is a new Sainsbury's superstore by
Nick Grimshaw in the 'portakabin' style of architecture.

A little further along the Canal towards Regent's Park another restaurant barge,
the Gallery Boat Chinese Restaurant, is moored (15 Prince Albert Rd, NW1, tel.
071-485 8137). There are guided walks along the Regent's Canal organised by
the Inland Waterways Association between May and December starting at
Camden Lock or Little Venice (tel. 071-586 2510).

Camden Palace in Camden High St, formerly a cinema, has been
transformed into one of the most exciting pop venues/night clubs in
London.

The *Round House* in Chalk Farm Road (nearest Underground
Chalk Farm) is a former engine shed of the London and Birmingham
Railway, built in 1847. Later it became a warehouse and factory and in
1967 a theatre; in 1984 it was saved from demolition by the GLC to
become a Centre for Black Ethnic Arts. This development collapsed in
1989 and the future of the building is unknown.

III THE RIVER THAMES

The **Thames**, once a busy highway, still provides a superb view of ⌐
capital and an insight into its history from the many sightseeing boa⌐
and the River Bus which operate from Westminster Pier, Charing
Cross Pier, and Tower Pier—downstream as far as Greenwich and the
Thames Barrier, all the year round. Upstream services from Westminster Pier to Kew, Richmond, Kingston and Hampton Court operate
during the summer. Full details of services on p 22.

The Roman armies founded Londinium on the N bank where a spur of gravel
provided the necessary foundation for a river-crossing. Caesar called the river
Tamesis and a wooden bridge was built between Southwark on the S bank and
the new settlement. Londinium became an important port and London Bridge in
various forms remained the only permanent crossing (other than Kingston
Bridge and Putney Bridge; see p 253) until Westminster Bridge was built in 1750.
Although the Thames was a royal river—royal barges proceeded regularly
between Whitehall Palace, the Placentia at Richmond, and Greenwich, and
Hampton Court—the City of London retained effective control of the port and
river as far W as Staines and E to the mouth of the Medway until the 19C. The
first Thames Conservancy Act established the Thames Commissioners and the
Port of London Authority was set up in 1909 with control of 135 miles of tidal river
from Teddington to the sea. The Thames Water Authority, established in 1974 to
take charge of water supply, drainage, recreation and sewerage, took over the
Thames Conservancy function in 1983, while the Port of London retained its
navigational role. In 1989 the Port of London Authority resumed control of the
piers and Thames Water, due to be privatised, retained responsibility for water
supply etc.
At times during the 18C and 19C the river would freeze and Frost Fairs were
held on the ice above London Bridge—the last in 1814. The removal of the old
London Bridge which acted as a dam accelerated the flow of the river and this
effect was intensified by the building of the Embankments. It is unlikely that the
river will freeze again. However, as SE England is sinking at a rate of about 12
inches every 100 years, the river has become more liable to flood its banks. In
1928 14 people died when Central London flooded and in 1953 300 people died
along the E Coast and the Thames Estuary. The Thames Flood Barrier,
completed in 1983, is intended to prevent this happening again (see below). In
1989 the River Thames claimed 47 lives when the pleasure boat, The
Marchioness collided with a barge during a night-time disco cruise.

33 Westminster to the Tower; to Greenwich and the Thames Barrier

This is a brief description of places of interest; for full details see under
the relevant area description.

Westminster Pier adjoins Westminster Bridge on the N bank; there
are plans to redevelop it.

Westminster Bridge, the second bridge to be built across the
Thames in Central London (London Bridge was the first), was
completed in 1750. When the old London Bridge was removed in 1831
the foundations of Westminster Bridge were undermined by the
increased waterflow and a new bridge (designed by Thomas Page)
replaced the old one in 1862. At the head of the bridge on the N side is
a statue of Boadicea and on the S side a White Lion, made of Coade
stone. Opposite Westminster Pier is **County Hall**, headquarters of the
former Greater London Council (see p 286), and above the bridge, the
Houses of Parliament on the N bank, with *St. Thomas's Hospital*
opposite.

ing downstream, the *Victoria Embankment* is on the N side.
was completed in 1870 to a design by Bazalgette and incorpo-
d the District Line Underground service as well as a new
verage system. The *RAF Memorial* was erected in 1923. Beyond
e the buildings of the former Scotland Yard, now the *Norman
Shaw Building* with offices for MPs, the plain white square of the
Ministry of Defence built on the site of old Whitehall Palace, and the
ornate Renaissance buildings of *Whitehall Court*, the *National
Liberal Club* and the *Royal Horseguards Hotel*. Moored along the
Embankment are the 'Tattershall Castle', a Clyde paddle-steamer,
now a pub, and the 'Hispaniola', a restaurant.

On the S bank between County Hall and Hungerford Bridge are
the *Jubilee Gardens*, laid out in the Queen's Jubilee Year of 1977
and the start of the 10-mile waymarked *Jubilee Walkway*.

Hungerford Bridge carries railway traffic to Charing Cross Station
and also pedestrians to and from the S Bank. The original suspension
bridge on this site was designed by Brunel but demolished in 1864.
Just beyond on the N bank is *Charing Cross Pier*.

The **Royal Festival Hall** on the S side is part of the **South Bank
Arts Complex**, opened in 1951 and designed by Robert Matthew and
Leonard Martin, for the Festival of Britain celebrations that year. It
seats 3400 and has restaurants, bars and changing art exhibitions.
The *Festival Pier* in front of it opened in 1983. The *Queen Elizabeth
Hall* and the *Purcell Room* are part of the South Bank Complex, as is
the *Hayward Gallery*, just beyond.

The Victoria Embankment continues along the N bank with
decorative dolphin lamp posts and moorings of lion heads with rings
along the river front. **Cleopatra's Needle**, a pink obelisk, is one of a
pair presented to Britain by Mohammed Ali and erected here in
1878. It stood at Heliopolis originally and dates to 1500 BC. Beyond
are the *Victoria Embankment Gardens*, with summertime music and
a statue of Burns. The old watergate of York House indicates that the
river used to be twice as wide at this point.

The clock on *Shellmex House* is the largest in London and dates to
1932. The *Savoy Hotel* founded by Richard d'Oyly Carte opened in
1889 on the site of the old Savoy Palace. Just before Waterloo Bridge
on the N side is moored the original 'Queen Mary', an attractive
turbine steamer built in 1933, now open as a restaurant ship.

Waterloo Bridge provides an excellent view-point as it is located
on the turn of the river. This concrete bridge was designed by Sir
Giles Gilbert Scott and opened in 1942. John Rennies' original
Waterloo Bridge which opened in 1817 started to sink in 1923.

Below Waterloo Bridge on the N side is the floating *Thames Police
Station* and on the S side the *National Film Theatre* (with an outdoor
restaurant) and the Museum of Moving Image.

Somerset House on the N side just past Waterloo Bridge was built
in 1776 with its own river entrance. The E wing is *King's College*,
part of the University of London; the N wing houses the Courtauld
Institute collection of paintings. The area called the TEMPLE takes its
name from the Order of Knights Templar. It is now used by the Inner
and Middle Temple, two of the four Inns of Court. The heraldic
dragons mark the boundary between the City of London and
Westminster. Ships moored along here are the 'Wellington', the
livery hall of the Master Mariners, and the Royal Navy training ship
'President'. The 'Discovery' moved first to St. Katharine's Dock and
then in 1986 to Dundee. The Thames barge, 'Wilfred', a winebar is
now moored here. Near the bridge are the Gothic buildings of *Sion*

College and the former *City of London School for Boys*.

On the S bank, the **Royal National Theatre**, concrete and stark on the outside, is open through the day and evening with comfortable bars, buffets and a restaurant. There are three theatres: the *Olivier*, the *Lyttelton* and the *Cottesloe*. Next to it are the buildings of London Weekend Television and IBM. The *Old Barge House* stairs can still be seen with *King's Reach Tower* beyond. These watermen's steps are a reminder of the days when passengers were carried across the river by ferrymen. The *Oxo Tower* has been preserved in the Coin St redevelopment which includes Gabriel's Wharf market. *Seacontainers House*, now offices, was supposed to become a hotel in 1974.

Next to Blackfriars Bridge, the modern *Doggetts Coat and Badge* pub takes its name from the red coat worn by the Thames Watermen who compete in the Doggetts Coat and Badge Race, established by Thomas Doggett, a comedian and manager of Theatre Royal Drury Lane in 1715. The 5-mile race from London Bridge to Cadogan Pier, Chelsea, takes place each year at the end of July.

Blackfriars Bridge and St. Paul's Cathedral by William Marlow (1740–1813), from the collection of the Guildhall Art Gallery, City of London

The Fleet River, now in a pipeway, enters the Thames on the N side just above **Blackfriars Bridge**, named after the Dominican Priory which stood here. The original bridge opened in 1769 and the new bridge, designed by Joseph Cubitt, was opened by Queen Victoria in 1869. The Blackfriars Railway Bridge beyond leads to Blackfriars Station and incorporates stones from the old Westminster Bridge.

Along the N bank between Blackfriars and Southwark bridges is the *Mermaid Theatre* at the former *Puddle Dock*; it opened in a converted warehouse in 1959 and was rebuilt in 1981. The new *City of London School* is here, and the *Samuel Pepys* pub is in a converted warehouse.

Vintners' Hall dates from 1671 and is the Livery Hall of the Vintners' company, one of two companies entitled to own swans on the Thames in addition to the Queen (the other is the Dyers'). Once a year during Swan Upping, usually in July, swans are counted and marked; two nicks in the beak for Vintners' swans and one for Dyers'—the Queen's swans are unmarked. This event now takes place up-river beyond Sunbury. On the S side along Bankside new developments have brought offices to an ancient area of London (see Rte 27). The *Founder's Arms* pub is part of a new development of flats and offices and has a riverside terrace looking out on the river and St. Paul's Cathedral opposite.

The redundant **Bankside Power Station** (1963) was designed by Sir Giles Gilbert Scott, who also designed Battersea Power Station. In Cardinal Cap Alley, No. 49 Cardinal's Wharf survives; Wren is said to have watched the rebuilding of St. Paul's from here.

BANKSIDE was a traditional place of entertainment and work to rebuild Shakespeare's Globe Theatre is due to be completed in 1993.

Southwark Bridge dates to 1921; first built by John Rennie in cast-iron in 1819. On the N bank is the *Riverside Inn* and on the S side the *Anchor*, a 300-year-old tavern in an 18C building. It has recently been restored and has a restaurant.

The massive decorative turrets of **Cannon St Station** remain at the N side of the *Cannon St Railway Bridge* (opened in 1866), while the station itself has been rebuilt further inland.

Past the railway bridge on the N side is the modern *Mondial House*, the international headquarters of British Telecom, and further along *Fishmongers' Hall*, a classical building completed in 1832. The fishmongers administer the Doggett's Coat and Badge Race, see above.

The 'Regalian' is moored at the old *Swan Pier* as a restaurant and bar.

On the S bank is the site of Winchester Palace and the old Clink Prison; a sign under the bridge tells the story. The gaol was built in the 16C in Clink St. In *St. Mary Overie Dock* is the 'Kathleen and May' schooner and further on Southwark Cathedral. The open space incorporates stones from the old London Bridge.

The first **London Bridge** was built by the Romans sometime after AD 43; remains have been uncovered on the N side. The wooden structure was renewed several times and a stone bridge was begun in 1176; it featured 20 arches and stone piers with a drawbridge. It took 30 years to complete and buildings were incorporated to pay for the bridge's upkeep. One of the pointed stone arches has been uncovered on the N bank. London Bridge, one of the wonders of the medieval world with its houses and shops, could not cope with increasing traffic in the early 19C. A new bridge designed by John Rennie opened in 1825 and this was widened in 1902. It was sold to Lake Havasu City, Arizona, for £1m in 1970 when a larger bridge was needed. This opened in 1973. The nursery rhyme 'London Bridge is falling down' probably refers to the earlier wooden bridges; one was apparently washed away in a flood and another was torn down by invading Vikings led by Olaf the Norseman in 1014.

Between London Bridge and Tower Bridge on the S bank, the new LONDON BRIDGE CITY is being built with Kuwaiti money; it includes office blocks, a private hospital and a park. *Hay's Wharf*, once used by giant tea clippers, has been filled in and a shopping 'Galleria' created with restaurants and the pub *The Horniman at Hays*.

On the N bank there is more redevelopment next to **Billingsgate Market** which closed in 1981 when the fish market moved to West India Docks. Archaeological excavations on the adjoining site revealed more information about London's Roman and Saxon past.

A glass encased office block now stands on the site. Jones's Billingsgate opened in 1877 on the site of an ancient r of 870. The free fish market was established in 1699 and the pc wore 'bobbing hats', round, hard-topped leather hats for ca ing loads of fish. The old building has a preservation order and h been developed for office use. **Custom House** next to it was designe by Laing and opened in 1817. Adjoining it is *Tate and Lyle's Sugar Quay*.

Tower Pier is just before the Tower of London, separated from the river by Tower Wharf leading to Tower Bridge and underneath it to St. Katharine's Dock.

HMS Belfast is moored on the S bank. This Royal Navy cruiser saw action in the Second World War and has been converted into a floating museum. There is a ferry from Tower Pier in summer but the ship is open all the year round; access from Tooley St (see p 296). Visiting naval ships often moor alongside HMS Belfast.

Tower Bridge, widely recognised as a symbol of London, with its two Gothic towers, is often mistakenly referred to as London Bridge. It opened in 1894 as the only moveable bridge on the river, designed by Sir Horace Jones and built by Sir John Wolfe Barry to blend with the Tower of London. The bascules, each weighing over 1000 tons, were originally raised by hydraulic power. The walkways were incorporated to allow pedestrian traffic to flow uninterrupted as the bridge was frequently opened. They became a haven for unsavoury characters and closed ten years after the bridge opened. The *Tower Bridge Walkway* reopened as a tourist attraction in 1982 (see p 268).

Along the river from the Tower to Greenwich and on to the Thames Barrier the largest redevelopment scheme in Western Europe is now under way under the direction of the London Docklands Development Corporation (see Rte 29). This means that the scene is changing fast, but the following would be seen on a river-trip (in 1989).

On the N side next to Tower Bridge is **St. Katharine's Dock**, already successfully redeveloped for business and tourism with its marina, the *World Trade Centre*, the *Tower Hotel*, the restored *Ivory House* and *Dickens Inn*, plus modern council housing. Recent additions include the new riverside offices and an extension of the Dickens Inn.

Opposite are the former *Courage Brewery, Butler's Wharf, St. Saviour's Dock* and *New Concordia Wharf* converted into attractive offices and housing. The Design Museum is in a bright, white converted '50s warehouse.

Also on the S bank is the *Cherry Garden Pier* where visiting ships sound a signal if they wish Tower Bridge to be raised—this now happens only two or three times a month. The *Angel* pub and restaurant is a fine 16C building with good views of the river.

Opposite is **Wapping** with the *Town of Ramsgate*, a 17C pub next to *Wapping Old Stairs*. Pirates tried by Judge Jeffreys were tied to the piles at low tide and suffered three tides before being untied. Judge Jeffreys is said to have watched from the Angel opposite. The modern headquarters of the Thames Division of the Metropolitan Police is here. Beyond Tunnel Pier is *Execution Dock* where Captain Kidd (died 1701) and other pirates were hanged. Brunel's first Thames tunnel was built from Rotherhithe to Wapping and is now used as part of the East London Line Underground.

On the S Bank Brunel's Engine House at *Rotherhithe—The Pumphouse* has an exhibition telling the story of the building of this tunnel, the first in the world under a river. Nearby is the *Mayflower* pub; 18C and renamed to commemorate the Pilgrim Fathers who

m the Thames near here; there is a restaurant and balcony
od views.

osite on the N Bank is the popular *Prospect of Whitby* pub
h dates from 1520 and has a restaurant.

*Once an isolated outpost to the East, the Prospect of Whitby is
now in the midst of growing Docklands developments*

The *Rotherhithe Road Tunnel* connects Rotherhithe and Stepney; the
circular air vents can be seen on either side of the river. It opened in
1908. The *Surrey Docks* on the S side are closed and are being
redeveloped with new housing along the River, industry and
shopping.

At *Shadwell* on the N side *King Edward Memorial Park* mar
place of the old Shadwell fish market and includes a memor.
Willoughby, Frobisher and other 16C navigators.

At *Limehouse* another redevelopment of flats and houses
underway along the Regent's Canal and Limehouse Basin. In the 19
this was London's notorious Chinese quarter and there are still some
Chinese restaurants in West India Dock Road. The *Grapes* pub
overlooks the river and was frequented by Dickens and Whistler.

As the river turns S the point on the S bank known as *Cuckold's
Point* is said to take its name from a Mr Cuckold who ducked his
unfaithful wife here; others followed suit. The river loops around the
Isle Of Dogs, part of the Docklands Redevelopment Scheme (see Rte
29). It was originally marshland and used as a hunting ground by
Henry VIII when at Greenwich. Along the river bank to the N are a
series of converted warehouses and new residential areas including
Cascades, with portholes and a stepped silhouette, overshadowed in
scale by Canary Wharf, overlooking West India Dock—the largest
commercial development in Europe. The *West India Docks* opened in
1802 and *Millwall Docks* in 1864.

The site of the dockyard where Brunel's 'Great Eastern', a ship
combining sail and steam, was built is marked on the N bank at
Burrells Wharf, another residential conversion.

On the S Bank Surrey Docks Farm has been relocated to a new
riverside location; a valuable resource to local schools and other
groups. At Nelson Dock the Scandic Crown Hotel and Conference
Centre opens in 1991. Further along at Greenland Dock, there is a
marina at South Dock. The *Royal Naval Victualling Yard* at **Deptford**
is now part of a housing estate. The depot was founded in 1513 and it
was here Queen Elizabeth I knighted Sir Francis Drake aboard his
ship, the 'Golden Hind', now kept in dry-dock. At Deptford Creek, the
Ravensbourne river enters the Thames.

At *Island Gardens* to the N is a small park opened in 1895 to provide
a good viewing point of the buildings of Greenwich. The small domed
buildings on either side of the river are the entrances to the
Greenwich pedestrian tunnel (opened 1902). The terminus of the
Docklands Light Railway opened in July 1987 is here.

On the S side are the historic buildings of **Greenwich**; on the
waterfront, the 'Cutty Sark' in its dry-dock; above on the hill the **Old
Royal Observatory** in *Greenwich Park*. The red time ball still drops at
13.00 each day, a signal since 1833 for ships passing on the river. Past
Greenwich Pier is the **Royal Naval College** and the **National
Maritime Museum** with the Palladian **Queen's House**.

The *Trafalgar Tavern* has a ship-style bar and a restaurant overlooking the river; the small balcony of the *Yacht* pub is just beyond,
and further on the picturesque Trinity Alsmhouses. From here the
route to the Thames Barrier is largely industrial, including the
Greenwich Power Station alongside the *Cutty Sark*—a Georgian pub
with a nautical theme.

Opposite on the N bank is the *Waterman's Arms*, followed by more
housing and then another entrance to the West India Dock marked by
a Blue Bridge with a view across the Isle of Dogs to the City.

On the S side is the *Victoria Deep Water Container Terminal*, one of
the few flourishing parts of the Port of London above Tilbury.

The *East Greenwich Gasworks*, founded in 1881, is now a redevelopment area. The *Blackwall Tunnel* crosses Blackwall Reach from E
Greenwich to Poplar. *Brunswick Power Station* on the S side has been
demolished (1989). From this site the Company of Merchant Ven-

departed to found the State of Virginia in three ships, 'God-
, 'Discovery' and 'Susan Constant', commemorated by a
cairn on the river front.

w Creek joins the River Lea to the Thames on the N bank;
ther along is the entrance to the large *Royal Docks*, now closed
nd the site for a huge redevelopment project and the already
opened London City Airport. Industries continue on the N Bank at
Silvertown.

The **Thames Barrier**, completed in 1983 and officially opened
the following year by HM The Queen, was designed to save
London from flooding. There is a Visitor Centre and river tours
(see p 321).

Beyond the Barrier on the S side is **Woolwich** with the *Woolwich
Free Ferry* established in 1889.

34 Westminster to Kew; Richmond, Kingston and Hampton Court

Upstream services from Westminster Pier to Kew, Richmond, Kingston and
Hampton Court operate daily in the summer and at weekends in spring and
autumn; check in advance as they are liable to change at short notice.

Travelling times: Westminster Pier to Kew 1hr 30 minutes; to Richmond 2hr
30 minutes; to Hampton Court 3hr 45 minutes (actual times depend on tides).
It is possible to walk along the towpaths from Putney to Hampton Court. See
p 22 for practical information.

Westminster Pier, at the N end of Westminster Bridge, is due to be
rebuilt in the near future as its structure is unsound; river services
may be transferred while work is being undertaken.

Opposite Westminster Pier is *County Hall*; *Westminster Bridge*,
only the second bridge to be built across the Thames in central
London, was designed by Thomas Page in 1862 when it replaced a
stone bridge of 1750. On the N bank is the terrace of the *Houses
of Parliament* where MPs and their guests enjoy tea during the
summer months. On the S bank is *St. Thomas's Hospital* with
several new buildings. Adjacent to it are the walls of **Lambeth
Palace**, the London residence of the Archbishop of Canterbury,
and *St. Mary's Church*, Lambeth, which is now a museum of
garden history.

On the N bank are *Victoria Tower Gardens*, with Westminster
Abbey beyond. *Lambeth Bridge* replaced an ancient horse-ferry in
1862. The present bridge was built in 1929. The HQ of the London
Fire Brigade is on the S side with two or more fire-boats moored
outside; on the N bank there are office blocks. The classical lines
of the Tate Gallery (1887) are in view on the N bank. Note the
Henry Moore statue outside Riverwalk House just before *Vauxhall
Bridge*. The first Vauxhall Bridge was built in 1811–16, the earliest
iron bridge to carry trams across the Thames. A new bridge
replaced it in 1906; the bronze figures alongside it represent Agriculture, Architecture, Engineering, Learning, the Fine Arts and
Astronomy—each holding an appropriate symbol. There are
redevelopments on the S bank at Vauxhall. Further along the S
bank is the redundant *Nine Elms Cold Store*, and the *New Covent
Garden Market* which moved here from Covent Garden in 1974.
This is London's main wholesale fruit and vegetable market.

On the N bank are the Dolphin Square Apartments. Villa de Cesari, a Roman-style restaurant is located in a converted riverside warehouse just in front of the the large apartment complex with the restaurant Elephant on the River alongside.

The future of *Battersea Power Station* on the S bank which was being converted into a leisure and entertainment centre is uncertain (1990).

The *Grosvenor Bridge* was the first railway bridge over the Thames; the first train crossed to Victoria Station in 1860. The bridge, rebuilt in 1967, has an attractive Victorian pumping station next to it on the N bank. On the S Bank can be seen the dramatic Marco Polo building (1988) which houses the Observer newspaper.

Chelsea Suspension Bridge, designed by Thomas Page, opened in 1858 and was replaced by another suspension bridge in 1937. (Other suspension bridges over the Thames are Albert Bridge and Hammersmith Bridge.)

Battersea Park is on the S side of the river; part of the pier has been removed to build the Festival Pier outside the Festival Hall. The Japanese pagoda was presented to the GLC in 1985 by a Buddhist sect.

On the N bank are the grounds of the **Chelsea Royal Hospital**, where the Chelsea Flower Show is staged annually in May, and the walled *Chelsea Physic Garden*. The attractive red-brick buildings of Cheyne Walk start here and continue towards World's End. *Cadogan Pier*, just before the Albert Bridge, is the finishing point of the Doggett's Coat and Badge Race. The attractive *Albert Bridge* was designed by Roland Mason Ordish in 1873 as a cantilevered structure; it was modified as a suspension bridge by Joseph Bazalgette. After strengthening it was reopened in July 1973 but still has a weight limit and 'troops must break step' before crossing the bridge, according to a notice. The toll booths also remain and the bridge is beautifully illuminated at night.

On the N bank in *Cheyne Walk* is the *King's Head and Eight Bells*, a 400-year-old pub. *Chelsea Old Church* in dour brick has been completely rebuilt after Second World War damage. A new statue of Sir Thomas More stands outside. Next to it is Crosby Hall, moved here from Bishopsgate in 1910.

The first *Battersea Bridge* was a wooden structure completed in 1772; it was portrayed by both Whistler and Turner. The replacement was designed by Bazalgette and opened in 1890. Houseboats are moored in front of Cheyne Walk before it swings away from the Thames beyond the tower blocks of the World's End Estate. *Chelsea Wharf* has been converted into workshops, offices and a restaurant; next to it Lots Road Power Station, built in 1904 to provide power for the Underground. The striking Chelsea Harbour development at Chelsea Basin includes a tower block with a red ball on top, a marina, hotel, offices and restaurants. The Thames riverbus operates a regular downstream service from here.

On the S side is the attractive church of *St. Mary Battersea* from where Turner painted Thames sunsets. The *Old Swan* is a modern riverside pub, and new housing has been built in this area. Just before the Westland Heliport at Battersea the river is crossed by the Battersea Railway Bridge. This part of the riverbank is mostly industrial, with the site of Fulham Power Station (demolished for redevelopment) on the N bank.

Wandsworth Bridge opened in 1873 and was rebuilt in 1938. The River Wandle enters the Thames here through a redeveloped indusial area. On the N bank the grounds of 18C *Hurlingham House* provide a refreshing green space; it is now home of the Hurlingham Club. Wandsworth Park is further along the S bank.

The *Fulham/Putney Railway Bridge* opened in 1899. The first *Putney Bridge*, also known as Fulham Bridge, was made of wood and opened in 1729. Bazalgette designed the replacement granite bridge in 1884; this incorporates an aqueduct. The old Putney Bridge was the first Thames bridge W of London Bridge, except Kingston Bridge, until Westminster Bridge was completed in 1750. It now carries more vehicle traffic than any other bridge over the Thames. The parish churches of Fulham and Putney are on either side of the bridge, which also marks the start of the Oxford and Cambridge Boat Race, first rowed in 1829 and now held annually in March/April. The start is marked by the Universities' Stone on the S bank near the *Star and Garter* pub. Putney Pier is nearby.

On the N bank is *Fulham Palace*, hidden by trees. Bishops Park skirts the river for half a mile, ending at *Craven Cottage*, Fulham's soccer ground.

On the S bank, past the attractive setting of Putney, is Barn Elms Park and sports centre. Further along in the great curve of the river are the Barn Elms Reservoirs. Here a memorial stone to Steve Fairbairn, rowing coach, marks 1 mile from the start of the Boat Race. The huge Harrods depository in terracotta dates to 1890.

Some of the wharves on the N bank have been restored as offices and workshops; they include the *Riverside Studios*, a theatre and arts centre located in a former BBC studio.

Hammersmith Bridge opened in 1827; the suspension bridge designed by Bazalgette replaced it in 1887. It has twice been strengthened, most recently in 1984 after great cracks opened up. The Lower Mall, Hammersmith, along the N bank, has some fine 18C houses as well as the *Rutland* and *Blue Anchor* pubs. In Upper Mall is *Kelmscott House*, where William Morris lived, just past the 17C *Dove Inn*. The *Old Ship*, an 18C pub, also overlooks the Thames. A small island, *Chiswick Eyot*, along the N bank, provides a sanctuary for birds.

On the S bank is *St. Paul's Boys School* which moved here from the City in 1968; famous former pupils include Milton, Pepys and Field Marshal Lord Montgomery.

Hammersmith Mall is continued on the N bank as Chiswick Mall, with attractive 18C mansions. The church of *St. Nicholas* dates from the 15C; nearby is the modern *Fuller's Brewery*.

On the S bank before *Barnes Railway Bridge* (opened 1849) is the large *Bull's Head* pub, well-known for jazz. Duke's Meadow on the N bank remains undeveloped. A wooden post marks the finishing point of the University Boat Race just before *Chiswick Bridge*, with Watney's Brewery and the *Ship Inn* conveniently sited on the S bank. Chiswick Bridge was one of three opened in one day in 1933 by Edward VIII (then Prince of Wales; the others were Twickenham and Hampton Court Bridges). The boathouse on the N bank beyond the Bridge is used by the Oxford and Cambridge teams after the Boat Race.

Industrial and then residential developments now occupy both banks. Just before *Kew Railway Bridge* is the large modern *Public Records Office*. Beyond the bridge on the N bank is the picturesque Strand on the Green, with two well-known pubs, the *City Barge*, with a charter granted by Elizabeth I and named after the Lord Mayor's official barge which was moored here, and the *Bull's Head*. The small island here is *Oliver's Ait*, supposedly named after Oliver Cromwell.

From the Toll House on the S bank the Port of London Authority controls the upper part of the Thames as far as Teddington. Kew Pier is just before *Kew Bridge*, opened in 1903 by Edward VII and originally named after him. It succeeded the original timber bridge of 1758 and a granite bridge of 1789, opened with a procession led by George III.

On the N bank is *Kew Bridge Pumping Station*, open to the public at weekends as the Living Steam Museum and containing the original beam engines. In the church of *St. George* is the Musical Museum.

Brentford Ait, another islet, is to the N; **Kew Gardens** on the S bank here cover 288 acres (open all year). The *Waterman's Art Centre* is on the N Bank. The River Brent and the Grand Union Canal enter the Thames here at the site of an ancient ford used by both Romans and Vikings. The once-busy Brentford Dock has been redeveloped with housing and a marina.

On the riverbank to the N is **Syon Park** with *Syon House* set back from the river, still occupied by the Duke of Northumberland (open to the public). In the grounds are the Butterfly House and the Heritage Car Collection.

On the S bank, in *Old Deer Park* is the King's Observatory. Opposite is *Old Isleworth*, with the river dividing around Isleworth Ait. The village has been redeveloped retaining its fine 17C and 18C houses and its modern church, *All Saints*, with a 400-year-old tower. Here is the *London Apprentice*, a 15C pub and restaurant with an Elizabethan interior.

The River Crane joins the Thames just past Isleworth Ait; further along on the S bank is *Richmond Lock*, footbridge and sluices, the first on the up-river journey. At high tide the lock is not used but at other times sluices control the water level. The lock was opened in 1894.

Twickenham Bridge opened in 1933; it features parapets, lamps and railings in bronze. Just beyond is *Richmond Railway Bridge*. Past the houses on the S bank—including Asgill House of 1760—is Richmond Green. A new development fronts the riverbank with *Richmond Ait* just before the picturesque *Richmond Bridge*; this is the oldest Thames bridge still in use in Greater London. Built by James Paine in 1774, when it was widened in 1937–39 the original stones were carefully replaced on the outside. The Richmond Landing Stage is just beyond the bridge.

The view of the Thames from Richmond Hill, by the Star and Garter Home opened in 1924, is one of the loveliest along the river.

Petersham Village is on the S bank just beyond Glover Island; on the opposite side are **Marble Hill Park and House**, an 18C Palladian mansion (open to the public). Nearby is the remnant of *Orleans House*, the Octagon Room, now used as an art gallery.

A ferry operates across the river to *Ham Common* and **Ham House**, a fine Jacobean mansion (1610) which now belongs to the National Trust and is open to the public.

Eel Pie Island divides the river; here are private houses and a former hotel where British rock music was developed in the 1960s.

Just before the island, on the N bank is the *White Swan* pub; further on is *York House* in the centre of Twickenham, set in an exotic garden, and used as council offices. *Pope's Grotto* pub on the N bank along Cross Deep takes its name from Alexander Pope's famous Grotto in the garden of his house at Strawberry Hill, now a school.

The turbulent waters of *Teddington Lock and Weir* lie ahead. Built in 1811, the lock marks the dividing line between the tidal and non-tidal waters of the Thames and an obelisk just before the lock marks the boundary between the National Rivers Authority, which has jurisdiction over the upper river, and the Port of London Authority which controls the River to its estuary. Just beyond the weir on the N bank are the studios of Thames Television; the *Angels* pub is nearby.

The Thames flows between Kingston on the S bank and Teddington to the N past two islands, Trowlock Island and Steven's Eyot, before reaching *Kingston Railway Bridge*, dominated by the two chimneys of Kingston Power Station, and Kingston town centre. There was a permanent bridge here in the 12C, the second bridge (London Bridge was the first) over the Thames. The present bridge is the third on the site and opened in 1828; its size was doubled in 1924. The remains of the medieval bridge and of the equally ancient Clattern Bridge over the Hogsmill tributary which enters the Thames here can still be seen in the new John Lewis department store development at Horsefair.

From Turks Boatyard there are services to Hampton Court during the summer; Kingston Pier is just beyond the bridge. The next island is *Raven's Ait*, with ferry access from the S bank to Hampton Court Park. Before reaching Hampton Court the river winds round *Thames Ditton Island* which has some houses and is linked by a suspension bridge to the S bank.

The Hampton Court Landing Stage is just before *Hampton Court Bridge*, designed by Lutyens in 1933 to harmonise with the palace. It is the fourth bridge on the site. **Hampton Court Palace**, begun in 1514, is on the N bank while the village of *Hampton* is further along the river.

Notes for Walkers: It is possible, and very pleasant, to walk along the banks of the Thames more or less continuously from Hampton Court to Putney. From Hampton Court use the towpath on the N side to Kingston Bridge with small diversions (3 miles). Cross to the S bank at Kingston Bridge and follow the towpath from the power station to Richmond, past Ham and Petersham (4.5 miles); Teddington is reached by using the footbridge at Teddington Lock and Marble Hill Park is reached via the ferry (in summer). From Richmond to Chiswick Bridge follow the S bank, past Kew on the S and past Hammersmith on the N to Putney Bridge (8 miles). From here there is no continuous towpath so use a detailed street-map. Putney Bridge to Westminster Bridge is 5.5 miles.

IV   OUTER LONDON: SOUTH EAST, SOUTH AND SOUTH WEST

35   Greenwich, Blackheath, Deptford, Surrey Docks, Rotherhithe, Woolwich, Bexley, Eltham

Greenwich on the S bank of the Thames, 4.5 miles from central London, was once a quiet fishing village whose location on the Roman Watling St and by the Thames brought it to royal attention in the 15C, when Humphrey, Duke of Gloucester, built himself a mansion and enclosed the park as a hunting ground. Today the magnificent buildings—the Old Royal Observatory, the Queen's House, the National Maritime Museum and the Royal Naval College—contrast strongly with the housing estates which followed in the 18th and 19th centuries, but still provide one of London's most impressive views from the N bank at Island Gardens (cross via the pedestrian tunnel) and from the top of Greenwich Park by the statue of General Wolfe. The view from here has been considerably changed by the Canary Wharf development. (See p 281). In 1991 Greenwich will be celebrating its connection with Henry VIII—500 years after his birth in Greenwich at the Palace of Placentia.

Access: BR (Charing Cross) to Greenwich or Maze Hill Stations; by river from Westminster, Charing Cross or Tower Piers to Greenwich Pier. Docklands Light Railway from Tower Gateway to Island Gardens, then by foot through the pedestrian tunnel.

The Royal Naval College—formerly the Greenwich Hospital— is in King William Walk on the site of Henry VII's Palace of Placentia, developed from Bella Court, Duke Humphrey's mansion built in 1426–34. It became a favourite residence of the Tudor sovereigns; Henry VIII and his daughters, Mary and Elizabeth, were all born at the Placentia and Edward VI died here. The palace also saw Henry VIII's weddings to both Katharine of Aragon and Anne of Cleves. Here he started the liaison with Anne Boleyn which led eventually to the breach with Rome. During the reign of the Stuarts the Placentia went into decline and was demolished by Charles II.

Royal Naval College, King William Walk, SE10. Tel. 081-858 2154. Open daily 14.30–17.00 (closed Thur); closed at short notice for functions.

The remains of the 15C Palace were found beneath the lawn of the Royal Naval College during excavations in 1970–71. The present buildings were begun for Charles II by John Webb (NW block) as part of a new royal palace. When William and Mary came to the throne Sir Christopher Wren was instructed to convert the buildings into a hospital for the benefit of seamen and Greenwich's royal connections effectively came to an end. The new buildings, mostly by Wren and Hawksmoor, were opened in 1704 with further additions in 1750. In 1869 the sick seamen were moved to more modest surroundings at the Dreadnought Seaman's Hospital (1763) in nearby Romney Road and the Royal Naval College moved here from Portsmouth. The Seamen's Hospital closed in 1988 and the site is being redeveloped.

Today, visitors can admire Wren's twin domes which carefully frame the Queen's House, just beyond, without obstructing its view from or of the river. The Painted Hall and Chapel are open to visitors. The *Painted Hall*, still used daily by the officers as a dining room and also available for functions, was decorated by Sir James Thornhill between 1707 and 1722. He and his assistants were paid £3 per square yard for the ceiling and £1 for the walls. They created one of the most impressive halls in England. At the focal point of the ceiling are William and Mary, waited upon by the Four Virtues. On the far wall Thornhill himself can be seen to the right of the family of George I. Nelson's body lay in state in this Hall after his death at Trafalgar in 1805 and thousands of Londoners came to pay their respects. Opposite the Painted Hall is the *Chapel*, its delicate Wedgwood blue and white in vivid contrast to the brown and gold of the Hall. The Chapel was rebuilt after a fire in 1779 to a new classical design by James 'Athenian' Stuart. The altarpiece is by Sir Benjamin West as are the statues in the vestibule of Faith, Hope, Charity and Humility, executed in Coade stone.

There are public services on Sundays and concerts during the Greenwich Festival in June and at other times. The statue of George II in the Grand Square of the four buildings is by Rysbrack.

On the other side of Romney Road, forming part of the Royal Naval College architecturally, are the buildings of the **National Maritime Museum**, including the **Queen's House**.

Queen's House, Romney Road, SE10. Tel. 081-858 4422. Reopened in summer 1990 after a six-year refurbishment programme. Open daily Mon to Sat 10.00–17.00, Sun 14.00–18.00 from April to October. During winter open for booked parties, receptions etc.

Queen's House, the first Palladian-style villa built in England, was designed by Inigo Jones and enlarged by Webb in 1662. It was built for James I's wife Queen Anne of Denmark (1616–35), begun in 1616 and completed in 1635, and faced the Placentia on one side and the park on the other; the main Dover Road went through the building. The Queen died before it was completed and it became the home of Henrietta Maria, Charles I's French wife, in 1635. After the Civil War, Charles II commissioned John Webb to enlarge the house; the road was diverted and the additions carefully matched Inigo Jones's original design. It was later used as a school and fully restored in the 1950s after wartime use by the Admiralty. It is now part of the National Maritime Museum.

From the Vaults the spiral Tulip Staircase, taking its name from the tulip motifs in the iron baluster, rises to the Great Hall—a perfect 40 foot cube occupying two floors of the building. It had a painted ceiling, reinstated with a photographic copy—the original is in Marlborough House. The floor is by Nicholas Stone. In the Orangery and ground floor galleries there are paintings by the De Veldes, father and son, invited to London from the Netherlands to record the great sea battles of Charles II and James II, and also paintings of Greenwich and a set of 17C navigational instruments made in ivory, the Barberini collection and 17C wall maps. Models of 17C ships are also on display. The brick-vaulted basement, open to the public for the first time, houses the Museum's Treasury of precious objects. The Royal apartments on the first floor have been returned to John Webb's 1660's arrangement of a Queen's and a King's side. Silk wallhangings, handwoven velvet cushioned furniture and 17C portraits and marine paintings recreate the period of Henrietta Maria with a replica of her bed in the Queen's bedroom and a portrait of her by Van Dyck.

National Maritime Museum, Romney Road, SE10. Tel. 081-858 4422. Open Mon to Sat 10.00–17.00, Sun 14.00–17.00 (winter); until 18.00 in summer; admission charge, includes Old Royal Observatory. Lecture theatre. Cafeteria.

The two museum buildings on either side of the Queen's House provide an unrivalled collection illustrating Britain's naval history. The E and W Wings were built after Trafalgar to the design of Daniel Alexander with flanking colonnades linking them to the Queen's House, then a school for seamen's children. In 1933 the school moved and the National Maritime Museum was established. The new Neptune Hall, a Victorian extension to the W Wing, was reopened in 1972 to illustrate the development of boat building. The main entrance is in the W Wing and here there is an information counter and shop. (There is another entrance to the E Wing from Park Vista.) The E Wing is used mainly for special exhibitions and also houses the lecture theatre.

The *W Wing* is on three floors; starting from top, i.e. the second floor, the displays here cover the Discoveries and Seapower from 1450 to 1700 and in a new display the Ship of War 1650–1815—an exhibition of models; stairs descend to the first floor and the *James Cook Gallery*, illustrating his explorations of the Pacific Ocean. 18C merchant trade and trade and communications lead to the French Revolutionary War and the *Nelson Galleries* with paintings, silver and relics. The most famous is the Vice-Admiral's undress uniform coat which he was wearing on 21 October 1805, showing the bullet hole in the left shoulder. The *Harrison Gallery* features Harrison's first chronometer and his other instruments.

On the ground floor is an exhibition of medals, the museum shop and bookshop, the library, open by appointment only, and the coffee shop. On the lower ground floor is the entrance to the *Neptune Hall* with a display of 19C merchant shipping artefacts and figureheads. Exhibits change regularly, but the hall contains the largest single collection of industrial maritime history including the complete fabric of the riveted steel steampaddle tug 'Reliant' built at South Shields in 1907; visitors can see the machinery in motion and walk through the stoke-hold, crew's forecastle and the master's cabin. This display on the mezzanine floor ends with the steam launch 'Donola', built in 1893. Another steam launch, 'Waterlily', and various engines complete the exhibits on steam. As a contrast to the cabins on the 'Reliant' visitors can enter a first-class cabin of a 1960s Atlantic liner.

Around the sides of the Hall there is a continuous display of the development of wooden boats from prehistoric times. Royal barges in the *Barge House* opened in 1978 include Prince Frederick's 18C barge. Under the 'Reliant' is a gallery devoted to the development of iron and steel shipbuilding.

The Yachting Gallery follows, covering aspects of the sport from the royal yachts of the 17C to the plastic yachts of today. Cargo and shipyards are covered in the basement gallery.

The National Maritime Museum stands at the edge of **Greenwich Park** which stretches up to the top of the hill and the Old Royal Observatory and beyond to Blackheath. This royal park was first enclosed by Humphrey, Duke of Gloucester, as a hunting ground in 1433. Today the park, with its steep topography, offers superb views of the Thames and is favoured by skateboarders, and in winter by tobogganers. During the last part of the 19C the park was the location for the increasingly unruly Greenwich Fairs, finally banned in 1870. There is a formal flower and water garden towards Blackheath and a 'wilderness' inhabited by a herd of 30 deer (not open to the public). Through the main gates on the Blackheath side thousands pour each May at the start of the London Marathon, first held in 1981. Refreshments are available during the summer and at weekends. The park was laid out by Sir William Boreman to a plan by André le Nôtre, commissioned by Charles II. The Versailles influence only remains in the southern section where an impressive chestnut avenue leads from Blackheath Gate to General Wolfe's statue by Tait Mackenzie (presented by the Canadian nation in 1930). The trunk of an oak survives where Henry VIII is said to have danced with Anne Boleyn, and where Queen Elizabeth picnicked as a child (250 yards SW of Maze Hill Gate). Near Queen Elizabeth's Bower (200 yards S of Maze Hill Gate) are the remains of a Roman Villa. On the side of the Park near Ranger's House are Ranger's Field, used for cricket matches, and the remains of Queen Caroline's Baths (W of Blackheath Gate). The statue of King William IV in the NW corner of the park came from King William St in the City. There is a Moore bronze sculpture, 'Standing Figure and Knife Edge' behind the tennis courts, NW corner.

The six buildings of the **Old Royal Observatory** are now part of the National Maritime Museum. The Royal Observatory moved to Herstmonceux Castle in Sussex in 1948 to benefit from less polluted and darker skies than those metropolitan London could provide but has since moved to the Canaries. The attractive outline of *Flamsteed House* with its Red Time Ball crowns the hill. The Red Time Ball was installed in 1833 to give a visual indication of the time to ships on the river; it still drops at 13.00 local time every day. The 24-hour clock by the gate is 120 years old and shows Greenwich Mean Time.

Old Royal Observatory, Greenwich Park, SE10. Tel. 081-858 1167. Opening hours as for National Maritime Museum. Admission charge (also for main Museum). Bookshop. Cafeteria in main Museum.
  Wren built Flamsteed House with 'a little pompe' for the first Royal Astronomer, Rev. John Flamsteed, appointed by Charles II in 1675; Astronomers Royal lived here until 1948. The rooms have now been restored to their appearance at the time of Flamsteed.

The *Octagon Room* was for general astronomical use, the *Sextant House* and *Meridian Building* were added in the mid 18C. They became the location for the most important work carried out here in the development of nautical astronomy. The Prime Meridian of the World established in 1884 traverses the Meridian Building.

Enter Flamsteed House across the courtyard, crossing the Meridian marked in the ground. The displays in the Octagon Room and adjoining galleries show the history of the nautical almanac and the measuring of longitude by observation of the moon, methods of finding time by the sun, moon and stars, and the history of the first instruments of navigation.

Flamsteed's living quarters have been authentically restored in their simplicity. The Meridian Building contains original instruments and replicas. The astrolabe collection in the Halley Gallery is one of the most important in the world; the Airy Transit Circle which defines the Prime Meridian of the World and Bradley's 12.5ft Zenith Sector with which he discovered the aberration of light and the mutation of the earth's axis are also on view. There is a bookshop.

The *South Building*, a planetarium, is used by school parties and there are public lectures during the school holidays. The striking onion dome of the Victorian *Great Equatorial Building* has been restored. This and the Altazimuth Pavilion are not open to the public.

On the E side of the Park in Maze Hill is *Vanbrugh Castle*, built in 1726 by Sir John Vanbrugh for himself, as Surveyor to the Royal Hospital, in a medieval style—now privately occupied. *Woodlands*, nearby at 90 Mycenae Road, was built in 1774 as a country house for John Julius Angerstein whose collection of paintings formed the basis for the National Gallery (buried in 1823 in St. Alfege Church). Woodlands (tel. 081-858 4631) is now a local history centre and art gallery, open 10.00–19.30 weekdays, 10.00–18.00 Sat, 14.00–18.00 Sun, closed Wed. Free.

Ranger's House in Chesterfield Walk on the W side of the Park houses the magnificent Suffolk Collection of family portraits by

William Larkin and others, famous for the details on costumes and furnishings, and musical instruments from the Dolmetsch Collection on the 1st floor. Recitals take place during the Greenwich Festival and in late summer and autumn. Ranger's House was built in the 1680s and later extended by the Earl of Chesterfield; it became the residence of the Ranger of Greenwich Park in 1814. In 1974 it was opened as an art gallery by the Greater London Council.

Ranger's House, Chesterfield Walk, SE10. Tel. 081-853 0035. Open daily 10.00–17.00 (Nov. to Jan. 10.00–16.00). Free.

Nearby in Croom's Hill is *Macartney House*, home of General Wolfe's parents, and some attractive 17 and 18C buildings along this winding road which leads down into central Greenwich.

The Fan Museum opens in Croom's Hill in 1990. The Fan Museum, 10-12 Croom's Hill, SE10. Tel. 081-305 1441. Open to pre-booked parties. Admission charge. The Museum shows a changing series of thematic exhibitions on the subject of fans through the ages with permanent exhibits on material from which fans are made. There is also a workshop.

The *Greenwich Theatre* (1969), Greenwich Church St tel. 081-858 7755, was built on the site of an old music hall. Opposite on a former car park, a new Ibis Hotel (100 rooms) opened in 1988. Adjoining is a multi-screen cinema. The Greenwich Antique Market (Sat and summer Sun 09.00—17.00) continues on part of the site. Bric-à-brac, genuine antiques, and second-hand books.

St. Alfege Church in the centre of Greenwich marks the spot where Alphege, Archbishop of Canterbury, was murdered by invading Danish Vikings in 1012. Henry VIII was baptised in the medieval church and Thomas Tallis, founder of English church music, was buried in the old church. The keyboard from the 16C organ is preserved in the nave of the new church designed by Hawksmoor and completed in 1714. It was restored after heavy war damage and is used for concerts during the Greenwich Festival as well as for regular services, although much work still remains to be done.

Greenwich had a traditional covered market in the centre; this is now closed and a craft market operates here on Sat and Sun. Along Greenwich High Road, near the station, are the Queen Elizabeth's Almshouses, the first to be founded after the Reformation, in 1576. The present buildings around an attractive courtyard were completed in 1819.

On the river-front, now known as *Cutty Sark Gardens*, the majestic 'Cutty Sark' rests in its own drydock. One of the last sailing clippers to make the voyage from China carrying tea, it was built in 1869 on the Clyde. The opening of the Suez Canal and the arrival of steam spelt the end for the sailing ships. The ship was rescued and restored and opened to the public in 1954. It now houses a fine collection of figureheads, and full-scale replicas of cabins of the period. Special exhibitions are held in the hold.

'Cutty Sark', Cutty Sark Gardens, SE10. Tel. 081-858 3445. Open Mon to Sat 10.00–18.00, Sun 12.00–18.00; winter until 17.00. Admission charge. Nearest BR station Maze Hill.

Cutty Sark Gardens also house 'Gipsy Moth IV', the yacht in which Sir Francis Chichester circumnavigated the world single-handed in 1968. It is open the same hours as the 'Cutty Sark'; admission charge.

The 'Cutty Sark', one of the last sailing clippers to make the voyage from China, built on the Clyde in 1869

The Gardens are used for open-air performances and art and crafts markets during the Greenwich Festival in June and the Greenwich Clipper Weeks in August. A bookboat is moored below the council estate to the W. There is a tourist information centre in Greenwich Church St. Tel. 081-858 6376.

The pedestrian tunnel completed in 1902 is 1200ft long with attractive domed entrances and solid Victorian lifts due to be replaced in 1990/91. The riverside walk past the pier towards the E provides good views of the Royal Naval College and the Park. From here the Court saluted Willoughby and Chancellor as they set off in search of the North-East Passage in 1553; Raleigh put down his cloak for Elizabeth I and was later arrested on his return from Guiana; and George I landed here from Holland on his way to claim the crown of the United Kingdom. Recently Prince Charles welcomed members of the Transglobe Expedition here (1983).

The *Trafalgar Tavern* (built 1837) has iron balconies resembling the inside of a man-of-war. It became famous for its whitebait dinners for the Government in Queen Victoria's reign; other famous customers included Dickens, Thackeray and George Cruickshank. It closed in 1915 and reopened, restored, in 1965.

Further along to E are the striking Trinity Alsmhouses, founded by Henry Howard, Earl of Northampton in 1613 and overlooking the Thames. 18 men were given their home here but according to the statutes should not include 'any idiot, nor any other that is not able to say, without book, the Lord's Prayer, the Creed and the Ten Commandments'. A passage beneath the clock tower, dwarfed by the nearby power station, leads to the courtyard with a fountain.

A regular river service by steamboat between Greenwich and Central London started in 1855; the railway link through Deptford was even earlier

making Greenwich as popular for Sunday outings among London's workers as i
is with tourists today.

Blackheath, S of Greenwich, is an attractive residential suburb with
claims of being S London's 'Hampstead'. The Roman Watling St
crossed Blackheath and both Roman and Saxon remains have been
found. During the Peasant's Revolt in 1381 Wat Tyler assembled his
supporters on the heath before proceeding towards London. It was the
scene of royal celebrations such as the welcome for Charles II in 1660,
and revivalist meetings in the 18C. The *Royal Blackheath Golf Club*
was the first in the country (founded 1608); the *Blackheath Rugby
Club* is also the oldest. But the heath had a bad reputation for highway
robberies until the late 18C.

Blackheath Village developed in the mid 19C with the arrival of the
railway and has retained its delightful, old-fashioned atmosphere.
Blackheath's intellectual reputation is based on educational institutions founded during the Victorian period; these include a conser-
vatoire of music and an art school. Blackheath Concert Halls are in
Lee Road, SE3.

Morden College, St. German's Place, SE3, was built in 1695 by
Wren with a colonnaded courtyard to house 'decayed Turkey Merchants who had fallen on hard times'. Sir John Morden, its benefactor,
was himself a 'Turkey merchant'. It continues today as a home for
elderly people. Nearby is *The Paragon*, a crescent of 14 semi-
detached villas linked by a single-storey colonnade, built by John
Cator and designed by Michael Searles who also designed Paragon
House and Colonnade House. The first tenants moved in around 1800
and it was not until earlier this century that the buildings started to
deteriorate as tenants added out-buildings. They were restored to
their original appearance after the Second World War.

Today the Heath is the venue for Bank Holiday fairs, football,
kite-flying and the start of the annual London Marathon in April or
May. The *Hare and Billet* (7A Elliot Cottages, SE3; formerly the
Harrow and Crooked Billet) is a 100-year-old village pub on the
heath.

To the S is Lee (in the London Borough of Lewisham, see p 303).

Deptford, W of Greenwich, a suburb based on the docks and
industries of the 19C, now in decline, started as a small fishing village
which rose to national importance when Henry VIII founded the Royal
Naval Dockyard here in 1573. The dockyard closed in 1869 and
became a foreign cattle market which survived until 1913. Sir Francis
Drake moored the 'Golden Hind' at the Dockyard in 1581 and
received his knighthood from Queen Elizabeth. Pepys recorded
regular visits in his diaries.

Adjoining it was the *Royal Victoria Victualling Yard*, established in
1742 and closed in 1961, now the site of the Pepys Housing Estate. A
colonnaded terrace and two handsome 18C rum warehouses with
arcaded ground floors have been restored for the *Pepys Library* and
Deptford Sailing Centre. At *Sayes Court* (now a small park) nothing
remains of the residence of John Evelyn (1620–1706) where Pepys
and Wren were entertained to dinner and where Wren was introduced to Grinling Gibbons, a local craftsman. Peter the Great was
Evelyn's guest in 1698 when working in the Royal Dock.

St. Nicholas, the old parish church of Deptford, stands just beyond
the busy High St. The 15C ragstone tower is surrounded by a
ed-brick building added in 1697 and restored after Second World

War damage. Grinling Gibbons' work can be viewed inside. Christopher Marlowe, the playwright, killed in a local tavern brawl in 1593, is buried here. *St. Paul's Church*, E of Deptford High St, is a perfect baroque building by Thomas Archer (1730), described by Sir John Betjeman as 'a pearl in the heart of Deptford'. It has giant Corinthian columns and a rich plaster ceiling, and houses a memorial to Dr Charles Burney, brother of Fanny Burney and a rector of Deptford. Workshops and flats have been built in the churchyard. In Albury St, the local authority has restored some 18C sea-captains' houses.

Deptford Market on Fridays and Saturdays (Douglas Way and the High St) is a lively S London event with some 250 stalls selling greengrocery, household goods, clothes and bric-à-brac.

The first London railway ran on arches between Deptford and Bermondsey in 1836 (extended to London Bridge in 1837). The Greenwich section added in 1838 involved building a bridge over the busy Deptford Creek (outlet of the Ravensbourne) with a drawbridge which took eight men to operate.

The *Albany Theatre*, Douglas Way, Deptford, SE8, Tel. 081-691 7223 is a multi-purpose arts centre and theatre in a new building opened by the Princess of Wales in 1982.

Between Deptford and Rotherhithe to the NW were the great Surrey Docks on a promontory of the River Thames. They were the only enclosed docks built on the S side of the river; the first were linked to various canals—the Croydon Canal and the Grand Surrey Canal—the first dock with a new lock was completed in 1860. The Greenland Dock covering 22 acres was operational from 1904 handling whale cargo and later softwood from Scandinavia. At Nelson Dock a Scandinavian hotel group, Scandic, is opening a 400-bedroom hotel and conference centre in 1991. Greenland Dock features award-winning housing and a marina at South Dock. The 300-acre Surrey Dock area was badly damaged in the Second World War and closed in 1970. As part of the regeneration of Docklands, see p 277, several of the docks have been filled in and the land used for housing and workshops; Associated Newspapers' printing plant opened here in 1989 and Surrey Quays shopping centre in 1988.

Rotherhithe, formerly *Redriffe*, was badly affected by the closure in 1970 of the Surrey Docks, but several Thames-side wharves and warehouses have been imaginatively restored for housing and workshops and further developments are under way.

Brunel's Engine House in Tunnel Road was built by Marc Brunel as part of the Thames Tunnel (1825–43), the first underwater tunnel in the world, which linked Rotherhithe with Wapping. The newly restored 1885 Rennie engine takes pride of place inside the small brick building which also houses an exhibition on the construction of the tunnelling, which cost many lives. However, Brunel's tunnelling shields had lasting impact on tunnel building in Britain and overseas. Brunel's Engine House is open Sundays, by appointment. Tel. 081-318 2489.

Brunel's *Thames Tunnel* was at first a foot tunnel but now forms part of the East London Underground line.

Nearby is *St. Mary's Parish Church* where the captain of the 'Mayflower', Christopher Jones, is buried. The church dates back to 1714; there are mast-like pillars inside and an organ by Byfield installed in 1764. Opposite is *Peter Hills School* (1797) with two attractively carved figures of pupils at the first floor level. Th

Mayflower pub, Rotherhithe St, overlooks the river and takes its
from the ship which sailed from the Thames to Portsmouth and t
Americas in 1620. There is a river-jetty and the pub is licensed to .
American and British postage stamps.

The *Hope Sufferance Wharf* by the river has been converted into craf
workshops and houses the London Glass-Blowing Workshop with daily
demonstrations. In the area are the *Finnish Seamen's Church*, the
Swedish Mission and the Norwegian church of *St. Olaf* which served
the sailors of the past and today's long distance lorry drivers (the A2 is
nearby). The *Prince of Orange* pub in Lower Road next to the Swedish
mission is a traditional jazz pub.

Woolwich, E of Greenwich (access: BR, Woolwich), is still dominated
by its naval and military past and famous for its football team, Arsenal
(which moved to Highbury, N London in 1913 in search of more space),
and the Woolwich Building Society founded after the Second World
War on the savings of the munition workers. Henry VIII established the
Dockyard here in 1513 (as at Deptford) to build the 'Great Harry', the
fleet's flagship, and later the 'Sovereign of the Seas', designed by
Phineas Pett and his son Peter in 1637 (both buried at Deptford). The
Dockyard closed in 1869; subsequently part of it was used by the Royal
Arsenal Co-operative Society, and for housing. Two of the dry-docks
have become swimming pools. The **Woolwich Arsenal** dates from
1716; after an explosion at Moorfields an out-of-London site was
essential. 40,000 workers were employed here during the Second
World War; the Arsenal closed from 1963. The main entrance by Sir
John Vanbrugh is in Beresford Square and the 1829 gateway survives.
The Brass Foundry (1717) is now used by the National Maritime
Museum and the Grand Store (built 1806–13) is used by the British
Library. Plans are being made for redevelopment.

Woolwich Market received its first Royal Charter in the 13C; today it
thrives in Beresford Square, in the shadow of the Arsenal gates
(Monday to Saturday), having abandoned Market Hill in the middle of
the 19C. Greengrocery, fresh fish and household goods are on sale with
cheap clothes in the nearby, covered market in Plumstead Road.
Woolwich was the home of Britain's first McDonald's restaurant in
Powis St in 1974. Nearby the former Granada cinema, now a bingo club,
has a Venetian Gothic interior of 1937. The *Tram Shed* (1908) at 51
Woolwich New Road was an electricity sub-station for London's
electric tramways and has been used as a theatre and music venue since
1973. The Waterfront Leisure Centre opened in the High St in 1988 with
a tropical pool complex and water features. Tel. 081-316 6600.

The **Thames Barrier** off Woolwich Road, crossing the Thames, was
completed in 1983 and officially opened by HM The Queen in May
1984. It is the largest moving flood barrier in the world with eight
gigantic piers which allow shipping to pass unhindered up and down
the river. The floodgates lie on the river-bed and take from one to three
hours to rise 65ft to protect London from flooding during a high winter
tide. In the *Barrier Centre*, a dramatic audio-visual presentation and
working models illustrate the history of the river and the threat of
flooding. There is a cafeteria. A walkway along the river gives good
views of the spectacular barrier and there are boat tours from the Barrier
Pier.

Thames Barrier, Unity Way, off Woolwich Road, SE18. Tel. 081-854 1373 Open
Mon to Fri 10.30–17.00, Sat, Sun 10.30–17.30. Admission charge. Access: BR to
Charlton or Woolwich Dockyard, then bus. Or by river from Westminster Pier
direct or via Greenwich. Buses from Greenwich.

The Thames Barrier, completed in 1983

The *Woolwich Free Ferry*, 1 mile further downstream (continue E along Woolwich Rd and Woolwich Church St to the A205 roundabout; the ferry pier is to the left), linking the S and N banks of the Thames, was probably established as a ferry crossing in the 15C. The present ferry service dates from 1889. The E London crossing, a new bridge across the Thames, will be built to link Woolwich and Newham and relieve the Dartford Tunnel.

The *Royal Military Academy* was founded in Woolwich Arsenal in 1721 but moved S to Woolwich Common in 1808. There are two museums of artillery, both worth exploring, the *Royal Artillery Museum* and the *Rotunda Museum of Artillery*.

The Royal Artillery Museum, Royal Military Academy, Woolwich Common, Academy Road, SE18. Tel. 081-854 2242. Open Mon to Fri 12.30-16.30, Sat & Sun 14.00-17.00 (until 16.00 winter). Free. Access: BR, Woolwich Arsenal, then bus 122/161.

The striking yellow brick Royal Military Academy was designed by James Wyatt; the central block was inspired by the White Tower. The Royal Military College at Sandhurst and the Academy were amalgamated in 1945. The Museum tells the history of the regiment of the Royal Artillery, with paintings by war artists and personal relics.

On the N side of the Common stands another impressive building, the *Royal Artillery Barracks* (not open to the public) completed in 1802 and featuring a triumphal arch and a frontage of 1000ft with a vast parade ground. Nearby is the *Museum of Artillery in the Rotunda* in Repository Road, SE18. Tel. 081-316 5402. Open weekdays 12.00–16.00, Sat, Sun 13.00–17.00 (winter until 16.00). Free. Access: BR, Woolwich Arsenal then bus 53, 54 or 75.

The Rotunda started its days as a pavilion in St. James's Park in 1814 and was removed here in 1819. Nash converted it into a permanent building with a striking concave copper roof. It contains the Royal Artillery's collection of guns. In the courtyard there are large tanks and armoured vehicles.

Charlton House, Hornfair Road, SE7 in the village of *Charlton* between Woolwich and Blackheath (1.5m SW of Woolwich Town Centre) is a Jacobean mansion completed in 1612 and now used as a community centre and library (open Mon to Fri 09.00–17.00. Tel. 081-856 3951 for other times; BR, Charlton). In red brick, with white stone balustrades, it is beautifully set against well-used grounds. In the village the *Bugle Inn* is at least as old and *St. Luke's* church dates back to 1630. It contains a bust by Chantrey of Spencer Perceval, the Prime Minister assassinated in 1812.

Charlton Athletic Football Club is returning to its Valley ground in Charlton in 1991 after two disappointing years sharing Crystal Palace F.C. ground in Norwood.

Greenwich Borough Museum in Plumstead Library, 232 Plumstead High St, SE18, contains local archaeological finds and sections on local history. The area is dominated by modest terraced housing of the late 19C and early 20C designed to meet the needs of the industrial and dock workers of the area.

Towards Belvedere, 3 miles E of Woolwich, the ruins of *Lesnes Abbey* are set into the hillside off Abbey Road with Abbey Woods beyond, overlooking the river and the huge new town of *Thamesmead*. The founder of the Abbey, Richard de Luci, dedicated it to Our Lady and St. Thomas Becket in 1178; the monastery was suppressed and dissolved in 1525. For a time the site was administered by Christ's Hospital but the old London County Council took it over in 1930 and excavations were carried out in 1951. The walls of the building with its refectory, cloisters and chapel are well preserved and include a doorway and some windows—all remain in the open air.

Basic refreshments are available in the attractively laid out park and Abbey Woods beyond is famous for its display of daffodils in spring.

Bexley (London Borough of Bexley) is 6 miles SE of Blackheath along the A2. Its mainly rural environs were sprinkled with a few mansions before suburban development got under way in the early part of this century. Recent developments include an impressive new shopping centre with indoor marbled malls at Bexleyheath Broadway, and Crook Log Sports Centre in Brampton Road, Bexleyheath.

Just a stone's throw from a huge roundabout and flyover system (1.5 miles SE of Bexleyheath Town Centre) carrying local traffic, above the busy A2, stands 16C **Hall Place**. (Approach along the A220 from Bexleyheath.)

Hall Place, Bourne Road, Bexley. Tel. 081-303 7777. Open Mon to Sat 10.00–17.00 (or dusk if earlier), Sun 14.00–18.00 (March–October). Free. Refreshments near car park.

The building is in two parts, local flint stone and red brick, and now belongs to the London Borough of Bexley. It is used for local exhibitions and the rooms have been restored. The garden features the traditional topiary work of the period, depicting coats of arms; there is a herb garden and cottage garden and formal rose plantation. A river meanders through the park. Hall Place was the family home of Sir John Champneys, Lord Mayor of London in 1534. Stone from local monasteries was used to build it. The Great Hall features a minstrel gallery, and the organ from nearby Danson Park is now housed here.

In Bexley High St (half a mile S along the A223, Bourne Rd) is 13C *St. Mary the Virgin*—the local parish church which retains its typical

Kentish shingled spire. Inside, monuments commemorate local families including the Champneys of Hall Place, William Camden, Henry Castilayn, and Thomas Sparrow, alias Lamendby (died 1513). John Styleman of Danson (died 1734), who endowed the almshouses still in the High St, is remembered by a large pyramid memorial. The 18C lychgate is in the SE corner of the churchyard.

Bexley Village retains many old buildings.

Two miles SW of Bexleyheath, *St. Paulinus* at **Crayford** is noted for its 12C Perpendicular style and important monuments. Amongst them are two life-sized alabaster figures of William Draper (died 1650) and his wife Mary (died 1652), surrounded by their children. This is an industrial area and *David Evans*, silk-printers, welcomes visitors to its silk printing plant and small museum. Tel. 0322 57526.

In **Bexleyheath** (half a mile SW of town centre) the **Red House** in Red House Lane (off Upton Road) reveals further aspects of William Morris, who also lived in Waltham Forest and Hammersmith. Here in 1860 he had built a Gothic L-shaped two-storey house which created a sensation with its medieval steep tiled roof and use of red bricks both outside and inside. Morris lived here for only five years but the original decorations have been retained by subsequent owners. Write to the Red House, Red House Lane, Bexleyheath, Kent, enclosing a stamped, addressed envelope to arrange a visit on the first weekend of each month. Admission charge.

Danson Park (1762) (1 mile W along the A207 from Bexleyheath town centre) stands on a hilltop in grounds laid out by Capability Brown and now a public park; access from the A207 into Danson Road. This elegant villa has stood empty for more than ten years in the care of the London Borough of Bexley. It is now in commercial use.

At *Avery Hill Park* (BR, Eltham) (3 miles SE of Blackheath and 1 mile E of Eltham) there is an outstanding collection of tropical and temperate plants in the Winter Garden conservatory, a collection second only to that of Kew. The Winter Gardens are open Mon to Fri 13.00–16.00, weekends 11.00–16.00 (18.00 in summer); free. A teacher training college occupies part of the grounds.

Eltham (2 miles SE of Blackheath and on the A210), a busy suburb, has retained some interesting buildings at the W end of the High St including *Cliefden House* (18C) with stable block and orangery, and the *Greyhound* pub with fireplaces removed from Eltham Palace. The *Bob Hope Theatre*, Wythfield Road, Eltham, SE9, was inaugurated by the 'local boy' himself in 1982. Court Yard just off the High St leads to **Eltham Palace**; although only open two days a week this medieval palace adds an interesting dimension to England's history. A 15C stone bridge leads over a moat to the courtyard and the Great Hall, the only remaining complete building. It is 100ft long and features a restored minstrel's gallery and oriel windows decorated with coats of arms. The magnificent hammer-beam roof is the third largest in England. The Palace and surrounding grounds are leased by the Crown to the army and the great Hall is frequently used for important banquets.

Eltham Palace, Court Yard, SE9. Tel. 081-854 2242 ext. 4232. Check opening hours. Open Thur and Sun 11.00–16.00 (winter), 11.00–19.00 (summer). Access: BR, Eltham. Free.

Eltham Palace's royal history dates back to 1300 when it was presented to Edward II by the Bishop of Durham. Edward III received the captive John II here and established the Order of the Garter during a tournament. Geoffrey Chaucer was Clerk of Works under Richard II. Henry VI added further buildings to create an outer and inner courtyard; some of the half-timbered houses of the former still survive outside the gate. The Great Hall was rebuilt in 1479. The Palace was not used after Cromwell and the Great Hall became a barn until it was restored in 1933 by Samuel Courtauld. Excavations in the grounds have exposed the W wall of the Palace.

Well Hall Road leads N from Eltham High St half a mile to *Well Hall Pleasaunce*, a small local park, formerly the grounds of Well Hall mansion (demolished 1931). (Access: BR, Eltham). The *Tudor Barn* survives as an art gallery and restaurant. Well Hall was the home of William Roper who married Sir Thomas More's daughter Margaret in 1521. The Barn, built c 1550, has a small stained-glass window featuring Margaret Roper.

36 Dulwich, Forest Hill, Sydenham, Norwood, Streatham, Wandsworth, Battersea, Brixton, Kennington, Camberwell, Peckham, Lewisham

Dulwich Village (nearest BR station West Dulwich) has a recorded history going back to 967 when King Edgar granted the manor to one of his followers; later it belonged to Bermondsey Abbey before the land was purchased by Edward Alleyn, the actor manager, in 1605. Alleyn founded **Dulwich College** (c 400 yards E from West Dulwich Station along the A205) partly as a school for the poor and partly as almshouses which are still in use. The *Old College Building* (N) in College Road is now the offices of the trust which administers Dulwich College, Alleyn's School and James Allen's Girls School. The new Dulwich College (S of A205 in College Road), designed by Charles Barry (son of the architect of the Houses of Parliament) in an ornate Italian style in 1842 with extensions in 1870, includes a *Chapel* in which Alleyn is buried; 800 pupils give thanks to him here daily. Famous former pupils include Raymond Chandler and P.G. Wodehouse. The College has suspended its right to collect the toll from cars using the privately-owned College Road alongside, the only toll-road remaining in the London area.

The **Dulwich College Picture Gallery** is next to the Old College Building in College Rd. The collection of outstanding Dutch Masters was bequeathed to the college at the beginning of the 19C. They belonged to Noel Desenfans, a French picture dealer who left them to his friend Sir Francis Bourgeois, who in turn left them to the College. Sir John Soane was commissioned to design the gallery, the first public art gallery in Britain, which also contains a mausoleum for its founders; it opened in 1817. Recent restoration work highlights the symmetry and beauty of this simple dome-topped building. The collection has been in the news as a result of several break-ins and most recently (in 1983) thieves removed Rembrandt's 'Jacob III de Gheyn'. This was returned in 1986.

Dulwich Picture Gallery, College Road, SE21. Tel. 081-693 5254. Open Tues to Fri 10.00–13.00, 14.00–17.00, Sat 11.00–17.00, Sun 14.00–17.00, closed Mon. Admission charge. Access: BR, West Dulwich.

Three hundred paintings are on view; particularly well represented is the 17C, with superb works by Claude, Cuyp, Hobbema, Murillo, Rembrandt, Reni, Rubens and Van Dyck. Highlights include: in Room I Gainsborough's portraits of the Linley family. In Room II Van Dyck's 'Madonna and Child'; 'Samson and Delilah' attributed to Rubens. In Room III Van Dyck's 'Lady Digby on her

..eathbed', painted two days after her death; Murillo's 'Flower Girl'. In Room IV, the two Veroneses, one a fragment of an altarpiece. In Room VI a notable group of works by Cùyp; in the centre is the Mausoleum with the tombs of Bourgeois (centre), Desenfans (right) and Mrs Desenfans (left) with busts. In Room VIII works by Rubens. Room IX, mainly 18C British portraits, followed by 17C portraits in Room X. In Room XI 17C Dutch pictures include 'Jacob's Dream', attributed to Rembrandt until 1914 but actually by De Gelder; Rembrandt's 'Girl leaning on a window-sill'. Room XII, Poussin's 'Return of the Holy Family from Egypt'.

Dulwich Park opposite the Picture Gallery covers 72 acres and is particularly noted for its fine displays of azaleas and rhododendrons in the spring. Charles I hunted in Dulwich Woods and Common, the remains of which are on the other side of the South Circular Road. Highway robberies and duels were common in the 18C. Dulwich Wells on the corner of Dulwich Common and Lordship Lane was a spa for a short time; only the *Grove Tavern* now marks the spot. Margaret Thatcher owns a house in a new development off Dulwich Common overlooking Dulwich and Sydenham Golf Course.

Dulwich Village has attractive cottages dating back to the 18C and a fine Victorian pub, *The Crown and Greyhound*; in its predecessor Dickens used to drink as a member of the Dulwich Club. There is a local art gallery and community centre at Belair, Gallery Road, SE21, a fine early 18C villa by Richard Shaw. Dulwich or Sydenham Hill Wood to the S, enter from Crescent Wood Road, is a remnant of ancient woodland providing sanctuary for birds and other wildlife.

Forest Hill (1.5 miles E of Dulwich Village) attracted many German exiles in the 19C and there is a new German church (1959), *Dietrich Bonhoeffer Church* in Dacres Road, off Perry Vale, half a mile S of Forest Hill Station.

The *Horniman Museum and Gardens* is at 100 London Road, SE23.Tel. 081-699 1872. Access: BR, Forest Hill. Open Mon to Sat 10.30–18.00, Sun 14.00–18.00. Library, Cafeteria. Free.

The striking art nouveau museum with a tall clock tower on the crown of the hill was designed by Harrison Townsend and opened in 1901. The mosaic on the façade is by Anning Bell. The park beyond features a sunken garden, rose and water gardens and has animal and bird enclosures as well as a wonderful view towards Central London. A carved totem pole was erected in the gardens in 1985 and a Victorian conservatory was added in 1989.

The collection was started by Frederick John Horniman, the tea merchant, and opened to the public at first in his own home, Surrey House, Forest Hill. He financed the building of the museum and gave it in trust to the benefit of Londoners; it was administered by the Inner London Education Authority, and from 1990 became an independent charitable trust. The museum features natural history including many stuffed birds, an ethnographic collection and a small section on the history of stimulants; a collection of 5000 musical instruments was presented to the museum in 1947 (some are now in Ranger's House, Blackheath) and sound tape tours of the instruments being played are available for hire. The education department arranges special programmes for children and there is a cafeteria.

The once quiet village of **Sydenham** was a spa—the health-giving water now flows in pools and streams in Sydenham Wells Park—but came to national attention when the Crystal Palace was moved to Sydenham Hill in 1854 after the Great Exhibition of 1851. Thousands of Londoners travelled to Crystal Palace's huge, newly built railway station to visit the new 'entertainment' centre. Many settled in big houses in the area of Sydenham and Norwood. By the time the Crystal Palace was destroyed by fire on 30 November 1936 the area was already in decline. It is now a tightly built-up suburb.

Crystal Palace Park and National Sports Stadium, Thicket Road, SE20. Tel. 081-778 7148 (Park), 081-778 0131 (Sports Centre). Access:

BR, Crystal Palace. Car park, cafeteria (March to October). Adjoining the car park the foundations of the Crystal Palace still remain. The huge glass and iron building designed by Sir Joseph Paxton was 1600ft long with aisles and two transepts. The 282ft-high water towers at either end survived the fire but were removed in 1940.

The 100-acre Crystal Palace Park is managed by the London Borough of Bromley and includes a boating lake and, on a series of artificial islands, models of huge prehistoric monsters designed by Waterhouse Hawkins in 1854; a black gorilla was added in 1961. A huge bust of Sir Joseph Paxton by W.F. Woodington (1869) stands on a red brick plinth below the site of the original palace. The Crystal Palace Museum is located in the last surviving building of the original Palace with displays on its history. Open Sat, Sun 1400-1700 (tel. 081-778 2173). A television transmitting mast crowns the hill; below is the National Sports Centre built between 1956 and 1964 and featuring an Olympic-size indoor swimming pool, a sports stadium with athletic track and a ski-training slope. Squash, badminton and other sports are also played here (membership fee). The concert bowl in the grounds is used for pop and symphony concerts during the summer. Planning permission has been granted for a 150-bed hotel and conference centre modelled on the old palace to be built on the site.

Norwood, to the S, once the haunt of highwaymen, including Dick Turpin, is now a closely built-up suburban area where the peace is more likely to be broken by football fans attending Crystal Palace Football Club home matches; the ground is at Selhurst Park, Whitehorse Lane, South Norwood (access: BR, South Norwood). Charlton F.C. shared this ground for two years but returns to the Valley in 1991.

The area enjoyed a period of fame in the 19C first as a spa based on the springs at Beulah Hill (the spa opened in 1831) and later with the arrival of Crystal Palace as a fashionable residential area; inns and hotels followed. Well-known residents included Madame Tussaud and (for a short time) Camille Pissarro who painted the Palace and South Norwood Station. Sir Arthur Conan Doyle lived and wrote some Sherlock Holmes stories at 12 Tennison Road, South Norwood, SE25, from 1891–94. Norwood today is a slightly neglected area overshadowed by the thriving commercial centre of Croydon to the S.

In Norwood High St, opposite the Greek Revival church of St. Luke's, are the impressive iron gates of Norwood or the South Metropolitan Cemetery, next to Highgate and Kensal Rise the most famous and still the most interesting in London. Founded in 1837, the main buildings were designed by Sir William Tite, but have now been mostly lost. However, the monuments survive despite past neglect and vandalism and include granite plinths, Gothic mausoleums and particularly in the Greek part an outstanding number of monuments. There is a large German section too based on the German community at Forest Hill, see above. The cemetery is now in the care of the London Borough of Lambeth. Among those buried there are a number of architects and engineers includings Sir Horace Jones (died 1887), Sir William Cubitt (died 1861) and builders Thomas Cubitt (died 1855) and William Colls (died 1893), as well as Mrs Isabella Beeton (died 1865), household and cook-book author.

Streatham, 2.5 miles W of Crystal Palace, also enjoyed short-lived prosperity at the end of the 18C as a spa, based on a spring on Streatham Common. But its growth depended more on its convenient location on the main road between Central London and Croydon; City merchants built villas here in the 18th and 19th centuries. At Streatham Park overlooking Tooting Bec Common, the Thrales acquired a large estate; between 1766 and 1782 Dr Samuel Johnson spent much time with them writing in the summer house, which is now at Kenwood. Other regular guests included Burke, Garrick, Fanny Burney and Joshua Reynolds. The house was demolished in 1863 and the grounds are now covered by a housing estate.

Streatham is now a busy suburb with good entertainment facilities, including *Streatham Ice Rink*, 386 Streatham High Road, SW16 (tel. 081-769 7861; access: BR, Streatham, Streatham Common). The *Leigham Arms*, Wellfield Road, Streatham, has 16C origins and a cobbled cellar.

Tooting, 1 mile S of Streatham, has two adjacent commons, *Tooting Bec* (150 acres) and the smaller *Tooting Graveney* (half a mile W in Upper Tooting) in a residential suburban setting. St. George's Hospital moved to Blackshaw Rd, Tooting, SW17 from Hyde Park Corner in 1980. *Tooting Bec Lido* at Tooting Bec Road, SW16 (tel. 081-871 7198) is London's largest open-air swimming pool (access: Underground, Tooting Bec).

Thomas Hardy lived at 172 Trinity Road, SW17 (1878–81) and the Scottish music hall star Sir Harry Lauder lived at 46 Longley Road, SW17 from 1903–11. Daniel Defoe's supposed residence in the area (see Wandsworth) is commemorated in the *Defoe Chapel* in Tooting High St (1766), now a betting shop.

Wandsworth, 2 miles NW of Tooting, was London's first industrial area. It was based on the Wandle river and boosted in the 18C by the arrival of Huguenot refugees, when the Wandle supported some 65 watermills between Wandsworth and Merton to the S. Local industries included bleaching and dyeing, iron and copperware and brewing which still continues at the large Young's brewery. Wealthy industrialists built large villas around Wandsworth Common. Today this is mainly a residential suburb with some recent landscaping by the council of the industrial wasteland. The history of the area can be explored at the new Wandsworth Museum, Disraeli Road, Putney, SW15, tel. 081-871 7074, open Mon to Wed, Fri to Sat, 13.00–17.00, Free. On show are old maps, paintings and photographs as well as objects from local collections.

A British Olympic Museum is planned for 1 Wandsworth Plain, SW18, tel. 081-871 2677, with Olympic memorabilia and archives on display.

King George V Park is the setting for the annual Wandsworth weekend in July. At *Book House*, 45 East Hill, SW18 (tel. 081-870 9055), the National Book League holds regular exhibitions and runs a reference library. Oscar Wilde was a prisoner for six months at *Wandsworth Prison* in Heathfield Road, SW18, which dates from 1851 as 'a house of correction'. Ronald Biggs, the train robber, staged a spectacular escape from the prison in 1965.

Daniel Defoe, Thackeray and Voltaire all lived in Wandsworth for a time as did John Wesley. David Lloyd George settled at 3 Routh Road, SW18 from 1904, when he first came to London, to 1908.

Clapham. **Clapham Common** (2 miles E of Wandsworth, 1 mile S of Battersea) (access: Underground, Clapham Common) covers 220 acres; around its perimeter are some of the most attractive private houses in London dating back to the late 18th and early 19th centuries when Clapham was 'a pretty suburb', according to Thackeray.

Samuel Pepys lived at the North Side of the Common, until his death in 1703, in a mansion demolished in 1754. On the site now stands *The Elms*, where Charles Barry lived and died in 1860, and *Gilmore House*, built in 1760 with busts of Shakespeare and Milton in niches on it façade. The Clapham Sect met here in the 19C. William Wilberforce lived in Broomwood which stood at the corner of Broomwood Road, and Henry Cavendish, philosopher, lived in Cavendish House, on the corner of Cavendish Road. Captain Cook is said to have lived at No. 22 North Side for a time and used the balcony on the third floor.

, Clapham developed rapidly in the late 19C with terraced housing built to meet the demands for cheaper accommodation. Recently, Clapham Common has once again become a fashionable residential area. On Clapham Common there are fairs and a horse show on August Bank Holiday Weekend. At 80b The Chase, SW4, a Soseki Museum established in a private house where Japanese novelist Soseki Natsume lived is open Wed and Sat 10.00–12.00 and 14.00–17.00, Sun 14.00–17.00. Free. (Access: Underground, Clapham Common.)

Clapham Junction, once the busiest railway junction in the world with 2500 trains a day, is still important. A memorial stone in Spencer Park, SW18 commemorates 35 people killed in the Clapham rail disaster in 1988. Nearby in St. John's Hill, SW11 is *Clapham Junction Market* (access: BR, Clapham Junction) on Fridays and Saturdays with new clothes and household goods. At Northcote Road, SW11, another popular market concentrates on fruit and vegetables in a road with many ethnic grocers reflecting the cosmopolitan mix of this part of London.

Battersea (1 mile N of Clapham Common, half a mile S of Battersea Bridge), on the Thames, is an ancient settlement as indicated by the recovery in 1857 of the Iron-Age Battersea Shield now in the British Museum; today its famous landmarks *Battersea Power Station* and *Battersea Park* overshadow the suburban area beyond.

In Old Battersea on the river stands *St. Mary's Church* in Battersea Church Road, SW11, built in 1777, on the foundations of an 11C church, in dark red brick with classical details. The E window has 17C heraldic glass and there are monuments from the earlier church and church bells from the 17C. J.M.W. Turner was inspired to paint his Thames sunset by the view from the church window and the poet William Blake married the daughter of a local market gardener here in 1792. The first *Battersea Bridge* was built in the 18C; the present bridge was built by Bazalgette in 1890 and replaced the wooden structure depicted in many paintings.

Before becoming an industrial area based on the Nine Elms railway yard, Battersea served as a market garden for London. The local manor house stood next to the church and is now demolished. But *Old Battersea House* in Vicarage Crescent, SW11, 200 yards from the church, built in the style of Wren, survives and houses the William de Morgan collection of paintings and ceramics. The house is open by arrangement; write to the De Morgan Trust, 21 St. Margaret's Crescent, SW15 6HL. It has been renovated by the London Borough of Wandsworth. The *Vicarage* and *Devonshire House* are also attractive 18C houses.

Battersea Arts Centre in Lavender Hill, opened in 1981 in the former Town Hall; it includes a modern purpose-built dance studio. Half a mile to the N along Latchmere Rd is the *Latchmere Leisure Centre* (tel. 081-871 7470).

Battersea Park, Battersea Park Road, SW11 (access: BR, Battersea Park or Underground to Sloane Square then bus 19 or 137) was laid out and opened in 1853 on the once notorious Battersea Fields where the Duke of Wellington fought a duel with Lord Winchilsea in 1829 and here the rough-necks of London used to go for illicit trading, shooting and entertainment, travelling by boat from London. The park lake was excavated in 1864 and the park was further improved as part of the Festival of Britain in 1951 with the addition of sports and entertainment facilities including a funfair which closed in 1975 when it became unsafe. There is a *Children's Zoo* (summer), an annual Easter Parade and many other events. The former owners, the GLC erected a Japanese Peace Pagoda here in 1985. The park is now managed by the London Borough of Wandsworth.

Battersea Power Station, a listed building, opened in 1933 to general public disapproval because of the fears of pollution as well as its gigantic size. Dubbed 'A Temple of Power', it was designed by Sir Giles Scott, architect of Liverpool's Anglican Cathedral, and phased out in the '70s. The four fluted chimneys are 335ft high and the interior could hold a 22-storey building. It was destined to become a leisure and entertainment centre but its future is now uncertain.

In Queenstown Rd is the dramatic Marco Polo building by Ian Pollard and Peter Argyrou Ass. opened in 1988. The S part houses 'The Observer' newspaper. Nearby in Ingate Place, SW8, the Fulham Pottery, Britain's oldest still working pottery, founded in 1672 in the New King's Road, across the River, is now established in a former warehouse.

At the former railway yard at *Nine Elms*, Battersea, is the new *Covent Garden Market* which moved here from Central London in 1974. This is a wholesale fruit and vegetable market and visits are by appointment only (tel. 071-720 2211). The *Dogs' Home*, Battersea, moved to Battersea Park Road, SW8 in 1871. It takes in both stray dogs and cats and finds new homes for them.

Brixton, to the N of Streatham, was a fashionable residential area in the 19C. Large villas along Brixton Hill and in Angell Town were built for City merchants in the late 18C but the arrival of the railway brought cheaper housing in densely built terraces. These proved ideal cheap rented accommodation for the large influx of Commonwealth immigrants in the 1950s and '60s. In between, Brixton had established itself as an important shopping centre for S London; Electric Avenue was one of the first city streets with electricity when it opened in 1888. The Ritzy cinema built in 1910 still survives. Large housing estates have replaced some of the older housing and the area's character is set by the large West Indian community, many now second and third generation families.

Brixton Market (Mon to Sat) in Electric Avenue, Pope's Road, and Brixton Station Road, SW9 (access: BR, Brixton, Underground, Brixton) started in the 1880s and now sells clothes, fruit, vegetables, fish, household goods and bric-a-brac.

Brixton Windmill in Blenheim Gardens, off Brixton Road, was built in 1816 and was in use until 1934 as a flour-mill. It has been restored by the council and surrounded by a small park.

Next to Brixton Station is the *Brixton Recreation Centre*, a new and impressive complex opened in 1985. It has a swimming pool and other facilities. *Brixton Prison* (1820) is in Jebb Avenue, SW2, off Brixton Hill. It once housed a treadmill. Van Gogh stayed in Brixton in 1872 at the age of 19.

Kennington. *Kennington Common* saw the assembly of the Chartists in 1848, quietly dispersed by the police as directed by the Duke of Wellington. Now a public park, it was used as a fairground but was

also Surrey's execution ground. *St. Mark's Church* stands on the s.
the gallows; the last execution was in the early 19C. The park lodge
the N side of the park is the Prince Consort's model house designed ,
the Great Exhibition by Henry Roberts and transferred here in 185'.

At 278 Kennington Road, Charlie Chaplin was born in 1889.
Attractive terraced houses of the 18th and early 19th centuries survive
in Kennington Park Road, Cleaver Square and Kennington Road. The
Surrey Cricket Club was established at *The Oval Cricket Ground*
(nearest Underground Oval) in 1845. It is surrounded by council flats
and new stands are under development.

Camberwell. *Camberwell Green* was once the site of fairs which
rivalled the popular events at Greenwich but these were stopped in
1855. Today it is a mere traffic island in a busy but neglected part of
London. Some impression of Camberwell's more fashionable past can
be glimpsed in *Camberwell Grove* where Joseph Chamberlain was
born (at No. 188) in one of the pleasant Georgian houses in 1836. Robert
Browning was born at nearby No. 179 Southampton Way in 1812. In
Meeting House Lane, running N from Peckham High St, stood the
Meeting House used by William Penn before his imprisonment in the
Tower in 1668. The parish church of *St. Giles* in Church St was built in
1844 by George Gilbert Scott on the site of an older church destroyed by
fire. The E window glass was designed by John Ruskin who lived
nearby at Herne Hill.

Camberwell School of Arts and Crafts was established in 1896 and
enjoys a high reputation. It is next to the *South London Art Gallery*
opened in 1891 with funds from Passmore Edwards.

South London Art Gallery, Peckham Road, SE3. Tel. 071-703 6120. Open during
exhibitions Tues to Sat 10.00–13.00, 14.00–18.00, Sun 15.00–18.00. Free. Access:
Underground, Elephant and Castle, then bus 12, 36.
    The gallery presents temporary exhibitions including those of the students as
well as displays from the permanent collection of 19th and 20th century British art.

At **Walworth** to the NE is the *Cuming Museum* on the first floor of the
Newington District Library, Walworth Road, SE17. Tel. 071-701 1342.
Open Thur to Sat 10.00–17.00. Free. The museum has a collection of
archaeological finds from Southwark, George Tinworth's Shake-
speare Monument and a photographic record of Dickens' Southwark.
The Tudor-style red-brick building is matched by the adjoining *Town
Hall* in Gothic style—both of Victorian origin. The headquarters of the
British Labour Party is at 150 Walworth Road.

St. Peter's Church in Liverpool Grove, SE17 (a turning E of Walworth
Road), was designed in 1825 by Sir John Soane; a few terraces of older
houses survive here in a sea of modern council housing. The great
attraction of Walworth is *East St*, a large 100-year-old market, with 250
stalls from Walworth Rd to Flint St. (Access: Underground, Elephant &
Castle, walk or bus down Walworth Rd.) The market is open on
Tuesdays to Saturdays for greengrocery, clothes, and household goods
and on Sunday mornings also for plants. This is S London's answer to
Petticoat Lane with a friendly atmosphere.

South of Albany St, stretching from the Walworth Rd to the Old Kent
Rd is *Burgess Park*, an imaginative development undertaken by the
former GLC in a heavily built-up area to create a park and leisure
facilities for local residents. Already there is a lake (with fishing),
football pitches and a nature centre. The park will eventually cover 135
acres, most of it reclaimed from industrial use but also from run-down
housing.

Denmark Hill (running S from Camberwell Green) are *King's College Hospital* (1913) and the *Maudsley Hospital* (1915); in Chamn Park is the *William Booth Memorial Training College*, designed by r Giles Gilbert Scott in 1932 with statues of the Salvation Army's ounders General and Mrs Booth, outside. John Ruskin lived at 28 Herne Hill, the continuation of Denmark Hill, and at 163 Denmark Hill; both houses have gone but he is remembered in *Ruskin Park*. Part of British Rail's *Denmark Hill Station* has been converted into a pub in the 'Firkin' brew-pub chain.

Peckham. The many thousands who rush down the A2 in cars to and from Dover hardly notice their historic surroundings as they pass along the now rather dingy Old Kent Road, formerly the Roman Watling St. This was the route taken by Chaucer's Canterbury Pilgrims who halted at 'St. Thomas a Watering', now a Victorian pub, the *Thomas a Becket*, at 320 Old Kent Road, SE1, with a boxing theme and museum housing some 1000 exhibits (access: Underground, Elephant and Castle; tel. 071-703 2644). Further along is the Henry Cooper pub. At the junction with Peckham Park Road stands the *North Peckham Civic Centre* with a library and theatre. The exterior mural by Polish artist Adam Kossowski attempts to capture the history of the Old Kent Road from Roman times to its recent past when costermongers sold their wares along the road.

The *Livesey Museum* is at 682 Old Kent Road, SE15. Tel. 071-639 5604, originally a library. It stages temporary exhibitions mainly on London themes for the benefit of the local community and schools.

Peckham itself is to the S of the Old Kent Road; once an area of market gardens it also had some grand houses. *Peckham Rye Common* was saved from encroaching developments in 1868 and now adjoins a park with sporting facilities. Some 19C houses survive in Peckham Rye where Elizabeth Cadbury, Quaker and wife of the chocolate manufacturer, was born.

Tilling's first omnibus service ran from Peckham to the City in 1851 and the railway arrived in 1862.

At *Nunhead*, the *Old Nun's Head* at 15 Nunhead Gardens, SE15, stands on the site of a nunnery; the Abbess's head was set on a stake on the Green, hence the name. Nunhead also has an interesting Victorian *Cemetery*, founded in Linden Grove near the Old Nun Head Tavern in 1840, with catacombs set on a hilltop wooded site. Between the wars it was completely neglected and the London Borough of Southwark took it over in 1975 to try to salvage at least a part. Among those buried here are Thomas Tilling (died 1893) who pioneered the horsedrawn bus, Robert Abel, cricketer (died 1936); the *Martyrs' Memorial*, an obelisk erected in 1851, commemorates five Scottish nationalists transported to Australia.

Lewisham is a busy shopping centre with a modern covered complex opened in 1975 and a lively street market in the High St (Mon to Sat). The *Clock Tower* at the junction of Lewisham High St and Lee High Road was built to commemorate Queen Victoria's 1897 Jubilee. At the corner of the High St and Ladywell Road stands Lewisham's oldest building, *The Vicarage*, built in 1692. The coping stones of the holy well at Ladywell can be seen outside *Ladywell Sports Centre*.

The *Fox and Firkin* at 316 Lewisham High St, SE13, was the first in a series of independent brewery pubs opened in the '70s. It features a stuffed fox and home-brewed ale.

To the N, at **Lee**, is the *Manor House and Library Gardens*, Old Road, SE13, with an 18C Adam ceiling, now housing a library and the borough archives. It was the home of the Baring banking family. In Lee Hr Road (corner of Brandram Road) are the *Merchant Taylor Almshouse* built in 1876 on the site of older almshouses, founded by Christophe Boone, a city merchant; the old chapel (1683) remains. The ruined tower of the old *St. Margaret's Church* in Lee Terrace stands in the churchyard on the other side of the road; here the astronomer royal, Edmund Halley (cf Halley's comet) is buried. In Belmont Hill, the Cedars, a Victorian House, has been converted from a convent to the headquarters for a Japanese Buddhist sect.

Lewisham Concert Hall and Theatre is to the S at *Rushey Green*, Catford, opened in 1932 with adjoining civic buildings and a shopping precinct.

Catford has a greyhound stadium. Going S towards Bromley is the large *Downham Estate* built by the London County Council in the 1920s to provide cottage-style houses for thousands of poor inner Londoners. On the way at *Southend* (crossroad leading to Beckenham) is *Peter Pan's Pool*, a visible sign of the Ravensbourne River which flows through this area on its way to the Thames, and which once powered numerous watermills supporting local industries. Sainsbury's has built a large Homebase store overlooking the pond in the likeness of the old Crystal Palace.

Penge just to the S of Crystal Palace, enjoyed a period of brief fashionableness before becoming a modest working-class suburb. In Penge High St are the striking *Free Watermen's and Lightermen's Almshouses*, designed by George Porter in Tudor style (1841), with an impressive gatehouse and quadrangle—still in use. Nearby in St. John's Road are the delightful *Queen Adelaide's Cottages*, designed by Philip Hardwick also in Tudor style (1847) for the benefit of naval widows, now used as council housing.

In **Beckenham** (part of the London Borough of Bromley) is *Beckenham Place Park* (managed by LB Lewisham); approach from Southend Road, nearest BR station Beckenham Junction. The mansion built in 1774 for John Cator is now used by players on the 18-hole public golf course. This is the home of the Mander and Mitchenson Theatrical Collection since 1988; open by appointment, tel. 081-658 7725. A new home is being sought for this personal collection of two devotees of the theatre: paintings, photographs, costumes, printed material and a comprehensive archive from the 17C to the present day.

In Bromley Road, just off Beckenham High St, are three 17C *Rawlins Almshouses*, built in 1649, next to Victorian *St. George's* parish church, which has a 13C lychgate, said to be the oldest in the country. The *George Inn*, further down in the main part of the High St, dates back to 1662 when it was a coaching inn. In Foxgrove Road, the annual Beckenham Tennis Championships take place in June, attracting international players heading for Wimbledon. On the corner of Brackley Road and Southend Road stands a rare Edward VIII pillar box made at Carron ironworks. Further down Brackley Road is St. Paul's Church built for the Cator Estate in 1864 and the oldest church in Beckenham.

In common with Beckenham, **Bromley** is a prosperous commuting suburb where the busy High St already established as a popular shopping centre is being further enhanced with a massive retail, leisure and commercial development to the E of the High St. It will include two department stores, shopping malls, restaurants, Queens Garden and a leisure centre with a swimming pool.

1.G. Wells was born in Bromley in 1866 and a blue plaque on ...lders department store in the Market Square marks the site of the ...amily home. The parish church of *St. Peter and St. Paul* nearby in Church Road was consecrated in 1957, replacing a 13C church destroyed by bombs in the Second World War. Dr Johnson's wife, Elizabeth (died 1752), is buried in the churchyard. St. Mary's Church in College Road retains rare Victorian murals undergoing restoration.

Bromley College in London Road was founded by Bishop Warner for poor widows in 1666; the design is attributed to Wren and is similar to Morden College, Blackheath, incorporating pillars from Gresham's Royal Exchange destroyed in the Great Fire.

Plaistow Lodge in London Lane was built for Peter Thellusson, an eccentric Huguenot millionaire, at the end of the 18C; it was the Quernmore secondary school and is now used by other schools. *Sundridge Park* houses a management centre. The house and grounds were designed by John Nash, Humphry Repton and Samuel Wyatt for corn merchant Claude Scott in 1801. In the grounds where the first 'bred' pheasants were shot by, among others, the Prince of Wales, there is now a golf course.

Bromley Palace belonged to Bishop of Rochester; the current building in Rochester Road, Bromley dates back to 1775 and used to be Stockwell College. It is now Bromley's *Civic Centre and Town Hall*. *St. Blaise's Well* in the grounds was reputed to have medicinal properties.

Among the new office blocks in the busy High St is *The Churchill Theatre* and new *Library* designed by Aneurin John and completed in 1975. The theatre restaurant overlooks *Library Gardens* (access: BR, Bromley South).

In nearby **Chislehurst** (to the W) a large *Common* creates a rural atmosphere in a wealthy suburban setting (access: BR, Chislehurst, bus 227 from Bromley). *Camden Place* on the NW side of the Common was the home of Napoleon III in exile after 1871. For a time after his death his body was buried in the Catholic church of *St. Mary's* in Hawkeswood Lane, in a specially erected mortuary chapel. Later his widow, Empress Eugénie, moved to Farnborough (Hants) and his body was reburied there.

In **Petts Wood** (between Bromley and Chislehurst; BR, Petts Wood); near Orpington Rd, Chislehurst a memorial in the form of a stone pillar was erected in 1927 to William Willett (died 1915) who conceived the idea of summer time (introduced as daylight saving in the First World War). Petts Wood is a 70-acre National Trust area in the middle of an attractive suburb.

Near Chislehurst station are the gigantic *Chislehurst Caves* (100 yards from station) which run for miles in the chalk hills; they are remains of chalk mines from Roman times and were used by thousands of Londoners as shelters during the Second World War.

Chislehurst Caves, Chislehurst (tel. 081-467 3264). Access: BR, Chislehurst, bus 227 from Bromley, turn into Old Hill from A222, 300 yards further on left. Open daily 11.00–17.00 summer; winter, Sat and Sun only. Guided tours. Admission charge.

In **Hayes** (SE of Bromley) William Pitt and William Pitt the Younger lived at Hayes Place, demolished in 1934. Sir Everard Hambro, the banker, was a later resident and benefactor to the growing village, now a residential suburb.

To the S of Bromley, at **Farnborough**, another privately owned 19C estate has become a public golf course and park. *High Elms* was the home of Sir John Lubbock, the first Lord Avebury, astronomer and mathematician (died 1865). He planted the grounds with an unusual collection of trees; there is a nature centre and a trail through the park. His son, Lord Avebury, is best known for the introduction of Bank Holidays in 1871. The manor house burnt down in 1967. Nearby is the village of *Downe* with its attractive flint and brick cottages and the family home of Charles Darwin.

Down House, Luxted Road, Downe, Orpington, Kent. Tel. 66 59119 or 0689 59119. Access: BR, Bromley South, bus No. 146 to Downe. Open Tues to Thur, Sat, Sun and Bank Holidays 13.00–18.00 (last admission 17.30). Closed all February, Mon and Fri.
    Down House became Charles Darwin's home in 1842 and he lived there until his death in 1882. In 1927 it became a museum run by the Royal College of Surgeons. Part of the house recreates the period with Darwin's study and his chair as the centre-piece. Exhibits show the developments of his theory of natural selection. In the garden visitors can trace Darwin's footsteps along the Sandy Walk. Plants, fossils and scientific instruments are also on display.

Further E, at **Keston** (3 miles S of Bromley) there is a hill-fort and windmill dating back to 1717 on the Common. The parish church in Westerham Road is in Norman style with Roman foundations. *Caesar's Well* on the Common is the source of the River Ravensbourne. At Holwood House in Westerham Road, Keston, William Pitt the Younger, who lived there from 1785 to 1803, met William Wilberforce in 1787 to decide on the abolition of slavery. The historic Wilberforce Oak on a public footpath between Westerham Road and Shire Lane marks the spot. At Pitt's Oak William Pitt used to catch the stage coach for Parliament. The manor dates from the 15C. The 18C house, extended by Pitt, was partially destroyed by fire in 1985. It has been restored and now belongs to the Seismographic Service.

West Wickham, towards Bromley and Beckenham, retains its castle-style manor house, *Wickham Court* (1480). Here Henry Heydon married Anne Boleyn. It is now a college.

Biggin Hill, 5 miles S of Bromley, annually in May or June, remembers the crucial role its airfield played in the Battle of Britain (1940–41) with a two-day airshow on what is now mainly a busy civil airport under the authority of the London Borough of Bromley. A permanent memorial in the form of model Spitfire and Hurricane aircraft can be seen outside the Memorial Chapel along the main road which becomes the very long Biggin Hill High St.

The Priory at **Orpington** (3 miles SE of Bromley) is an excellent example of a pre-Reformation Rectory House, dating back in part to 1270. It was the home of rectors of St. Mary's Church until 1600 and has been restored as a local meeting place with a small museum.

Bromley Museum, The Priory, Church Hill, Orpington, Kent. Tel. 0689-31551. Access: BR, Orpington. Open Mon to Wed, Fri, Sat 09.00–17.00. The museum tells the story of the area—the largest of the London boroughs—through archaeological exhibits including Stone Age, Roman and Saxon. It also features the Avebury collection.

The Walnuts Sports Centre adjoins the new shopping centre in the High St offers swimming, squash and other sports.

37 Croydon, Carshalton, Cheam, Sutton, Wimbledon, Merton, Kingston

Croydon now has the largest concentration of office space in Britain outside Central London but its origin lies in the church. The Archbishop of Canterbury took over the local manor house in the 14C to create a convenient staging post between Lambeth Palace and Canterbury. Today the *Archbishop's Palace* (or *Old Palace*), now a girls' school, is overshadowed by office blocks, the result of a massive expansion of the town centre since 1954. At the heart is the *Whitgift shopping centre*—a '60s complex in plain concrete (recently refurbished)—which takes its name from Archbishop Whitgift, who founded the Grammar School, and almshouses.

The Old Palace, Old Palace Road, Croydon, tel. 081-680 5877, is open on certain days during school holidays; tours 13.35 to 14.30 (access: BR, East Croydon). Approach via Church St, a turning off the High St, opposite George St (400 yards). It retains a 12C undercroft and the Great Hall dates back to 1390, rebuilt with a Spanish chestnut wood roof in 1452. Queen Elizabeth stayed here and her bedchamber is on view as is the original Chapel. Earl Rothesay, later James I of Scotland, spent six years in captivity in the Palace before becoming King.

The parish church of *St. John the Baptist*, in Church St next to the Old Palace, retains its medieval porch but was rebuilt after a fire in 1867 by Sir George Gilbert Scott. Many of the original memorials and brasses were saved as was Archbishop Whitgift's tomb and those of five other archbishops. In the High St on the corner with George St are the *Whitgift Almshouses* which still provide accommodation for the poor and elderly. They date back to 1599 and some of the original furniture can be seen in the Audience Chamber. Whitgift's portrait hangs in the Chapel and there is a 16C clock in the quadrangle. (For details of access to these historic buildings contact Croydon Tourist Information Centre, Central Library, Katharine St, Croydon. Tel. 081-760 5630.)

The Victorian Town Hall is being redeveloped to include a new central library, a museum and art gallery. In Central Croydon there is a daily street market in Surrey St going back 700 years.

The first public railway in the world opened in 1803 between Croydon and Wandsworth—the wagons were drawn on rails by horses. *West Croydon* railway station opened in 1839 and *East Croydon* in 1841, signalling the start of the area's rapid growth as a commercial and residential centre.

Croydon was also in the forefront of aviation. At the original *Croydon Aerodrome* building, 2.5 miles S of the town centre along Purley Way, the A23, part of the original building is due to become a museum in 1991, tel. 081-654 4620. A housing estate covers the airfield, which closed in the 1950s. Military flights started in 1915; George VI gained his wings as Prince Albert in 1919. It became London's first airport officially in 1928 and until 1959 it was used for civil and military flights; it was the base of Imperial Airways. Pioneering flights from here include Amy Johnson's record breaking flight to Australia in 1930.

Fairfield Halls were completed in the 1960s and include a 2000-seat concert hall, 800-seat theatre, the Ashcroft, an art gallery and restaurant. Nearby is a new Holiday Inn hotel. Notable among the many office blocks is the octagonal, 23-storey high *NLA House*

designed by Richard Seifert and completed in 1970. The Wa⬛
Palace, a leisure complex, opened in Purley Way, S of the tow⬛
centre, in 1990.

Between Shirley and Beckenham, 3 miles E of Croydon in Monks
Orchard Rd, is the *Bethlem Royal Hospital*. This, the oldest hospital
in the world for the treatment of the mentally ill, was founded in
Bishopsgate in 1247. It moved to Moorgate in 1675 where it became
known as Bedlam, attracting visitors who watched the inmates from
the gallery. In 1815 a specially designed building at Lambeth, now
the Imperial War Museum, became the Bethlem and it moved from
there to Shirley in 1926. A museum at the Hospital houses the
archives of this and the Maudsley Hospital and a collection of
pictures. Open by appointment tel. 081-777 6611.

In the grounds of the John Ruskin School in Upper Shirley Road
is a restored Victorian windmill.

The archbishops of Canterbury left Croydon for *Addington
Palace* in 1808, taking over a manor house in Coombe Road, until
1897 when Canterbury and Lambeth became the only two
residences of the archbishops. The Palace was reconstructed by
Norman Shaw for private use; in 1951 it became the home of the
Royal School of Church Music. The Great Hall features Italian
walnut panelling, a grand fireplace and a gallery; tel. 081-654 7676
to view. In the grounds is the Addington Palace Golf Course.
(Access: BR, East Croydon, then bus; 3 miles SE of Croydon.)

At *Selsdon Park*, 3 miles SE of the centre of Croydon, another
golf course occupies the grounds of the former Selsdon Court, now
Selsdon Park Hotel which incorporates some medieval parts of the
original building with 19C additions. It overlooks the grounds, the
golf course, and Selsdon Wood, National Trust land.

In this area several nature trails and reserves reveal some of the
original Surrey countryside; details from the London Borough of
Croydon, Central Library, Katharine St, Croydon.

Sanderstead (3m S), Purley (2m S), Kenley (4m S) and Coulsdon
(5m SW of Croydon) are attractive residential suburbs developed
mainly in the early and middle part of this century.

At *Beddington*, 2 miles to the W of Croydon (in the London
Borough of Sutton) excavations (in 1873) revealed the bath-house of
a Roman villa at Beddington Park. Later Roman remains include a
coffin (1930) and a cinerary urn (1974). Approach via Beddington
Lane S from Mitcham Rd (A236), turn left into Bath House Rd, 1
mile S of BR Beddington Lane. The manor house, Carew Manor,
has been largely rebuilt but in the Great Hall, an impressive
hammer-beam roof dating back to the early 15C remains. It is now
a school, next to *St. Mary the Virgin*, the local parish church in
Church Road, off Croydon Road (A232). This is of pre-Norman
origin; it contains a fine organ-case designed and painted in the
William Morris workshop at Merton Abbey, decorated with flowers,
leaves and angels.

In the centre of **Carshalton** (3.5 miles W of Croydon. Access: BR,
Carshalton) is the source of the Wandle river, surrounded by
attractive houses, some weatherboarded, in what is now a conservation area. From here the river flows through Sutton, Merton,
Croydon and Wandsworth; the Wandle valley provided an early
start for industrialisation (at the beginning of the 19C) with more
than 80 mills (in 1831) along its banks providing power for a variety
of industries (see also Wandsworth). Mill-wheels and mill-stones

. be seen in *The Grove* public gardens, where the former manor house, *Stonecourt*, is now council offices.

Carshalton House, Pound St, was built in 1714 and is now a convent school. *Carshalton Park* has a brick grotto and a dry canal; the new house intended for the grounds was never built. The manor house which stood near the High St was pulled down in 1927. At *Little Holland House*, 40 Beeches Avenue (tel. 081-647 5168) the hard work of one Frank Dickinson (died 1961) self-taught craftsman, can be admired. He took nearly 60 years to make every part of the house, begun in 1904, working in the tradition of the self-sufficiency movement created by John Ruskin and William Morris. He left the house to the Arts and Crafts movement and it is run by the LB of Sutton. Open: 1 March–31 Oct; 1st Sun in each month and BHs, 12.00–18.00. Free (BR, Carshalton Beeches).

At **Cheam**, *Nonsuch Park* (1.5 miles N of Sutton) serves as a reminder of Henry VIII's last palace, Nonsuch, built in 1538 and demolished in 1688. Three pillars mark the site of the palace, unearthed in 1959. Archaeological finds including stone, gilded slate, glass and pottery from the site are now in the Museum of London and at Bourne Hall Museum in Ewell.

Nonsuch Palace was a Tudor extravaganza, a two-storey building around open courtyards in the Renaissance style, decorated by Italian craftsmen, with two towers topped by onion-shaped cupolas. Stone from Merton Priory, dissolved by Henry VIII, was used in the construction. In 1556 it passed to the Earl of Arundel, and then back to Queen Elizabeth I who stayed here frequently, using it for hunting. Later both James I and then Charles I stayed here. During Charles II's reign it was given to Barbara Villiers, Countess of Castlemaine who sold it for building material. Excavations in 1960 revealed the foundations. An 18C mansion house stands in the Park.

Nonsuch Park is between London Road and Ewell Road, Cheam; approach along The Avenue. Nearest BR station Cheam. A Roman road, Stone St, runs along the W side of the Park.

On the corner of Park Lane and Malden Road, just off Cheam High St, stands **Whitehall**, a weatherboarded house typical of the area, which has been restored and is open to visitors.

Whitehall, 1 Malden Road, Cheam, Sutton, Surrey. Tel. 081-643 1236. Access: BR, Cheam; bus 213A. Open Apr to Sept Tues to Thur, Sun 14.00–17.30, Sat 10.00–17.30, Oct to Mar Wed, thur, Sun 14.00–17.30, Sat 10.00–17.30.

The house dates back to c 1500 and is one of the earliest surviving two-storey buildings in England. The weatherboarding was added in the 18C to cover the gaps between the original timbers as the mixture of straw and plaster dried out. It was once Cheam School (now in Berkshire) whose famous pupils have included the Duke of Edinburgh and Prince Charles. The London Borough of Sutton organises exhibitions and concerts here.

Set back from Malden Road in Church Road is the Victorian Gothic parish church of *St. Dunstan*. The Lumley Chapel in the churchyard dates from the 13C and was turned into a memorial to Lord Lumley and his wife Jane Fitzalan in 1592 (non-royal occupants of Nonsuch Palace). Her alabaster tomb includes the children portrayed against a background of a room in the Palace. Lord Lumley's memorial depicts him as a scholar; his second wife, Elizabeth Darcy, is also included.

Cheam became a busy suburb only in the 1920s and '30s with Tudor-style shopping centre and remains of the old village in the centre.

Sutton (4.5 miles W of Croydon) is the commercial centre of the area first established when the London to Brighton Road was built through the small village in 1755; a residential suburb developed here with the arrival of the London to Epsom railway in 1847. Further house building followed in the early 20C and more recently a library, civic centre and art college were built in the centre, including the Secombe Centre with its theatre, named after singer Harold (Harry) Secombe. *St. Nicholas*, the parish church, has Saxon origins but the present building was designed by Edwin Nash in 1864. There is a lively street market on Tuesdays and Saturdays in West St (fashion, leather and jewellery).

Wimbledon (access: BR, Wimbledon; Underground, Wimbledon, Southfields, Wimbledon Park). The remains of a pre-Roman fort known as Caesar's Camp can still be seen on what is now the Royal Wimbledon Golf Club, part of Wimbledon Common. But it was not until the 16C that Wimbledon Village came to prominence when the Earl of Exeter built Wimbledon House—later demolished.

Wimbledon Common covers, with Putney Lower Common, 1100 acres; special features include Rushmere and King's Mere ponds, the golf course and the windmill. *Wimbledon Windmill* was built in 1817 and is believed to be the only remaining hollow-post flour mill in this country. It has been restored and a small museum is open to the public on Saturdays, Sundays and Bank Holidays, 14.00–17.00 (April to October); admission charge. Approach along Parkside and turn into Windmill Road (nearest Underground Southfields).

Wimbledon Common has a history of duels, the first recorded in 1652. In 1798 the Prime Minister, William Pitt fought George Tierney, MP, and in 1809 Lord Castlereagh and George Canning duelled here. The last duel was in 1840 when Lord Cardigan wounded Captain Harvey Tuckett. The Common's fictional inhabitants, the Wombles, are known to millions of children.

The *Fox and Grapes* pub in Camp Road, off the Common, has one bar named after Caesar's Camp; the 300-year-old pub is in a mock-Tudor style.

Southside House, Wimbledon Common, SW19 is a 16C farm building with a Dutch brick façade added in 1687, now the Headquarters of the School Teachers Cultural Foundation. It is the former home of the Pennington Mellor family and contains many treasures of the family as well as of the Swedish philanthropist and writer, Axel Munthe, whose wife, Hilda Pennington Mellor Munthe, and children lived here. After war damage the LCC assisted with its restoration on condition that it remained accessible to the public. In the Music Room is a portrait of Emma Hamilton who often visited from her nearby home in Merton. Visits on guided tours only from 1 October to 31 May, Tues, Thurs and Sat 10.00–17.00 or by appointment to the Administrator, Pennington Mellor Charity Trust, Southside House, Wimbledon Common, SW19. Tel. 081-946 7643.

Cannizaro House, West Side, Wimbledon Common, a Georgian mansion, was substantially rebuilt in 1901; it is has been converted into a country house hotel.

Wimbledon Village, now a large and thriving suburb, enjoys a hilltop location and some attractive early buildings survive, including

…*gle House* with its distinctive gables (1613) and *Claremont*, a late 7C building. The *Rose and Crown*, also in the High St, is 17C; the poet Swinburne drank here.

In Wimbledon Broadway stands the *Wimbledon Theatre* (1910), tel. 081-543 4549, with a green cupola restored in 1968, showing pre-West End productions and Christmas pantomimes. The theatre is due to close for some time in 1990 while the town centre is redeveloped. Nearby is the *Polka Theatre*, tel. 081-543 4888, with a programme of children's plays and a large collection of puppets. *Wimbledon Stadium*, tel. 081-946 5361, in Plough Lane is used for dog-racing, speedway and stock-car racing. There is a local history museum run by the Wimbledon Society in The Ridgway, Wimbledon.

Wimbledon's international fame is founded on the annual tennis championships at the *All England Club* in Wimbledon Park, Church Rd, held in June, since 1877.

Access: Wimbledon (BR and Underground), special buses during the championship along the High St into Church Rd (1.5 miles).

There are 16 outside courts and two under-cover courts including the Centre Court which seats 14,000 (all grass—there are no clay courts). The *Wimbledon Lawn Tennis Museum*, Church Road, Wimbledon, SW19, overlooks the Centre Court. Open Tues to Sat 11.00–17.00, Sun 14.00–17.00 and during the championships (to those attending matches). Admission charge. Tel. 081-946 6131. Parking. The museum has a large collection of ladies tennis fashion through the last 100 years, life-size models of well-known players, a reconstruction of a racquet-maker's workshop and men's dressing-room, tennis bric-à-brac and a library.

One mile SE of Wimbledon lies **Merton** which has given its name to the London borough. It was a pioneer among garden suburbs but its history dates back to the 12C when Merton's Augustinian priory was founded. Students included Thomas Becket and Walter of Merton, who later founded Merton College at Oxford. Stone from the demolished priory after its dissolution was used to build Nonsuch Palace (see above). Some remains can still be seen in Station Road. Lord Nelson visited Sir William and Lady Hamilton at Merton Place from 1801 to 1805. The house has been demolished. His pew is preserved in the parish church of *St. Mary the Virgin*, Merton Park. The Wandle flows through Merton and provided power for early industries including Liberty's fabric-printing workshops which remained here until 1972. William Morris established a workshop here in 1887 to manufacture textiles, tiles and furniture. It was destroyed in the Second World War.

At Priory Park, the listed Liberty Board Mill has been developed into a waterside attraction with a crafts centre and museum on a site shared with Sainsbury's Savacentre; archaeological remains discovered during the development are also on view. Also planned is a leisure pool, entertainment centre and multi-screen cinema. Access Underground, Colliers Wood.

John Innes, another household name, established his Horticultural Institute at Merton Park in 1909; he first bought the estate in 1867 and transformed the farmhouse into a manor house and the surrounding grounds, now a public park, with avenues of trees and holly hedges. *John Innes Park* is at Water Lane, SW19 (nearest BR station is Wimbledon Chase— approach along Kingston Road).

In *Morden Hall Park*, linked to Priory Park by a riverside walkway along the Wandle, 0.5 miles to the S, is a weatherboarded *snuff-mill* (early 19C) in the grounds of *Morden Hall*, owned by the National Trust, set in a new environmental centre. There is also a nature

reserve. Morden Hall is a 17C building now used by the co▮
(nearest Underground Morden). The parish church of St. Lawrenc▮
London Road was built in 1636 on 11C foundations; nearby is ▮
300-year-old George Inn. Beyond is Morden Park, with a Georgi▮
mansion also used by the local council. The Underground railway wa▮
extended to Morden in 1926; this spurred extensive housing developments.

Mitcham, 1 mile to the E of Morden, claims the second oldest village
cricket green in the country (cricket was played here before 1720). A
Saxon cemetery was excavated at Ravensbury Park (half a mile S of
town centre, off London Road, A217) earlier this century and the finds
(including weapons and brooches) can be seen in the Museum of
London. **Mitcham Common** covers 460 acres and joins with Beddington (see p 337). Two pubs remain from Mitcham's turnpike days, the
White Hart and Burn Bullock (formerly the King's Head) from the 18C.
The council owns three mansions, Eagle House (1705), Park Place
(1780) and The Canons; the last built in 1680 and now a centre for
recreation, indoor and outdoor sports, antique fairs and other events.

Canons Leisure Centre, Madeira Road, Mitcham, Surrey. Tel. 081-640 8544.

Kingston upon Thames is 10m SW of Central London; on the Thames
opposite Hampton Wick (BR; Kingston). This is one of only two royal
boroughs in London (the other is Kensington and Chelsea). The town
centre is undergoing major redevelopment due to be completed in the
90s, and a new relief road opened in 1989. Kingston is the most historic
of outer London boroughs with the best preserved medieval street plan
around the Market Place. Kingston became the coronation place for
seven Anglo-Saxon rulers from Edward the Elder in 900 to Ethelred the
Unready in 979; seven silver pennies are set into the base of the
original Coronation Stone outside the Guildhall (1935), High St. After
the Norman Conquest Kingston's economy changed as Westminster
became the royal base. The first Kingston Bridge dates from around
1100. As the second bridge over the Thames after London Bridge, it
ensured Kingston's growth as a market town. The present bridge dates
to 1828 and was doubled in size in 1914. The remains of the medieval
bridge will be incorporated in the new John Lewis department store at
Horsefair, see below. Beyond Horsefair is Turks Boatyard, founded in
1710, still building boats and providing a local passenger boat service.

A tributary of the Thames, the Hogsmill flows through the borough;
the ancient arches of the Clattern Bridge (1175) can be seen next to the
Guildhall (a gate leads down to the water-level; High St/Market
Square).

The Ancient Market dates to the 13C or even earlier; fresh food is
sold here, Monday to Saturday. The Royal Charter granted in 1628
prevents any other markets from opening within seven miles; this
restriction has been eased to allow markets at Sutton and Putney. Near
the Market Place is the Apple Market with a smaller range of stalls.

Two major new developments dominate the town centre. The new
John Lewis department store on the banks of the Thames with a huge
glass roof opens in 1990 incorporating archaeological remains of a
medieval undercroft and the ruins of the old bridge, as well as
restaurants and cafes along the river. On the other side of the road is
the new Bentall Centre incorporating a new Bentall department store
retaining the Aston Webb façade of this 120 year old store, and
including 100 shops and restaurants around a central atrium, opening
in mid 1990. In the historic Market Place, Chieseman's department

with a listed Jacobean staircase). No. 14 preserves an original
r façade dating to the 16C; No. 15 and 16 are reproductions.
in the Market Place is the *Market House* (1840), formerly the
wn Hall, and the site of the Guildhall from 1500. A statue of
Queen Anne (1706) by Francis Bird stands in the S end of the
Market Place. One of the two historic inns, the *Griffin Hotel* has
been converted into shops and a restaurant; the *Druid's Head*
retains its Stuart staircase and late 17C interior. The restored *All
Saints' Church* in the Market Place has four arches supporting the
13C tower. The original church dates from before the Conquest and
was the location of the Saxon coronations (as illustrated in the
windows of the N aisles of the present church). Another 13C
building, *King John's Palace*, stood at the site of the present police
station.

Both Thames St and Clarence St reveal interesting façades above
the shop-fronts. Further historic buildings survive in the High St;
Eadweard Muybridge, see below, was born at 30 High St.

At the *Kingston Museum and Heritage Centre*, Wheatfield Way,
Kingston (half a mile E of town centre; open Mon to Sat 10.00–
17.00 tel. 081-546 5368) local history is displayed, including archaeological finds and Martinware pottery.

Eadweard Muybridge, founder of modern cinematography, was born in Kingston in 1830 and made his career in the United States. He bequeathed his
collection of apparatus and photographs to Kingston in 1904. It is now on view
in the Museum which is also a tourist information centre.

Kingston's biggest market is at Fairfield West on Mondays (until 13.00) with
bric-a-brac, household goods, clothes, etc.

The *Kingfisher* in Fairfield Road, Kingston (tel. 081-546 1042) is a
new leisure centre with swimming and sporting facilities. Near the
Heritage Centre, in London Road is a row of almshouses founded
by William Cleave in 1669 and still in use. Kingston's grammar
school uses the Lovekyn chapel founded in 1309.

The thriving residential surroundings of Kingston continue 3 miles
S to **Surbiton**, a Victorian suburb established after the arrival of the
railway in 1838, which at first by-passed Kingston.

Three miles to the S is **Chessington**, best known for its zoo, but
with a medieval village church, *St. Mary the Virgin* (Garrison Road,
off Leatherhead Road), which holds the smallest silver chalice in
England, 3.5 inches high and hallmarked 1568.

Chessington World of Adventures, Leatherhead Road, Chessington. Tel. Epsom (03727) 29560 Open daily 10.00–17.00 (April to
October), 10.00–16.00 (November to March). Access: Bus 65 or 71
from Kingston; BR, Chessington South, Green Line 777. Admission
charge. Car and Coach Park.

Chessington Zoo, established in 1931, became the Chessington World of
Adventures in 1987, owned by Madame Tussaud's. The zoo remains and
includes a new area with a bird garden. A monorail carries visitors over the
animal enclosure and through the themed areas which include a Western
town, the Rocky Mountains, the 'Mystic' East, and an old English village.
Exciting rides and themed catering is provided in each area. In 1990 the
world of Transylvania opens with a Count Dracula Castle and a vampire
horror ride. Circus World is a participatory, non-animal circus. *Burnt Stub
Manor* (17C) is available for functions and Elizabethan evenings.

Just to the NE of Kingston town centre is *Coombe* where John Galsworthy
(1867–1933) was brought up and which he referred to as 'Robin Hill' in The
Forsyte Saga.

38 Richmond, Putney, Barnes, Mortlake, Kew, Ham and Petersham, Teddington, Twickenham, the Hamptons and Hampton Court Palace

Richmond upon Thames, a flourishing suburb and growing commercial centre, has a delightful riverside location and a royal past which can still be traced at Richmond Green and in Richmond Park.

Access: BR or Underground to Richmond; by river from Westminster Pier (Easter to September only).

Edward III built Sheen Palace here in the 14C but as early as 1125 Henry I had stayed here. Sheen Palace was destroyed by fire in 1499; Henry VII had it rebuilt and renamed Richmond Palace after his Yorkshire earldom. It became one of the favourite palaces of the Tudor monarchs. Henry VII and Elizabeth I died here. After the execution of Charles I the main buildings were demolished. Royalty returned to Richmond in 1720 when George, Prince of Wales, the future George II, took over Richmond Lodge in Old Deer Park. George III also used the lodge but preferred Kew Palace.

The remains of **Richmond Palace** are in Old Palace Yard off Richmond Green and include the *Gate House*, with Henry VII's coat of arms, and the *Wardrobe*, reconstructed from the original Tudor building. At *Trumpeter's House* in Old Palace Yard, built c 1710, Metternich once stayed and was visited by Disraeli in 1849.

The four well-proportioned houses in *Maids of Honour Row* fronting the Green nearby were built in 1724 for the Ladies in Waiting of the then Princess of Wales. Old Palace Lane leads down to the Thames past the imposing *Asgill House* on the site of the watergate of Richmond Palace. This fine mansion was designed by Sir Robert Taylor for Sir Charles Asgill, Lord Mayor of London, in 1760. It is privately owned but can be viewed by appointment. A tiny public house, the *Swan*, is on the way. On two sides of the Green and in adjoining alleyways are attractive 17C and 18C houses including in Greenside, *Oak House* (1760), *Old Palace Place* (1700) and *Old Friars* (1687), on land which was once the monastery of the Observant Friars. This architectural heritage makes Richmond Green one of the most unspoilt and attractive 'squares' in Greater London. On the Green there was jousting in Tudor times, and two centuries later cricket—the *Cricketer's Inn* is on the E side of the Green. Antique and gift shops, and boutiques now fill the alleyways which lead through to George St and the Quadrant, the main shopping area.

On the Little Green to the E is the *Richmond Theatre*, tel. 081-940 0088, built by Frank Matcham in 1899, its gaudy Victorian terracotta façade and green cupola somewhat out of keeping with the restrained 17C and 18C architecture. There was a Theatre Royal, known as the Theatre on the Green, on the other side from 1765 to 1884. The present theatre maintains this long theatrical tradition with pre-West End productions and Christmas pantomimes; there is fringe and cabaret at the nearby *Orange Tree Pub Theatre*. The Richmond Festival is centred on the Green and its theatres in June or July. The local tourist information centre is the Old Town Hall, Whittaker Avenue, tel. 081-940 9125. There are walking tours of Richmond in the summer. A local museum has been established in the Old Town Hall.

Richmond Bridge (Bridge St off Hill St from the town centre—A305 to St. Margaret's) is the oldest bridge still standing over the Thames in

eater London area and was built between 1774 and 1777 by
s Paine. Its five arches and graceful curve make it one of the most
active as well, and it is popular with artists. Two pubs overlook the
ames here but the river frontage is liable to flooding. The major
verside redevelopment (1988) including shops and offices to the N
of the bridge was designed by architect Quinlan Terry and comprises
some 20 buildings in different classical styles, pleasing in scale and
arranged around four courtyards, with a restaurant overlooking the
river. The local parish church, *St. Mary Magdalen*, in the centre of the
town, has a 15C flint and stone tower. It is set back in Church Walk.

*A return to classicism—the Quinlan Terry development
overlooking the River Thames at Richmond*

The view from *Richmond Hill* is famous and is best reached from the
town centre via Paradise Road, Mount Ararat Road, and the Vineyard.
In Paradise Road is *Hogarth House* (1748), the home of Leonard and
Virginia Woolf from 1915 to 1924, where they founded the Hogarth
Press. In the Vineyard are three groups of almshouses, *Michel's*
(1811), *Bishop Dippa's* (1667, rebuilt in 1850) and *Queen Elizabeth's*
(1767, founded in 1600), and in Ormond Road, just off Hill Rise,
attractive 18C houses.

Below Richmond Hill are the *Terrace Gardens*, laid out as a public
park in 1887 with the famous view of the Thames winding S and W,
Petersham Meadows and Ham Common on one side and Marble Hill
House and Park on the other. The *Richmond Gate Hotel* occupies
several 18 and 19C buildings and its restaurant enjoys the same view
The *Star and Garter Home* for disabled seamen was built in 1924 in
bright red brick and stands on the site of the famous inn connected
with Charles Dickens and Thackeray. The nearby pub is the *Lass of
Richmond Hill*. Attractive houses along Richmond Hill include *The
Wick*, built in 1775 by Robert Mylne, and *Wick House*, built a few
years earlier for Sir Joshua Reynolds by Sir William Chambers.

Here is the entrance to **Richmond Park**, although the 2500-acre
park can be approached from several different directions.

This was a royal hunting ground enclosed in 1637 by Charles I.
Some oak trees date back to the Middle Ages and there are about 600

red and fallow deer which now roam freely in this natural parklar.
the centre are the man-made *Pen Ponds* and the beautiful *Isab*
Plantation and Woodland Gardens, most impressive from mid Aprir
the end of May when hundreds of azaleas and rhododendrons bloom
Several buildings stand within the Park although nothing remains of
the royal Richmond Lodge in Old Deer Park (on the other side of
Twickenham Road and fronting the river) except the *King's Observa-*
tory, built by Sir William Chambers (1769) and now offices. To view
write to King's Observatory, Old Deer Park, Richmond.

In Richmond Park is the *White Lodge* (three-quarters of a mile NW
of the Robin Hood Gate in Roehampton Vale), built in 1727 as a
hunting lodge for George I, influenced by Chiswick House across the
river. Queen Mary, George V's consort, grew up here and her eldest
son, later Edward VIII, was born here. It was the first married home of
Queen Elizabeth, the Queen Mother. It is now the Royal Ballet Junior
School, and is open to the public in August only, daily 14.00–18.00.

Pembroke Lodge (half a mile S of Richmond Gate—Richmond Hill) was the
home of Lord John Russell and the childhood home of his grandson, the
philosopher Bertrand Russell; it is now a restaurant and cafeteria (tel. 081-940
8207; open January to October daily, November to December, weekends only.)

Thatched House Lodge (1.5 miles S from Richmond Gate) was built by Sir
Robert Walpole and is now the home of Princess Alexandra. It stands on the
mound of a former icehouse.

Near Pembroke Lodge a prehistoric barrow provides the high ground from
which it is said that Henry VIII watched for the rocket announcing Anne Boleyn's
execution—St. Paul's Cathedral can be seen from here among high-rise office
blocks.

There is access nowadays for cars (except commercial vehicles) through the
park from 07.00 in March to November and from 07.30 from December to
February until 30 minutes before lighting-up time. There are gates at East
Sheen, Roehampton, Kingston Hill, Kingston and Ham in addition to Richmond
Gate.

Richmond Ice Rink is on the other side of the river, in Clevedon Road,
Twickenham (tel. 081-892 3646), moving to a new site in December
1991.

Putney, **Barnes** and **Mortlake**, to the NW of Richmond and on the S
bank of the Thames, are attractive residential suburbs in the news
once a year during the Oxford and Cambridge boat race in March,
rowed from Putney to Mortlake. Putney furthest W is actually in the
London Borough of Wandsworth. Near the start of the Boat Race is the
Duke's Head (Lower Richmond Road) with attractive Victorian
engraved glass. Nearby is the jazz-pub, the *Half Moon*. **Putney** itself is
a growing commercial centre with a large heath to the S adjoining
Wimbledon Common; this is the setting for the annual Putney Show in
June. *St. Mary's Church* by Putney Bridge has been restored after a
fire in 1977; the 15C tower and fan-vaulted chantry chapel survive but
the brasses are lost. The first *Putney Bridge*, a wooden structure
erected in 1729, was only the third bridge over the Thames (after
London Bridge and Kingston), preceding Westminster Bridge built in
1750. The present bridge was built by Bazalgette in 1886.

The Wandsworth Museum, Disraeli Road, Putney SW15, tel. 081-
871 7074, tells the story of the area (LB Wandsworth) from pre-historic
times to the 20C and includes temporary exhibitions. Open Mon to
Wed, Fri, Sat, 13.00–17.00. Free.

In Putney Hill, Algernon Swinburne lived at The Pines for 30 years
from 1879, with members of the Pre-Raphaelite Brotherhood as
frequent guests. Putney Hill leads S to Kingston Road and the *Putney*

Cemetery, established in 1887; one of the more fashionable eteries in London with some interesting monuments erected ore restrictions were introduced. Among those buried here are cob Epstein, sculptor (died 1959), Sir George Reid, Australian politician (died 1918), and William Routledge, the explorer (died 1939).

The village atmosphere survives in **Barnes** to the W of Putney with an attractive green and duck-pond. *St. Mary's Church*, Church Road, SW13, damaged by fire in 1978, has been rebuilt—a Norman wall was exposed by the fire and the 15C brick tower survives.

The estate of *Barn Elms* in Rooks Lane, the former manor of Barnes, was leased to Sir Francis Walsingham in 1579 by the Crown; Elizabeth I stayed here. In 1884 it became the base for the fashionable Ranelagh Club (closed in 1939). Another house in the grounds was occupied by Jacob Tonson, the publisher, who hosted the meetings of the Kit-Cat Club from 1700–20 and also built a gallery for Sir Godfrey Kneller's portraits of its illustrious members (see National Portrait Gallery). Nothing remains of the houses but the grounds were used by William Cobbett in 1827–31 for a variety of farming experiments including the growing of maize. It is now *Barn Elms Park*, and school playing fields.

In Castlenau Road, Barnes, there are some imposing Victorian villas, and in the 18C Barnes Terrace the writer Henry Fielding lived at Millbourne House in 1750; later the actor Tom Sheridan lived in the same house. The composer Gustav Holst lived at No. 10 from 1908 to 1913. Actors and television personalities are the local residents of today and Barnes sports one of London's best-known jazz-pubs, the *Bull's Head*, in Lonsdale Road, SW13.

To the N is Barn Elms Reservoir alongside the Thames due to become a nature reserve, with the imposing Harrods Depository on the Riverbank in terracotta to match the store, see p 129.

At **Mortlake** (including East Sheen), James I established a tapestry workshop in 1619 staffed by Flemish weavers. The workshop went into decline after the Civil War and by 1703 Queen Anne closed it down. Mortlake tapestry can be seen at Ham House, Hampton Court, and in the back of the priest's chair at *St. Mary's*, the parish church in the High St, where there is also some local pottery on view. The church (1543) was rebuilt to a design by Sir Arthur Blomfield in 1905. There are monuments to Henry Addington, later Viscount Sidmouth, Prime Minister and to his wife. John Dee (died 1608), a local resident and Elizabethan astrologer, was buried in the chancel of the old church. In *St. Mary Magdalene's*, North Worple Way, the explorer, traveller, and translator of 'The Arabian Nights', Sir Richard Burton lies buried in an exotic tomb shaped like an Arabian tent.

From the garden of *The Limes*, Mortlake High St, Turner painted two views of the Thames. The house, now used as offices, was built in 1720 for Countess Stafford. The *Ship* in Ship Lane, SW14, is a 16C terraced pub, at the end of the Boat Race (see above).

Watney's Brewery by the river occupies land previously part of the grounds of Mortlake Manor, once a residence of the Archbishops of Canterbury. The Earl Spencer, father of the Princess of Wales, is the present Lord of the Manor and keeper of the Court Rolls. Tours of the brewery can be arranged (tel. 081-876 3434).

East Sheen on the higher ground to the W has attractive houses in Christ Church Road; only the old stables and clock tower survive of *Sheen House*, built in 1786 and occupied by Lord Grey in 1830.

Kew (1.5 miles NE of Richmond by road, and on the Thames) owes both its botanic garden and attractive village setting at Kew Green to the existence of nearby royal Richmond Palace. The large Georgian houses around the Green were built for members of the King's Court in the reign of George III. The parish church of *St. Anne's* dates to 1714 and features a distinctive octagonal cupola. Thomas Gainsborough (died 1788), the painter, is buried here, and so are John Kirby, the architect, and Jeremiah Meyer, miniature painter to Queen Charlotte, Francis Bauer, George III's botanical artist (died 1840) and John Zoffany, painter (died 1810).

The *Herbarium* of the Royal Botanic Gardens on the Green houses the largest collection of dried plants in the world and is open by appointment to students. Near Kew Bridge is the new **Public Record Office**, Ruskin Avenue, Kew—the national repository of central government records (open 09.30– 17.00. Tel. 081-876 3444).

Royal Botanic Gardens, Kew, Richmond, Surrey. Tel. 081-940 1171. Open daily 09.30–16.00 (November to January); 09.30– 17.00 (February); 09.30–18.00 (March, September to October); 09.30–18.30 (April to August) and –20.00 on Sunday and Bank Hols. Admission charge. Access: Underground, Kew; BR, Kew Bridge. Car and coach parking.

Kew Gardens started as a small botanic garden in 1759 when Princess Augusta, mother of George III, was living on the Kew Estate in the White House (later renamed Kew Palace). Sir William Aiton was her head gardener and Sir William Chambers was employed to design several of the distinctive buildings which survive in the grounds today, including the Great Pagoda, the Orangery and three temples. The 9-acre site was considerably enlarged by George III who combined it with the Richmond Lodge estate. He and Queen Charlotte frequently stayed at Kew Palace (Richmond Lodge was then demolished). This was in turn demolished in 1802 and its position marked by the sundial in front of the present Kew Palace (formerly the Dutch House). In 1841 the now extensive Kew Gardens were handed to the nation and expanded to 300 acres. Sir Joseph Banks, who accompanied Captain Cook on his first round-the-world voyage, was the gardener from 1772 to 1819 when plants were collected from South Africa, Australia, and the Pacific. William Cobbett was a gardener here about 1775.

Sir William Hooker became the Director of the new National Botanic Institute and the Royal Botanic Gardens in 1841. Among its historic achievements are the introduction of the bread-fruit tree to the West Indies in 1791 (the purpose of the 'Bounty' voyage), quinine to India in 1860 and rubber-trees to Malaysia in 1875; in the late 19C Kew played an important part in restoring the European wine growing industry with imported American rootstock after it was wiped out by phylloxera.

The red-brick **Kew Palace**, formerly the Dutch House, is close to the main gates. It was built in 1631 by a London merchant of Flemish descent, Samuel Fortrey. From 1727 it was leased by the Crown and became England's smallest royal residence. It is open to the public and furnished in the style of the period of George III. Queen Charlotte died here in 1818. Among the splendid paintings and furniture is a small collection of royal toys of the past. A formal garden in the 17C style lies behind the palace; the herb garden is most attractive.

The **Orangery**, built in 1761 to Sir William Chamber's design and one of the finest buildings at Kew, has windows only to one side. It was converted into an exhibition centre in the 1960s and provides a useful history of Kew Gardens as well as space for temporary exhibitions.

Museum No. 1, opposite the Palm House, opened in 1857. It contains information on commercially important plants such as rubber, and medicinal plants. Wood and wood products can be seen at *Cambridge Cottage*. A most remarkable display of paintings of plants can be seen in the *Marianne North Gallery*. The small red-brick building was designed in 1882 by James Ferguson to hold the collection of 832 oil paintings presented to Kew by the artist. Marianne North (died 1890) was an intrepid Victorian travelling painter and the colourful and intricate paintings overwhelm the visitor.

Kew Gardens' greenhouses are world-famous; the oldest remaining structure is the *Aroid House*, designed by John Nash in 1825 and moved here from Buckingham Palace in 1836; it houses tropical plants.

The *Palm House*, the most beautiful of all, covers 2248 square metres (24,000 sq. ft), larger than the demolished palm house at Chatsworth but only half the size of the Temperate House. It was completed in 1848 to a Decimus Burton design, built by Richard Turner. (Closed in 1984 for major repairs and refurbishments; reopened in 1990 after replanting.)—The *Waterlily House* at the N end of the Palm House was built in 1852.

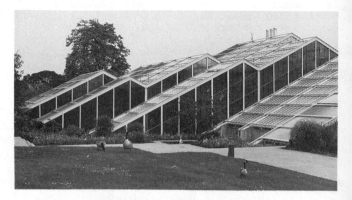

The Princess of Wales Conservatory opened in 1987

The *Temperate House* was designed by Decimus Burton. Building started in 1860 and was not completed until 1899. It covers 5209 square metres (48,392 sq. ft). New boilers, ventilators and clean glass have greatly improved the growing conditions since it re-opened in 1982. It contains some 3000 species. The former T-ranges and Ferneries were the site for the new tropical conservatory, the *Princess of Wales Conservatory*, opened in 1987. Designed by the Property Services Agency, it covers an area of 4490m^2; its diamond shape and part-underground location conserve energy.

Other historic buildings include *Queen Charlotte's Cottage*, built in the 1770s as a summerhouse for the royal family and containing an exhibition of contemporary engravings.

South of Richmond lie two attractive river-side villages, **Ham** (2 miles S) and **Petersham** (1 mile S). The manor of Ham was royal land from the 12C and was included with the estate of Petersham, which belonged to Chertsey Abbey, in the dowry of Elizabeth Woodville who married Edward IV. Later the two estates passed to the Dysart family who retained possession until 1948. In 1610 Thomas Vavasour was granted permission to build Ham House within the Petersham boundary. In addition to Ham House (see below) there are attractive 17 and 18C houses in Petersham Road and River Lane. John Gay, author of 'The Beggar's Opera', lived at Douglas House from 1720 and Dickens first rented Elm Lodge in the summer of 1839. *Sudbrooke Park* in Sudbrooke Lane was completed in 1728 for the Duke of Argyll by James Gibbs. Now used by the Richmond Golf Club, it has a fine 30ft

cube room and portico of Corinthian pillars. Captain Geo
Vancouver, explorer of the Pacific coast of North America, lived
River Lane and is buried in the parish church of *St. Peter*. His death i
1798 is commemorated with an annual service in May. The church
has a 13C chancel, a red-brick nave of the 16C with many later
additions.

Petersham Meadows and *Ham Common* (125 acres) form part of the
famous river view from Richmond Hill. Ham Common and its pond
are surrounded by fine houses and charming cottages and the area is
now a popular residential suburb with much 20C detached and
semi-detached housing.

There is a ferry service across the river from the bank near **Ham
House** to Orleans House and Marble Hill House on the opposite bank.

Ham House, Ham St, Petersham, Richmond. Tel. 081-940 1950. Open Tues to
Sun 11.00–17.00. Owned by the National Trust, managed by the Victoria and
Albert Museum. Admission charge. Cafeteria. Access: Underground or BR
Richmond; then Bus 65 or 71 to Ham House. Car park.

Ham House was built in 1610 by Sir Thomas Vavasour, Knight Marshal to
James I; successive owners altered the H-shaped building but it has been
restored to its 17C appearance with original furnishings. In 1637 it became the
property of Earl Dysart and passed on his death to Elizabeth, who married the
Duke of Lauderdale in 1672. They enlarged and furnished the house so
ostentatiously it became famous throughout the country.

Ham House is approached through a terraced garden; the doorway,
surrounded by Corinthian pillars, leads into the Great Hall. The
figures of Mars and Minerva on the fireplace are believed to represent
the first Earl of Dysart and his wife. This floor contained the private
apartments of the Lauderdales—the first floor was used for state
occasions and approached via the Great Staircase from the Inner Hall.
The elaborately carved staircase dates to 1637; baskets of fruit top the
newel posts and the ceiling above in the Italian style is by Joseph
Kinsman.

In the first floor rooms there are displays of costumes, textiles and
miniature paintings, including Hilliard's portrait of Queen Elizabeth
and David des Granges' of Charles II. In the Round Gallery there are
portraits of Elizabeth Dysart by Lely, one as a young lady and another
as the Duchess of Lauderdale. In the North Drawing Room local
tapestries from Mortlake adorn the walls; the plaster ceiling and
frieze are by Kinsman. The dolphin-carved chairs retain their original
silk covers. There are Lely portraits in the Long Gallery. The Queen's
Bedchamber was prepared for Catherine of Braganza, Charles II's
consort—later it became a drawing room with fine tapestries by
Bradshaw. The ceiling in the Queen's Closet is by Verrio and the
landscapes by Thomas Wyck.

In the Duchess's Bedchamber on the ground floor there are four
sea-paintings by Willem van de Velde and a painted ceiling by
Verrio—others are in the White Closet and Private Closet. In the
Withdrawing Room the furniture is covered in Spitalfields silk. The
Chapel retains its original altar cloth; the furniture was carved by
Henry Harlow. Paintings at Ham House in other rooms are by
Cornelius Johnson, John Michael Wright, Sir Godfrey Kneller, Sir
Joshua Reynolds and John Constable. The gardens in the 17C style
are most attractive and there is a pleasant cafeteria in the Orangery.

Twickenham is on the N bank of the Thames but SW of Richmond, as
the river twists and turns S and W from this point. Like neighbouring
Teddington it was once part of County of Middlesex and a known

on settlement in 704. Today it is a flourishing residential suburb, ll-known for its rugby ground and some attractive historic houses of the 18C. Access: BR, Twickenham.

York House in York St is a late 17C building now used as council offices by the London Borough of Richmond upon Thames. It was once the property of Lord Clarendon (until 1689) and former illustrious residents include Anne Damer (from 1817), the sculptress, the Comte de Paris (from 1864) and the Indian merchant, Sir Ratan Tata who designed the gardens (1906–13) in the Italian style. The gardens are in two parts with a nymph fountain and a stone bridge across Riverside Road to a Grotto and a fine Italian sculpture group. Sion Road contains a fine terrace of 1720s houses.

St. Mary's Church in Church St has a medieval tower and an 18C galleried interior. Alexander Pope (died 1744) is buried here; his monument reads 'to one who would not be buried in Westminster Abbey'. Further epitaphs by him and by Dryden to others commemorated in the church include one to Mary Beach, Pope's nurse and servant, Kitty Clive, the actress, and Thomas Twining of the tea family. From the embankment it is possible to cross to *Eel Pie Island*, mentioned in Dickens' 'Nicholas Nickleby'; in the 1960s rock and roll artists such as the Rolling Stones and the Who made the now closed hotel famous.

Follow Whitton Road, N from the town centre, past Chertsey Road to Rugby Road and *Twickenham Rugby Ground*—headquarters of the Rugby Football Union and the site of England's home internationals since 1910. Further along in Kneller Road is *Kneller Hall* (tel. 081-898 5533) built for Sir Godfrey Kneller, the royal portrait painter, in 1709–11; the house was remodelled by George Mair in 1848 and imposing turrets and pillars in the neo-Jacobean style added. It is now used by the Royal Military School of Music and there are open air concerts here on Wednesday evenings from May to August. (In a cost-cutting exercise it is proposed to move the School to Chatham.) *Twickenham Tourist Information Centre* in the Civic Centre, York Street (tel. 081-891 1411), can provide more information. Church St in the centre of Twickenham is now partially pedestrianised and there is a variety of speciality shops and boutiques. The Church St Fair is held here during Twickenham Week in May.

To reach the site of Alexander Pope's villa head S from Twickenham towards Strawberry Hill along Crossdeep (about half a mile). A girls' school, *St. Catherine's Convent*, occupies the present building of 1842. Pope lived here from 1719 to 1744 and the fantastic garden became famous, designed to match the Gothic splendour of the house. *Pope's Grotto* survives and can be visited by prior application on Saturday mornings (tel. 081-892 5633).

Further along Crossdeep is *Radnor Gardens*, now a bowling green, and then **Strawberry Hill**, Horace Walpole's famous house. This is now *St. Mary's Training College* (Waldegrave Road, Twickenham) but the Gothick interior has been carefully preserved. The house can be visited by prior application on Wednesdays and Saturdays (tel. 081-892 0051). It took Horace Walpole 30 years from 1747 to turn this simple 'plaything' house into a magnificent castle with details copied from famous buildings throughout Britain, including Old St. Paul's, Canterbury Cathedral and Westminster Abbey. Walpole wrote 'The Castle of Otranto' while living here (1754–76).

Marble Hill House is in Richmond Road, Twickenham, three quarters of a mile to the N of the town centre (tel. 081-892 5115). Open daily Easter to Sept 10.00–18.00, Oct to Easter 10.00–16.00 (closed Fri). Access: Underground to Richmond, BR, St. Margarets. Buses. Car park

Marble Hill House in its 66-acre park is owned by the English Heritage; there a cafeteria in the stable block (open April to September).

The house was built in the Palladian style in 1729 for Henrietta Howard Countess of Suffolk and mistress of George II. The final design was by the Earl of Pembroke; the builder was Roger Morris. The ground floor rooms are now used for exhibitions and the first floor has been furnished in the style of the period. An impressive mahogany staircase leads from the hall to the Great Hall on the first floor with carvings by James Richards. Two views of Rome painted by Pannini in 1738 for the House were reinstated in 1989. Small arcades and columns divide the rooms. Lady Suffolk received John Gay and her neighbours Alexander Pope and Horace Walpole here. Pope helped to plan the garden.

Lord Tennyson lived in nearby 18C *Chapel House*, Montpelier Row, in 1851–52, and *South End House*, Montpelier Row was the home of Walter de la Mare in 1950–56.

The remnant of *Orleans House*, the *Octagon Room*, is in Lebanon Park Road and houses the *Orleans House Gallery*, (tel. 081-892 0221) open from April to September, Tues to Sat, 13.00–17.30, Sun and Bank Holidays 14.00–17.30, October to March 13.00–16.30, and Sun and Bank Holidays 14.00–16.30. Admission free. Access as for Marble Hill House.

On view is the Ionides Collection of 400 topographical works of Richmond and Twickenham as well as temporary exhibitions which sometimes take over the complete gallery. Orleans House was built in 1710 by John James and the Octagon added in 1720 by James Gibbs for James Johnston, Secretary of State for Scotland. The elaborately decorated stucco walls and ceilings were carved by Guiseppe Artaria and Giovanne Bagutti. From 1814 to 1817 Louis-Philippe, Duc d'Orleans (King of France in 1830–48) lived here. A woodland garden surrounds the Octagon which is all that remains of the house.

A ferry operates from here to Ham House on the other side of the Thames daily 10.00–18.00.

Teddington, 1.5 miles SW of Twickenham (access: BR, Teddington), was a fashionable residential area in the 19C with large houses whose grounds stretched down to the Thames. Most of these are now gone and have been replaced by substantial suburban houses. Thames Television has large studios in Broom Road by the river and other film and video companies are established nearby. *The Anglers* pub is a popular venue for the television community.

There is a footbridge from Ferry Road to Ham with a good view of Teddington Lock and Weir, the highest tidal point of the Thames.

Teddington has two parish churches: *St. Albans*, at the Twickenham Road/Ferry Road junction, was begun in 1887 to a grandiose design by W. Niven but left half finished. It overshadows the old *St. Mary's*, opposite, of 16C origin. The actress Margaret Woffington (died 1760) is buried in the church and has given her name to a row of 18C cottages nearby. Sir Orlando Bridgeman, Charles II's Lord Keeper of the Great Seal is also buried in the church and the author of Lorna Doone, R.D. Blackmore (died 1900) who lived in Teddington, is buried in the nearby Victorian cemetery.

All Hallows church, in Chertsey Road towards Twickenham, is a modern building completed in 1940 but with an ancient tower moved stone by stone from All Hallows, Lombard St in the City, when the 17C Wren church was demolished (1938–39). Memorials and furnishings also moved to the new church include a carved pulpit from which John Wesley preached his first sermon (in 1735), and the 18C organ.

At Normansfield Hospital in Teddington, previously a mental asylum, a small private theatre of 1866 has survived virtually unaltered.

Bushy Park, half a mile S of Teddington, can be reached from the
wn centre via Park Road, or from Hampton Court (BR, Hampton
Court). It covers 1000 acres and opened to the public in 1838. The
former home of the park ranger, *Bushy House* at the Teddington end,
is now the *National Physical Laboratory*. The attractive Orangery was
recently restored. The one-mile-long Chestnut Avenue which leads
from Teddington to Hampton Court is edged by 274 horse chestnut
trees. The Diana Fountain near Hampton Court was designed by
Francesco Fanelli and placed here by Wren in 1714. To the W of
Chestnut Avenue are the *Waterhouse Woodland Gardens*, Lime
Avenue, and the artificial Longford River.

The Hamptons. ****Hampton Court**, 13m W of Central London, stands
on the site of an early Saxon settlement. The manor established here
at the time of the Domesday Book (1086) was vested in Walter de St.
Valery and acquired by the Knights Hospitaller of St. John of
Jerusalem in 1236. They sold the lease to Thomas Wolsey in 1514. A
small village developed around the manor but 1m further W the
village of Hampton became established, while 1m downstream to the
E, Hampton Wick formed its own parish. During the 19C Hampton
developed northwards towards Twickenham and the area here (just
1m W of Teddington) became known as New Hampton and later
Hampton Hill. Today Hampton Court refers just to the area around
the Palace, and the Hamptons have developed into separate suburbs.
As late as 1980 former market gardens to the NW of Hampton were
developed for housing.

HAMPTON COURT PALACE.

Access: BR, Hampton Court; Green Line, 716, 718 and 726; river
services during summer from Westminster Pier and Kingston. Tel.
081-977 8441. Open daily 09.30-18.00 (Summer); 09.30–16.30 (Winter). Maze same hours. Admission charge. Car and Coach park. Free
daily guided tours May to Sept (except Sunday) at 11.15 and 14.15.
Restaurant and Cafeteria in the grounds.

Hampton Court Palace is one of the most attractive historic buildings
in Greater London, with delightful gardens, a large park, and
riverside walk (administered by the Department of the Environment).

The Palace was begun in 1514 by Cardinal Wolsey, who intended a building
surpassing in splendour every other private residence. In 1529, as the Cardinal
fell from favour, he was obliged to surrender his Palace to Henry VIII, who added
the Great Hall and the Chapel. From that time, for two centuries Hampton Court
was a favourite royal residence conveniently located on the Thames. Edward VI
was born here in 1537 and William III, who died in 1702 after a fall from his horse
in the Home Park, employed Sir Christopher Wren to substitute the present East
and South Wings for three of Wolsey's courtyards. After the death of George II
the Palace ceased to be a royal residence but state functions still take place here
occasionally. The 'Grace and Favour' apartments surrounding the smaller courts
are still the residences of pensioners of the Crown and others. A Son-et-Lumiere
production was held here in 1984 over two months in the summer, recreating the
history of the Palace. A fire severely damaged part of the Great Hall in summer
1986. Reconstruction work may alter the layout as described below.

In the mellow red brick front of the Palace stands the *Great Gatehouse*
with oriel windows from Wolsey's time, terracotta medallions of
Roman emperors attributed to Giovanni da Maiano, and the arms of
Henry VIII. The moat in front is crossed by a fine bridge, added by
Henry VIII and guarded by the 'King's Beasts'. The *Base Court*
beyond the Gatehouse is the largest court and survives from the

The Great Gatehouse at Hampton Court Palace

original Palace. To the left are several smaller courts, recreating the atmosphere of Tudor domestic architecture. Anne Boleyn's Gateway leads to the *Clock Court*, named from the curious astronomical clock made for Henry VIII. The graceful colonnade on the right was added by Wren. The entrance to the State Apartments is at the end; before it is a small exhibition on the history of the Palace in one of the former 'Grace and Favour' apartments.

The **State Apartments** in the East and South Wings contain some 500 paintings, among which the Italian School is best represented, and much of the original furniture and decorations.

Enter via the *King's Staircase*, with walls and ceilings by Verrio, to the *Guard Chamber* which contains more than 3000 pieces of arms. Opening off this are the panelled *Wolsey Rooms*, used by members of his household, with a charming view of the Knot and Pond Gardens and fine ceilings. The portraits here include: William Scrots, *Edward VI*; Gheeraerts, *Portrait of a Lady*, and Mytens, *Charles I and Henrietta Maria*. The *First Presence Chamber* contains a portrait of William III by Kneller. In the *Second Presence Chamber* are paintings by Tintoretto, Bordone and Bassano. In the *Audience Chamber*, with a view of the Privy Gardens, are: Tintoretto, *Knights of Malta*, *Nine Muses* and *Portrait of a Man*, and Lotto, *Andrea Odoni*. In the *King's Drawing Room*: Lotto, *Portrait of a Man*; Titian, *Portrait of a Man*, and Tintoretto, *Venetian Senator*. In *William III's Bedroom*, with a ceiling by Verrio, are the King's Bed and a clock by Quare which goes for a year without winding. The *King's Dressing Room* contains works by Holbein. The *King's Writing Room* contains: Pontormo, *Madonna and Child*; Parmigianino, *Portrait of a Boy*, and Andrea del Sarto, *Holy Family*.

Enter the Queen's Rooms, starting at *Queen Mary's Closet*. Paintings include: Pieter Brueghel the Elder, *Massacre of the Innocents*.

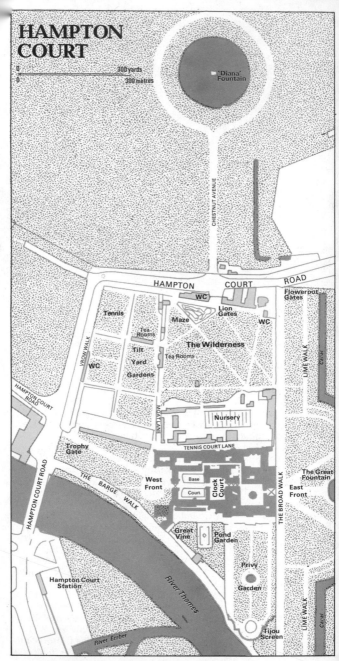

HAMPTON COURT

0   300 yards
0   300 metres

'Diana' Fountain

CHESTNUT AVENUE

HAMPTON COURT ROAD

WC

Flowerpot Gates

Tennis

Maze

Lion Gates

WC

Tea Rooms

The Wilderness

VROW WALK

Tilt Yard Gardens

Tea Rooms

WC

LIME WALK

Canal

HAMPTON COURT ROAD

MOAT LANE

Nursery

TENNIS COURT LANE

Trophy Gate

THE BROAD WALK

The Great Fountain

HAMPTON COURT ROAD

THE BARGE WALK

West Front

Base Court

Clock Court

East Front

Great Vine

Pond Garden

Privy Garden

Hampton Court Station

River Thames

LIME WALK

Canal

River Ember

Tijou Screen

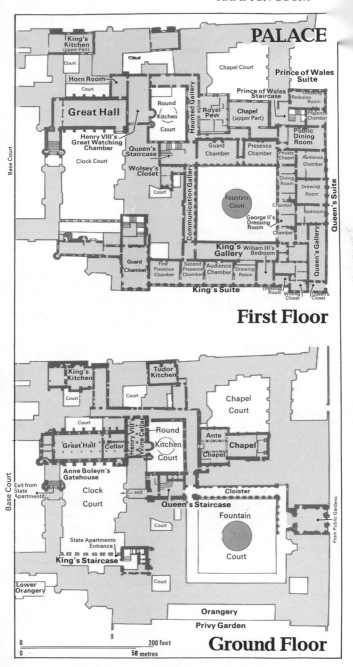

PALACE

King's Kitchen (upper Part)

Court

Court

Chapel Court

Prince of Wales Suite

Horn Room

Court

Great Hall

Round Kitchen Court

Haunted Gallery

Royal Pew

Chapel (upper Part)

Prince of Wales Staircase

Dressing Room

Bedroom Room

Presence Chamber

Henry VIII's Great Watching Chamber

Clock Court

Queen's Staircase

Wolsey's Closet

Court

Communication Gallery

Guard Chamber

Presence Chamber

Private Chapel

Public Dining Room

Audience Chamber

Dining Room

Drawing Room

Fountain Court

George II's Dressing Room

Chamber

Bedroom

Queen's Suite

Chamber

Guard Chamber

First Presence Chamber

Second Presence Chamber

Audience Chamber

Drawing Room

King's Gallery

William III's Bedroom

Queen's Gallery

King's Suite

Dressing Room

Writing Closet

Queen's Closet

Base Court

First Floor

King's Kitchen

Court

Tudor Kitchen

Court

Chapel Court

Great Hall

Cellar

Henry VIII's Wine Cellar

Round Kitchen Court

Ante Chapel

Chapel

Anne Boleyn's Gatehouse

Exit from State Apartments

Clock Court

exit

Queen's Staircase

Cloister

Fountain

Court

From Public Gardens

Court

State Apartments Entrance

King's Staircase

Court

Lower Orangery

Base Court

Orangery

Privy Garden

0   200 feet

0   50 metres

Ground Floor

e *Queen's Gallery*, completed for Queen Anne, has Brussels pestries depicting the story of Alexander the Great and a mantelpiece y Nost. In the *Queen's Bedroom* is the State Bed in crimson silk; the ceiling is by Thornhill. The walls and ceiling of the *Drawing Room* were painted by Verrio—the windows command a fine view of the gardens. In the *Queen's Audience Chamber* there are Dutch and Flemish portraits. The *Public Dining Room*, decorated by William Kent, contains paintings by Sebastiano, and Mytens, *Charles II and the Dwarf*.

The three small rooms to the N form a suite once occupied by Prince Frederick, son of George II. The *Prince of Wales Presence Chamber* contains fine Italian paintings. The *Prince of Wales Drawing Room* has a portrait by Gheeraerts, *Louis Frederick*. The *Prince of Wales Bedroom* contains Queen Charlotte's bed, designed by Robert Adam, and some of Kneller's Hampton Court Beauties.

Cross the *Prince of Wales Staircase* with its elaborate balustrade and Mortlake tapestries depicting the Battle of Solebay (1672), and enter a lobby with a charming portrait of Henry, Prince of Wales with the Earl of Essex (1605). Beyond the Queen's Presence Chamber, enter the *Queen's Private Chapel* where the paintings include *St. Jerome* by Georges de la Tour. In the *Private Dining Room* is Van Eden's *Landscape with Waterfall*. The *Queen's Private Chamber* has works by Jan Brueghel the Elder.

A series of small rooms leads to the *Cartoon Gallery*, designed by Wren for the Raphael Cartoons now in the Victoria and Albert Museum. It contains 17C Brussels tapestries copied from the cartoons, below which are paintings illustrating the life of Henry VIII. The *Communications Gallery* contains the *Windsor Beauties* by Sir Peter Lely, portraits of the ladies of Charles II's court.

The gallery leads to three small rooms including *Wolsey's Closet*, the only remaining room of his personal apartment with good linen-scroll panelling and vivid painted decorations. The *Cumberland Suite* was designed by William Kent in 1732.

Cross the upper landing of the Queen's Staircase with fine ironwork by Tijou and a brilliant allegorical painting by Honthorst of Charles I and his Queen as Apollo and Diana. Enter the *Haunted Gallery*, built by Wolsey, where the ghost of Catherine Howard is said to walk. The tapestries probably belonged to Elizabeth I.

Off it opens the *Holy Day Closet*, leading to the upper part of the *Royal Chapel*, with a fine ceiling and woodwork.

From the end of the Haunted Gallery enter Henry VIII's *Great Watching Chamber*, hung with Flemish tapestries which once belonged to Wolsey, then pass through the Horn Room to enter the **Great Hall** (106ft long by 40ft wide and 60ft high), built by Henry VIII in 1531–36 with one of the finest hammerbeam roofs in existence. The walls are hung with beautiful Brussels tapestries.

From its furthest end a flight of steps descends to Anne Boleyn's Gateway: turn right into *Base Court*.

In the right-hand corner of the Base Court is the entrance to the King's Beer Cellar and Henry VIII's New Wine Cellar; on leaving the wine cellars, turn left then right to reach the *Serving Place* and the *Tudor Kitchens* with huge fireplaces and ancient utensils. From the Serving Place dark corridors lead to *Fountain Court*, designed by Wren who occupied rooms off the W side of the walk. To the N is the entrance to the Royal Chapel (open for services on Sunday at 11.00 and 15.30).

The **Gardens**, entered from the E walk of the cloister, were laid out in their present formal style under William III. At right-angles to the Broad

Walk, which skirts the E front of the Palace, is the Long Water w. bisects the Home Park. To the left is the entrance to the old *Ten Court* (open April to Sept), rebuilt by William III on the site of the cou. built by Henry VIII in 1529. Real tennis is played here occasionally. On the S side of the Palace are the *Privy Gardens*, at the end of which, near the river, is a fine iron gate by Jean Tijou, the *Elizabethan Knot Garden* of aromatic herbs, the *Pond Garden*, a sunken garden laid by Henry VIII and a later *Sunk Garden* in formal 17C style. Beyond is the *Great Vine*, planted in 1768 and still producing a crop of finest Black Hamburg grapes each year.

To the right is the *Orangery* with an exhibition of horsedrawn vehicles from the Royal Mews; further on is the *Lower Orangery* with the famous series of tempera paintings, the *Triumph of Julius Caesar*, painted by Mantegna (1485–94) for the Duke of Mantua and bought by Charles I in 1629 for £10,500; they have now been restored. Opposite, overlooking the river is *William III's Banqueting House* (c 1700), decorated by Verrio (open April to September).

On the N side of the Palace is the *Wilderness*, laid out by William III with the famous *Maze* planted in his reign also. The Lime Trees in the Great Fountain Gardens were replaced in 1987.

There is a restaurant and cafeteria in the Tiltyard Gardens.

On *Hampton Green*, W of the Palace-approach, are the *Old Court* House, where Sir Christopher Wren died in 1723, and *Faraday House*, where Michael Faraday died in 1867. The *Royal Mews* and the 16C *Barn* are still in use. *Hampton Court House* on the side of the Green was built in 1757; the concert room added in the late 19C by the Twinings is now the *Hampton Court Theatre*. Along Hampton Court Road to the W is *Garrick's Villa*, given a new façade by Robert Adam when the actor came to live here in the middle of the 18C. On Garrick's Lawn, approached from Hogarth Way, a turning off Hampton Court Road, is *Garrick's Temple to Shakespeare* (1755) an Ionic Temple which housed the Roubiliac statue of Shakespeare now in the British Library. It is open by appointment (tel. 081-892 0221).

St. Mary's parish church is 14C but rebuilt in the 19C, with a chancel by Sir Arthur Blomfield. Antonio Verrio, who decorated the walls and ceilings of Hampton Court Palace, is buried here.

39 Fulham, Hammersmith, Brentford, Hounslow, Uxbridge, Ealing, Acton and Southall

Hammersmith and Fulham are somewhat uncomfortably joined in a London Borough which stretches along the river from Chelsea to Chiswick (LB Hounslow). The Bishops of London had an official residence at Fulham Palace until 1973; the present building overlooking the Thames in Bishops Park dates from the 16C and is currently being restored. The parish church of All Saints by Putney Bridge has a medieval tower in Kentish ragstone (refaced); the church was rebuilt in 1800 and has many interesting monuments associated with the Bishops of London, including ten of their tombs. Fulham Pottery was established in the New King's Road in 1672; white earthenware vases—Fulham Vases—were made here until the 1970s. The Pottery has been re-established across the Thames in Battersea, see p 330. The gigantic am Power Station (1936) is being redeveloped. Fulham Football o's ground at Craven Cottage (1879) is also part of a redevelopment oject. On the other side of Putney Bridge approach, Ranelagh Gardens ead to the Hurlingham Club, where sport is still the main activity, although Hurlingham House (1760) is increasingly used for functions of various kinds. The grounds, which became famous first for pigeon shooting and later for polo, first played in 1874, were considerably reduced in size when the LCC acquired part for housing in 1946.

Fulham is popular residential area with a wide range of shops and restaurants in the Fulham Road and New King,s Road. The Fulham Broadway Piazza pedestrianised shopping area opened in 1988. (Access: Underground, Fulham Broadway.)

Hammersmith (access: Underground, Hammersmith) is a busy commercial and residential suburb by the Thames; a major redevelopment of the centre is going ahead after years of controversy. Once an agricultural community supplying the City of London with vegetables, Hammersmith grew into a suburb with the arrival of the railway in the 19C. Today it supports two theatres, many historic houses and several attractive riverside pubs.

The *Lyric Theatre*, Hammersmith is in King St, W6 (tel. 081-741 2311), in a new and otherwise undistinguished shopping centre; the interior is that of the 1895 theatre which stood in Broadmore Grove. Its greatest director was Nigel Playfair (1918–33) whose most successful production, 'The Beggar's Opera', ran for three years from 1920. The theatre closed in 1966 and was demolished in 1974. The plasterwork interior by Frank Matcham was saved and included in the main auditorium of the new theatre, designed by Derek Wool, which opened in 1979. There is a smaller theatre for experimental works, a bar and buffet.

The *Riverside Studios*, Crisp Road, W6 (tel. 081-748 3354), Hammersmith's second theatre, is located in former television studios. (Approach along Queen Caroline St from town centre.) The modest facilities are used effectively for dance, theatre and music, against a constant struggle for funding.

The *Hammersmith Odeon* in Queen Caroline St (tel. 081-748 4081) is used for pop-concerts and the *Hammersmith Palais* for dancing and concerts (Shepherds Bush Road, Hammersmith, W6. Tel. 081-748 2812). The local parish church of *St. Paul's* in Queen Caroline St dates to 1883; its Gothic structure is just visible above the Hammersmith flyover carrying the Great West Road. The font comes from an older church on the same site and the carved pulpit from Wren's All Hallows, Thames St. There are memorials to William Tierney Clark, who built the first Hammersmith Bridge in 1827—London's first suspension bridge—and to Charles II, erected by royalist and adventurer Nicholas Crisp (died 1665).

Bradmore House (1739), once part of the bus station, will be partly incorporated in the new town centre. It was designed by Thomas Archer; some of the panelling from the house is in the Geffrye Museum. Queen Caroline, wife of George IV, died in this house in 1821. Lucien Pissarro, son of Camille Pissarro and also a painter, lived at 27 Stamford Brook Road, Hammersmith, W6 (1900–44); his house became a meeting place for artists of the day, including Sickert, William Rothenstein, Charles Ricketts and Charles Shannon. The last two shared the studios at Landsowne House, Landsowne Rd, W11, with Glyn Philpot (died 1937).

From the present **Hammersmith Bridge**, designed by Sir Joseph Bazalgette (1887) and now closed to heavy traffic, Lower and Upper Mall stretch to the W, forming a delightful 2-mile-long river-walk towards Chiswick. Among the interesting houses are (from Hammersmith Bridge), the headquarters of the Amateur Rowing Association with a distinctive blue balcony, the *Blue Anchor* pub next door, and *Westcott Lodge*, an 18C house owned by the Borough Council. At *Furnivall Gardens*, attractive flower beds provide a breathing space between the river and the constant traffic on the Great West Road. The gardens are named after Dr F.J. Furnivall, the social reformer (1825–1910), whose sculling club was based at Hammersmith Pier and Creek. Privately owned boats moored here are the only reminders of the busy Creek where Stamford Brook joined the Thames; commercial river-traffic was heavy until 1921 when the Creek was filled in.

The 16C *Dove Inn* is one of London's most famous pubs; half of the building was used for the Dove's Press. Charles II and Nell Gwynn are supposed to have met here. Names of other famous customers are displayed above the great fireplace. There is a good view of the river and the boat race from the balcony. William Morris lived at *Kelmscott House*, Upper Mall, from 1878 to 1896; he named the house after his country home in Oxfordshire. Earlier it was the home of Sir Francis Ronalds, inventor of the telegraph, who laid cables in the garden in 1816 as part of his experiments. Part of his original telegraph can now be seen in the Science Museum. Morris set up the Kelmscott Press in nearby Sussex House. Plans were made in 1985 to turn Kelmscott House into a William Morris museum but it was sold into private ownership.

House-owners along the Upper Mall have secluded gardens along the river, some of which are open to the public on certain days under the National Gardens Scheme. At Rivercourt Road two large bastions mark the site of the house of Catherine of Braganza; she lived here after the death of her husband, Charles II. The *Old Ship Inn* and the *Black Lion* stand on either side of the *West Middlesex Pumping Station* (1806) designed by Tierney Clark. Past famous residents of Hammersmith Terrace include the artist Philip de Loutherbourg (died 1812), Sir Emery Walker, the antiquary (1903–33 at this house) and Sir Alan P. Herbert.

Chiswick. Hammersmith Terrace leads into *Chiswick Mall*, one of the most attractive groups of 18C houses in London, including Lingard House, Thames View, Strawberry House, Morton House, Eynham House, Bedford House, Red Lion House, once the home of Nigel Playfair, and Woodroffe House. *Walpole House* was the home of Barbara Villiers, Duchess of Cleveland, Charles II's mistress, who died here in 1709. It is a fine example of the Restoration period. At the *Fox and Hound* pub, Alexander Pope lived with his parents until he moved to Strawberry Hill in 1719.

Past Fuller's Brewery, with its cobbled yard, 200 yards into Church St is the parish church of *St. Nicholas*. All that remains of the old church is the 15C tower, the rest was rebuilt in 1884. William Hogarth's grave is marked by a pedestal and urn with an epitaph by Garrick; nearby is the tomb of the artist James Whistler (died 1903). Others buried here and in the adjoining cemetery include Philip de Loutherbourg, the artist (1740–1812); William Kent (died 1748) and Colen Campbell, architects to Lord Burlington are also buried here, as is the Duchess of Cleveland (1641–1709).

Church St leads to the busy Hogarth Roundabout—well-known from London traffic reports. Chiswick Square, with *Boston House* (1740), is nearby (left off roundabout).

Strand-on-the-Green, another stretch of fine riverside houses, is best approached from Kew Bridge (access: BR, Kew Bridge) eastwards towards Chiswick. Among famous residents of the 18C houses were the artist John Zoffany at No. 65 (1790–1810), Nancy Mitford, the writer, at Rose Cottage, Dylan Thomas at Ship House Cottage and Lord Cudlipp, newspaper owner, at No. 14. The *City Barge* at No. 27 has a 15C charter—the Lord Mayor's barge used to be moored nearby, hence the name—and the *Bull's Head* at No. 15 is 350 years old, as the exposed, blackened beams indicate.

Of great historic interest is **Chiswick House**.

Chiswick House, Burlington Lane, Chiswick, W4. Tel. 081-995 0508. Open mid-March to end Sept daily 10.00–18.00; 1 Oct to mid March daily 10.00–16.00.

Main entrance from Great Chertsey Road. Access: Underground, Turnham Green, then bus; BR Chiswick. Car park in grounds from Great West Road. Modest cafeteria in park (summer and weekends). Admission charge. Grounds open daily.

Chiswick House was built by the third Earl of Burlington in the grounds of his then principal residence. As one of the greatest patrons of the arts of his day, he planned the house as 'a temple to the arts', influenced by two visits to Italy. The design was based on Palladio's Villa Capra near Vicenza but is not a copy. The summer parlour was built first and completed in 1729. William Kent was responsible for the interior and the garden. The old Jacobean mansion to which the villa was attached when completed was demolished in 1788 and the Duke of Devonshire (his mother was Burlington's only child) enlarged the house with wings designed by James Wyatt. In 1892 the Duke removed his treasures to Chatsworth and the house became a private lunatic asylum until it was purchased by Middlesex County Council in 1928. During restoration work after the Second World War the wings were removed and the house returned to its original design in 1958. It is now owned and run by the Department of the Environment.

Burlington's villa was a sensation when it was completed and influenced the architecture of private mansions throughout Britain. Artists and writers of the day were regular visitors, including Alexander Pope who lived nearby. Joseph Paxton, designer of Crystal Palace, worked when a boy in the gardens. Charles James Fox died here in 1806 and King Edward VII spent time here as the Prince of Wales in 1866–79, guest of the Duke of Devonshire.

The striking exterior design is best appreciated from the courtyard. Double staircases flanked by statues of Palladio and Inigo Jones by Rysbrack (c 1730) lead to the first floor entrance of the two-storey square, dome-topped building. Six Corinthian pillars adorn the portico, below which is the public entrance. In 1989 a new exhibition was installed introducing the history of the house through a short audio visual presentation. Below are some of the highlights of the interior.

The ground floor was Lord Burlington's private apartments and the layout radiates from an octagonal hall directly underneath the dome. The *Library* is to the left; a wine cellar below the hall. The *Summer Parlour* is the link building with the earlier, now demolished house.

A concealed spiral staircase leads to the first floor; the *Dome Saloon* now houses the paintings which were removed to Chatsworth; *Charles I and family* (probably a copy of the Van Dyck in the Royal Collection); the *Moroccan Ambassador* by Kneller, *Louis XIII* and *Anne of Austria*, both by Ferdinand Elee, plus four allegorical and classical paintings by Guido Reni, Anthonie Schoonjans and Danielo da Volterra. The dome has been restored to its original colour and the busts are all replacement copies.

On the left is the *Red Velvet Room*, originally covered in velvet. The richly carved chimney pieces date to 1729 with paintings by Sebastiano Ricci.

The *Blue Velvet Room* has an elaborate marble chimney piece and a richly decorated ceiling by Kent. The Red Closet beyond also has an elaborate panelled ceiling. The *Gallery* runs the full length of the house overlooking the gardens. Despite its relatively small dimensions, it has been carefully proportioned with two arches to increase its grandeur. Statues of Mercury, Venus, Apollo and a muse adorn the central section. The central ceiling panel is probably a copy by Ricci of a work by Veronese. The *Green Velvet Room* has fine chimney pieces and a restored Venetian window. Above the doorways in the bedchamber are portraits of the Earl of Cumberland, Lady Burlington and Lady Thanet.

The *Gardens*, laid out by William Kent, marked a departure in garden design, away from the formal layout inspired by Le Nôtre towards an Italian style based on radiating paths, each revealing a different vista.

To the S a temple and a bridge by James Wyatt over a cascade are being restored. A tall obelisk incorporates a Roman tombstone. Most striking is the small-scale turfed amphitheatre with a pond in its centre and a small Ionic temple. N of the Summer Parlour stands the Inigo Jones gateway brought from Beaufort House, Chelsea, to Chiswick in 1736 as the stone tablets record. The path leads towards the Orangery, cafeteria and conservatory with formally planted Victorian-style flower beds in front.

Return to the Hogarth Roundabout to explore **Hogarth's House** on the Great West Road. The house survives behind a large office block.

Hogarth's House, Hogarth Lane, Great West Road, Chiswick, W4. Tel. 081-994 6757. Open April to Sept, Mon to Sat 11.00–18.00, Oct to March 11.00–16.00, Sun 14.00– 18.00 (16.00 in winter) (closed Tues first two weeks of Sept and last three weeks of Dec). Admission free. Car park in W-bound layby of Great West Road. Access: Underground, Turnham Green; Chiswick. Bus E3.
 William Hogarth, the 18C cartoonist, painter and illustrator, used Hogarth House as his summer residence from 1749 until his death in 1764, and referred to it as 'the little country box by the Thames'.
 Following a period of neglect, a public appeal to buy the house in 1900 failed. Local benefactor Lt. Col. Robert Shipway stepped in, and restored and opened it to the public in 1902 as a Hogarth Museum. He presented it to Middlesex County Council seven years later. It was seriously damaged by bombs in 1940 and reopened after restoration in 1951. It is now run by the London Borough of Hounslow.

Hogarth House contains a selection of Hogarth prints and 18C furniture, revealing interesting glimpses of London life as well as reflecting Hogarth's strong social and moral conscience. In the Kitchen, now a gallery, three of the well-known moral series are shown: 'A Harlot's Progress', 'An Election' and 'Marriage á la Mode'. In the Dining Room hang the contrasting 'Beer St' and 'Gin Lane' extolling the virtues of beer as opposed to gin. Hogarth's contempt for the papacy can be seen in 'O, the Roast Beef of Old England' or 'Calais Gate'. In the Best Parlour with its triple bay window, the rural view of the 1750s as shown in 'Mr Ranby's House' (Room 3) can be compared with the view of today. Hogarth's portrait is over the mantelpiece and the prints 'Industry and Idleness' show interesting glimpses of the Lord Mayor's show and an execution at Tyburn.
 In the garden a mulberry tree planted by the artist still flourishes.

Brentford (1 mile W of Kew Bridge and 3 miles W from the Hogarth Roundabout), as the name suggests, was an important river-crossing and inhabited well before London itself. Julius Caesar is said to have first crossed the Thames at this point and archaeological finds from the riverbed collected by Thomas Layton (1882–1964), local archaeologist, are in the Museum of London.

The Battle of Brentford between Charles I and the Parliamentary forces in 1642 ended at Turnham Green with the royalists turning back from London. Today Brentford is recovering from its industrial growth in the late 19C which later left large areas derelict as heavy industry moved elsewhere. E.M. Forster, the novelist, lived at Arlington Park Mansions, Turnham Green (1939–70) and described the bombing of London's docks from his top-floor flat.

As part of the regeneration of the riverside, the London Borough of Hounslow and commercial interests have built housing, and in 1984 the *Waterman's Art Centre* opened. Purpose-built on the site of the old gasworks in Brentford High St, the Centre overlooks the river and includes a 240-seat theatre, a cinema, art gallery, bar and restaurant with open air terraces. Waterman's Arts Centre is at 40 High St, Brentford. Tel. 081-586 3312. *Waterman's Park* has been laid out on derelict ground nearby. (Access: Underground, Gunnersbury; BR, Kew Bridge.)

The *West London Pumping Station* which dominates the area visually was converted into a steam museum by enthusiasts who in 1975 formed the Kew Bridge Engines Trust.

Kew Bridge Steam Museum, Green Dragon Lane, Brentford. Tel. 081-568 4757. Open daily 11.00–17.00; steaming of the original beam engines at weekends. Admission charge. Car park. Access: Underground, Gunnersbury; BR, Kew Bridge.

The West London Pumping Station supplied London with fresh water from 1852 to the 1960s. On view are the Cornish beam engines dating from 1845 and 1869; the main beams are over 30ft long and they are steamed at weekends. Electric pumps took over in 1944.

The *Musical Museum* in the former St. George's Church at 368 High St, Brentford, Middlesex (081-560 8108); open April to October, Sat and Sun, 14.00–17.00, Wed to Fri July and Aug 14.00–17.00. Admission charge. Car park in North Road. Access: Underground, Gunnersbury; BR, Kew Bridge.

The Musical Museum contains Frank Holland's life-long collection of automatic musical instruments. There are ten reproducing piano systems and three reproducing pipe organs, including a giant Wurlitzer, as well as 30,000 music rolls. Frank Holland will demonstrate the instruments—allow one hour for a nostalgic session of early 20C popular and classical music.

In the centre of Brentford stands the parish church of *St. Paul's* (St. Paul's Road), built in 1867 with a noteworthy painting of the Last Supper by Zoffany. The older parish church, *St. Lawrence*, at the western end of the High St, was closed in 1976. The Butts, just off Halfacre, was the site of parliamentary elections but is now a car park. There are some fine early 18C houses here, including *Beaufort House*.

The *Grand Union Canal* opened between Brentford and Uxbridge in 1794 and Brentford, as an important trans-shipment point for goods from the N, laid the foundations for its early industrial development. The Canal can be explored by walking along the tow-path. Access from Brentford High St into Dock Road with a view over Thames tidal lock. Several pubs survive along the canal. At *Hanwell* there is a flight of six locks raising the canal 50ft in a third of a mile.

NW of Brentford is *Boston Manor Park* with a fine mansion house, *Boston Manor House*, Boston Manor Lane, Brentford.

Open Sun only 14.00–16.00, (May to September). Free. Park open daily 08.00 to dusk. Tel. 081-862 5809. Admission charge. Access: Underground, Boston Manor.

This attractive Jacobean manor house was built in 1622, on the 14C estate and passed to the Clitheroe family in 1670. They owned it until 1924 when Brentford Council took it over and restored it. The red-brick house is well furnished. The beautiful ceiling in the first floor drawing room which depicts the senses and the elements is particularly noteworthy. The grounds, with 17C cedars, are a public park divided in two by the M4 motorway.

1 mile NE of Brentford is *Gunnersbury Park* with the *Gunnersbury Park Museum* covering the history of the area.

Gunnersbury Park Museum, Pope's Lane, W3. Tel. 081-992 1612. Open March to October, Mon to Fri 13.00–17.00, Sat, Sun 14.00–18.00; closes 16.00 in winter. Park open daily. Admission free. Cafeteria (summer and weekends).
   The museum consists of two 19C villas which were the property of the Rothschild family. It became a museum in 1925 and contains a collection of flint instruments, other archaeological finds, exhibits on transport, domestic life, costumes and local views. The Victorian kitchens have been restored.

The centre of the former village of **Old Isleworth**, 1.5 miles SW of Brentford by the River Thames (access: BR, Isleworth) has been imaginatively transformed in a major redevelopment which has restored old buildings and added others in a mixed housing and commercial development. The modern church of *All Saints* by Michael Blee opened in 1969 with the 14C tower from the old church, which burnt down, incorporated. Part of the 18C aisle walls have been preserved in the open courtyard. A fountain has been added, and there are views of the Thames from inside the vaulted church. There has been a church on the site since 695. Nearby is the *London Apprentice* (1741), Church St, Old Isleworth, a famous river pub with original Hogarth prints on display, named after the apprentices who rowed upstream from the City on their day off. In the river is Isleworth Ait and on the other side *Old Deer Park*.

Isleworth became fashionable in the 18C when large residential properties were built along the river. But industry spread from Brentford; Pears Soap had a factory here until 1962. Council housing followed. At Mill Platt (off Twickenham Rd) there are 17C almshouses founded by Lord Ingason next to the West Middlesex Hospital which was based on the former workhouse (1837).

On the river between Brentford and Isleworth is Syon House and Park. **Syon House and Park**, including the Heritage Motor Museum and Butterfly House, are in Park Road, Brentford.

Access: Underground, Gunnersbury, then Bus 237, 267. Car park. Syon House, tel. 081-560 0881. House open Sun to Thur 12.00–17.00 (Easter to September). October, Sun only 12.00– 17.00. Last admission 16.15. Admission charge. Park gardens open daily 10.00–18.00 (Easter to September) 10.00–dusk (October to March). Admission charge. Cafeteria and Camellia Restaurant, tel. 081-568 0881.

Syon House, the property of the Duke of Northumberland who still lives here, was remodelled for the family in the mid 18C by Robert Adam. The exterior retains the simplicity of the original Tudor building constructed for the Protector Somerset after the Dissolution when he took over the Brigettine convent founded on the site in 1415. Queen Elizabeth granted the estate to the Percy family, Dukes of Northumberland.

Dramatic events from the past of Syon House include Queen Katherine Howard being confined here before her execution in 1542. Lady Jane Grey accepted the crown in 1553 and lived here for nine days before being taken to the Tower. Today's visitors can admire some of the best work of Robert Adam produced at the height of his creativity.

The public entrance leads to the hall in pale colours with a diamond patterned ceiling by Joseph Rose. A large bronze, 'The Dying Gaul', a copy of an antique statue, is by the stairs which lead to the Anteroom, perhaps the finest room in the house, converted into a square by the addition of a screen of columns. The vivid colours are offset by the scagliola floor and rich gilding on the ceiling and on the capitals of the columns. The dining room is white with liberal gilding; the rich ceiling features arabesques, fans and flower motifs. The Three Graces in marble are in a panel above the fireplace. Red Spitalfields silk still covers the walls in the Red Drawing Room with paintings by Lely of Charles I and the Duke of York. The deep-coved ceiling is decorated in Renaissance style with octagons and squares containing medallions of classical scenes by Cipriani in gold, yellow, pink and green. These colours, repeated in the Thomas Moore carpet, add lustre to the room. Two sideboard tables display mosaics from the Baths of Titus in Rome. In the gallery, designed to provide 'variety and amusement' for the ladies, Adam created a wide space with the use of geometric ceiling features. Authentic Adam furniture includes the marquetry tables. The Oak Passage leading to the exit is lined with 17C carved oak panels, paintings and a pictorial map of the Hundred of Isleworth, painted in 1653 by Moses Glover.

The gardens, laid out by Capability Brown in 1762 at the same time as Adam worked on the house, feature the (artificial) Long Lake, Flora's Lawn against a Doric column and mulberry trees planted during the Protector Somerset's residence here in the 16C. The *Great Conservatory* was added in 1827, designed by Charles Fowler. Paxton is said to have used it as a model for his conservatory at Chatsworth and later for the Crystal Palace. There is an aviary, aquarium and a Garden Centre selling house and garden plants but also including an exhibition of toys.

In the grounds of Syon Park are the *British Heritage Motor Museum*, in the stable block, and the *Butterfly House*.

Heritage Motor Museum, Syon Park, Brentford. Tel. 081-560 1378. Open daily 10.00–17.30, Nov to Feb closes 16.00. Admission charge. Access as for Syon House.
This is the world's largest collection of historic British cars, showing production cars from 1895 to the present day including prototypes, rally and racing cars. Rides in historic cars can be arranged.

Butterfly House, Syon Park, Brentford. Tel. 081-560 7272. Open daily 10.00–17.00 (15.30 in winter). Admission charge.
A large number of different species of butterfly fly freely in a 'natural' indoor setting. During the winter months the display is limited. Good bookshop with specialist literature.

3 miles W along the Great West Road (turn right into Syon Lane, then Osterley Lane) is **Osterley Park House**, also of Adam design but overshadowed by its illustrious neighbour, Syon House.

N of the Great West Road in the LB of Hounslow is Osterley with its huge park, again split by the motor way and Osterley Park House.

Osterley Park House, Osterley Lane, Osterley, Middlesex. Tel. 081-560 3918. House open Tues to Sun 11.00–17.00 (last admission 16.30). Park open 10.00 to dusk. Open Bank Hols in summer. Admission charge. National Trust. Car Park. Access: Underground, Osterley. Cafeteria in stable block.
Sir Thomas Gresham, city gentleman, built the house in 1576 and received Queen Elizabeth I here. It became the property of the Child family of bankers in 1711 and they remodelled it between 1750 and 1780. First Sir William Chambers then Robert Adam took up the commission. The lavish interior which has survived intact is mostly the work of Adam. The Earls of Jersey left Osterley to the nation in 1923 and it is now owned by the National Trust and managed by the Victoria and Albert Museum.

The Elizabethan exterior of the building features prominent corner towers round a raised courtyard. Adam added the entrance with a six-column portico. The public rooms are on the ground floor with the private apartments above. The hall is decorated with low-relief wall panels portraying trophies of war. The gallery was probably designed by Chambers, and Adam's contribution consists of the mirrored candle brackets. The original paintings have been removed and replaced by some from the Victoria and Albert Museum. The Eating Room is formally arranged with lyre-backed chairs along the walls. The rococ ceiling has a Bacchic theme, decorated with grapes and vines. The staircase is guarded by columns and designed as a frame for the ceiling, 'The apotheosis of a Hero' by Rubens, removed and since lost in a fire. The Library ceiling has been restored to its original bright colours; wall paintings are by Zucchi and Cipriano and the furniture is by John Linnel. The plain Breakfast Room has a rococo ceiling. The drawing room, described by Walpole as 'worthy of Eve before the Fall', features a great sunflower in the centre of the ceiling with radiating panels in green and gold; the sunflower theme is repeated in the carpet by Thomas Moore. The walls have been restored in 'pea-green silk damask'. There are two portraits by Reynolds. The tapestries commissioned for the house from the Gobelins factory to the designs by Boucher are in the Tapestry Room. In the State Bedchamber the four-poster bed designed by Adam has a small dome and a bedhead decorated with small boys riding dolphins. In the well-known Etruscan Room Adam introduced a design reminiscent of Greek vases.

The park is one of the largest estate parks still surviving in London. There is a Doric temple by John James (c 1720), the interior by Chambers, and a lake. The Elizabethan stables and two summer houses are private residences.

The LB of Hounslow which includes Chiswick, Brentford, Isleworth, Hounslow, Osterley, Heston, Cranford, Bedfont and Feltham is a multi-racial borough servicing a great industrial area around the Great West Road, M4 motorway and Heathrow Airport (actually in the LB Hillingdon). Brentford High St, now a quiet backwater in Brentford, became a notorious bottleneck in the 19C as the main artery to the W. The *Great West Road* was built in 1925 to relieve this congestion and, with Western Avenue completed further to the N in 1921 (now the A40), this part of London became a major industrial growth area in the 1920s and '30s based on the large-scale use of electricity as a source of power. Along the 'Golden Mile' of the Great West Road between Hammersmith and Osterley some of the great factories of this era still survive. Wallis, Gilbert and Partners designed the art deco façades of the *Pyrene* building (1929), the *Hoover* building (1932) in Western Avenue, Perivale and the even more striking *Firestone* factory (1928), demolished in the teeth of a preservation order in 1980. The Fiat Tower (1930s) is being preserved in a new building.

Striking London Transport architecture of the period, pioneered by Charles Holden, can be seen at *Osterley Station* (1934) with its curving walls and elongated 'Star Wars' pinnacle. After a period of decline, the 'high tech' industries are moving into glass-fronted new buildings (Honeywell, Mowlem and Wang), although the Gillette Factory of 1936 survives.

Hounslow centre is split in two by its lengthy High St which once carried travellers on their way to Bath. Today it is dominated by the Indian and Pakistani communities which settled here in the 1950s and '60s with specialist shops, temples, mosques and cinemas.

The parish church of *Holy Trinity* in the High St was destroyed by fire in 1943; the new church was designed by Lt. Col. W.E. Cross. Beyond lies *Hounslow Heath*, once covering 4000 acres; the 200 acre park is now an urban wildlife refuge with a mixture of heathland, woods, water and grassland; it was notorious for highwaymen. For a hort time after the First World War London's first air terminal was

.tablished on the Heath and the world's first regular commercial
passenger flight took off on 25 August 1919 followed by the first regular
airmail service on 11 November 1919—both to Paris. Croydon took over
in 1920. The River Crane flows through Hounslow for 6 miles; some of
the riverside has been opened up to the public in the last few years
revealing its history of gunpowder manufacture and sawmills.

The new Treaty Centre in Hounslow Town Centre features a covered
shopping mall, department stores and a new central library.

At *Heston*, 2 miles NW of Hounslow centre, *Heston Aerodrome* was
used for private flying from 1929 to 1939. In the 19C *St. Leonard's*
church, Heston, there is an Adam monument to Robert Child of
Osterley Park; the tower is 15C and the lychgate a reconstruction from
15C material.

Heathrow, 15m to the W of Central London—5 miles from
Hounslow—one of the three London airports operated by the British
Airports Authority, was established in 1929 as a test flight base, and was
used in the Battle of Britain (1941). It opened to international traffic in
1946. In 1953 it handled one million passengers and in 1988 38.5
million, making it the world's busiest international airport. There are
four terminals and two runways. The Piccadilly Line Underground was
extended to Heathrow Terminals 1,2,3 in 1977 and to the new Terminal
4 in 1987. A direct railway link is planned to Paddington Station.

The *Queen's Building Roof Gardens* give good views over the airport.
Open daily, July to September 09.00–19.00, October to June 09.30–
16.30. Admission charge. Tel. 081-759 4321. Access: Underground,
Heathrow 1, 2, 3.

Two and a half miles S of Hounslow at **Hanworth** the remains of Henry
VIII's hunting lodge and the residence of Katherine Parr can be seen in
the entrance of *Tudor Court* (Castle Way), a block of flats overlooking
Hanworth Park. *Hanworth Park House* dates to 1820 and stands on part
of the former manor, now a public park. *Hanworth Airport* was
operational between 1929 and 1946 when it closed as Heathrow grew.
St. George's church has medieval origins but was rebuilt in 1812; 16C
stained glass survives in the N chapel.

One mile to the NW is **Feltham**; the *Feltham Arena* is used for sporting
events. At *East Bedfont* 1.5 miles further NW, almost on top of the
airport, *St. Mary's* church retains its Norman doorway in a 19C
building; restoration work has revealed wall-paintings of c 1250. The
'king' of the gypsies, John Stanley, was buried here in 1766.

Cranford, 2 miles further N towards the M4, has a village 'lock-up' in
the High St, the Round House, built in the 19C to detain prisoners before
their appearance at the local court. *St. Dunstan's* church (15–18C), on
the Feltham exit of the M4, stands in the former grounds of Cranford
House, now *Cranford Park*, somewhat overshadowed by the
motorway.

Harmondsworth and **Harlington** are within half a mile of each other
just to the N of Heathrow and W of Cranford, between the A4 and M4
and within the London Borough of Hillingdon in a virtual no man's land
created by the airport. The church of *St. Peter and St. Paul* in Harlington
is separated from its parish of Harlington by the motorway. The chancel
is 12C and there is a notable carved Norman door. In Harmondsworth
there are several listed cottages, a 17C pub, the *Five Bells*, and *St.
Mary's* church (12–16C). Richard Cox, famous for the Orange Pippin
apple, is buried here. Behind the church is a huge tithe barn, 190ft long
and 36ft wide, built in the 14C on a disused farm, and said to be one of
the finest in Europe.

West Drayton, 1 mile further N, has a traditional village green. The gatehouse is all that remains of the 16C manor house, which belonged to Sir William Paget, secretary to Henry VIII, and was demolished in 1750. The nearby Drayton Hall was built by the de Burgh family in 1786. Napoleon III was entertained here in 1871. The house is now used as offices. The family monuments are in the 15C flintstone church of *St. Martin*. Brunel tested his Great Western Railway between West Drayton and Langley, in 1837. It opened the following year, and the technical college named after him, founded in 1957, now *Brunel University*, moved to Uxbridge in 1968.

In **Hayes**, 2 miles N of Harlington, another village centre has been preserved although the area is now mainly industrial with new factories such as the Heinz building. The local manor house in the High St is used for sheltered housing. (Access: BR, Hayes & Harlington.) Opposite stands the church of *St. Mary's*, restored by Sir George Gilbert Scott in 1873 but retaining many of its original features and some Middlesex brasses. There is a life-size sculpture of Sir Edward Fenner, a judge, in his legal robes.

The Beck Theatre, the lively local arts centre, is in Grange Road, Hayes (tel. 081-561 7506); it provides entertainment, films, theatre and facilities for the local community. At Christmas there is traditional pantomime.

From Hayes it is possible to walk along the Grand Union Canal to Uxbridge (5m). Access in Station Road next to the Old Crown pub. It passes the *West Drayton Pumping Station* (1890) and the *Packet Boat Inn* where passengers used to depart for Paddington on barges drawn by horses.

Hillingdon, 3 miles NW of Hayes, has given its name to the whole borough. The church of *St. John the Baptist* is cut off from the town centre by the busy Uxbridge Road at Royal Lane. The 13C church was rebuilt in 1848 by Sir George Gilbert Scott. Brasses include a magnificent one commemorating Lord and Lady Estrange (d 1479). Lady Estrange was the aunt of the little princes who died in the Tower. In Vine Lane on the other side of the main road is *The Cedars*, a 16C house which belonged to Samuel Reynardson, the botanist—he planted the cedar tree by the house in 1683. *Hillingdon Court* built in the 1850s for the Mills family is now an American Community School and *Hillingdon House*, built in 1844 for the Cox family, is now owned by the RAF.

Uxbridge 1 mile to the W, once an important market town and coaching post, is now a busy commercial and industrial centre. It lies at the foot of the Colne Valley which is traversed by the *Grand Union Canal*. Villages developed into prosperous suburbs on both sides, now the London Borough of Hillingdon. Hillingdon has built its new *Civic Centre*, here; completed in 1977, it has 700 windows set into its red-brick walls and striking sloping roofs topped by a cupola. Modern works of art inside include a stained glass window depicting Hillingdon's links with its twin towns. Access: Underground, Uxbridge.

In a conservation area in the High St the *Market House* of 1788 has a fine hammerbeam roof dating back to the 14C. The *Treaty House* to the W was owned by Sir Edward Carr in the 17C when it was used for (unsuccessful) negotiations between Royalists and Parliamentarians in 1645. The panelling was sold to the Empire State Building in 1929 but returned as a gift to the Queen in 1955 and installed in the house which is now a pub. There is a market in the Pavilion Shopping Centre on Fridays and Saturdays.

Brunel University was moved to the outskirts of Uxbridge from Ealing in 1968.

Ickenham, 2 miles to the NE of Uxbridge, retains its village centre, green, pond and an old inn in an increasingly modern environment. The former manor house, *Swakeleys*, is half a mile from the town centre (Long Lane, turn into Swakeleys Road). It was the headquarters of a sports club, but in recent years a consortium of local residents bought it and converted into luxury offices; open to the public three days a year. The gardens are accessible. Swakeleys is a 17C building designed for a Lord Mayor of London, Sir Edmund Wright. Another Lord Mayor, Sir Robert Vyner, lived here at the time of the Great Fire of London when Pepys visited him. A mile S from the parish church of *St. Giles*, part of which is 14C, at the corner of Swakeleys Rd and Long Lane, is a 15C moated *Manor Farm* (in private ownership).

The manor of **Ruislip**, 3 miles NE of Uxbridge, was established in the 11C. Ruislip is now a residential suburb with large areas of open land to the N. Old village buildings remain: *Manor Farm House* is now offices with one of the ancient timber barns used as the local library. The *Great Barn* is 13C, as is part of the parish church of *St. Martin*. The wall-paintings are from the 15C. The *Swan* is a 16C coaching inn.

At *Ruislip Common*, N of the town centre, a *Lido* has been created on the side of a 40 acre stretch of water—a feeder of the Grand Union Canal. There are sandy beaches, a play area, a miniature railway and a water-ski club.

Eastcote Village, 2 miles NE of Ruislip (access: Underground, Eastcote), has some good examples of 18C and 19C building in the High Road. *Eastcote House* (demolished) belonged to the Hatreys who also owned Chequers, now the Prime Minister's official residence; a park survives.

Northwood, 2 miles to the N, is a pleasant suburb with mainly 20C housing, several old farm houses and the former manor, the *Grange*, now public offices. *Mount Vernon Hospital* has an art nouveau church of 1905, designed by F.H. Wheeler.

At **Harefield**, 3 miles NW of Ruislip, *St. Mary's* church retains its 12C walls. It is rich in monuments, including those to the local Newdigate family. Grinling Gibbons carved the marble statue of Mary Newdigate. Alice, Countess of Derby, rests in her monument on a four-poster bed, sculpted by Maximilian Colt in 1637. She is surrounded by her three daughters. Countess Alice built the nearby almshouses in the early 17C when she lived at the local manor house. Queen Elizabeth I visited her at the manor. In the rural churchyard there is an *Australian Memorial Cemetery* to 110 soldiers who died at the temporary hospital during the First World War; a special service is held on Anzac Day (25 April). At Park Lodge Farm, Harvil Road, Harefield, there is an educational centre where city children can learn about farming.

Harefield Chest Hospital is based on the former Belhamonds Mansion. Another war memorial stands near *Northolt Aerodrome* (RAF) on the busy A40, 2m S of Ruislip at Northolt. This is the *Polish War Memorial*, dedicated to the memory of 546 Polish pilots killed in action with the RAF in 1939–45. It was at Northolt Aerodrome that Chamberlain landed in 1938 after negotiating the Munich Agreement and promised 'peace in our time'. **Northolt** itself is a busy suburb which has expanded rapidly since the 1920s. There was a pony race track here in the 1930s but it has been built over. The 14C *St. Mary the Virgin* church overlooks the Green, off Mandeville Road.

Ealing, 7 miles W of Central London, was part of the Bishop of Lond manor of Fulham, and was mainly farmland with residential devel ment from the 18C. In the 1880s it was dubbed 'Queen of Suburbs' as th arrival of the railway and a tram-connection made it a popula residential area for city-workers. The Great Western Railway traversed Ealing in 1838 and the *Wharncliffe Viaduct*, Brunel's masterpiece, still spans the Brent river at the southern tip of *Brent River Park*. Industrial expansion followed with the building of Western Avenue. Some of the old coaching inns survive, including the *Old Hatte*, the *Bell*, and the *Green Man*. Today there is an attactive modern shopping centre at Ealing Broadway, opened in 1985 and designed in consultation with local residents, blending with the Victorian solidity of the Town Hall with its tower, spire and archway. (Access: Underground, BR, Ealing Broadway.)

St. Mary's church in St. Mary's Road has 12C origins but was rebuilt in 1740 and remodelled in 1866. Among the older monuments is one to the assassinated Prime Minister, Spencer Perceval, who lived at Elm Grove until his death in 1812. At *Ealing Green*, S from the High St, some Georgian cottages survive and in nearby *Walpole Park*, *Pitshanger Manor* was until recently used as a library; it is now open to the public.

Pitshanger Manor Museum, Mattock Lane, Ealing, W5. Tel. 081-579 2424. Open Tues-Sat 10.00-17.00. Free.

The manor was built in 1770 and remodelled by Sir John Soane in 1801–02. He lived here himself until he moved to Lincoln's Inn Fields in 1811. Later Spencer Perceval's daughters lived here. The Borough took it over in 1900.

After careful restoration, two rooms designed by George Dance—the Drawing Room and Eating Room of 1768—are on view in their original colours. The Soane Breakfast Room of 1810 with its unique marbled decorations will be followed by additions of Soane furniture in other rooms. A Victorian Room shows the Martinware pottery collection (Hull Grundy Estate); the Martin brothers made their grotesque and humourously decorated pottery at their factory at Southall from 1877–1923, see below.

Rochester House at Little Ealing Lane, South Ealing, now a conference centre, belonged to the Bishop of Rochester, Zachary Pearce, and was built in 1712. *Ealing Park*, another attractive 18C house, was the home of Lord Warwick but is now a convent school. *Ealing Abbey* (Charlbury Grove off Castlebar Rd, SW6) the Catholic church, was begun in 1897 by Frederick Waters; damaged in the Second World War, it was restored and reopened in 1965 with a new chapel of St. Boniface funded by the West German government.

Ealing Studios on The Green, Ealing, are now used by the BBC but were the location for the many famous Ealing comedy films of the 1950s and '60s. Ealing's *Questors Theatre* in Mattock Lane was founded in 1921 and has a 400-seat playhouse opened in 1964 for amateur productions.

The leader of the Labour Party, Neil Kinnock, lives with his family in Clovelly Road, Ealing (1989).

Acton, 2 miles E of Ealing towards Central London, has a long history. The manor of Acton was created in the 13C and at one time belonged to the Earl of Bedford. The manor house of Berrymead was renamed the *Priory* in 1802 and is now used as borough council offices (Salisbury St). The Tudor-style building retains some of its 16C interior features.

Turnham Green, which once joined Acton Green, was the location of a battle in 1642 during the Civil War when Charles I's forces caught up with the Parliamentarians after the Battle of Brentford (see p 361). Acton became a spa in the 18C and has three medicinal wells. It was soon abandoned for more fashionable resorts and the assembly rooms turned into tenements. Spurred on by the building of the Grand Union al, Acton developed rapidly in the 19C with industrial and dential building. *Bedford Park*, the first planned garden suburb, as built from 1876, under the supervision of the architect Norman haw, in Queen Anne style. It is now a conservation area.

On the N side of the 25-acre *Acton Park* (with sports facilities) are the *Goldsmiths' Almshouses*, built in 1811 by the Goldsmiths' Company and distinguished by their coat of arms and clock. They still provide a home for 20 families and widows. *St. Aidan*, the local Roman Catholic church, was designed in 1961 by A.J. Newton; paintings include a Crucifixion by Graham Sutherland and 'Christ preaching to the People' by Carel Weight.

In **Shepherds Bush** 1.5 miles E of Acton and 5 miles from Central London is the former *White City Stadium* (Wood Lane, W12) closed in 1984. It was the venue for the fourth Olympic Games in 1908 and in the same year it was used for the Franco-British exhibition which attracted a million visitors. Greyhound racing was introduced in 1927 while the Stadium continued to be used for athletics. It was also the home ground of Queen's Park Rangers football club, now based at Loftus Road. W12. This is the site for the BBC's new corporate headquarters due for completion in the early 1990 designed by Scott, Brownrigg and Turner. A BBC news and current affairs building is due to open in 1994 and new radio headquarters may follow.

The main *BBC TV Studios* are in Wood Lane, W12 (nearest Underground White City).

Between Shepherds Bush and East Acton along Du Cane Road is *Wormwood Scrubs*, the largest prison in Britain, housing 1200 prisoners. It was built by prisoners between 1874 and 1890 to a design by Sir Edmund Du Cane. George Blake, the spy, escaped from here in 1966. Next to it is *Hammersmith Hospital*. *Wormwood Scrubs Common* is used for fairs on Bank Holidays.

Southall (BR, Southall), 3 miles W of Ealing, is dominated today by its Asian community which settled here from the early 1950s. Asian shops, restaurants and Sikh and Hindu temples and mosques line the High St; local cinemas show Indian films.

Southall was granted a market charter in the 17C and still supports a thriving market on Wednesdays, Fridays and Saturdays. The historic cattle market survivies as a horse market on Wednesdays, the only one remaining in London (Southall Horse Market, Southall High St. Tel. 081-574 1611). There is also a Sunday morning market, Western International, in Hayes Road, specialising in clothes and household goods.

Southall Manor on the Green is in Tudor style with 17C interior panelling; it is now used by the Chamber of Commerce. Southall's parish church of *St. Mary's* at Norwood Green has Norman origins but was rebuilt in the 15C. The altar tomb is dedicated to the family of Edward Cheseman, of Norwood Manor.

The Martin brothers were born in Southall and moved their pottery here from Fulham in 1877, creating the distinctive Martinware at their workshop until 1923. There is a collection of Martinware on view at Pitshanger Manor, see p 369. A new town centre development will include shops, offices, a new public library and a Sikh Temple.

At *Southall Railway Centre*, Merrick Road, (tel. 081-574 1529) a former railway engine shed houses a collection of steam and diesel locomotives and rolling stock. Open Saturday and Sunday 11.00–18.00. Admission charge.

Norwood, 1 mile S of Southall, was well-known for its b. fields which can still be seen. The bricks for the building Buckingham Palace came from Norwood.

At **Greenford**, 1.5 miles NE of Southall, the old church stands next to a new church of the *Holy Cross*. The old church is 14C and features some excellent glass including the coat of arms of Henry VIII and Katherine of Aragon in the E window as well as the arms of Eton and King's colleges. In common with St. Mary's at Perivale, the oldest church in the borough, it has a weatherboarded tower. **Perivale**, 2 miles NE of Greenford, is an industrial suburb of the 1920s and '30s characterised by the gleaming white *Hoover* building and the *Sanderson* factory, among many others.

40 Windsor and Eton

WINDSOR, 21 miles W from Central London, is not within the Greater London area but, as it is the most popular day-trip from London, it is included here.

Access: by road, M4, junction 6; BR, from Waterloo or Paddington (change at Slough); Green Line Coach, 700 (May–Oct), 702, 704, 718 (all year) from Eccleston Bridge, Victoria; guided tours (see below).

Tourist Information Centre at Windsor and Eton Central Station, tel. 0753 852010.

Tours of Windsor: during the summer there are guided walking tours from the Central Station's tourist information centre, open-top bus tours from Castle Hill, and river trips from the Promenade.

English kings and queens have lived at Windsor for 900 years; Saxon kings first settled at Old Windsor but their palace of Kingsbury was allowed to crumble after William I built a wooden fortress at New Windsor in 1066. In 1276 the borough received its royal charter and in 1974 it became the Royal Borough of Windsor and Maidenhead. It is sited on the S bank of the Thames, and connected by footbridge to Eton.

Thames St ascends from the river and car park (there is direct access from the new car/coach park to Windsor Railway Station via lift and footbridge); on the corner is a memorial to George V by Lutyens (1937). Here also is a modern shopping precinct. The High St climbs between the Castle Bastions and 18C houses, now shops. The statue of Queen Victoria at Castle Hill is by Sir Edgar Boehm and was erected to celebrate her Diamond Jubilee—it was unveiled by the Queen in 1887. Castle Hill leads to the entrance to **Windsor Castle**.

Windsor Castle: precincts open daily except Garter Day; the Castle is open March to Oct 10.30–17.00, Nov to Feb 10.30– 15.00. State Apartments, open as for Castle but closed when the royal family is in residence; check on 0753 868286. Dolls' House open as State Apartments. St. George's Chapel open in winter 10.45–15.45 (Sundays 14.00–15.45) and in summer 10.45–16.00 (Sundays 14.00–16.00). Admission charge.

The ceremony of the Changing of the Guard takes place daily (except Sun) at 11.00 by the Castle entrance. The Garter Service is held in St. George's Chapel in June (tickets for the precinct: write to the Lord Chamberlain's Office, St. James's Palace, London SW1). Major refurbishment of the Royal Apartments continues during 1990.

Windsor Castle is built on a chalk cliff rising abruptly above the Thames. It was rebuilt in stone by Henry II and then improved and extended by Henry III and Edward III, preserving, however, the original plan of two baileys and a mote-hill. Henry I's marriage to Adeliza of Louvain (1121) was the first royal wedding to be celebrated here. Edward III was born in the castle in 1312 and Henry IV in 1421. Three kings, David II of Scotland, John of France, and

s I of Scotland, have been imprisoned within its walls; from his cell window
es first saw his future wife, Jane Beaufort. Edward III's queen, Philippa of
nault, died here in 1369. The present appearance of the building dates from
e extensive restorations undertaken by Wyatville under George IV.

Enter the *Lower Ward* from *Henry VIII's Gateway*. In front is the
entrance to the *Horseshoe Cloisters*, built during Edward IV's reign, at
the NW angle of which stands the *Curfew Tower* with a 13C interior.
The tower houses eight chapel bells and an unusual clock of 1689
which chimes every three hours. On the right are the houses of the
Military Knights of Windsor, an order founded by Edward III as the
'Poor Knights of Windsor' at the same time as the Order of the Garter.
They were given their present name by William IV in 1833. The central
tower (1359) bears the arms of Philip and Mary.

St. George's Chapel is a superb Perpendicular building, begun in
1478 by Henry Janyns for Edward IV and continued in 1503–11 by
William Vertue. As one of the most perfect specimens of 15–16C
Gothic work, it ranks with King's College Chapel, Cambridge and
Henry VII's Chapel at Westminster.

Enter by the S door and walk through the choir and the nave. The
Nave has a fine lierne vault with carved bosses. At the SW corner is the
Beaufort Chapel where the tomb of the Earl of Worcester (died 1526)
has a Flemish bronze grating, unusual in Britain. The great West
Window contains fine glass of 1503–09. In the NW corner is the tomb of
George VI (died 1936) by Lutyens and Reid Dick, and of Queen Mary
(died 1953), with the theatrical tomb of Princess Charlotte (d 1817) in
the Urswick Chapel behind.

The *Choir* is separated from the nave by a Gothic screen (c 1785) by
Henry Emlyn. The organ, originally centrally placed (as in King's
College Chapel), was rebuilt in flanking sections to give a better view
of the fan vaulting. In the *North Choir Aisle* is (left) the *Rutland Chapel*
(1481) with effigies of George Manners (died 1513) and his wife. To the
right is the *Chantry Chapel of William, Lord Hastings* with contemporary paintings of his execution in 1483; to the left is the memorial
chapel of George VI (1969). To the N of the High Altar a superb pair of
gates (1482) fronts the tomb of Edward IV. Above is the Royal Pew, a
splendid wooden oriel provided by Henry VIII for Catherine of
Aragon. In the centre of the floor is a vault containing the remains of
Henry VIII, Jane Seymour and Charles I. The Stalls, in three tiers, are
surmounted by the helmets, crests and banners of the 26 Knights of the
Garter, whose installations have taken place at Windsor since 1348.
The reverse stalls are those of the royal family, the Sovereign's Stall
marked by the Royal Standard.

Past the Screen turn left; the Bray Chapel contains the cenotaph of
the Prince Imperial, son of Napoleon III, killed in S Africa in 1879. In the
South Choir Aisle the *Chantry of John Oxenbridge*, with paintings of
1522, is on the left; it also contains the great sword of Edward III and the
simple slab marking the tomb of Henry VI. On the S side of the altar is
the tomb of Edward VII and Queen Alexandra (by Mackennal). The SE
Chapel, with the tomb of the Earl of Lincoln (died 1585), is called the
Lincoln Chapel or *John Schorne's Tower*, from the relics of Sir John
Schorne (died 1314) brought here in 1478 from North Marston in
Bucks.

The E wall of the ambulatory once formed the W front of Henry III's
Chapel (1240–48) and retains its original doors. Beyond the floor slab of
Sir Jeffry Wyatville the NE door leads through a slype, or passage, to
the *Dean's Cloister*, preserving arcading of Henry III's chapel and a
piece of fresco. To the N is the picturesque *Canon's Cloister* of 1353–56.

The **Albert Memorial Chapel** was rebuilt by Henry VII as a bu
place for Henry VI but later completed by Wolsey—his tomb w
never used and was broken up during the Civil War. Queen Victori
had the chapel converted into a splendid memorial to Prince Albert
(died 1861) who is buried at Frogmore. The cenotaph of Prince Albert
is by Baron Triqueti. The chapel also contains the tombs of the Duke
of Clarence (died 1892), the elder son of Edward VII, by Alfred
Gilbert, and of the Duke of Albany (died 1884), Queen Victoria's
youngest son. Beneath the chapel George III, Queen Charlotte, and
six of their sons (including George IV and William IV) are buried.

To the left of the entrance to the N Terrace is the *Winchester Tower*,
where Chaucer may have lived in 1390 when Master of the Works at
Windsor. From the N Terrace there is a view of the Home Park, Eton,
and Stoke Poges church.

Below is St. George's School, the choir school in the building (1802) of Travers
College, founded in 1795 from a bequest of Samuel Travers (died 1725) for
'Naval Knights', an order corresponding to the Military Knights (see above) but
disbanded in 1892.

From the N Terrace enter the *State Apartments*, which occupy the N
wing of the Upper Ward. These are used mainly for royal functions
and contain many notable paintings from the royal collections, superb
furniture, and other treasures.

From the China Gallery ascend the *Grand Staircase*, with a statue of George IV
by Chantrey, and armour made for Henry VIII and the sons of James I. *Charles
II's Dining Room* has a ceiling by Verrio and carvings by Grinling Gibbons. In the
King's Drawing Room, or *Rubens Room*, is a series of noble works by Rubens
(Holy Family, etc.) and a St. Martin by Van Dyck. The *State Bedchamber*
contains a fine Louis Seize bed; in the adjoining *Dressing Room*, or *Lesser
Bedroom*, are a painting by Van Dyck (Charles I, from three points of view, for
use in the execution of a bust), and many smaller paintings: portraits by Clouet,
Memling, Dürer, and And. del Sarto; by Rubens (of himself and of Van Dyck),
and by Holbein. In the *King's Closet* are Venetian views by Canaletto and
portraits of David Garrick by Hogarth and Reynolds. The *Queen's Drawing
Room* contains an unequalled array of portraits by Van Dyck: Charles I,
Henrietta Maria, their children, and members of the court, also James II as Duke
of York (Dobson); 17C French and English furniture.

Continue into an older wing (renewed by Charles II), where the *Queen's
Ballroom* has more characteristic views by Canaletto. The *Queen's Audience
Chamber* has Gobelins tapestries, and portraits of the Princes of Orange (by
Honthorst) in frames carved by Grinling Gibbons; the *Queen's Presence
Chamber* continues the series of tapestries. Both these rooms have ceilings by
Verrio glorifying Queen Catherine of Braganza. Here also is a bust of Handel by
Roubiliac. The *Queen's Guard Chamber* displays a fine suit of armour (1585)
made for Sir Christopher Hatton, and busts (Philip II, Charles V) by Leone Leoni.
Above busts of Marlborough and Wellington hang the replica standards that
constitute the annual rent for Woodstock and Stratfield Saye. A bust of Churchill
was commissioned from Oscar Nemon (1953). The noble *St. George's Hall*, 185ft
long, in which the festivities of the Order of the Garter are held, bears on the
ceiling and walls the coats-of-arms of the knights since 1348. The portraits of
English sovereigns from James I to George IV are by Van Dyck, Kneller, etc.
Among the parallel range of busts (by Nollekens, Chantrey, etc.) that by
Roubiliac represents George II (*not* I). The *Grand Reception Room* has fine
Gobelins tapestries; the *Throne Room* or *Garter Room* contains portraits of
sovereigns in their Garter robes. The large *Waterloo Chamber*, constructed in
1830 inside a 12C court, contains portraits, mostly by Lawrence, of people who
were instrumental in the downfall of Napoleon. From the *Grand Vestibule*
beyond, with relics of Napoleon and the Japanese surrender sword (early 15C) of
1945, descend by King John's Tower to the Quadrangle.

In a room to the left of the entrance is *Queen Mary's Dolls' House*. The Dolls'
House was given to the nation by Queen Mary in 1923. It was designed by
Lutyens and measures 8ft by 5ft. Details include books and paintings by
contemporary authors and artists, working plumbing and electric lighting.

Round Tower or *Keep* provides a magnificent view (220 steps); ~ptical in plan, its lower half of 1170 was heightened by ~ yatville.—The *Private Apartments of the Queen* are on the E side of ~he Upper Ward (no admission). The passage between the Round Tower and the Upper Ward leads through St. George's Gateway to Castle Hill, near the entrance to the *Royal Stables*.

To the N and E of the Castle is the *Home Park*; in the S part are *Frogmore House* and *Mausoleum*. The latter contains the remains of the Prince Consort and Queen Victoria. Also buried here is the Duke of Windsor, King Edward VIII (1894–1972). It is usually open on the first Wednesday and Thursday in May, 10.00–dusk, and on the Wednesday nearest to 24 May (Queen Victoria's birthday).

Windsor *Guildhall* off Castle Hill was designed by Sir Thomas Fitch in 1687 and finished by Sir Christopher Wren in 1707. Wren completed the Market House and the Guildhall Chamber, supported on Portland stone pillars. It is adorned with statues of Queen Anne and Prince George of Denmark and contains royal portraits and collections of Windsor's silver plate.

The parish church of *St. John the Baptist* in the High St was rebuilt in 1822; it contains a Last Supper ascribed to Franz de Cleyn (1588–1658) and carvings by Grinling Gibbons and others. There is a large brass-rubbing centre (open daily, Easter to November) with reproduction brasses from all over S England. Market St and Church St are both cobbled and have attractive houses.

In the *Royal Mews*, St. Albans St, visitors can see the Queen's horses and carriages, including the Scottish State Coach, used at the 1981 royal wedding. Also on display is a selection of gifts presented to the Queen for her Silver Jubilee in 1977. The Royal Mews is open Mon to Sat all the year round and Sun 13.30–16.30.

Opposite Castle Hill is *Windsor and Eton Central Station*, half of which has been converted into *Royalty and Empire* (by Madame Tussaud's), tel. 0753 857837. Open daily 09.30–17.30. Admission charge).

The original Royal Waiting Room and large Jubilee Glass Canopy built for the present station by the Great Western Railway Company to celebrate Queen Victoria's Diamond Jubilee have been restored. Madame Tussaud's have added life-like figures of all the personalities involved; they have restored railway carriages and built a full-size replica of the Queen-class locomotive, one of the most powerful engines of the time, which pulled the train in which the foreign royal guests arrived to be received by Queen Victoria.

In Thames St is the *Theatre Royal, Windsor*, founded in 1792; George III was its royal patron. The present building dates from 1815. The theatre is the centre of the Windsor Festival, held annually in September with concerts in St. George's Chapel and Eton College.

The *Household Cavalry Museum*, Combermere Barracks, is in St. Leonards Road, just S of central Windsor on the way to Windsor Safari Park. The museum is open Monday to Friday all year, and on Sundays from Easter to September. It contains one of the country's most comprehensive collections of arms, saddlery, standards and uniforms.

S of Windsor is **Windsor Great Park** (nearly 2000 acres), traversed by the road to Ascot and the Long Walk. The latter, planted with elms by Charles II and replanted after 1945 with horse chestnut and plane trees, stretches straight from the Castle to *Snow Hill* (2.75 miles) which bears a huge statue of George III ('The Copper Horse') by Westmacott. Still within the park, best approached via Old Windsor village, along winding Crimp Lane (where Shelley had a cottage in

1816) is (4.5 miles) the *Savill Garden*. Open 10.00–18.00 in summer, 10.00–dusk in winter. The garden comprises 20 acres of lovely woodland named after a former park ranger.

The *Windsor Safari Park* (open daily 10.00–dusk, admission charge) includes a drive-round section (bus tours available) where wild animals such as lions, cheetahs, baboons and camels wander freely. There is a children's zoo, picnic areas and a dolphinarium, as well as restaurants.

Across Windsor Bridge (access from Thames Avenue; no cars) is **Eton**, a town with several attractive antique shops and **Eton College**, founded by Henry VI in 1440 and perhaps the best-known of all English schools. Famous Etonians include Fielding, the elder and younger Pitt, the Walpole brothers, Gray, Shelley, Wellington, Canning and Gladstone.

Eton College is open 14.00–17.00 during school terms, daily 10.30–17.00 during holidays (April to October, closed in winter). For guided tours contact Eton College Tourist Manager, tel. 0753 869991.

The main block of fine mellow brick includes two courts or quadrangles. The larger—School Yard—contains a statue of Henry VI (1719). A frieze commemorates 1157 Etonians who fell in the First World War and 748 killed in the Second. Above is the *Upper School* (1689–94) with busts of eminent Etonians, damaged in 1941 but restored; the panelled walls and staircases are covered with names of boys going on to King's (earliest 1577), with wooden pillars of c 1625. The *Chapel, a Perpendicular structure begun in 1441 and completed in 1483, has a fan vault added in 1958 by Sir William Holford. A superb series of wall-paintings (1479–88) of British workmanship was discovered in 1847 and has been restored; the stained-glass E window is by Evie Hone (1952) and the clerestory windows are by John Piper. A museum describing the history of the college, personalities and games opened in 1985.

A fine gatehouse of c 1517 erected by Provost Lupton leads to the second court or *Cloisters*, with the Collegers' *Dining Hall* (1450) and the *College Library* (1725–29) above it.—In the playing fields beyond is the 'wall' which gives its name to the 'wall-game', a style of football peculiar to Eton.

Between Windsor and Staines is *Runnymede*, where King John signed the Magna Carta, the great charter of English liberties, on 15 June 1215. Runnymede was given to the nation in 1921; Sir Edwin Lutyens designed the commemorative pillars and flanking lodges which were unveiled by the Prince of Wales, later Edward VIII, in 1932. Further memorials include the Magna Carta Memorial (1957), the John F. Kennedy Memorial (1965) and the Commonwealth Air Force Memorial (1953).

V OUTER LONDON: NORTH WEST, NORTH, NORTH EAST AND EAST

41 Wembley, Willesden, Brent Cross, Harrow, Pinner, Stanmore

Wembley, in many ways a typical suburb of the 1920s and '30s, is best known for *Wembley Stadium,* built in 1923 for the British Empire Exhibition which opened in 1924, attracting some 27 million visitors in two years. It now holds up to 80,000 spectators and is the venue for the annual Football Association Cup Final (in May), other sports events and pop concerts.

Tours of the stadium (tel. 081-903 4864) include a visit to the changing rooms, a walk through the Players' Tunnel with sound effects of cheering crowds, and a visit to the Royal Box. Tours are on Monday to Wednesday and Friday to Sunday except when the stadium is being used. Admission charge. Suspended until 1991.

The Palaces of Industry and Arts built as part of the British Empire Exhibition are now used as industrial warehouses in the area N of the *Empire Pool,* now known as *Wembley Arena* (1934). The arena has a spectacular 240ft-high roof; it is used for show-jumping, ice-shows and concerts. Refitting here has taken the seating to 13,000.

The *Wembley Conference Centre,* opened in 1976, seats 2700. An exhibition hall was added in 1986 and further halls are planned. A 12-screen multiplex cinema is now being added and a Museum of Sport and theme restaurants may follow.

Wembley Stadium car park (6000 spaces) is the location for a popular Sunday market; mainly new goods on sale.

The *Grange Museum* is in Neasden Lane, **Willesden,** NW10, 2 miles E of Wembley. (Tel. 081-908 7432.) The museum, in an early 18C stableblock, has a collection of local Brent artefacts and documents, a Victorian parlour, a 1930s sitting room, drawings and maps, and temporary exhibitions.

Open Tues to Thur 12.00–17.00, Sat 10.00–12.00, 13.00–17.00. Tel. 081-908 7432. Access: Underground, Neasden.

In *Gladstone Park,* Dollis Hill Lane, NW2 (half a mile further E) stands Dollis Hill House (not open to the public), built in 1823 and the former home of Lord Aberdeen; here Mark Twain and Gladstone were among the guests. In 1941 the War Cabinet met here and an underground control centre was planned but never built (cf. Cabinet War Rooms in Horse Guards). The park has an attractive walled garden; a recent addition is a sculpted memorial (by Fred Kormis) to those who suffered in prisoner-of-war camps.

Willesden's parish church, *St. Mary,* stands high above the surrounding area on the corner of Neasden Lane and the High Road, half a mile S of Neasden. It dates to the 13C with a 14C tracery door, a Norman font, and an Elizabethan communion table. The novelist Charles Reade (died 1884) is buried in the churchyard.

S of Willesden along the industrial wasteland created by the Grand Union Canal and railway lines is the **Kensal Green Cemetery,** probably the best-known in London and with some of the most

interesting monuments still standing in a London cemetery. (.
Harrow Road; Underground, BR, Kensal Green.)

The cemetery was founded in 1832. It has chapels in a classical
and its main gateway is a triumphal arch. Towering Gothic monume.
obelisks, mausoleums and modest statues abound, and the neglect
the past may finally have been halted with the formation of c
preservation society. Among the illustrious burials here are Marc
Brunel (died 1849) and his son Isambard (died 1859), engineers;
Princess Sophia (died 1848), daughter of George III; William Thackeray
(died 1863), and Anthony Trollope (died 1882), novelists; Mary Hogarth
(died 1837), Dickens' sister-in-law, and Emile Blondin (died 1897) who
crossed Niagara Falls on a tightrope.

The cemetery is bounded to the S by the Grand Union Canal,
Paddington Arm, which used to allow direct access by barge. Today it is
possible to walk along the towpath from Warwick Avenue, Little Venice
(see p 176) to Willesden Junction, passing the cemetery on the N bank
and, further along to the S, Wormwood Scrubs Common, used by
pioneers of flying in the early part of this century but now better-known
for the prison. See p 370.

St. Augustine's Church in Kilburn Park Road (off Kilburn High Road), 2
miles SE of Willesden, is one of London's largest Victorian churches,
designed by J.L. Pearson and completed in 1898. The 250ft tower is an
architectural triumph.

Within the London Borough of **Brent** there are recreational facilities at
Roundwood Park to the S and the *Welsh Harp Reservoir* to the N. The
latter takes its name from an old pub, demolished to make way for the
main road, and not from its shape. There is a nature centre here.

At the junction of the North Circular Road and the start of the M1 is the
Brent Cross Shopping Centre which opened in 1976 on a 52-acre site.
(Access: Underground, Brent Cross; Bus, 16.) The centre includes two
department stores, shops and a supermarket under cover in a
landscaped setting with car parking.

Edgware Road follows the line of the Roman Watling St which leads to
St. Albans. The tower of the red-brick church of *St. Margaret's*, on the
corner of Watling St and Station Road, Edgware, is 14C. There are
almshouses of the 1680s further along Watling St, and timber-framed
buildings survive along the W side of the High St, including a 17C
coaching inn, the *White Hart*.

Harrow, Hampstead and Highgate all occupy high ground to the N of
central London. **Harrow** and the surrounding area were important
Saxon settlements, as is shown by the earthworks at Grims Dyke.
Harrow was a residence of the Abp of Canterbury and the hunting
grounds attracted poachers as well as his guests. Headstone became the
local manor in the 14C.

Today Harrow on the Hill is still dominated by the 16C *Harrow School*,
established by a charter from Elizabeth I to a John Lyon (a yeoman of
Preston, Middlesex) in 1572. There are tours of the school (tel. 081-422
2196). The school, built in 1615, was expanded in the 18C but the Fourth
Form Room in the Old Schools retains oak panels scored with the names
of former pupils. Across Church Hill are the Chapel and the War
Memorial Building added in neo-Jacobean style in 1926 (Herbert
Baker). It incorporates 16C panelling from Brooke House, Hackney, in
the Fitch Room, and other historic relics. The dramatist Sheridan, a
former pupil, returned to live just behind the church in 1781—
'Sheridan's stables' have been incorporated in the new Leaf Schools

g. The Vaughan Library and the Chapel were designed by Sir e Gilbert Scott. The Speech Room in the High St, built in 1874, has ue of Elizabeth I in a niche over the street. The Old Speech Room, a Tudor-style windows, is now an art gallery and museum of the ool.

Harrow can count seven prime ministers among former pupils including Spencer Perceval, Sir Robert Peel, Palmerston, Baldwin and Churchill. Other famous pupils include Byron, Cardinal Manning, the Earl of Shaftesbury, Trollope, Galsworthy, G.M. Trevelyan, Pandit Nehru, and Kings Faisal II of Iraq and Hussein of Jordan.

The parish church of *St. Mary* at the crown of the hill is 400ft above sea level and 200ft above the surrounding area. The view from the terrace is associated with Byron who used to sit on the flat tombstone of John Peachey 'for hours and hours'. The Harrow School song recalls 'Byron lay lazily lay, Hid from lesson and game away, Dreaming poetry all alone, Up-a-top of the Peachey stone'. The church was founded by Lanfranc, Abp of Canterbury, and consecrated by Anselm in 1094, probably on Saxon foundations. The structure is 12 and 13C and was restored by Sir George Gilbert Scott in the 19C. Fittings include a 12C font and fine brasses, including one to John Lyon (died 1592), founder of the school, shown with his wife Joan. A memorial to John Lyon by Flaxman was added in the 19C. Byron's daughter Allegra lies in an unmarked grave beneath the church porch.

In the High St is the *King's Head*, a 16C pub.—Modern Harrow lies 1 mile to the N and has a new shopping centre, civic centre and a leisure centre. Tourist Information is available at Harrow Civic Centre, Station Road, Harrow, tel. 081 863 5611. The new Harrow Arts Centre is in Uxbridge Road, Hatch End. There is a local museum at Headstone.

Harrow Museum and Heritage Centre, Headstone Lane, Harrow. Tel. 081-861 2626. Open Wed, Thurs, Fri 12.30-1700, Sat, Sun and BH 10.30-17.00. (Tithe Barn only, Manor House by appointment). Access: Underground, North Harrow, BR Headstone Lane.

Moated *Headstone Manor* dates to the 14C and was a residence of the Abp of Canterbury from 1344. The House is being restored. The Tithe Barn is 150ft long, 30ft wide, and dates from 1533–55. It was first restored in 1973 and features an exhibition of local history. It is also used for meetings and entertainment. A historic granary from Halls Farm is being moved and rebuilt on the site to recreate a 19C farmyard.

Pinner, NW of Harrow, was once a chalk-mining area but is now a prosperous suburb built largely in the 1930s. The Pinner Fair, granted its charter in 1336, continues once a year on the Wednesday following the Spring Bank Holiday. It is held in the High St, where some half-timbered 16C houses survive, including the *Queen's Head* and *Victory Hotel*. The 15C church of *St. John the Baptist* in the High St was consecrated in 1321 and restored in 1880.

In Moss Lane, Pinner, stands the oldest surviving timber-framed house in the old county of Middlesex, 15C *East End Farm Cottage*. Nearby is Tudor Cottage, a half-timbered 16C farmhouse.

The Kodak company established itself in this part of London in 1887 with a factory in Headstone Drive, Wealdstone. The Kodak Museum located here closed in 1984 and the collection is now housed in the National Photographic Museum, Bradford. HMSO has printing works in Wealdstone. The stone of Wealdstone is outside the *Red Lion Hotel*, Harrow Weald, 2 miles N of Harrow on the Hill. It is one of several stones in the area which probably marked parish boundaries.

Stanmore, 3.5 miles NE of Harrow on the Hill, now a busy commercial and shopping centre with a large residential population, lies at the N end of the Bakerloo Line. Its ancient history is commemorated by obelisk now in the grounds of the Royal National Orthopaedic Hospital and originally erected in 1750 to mark a battle between the Celts and Romans. The pond on Stanmore Common is popularly known as 'Caesar's Pond'. Two churches, both dedicated to St. John, stand in the churchyard of Great Stanmore. The medieval church was rebuilt and consecrated by William Laud, later Abp of Canterbury, in 1632. It was declared unsafe in the 19C and left as a ruin overgrown with ivy. The new church, completed in 1850, incorporates some of the monuments from the old church and includes a Nicholas Stone font with the Wolstenholme crest and arms. Sir John Wolstenholme, the church's benefactor, is also represented in life-size effigy. Outside, a white marble angel marks the grave of Sir William Gilbert.

On *Stanmore Common*, Common Road, stands *Bentley Priory*, established in the 12C and dedicated to St. Mary Magdalene.

In the 18C the manor house built on the site was pulled down and Sir John Soane designed a new mansion for the Marquess of Abercorn. In this celebrated house he entertained political and literary figures of the time. Queen Adelaide, William IV's widow, died here in 1849. The house was sold to the Air Ministry in 1925 and it was from here that the RAF staff, under Sir Hugh Dowding, controlled the British forces in the Battle of Britain in 1940.

Stanmore Hall in Wood Lane was built in 1843 and has some fine Morris interiors. It was badly damaged by fire in 1979 and is being restored.

Off Old Redding, Harrow Weald, another mansion, *Grims Dyke*, has become a hotel. The house was built in 1872 for Frederick Good, a painter, designed by Norman Shaw in Tudor style with gables, half-timbering and tall chimneys.

W.S. Gilbert lived here from 1890 until his death in 1911 (most of his work with Arthur Sullivan dates from before this period). In the Iolanthe Room a 15ft-high pink alabaster fireplace remains of the original fittings. The hotel holds regular Gilbert and Sullivan evenings in this room.

The *Grims Ditch earthworks* are 5 miles long; they are probably of Saxon origin, and possibly designed to defend London. They may also be of agricultural origin. They can best be seen at the junction of Oxhey Lane and Old Redding.

The *George V Memorial Gardens* in Whitchurch Lane, Stanmore, are all that remains of Canon Park. A mansion stood here from 1725, built for the Duke of Chandos. The family ran out of money and the estate was broken up in the mid 18C; parts of the house were sold all over the country. Some were used for a modest country house on the site, now the North London Collegiate School for Girls, established in Camden Town in 1850 by Frances Mary Buss, a pioneer of education for women. The parish church of *St. Lawrence*, Whitchurch, has survived. The Chandos monument includes representations of two of the duke's three wives and is adorned with grisaille paintings, as are the walls and the vaulted roof, by Louis Laguerre. Bellucci was responsible for the altar paintings and the small organ was played by Handel who was the duke's private choirmaster and composed the Chandos Anthem for him in 1718.

42 Hendon, Mill Hill, Barnet, Finchley

Hendon, 7 miles NW of central London, well-known from its early aviation connections, has a history dating back to a Benedictine settlement in the Middle Ages; its woods are said to have provided

oak for the construction of Westminster Abbey. Among the
.asant suburban housing of this century there are older buildings at
.e Burroughs, including 18C cottages and, beyond, *Burroughs
House*, owned by All Souls College, Oxford. The centre of the old
village is in Church End Road where *St. Mary's Church* stands on
medieval foundations. It has an 11C tower, a fine square, arcaded
Norman font, and brasses and tombs including that of Sir Stamford
Raffles (1781–1826), founder of Singapore and of London Zoo.

The oldest house in the area (near the *Greyhound* pub) is *Church
Farm House* which belonged to the Kempe family. The main part of
the building dates from the mid 17C but there is some 16C panelling
inside. The house opened as a local museum in 1955; temporary, local
exhibitions are held on the first floor. The ground floor is furnished in
period style; the central chimney stack has a passage through it and
the large kitchen is set up as it would have been at the end of the 18C
with a mechanical spit and large kettles.

Church Farm House Museum, Greyhound Hill, Hendon, NW4. Tel. 081-203
0130. Open Mon, Wed to Sat 10.00–13.00, 14.00–17.30, Tues 10.00–13.00, Sun
14.00–17.30. Admission free. Access: Underground, Hendon Central.

All that remains of Church End Farm opposite is part of a model dairy
added in the 19C.

Hendon's fame as an aviation centre started with the opening of the
London Aerodrome factory and flying field in 1910 by Claude
Grahame-White. From here Pierre Prier made the first non-stop
London-Paris flight (3 hours 56 minutes) in 1911, and from here the
first official mail flight, to Windsor, took off on 9 September 1911. The
aerodrome was commandeered in 1914 by the Royal Naval Air
Services and became the Royal Air Force Station Hendon in 1918.
From 1920–37 annual air displays in aid of RAF charities attracted
many thousands of spectators.

Most of the aerodrome land has been redeveloped as a housing estate by the
GLC; this has been named after the aerodrome's founder as the Grahame Park
Estate.

Two of the remaining hangars form the main building of the *RAF
Museum* which opened in 1972 and which includes the *Battle of
Britain Museum* (1978) and the *Bomber Command Museum* (1983).

RAF Museum, Grahame Park Way, Hendon, NW9. Tel. 081-205 2266. Access:
Underground, Colindale. Car park. Open daily 10.00–18.00. Admission charge.
Roundel Buffet.

The RAF Museum tells the story of the RAF and its forerunners and
illustrates the development of its aircraft, armaments and equipment
to the present day. The collection includes some 60 historic aircraft.
Considerable changes and improvements are planned for the displays including more interactive opportunities. In 1990, the 40th
anniversary of the Battle of Britain is being marked by a special
exhibition.

From the entrance hall explore the galleries on the first floor. On the right is the
Art Gallery with a changing display of works relating to aviation by 20C artists,
as well as commemorative and decorative RAF silver. Gallery 2 shows a detailed
reconstruction of a Royal Flying Corps and Royal Naval Air Services workshop
with the fuselage of a De Havilland BE2a of 1911 as its centrepiece. There is a
viewing platform here on to the Aircraft Gallery below. Gallery 3 features a
reconstruction of a workshop in a Bessoneau hangar in France. A case contains
relics of the celebrated German ace, Baron von Richthofen, including his flying
helmet and lucky dog mascot. Gallery 4 is devoted to Lord Trenchard (1873–

1956), first Marshal of the RAF, appointed Chief of Air Staff in 1918. Other personalities are commemorated in Gallery 5. Gallery 6 has a display of Victoria Cross and George Cross medals. Inter-war aircraft components are shown Gallery 7—a diorama shows a Hendon Air Display (see above). Gallery 8 has changing displays illustrating the early part of the Second World War; Gallery 9 is also devoted to this war and includes escape aids used by prisoners-of-war. Gallery 10 includes a tribute to Sir Frank Whittle, inventor of the jet engine. Gallery 11 shows sophisticated equipment of the 1980s.

Enter the Aircraft Hall via the entrance hall; here is a display of 30 historic aircraft, regularly rearranged but likely to feature the Blériot XI, Vickers Gunbus, Sopwith Triplane, Vickers Vimy, Sopwith Camel and the Hawker Sea Fury. At the far end of the hall is the Dermot Boyle Wing housing temporary exhibitions. Aviation records and the Library are on the second floor (visits by appointment).

The Battle of Britain section was opened by the Queen Mother in 1978. It commemorates the battle fought over SE England during the summer of 1940 in which 640 British and Allied fighter planes and their pilots ('the Few'), overcame 2400 bombers and fighters of the German Luftwaffe.

By the entrance in the Ground Floor Gallery is the wreckage of a crashed Hawker Hurricane; nearby is a tableau of a bombed street. The collection of aircraft includes two British fighters, the Vickers Supermarine Spitfire and Hawker Hurricane, and German and Italian aircraft including the Heinkel III, two Junkers, two Messerschmitts and a Fiat Falcon. In the Eastern Aircraft Hall there is a Westland Lysander, a Supermarine Seagull, a Gloster Gladiator and a Sunderland flying boat of 1944, the only one of its kind to survive. From the First Floor Gallery there is a good view of the aircraft below as well as a collection of newspaper cuttings from the period May to October 1940, and a recreation of an Underground station used as a shelter. The reconstruction of the Group Operations Room at RAF Uxbridge shows the battle situation at the height of the conflict.

The Bomber Command section opened in 1983. It is dedicated to the memory of the thousands of aircrew who died in the Second World War.

Displays illustrate the history of Bomber Command, formed in 1936. The collection of historic aircraft includes the sole surviving De Havilland 9a, a Hawker Hart (1930), Vickers Wellington (1944), Handley Page Halifax (1942), De Havilland Mosquito (1946), and Vickers Valiant (1956).

The original Tudor building of *Hendon Hall* was demolished and rebuilt in the 17C and is now the *Hendon Hall Hotel*, at the junction of Ashley Lane and Parsons St, half a mile N of Hendon Central. David Garrick lived here (1756–79) and erected an obelisk in the grounds dedicated to Shakespeare; another was put up to Garrick after his death, marked now by the small Garrick Park. Many additions have been made to Hendon Hall but a special feature is the painted ceiling by Tiepolo rediscovered in 1954. The portico and Corinthian capitals are said to come from the Canons and were added by Samuel Ware, the architect and builder, in the 19C.

In *Colindale* on the other side of the Grahame Park Estate is the *British Library Newspaper Collection*.

British Library Newspaper Collection, Colindale Avenue, NW9. Tel. 081-323 7353. Open Mon to Sat 10.00–16.45. Free. Over 21s only, identification necessary. Access: Underground, Colindale.

Originally housed in the British Museum, the collection had filled all the available space by 1897; the Colindale Repository was completed in 1903. Its 20 miles of shelving hold daily and weekly newspapers from 1801, with English, provincial, Scottish and Irish newspapers from 1700, plus a large collection of Commonwealth and foreign newspapers. A bomb demolished the original building in 1940 and part of the collection was destroyed. The library is geared search. (The Burney Collection of Newspapers is still at the British Library in Bloomsbury.)

The old village of **Mill Hill** is separated from the modern suburb by the A1 from Mill Hill Broadway, squeezed in next to the M1. The old village to the E is centred on The Ridgeway (nearest Underground Mill Hill East). It has associations with Sir Stamford Raffles and William Wilberforce. *Highwood House* in Highwood Hill, now a residential home, has a plaque marking Raffles' residence here; before that it was the home of Sir William Russell, one of the Bedfords. He was captured trying to escape through a circular window (still a feature) and executed for his part in the Rye House Plot aimed at Charles II.

William Wilberforce, a contemporary of Raffles, lived at *Hendon Hall*, also in Highwood Hill. He designed and built *St. Paul's Church* in The Ridgeway with support from Raffles. It was completed in 1836; the work of the painter Charles Muss can be seen in the glass of the E window. There are slave graves in the crypt.

Holcombe House in Holcombe Hill, now a convent school, was the home of Sir John Anderson, a Lord Mayor of London. Cardinal Vaughan stayed here while planning St. Joseph's College (see below). Some Georgian features survive, the fine portico and fanlight, and the staircase and murals by Angelica Kauffmann.

St. Joseph's in Lawrence St (reached from Mill Hill Circus) is still a missionary college, founded in 1866 by Cardinal Vaughan. An impressive campanile is topped by a statue of St. Joseph, 100ft above ground. In the High St, possibly the shortest in London, a weather-boarded Quaker meeting-house, Rosebank, survives; it was in use from 1678 to 1719.

The best-known educational establishment in the area is *Mill Hill School* in The Ridgeway, built in the grounds of a house which belonged to the botanist Peter Collinson; some of the trees and a gate from the old garden remain.

The school was founded in 1807 as a Nonconformist institution; the classical building was designed by Sir William Tite in 1825. Among famous pupils have been the broadcaster Richard Dimbleby, fashion designer Norman Hartnell, and the architect Martin Shaw Briggs who is responsible for some of the new buildings.

At Angel Pond Green the 17C Nicol Almshouses contrast with the modern cottages designed by Richard Seifert in the 1960s. Seifert himself, architect of many London tower blocks including Centre-point, lives in a 1930s house in Milespit Hill, Mill Hill.

Three miles N of Mill Hill is **Barnet**, which has given its name to the London Borough. High, or Chipping Barnet, set on high ground, is a thriving suburb with a small street market in St. Albans Road. The principal market for which a charter was granted in the 12C was held next to the church of *St. John the Baptist*. This has a distinctive chequer-work tower rebuilt in 1875 by Butterfield. The nave and N aisle are from the 15C. Memorials to the Ravenscroft family include an alabaster statue and the tomb of Thomas Ravenscroft (died 1630). The red-brick *Tudor Hall* (1577) nearby in Wood St was once part of the Queen Elizabeth Grammar School, granted a charter in 1573; the building is now used by Barnet College. Also in Wood St is *Barnet Museum*.

Barnet Museum, 31 Wood St, Barnet. Tel. 081-449 0321. Open Tues and Thur 14.30–16.30 (16.00 in winter), Sat 10.00–12.00, 14.00–16.00. Free. Access: Underground, High Barnet.

The museum contains relics of the Battle of Barnet fought on nearby Ha~~
Common in 1471. Horseshoes, local photographs, household impleme.
clothes and other artefacts from the area form the rest of the collection. Part of t.
panelling from Tudor Hall (see above) has been preserved here.

An obelisk commemorating the Battle of Barnet stands at *Hadley High Stone*, 1.5 miles from High Barnet (Underground) past Hadley Green. It was erected in 1740 by Sir Jeremy Sandbrook to mark the one of the battles of the Wars of the Roses, in which Edward IV defeated the Lancastrians and the Earl of Warwick died. At *Hadley Green* the explorer David Livingstone lived in 1857 in one of the attractive Georgian houses. The nearby *Wilbraham Almshouses* date to 1612; Sir Roger Wilbraham's good deeds are commemorated in the Monken Hadley parish church of *St. Mary the Virgin* on a monument by Nicholas Stone. The 15C church is distinguished by a flint and ironstone tower topped by a beacon.

High Barnet's situation on the N route from London stimulated local trade and many coaching inns were located along the main road; one, the *Red Lion* at the foot of Barnet Hill, was established in the 16C. The former cattle market survives as the September Fair. The coming of the railway led to Barnet's development as a suburb, but it also killed off much of the trade engendered by the road. The Old Bull Arts Centre is at 68 High St, tel. 081 449 5189, with a small theatre and regular exhibitions.

Friern Barnet, 3.5 miles SE of High Barnet, was mainly woodland— Elizabeth I hunted here—until the mid 19C when it developed with the railway. *East Barnet*, 2 miles SE of High Barnet, developed in a similar way from an arable past. It has an 11C church, St. Mary the Virgin.

Totteridge between High Barnet and Friern Barnet is a small suburban village surrounded by parkland and a golf course. Outside the parish church, *St. Andrew's*, at the E end of the attractive Totteridge Lane, stands a 1000-year-old yew tree. The church, rebuilt in brick in 1790, retains the weather-boarded bell turret of the older structure. Members of the Pepys family are buried in the churchyard.

Finchley, in two distinct parts—Church End and East Finchley— straddles the North Circular Road 6 miles from central London. *Finchley Manor House* at 80 East End Road was built in 1723 by Thomas Allen. It is now used as a synagogue (there is a large Jewish community in this part of London) and as the HQ of the Reformed Synagogues of Great Britain. Here is the London Museum of Jewish Life (tel. 081-346 2288) which has a collection of material relating to Jewish social history in England. Open Mon–Thur 10.30–17.00, Sun 10.30–16.30 (closed Bank Holiday Sun and Mon, Jewish Holidays and Festivals and Suns in Aug.)

The local borough council recently restored and opened to the public the grounds of *Avenue House* in East End Road (tel. 081-346 4841. Access: Underground, Finchley Central) with a fine collection of rare trees. The house was damaged by fire in 1989.

The house (open by appointment) was built on land originally owned by the Knights Templar. In 1874 Henry Charles Stephens, son of the inventor of modern ink and also known as 'Inky' Stephens, came to live here and established a laboratory (restored) on the first floor. He later became an MP for Finchley (now Margaret Thatcher's constituency) and made various improvements to the house including the addition of a stable block in a French Gothic style which houses the mayoral car.

Also at Church End is the parish church of *St. Mary*, much altered after bomb damage but with a surviving 12C font. In Hendon Lane is

st's College with a distinctive green copper roof and pepper-pot
ers.

At the junction of the North Circular Road and Regent's Park Road
o the S there is a statue by Emile Guillaume, La Délivrance, a
woman holding a sword, donated to the borough to commemorate the
Battle of the Marne.

43 Highgate, Hampstead, Golders Green

There is so much to see in Highgate and Hampstead that the first part of this
section has been arranged as a route from Archway Underground to Hampstead
Underground to be explored on foot, or possibly using the local buses or a car.

Hampstead and Highgate, separated by Hampstead Heath, are two of
London's most attractive suburbs, still retaining much of their village
charm.

Highgate (access: underground, Archway; bus C11 to South Grove,
or walk) takes its name from a tollgate sited along the Old North Road,
its site marked today by the *Gate House* pub. Sir William Cornwallis
became Lord of the Manor in the 1580s, succeeding the Bp of London,
and many famous people passed through the growing village along
the road to the N, including Richard Whittington, three times Lord
Mayor of London.

At the start of Highgate Hill, where the traffic whirls around a busy
one-way system, Archway Road leads N to A1 and Highgate Hill NW
to Highgate. The Whittington Stone (W side of road) marks the spot
where he is said to have stood and listened to the bells of Bow Church
summoning him back to London. His famous cat is sculpted on top of
the stone which was erected in 1821—the cat was added in 1964.
Whittington bequeathed money for almshouses which stood here
until 1970 when they were removed to Surrey; a pub and a hospital
here have taken his name.

Highgate Hill became such a busy thoroughfare that a cable
tramway was introduced in 1884—Europe's first. Trams followed but
now there are only buses and much of the traffic has been diverted
along Archway to the NE. The viaduct above Archway Road dates to
1897 and replaced the Nash original. From it there is a good view of
London and of the tortuous traffic system which has been the subject
of a lengthy, inconclusive planning enquiry.

Along Highgate Hill, heading N towards the village centre, there
are several attractive 17 and 18C houses. On the W side is *Waterlow
Park* with the white stucco *Lauderdale House*, dating from the mid
17C and open to the public.

Lauderdale House, Waterlow Park, N6. Tel. 081-348 8716. Open Tues to Fri
11.00–16.00, Sun 12.00–17.00, (Sat—please contact the house—closed for
private functions).
    Lauderdale House was built for the Duke of Lauderdale in 1645; Nell Gwynn
is said to have stayed here. It later became a boarding-house and where John
Wesley stayed. In 1871 the philanthropist Sir Sidney Waterlow bought it. He
opened the grounds to the public and later presented it to the London County
Council; the park is named after him. The London Borough of Camden now
owns the building which is run as a community arts centre with musical and
theatrical events and exhibitions (cafeteria).
    Waterlow Park is open daily from 07.30. Its 27 acres are laid out as 'a garden for
gardeners'; there are ponds with wildlife and an aviary.

The Egyptian Avenue, Highgate Cemetery

On the E side of the hill is *Cromwell House*, an attractive Dutch-style red-brick building of the 17C. It is now used by a missionary society. (The house has no connection with Oliver Cromwell.) *St. Joseph's Church*, below, with two distinctive onion-shaped copper domes, has a monastery adjoining. Sir Francis Bacon is said to have stayed in a house in Highgate Hill in 1626 when he conducted his famous experiment in refrigeration by stuffing chickens with snow; the consequent chill killed him.

Highgate Hill becomes Highgate High St with a coaching inn, the *Duke's Head*, of 16C origin with village prints on its walls. Charles I is said to have used the *Rose and Crown* also in the High St when visiting Nell Gwynn at Lauderdale House. South Grove and Pond Square are to the W. S.T. Coleridge lived at No. 3 The Grove from 1816 until his death in 1834 and he is very much associated with the area. At the Highgate Literary and Scientific Institute (tel. 081-340 3343; founded 1839) in South Grove there is an annual Coleridge

..ival in July. The Institute stages occasional local exhibitions and
..so houses the royal coat of arms from the former *Fox and Crown* pub
..1 West Hill, and many important documents relating to the area.
Coleridge is buried in the church of *St. Michael* in South Grove. Its
conspicuous spire towers high above London—inside, a line on the
vestibule wall shows that the church is level with the top of St. Paul's
Cathedral. Coleridge's body was originally interred in the chapel of
Highgate School, and was moved here in 1961.

Highgate School in North Road was founded in 1565; it declined in
the 17C when most of its funds were spent on its chapel, but revived in
the 19C and continues to thrive. Well-known former pupils include Sir
John Betjeman, who lived in West Hill as a child. Artist and art critic,
Roger Fry, was born at No. 6 The Grove in 1866.

The ponds of Pond Square were in-filled in 1864; the *Flask* pub in
Highgate West Hill (not to be confused with the Flask in Hampstead)
is one of the highway taverns at which travellers would stop to fill
their flasks. Turpin is said to have hidden in the cellar.

From South Grove Swains Lane descends to the S, past a tall radio
mast, to **Highgate Cemetery**.

Eastern section: open 10.00–16.00 daily October to March; 10.00–17.00 April to
September. Western section: Tours Mon to Fri at 12.00, 14.00, 15.00, weekends
hourly 10.00–16.00 inclusive. Tel. 081-340 1834.
   The cemetery was founded in 1838 and originally run for profit. It is in two
parts; the Western Cemetery is no longer in use and is maintained by the
'Friends of Highgate'. Among the overgrown vegetation there are huge ornate
tombs and catacombs, and fascinating marble and stone statues including a
horse, a lion and a dog.

Those buried in the Western Cemetery include the inventor Michael Faraday
(died 1867), the novelist Mrs Henry Wood (died 1887), the poet Christina Rossetti
(died 1894), Elizabeth Siddal, wife of D.G. Rossetti, and the scientist Jacob
Bronowski (died 1974).

In the public Eastern Cemetery is the famous grave of Karl Marx (died
1883)—a place of pilgrimage for visitors from all over the world. The
inscription on the stone reads 'Workers of the World Unite' and the
large bust by Laurence Bradshaw, which dominates the cemetery
here, was added in 1956. Also buried here are Herbert Spencer (died
1903), George Eliot (as Mary Ann Cross; died 1880) and many other
illustrious literary figures.

At the *Wrestler's Tavern* in Swains Lane the tradition of 'the Swearing
of the Horns' has been revived. Visitors are invited to take an 'oath of
merriment'. In the 18C visitors were required to 'swear the horn' at
Highgate's 20 local taverns before drinking and 'merrymaking'.
Various animal horns were used.

Parliament Hill, 270 acres of open land, is just W of Highgate Road
and may have taken its name from the Gunpowder Plotters who were
to meet here to watch Parliament go up in flames. The excellent view
of London remains, as does, of course, Parliament. Highgate Ponds
are popular with anglers.

Between Swains Lane and Highgate West Hill is the Holly Lodge
Estate, once the suburban home of one of the 19C's wealthiest
women, Angela Burdett Coutts, heiress to the banking fortune. The
house was demolished to make way for a planned housing development, Holly Village, conceived by her as a 'rustic fantasy for the
working class'.

Off West Hill is Millfield Lane, leading towards the Heath and Hampstead. Here
the famous first meeting took place between Keats and Coleridge.

Hampstead is reached along Hampstead Lane from Highgate (bus 210). Fro[m]
central London access is via Haverstock Hill (Underground, Hampstead).

Kenwood House on Hampstead Heath lies half a mile from Highgate along
Hampstead Lane. It takes its name from the Caen river, an old tributary of the
Fleet. It is open to the public and houses the *Iveagh Bequest*.

Kenwood House, Hampstead Lane, NW3. Tel. 081-348 1286. Open daily Easter
to Sept 10.00–18.00, Sept to Easter 10–4. Admission free. Park open daily
08.00–dusk. Tea rooms in Coach House. Access: Underground, Golders Green;
bus, 210).

Kenwood House which houses the Iveagh Bequest

Kenwood House, once the seat of the Argylls, passed to the Earl of Mansfield
in 1754, who was then Lord Chief Justice to George III. He commissioned Robert
Adam to remodel the house; he added a further storey and a library, encased it in
stucco and added ornamental details such as the Ionic portico. The flanking
wings were added later by George Saunders. The grounds were laid out in 1797
by Humphry Repton; they include the lake, now the setting for summer evening
concerts. Spring concerts take place in the Adam Orangery. Also in the grounds
is Dr Johnson's thatched summerhouse, brought here in 1968 from Thrale Place
in Streatham (see p 328).

During the First World War the Grand Duke Michael of Russia lived at
Kenwood. The contents were sold in 1922 and the land was marked up as
building plots when Edward Guinness, Earl of Iveagh, bought the house and
created his famous collection of paintings. As the Iveagh Bequest, all of this was
left to the nation (in the guise of the London County Council) on his death in
1927. It is now owned and managed by English Heritage.

Kenwood is an attractive house with an important collection of
paintings in an enviable setting. The Entrance Hall has an Adam
ceiling representing Bacchus and Ceres; the painting was thought to
be by Biagio Rebecca but has now been identified as the work of
Antonio Zucchi, husband of Angelica Kauffmann, whose work is also
to be seen here. Note among the paintings Reynolds' 'Venus Chiding
Cupid', a portrait of the first Earl of Iveagh, and a bust of Lord
Mansfield. By the main staircase in a display case is the Titus Clock,
made for George III. The Marble Hall was added by Saunders and
leads to the Dining Room, where the most important pictures hang:
Rembrandt, 'Portrait of the Artist', Bol, 'Portrait of a Woman',
discovered to have a false Rembrandt signature when cleaned in

1; over the fireplace is Rubens' 'Madonna and Child and St. Joseph'. In the Vestibule there are paintings by Angelica Kauffmann. From here a door leads to the extremely attractive Library, one of Adam's finest interiors. Plasterwork decorations are by Joseph Rose and the paintings are by Zucchi. It is said that he met his future wife, Angelica Kauffmann, while both were working here.

In Lord Mansfield's Dressing Room there are works by Reynolds, and Gainsborough's 'Going to Market'. In the Parlour is an early Turner sea-picture, 'Fishermen upon a Lee Shore', and a Van Dyck, 'James Stuart, Duke of Richmond, and Lennox'. In Lady Mansfield's Dressing Room there is a display of Adam's designs for Kenwood. Fine paintings in the Orangery include Van Dyck, 'Henrietta of Lorraine' and Gainsborough, 'Lady Howe'. The sofas were designed by Adam. In the Lobby, Romney's 'Lady Hamilton at Prayer' and two Reynolds portraits are noteworthy, as is the elaborate John Sandforth clock (late 18C). In the Music Room there are fine portraits by Reynolds, and in the West Hall two paintings by Landseer.

The shop stocks postcards and books. Temporary exhibitions are held on the first floor.

From the grounds of Kenwood (Pope particularly enjoyed the avenue of limes), it is possible to walk across the Heath to Hampstead Village. Hampstead Lane to the N leads into Spaniards Road; the road narrows where an old tollgate stood. Here is *Spaniards Inn* (1630) once owned by the Spanish ambassador to James II. In this tavern the Gordon rioters (1780) were plied with drink by the landlord on their way to burn Kenwood—a successful diversion. Others who have enjoyed drinking here include Keats, Shelley and Byron, as well as Dickens. Dick Turpin's guns are displayed; he used the inn as a hide-out.

At the cross-roads at Whitestone Pond a flagpole marks the summit of Hampstead Heath, 443ft above sea-level. Children still sail boats in the pond as Shelley did at the end of the 18C. Craft products and paintings are displayed and sold here on summer weekends.

Jack Straw's Castle pub and restaurant has medieval origins; its name comes from one of Wat Tyler's accomplices who was executed after the 1381 rebellion. The white weather-boarding and castellation were added in the 1960s. The banker Samuel Hoare lived at nearby Heath House.

Hampstead Heath (825 acres), could easily have disappeared during the 19C, only being saved by fervent local preservationists. Until 1986 it was owned by the GLC; the City of London has now taken over the management of the Heath.

The village of Hampstead began to develop in the 18C when the quality of its spring water was recognised. Well Walk and Flask Walk recall Hampstead's relatively short period as a spa with its own Assembly Rooms, now demolished. Hampstead's popularity inspired the lord of the manor, Sir Thomas Maryon Wilson, to develop the heathland beyond the village. The local community was in uproar and the struggle to prevent development continued from 1829 until Wilson's death in 1869 when his son gave in and sold 240 acres to the Metropolitan Board of Works. Further areas, including Parliament Hill Fields, were added over the next century. The sandy, wild heath was a popular excursion for 19C city-dwellers crowded into Islington and the City. Karl Marx took his family and friends for regular Sunday picnics on the Heath which even then offered donkey rides. Notable among painters of the Heath Constable.

Activities on the Heath today include fishing, boating, dry-skiing, horseriding, and swimming in three ponds—Hampstead Pond (mixed), Highgate Pond (men), Kenwood Pond (women).

From the cross-roads at Jack Straw's Castle North End Way leads N to Golders Green (see below) and S into Heath St and the old village. To the E is the *Vale of Health* with attractive 19C houses; while living at South Villa in 1816 Leigh Hunt was visited by Keats, Byron, Coleridge, Shelley and Lamb. D.H. Lawrence, Edgar Wallace and Compton Mackenzie later lived here for short periods. The area's name may be an attempt by the developers to counteract the associations of its origin as a drained swamp. Willows now surround a small pond, all that remains of the swamp. The nearby fairground on the Heath expands into the car park for a fair three times a year on Bank Holidays.

East Heath Road continues along the E side of the Heath to Downshire Hill; here Michael Hopkins won a RIBA award in 1977 for his house of glass added unobtrusively in an 18C setting.

On the corner of Keats Grove and Downshire Hill is *St. John's Church* (1818) with old box pews and Georgian galleries. Keats Grove was known as Wentworth Place when John Keats came to live here in 1818. **Keats House** was originally two semi-detached houses; one was occupied by Mrs Brawne and her three children, the other by Keats's friend Charles Armitage Brown. Keats fell in love with Fanny Brawne and they became engaged in 1819; in 1820 illness forced him to travel to Italy where he died. He spent two of his most creative years at the house which is now a place of pilgrimage for his admirers. Keats House was saved from demolition in 1925 after a public appeal; it is now owned by the London Borough of Camden.

Keats House, Keats Grove, NW3. Tel. 071-435 2062. Open Mon to Fri 14.00–18.00, Sat 10.00-17.00 Sun 14.00–17.00, shorter hours in winter. Free. Access: Underground, Hampstead, BR Hampstead Heath.

The Regency house contains memorabilia of the poet's life. From the entrance hall enter the Brawne Room where Keats first met Fanny in October 1818. The room is furnished in period style, with a painting of 'Keats Listening to the Nightingale on Hampstead Heath' by John Severn (1845) and a marble bust of Keats by the American sculptor Anne Whitney (1873; exhibited here since 1933; see also St. John's Church, below). In a glass case is a lock of Fanny's hair and other relics. Brown's Sitting Room, on the other side of the hall, contains the sofa on which Keats lay during his illness, and a set of Hogarth's Rake's Progress prints. In Keats' Sitting Room are his books and another portrait. A display case here contains letters and a lock of his hair. There are more letters and MSS in the Chester Room, added to the house later.

On the first floor is Keats' bedroom, with a Regency-style tent-bed similar to the one he may have slept in when he first realised he had contracted consumption. The Keats Memorial Library is open by appointment.

In the basement are two kitchens and a wine cellar. The small garden features an ancient mulberry tree and a recent replacement of the plum tree under which Keats wrote 'Ode to a Nightingale'. The adjoining public library has a large collection of Keats's works and books relating to his life.

Keats House is now the HQ of the Keats-Shelley Memorial Association; occasional poetry readings are held here.

Downshire Hill leads W into Rosslyn Hill and Hampstead High St. The redundant church of St. Stephen's by S.S. Teulon (1869) is in Rosslyn Hill. Old Hampstead may be explored from Hampstead Underground Station in the centre of the village.

Hampstead retains its reputation acquired over the last two centuries as a centre for artists, writers and intellectuals, bolstered by actors, journalists and broadcasters, and a sprinkling of foreign diplomats and other expatriates. The

ography of the village on its steep hill and strong local interests have ensured
e preservation of many attractive houses and restricted new developments
hough there are blots, such as the massive Royal Free Hospital in Pond St; it
moved here from Grays Inn Road in 1974.

Hampstead Underground Station opened in 1907 on the Northern
Line; at 181ft its lift-shaft is the deepest in London. From here Heath
St climbs N to the Heath and S to Church Row (turning to the W).
Church Row has attractive brown-brick Georgian houses with iron
railings. The parish church, *St. John's*, on the corner of Frognal Way,
has a distinctive spire; the decorative iron gates came from the
Canons in Stanmore. The church (begun 1744) has a barrel vault;
monuments include a bust of Keats by Anne Whitney (a replica of the
original in Keats House), presented by American admirers in 1894,
and memorials to Constable, Norman Shaw and George du Maurier.
    Nearby in Holly Place (up Holly Walk) stands *St. Mary's Catholic
Church*, at the centre of what was a community of refugees from the
French Revolution. The church was built in 1816, one of the first new
Catholic churches in London since the Reformation.
    Frognal, parallel with and W of Holly Walk, leads to Arkwright
Road and the *Camden Arts Centre*. To the E Fitzjohn's Avenue
continues S to Swiss Cottage. Near Swiss Cottage Library in Adelaide
Road there is an impressive, seated, bronze statue of Sigmund Freud
by Oscar Nemon (1930); it was unveiled in 1970. In *Maresfield
Gardens*, parallel with Fitzjohn's Avenue, was the home of Sigmund
Freud who died here in 1939. It was here that Salvador Dali sketched
Freud. The House opened as a museum in 1986, four years after
Freud's daughter Anna who lived here, died.

Freud Museum, 20 Maresfield Gardens, Hampstead, NW3. Tel. 071-435 2002.
Open Wed to Sun 12.00–17.00. Admission charge. Underground Finchley Road.
Freud's study has been recreated including his famous couch and desk with
collection of antiquities. Lecture room and garden.

In Frognal are the buildings of *University College School* (1907); the
school moved here from Gower St, Bloomsbury. Upper Frognal Lodge
was the last home of Ramsay MacDonald.
    Turn back towards Heath St along Mount Vernon where the house
of a former governor of the Tower of London is hidden behind a high
wall. In Holly Hill is the striking façade of the *National Institute for
Medical Research* and, opposite, the much-altered house built by the
painter George Romney in 1796. Later the house became lecture
rooms; Constable and Faraday were among the speakers here. Steps
lead down Holly Mount back into Heath St past the picturesque *Holly
Bush* pub (1796). Continue N along Hampstead Grove; the cottages at
Nos 4–14 have medieval foundations. Opposite is 17C **Fenton House**,
open to the public.

Open Apr to Oct, Sat to Wed 11.00–17.00, Oct to Mar Sat, Sun only 14.00–17.00,
last admission 17.00. Tel. 071-435 3471. Admission charge. Access: Underground, Hampstead.
    The William-and-Mary style red-brick house was built in 1695 and became
known as Fenton House in the early 19C when a merchant family of that name
owned it. In 1936–52 it was the home of Lady Binning who bequeathed the house
and its contents to the National Trust. On view is a collection of European and
Oriental ceramics and the important Benton Fletcher Collection of musical
instruments, left to the Trust in 1937. Music students are invited to play these,
and this adds greatly to the atmosphere of the house.
    The original entrance from Holly Hill is graced by decorative iron gates by
Jean Tijou. The present entrance is in the E front through a Regency loggia. In
the entrance hall (original panelling) are 17C needlework pictures—the Dining
Room contains a number of Regency pieces and a Burkat Shudi harpsichord of

1770. The Porcelain Room contains fine English and continental porcelain, and a pair of Sheraton armchairs. Sung and Ming dynasty china is displayed in the Oriental Room; Chinese snuff bottles (17–20C) are in a hanging cabinet. There are Staffordshire figures on the first floor landing and others in the Rockingham Room, where there is more needlework. Chinese blue-and-white porcelain is shown in the Blue Porcelain Room which also contains a two-manual harpsichord by J. and A. Kirckmann (1777).

In the Drawing Room Worcester porcelain is displayed in the alcoves by the fireplace. An early, grotesque Meissen teapot and cover and a pair of parrots are in the display cabinet on the N side of the room. The walnut-veneered spinet in the Pink Room is early 18C and was made in London. The service staircase leads to the Attic Floor with several musical instruments including a Dolmetsch clavichord, a painted Italian harpsichord, the earliest existing English grand piano (made by Bakers in Jermyn St; 1763–78), and a Robert Hatley virginals (1664) with traditional flower and fruit decoration, a rare survivor of the Great Fire of London.

Concerts are given in the main dining room on the harpsichord (see above), the largest ever made in England. A harpsichord of 1612 on which Handel is said to have played is also used occasionally. The high-walled garden is attractively laid out.

George du Maurier lived further along Hampstead Grove in New Grove House, attached to Old Grove House, an impressive Georgian mansion. Opposite the Mount, Admiral's House is distinguished by the bridge-like balcony added by Admiral Matthew Barton (died 1795). Later the Victorian architect Sir George Gilbert Scott lived here. At Grove Lodge a blue plaque marks the home of John Galsworthy (died 1933) who completed the Forsyte Saga here. There are no windmills left on Windmill Hill, nor are there judges in Judge's Walk. The latter takes its name from the High Court judges who held court sessions here when the plague was prevalent in the City. Judge's Walk leads back to the Heath. At the little cottage called Capo di Monte, the actress Sarah Siddons stayed and is remembered by an S over the door. From this vantage point at the top of Heath St Constable painted several views of Hampstead.

Heath St leads back down the hill past the Quaker Meeting House of 1907. To the E is New End with council flats and *Burgh House*, a local community centre run by the Burgh House Trust.

Burgh House, New End Square, NW3. Tel. 071-431 0144. Open Wed to Sun 12.00–17.00, Bank Holidays 14.00–17.00. Free. Cafeteria. Access: Underground, Hampstead.

The house, built in Queen Anne style in 1703, belonged to Dr Gibbons, physician of the wells. It takes its name from a later owner, the Rev. Allotson de Burgh, the musicologist. It was recently restored by the London Borough of Camden and opened to the public in 1979. Fine internal features include a carved staircase, fireplaces and some original plasterwork. The Exhibition Room is used for changing exhibitions of local artists' work. On the first floor is the Hampstead Museum of Local History. Rooms are used for lectures, concerts and private functions.

That this is the former spa area is reflected in the names of Well Walk and Flask Walk; the Victorian fountain in Well Walk marked 'not drinking water' is opposite the site of the original Pump House and Assembly Rooms. Keats lived at 30 Well Walk in 1816 before moving to Keats Grove; Constable lived at No. 40 in 1826–37.

Flask Walk leads back to Heath St past the *Flask Tavern* where the Kit-Cat Club (1700–20) met during the summer; members included Walpole, Vanbrugh, Congreve and Kneller (see also p 98). More of 20C Hampstead is found along the High St and down Rosslyn Hill with its healthfood restaurants, bookshops and boutiques.

N of the cross-roads at Whitestone Pond, North End Way leads to Golders Green and Hampstead Garden Suburb. Not far along the road is the *Old Bull and Bush* pub, made famous by the music-hall song. The pub's 17C building was once the country home of William Hogarth. Opposite is *Golders Hill Park* with an attractive walled garden, a deer enclosure, and a children's zoo. A turning to the E leads to a preserved working farm, *Wyldes Farm*, often used in films. In North End Avenue, another turning to the E, is *Byron Cottage*, once the home of Lady Houston, who progressed from chorus girl to possession of three aristocratic husbands, and used her fortune for the benefit of women's suffrage as well as for the development of the Spitfire and Hurricane fighter planes. *Pitt House* marks the site of a house demolished in 1952. Here in 1766–67 the Earl of Chatham, then prime minister, lay ill for 18 months, refusing to see anyone, while George III and his ministers alienated the American colonies by the imposition of unfair taxes.

Sir Nikolaus Pevsner, cataloguer of England's architectural heritage, lived at North End from 1935 until his death in 1984. Further along North End Road towards Golders Green is *Ivy House*, where the ballerina Anna Pavlova lived (1912–31). There is now a small museum here (open Sat 14.00–17.00. Free). The museum, set in the studio which overlooks the gardens and lake in which she kept tame swans, contains photographs, programmes, furniture, books, and other personal effects. The main building is used as a speech and drama college.

Two miles E of North End Road is the large and well-planned **Hampstead Garden Suburb**. It was conceived by Dame Henrietta Barnett, inspired by the poverty and slums of London's East End, where she was the wife of the vicar of St. Jude's. She purchased 20 acres of land and construction started in 1907 under the guidance of the architects Barry Parker and Raymond Unwin. Sir Edwin Lutyens designed the Central Square, including the parish church, St. Jude's, in brick with a steeply pitched roof.

The mixed architecture of the area, now mostly middle class in character rather than socially mixed as Dame Henrietta intended, is best appreciated by walking from Wyldes Farm off the North End Road, through the Heath extension, emerging at the junction of Finchley Road and Hampstead Way. A Town Trail leaflet of the area is available from the London Borough of Barnet Library Department.

Golders Green developed rapidly this century following the arrival of the Northern Line Underground. It is now a wealthy residential suburb with a strong Jewish community. The Golders Green Hippodrome opened as a music hall in 1913 but is now used as studios by the BBC. Anna Pavlova gave her final performance here. The *Golders Green Crematorium* opened in 1902 and is one of the biggest in London with 12 acres and landscaped gardens behind the Romanesque-style buildings. Among those cremated here and commemorated by a plaque or casket are Sigmund Freud (died 1939), Kathleen Ferrier (died 1953), Ivor Novello (died 1951), Anna Pavlova (died 1931), Marie Stopes (died 1958), and R. Vaughan Williams (died 1958).

44   Wood Green, Tottenham, Stoke Newington, Hackney, Enfield, Lea Valley, Epping Forest, Walthamstow

Wood Green, in the heart of the London Borough of Haringey, has the heights of Hampstead and Muswell Hill to the W and the valley of the River Lea to the E. Haringey is said to be the Saxon name, and this later merged with Hornsey; just to the S. *Alexandra Park*, on high ground in the centre of Wood Green, has good views over central London. (Access: BR, Alexandra Palace; shuttle bus during exhibitions.)

The 480-acre park was laid out in 1863; 10 years later Alexandra Palace was built to match the Crystal Palace at Sydenham. It burnt down almost immediately, and though it was rebuilt with a circus and a racecourse in the grounds it never quite matched the glamour of Crystal Palace. In 1936 it became a household name when the first scheduled live television transmissions were made from here by the BBC. The park passed to the GLC in 1956 when the BBC moved most of its TV activities to the new Television Centre at Shepherd's Bush. It was used as an exhibition centre until again gutted by fire in 1980. While the London Borough of Haringey planned and executed the £35m rebuilding of the Palace, a temporary Pavilion was used for exhibitions. The new Alexandra Palace opened, with its Palm Court fully restored, as a major exhibition centre in 1988. A sports centre, museum of television history and a hotel will complete the development. Alexandra Palace is used for a variety of events from antique fairs to major commercial exhibitions. A shuttle bus service operates from Alexandra Park BR Station during events.

Wood Green's new shopping centre was opened by the Queen in 1981; it includes department stores, shops, a market and restaurants, all in an air-conditioned environment. The *New River Sports Centre*, home of the Harringey Athletics Club, has an all-weather outdoor track and a 1000-seat stadium in Harringey itself to the S.

Tottenham, 2 miles E of Wood Green, is a mixed industrial and residential area. The manor of Tottenham has Scottish antecedents and was once owned by Robert Bruce, king of the Scots. Edward I confiscated the manor from the Scottish Pretender and Sir William Compton replaced the old dwelling with the present mansion in 1514; it has since been altered many times. The local borough took over the building in 1891 and it is now the *Bruce Castle Museum*.

Bruce Castle Museum, Lordship Lane, N17. Tel. 081-808 8772. Open daily 13.00–17.00, (Museum of Middlesex Regiment open Tues to Sat 13.00–17.00). Access: Underground, Seven Sisters.
   During the 19C the house was run as a school by Sir Rowland Hill, inventor of the adhesive postage stamp. As a result the museum has a large collection of postal memorabilia (1700–1840), including Victorian pillar-boxes, a postboy's riding boots and hat, and reports of mail robberies. The history of the Middlesex Regiment and changing exhibitions on local history make up the other sections of the museum.

Near the museum in Church Lane is the church of *All Hallows*, with a 14C tower; the adjoining vicarage, the Priory, dates from 1620. Several imposing Victorian buildings survive, including the former Tottenham Palace where Marie Lloyd sang (now a bingo club).
   Tottenham Hotspur's Football Club, with its ground in White Hart Lane, was founded in 1882; current developments aim to preserve some of the original buildings (access: BR, White Hart Lane).
   The Cross in Tottenham's High Road is probably a medieval market cross rebuilt in 1600 and covered with Gothic stucco in the 19C.
   Stoke Newington, 2 miles S of Tottenham, now a rather shabby but improving residential area, preserves some of its ancient village atmosphere. The village predates the Saxon settlement in Stoke Newington Church St and at Newington Green. Nos. 53, 54, and 55 Newington Green, all 17C houses, are now owned by English Heritage. Stoke Newington's most famous resident was Daniel Defoe who went to school at Newington Green and wrote 'Robinson Crusoe' while living at 95 Stoke Newington Church St (blue plaque). His family was part of a Nonconformist settlement of the area, later

1owed by a Jewish community and more recently by immigrants
om the Commonwealth. Defoe's tombstone from Bunhill Fields is
preserved in the local library. Red-brick *St. Mary's Old Church*, also
in Stoke Newington Church St, dates from 1560, but there has been a
church on this site for 1000 years. The 'new' church of St. Mary was
designed by Sir George Gilbert Scott in 1858. Nearby Nonconformist
Abney Park Cemetery was established in the wooded grounds of
Abney House in 1840; the popular cemetery fell into decay and was
taken over by Hackney Borough Council in 1974 for preservation.
General William Booth and his wife Catherine, founders of the
Salvation Army, and their son Bramwell Booth are buried here.
Clissold Park has a small zoo.

Stoke Newington Pumping Station in Green Lanes (skirting the W
side of Clissold Park), a castle-like structure, is an interesting example
of Victorian industrial architecture, designed in 1854–56 by Chadwell
Mylne. It is due to be redeveloped.

This is the LB of Hackney; *Hackney* itself is to the SE (See also p 274.)
Hackney's oldest surviving house, Sutton House, is in Homerton High
St. Thomas Sutton, founder of Charterhouse, lived here in at the
beginning of the 17C. It now belongs to the National Trust and is due
to be restored. Hackney developed quickly in the late Victorian
period and early part of the 20C. It is now dealing with the problems of
modern housing built after the Second World War. The Hackney
Museum illustrates the history of the area. It is at Central Hall, Mare
St, E8, opposite the Town Hall. The Sam Uriah Morris Society runs a
museum of the history of black people at Harriet Tubman House, 136
Lower Clapton Road, E5. Tel. 081-986 4121. The Hackney Empire,
designed by Matcham, has been rescued from its second life as a
bingo-hall to become once again a music-hall at 291 Mare St, E8. Tel.
081-985 2424. Ridley Road street market offers fruit and veg' and
clothes and household items.

Hackney Marshes to the NE covers an area of 330 acres; when first
drained in the 18C Roman remains were found. Dick Turpin is said to
have visited the White House pub. The Marshes are now used for
cricket and football.

The River Lea leads to Tottenham and Edmonton; industrial and
heavily built-up areas. (See below). Three miles N of Edmonton, on
the outer edge of Greater London and with a country-town atmosphere, is **Enfield**. Its past as a royal hunting-ground, Enfield Chase,
survives in the open parkland at Forty Hill, White Webbs and Trent
Park. Elizabeth I spent some of her childhood at Elsyinge Hall, which
stood on Forty Hill, just N of Forty Hall. *Forty Hall* was built for Sir
Nicholas Raynton in 1629 and it remains a fine example of Jacobean
architecture, showing the influence of Inigo Jones. It is now a local
museum with several rooms restored to their original splendour and
reopened by the local Council in 1966.

Forty Hall, Forty Hill, Enfield, Middlesex. Tel. 081-363 8196. Open Tues to Sun
10.00–18.00, (Easter to September), Tues to Sun 10.00–17.00 (October to Easter).
Cafeteria open Easter to September. Car park. Access: BR, Enfield Town.
    The drive leads past a duck-pond by the N entrance and an attractive porch
with carved turtle doves above. The entrance hall features fine plasterwork from
1787; in the dining room is the original screen with a striking shell motif. There
are ornate fireplaces here and in the drawing room which has a plaster ceiling
with a bold strapwork design. In the Raynton Room the portrait of Sir Nicholas
Raynton may be by William Dobson. The plasterwork ceiling continues in the
attractive staircase hall. From the first landing there is a good view of a
200-year-old cedar of Lebanon in the grounds. The first floor rooms contain

furnishings and pictures of the 17 and 18C, local antiquities and maps. Forty Hall has been extended and an exhibition gallery created in the outbuildings where temporary exhibitions are held.

To the N of the house is the home park with a lime-tree avenue. In the SW corner of the grounds a pleasant rose garden is protected by high brick walls.

In Forty Hill, the *Goat* pub has a striking exterior and comfortable bars.

Sir Nicholas Raynton, a Lord Mayor of London (died 1646) is commemorated in the parish church of *St. Andrew*. His massive marble family monument dominates the N chapel of the 13C church, rebuilt in 1824.

Enfield used to be an important market town; a weekly market has been held here since 1632 and now takes place on Saturdays in the Market Place, near the church and the King's Head Hotel. Picturesque Gentleman's Row to the W of the church, with 17 and 18C houses, is now a conservation area. At No. 17, Clarendon Cottage, Charles Lamb and his sister lived in 1827. The New River, a 20-mile system of canals and aqueducts engineered by Sir Hugh Myddleton in 1613 to bring fresh water to the City of London, has been landscaped in front of the gardens. Sir Hugh has given his name to Myddleton House (1818), the mansion in Forty Hill, which is now the HQ of the Lee [sic] Valley Regional Park (see below). The Myddleton House Garden, Bulls Cross, Enfield, designed by the great botanist Edward A. Bowles in 1890, is open to the public 10.00–15.30 Mon to Sat and Sun in summer (tel. 0992 717711).

Enfield Grammar School, in the Market Place, was established in 1555; John Keats was a pupil here. The compiler of Whitaker's Almanack lived at White Lodge, a weather-boarded 18C house in Silver St, near the modern Civic Centre, which has a sculpture of the Enfield Beast of Enfield Chase outside.

In *Edmonton* to the S, the Council has established a local arts centre in a 16C building, *Salisbury House*, Bury St. Tel. 081-360 5306. Access: BR, Lower Edmonton. Some original panelling remains. Charles Lamb lived at Lamb's Cottage, Church St, moving here from Enfield (see above). He died in 1834 and is buried in the local churchyard of All Saints. There is another arts centre at Millfield House, Silver St. Tel. 081-803 6213. Access: BR, Silver St.

At *Southgate* there are attractive houses by the Green including the *Olde Cherry Tree Inn*, and Southgate House, built in the 1720s and now known as *Arnos Grove*. It is decorated in the Adam style and used as offices.

In *Palmers Green*, 17C *Broomfield House* was a local museum. The entrance hall had a fine staircase, an 18C fireplace and murals attributed to Gerrard Lanscroon (early 18C). A fire in 1984 destroyed a large part of the building and the museum is closed indefinitely (further information from the London Borough of Enfield on 081-886 6555).

The poet Stevie Smith (1902–71) lived at Palmers Green, and described the area in some of her work.

NW of Enfield is *Trent Park*, a training college with attractive grounds, including a nature trail, open to the public (access: Underground, Cockfosters). The main building was refaced with bricks from William Kent's Devonshire House in Piccadilly, demolished in 1962. During the Second World War it was used as an interrogation centre and internment camp.

To the N is the remaining land of Enfield Chase and to the W are Hadley Wood and Hadley Common.

Lee Valley Regional Park. The Lee Valley Regional Park Authority was established in 1967 to develop the leisure potential of the River Lea [sic] along 23 miles from Ware (Herts) to London's East End once its useful commercial life had ended. The Lea was the ancient frontier between King Alfred's Wessex and the Danelaw, and later the boundary between Essex and Middlesex. During the Great Plague in 1664–65 the watermen of Ware brought fresh water supplies to the City down the river (see also Epping Forest, below). Today it is possible to follow the course of the Lea on foot past its many locks and reservoirs; by car the river-bank and individual leisure facilities are best approached from the A1010 to the W.

At the Greater London boundary to the N is *Waltham Abbey*, built by Harold II; he was buried here after his death at the Battle of Hastings in 1066. The abbey was the last to surrender to the authority of Henry VIII after the dissolution of the monasteries. The present church (open 10.00–15.00 in winter, 10.00–16.00 in summer, depending on services) includes the Nave begun by Harold, the Lady Chapel of 1316 and a West Tower of 1558. The massive columns of the nave are channelled with chevrons and spirals. Henry II extended the abbey to the E. The fine windows in the Victorian E end are by Burne-Jones. The raised chapel on the right has a fresco of the Last Judgment of c 1430 and a W window with tracery. The 16C tower has an impressive peal of 12 bells, the 'wild bells' of Tennyson's 'In Memoriam'. In the crypt there is a small exhibition of historical interest.

The Abbey Gardens contain remains of the monastic buildings; a stone marks the site of the high altar and Harold's tomb. Part of the moat also remains as does the ancient Harold's Bridge. There is a beautiful rose garden and a Country Park with 70 acres of water meadows. The *Epping Forest District Museum* at 39–41 Sun St, Waltham Abbey, is open Mon, Fri to Sun 14.00– 17.00, Tues 12.00– 17.00 (free). Tel. 0992 716882. It is housed in a timber-framed Tudor building with an exhibition of local history.

In Stubbins Hall Lane, Crooked Mile, half a mile from Waltham Abbey, Hayes Hill and Holyfieldhall Farms are open to visitors. Farm animals, milking, sheep-shearing and crafts demonstrations can be seen. There is a shop and light refreshments at Hayes Hill Farm (more information on Nazeing 2291).

Across the Lea (1 mile W) is *Waltham Cross* which takes its name from the Eleanor Cross (heavily restored), the last but one in the series of crosses erected by Edward I in 1291 (see p 93). It stands on a traffic island, with a modern shopping centre behind. Eleanor's body rested at Waltham Abbey.

Anthony Trollope lived at Waltham House in 1859–71. To the NW is *Theobalds Park*, outside the Greater London boundary, where the Temple Bar (see p 215) from the City was erected in 1888. Proposals for its return are made from time to time.

S of Waltham Cross is the King George Reservoir (sailing club). Further S at *Picketts Lock* there is a large and well-equipped sports and leisure centre.

Picketts Lock Centre, Picketts Lock Lane, Edmonton. Tel 081-803 4756. Access: BR, Lower Edmonton, then bus W8. Open daily. Facilities include golf, squash, badminton, roller-skating, bowls, and a swimming-pool; there are floodlit pitches for football and hockey and tennis courts. Within the grounds is a camping and caravan site. Day tickets and season permits to fish the River Lea may be obtained from the Park Authority (call Lea Valley 717711).

Further S in *Leyton* (Lea Bridge Road) is the new *Lee Valley Ice Centre* with facilities for skating, training, ice-hockey, and seating for 1000 spectators. Skates can be hired (tel. 081-533 3151. Access: Underground, Leytonstone). Also in Leyton is the *Eastway Sports Centre* (Quarter Mile Lane, tel. 081-519 0017) with badminton, basketball, volleyball amd squash courts, as well as the Eastway Cycle Circuit.

The *Banbury Sailing Centre*, Greaves Pumping Station, North Circular Road, E4 (tel. 081-531 1129) offers dinghy and board sailing on Banbury Reservoir.

Epping Forest. In 1878 Epping Forest, threatened by enclosure, was saved for Londoners by an Act of Parliament initiated by the City of London Corporation which has since managed the 6000 acres of deciduous forest, spread over some 11 miles between the Lea and Roding river valleys. Queen Victoria visited the forest on 6 May 1882 and declared it to be for 'the use and enjoyment of my people for all time' from a specially constructed grandstand in the centre of the forest at High Beach. An estimated half million Londoners came to cheer her as she travelled by train to Chingford Station, and on by open carriage.

Epping Forest originally covered a huge area of Essex. Archaeological evidence shows Stone Age settlements; there are two Iron Age earthworks, Loughton Camp (SW corner, at the junction of Green Ride and Clay Road at Sandpit Plain, NW of Loughton) and Ambresbury Banks (by the B1393, S of Epping). There are Roman remains in Wanstead Park and the site of a Roman tile kiln near St. Margaret's Hospital. Later the forest became a Saxon stronghold, although one Viking incursion up the River Lea penetrated as far as Hertford; there have been Viking finds in the Walthamstow Marshes.

The Normans introduced the Forest Law and the office of Verderer to administer it; the office survives as an honorary appointment. The N part of the forest became known as Waltham Forest as the importance of Waltham Abbey grew, while Barking Abbey came to own most of Hainault Forest. During the Tudor period Waltham Forest became a favourite royal hunting ground. Henry VIII built the pavilion at Chingford which in 1581 Elizabeth I converted into the present Hunting Lodge. Deer were introduced at this time and Chingford Plain was cleared of trees. Elizabeth also visited Wanstead House (to the S), owned by Robert Dudley, Earl of Leicester; the remains of the house can be seen in Wanstead Park (see below). At the beginning of the 18C Dick Turpin robbed travellers through the forest. He is said to have hidden in a 'cave'—more of a hollow in fact—against the bank of Loughton Camp, now known as Turpin's Cave.

Epping Forest was an important source of timber and trees were 'lopped' to promote new growth; this pollarding did not stop until 1878 and some typical 'bushed' trees can still be seen. Oak, beech, lime, hornbeam, birch and holly grow freely. The fallow deer are confined to a sanctuary at Birch Hall but other wildlife includes badgers, foxes, weasels and squirrels. Cows also wander freely at certain times of the year—a privilege granted to farmers on forest land—drivers through Chingford and Woodford should look out for cattle on road verges in this area, particularly during autumn when grass in the forest is sparse.

During the 19C Epping Forest became a popular destination for Sunday outings from the City and East End. 'Retreats' were established to serve large numbers of meals for the day-trippers; the Turpin pub could serve up to 500 meals at a sitting and another retreat at High Beach served teas for up to 4000 children. Most then would have arrived by train but the tradition continues today; families arrive by car and picnic in the forest. Horse-riding is also popular.

Places of interest.
Queen Elizabeth Hunting Lodge, Epping Forest Museum, Rangers Road, Chingford (tel. 081-529 6681). Open Wed to Sun 14.00–18.00 (or dusk if earlier) and Bank Holidays. Admission charge. Parking. Access: Underground, Chingford. This 16C timber-frame building has been carefully restored. The two upper storeys were originally open platforms with uninterrupted views of the forest and

˞e progress of the deer hunt. The museum contains exhibitions on the history ˞nd natural history of Epping Forest.

The Royal Forest House next to it occupies a neo-Tudor building; it serves light refreshments and full meals.

Beyond the Hunting Lodge is *Chingford Plain*, site of the Bank Holiday Chingford Fair. It is also a public golf course and the location of Gilwell Park, HQ of the Scout movement.

The *Epping Forest Conservation Centre*, High Beach, Loughton (tel. 081-508 7714), open Easter to end October, Wed to Sun (winter weekends only) 10.00–12.30, 14.00–17.00 weekdays; 11.00–12.30, 14.00–17.00 (or –dusk) Sun. Free. Access: Underground, Loughton. This is an educational centre offering adults' and children's study courses, guided walks through the forest, and displays, maps and publications in the centre itself.

Nearby is the pretty Victorian church of *High Beach*. Tennyson lived at High Beach House. Near Epping Copped Hall, a mansion with Tudor origins rebuilt in the 18C, has burnt down. Amberbury Banks and Loughton Camp, see above.

To the S the forest is broken up by residential development. Higham House, a mansion of 1768, now a school, overlooking the Higham Lake is at Woodford; Hollow Ponds, an attractive lake landscape, is by Whipps Cross; nearby is Eagle Pond, home of wild geese and other wildfowl (nearest Underground, Snaresbrook).

In *Wanstead Park* there are three attractive lakes, the Ornamental Water, Heronry Pond and Perch Pond. The remains of Wanstead House are in the grounds; it was designed and built in 1715 by Colen Campbell and set a new fashion in country houses with its severe Classical exterior contrasting with a sumptuous interior. Robert Dudley lived here in the 16C and Queen Elizabeth I visited him in 1578. Later the house was owned by the Child family. It was demolished in 1822, sold to meet the debts of William Pole Tylney Long-Wellesley, who had assumed the title of Lord Warden of Epping Forest and led an extravagant life-style, even closing the Park to the public. The City Corporation acquired the Park as part of the Epping Forest Act of 1878 when his descendents attempted to enclose land in the Forest. Lord Mayors of London have added new trees to the forest at Wanstead Park.

S of Wanstead Park, off Aldersbrook Road, E12, is the *City of London Cemetery*, established by the Corporation in 1856 and still well maintained. It is the second largest cemetery in London, designed by William Haywood 'for posterity'. Thousands of graves have been moved here from City churchyards; many feature impressive monuments.

Epping itself is to the N, outside the Greater London area; the new M25 motorway passes under Epping Forest where it crosses the A104.

Walthamstow, 2 miles SW of Woodford and on the edge of Epping Forest, was in the 18 and 19C a desirable suburb with many large houses. Its character changed as industrialisation spread to nearby areas and with the establishment of working-class housing in modest terraces. Today it boasts one of the longest street markets in the country, stretching half a mile along the High St on Thursday, Friday and Saturday (access: Underground, Walthamstow), with nearly 500 stalls selling everything from jewellery, records, wholefoods and plants to live trout.

Walthamstow Village reflects the area as it was before the first suburban dwellers arrived. Approach via St. Mary's Road off Hoe St.

This leads to St. Mary's Church in Church Lane. Opposite is the 15 *Ancient House*. During the 19C this was divided into four shops but r is now reunited as a private dwelling, its timber frame somewhat askew. Further along are the *Squires Almshouses*, founded in 1795 'for the use of six decayed tradesmen's widows and no others', as the inscription outside says. *Sir George Monoux's Almshouses* are on the other side; both are still used. *St. Mary's Church* of 1108, which Pepys describes visiting, has its original brickwork encased in cement. Inside are two brasses and a striking monument to Lady Stanley (died 1630) surrounded by four of her daughters. The memorial to Lord and Lady Merry was sculpted by Nicholas Stone in 1633.

On the corner of Church Lane and Vestry Road a huge carved capital marks the entrance to the *Vestry House Museum*. The column once formed part of the façade of the Post Office in St. Martin's le Grand, demolished in 1913 and purchased by a local builder. Vestry House is a workhouse of 1730 which has also served as a police station (one cell remains outside and there is another within); it became a local museum in 1931.

Vestry House Museum, Vestry Road, E17. Tel. 081-509 1917. Open Mon to Fri 10.00–13.00, 14.00–17.30, Sat 10.00–13.00, 14.00–17.00. Free.
  Displays include local archaeological exhibits, a reconstructed Victorian parlour, costumes, local crafts, and exhibits of Victorian domestic life. Also on display is the Bremer Car, built in Walthamstow in 1895 and the earliest British car with an internal combustion engine. Panelling from Essex Hall, demolished in 1932, can be seen in the rear gallery.

One of Walthamstow's most illustrious residents was William Morris, born at Elm House in 1834. The family moved to Woodford Hall in 1847 but returned to *The Water House*, Walthamstow, in 1847. The house (c 1750) took its name from a moat in the grounds, now a park. The Morris family lived here until 1856. The house was presented to the local Council in 1898 by a later occupant, the publisher Edward Lloyd, who has given his name to the park. The house finally opened to the public in 1950 as the *William Morris Gallery*; as well as the Morris collection it includes the Brangwyn Gift. Frank Brangwyn, the artist, was a pupil of Morris and donated his collection in 1935.

William Morris Gallery, Lloyd Park, Forest Road, E17. Tel. 081-527 3782. Open Tues to Sat 10.00–13.00, 14.00– 17.00, first Sun of each month 10.00–12.00, 14.00–17.00. Free. Access: Underground, Walthamstow Central. Limited parking.
  Ground floor displays show the development of Morris's career and the work of the Century Guild, including wallpapers, textiles, embroidery, rugs and carpets, furniture, stained glass and ceramics. Among the highlights are the helmet and sword designed for the Oxford Union murals, the Beauty and Beast tile panel designed by Burne-Jones, the Woodpecker tapestry and the Kelmscott Chaucer. In the upper gallery are some stunning Pre-Raphaelite paintings, including works by Rossetti and Burne-Jones.

Lloyd Park is a small park with the old moat of The Water House surviving as a pond. The Walthamstow Theatre in the park is used for light entertainment.

In *Chingford*, to the N of Walthamstow, an obelisk was erected at Pole Hill in 1824 to mark the Greenwich Meridian. After the international agreement of 1884 the Meridian was realigned 19ft E of the pillar. *All Saints Church* was established in the 12C; it decayed and in the 19C was known as the Green Church—overgrown with ivy it became a popular subject for painters (cf. 'Home from Sea' by Arthur Hughes). The church was restored in 1929. The 'new' church of *St. Peter and St. Paul* was built next to Chingford Green in the mid-

C and houses the 12C marble font from the old church.

Friday Hill House in Simmons Lane, the work of Lewis Vulliamy (1839), was built on the site of Chingford Manor.

Leyton and *Leytonstone*, S of Walthamstow, are mixed industrial and residential areas. *Etloe House* in Church Road, Leyton, dates to 1770 and has a striking Gothic façade; it was once the home of Cardinal Wiseman. The church of *St. Mary the Virgin* is 11C.

Woodford, a prosperous and leafy suburb, traces its origins to Saxon times. It developed as a suburb with the arrival of the railway in the mid 19C. From 1924 to 1964 Sir Winston Churchill was Woodford's MP and his statue (by David McFall) was erected on Woodford Green (Woodford High Road) in 1959 by his constituents. Dr Barnardo opened a home for orphans at Manor Road, Woodford Bridge, in 1910. At Whipps Cross are the Hollow Ponds and at Snaresbrook Road is Eagle Pond, overlooked by Sir George Gilbert Scott's Royal Wanstead School (1843). (See above.)

Woodford's parish church, *St. Mary*, was completed in 1972 following the destruction by fire in 1969 of the old church. The 18C vicarage survives and is now the Crown Court.

At *Wanstead* the Child family, of East India Company fame, are remembered in *St. Mary's*, the parish church. This was built by Thomas Hardwick in 1790; the church is dominated by an elaborate 20ft monument to Sir Josiah Child, portrayed in Roman armour.

In *Ilford*, 3.5 miles SE of Woodford, the 17C mansion of *Valentines*, in Valentines Park, 1 mile N of Ilford Station (BR), survives as council offices, while the grounds have become a spacious park. Ilford is a 20C suburb devoid of much character. To the N was *Hainault Forest* but only a fragment has survived.

The London Borough of Redbridge, which includes Woodford, Wanstead and Ilford, takes its name from a red-brick bridge over the River Roding.

45 Stratford, Bow, Newham, Barking and Dagenham, Romford, Hornchurch, Upminster

The London Borough of Newham lies to the E of what is traditionally regarded as London's East End (see Rte 28) and includes East Ham, West Ham, Beckton and Stratford. The area is still dominated by the docks and the industrialisation they encouraged, but it is now undergoing a transformation which will give a much-needed economic lift to a depressed part of London (see also Docklands, p 277).

Stratford in the N part of the borough has a modern shopping centre, including a market, surrounded by a busy traffic system. Just off the Great Eastern Road is the *Theatre Royal, Stratford East*, built as a music-hall in 1884 and carefully preserved. As director, Joan Littlewood put the theatre on the map in the 1950s and '60s with a string of controversial productions; there is an attempt to maintain this tradition today.

The parish church of *St. John* in Stratford Broadway was built in 1834 in the Gothic Revival style; in the churchyard is a memorial to 18 Protestants burnt at the stake on Stratford Green in 1555. An obelisk in the Broadway was erected in 1861 in memory of a local banker, Samuel Gurney.

Along Romford Road, just out of the centre of Stratford, is *Passmore Edwards Museum*, housed in a striking group of buildin which include the public library and a college of technology, designe by Gibson and Russell in 1898. At the time this was the only purpose-built museum in Essex and it was intended to have comprehensive collections. It now extends to an 18C weather-boarded annexe—a former hospital for the poor. It re-opens in October 1990 after major refurbishment both inside and out including work on the natural history display.

Passmore Edwards Museum, Romford Road, E15. Tel. 081-534 2274. Open Mon to Fri 10.00–17.00 Sat 10.00–13.00, 14.00-17.00, closed Sun. Free. Access: Underground, Stratford.
The attractive Rotunda Gallery houses the Victorian collection illustrating the growth of Essex and local industry and crafts. The Natural History Gallery includes a pond with local fish; other exhibits cover archaeology and geology. Special exhibitions are held regularly and the museum has expanded to North Woolwich Railway Station (see below).

Little remains of Stratford's ancient past except a few street names. Stratford Langthorne Abbey was founded in 1135 and dissolved in 1538. It has given its name to Abbey Lane to the W of Stratford where an early industrial area developed along the River Lea. This area borders on Bow on the other side of the River Lea. It took its name from a 12C arched bridge over the Lea. Elizabeth of Hainault died (1375) in the Benedictine Nunnery of St. Leonard's at 'Stratford-atte-Bowe'. The church of St. Mary Stratford Bow in Bow Road dates from the early 14C (tower rebuilt after 1948). Here is a statue of Gladstone by Albert Bruce-Joy erected in 1882. Industries flourished along the banks of the River Lea from the 18C. The ornate *Abbey Mills Pumping Station*, designed by Bazalgette and Cooper in 1864, is a marvellous example of the Byzantine style applied to a mundane purpose; the pumping station can be visited by appointment with the Thames Water Authority (tel. 081-534 6717), Mon to Fri 09.30–16.00. Charrington's has restored the *Clock Mill* of 1817 as offices in the *Three Mills Conservation Area*, Three Mills Lane, Bromley by Bow. The derelict House Mills (1776) may be developed as a working museum.

The Bryant & May match factory was the largest of the 19C manufacturing industries set up here, the scene of the successful match-girls' strike in 1888. The tall red brick building in Fairfield Road, E.3 has been converted into housing, the Bow Quarter, using partly the original, now listed, buildings. A memorial to the match-girls is planned on the site.

In Grove Rd, Bow (E3) a blue plaque on the railway bridge marks the site where the first 'doodle bug' (V1) struck in 1944.

At the *Widow's Son Inn*, Devon's Rd, Bow, the collection of blackened hot cross buns grows each Good Friday when another one is presented by the Navy in recognition of a widow's son lost at sea some 200 years ago.

Nearby in Copperfield Rd is the new Ragged School Museum, 46-48 Copperfield Road, Bow, E3, tel. 071-232 2941 for opening hours. The Museum is housed in the warehouse where Dr. Barnardo opened his 'Ragged School' in 1877, providing free schooling, breakfast and dinner for the poorest children of the area. The Museum recreates the life of the children as it was in the classroom and also illustrates the daily life of the poor in the East End. The Isle of Dogs is to the S, see Rte 29.

In *West Ham*, SW of Stratford, the parish church of *All Saints* was built in the 12C; the ragstone tower is 14C and inside there are Tudor

Stuart brasses and monuments. At *West Ham Park* there are
ranical Gardens. West Ham United's football ground is at Upton
ark, Green St (access: Underground, Upton Park).

East Ham, E of Stratford, has a Grade I listed church, *St. Mary
Magdalen*, which has survived virtually unaltered since the 12C. The
Norman aisleless church ends with a narrow apse; the tower was
rebuilt in the 16C. Rubbings can be made from replicas of the original
brasses in the church (tel. 081-470 4525). The large churchyard is now
a nature reserve with its own Interpretative Centre (entrance in
Norman Road; access: Underground, East Ham, then bus to Beckton).

The huge Royal Docks dominate the area to the S. They form part of
the LDDC redevelopment programme and a 500 acre 'Water City'
with an industrial park, hotels, offices, housing, shopping, marina,
museum, an exhibition centre and sports arena (London Dome)
seating 25,000 all form part of the initial plans to be built over 10 years.
Included is an extension to the Docklands Light Railway due to open
in 1991.

The Royal group of Docks were the last to be built between 1855
and 1921, together they cover 254 acres of water. The Royal Victoria
Dock (1850–55); The Royal Albert Dock (1880); King George V Dock
(1912–1921). The Royal Docks were still in use in the '70s. The
Museum of London is planning a Docklands Museum and already
part of its growing collection is on view in a warehouse near Custom
House Station by the Royal Victoria Dock, tel. 071-600 3699 for
opening hours.

The London City Airport (see also p 14) is situated between the
Royal Albert Dock and King George V Dock with a mile-long runway.
It opened in October 1987 and includes a restaurant and exhibition
area. There are regular services to provincial cities and European
capitals.

At Silvertown is the redundant church of St. Mark by S.S. Teulon
(1862); the heavily decorated exterior has been restored and a
museum of local history is planned (part of Passmore Edwards
Museum).

At *North Woolwich Old Railway Station* on the Thames a new
museum has been established in a listed building of 1847 in the
Italianate style. Historical displays on the Great Eastern Railway are
featured and include original steam engines.

North Woolwich Old Railway Station Museum, Pier Road, North Woolwich. Tel.
081-474 7244. Open Mon to Fri 10.00–17.00, Sat 10.00–13.00, 14.00–17.00, Free.
Access: BR, North Woolwich.

From here there are good views of the Thames Barrier, the Woolwich
Ferry and a pedestrian tunnel to Woolwich. The Thames Barrier
Visitor Centre is on the S side and best approached from Greenwich
(see p 131). Another fine view of the Thames Estuary and the Barrier is
obtained from the top of Beckton's dry-ski slope, created from rubbish
on reclaimed land and opened in 1985 (access: by car, A13 to
Beckton; Underground, East Ham, then bus to Beckton). It now
includes a Mountaintop Ski Village (tel. 081-511 0351) with ski
facilities and a cafeteria.

British Telecom satellite dishes overlook the river.

Barking and **Dagenham** are important industrial centres with factories to the S on reclaimed marshland along the Thames, including the
vast Ford works at Dagenham.

The land used to belong to Barking Abbey, founded in 666 by Kr Erkenwald who established his sister Ethelburga as abbess. By th 10C the Benedictine nunnery was the most important in the country and William the Conqueror made it his base while building started on the Tower of London. The abbey buildings were demolished after dissolution in 1539 but there are remnants in the grounds of 13C *St. Margaret's Church* (access: BR, Barking). Remains of walls have been excavated in the grounds; the Curfew or Fire Bell Gate of 1460 and the NE Gate can be seen. Some Norman masonry has also been used for the outer wall of the N aisle of the church itself. Captain James Cook, the circumnavigator, married Elizabeth Batts of Barking here in 1762 and is commemorated on a modern carved screen. The church also contains the marble tomb of William Pownsett (died 1553) by Nicholas Bellin of Modena. Elizabeth Fry (died 1845), the prison reformer, spent many summers in nearby Dagenham and is remembered on a modern carved screen in the church. She is buried in the Quaker Burial Ground in Barking, now a park.

Barking Power Station, once one of the largest in Europe, closed in 1981.

Eastbury House in Ripple Road, Barking, is a good example of a medium-sized manor house of the late 16C. It is owned by the National Trust and used as the HQ of the Barking Arts Council. Open by appointment, tel. 081-592 4500. The red-brick three-storey gabled house has black decoration and has its origins in 1321.

Vicarage Field is a new shopping centre at Barking Town, and at Barking Reach a major new development of over 800 acres includes housing and industry.

There is a large Sunday market at Dagenham Dock.

Opposite the 13C church of *St. Peter and St. Paul* in Dagenham is the *Cross Keys* pub (Church Elm Lane), of 15C origin and retaining its Tudor exterior.

At *Dagenham*, 4m E of Barking, the manor house of *Valence* survives as a local museum. The timberframe building dates mainly from the late 17C and was partly moated. It became council offices in 1926 and a local history museum in 1974.

Valence House Museum, Becontree Avenue, Dagenham. Open Mon to Fri 09.30–13.00, 14.00–1630 (Tel. 081-592 2211). Access: Underground, Becontree.
In addition to the local history collection of maps, archaeological finds and exhibits on the former ship-building industry at Canning Town, the museum houses the important Fanshawe Collection of 48 family portraits by Lely, Dobson, Kneller and others.

Romford, 2 miles N of Dagenham, is proud of its status as an ancient market town with a charter of 1247. The cattle market continued until 1958 but Romford Market today is a mixture of antiques, bric-a-brac, and stalls selling new goods. It is one of Britain's longest markets (cf. Walthamstow), and is held on Wednesdays, Fridays and Saturdays (nearest station BR Romford). The large estates in the area house many resettled East Enders, who give this market a 'Cockney' flavour.

Romford's historic past is well-disguised by its modern shopping centre and the *Dolphin Leisure Centre* (1983) which features a leisure pool with wave machine, bar, restaurant, and banqueting hall. Water for the pool is heated by solar energy gathered by the aluminium-framed pyramidical roof; the banqueting hall has a stage and seating for 400. Romford also has an ice rink.

St. Edward's, the parish church, was rebuilt in 1850, but the 15C Church House (once a coaching inn), next to it, survives.

Havering atte Bower, which gives its name to the London Borough

Havering, is 4 miles NE of Romford. It once had a small medieval royal palace, known as The Bower, which fell into decay in the 17C. It was the official residence of Queens of England, including three of Henry VIII's wives, and stood near the present Village Green. Nearby is the present *Bower House*, built in 1729 and incorporating the coat of arms from the ancient palace—it is used by the Ford Motor Company. The house was designed by Henry Flitcroft; there are murals by Sir John Thornhill in the stairwell.

On the Village Green the village stocks and whipping post (not originals) set up in the 1700s can be seen.

Hornchurch, SE of Romford, is a 20C suburb with the modern Queen Theatre. It has 12C origins; the parish church of *St. Andrew* dates to that time but is now mainly 15C. It is the only church in Britain with a bull's head and horns at the E end instead of a cross—the town's seal, symbolising the early importance of its leather industry. Elizabeth Fry's son Joseph is buried in the churchyard; he lived at Fairkytes, a 17C mansion.

At *Upminster*, to the SE, a fine smock-mill, built in 1803 and in use until 1934, survives in St. Mary's Lane. The windmill has been restored and is open from April to September, the third Sat & Sun of the month from 14.00–1730. Free, guided tours. Nearby is the 12C church of *St. Laurence*, rebuilt in the 18 and 19C. The *Clock House*, also in St. Mary's Lane, is the original stable block of New Place—a mansion now demolished—and is dated 1775. Nearby in Hall Lane the Council has converted a 15C tithe barn into a the *Upminster Tithe Barn Museum*, a local history museum run by the Upminster and Romford Historical Society. Open by arrangement and the first weekend in month from April to Oct 13.30 to 18.00. (Check by tel. 0708 44297, also for windmill).

Upminster is now a prosperous commuting suburb with pleasant houses and gardens, mostly dating to the inter-war period. 15C Upminster Hall is used as the club-house of Upminster Golf Club.

INDEX

Topographical names and subjects are indexed in roman type; names of emine[...]
people are in *italic* type. Names beginning with Saint (St.) are indexed unde[...]
that heading.

Abbey Road 182
Abbey Mills Pumping
    Station 401
Abney Park Cemetery
    394
Academy of St. Martin
    in the Fields 94
Accademia Italiana 132
Acton 369
Adam, Robert 169, 198,
    364, 387
Addington Palace 337
Adelphi, The 198
Admiralty Arch 100
Africa Centre 204
Albany 115
Albany Theatre 320
Albert Bridge 161, 309
Albert Memorial 132
Albert, Prince 131, 132,
    137, 151, 228, 246
Albery Theatre 167
Aldgate 259
Aldwych Theatre 202
Alexandra Palace 393
Alleyn, Edward 325
All Hallows
    (Teddington) 351
All Hallows London
    Wall 248
All Hallows Staining
    258
All Hallows by the
    Tower 261
All Saints (Chingford)
    399
All Saints (Isleworth)
    363
All Saints (Kensington)
    132
All Saints (Kingston) 342
All Saints (Margaret St)
    176
All Soul's (Langham
    Place) 169
Almshouses 291, 318,
    319, 330, 333, 334,
    368, 370
Alsatia 217
Amen Court 221
American Club 118
American Embassy 122
Anchor Inn (Southwark)
    292
Ancient House 399
Angel Pond Green 382
Angel Pub 297
Angerstein, J.J. 95, 316
Apothecaries Hall 219
Apsley House 118
Architectural
    Association 183

Armourers' Hall 248
Army and Navy Club
    109
Arts Council, The 118
Asgill House 343
Ashburnham House 63
Astor, Lady 110
Athenaeum 108
Attlee, Clement 280
Austen, Jane 125
Australia House 201
Australian Memorial
    Cemetery 368
Ave Maria Lane 221
Avenue House 383
Avery Hill Park 324

Bacon, Sir Francis 298,
    385
Baden-Powell House
    131
Baker Street 174
Bakers' Hall 254
Baltic Exchange 256
Banbury Sailing Centre
    397
Bank of England 245
Bankside 291
Bankside Gallery 291
Bankside Power Station
    291
Banqueting House 91
Barbican 238
Barbican Art Gallery
    241
Barbican Centre 241
Barking 402
Barking Abbey 403
Barnard's Inn 228
Barn Elms 346
Barnes 346
Barnes Railway Bridge
    310
Barnet 382
Barnet Museum 382
Barnett, Dame Henrietta
    392
*Barrett Browning,
    Elizabeth* 171, 196
Battersea 329
Battersea Arts Centre
    329
Battersea Bridge 163,
    309
Battersea Dog's Home
    330
Battersea Park 329
Battersea Power Station
    330
Battle of Barnet 383
Battle of Britain
    Museum 380

Bayliss, Lilian 235, 289
Baynard Castle 219
Bayswater Road 136
BBC TV Studios 370
Beauchamp Place 130
Beaverbrook, Lord 110
Beckenham334
Beckenham Place Park
    333
Beckton Dry-Ski Slope
    402
Beddington 337
Bedford Park 370
Bedford Square 183
'Beefeaters' 262
Beerbohm, Tree 107
'Belfast', HMS 296
Belgrave Square 124
Belgravia 124
Bennett, Arnold 125,
    175
Bentham, Jeremy 185,
    260
Bentley Priory 379
Bermondsey 297
Bernhardt, Sarah 167
Berkeley Square 122
Berlioz, H. 170
Bethlem Hospital 271,
    284, 337
Bethnal Green 274
Bethnal Green Museum
    of Childhood 274
Beulah Hill 327
Bexleyheath 324
'Big Ben' 85
Biggin Hill 335
Billingsgate Market 254,
    281
Birdcage Walk 104
Birkbeck College 184
Bishopsgate 272
Blackfriars 219
Blackfriars Bridge 303
Blackheath 319
Blackwall Tunnel 307
Blake, William 112, 155
Blewcoat School 151
Bloomsbury 182
Bloomsbury Square 184
Blunt, Anthony 170
Boadicea 62, 301
Boilerhouse Project 137,
    296
Bomber Command
    Museum 380
Bond Street 117
Boodle's 111
Borough High Street
    295
Borough Market 294
Boston Manor House 362

ll, James 118
401
ater House 126
w Church, see St.
  Mary-le-Bow
ow Street 206
Bow Street Runners 207
Bracken House 250
Brangwyn Gift 399
Brent 377
Brent Cross Shopping
  Centre 377
Brentford 361
Brick Lane 272
Bridewell 218
British Council 109
British Empire
  Exhibition 376
British Heritage Motor
  Museum 364
British Library 188
British Library
  Newspaper Collection
  381
British Museum 188
British Telecom Tower
  177
Britten Opera Theatre
  131
Brixton 330
Brixton Prison 330
Brixton Recreation
  Centre 330
Brixton Windmill 330
Broadcasting House
  169, 370
Broadgate Square 271
Broad Sanctuary 64
Bromley 333
Bromley College 334
Bromley Museum 335
Bromley Palace 334
Brompton Cemetery 136
Brompton Oratory 130
Brompton Road 130
Broomfield House 395
Brown Hart Gardens 169
Browning, Robert 171,
  176, 196
Brown's Hotel 118
Bruce Castle Museum
  393
Brunel, I.K. 163, 307,
  367
Brunel, M.I. 163, 278,
  305, 320
Brunel's Engine House
  320
Brunswick Square 187
Buckingham Palace 105
Bunhill Fields 250
Burgess, Guy 170
Burgess Park 331
Burgh House 391
Burlington Arcade 117
Burlington House 116
Burney, Fanny 167
Bush House (BBC) 202
Bushy Park 352

Business Design Centre
  298
Butler's Wharf 296
Butterfly House (Syon
  Park) 364
Byron, Lord 124, 171, 378

Cabinet War Rooms 89
Cable Street 275
Cadogan Hotel 125
Cadogan Pier 309
Café Royal 168
Caledonian Market 297,
  299
Camberwell 331
Cambridge Circus 166
Camden Lock 300
Camden Passage 298
Camden Place 334
Camden Town 299
Campbell, Mrs Patrick
  134
Campden Hill 135
Canada House 94
Canada Walk 211
Canary Wharf 281
Cannon Street 250
Cannon Street Railway
  Bridge 304
Cannon Street Station
  252
Canonbury Tower 298
Canon Park 379
Cardinal's Wharf 291
Carew Manor 337
Carey Street 208
Carlton Club 111
Carlton Gardens 109
Carlton House Terrace
  108
Carlyle's House 161
Carnaby Street 168
Carshalton 337
Catford 333
Cathedral of the Holy
  Wisdom 137
Catherine of Braganza
  359
Cato Street 175
Cavalry and Guards
  Club 118
Cavel, Edith 94
Caxton Hall 151
Cecil Court 167
Cenotaph 89
Central Criminal Court
  229
Central Hall 64
Central Market (Covent
  Garden) 203
Central Mosque 178
Central Synagogue 176
Centre Point 182
Chancery Lane 212
Chandos House 170
Change Alley 255
Changing the Guard 106
Channel Tunnel
  Terminal 288

Chapel Market 298
Chapel Royal 102
Chapel Royal of St.
  Peter ad Vincula 267
Chaplin, Charles 166,
  284, 331
Charing Cross 93
Charing Cross Road 165
Charlotte Street 176
Charlton 323
Charlton F.C. 36, 323
Charlton House 323
Charrington's Anchor
  Brewery 277
Chartered Insurance
  Institute Museum 243
Chartered Accountants'
  Hall 248
Charterhouse Square
  232
Chaucer, Geoffrey 77,
  253, 294, 325
Chaucer Theatre 260
Cheam 338
Cheapside 236
Chelsea 157
Chelsea Bridge 159, 309
Chelsea Embankment
  159
Chelsea Flower Show
  159
Chelsea Harbour 163
Chelsea Old Church
  (All Saints) 162
Chelsea Physic Garden
  161
Chelsea Royal Hospital
  159
Chessington World of
  Adventures (Zoo) 342
Chesterton, G.K. 136
Cheyne Walk 161
Chinatown 164
Chingford 399
Chislehurst 334
Chislehurst Caves 334
Chiswick 359
Chiswick Bridge 310
Chiswick Eyot 310
Chiswick House 360
Christ Church
  (Kennington Rd) 286
Christ Church
  (Kensington) 136
Christ Church (Mayfair)
  121
Christ Church
  (Newgate) 233
Christ Church,
  Spitalfields 272
Christ's Hospital 235
Christie's 111
Church Farm House 380
Churchill, Sir Winston
  61, 89, 132, 400
Churchill Theatre 334
Church House 64
Church of Christ and St.
  John 282

Church of Christ the King 185
Citadel, The 100
City Barge 360
City Business Library 243
City Information Centre 208
City of London 207
City of London Cemetery 398
City of London Club 247
City of London Festival 207
City of London School for Boys 218
City Road 248, 250
Clapham 328
Clarence House 103
Cleopatra's Needle 198, 302
Clerkenwell 234
Clink Street 292
Clissold Park 394
Clore Gallery 156
Cloth Fair 232
Coade, Eleanor 286
Cobbett, William 346
Cock Tavern 216
Coin Street 290
Coleridge, S.T. 385
Colindale 381
Coliseum Theatre 167
College of Arms 219
Columbia Road 274
Commonwealth Institute 136
Connaught Hotel 122
Connaught Rooms 206
Constable, J. 177
Constitution Hill 103
Conway Hall 188
Cook, Captain James 329, 403
Coombe 342
Copenhagen Fields 299
Coram's Fields 187
Cork Street 117
Corn Exchange 258
Cornhill 255
County Hall 286
Courtauld Institute Galleries 200
Coutts, Angela Burdett 386
Covent Garden 202
Crafts Council Gallery 108
Crane River 366
Cranford 366
Craven Cottage 310
Cremorne Gardens 163
Cricket Museum 181
Crewe House 121
Cromwell House 385
Cromwell, Oliver 200
Cromwell Road 130
Crosby Hall 162
Croydon 336

Croydon Aerodrome 336
Crystal Palace 326
Crystal Palace Museum 327
Cubitt, Thomas 124
Cubitt Town 282
Cuming Museum 331
Curtain Theatre 273
Curzon Street 121
Custom House 254
Cutlers' Hall 235
'Cutty Sark' 317
Czechoslovak Centre 137

Dagenham 402
Danish Seamen's Church 280
Danson Park 324
Darwin, Charles 184, 335
Darwin Museum 335
David Evans Silk 324
Dean's Yard 63
De Beauvoir Town 274
Defoe, Daniel 250, 259, 393
de Gaulle, Charles 109, 122
Denmark Hill 332
Deptford 319
Design Centre 107
Design Museum 296
Dickens, Charles 137, 162, 185, 187, 198, 228
Dickens House 187
Diorama, Regent's Park 178
Dirty Dicks 272
'Discovery' RRS 121, 270
Disraeli, Benjamin 61, 188, 229
Dr Johnson's House 217
Docklands Arena 282
Docklands Light Railway 260, 277
Doggett's Coat and Badge Race 303
Dollis Hill House 376
Dolphin Square 153
Dorchester Hotel 121
Doughty Street 187
Dove Inn 359
Dowding, Lord 201
Down House 335
Downing Street 90
Doyle, Sir Arthur Conan 175, 327
Drapers' Hall 247
Drayton Hall 367
Drury Lane 205
Duke of York's Column 108
Duke of York's Theatre 167
Duke Street 112

Dulwich 325
Dulwich College 325
Dulwich Picture Gallery 325
du Maurier, George 136, 391
Dutch Church 247

Ealing 369
Ealing Studios 369
Eastbury House 403
Eastcote 368
East Ham 400
East London Crossing 322
East London Mosque 276
Eastway Cycle Circuit 397
Eaton Square 124
Ebury Street 150
Economist Building 111
Edmonton 395
Eel Pie Island 311
Eisenhower, General 121, 122
Eleanor's Cross 93, 197, 396
Electric Avenue 330
Elephant and Castle 295
Elgin Marbles 192
Eliot, George 161
Elizabeth Garrett Anderson Hospital 186
Elizabeth I, Queen 73, 200, 216, 313, 338, 397
Elsing Spital 243
Eltham 324
Eltham Palace 324
Ely Chapel 228
Ely House 118
Ely Place 288
Enfield 394
English Speaking Union 122
Epping Forest 397
Etloe House 400
Eton 375
Eton College 375
'Eros' 113
Euston Station 186
Evelyn, John 319
Execution Dock 305

Fairfield Halls 336
Fan Museum 317
Faraday Building 219
Faraday Museum 117
Farm Street 123
Farnborough 335
Farrell, Terry 197, 238, 278, 289, 300
Farringdon Road 234
Fawcett, Millicent 183
Feltham 366
Festival of Britain 287, 330

Fenton House 390
Finchley 383
Finchley Manor House 383
Finsbury Circus 248
First Church of Christ Scientist 125
Fishmongers' Hall 253
Fitzrovia 177
Flamsteed House 316
Flaxman Gallery 185
Fleet Prison 220
Fleet River 215
Fleet Street 215
Floral Hall 206
Florence Nightingale Museum 286
Flower Market (Covent Garden) 204
Foreign and Commonwealth Office 89
Foreign Press Association 109
Forest Hill 326
Fortress House 117
Forty Hall 394
Foundling Hospital, *see* Thomas Coram Foundation for Children
Foyles 166
Franklin, Benjamin 112, 197, 232, 236
Freemason's Hall 205
French House 165
French Protestant Church 165
Freud, Sigmund 390
Friday Hill House 400
Friends' Burial Ground 250
Friends' House 186
Friern Barnet 389
Frost Fairs 301
Fry, Elizabeth 230
Fulham 351
Fulham Palace 310
Fulham Pottery 330, 357
Fulham/Putney Railway Bridge 310
Fuller's Brewery 359
Furnivall Gardens 359
Furnival's Inn 228

Gaiety Theatre 202, 205
Galsworthy, John 343, 391
Gandhi, Mahatma 185
Garibaldi, G. 102, 228
Garlick Hill 251
Garrick Club 203
Garrick, David 198, 205, 381
Garrick's Villa 357
Gaskell, Mrs E. 163
Gay, John 349, 358
Geffrye Museum 273
Gentleman's Row 395

Geological Museum 146
George and Vulture 255
George Inn (Southwark) 294
Gibbons, Grinling 200
Gilbert, W.S. 131, 379
'Gipsy Moth IV' 317
Gladstone, W.E. 109, 110, 201
Globe Theatre 163, 291
Golden Square 164
Golders Green 392
Golders Hill Park 392
Goldsmiths' Hall 237
Goodwin Court 167
Gordon Riots 220, 245, 261, 388
Government Offices Building 61
Grand Union Canal 187, 362, 367, 377
Grange Museum 376
Gray's Inn 212
Great Equatorial Building 316
Great Fire 239, 253
Great Ormond Street 188
Great Scotland Yard 91
Great Synagogue 259
Great West Road 365
Greater London Council 286
Greek Street 165
Greenaway, Kate 297
Greenford 371
Greenland Dock 320
Green Park 103
Greenwich 313
Greenwich Antique Market 317
Greenwich Foot Tunnel 318
Greenwich Hospital, *see* Royal Naval College
Greenwich Mean Time 316
Greenwich Park 315
Greenwich Theatre 317
Gresham, Sir Thomas 244, 245, 364
Grey Coat Hospital 157
Grimaldi, Joseph 187, 234
Grims Dyke 379
Grocers' Hall 244
Grosvenor Bridge 309
Grosvenor Chapel 123
Grosvenor Gardens 149
Grosvenor House 121
Grosvenor Square 122
Groucho Club 165
Guard's Chapel 104
Guards' Monument 108
Guards' Museum 104
Guildhall 243
Guildhall Clock Museum 244
Guildhall Library 244

Gunnersbury Park Museum 363
Gwydyr House 91

Hackney 274, 394
Hackney Empire 394
Hadley Green 383
Hainault Forest 400
Hall of the Clothworkers 258
Hall of the Painter-Stainers 251
Hall of the Watermen and Lightermen 254
Hall Place 323
Ham 348
Ham House 349
Hammersmith 358
Hammersmith Bridge 310, 358
Hammersmith Odeon 358
Hampstead 388
Hampstead Garden Suburb 392
Hampstead Heath 388
Hampton Court 352
Handel, G.F. 78, 168, 379
Hanover Square 168
Hanworth 366
Hardy, Thomas 328
Harley Street 170
Harmondsworth 366
Harrods 129
Harrods Depository 310
Harrow 377
Harrow Museum 378
Harrow School 377
Harvard, J. 293, 294
Hatchard's 115
Hatton Garden 228
Havering atte Bower 403
Hayes 334, 367
Haymarket 107
Haymarket Theatre 107
Hay's Wharf 296, 304
Hayward Gallery 287
Headstone Manor 378
Heathrow 366
Heinz Gallery 175
Hendon 379
Henry Wood Promenade Concerts 33, 131
Her Majesty's Theatre 107
Hertford House 171
Heston Aerodrome 366
High Elms 335
Highgate 384
Highgate Cemetery 386
Highgate School 386
Highway, The 278
Highwood House 382
Hillingdon 367
Hill, Sir Rowland 137, 393

Hoare's Bank 216
Hogarth's House 361
Holborn 227
Holborn Viaduct 229
Holland House 135
Holland Park 135
Hollow Ponds 398
Holly Village 386
Holy Cross (Greenford) 371
Holy Trinity (Brompton Sq.) 130
Holy Trinity (Dalston) 274
Holy Trinity (Sloane St) 125
Home House 174
Home Office 152
Honourable Artillery Company 248
Hoop and Grapes 259
Hoover Building 371
Hope Sufferance Wharf 321
Hopton's Almshouses 291
Hornchurch 404
Horniman Museum 326
Horse Guards 91
Horse Guard's Parade 92
Houndsditch 260
Hounslow 365
Hounslow Heath 365
House of St. Barnabas-in-Soho 165
Household Brigade Cenotaph 104
Household Cavalry Museum 374
Houses of Parliament 84
Huggin Hill 251
Hungerford Bridge 197, 302
Hunterian Museum 209
Hyde Park 125
Hyde Park Corner 123
Hyde Park Hotel 124

Ickenham 368
Ilford 400
Imperial College 131
Imperial War Museum 284
India House 202
India Office Library 290
Institut Français du Royaume Uni 130
Institute of Contemporary Arts 101
Institute of Directors 108
International Press Centre 220
Iranian Embassy 132
Ironmongers' Hall 240
Irving, Henry 200
Isabella Plantation and Woodland Gardens 345

Islamic Cultural Centre 130
Island Gardens 282
Isle of Dogs 277, 307
Isleworth 363
Islington 297
Iveagh Bequest 387
Ivy House 392

Jack Straw's Castle 388
Jack the Ripper 272
Jeffreys, Judge 243, 278
Jermyn Street 112
Jewel Tower 63
Jewish Cemetery (Whitechapel) 277
Jewish Museum 185
John, Augustus 158, 165
John Innes Park 340
Johnson, Dr, House 217
Johnson, Dr Samuel 201, 215, 217, 228, 328
Jubilee Gardens 287
Jubilee Hall 202
Jubilee Market 202
Junior Carlton Club 109

'Kathleen and May' schooner 292
Kauffmann, Angelica 164, 382, 387
Keats House 389
Keats, John 248, 389
Kelmscott House 359
Kennedy, J.F. 132, 177
Kennington 330
Kensal Green Cemetery 376
Kensington 128
Kensington Exhibition Centre 134
Kensington Gardens 132
Kensington Gore 131
Kensington High Street 134
Kensington Palace 133
Kensington Palace Gardens 133
Kenwood House 387
Keston 335
Kew 347
Kew Bridge 311
Kew Bridge Engine Museum 362
Kew Gardens 347
Kew Palace 347
Kew Railway Bridge 310
King's Bench Walk 214
King's College 200, 332
King's Observatory 345
King's Road (Chelsea) 157
Kingston Railway Bridge 312
Kingston upon Thames 341
Kingston Museum 342

Kipling, Rudyard 176, 198
Kit-Cat Club 98, 346, 391
Kitchener, Lord 92
Kneller Hall 350
Knightsbridge 124
Knightsbridge Barracks 126

Lambeth Bridge 157
Lambeth Palace 283
Lambeth Walk 284
Lancaster House 102
Landseer, Sir E. 94, 176
Langham Place 169
Langtry, Lily 125, 167
Latchmere Leisure Centre 329
Lauderdale House 384
Lawrence, T.E. 63
Leadenhall Market 256
Lear, Edward 175
Leather Lane 228
Leathersellers' Company Hall 271
Lee 332
Lee Valley Ice Centre 397
Lee Valley Regional Park 396
Leicester Square 166
Leighton House 135
Lenin, V.I. 187, 234
Lesnes Abbey 323
Lewisham 332
Leyton 400
Leytonstone 400
Liberty's 168
Libyan Embassy 110
Limehouse 280
Lincoln's Inn 209
Lincoln's Inn Fields 209
Linley Sambourne House 136
Little Angel Theatre 298
Little Holland House 338
Little Italy 228
'Little Venice' 176
Liverpool Street Station 271
Livesey Museum 332
Livingstone, David 383
Lloyd Park 399
Lloyd's of London 256
Lloyd's Register of Shipping 259
Lombard Street 255
London Bridge 252, 304
London Bridge City 296, 304
London Bridge Station 296
London City Airport 14, 402
London Commodity Exchange 270

London Derivatives Exchange 247
Londonderry Hotel 121
London Docklands Development Corporation 279, 307
London Dungeon 296
London Hospital 276
London Library 110
London Marathon 315
London Museum of Jewish Life 383
London Palladium 169
London Pavilion 113
London Planetarium 182
London School of Economics 202
London Sessions House 295
London Silver Vaults 213
London Stone 252
London Transport Museum 204
London Wall Walk 237, 260
London Zoo 178
Long Acre 206
Long Water 125, 132
Lord Mayor's Show 207, 246
Lord's Cricket Ground 179
Lots Road 163
Lower Thames Street 253
Ludgate Circus 220
Lyceum 200
Lyric Theatre 163, 358

Macartney House 317
Machine Gun Corps War Memorial 123
Madame Tussaud's 182
Magna Carta 196, 375
Maida Vale 176
Maids of Honour Row 343
Mall, The 101
Mall Galleries 101
Manchester Square 171
Mander and Mitchenson Theatrical Collection 334
Mansion House 246
Marble Arch 128
Marble Hill 311
Marble Hill House 350
Marco Polo Building 330
Marlborough House 101
Marshalsea 295
Martinware Pottery 369, 370
Marx, Karl 165, 299, 386
Marx Memorial Library 234
Marylebone Cricket Club 179

Marylebone High Street 171
Maundy Service 64
Mayfair 120
Mazzini, G. 184, 228
Mercantile Marine War Memorial 261
Mercers' Hall 237
Mercant Taylors' Hall 248
Mermaid Theatre 219
Merton 340
Merton Priory 340
Metropolitan Police Historical Museum 206
Metropolitan Tabernacle 295
Michelin Building 130
Midland Grand Hotel 186
Middlesex Crown Court 61
Middlesex Hospital 176
Middlesex Street 260
Middle Temple Hall 214
Millbank 153
Millbank Tower 153
Mill Hill 382
Mill Hill School 382
Milton, John 196, 230, 236, 240, 243, 250
Mincing Lane 258
Ministry of Defence 90
Minories 260
Mitcham 341
Mitford sisters 132
Montague Square 175
Monument, The 253
Moore, Henry 117, 127, 153, 247
Moorfields 249
Moorgate 248
Mordern College 319
Mordern Hall Park 340
More, Sir Thomas 157, 162, 163, 236, 283
Morley College 286
Mormon Chapel (Kensington) 131
Morris, William 188, 234, 324, 340, 359, 399
Morse, Samuel 176
Mortlake 346
Mountbatten, Lord 89
Mount Pleasant 235
Mount Vernon Hospital 368
Mozart, W.A. 150, 165, 167
Munthe, Axel 339
Museum of Cricket 179
Museum of Garden History 283
Museum of London 238
Museum of Mankind 117
Museum of Moving Image 288

Museum of the Order of St. John 233
Musical Museum 362
Muybridge, Eadweard 342
Myddleton, Sir Hugh 395

Nash House 101
National Army Museum 160
National Art Library 137
National Film Theatre 287
National Gallery 95
National Maritime Museum 314
National Portrait Gallery 98
National Postal Museum 235
National Theatre *see* Royal National Theatre
National Westminster Tower 248
Natural History Museum 144
Naval and Military Club 118
Nelson Monument 94
New Caledonian Market 297
New Concordia Wharf 297
New Covent Garden Market 308
Newgate Prison 230
Newham 400
Newman, Card. 130
New Oxford Street 183
New River 297, 395
New River House 235
New River Sports Centre 393
New Scotland Yard 151
New Square 209
Newton, Sir Isaac 201
New West End Synagogue 137
New Zealand House 107
Nightingale, Florence 286
Nine Elms 330
NLA House 336
Nonsuch Park 338
Normansfield Hospital 351
Northolt 368
Northolt Aerodrome 369
Northwood 368
North Woolwich Old Railway Station 402
Norwood 327, 371
Notting Hill Carnival 137
Notting Hill Gate 137
Nunhead 332

Observer, The 330
Old Admiralty 92
Old Bailey 230
Old Battersea House 329
Old Deer Park 345
Old Jewry 237
Old Kent Road 332
Old Operating Theatre 294
Old Palace, Croydon 336
Old Park Lane 120
Old Royal Observatory 316
Old Treasury 90
Old Vic Theatre 289
Oliver's Ait 311
Omega Workshops 177
Oratory of St. Philip Neri, *see* Brompton Oratory
Orleans House Gallery 351
Orpington 335
Orton, Joe 298
Osterley House 364
Osterley Park 364
Osterley Station 365
Oxford Circus 169
Oxford Street 169
Oxo Tower 303

Paddington Station 175
Palace of Westminster, *see* Houses of Parliament
Palace Theatre 166
Pall Mall 108
Palmers Green 395
Palmerston, Lord 104, 118
Palumbo, Peter 179, 246
Pankhurst, Emmeline 63, 136
Paragon, The 319
Park Crescent 177
Park Lane 120
Parliament Hill 386
Parliament Square 61
Passmore Edwards Museum 401
Passport Office 152
Patent Office Library 213
Pater, Walter 136
Paternoster Square 221
Pavlova, Anna 392
Paxton, Joseph 360
Pembroke Lodge 345
Peckham 332
Peckham Rye 332
Penn, William 331
Penge 333
Pentonville Prison 299
Pepys Library 319
Pepys, Samuel 61, 93, 103, 107, 198, 203, 216, 218, 256, 258, 259, 328, 383

Percival David Foundation 185
Perivale 371
'Peter Pan' 132
Petersham 348
Petrie Museum 185
Petticoat Lane 260
Petts Wood 334
Petty France 152
Pevsner Sir Nikolaus 392
Photographers' Gallery 166
Piccadilly 115
Piccadilly Arcade 117
Piccadilly Circus 112
Picketts Lock 396
Pilgrim Fathers Memorial Church 295
Pimlico 153
Pinner 378
Pissarro, Lucien 358
Pitshanger Manor 369
Pitt House 392
Pitt, William 335
Placentia 313
Plaistow Lodge 334
Players Theatre 197
Playhouse Theatre 93
Polish Institute 132
Polish War Memorial 369
Polka Theatre 340
Pollock's Toy Museum 117
Polytechnic of Central London 169
Pond Square 386
Pope, Alexander 350, 359
Pope's Grotto 350
Porter Tun Room 241
Portland Place 169
Portman Square 175
Portobello Road 137
Post Office, The 235
Post Office Railway 235
Pratt's Club 111
President, HMS 218, 302
Prince Henry's Room 216
Printing House Square 219
Priory Church of St. John 234
Prospect of Whitby 279
Prudential Assurance Co. 228
Public Record Office 213
Puddle Dock 303
Pump House (Hampstead) 391
Punch and Judy Festival 203
Purcell, Henry 112
Purcell Room 287
Putney 345

Putney Bridge 345
Putney Vale Cemetery 346
Pye Corner 230
Pyx Chamber 80

Queen Adelaide's Cottages 333
Queen Anne's Gate 104
Queen Elizabeth Hall 287
Queen Elizabeth Hunting Lodge 397
Queen Elizabeth II Conference Centre 64
Queenhithe 251
Queen Mary College 277
Queen Mary's Gardens 178
Queen Mother Sports Centre 153
Queen's Building Roof Garden 366
Queen's Chapel 101
Queen's College 171
Queen's Gallery 106
Queen's House (Greenwich) 314
Queen Victoria Memorial 104

RAF Museum 380
Raffles, Sir Stamford 178, 382
Ragged School Museum 401
Raleigh, Sir Walter 236
Ranelagh Gardens 159
Ranger's House 316
Ratcliff Highway, *see* Highway, The
Ravensbourne, River 333
Red House 324
Red Lion Square 188
Reform Club 109
Regent's Canal 176, 280, 297, 300
Regent's Park 177
Regent's Park Zoo 178
Regent Street 168
Reuter's 217
Richmond Ait 311
Richmond Bridge 311, 343
Richmond Hill 344
Richmond Lock 311
Richmond Museum 344
Richmond Park 344
Richmond Railway Bridge 311
Richmond upon Thames 343
Richmond Theatre 343
Rifleman's War Memorial 149
Ritz Hotel 118
Riverside Studios 358

Rock Circus 113
Romford 403
Ronalds, Sir Francis 359
Ronnie Scott's 165
Roosevelt, F. 122
Rose Theatre 292
Rossetti, Christina 184
Rossetti, D.G. 161, 177, 188
Rotherhithe 306, 320
Rotherhithe Tunnel 280
Rotten Row 125, 126, 127,
Rotunda Museum of Artillery 322
Round House (Chalk Farm) 300
Round Pond 132
Royal Academy of Arts 116
Royal Academy of Dramatic Art (RADA) 183
Royal Academy of Music 171
Royal Aeronautical Society 120
Royal Agricultural Hall 298
Royal Albert Hall 131
Royal Armouries 263
Royal Army Medical College 153
Royal Artillery Museum 322
Royal Artillery War Memorial 123
Royal Automobile Club 109
Royal Ballet Junior School 345
Royal Botanic Gardens, Kew 347
Royal British Legion 110
Royal College of Art 131
Royal College of Music 131
Royal College of Organists 131
Royal College of Pathologists 109
Royal Commonwealth Society 93
Royal Court Theatre 158
Royal Courts of Justice 208
Royal Docks 308, 402
Royal Exchange 245
Royal Festival Hall 287
Royal Geographical Society 132
Royal Horticultural Society 157
Royal Hospital, Chelsea 159
Royal Institute of British Architects 169

Royal Institute of Chartered Surveyors 61
Royal Institution 117
Royal Mews 106
Royal Mews (Windsor) 374
Royal Military Academy 322
Royal Mint 261
Royal National Theatre 288
Royal Naval College 313
Royal Naval Dockyard 319
Royal Opera Arcade 107
Royal Opera House 206
Royal Over-Seas League 111
Royal Shakespeare Company Theatre 241
Royal Society 109
Royal Society of Medicine 170
Royal Victoria Victualling Yard 319
Royalty and Empire, Windsor 374
Rubens, P.P. 91
Ruislip 368
Runnymede 375
Ruskin, John 332
Russell Square 184
Rye House Plot 382

Saatchi Gallery 182
Saddlers' Hall 236
Sadler's Wells 234
St. Alfege (Greenwich) 317
St. Alphage 243
St. Andrew by the Wardrobe 219
St. Andrew (Holborn) 229
St. Andrew (Hornchurch) 404
St. Andrew's (Totteridge) 383
St. Andrew Undershaft 256
St. Anne (Limehouse) 280
St. Anne and St. Agnes 237
St. Anne's Soho 164
St. Augustine's (Kilburn) 337
St. Barnabas (Pimlico) 153
St. Bartholomew the Great 231
St. Bartholomew the Less 231
St. Bartholomew's Hospital 231
St. Benedict 273
St. Benet 220

St. Boniface 276
St. Botolph Aldgate 259
St. Botolph Bishopsgate 271
St. Botolph without Aldersgate 240
St. Bride 218
St. Bride Institute 218
St. Catherine's House 202
St. Christopher's Place 170
St. Clement Danes 201
St. Clement Eastcheap 252
St. Columba's 125
St. Dunstan (Cheam) 338
St. Dunstan in the East 254
St. Dunstan in the West 216
St. Dunstan's 277
St. Edmund the King and Martyr 255
St. Ermine's Hotel 146
St. Ethelburga 271
St. George in the East 279
St. George's (Beckenham) 333
St. George's Bloomsbury 183
St. George's Cathedral 286
St. George's Hanover Square 168
St. George's Hospital 123
St. George's Theatre 299
St. Giles Circus 182
St. Giles in the Fields 183
St. Giles without Cripplegate 240
St. Helen's (Bishopsgate) 270
St. James's 107
St. James's Church 112
St. James's Churchyard 187
St. James's (Clerkenwell) 234
St. James Garlickhithe 251
St. James's Palace 101
St. James's Park 103
St. James's Place 111
St. James's, Spanish Place 171
St. James's Square 109
St. James's Theatre 111
St. John (Clerkenwell) 234
St. John (Hoxton) 273
St. John (Regent's Park) 179
St. John (Stratford) 400

St. John's (Bethnal Green Road) 274
St. John's (Hampstead) 390
St. John's (Keats Grove) 389
St. John's Gate 233
St. John's (Ladbroke Grove) 137
St. John the Evangelist (St. John's, Smith Sq.) 63
St. John's Wood 179
St. John the Baptist (Barnet) 382
St. John the Baptist (Croydon) 336
St. John the Baptist (Hillingdon) 367
St. John the Baptist (Windsor) 374
St. Joseph's (Highgate) 384
St. Joseph's (Mill Hill) 382
St. Katharine's Dock 269, 305
St. Katharine's Yacht Haven 270
St. Katharine's (Regent's Park) 178
St. Katharine's Royal Foundation 279
St. Katherine Cree 258
St. Laurence (Upminster) 404
St. Lawrence (Brentford) 362
St. Lawrence (Morden) 338
St. Lawrence (Whitchurch) 379
St. Leonard's (Heston) 366
St. Leonard's (Shoreditch) 290
St. Luke's (Charlton) 323
St. Magnus Martyr 253
St. Margaret Lothbury 247
St. Margaret Pattens 254
St. Margaret's (Barking) 403
St. Margaret's (Lewisham) 333
St. Margaret's (Westminster) 61
St. Mark's (Kennington) 331
St. Mark's (Mayfair) 122
St. Mark's (Silvertown) 402
St. Martin's Court 167
St. Martin in the Fields 94
St. Martin Ludgate 220
St. Mary (Finchley) 383

St. Mary (Harrow) 378
St. Mary (Paddington Green) 176
St. Mary (Willesden) 376
St. Mary Abbots 134
St. Mary Abchurch 252
St. Mary Aldermary 251
St. Mary at Hill 254
St. Mary Lambeth 283
St. Marylebone 171
St. Mary-le-Bow 236
St. Mary-le-Strand 201
St. Mary Magdalen (Bermondsey) 297
St. Mary Magdalen (East Ham) 402
St. Mary Magdalen (Richmond) 344
St. Mary Magdalene (Barnes) 346
St. Mary Overie Dock 292
St. Mary's (Barnes) 346
St. Mary's (Battersea) 329
St. Mary's (Bromley) 334
St. Mary's (Chislehurst) 334
St. Mary's (Feltham) 366
St. Mary's (Hampton) 357
St. Mary's (Harefield) 368
St. Mary's (Hayes) 367
St. Mary's (Hendon) 380
St. Mary's (Islington) 298
St. Mary's (Mortlake) 346
St. Mary's (Putney) 345
St. Mary's (Rotherhithe) 320
St. Mary's (Twickenham) 350
St. Mary's (Walthamstow) 399
St. Mary's (Wanstead) 400
St. Mary's Catholic Church 390
St. Mary Somerset 251
St. Mary's Old Church (Stoke Newington) 394
St. Mary Stratford Bow 401
St. Mary the Virgin (Bexley) 323
St. Mary the Virgin (Beddington) 337
St. Mary the Virgin (Chessington) 342
St. Mary the Virgin (Merton) 340
St. Mary the Virgin (Monken Hadley) 383
St. Mary the Virgin (Northolt) 368

St. Mary Woolnoth 255
St. Marylebone 171
St. Matthew's 137
St. Matthew's (Bethnal Green) 274
St. Michael's (Cornhill) 255
St. Michael's (Highgate) 386
St. Michael Paternoster Royal 252
St. Mildred's 251
St. Nicholas (Chiswick) 359
St. Nicholas (Deptford) 319
St. Nicholas (Sutton) 339
St. Nicholas Cole Abbey 220
St. Olave 258
St. Olave, Old Jewry 237
St. Pancras Church 186
St. Pancras Old Church 186
St. Pancras Station 186
St. Patrick's (Soho) 165
St. Paul's (Brentford) 362
St. Paul's (Covent Garden) 203
St. Paul's (Deptford) 320
St. Paul's (Hammersmith) 358
St. Paul's (Mill Hill) 382
St. Paul's (Shadwell) 279
St. Paul's Cathedral 221
St. Paul's Churchyard 221
St. Paul's Knightsbridge 124
St. Paul's, Portman Square 175
St. Paulinus 324
St. Peter (Ham) 349
St. Peter and St. Paul (Bromley) 334
St. Peter and St. Paul (Chingford) 399
St. Peter and St. Paul (Harlington) 366
St. Peter's (Belgravia) 124
St. Peter's (Cornhill) 255
St. Peter, Vere Street 170
St. Sepulchre 229
St. Stephen (Walbrook) 246
St. Thomas (Southwark) 294
St. Thomas's Hospital 286
St. Vedast 237
Salvation Army HQ 220
Savile Row 117, 168
Savill Garden 375
Savoy Chapel 199

Savoy Hotel 199
Savoy Theatre 199
Sayes Court 319
School of Oriental and African Studies 184
Science Museum 146
Sedgwick Centre 260
Selfridge's 169
Selhurst Park 327
Selsdon Park 337
Selwyn House 110
Senate House 184
Serpentine 126
Serpentine Gallery 126
Sessions House 234
Seven Dials 167, 206
Shaftesbury Avenue 163
Shakespeare, William 236, 291, 293
Shakespeare Globe Museum 291
Shaw Theatre 186
Sheen House 346
Sheen Palace 343
Shell Centre 287
Shelley, P.B. 118, 126, 165, 186, 251
Shepherd Market 121
Shepherd's Bush 370
Sheridan, R.B. 171, 205
Sherlock Holmes 93, 175
Siddons, Sarah 176, 391
Sidney Street 276
Sikorski Museum 132
Simpson, Wallis 175
Simpsons in the Strand 199
Sion College 218
Sir John Cass Foundation School 259
Sir John Soane's Museum 211
Slade School of Art 185
Sloane, Sir Hans 144, 161, 162, 189
Sloane Square 125, 158
Smithfield 230
Smith Square 63
Smith, Stevie 395
Snow Hill Tunnel 229
Soane, Sir John 187, 211, 332, 369, 379
Soho 174
Somerset House 200
Soseki Museum 329
Sotheby's 117
South Africa House 94
Southall 370
Southall Railway Centre 370
Southampton Row 188
South Bank 287
Southgate 395
South London Art Gallery 331
South Metropolitan Cemetery 327

'South Sea Bubble' 248, 255
Southside House 339
Southwark 280
Southwark Bridge 252
Southwark Cathedral 293
Spaniards Inn 388
Spanish and Portuguese Synagogue 259
Speakers' Corner 127
Spencer House 111
Spitalfields 272
'Spital Sermon' 255
Squires Almshouses 399
Stable Yard 102
Stag Place 149
Stamford Brook 359
Stanmore 378
Stanmore Hall 379
Staple Inn 227
Stationers' Hall 221
Steele, Sir Richard 198
Stepney Green 277
Stock Exchange 247
Stoke Newington 393
Stoke Newington Pumping Station 394
Stornoway House 110
Strachey, Lytton 182, 185
Strand-on-the-Green 360
Strand, The 197
Stratford 400
Stratford House 170
Stratford Place 170
Strawberry Hill 350
Streatham 327
Strutton Ground 157
Sun Yat Sen 212
Surrey Docks 306
Sutton 339
Swakeleys 368
Swan Upping 304
Swedenborg, Emanuel 279
Swedenborg Square 279
Swinburne, A.C. 345
Sydenham 326
Syon House 363
Syon Park 311, 363

Tallis, Thomas 317
Tate Gallery 153
Tavistock Square 185
Teddington 351
Teddington Lock 311
Telecom Technology Showcase 219
Temple, The 213
Temple Bar 213, 215, 396
Temple Bar Monument 215
Temple Church 214
Temple of Mithras 251
Tennyson, Alfred, Lord 398

Terry, Ellen 158, 167, 203
Thackeray, W.M. 108, 111, 134, 214, 316
Thames Barrier 313, 321, 402
Thames Ditton Island 312
Thamesmead 323
Thames, River 301
Thames Tunnel 320
Thatcher, Margaret 161, 250
Theatre Museum 204
Theatre Royal, Drury Lane 204, 205
Theatre Royal, Stratford East 400
Theatre Royal, Windsor 374
Theobalds Park 396
Third Church of Christ Scientist 121
Thomas Coram Foundation for Children 187
Thomas, Dylan 78, 165, 360
Three Mills Conservation Area 401
'Times, The' 187, 279
Tobacco Dock 279
Tonson, Jacob 346
Tooting 328
Tottenham 393
Tottenham Court Road 182
Totteridge 383
Tourist Information Centre (Victoria) 148
Tower Bridge 268, 305
Tower Green 267
Tower Hill 261
Tower of London 262
Tower Wharf 268
Toynbee Hall 275
Tradescant Trust 283
Trades Union Congress 183
Trafalgar Square 93
Travellers' Club 109
The Treasury, Westminster Abbey 80
Treaty House 367
Trent Park 395
Trinity Almshouses 276
Trinity Almshouses (Greenwich) 318
Trinity House 261
Trocadero 113
Trollope, Anthony 170, 175, 396
Trooping the Colour 92
Truman Brewery 272
Trumpeter's House 343
Tudor Barn (Eltham) 325

Tudor Hall 382
Tufnell Park 299
Turf Club 109
Turner, J.M.W. 163, 171
Turnham Green 369
Turks Boatyard 312, 341
Twain, Mark 161
Twickenham 349
Twickenham Bridge 311
Tyburn (gallows) 128
Tyburn (river) 103, 171
Tyler, Wat 234, 253, 319

Unilever House 218
Union Chapel 298
United Oxford and
    Cambridge Clubs 110
University College 185
University College
    Hospital 185
University College
    School 390
Univeristy of London
    184
Upminster 404
Upminster Tithe Barn
    Museum 404
Uxbridge 367

Valence House Museum
    403
Valentines 400
Vale of Health 389
Vanbrugh Castle 316
Vancouver, George 349
Vaudeville Theatre 199
Vauxhall Bridge 153
Vestry House Museum
    399
Victoria and Albert
    Museum 137
Victoria Coach Station
    148
Victoria Deep Water
    Container Terminal
    307
Victoria Embankment
    302
Victoria Palace Theatre
    148
Victoria Park 275
Victoria Plaza 148
Victoria Station 148
Victoria Street 148
Victoria Tower Gdns 62
Villiers, Barbara 359
Vincent Square 157
Vintners' Hall 251

Walking along the
    Thames banks 312
Wallace Collection 171
Walpole, Horace 351
Walpole House 359
Waltham Abbey 396
Waltham Cross 396
Walthamstow 398
Walworth 331
Wandle, River 338

Wandsworth 328
Wandsworth Bridge 309
Wandsworth Museum
    328, 345
Wandsworth Prison 328
Wanstead 400
Wanstead Park 398
Wapping 278
Wapping Old Stairs 305
Warburg Institute 184
War Memorial of the
    Royal Fusiliers 227
Warwick Arts Trust 153
Warwick House 103
Watch House 229
Water House 399
Waterloo Station 288
Waterlow Park 384
Waterman's Art Centre
    362
Watling Street 377
Watney Mann Brewery
    276
Wellcome Institute 186
Wellcome Museum 147
Well Hall Pleasaunce
    325
Wellington, Duke of 244
'Wellington', The 302
Wellington Arch 123
Wellington Barracks 104
Wellington Museum,
    see Apsley House
Wells, H.G. 334
Wembley 376
Wesley, John 250, 353
Wesley's Chapel 250
Wesley's House 250
West Drayton 367
West Drayton Pumping
    Station 367
West End 61
Western Avenue 365
West Ham Park 402
West London Pumping
    Station 362
West Middlesex
    Pumping Station 359
Westminster 61
Westminster Abbey 64
Westminster Bridge 286,
    301
Westminster Cathedral
    150
Westminster City Hall
    150
Westminster Column 64
Westminster Hall 61, 62,
    81
Westminster Pier 301,
    308
Westminster Theatre
    149
Westminster Reference
    Library 167
Westminster School 63
Westminster Synagogue
    132
West Wickham 336

Wharncliffe Viaduct 369
Whitechapel 275
Whitechapel Art Gallery
    275
Whitechapel Bell
    Foundry 276
White City Stadium 370
Whitefield Memorial
    Church 183
Whitefriars 217
Whitehall 88
Whitehall (Cheam) 338
White Lodge 345
White's 111
Whitestone Pond 388
Whitgift Almshouses
    333
Whitgift Shopping
    Centre 336
Whittingdon, Richard
    252
Whittington Stone 384
Wig and Pen Club 215
Wigmore Hall 170
Wigmore Street 170
Wilberforce, William
    255, 329, 382
Wilbraham Almshouses
    383
Wilde, Oscar 160, 328
Willesden 376
William Booth Memorial
    Training College 332
William Morris Gallery
    399
Wimbledon 339
Wimbledon Lawn
    Tennis Museum 340
Wimpole Street 170
Windsor 371
Windsor Castle 371
Windsor Great Park 374
Windsor Guildhall 374
Windsor Safari Park 375
Woburn House 185
Woburn Square 184
Wollstonecraft, Mary
    186
Woodford 400
Wood Green 392
Woodlands 316
Woolf, Virginia 182, 185
Wool House 109
Woolwich 321
Woolwich Arsenal 321
Woolwich Free Ferry 322
Woolwich Market 321
World Trade Centre 270
Wormwood Scrubs 370
Wren, Sir Christopher
    133, 254, 357
Wyldes Farm 392

York House,
    Embankment 197
York House, St. James's
    102
York House,
    Twickenham 350

Young Vic 290

Zimbabwe House 197
Zoological Gardens, *see*
  London Zoo

ATLAS

Key to Sectional Plan	2–3
Sectional Plan of Central London	4–21
Hampstead and Highgate	22–23
Greenwich	24
Windsor Castle	25
Sectional Map of Outer London	26–30
London Underground	At the end of the book

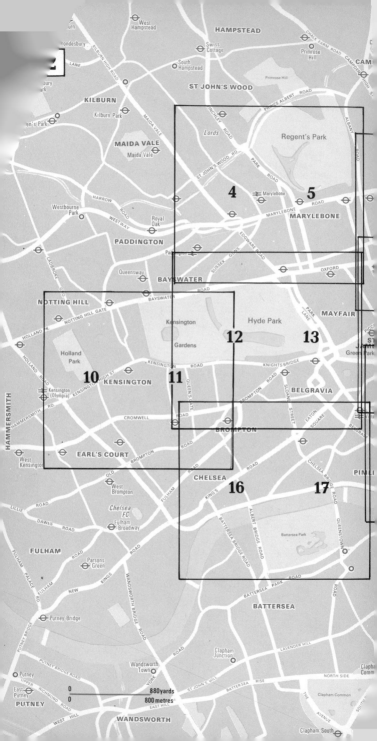

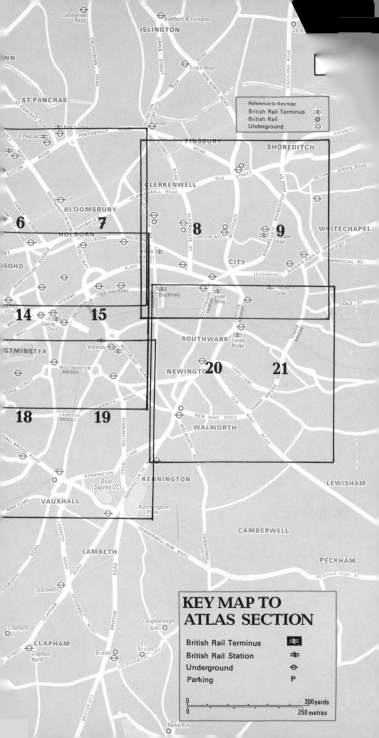

KEY MAP TO
ATLAS SECTION

British Rail Terminus ≱
British Rail Station ≹
Underground ⊖
Parking P

0   300 yards
0   250 metres

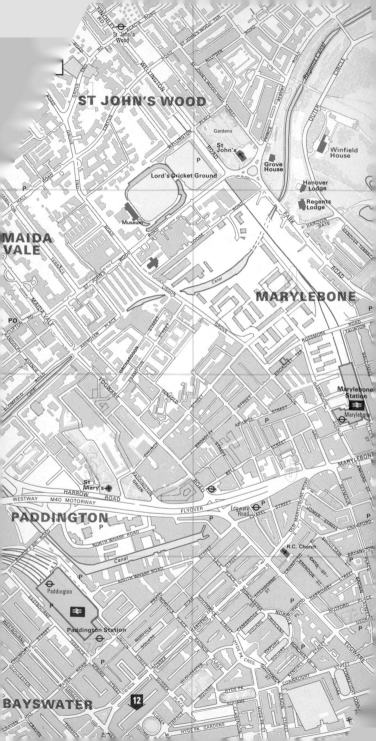

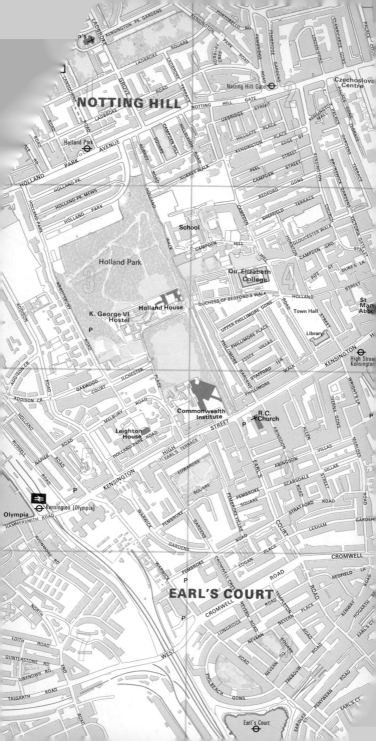

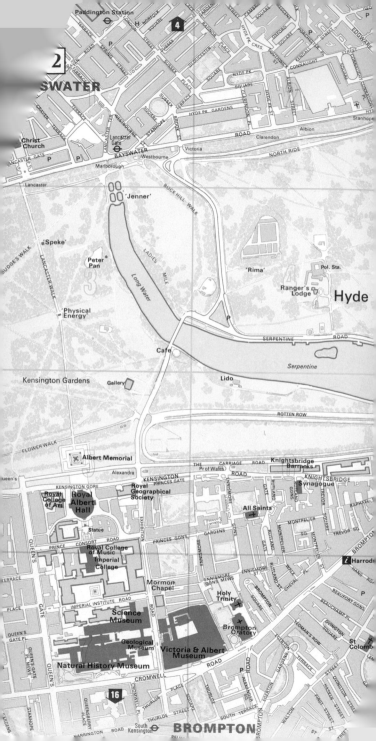

SWATER

Paddington Station

4

Christ
Church

Lancaster
Gate
BAYSWATER
Westbourne

Marlborough

NORFOLK STREET

SUSSEX SQUARE
STANHOPE

HYDE PK.
SQUARE

HYDE PK. GARDENS

Victoria

Clarendon

Albion
Stanhope

NORTH RIDE

Lancaster

'Jenner'

BUCK HILL WALK

'Speke'

Peter
Pan

'Physical
Energy'

LADIES
MILE

Long Water

'Rima'

Ranger's
Lodge

Pol. Sta.

Hyde

JUDGE'S WALK

LANCASTER WALK

Cafe

SERPENTINE   ROAD

Serpentine

Kensington Gardens

Gallery

Lido

ROTTEN ROW

FLOWER WALK

Albert Memorial

Alexandra

THE
CARRIAGE   ROAD
Pr of Wales
KENSINGTON   ROAD

Knightsbridge
Barracks

KNIGHTSBRIDGE

Queen's

KENSINGTON GORE

Royal
College
of Art

**Royal
Albert
Hall**

Royal Geographical
Society

PRINCES GATE

ENNISMORE

All Saints

Synagogue

RUTLAND GATE

MONTPELIER SQUARE

MONTPELIER

RAPHAEL

Statue

PRINCE CONSORT ROAD

Royal College
of Music
**Imperial
College**

EXHIBITION   ROAD

PRINCES GDNS.

BROMPTON

RUTLAND

TREVOR SQ.

CHEVAL

BROMPTON

i Harrods
HANS RD.

QUEEN'S GATE

Mormon
Chapel

ENNISMORE GDNS. MEWS

ENNISMORE
ST.

Holy
Trinity

BROMPTON

BEAUFORT GDNS.

OVINGTON
SQUARE

St
Colomb

IMPERIAL INSTITUTE ROAD

**Science
Museum**

Geological
Museum

Natural History Museum

Victoria & Albert
Museum

Brompton
Oratory

YEOMAN'S ROW

EGERTON GARDENS

EGERTON TERRACE

FIRST STREET

HASKER STREET

QUEEN'S
GATE
PLACE

QUEEN'S
GATE
PL. MEWS

CROMWELL   ROAD

16

THURLOE
PLACE

THURLOE
STREET

CROMWELL
PLACE

THURLOE
SQUARE

ALEXANDER
SQUARE

WALTON

SOUTH TERRACE

QUEENSBERRY
PLACE

HARRINGTON
ROAD

South
Kensington

BELL

BROMPTON

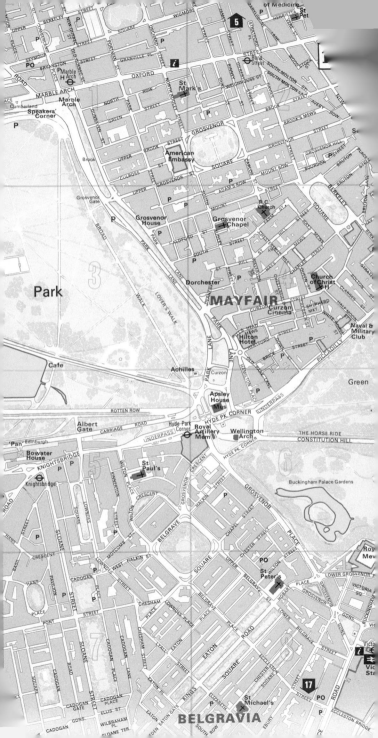

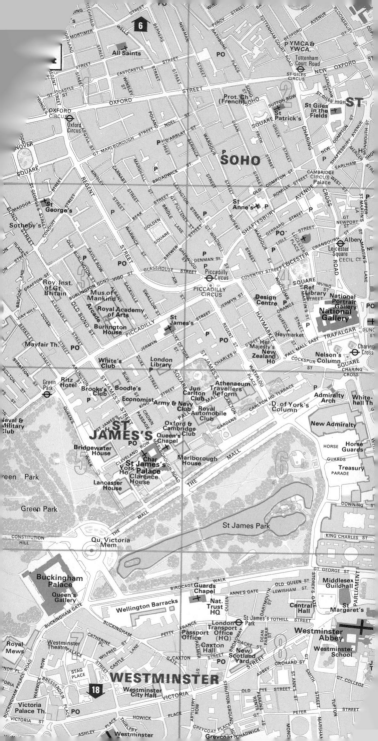

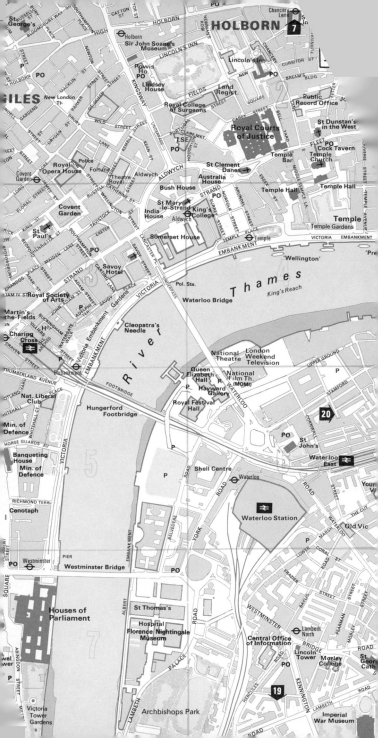

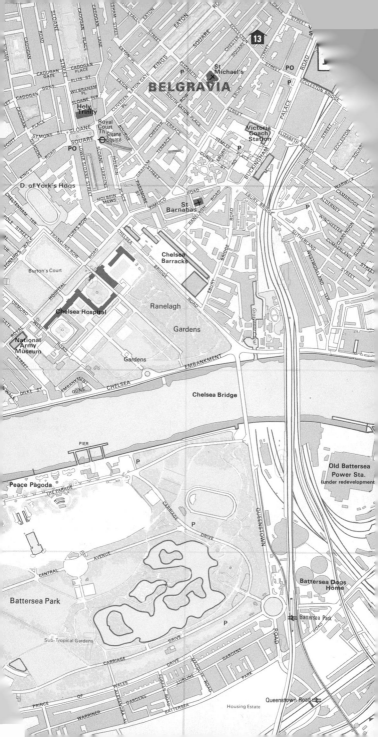

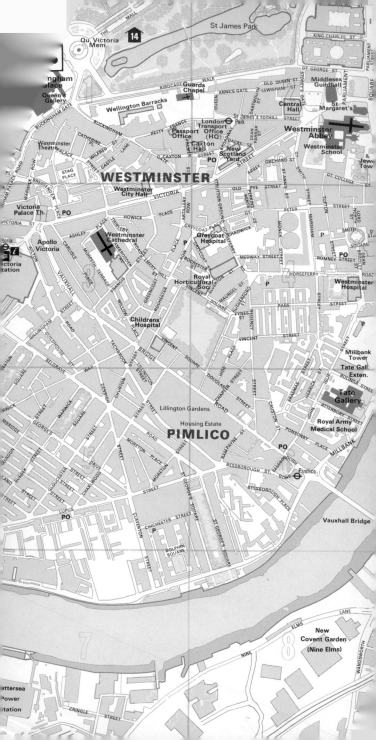

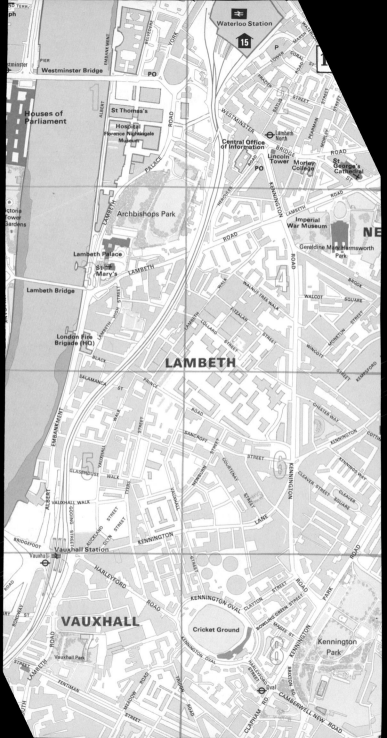

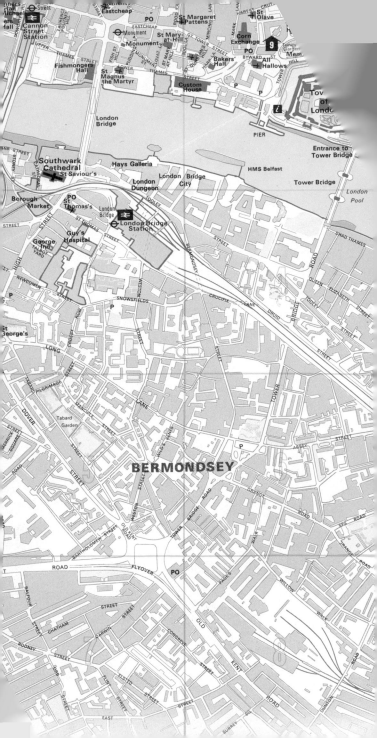

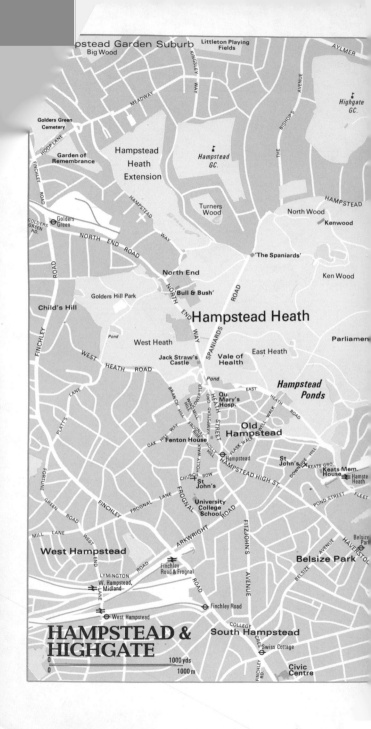

pstead Garden Suburb

Littleton Playing Fields

Big Wood

AYLMER

KINGSLEY WAY

MEADWAY

BISHOP'S AVENUE

Highgate G.C.

Golders Green Cemetery

HOOP LANE

Garden of Remembrance

Hampstead Heath Extension

Hampstead G.C.

THE

FINCHLEY ROAD

HAMPSTEAD

GOLDERS GREEN RD

Golders Green

Turners Wood

North Wood

Kenwood

ROAD

NORTH END ROAD

WAY

'The Spaniards'

Ken Wood

North End

Golders Hill Park

NORTH END WAY

'Bull & Bush'

SPANIARDS ROAD

Hampstead Heath

Child's Hill

FINCHLEY

Pond

West Heath

Vale of Health

East Heath

Parliamen

WEST HEATH ROAD

Jack Straw's Castle

LANE

Pond

Hampstead Ponds

PLATT'S

BRANCH HILL

NORTH END

WINDMILL HILL

EAST

HEATH ROAD

OAK HILL WAY

HEATH STREET

HAMPSTEAD GRO

FROGNAL

Qu... Mary's Hosp.

HILL WALK

HOLLY

Old Hampstead

HOLLY WALK

FLASK WALK

Fenton House

Hampstead

HIGH ST.

St John's

KEATS GRO.

FORTUNE GREEN ROAD

CHURCH ROW

HAMPSTEAD

DOWNSHIRE HILL

Keats Mem. House

Hampste Heath

St John's

HAMPSTEAD HIGH ST.

FROGNAL LANE

FROGNAL

University College School

POND STREET

FLEET

MILL LANE

FINCHLEY

ROAD

ARKWRIGHT

FITZJOHN'S

AVENUE

Belsize Park

WEST END

West Hampstead

LYMINGTON

ROAD

Finchley Road & Frognal

HAVERSTO

LANE

W. Hampstead, Midland

BELSIZE

AVENUE

Belsize Park

FINCHLEY ROAD

Finchley Road

West Hampstead

COLLEGE

South Hampstead

CRES.

Swiss Cottage

HAMPSTEAD & HIGHGATE

0   1000 yds
0   1000 m

FINCHLEY RD

Civic Centre

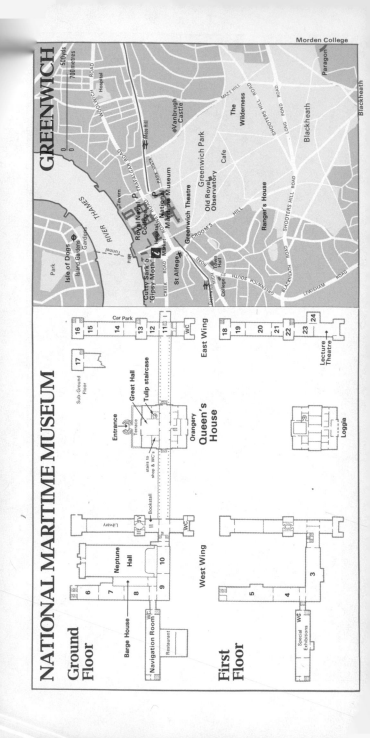

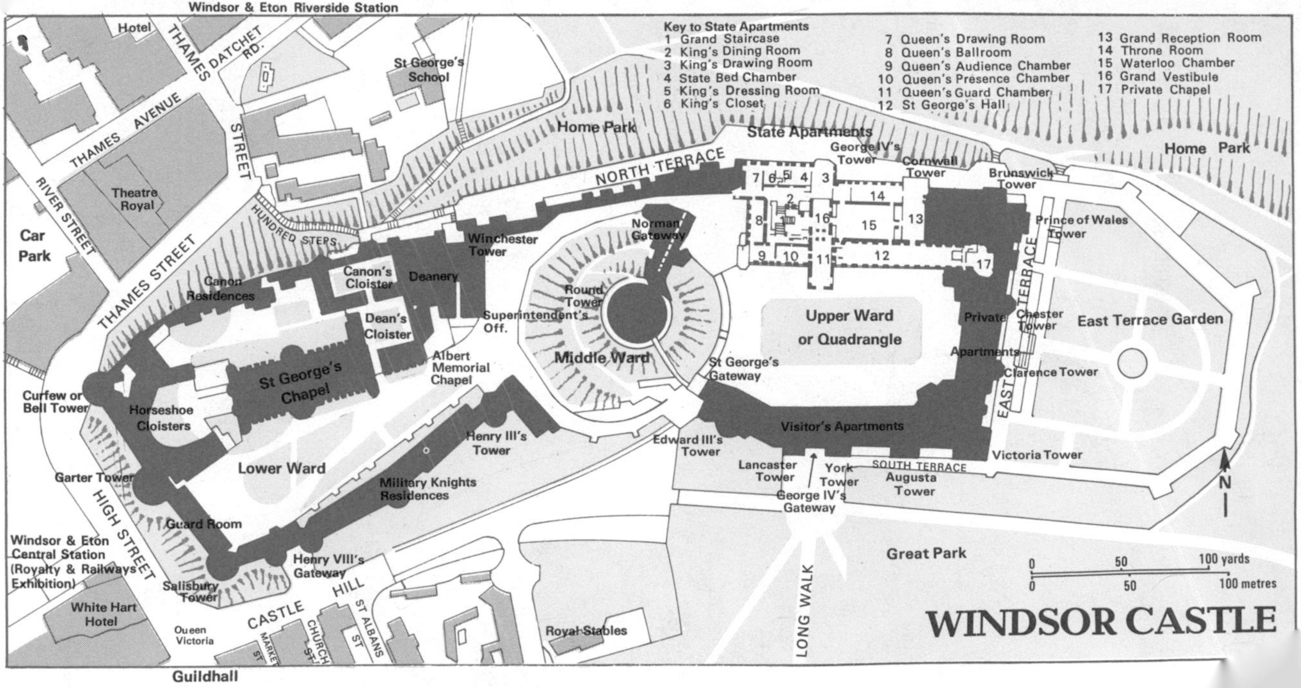

WINDSOR CASTLE

Key to State Apartments
1 Grand Staircase
2 King's Dining Room
3 King's Drawing Room
4 State Bed Chamber
5 King's Dressing Room
6 King's Closet

7 Queen's Drawing Room
8 Queen's Ballroom
9 Queen's Audience Chamber
10 Queen's Presence Chamber
11 Queen's Guard Chamber
12 St George's Hall

13 Grand Reception Room
14 Throne Room
15 Waterloo Room
16 Grand Vestibule
17 Private Chapel

N

0   50   100 yards
0   50   100 metres

Home Park

East Terrace Garden

State Apartments

EAST TERRACE

Prince of Wales Tower
Brunswick Tower
Chester Tower
Private Chamber
Clarence Tower
Victoria Tower

George's Tower
Cornwall Tower

Upper Ward or Quadrangle

SOUTH TERRACE
Augusta Tower
Lancaster Tower
York Tower
George IV's Gateway
Visitor's Apartments
St George's Gateway
Edward III's Tower

Great Park

LONG WALK

Home Park

NORTH TERRACE

Winchester Tower
Superintendent's Off.
Round Tower
Norman Gateway
Middle Ward

Royal Stables

Deanery
Canon's Cloister
Dean's Cloister
Albert Memorial Chapel
Military Knights Residences
Henry III's Tower

Windsor & Eton Riverside Station

St George's School

Hotel
THAMES AVENUE
THAMES
DATCHET RD.

STREET

HUNDRED STEPS

Canon Residences
THAMES STREET
St George's Chapel
Horseshoe Cloisters

RIVER STREET

Car Park

Theatre Royal

Curfew or Bell Tower
Garter Tower
Lower Ward
Guard Room
Salisbury Tower
Henry VIII's Gateway

HIGH STREET

Windsor & Eton Central Station (Royalty & Railways Exhibition)

White Hart Hotel
Queen Victoria
Guildhall

CASTLE HILL
MARKET ST
CHURCH ST
ST ALBANS ST

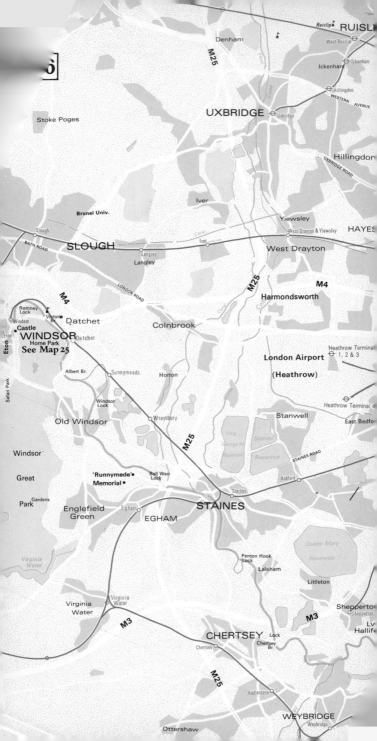

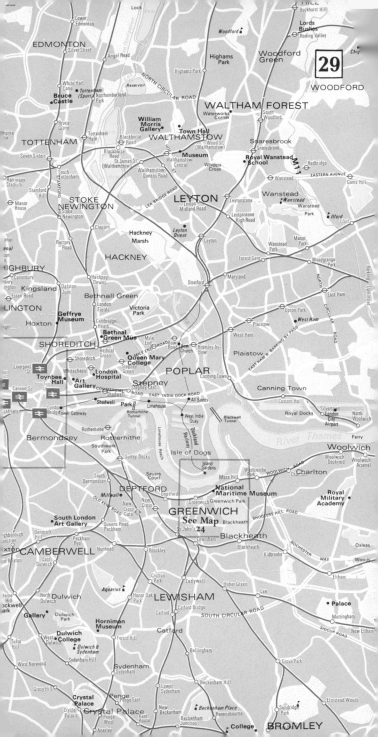

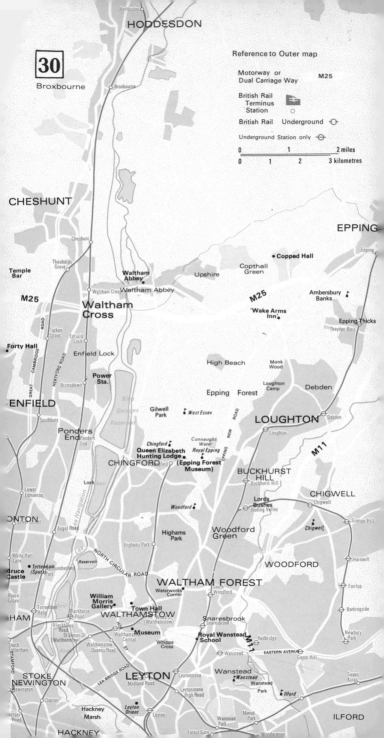